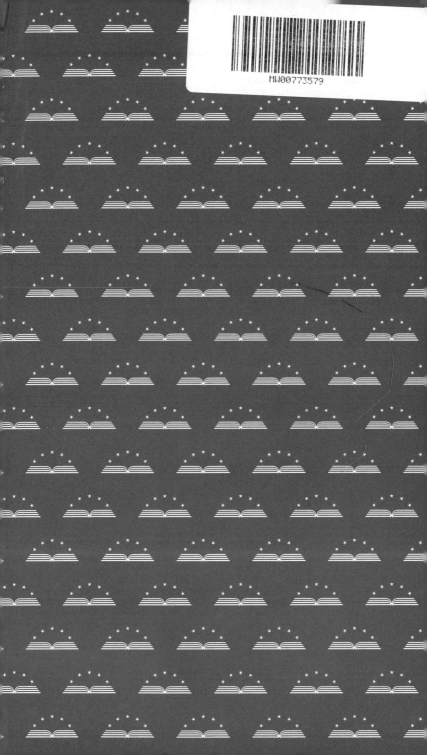

ALDO LEOPOLD

Aldo Leopold

A SAND COUNTY ALMANAC &
OTHER WRITINGS ON ECOLOGY
AND CONSERVATION

Curt Meine, *editor*

THE LIBRARY OF AMERICA

———

First Printing
The Library of America—238

Aldo Leopold:
A Sand County Almanac & Other Writings
on Ecology and Conservation
is published with support from

THE GOULD FAMILY FOUNDATION

Contents

A SAND COUNTY ALMANAC

and

SKETCHES HERE AND THERE

Illustrated by Charles W. Schwartz

To my ESTELLA

Foreword

THERE are some who can live without wild things, and some who cannot. These essays are the delights and dilemmas of one who cannot.

Like winds and sunsets, wild things were taken for granted until progress began to do away with them. Now we face the question whether a still higher 'standard of living' is worth its cost in things natural, wild, and free. For us of the minority, the opportunity to see geese is more important than television, and the chance to find a pasque-flower is a right as inalienable as free speech.

These wild things, I admit, had little human value until mechanization assured us of a good breakfast, and until science disclosed the drama of where they come from and how they live. The whole conflict thus boils down to a question of degree. We of the minority see a law of diminishing returns in progress; our opponents do not.

*   *   *

One must make shift with things as they are. These essays are my shifts. They are grouped in three parts.

Part I tells what my family sees and does at its week-end refuge from too much modernity: 'the shack.' On this sand farm in Wisconsin, first worn out and then abandoned by our bigger-and-better society, we try to rebuild, with shovel and axe, what we are losing elsewhere. It is here that we seek—and still find—our meat from God.

These shack sketches are arranged seasonally as a 'Sand County Almanac.'

Part II, 'Sketches Here and There,' recounts some of the episodes in my life that taught me, gradually and sometimes painfully, that the company is out of step. These episodes, scattered over the continent and through forty years of time, present a fair sample of the issues that bear the collective label: conservation.

Part III, 'The Upshot,' sets forth, in more logical terms, some of the ideas whereby we dissenters rationalize our dissent. Only the very sympathetic reader will wish to wrestle with the philosophical questions of Part III. I suppose it may be said that these essays tell the company how it may get back into step.

*   *   *

Conservation is getting nowhere because it is incompatible with our Abrahamic concept of land. We abuse land because we regard it as a commodity belonging to us. When we see land as a community to which we belong, we may begin to use it with love and respect. There is no other way for land to survive the impact of mechanized man, nor for us to reap it from the esthetic harvest it is capable, under science, of contributing to culture.

That land is a community is the basic concept of ecology, but that land is to be loved and respected is an extension of ethics. That land yields cultural harvest is a fact long known, but latterly often forgotten.

These essays attempt to weld these three concepts.

Such a view of land and people is, of course, subject to the blurs and distortions of personal experience and personal bias. But wherever the truth may lie, this much is crystal-clear: our bigger-and-better society is now like a hypochondriac, so obsessed with its own economic health as to have lost the capacity to remain healthy. The whole world is so greedy for more bathtubs that it has lost the stability necessary to build them, or even to turn off the tap. Nothing could be more salutary at this stage than a little healthy contempt for a plethora of material blessings.

Perhaps such a shift of values can be achieved by reappraising things unnatural, tame, and confined in terms of things natural, wild, and free.

ALDO LEOPOLD

Madison, Wisconsin
4 March 1948

January Thaw

EACH YEAR, after the midwinter blizzards, there comes a night of thaw when the tinkle of dripping water is heard in the land. It brings strange stirrings, not only to creatures abed for the night, but to some who have been asleep for the winter. The hibernating skunk, curled up in his deep den, uncurls himself and ventures forth to prowl the wet world, dragging his belly in the snow. His track marks one of the earliest datable events in that cycle of beginnings and ceasings which we call a year.

The track is likely to display an indifference to mundane affairs uncommon at other seasons; it leads straight across-country, as if its maker had hitched his wagon to a star and dropped the reins. I follow, curious to deduce his state of mind and appetite, and destination if any.

*   *   *

The months of the year, from January up to June, are a geo-metric progression in the abundance of distractions. In January one may follow a skunk track, or search for bands on the chicka-dees, or see what young pines the deer have browsed, or what muskrat houses the mink have dug, with only an occasional and mild digression into other doings. January observation can be almost as simple and peaceful as snow, and almost as continu-ous as cold. There is time not only to see who has done what, but to speculate why.

*   *   *

A meadow mouse, startled by my approach, darts damply across the skunk track. Why is he abroad in daylight? Probably because he feels grieved about the thaw. Today his maze of secret tun-nels, laboriously chewed through the matted grass under the snow, are tunnels no more, but only paths exposed to public

5

view and ridicule. Indeed the thawing sun has mocked the basic premises of the microtine economic system!

The mouse is a sober citizen who knows that grass grows in order that mice may store it as underground haystacks, and that snow falls in order that mice may build subways from stack to stack: supply, demand, and transport all neatly organized. To the mouse, snow means freedom from want and fear.

*   *   *

A rough-legged hawk comes sailing over the meadow ahead. Now he stops, hovers like a kingfisher, and then drops like a feathered bomb into the marsh. He does not rise again, so I am sure he has caught, and is now eating, some worried mouse-engineer who could not wait until night to inspect the damage to his well-ordered world.

The rough-leg has no opinion why grass grows, but he is well aware that snow melts in order that hawks may again catch field mice. He came down out of the Arctic in the hope of thaws, for to him a thaw means freedom from want and fear.

*   *   *

The skunk track enters the woods, and crosses a glade where the rabbits have packed down the snow with their tracks, and mottled it with pinkish urinations. Newly exposed oak seedlings have paid for the thaw with their newly barked stems. Tufts of rabbit-hair bespeak the year's first battles among the amorous

bucks. Further on I find a bloody spot, encircled by a wide-sweeping arc of owl's wings. To this rabbit the thaw brought freedom from want, but also a reckless abandonment of fear. The owl has reminded him that thoughts of spring are no substitute for caution.

* * *

The skunk track leads on, showing no interest in possible food, and no concern over the rompings or retributions of his neighbors. I wonder what he has on his mind; what got him out of bed? Can one impute romantic motives to this corpulent fellow, dragging his ample beltline through the slush? Finally the track enters a pile of driftwood, and does not emerge. I hear the tinkle of dripping water among the logs, and I fancy the skunk hears it too. I turn homeward, still wondering.

Good Oak

THERE ARE two spiritual dangers in not owning a farm. One is the danger of supposing that breakfast comes from the grocery, and the other that heat comes from the furnace.

To avoid the first danger, one should plant a garden, preferably where there is no grocer to confuse the issue.

To avoid the second, he should lay a split of good oak on the andirons, preferably where there is no furnace, and let it warm his shins while a February blizzard tosses the trees outside. If one has cut, split, hauled, and piled his own good oak, and let his mind work the while, he will remember much about where the heat comes from, and with a wealth of detail denied to those who spend the week end in town astride a radiator.

*   *   *

The particular oak now aglow on my andirons grew on the bank of the old emigrant road where it climbs the sandhill. The stump, which I measured upon felling the tree, has a diameter of 30 inches. It shows 80 growth rings, hence the seedling from which it originated must have laid its first ring of wood in 1865, at the end of the Civil War. But I know from the history of present seedlings that no oak grows above the reach of rabbits without a decade or more of getting girdled each winter, and re-sprouting during the following summer. Indeed, it is all too clear that every surviving oak is the product either of rabbit negligence or of rabbit scarcity. Some day some patient botanist will draw a frequency curve of oak birth-years, and show that the curve humps every ten years, each hump originating from a low in the ten-year rabbit cycle. (A fauna and flora, by this very process of perpetual battle within and among species, achieve collective immortality.)

It is likely, then, that a low in rabbits occurred in the middle 'sixties, when my oak began to lay on annual rings, but that the acorn that produced it fell during the preceding decade, when the covered wagons were still passing over my road into the Great Northwest. It may have been the wash and wear of the emigrant traffic that bared this roadbank, and thus enabled this particular acorn to spread its first leaves to the sun. Only one acorn in a thousand ever grew large enough to fight rabbits; the rest were drowned at birth in the prairie sea.

It is a warming thought that this one wasn't, and thus lived to garner eighty years of June sun. It is this sunlight that is now being released, through the intervention of my axe and saw, to warm my shack and my spirit through eighty gusts of blizzard. And with each gust a wisp of smoke from my chimney bears witness, to whomsoever it may concern, that the sun did not shine in vain.

My dog does not care where heat comes from, but he cares ardently that it come, and soon. Indeed he considers my ability to make it come as something magical, for when I rise in the cold black pre-dawn and kneel shivering by the hearth making a fire, he pushes himself blandly between me and the kindling splits I have laid on the ashes, and I must touch a match to them by poking it between his legs. Such faith, I suppose, is the kind that moves mountains.

It was a bolt of lightning that put an end to wood-making by this particular oak. We were all awakened, one night in July, by the thunderous crash; we realized that the bolt must have hit near by, but, since it had not hit us, we all went back to sleep. Man brings all things to the test of himself, and this is notably true of lightning.

Next morning, as we strolled over the sandhill rejoicing with the cone-flowers and the prairie clovers over their fresh accession of rain, we came upon a great slab of bark freshly torn from the trunk of the roadside oak. The trunk showed a long spiral scar of barkless sapwood, a foot wide and not yet yellowed by the sun. By the next day the leaves had wilted, and we knew that the lightning had bequeathed to us three cords of prospective fuel wood.

We mourned the loss of the old tree, but knew that a dozen of its progeny standing straight and stalwart on the sands had already taken over its job of wood-making.

We let the dead veteran season for a year in the sun it could no longer use, and then on a crisp winter's day we laid a newly filed saw to its bastioned base. Fragrant little chips of history spewed from the saw cut, and accumulated on the snow before each kneeling sawyer. We sensed that these two piles of sawdust were something more than wood; that they were the integrated transect of a century; that our saw was biting its way, stroke by stroke, decade by decade, into the chronology of a lifetime, written in concentric annual rings of good oak.

*   *   *

It took only a dozen pulls of the saw to transect the few years of our ownership, during which we had learned to love and cherish this farm. Abruptly we began to cut the years of our predecessor the bootlegger, who hated this farm, skinned it of residual fertility, burned its farmhouse, threw it back into the lap of the County (with delinquent taxes to boot), and then disappeared among the landless anonymities of the Great Depression. Yet the oak had laid down good wood for him; his sawdust was as fragrant, as sound, and as pink as our own. An oak is no respecter of persons.

The reign of the bootlegger ended sometime during the dust-bowl drouths of 1936, 1934, 1933, and 1930. Oak smoke from his still and peat from burning marshlands must have clouded the sun in those years, and alphabetical conservation was abroad in the land, but the sawdust shows no change.

Rest! cries the chief sawyer, and we pause for breath.

*   *   *

Now our saw bites into the 1920's, the Babbittian decade when everything grew bigger and better in heedlessness and arrogance —until 1929, when stock markets crumpled. If the oak heard them fall, its wood gives no sign. Nor did it heed the Legislature's several protestations of love for trees: a National Forest and a forest-crop law in 1927, a great refuge on the Upper Mississippi bottomlands in 1924, and a new forest policy in 1921. Neither did it notice the demise of the state's last marten in 1925, nor the arrival of its first starling in 1923.

In March 1922, the 'Big Sleet' tore the neighboring elms limb from limb, but there is no sign of damage to our tree. What is a ton of ice, more or less, to a good oak?

Rest! cries the chief sawyer, and we pause for breath.

*   *   *

Now the saw bites into 1910–20, the decade of the drainage dream, when steam shovels sucked dry the marshes of central Wisconsin to make farms, and made ash-heaps instead. Our marsh escaped, not because of any caution or forbearance among engineers, but because the river floods it each April, and did so with a vengeance—perhaps a defensive vengeance—in the years 1913–16. The oak laid on wood just the same, even in 1915, when the Supreme Court abolished the state forests and Governor Philip pontificated that 'state forestry is not a good business proposition.' (It did not occur to the Governor that there might be more than one definition of what is good, and even of what is business. It did not occur to him that while the courts were writing one definition of goodness in the law books, fires were writing quite another one on the face of the land. Perhaps, to be a governor, one must be free from doubt on such matters.)

While forestry receded during this decade, game conservation advanced. In 1916 pheasants became successfully established in Waukesha County; in 1915 a federal law prohibited spring shooting; in 1913 a state game farm was started; in 1912 a 'buck law' protected female deer; in 1911 an epidemic of refuges spread over the state. 'Refuge' became a holy word, but the oak took no heed.

Rest! cries the chief sawyer, and we pause for breath.

*   *   *

Now we cut 1910, when a great university president published a book on conservation, a great sawfly epidemic killed millions of tamaracks, a great drouth burned the pineries, and a great dredge drained Horicon Marsh.

We cut 1909, when smelt were first planted in the Great Lakes, and when a wet summer induced the Legislature to cut the forest-fire appropriations.

We cut 1908, a dry year when the forests burned fiercely, and Wisconsin parted with its last cougar.

We cut 1907, when a wandering lynx, looking in the wrong direction for the promised land, ended his career among the farms of Dane County.

We cut 1906, when the first state forester took office, and fires burned 17,000 acres in these sand counties; we cut 1905 when a great flight of goshawks came out of the North and ate up the local grouse (they no doubt perched in this tree to eat some of mine). We cut 1902–3, a winter of bitter cold; 1901, which brought the most intense drouth of record (rainfall only 17 inches); 1900, a centennial year of hope, of prayer, and the usual annual ring of oak.

Rest! cries the chief sawyer, and we pause for breath.

*   *   *

Now our saw bites into the 1890's, called gay by those whose eyes turn cityward rather than landward. We cut 1899, when the last passenger pigeon collided with a charge of shot near Babcock, two counties to the north; we cut 1898 when a dry fall, followed by a snowless winter, froze the soil seven feet deep and killed the apple trees; 1897, another drouth year, when another forestry commission came into being; 1896, when 25,000 prairie chickens were shipped to market from the village of Spooner alone; 1895, another year of fires; 1894, another drouth year;

and 1893, the year of 'The Bluebird Storm,' when a March blizzard reduced the migrating bluebirds to near-zero. (The first bluebirds always alighted in this oak, but in the middle 'nineties it must have gone without.) We cut 1892, another year of fires; 1891, a low in the grouse cycle; and 1890, the year of the Babcock Milk Tester, which enabled Governor Heil to boast, half a century later, that Wisconsin is America's Dairyland. The motor licenses which now parade that boast were then not foreseen, even by Professor Babcock.

It was likewise in 1890 that the largest pine rafts in history slipped down the Wisconsin River in full view of my oak, to build an empire of red barns for the cows of the prairie states. Thus it is that good pine now stands between the cow and the blizzard, just as good oak stands between the blizzard and me.

Rest! cries the chief sawyer, and we pause for breath.

* * *

Now our saw bites into the 1880's; into 1889, a drouth year in which Arbor Day was first proclaimed; into 1887, when Wisconsin appointed its first game wardens; into 1886, when the College of Agriculture held its first short course for farmers; into 1885, preceded by a winter 'of unprecedented length and severity'; into 1883, when Dean W. H. Henry reported that the spring flowers at Madison bloomed 13 days later than average; into 1882, the year Lake Mendota opened a month late following the historic 'Big Snow' and bitter cold of 1881–2.

It was likewise in 1881 that the Wisconsin Agricultural Society debated the question, 'How do you account for the second growth of black oak timber that has sprung up all over the country in the last thirty years?' My oak was one of these. One debater claimed spontaneous generation, another claimed regurgitation of acorns by southbound pigeons.

Rest! cries the chief sawyer, and we pause for breath.

* * *

Now our saw bites the 1870's, the decade of Wisconsin's carousal in wheat. Monday morning came in 1879, when chinch bugs, grubs, rust, and soil exhaustion finally convinced Wisconsin farmers that they could not compete with the virgin prairies further west in the game of wheating land to death. I suspect that this farm played its share in the game, and that the sand blow just north of my oak had its origin in over-wheating.

This same year of 1879 saw the first planting of carp in Wisconsin, and also the first arrival of quack-grass as a stowaway from Europe. On 27 October 1879, six migrating prairie chickens perched on the rooftree of the German Methodist Church in Madison, and took a look at the growing city. On 8 November the markets at Madison were reported to be glutted with ducks at 10 cents each.

In 1878 a deer hunter from Sauk Rapids remarked prophetically, 'The hunters promise to outnumber the deer.'

On 10 September 1877, two brothers, shooting Muskego Lake, bagged 210 blue-winged teal in one day.

In 1876 came the wettest year of record; the rainfall piled up 50 inches. Prairie chickens declined, perhaps owing to hard rains.

In 1875 four hunters killed 153 prairie chickens at York Prairie, one county to the eastward. In the same year the U.S. Fish Commission planted Atlantic salmon in Devil's Lake, 10 miles south of my oak.

In 1874 the first factory-made barbed wire was stapled to oak trees; I hope no such artifacts are buried in the oak now under saw!

In 1873 one Chicago firm received and marketed 25,000 prairie chickens. The Chicago trade collectively bought 600,000 at $3.25 per dozen.

In 1872 the last wild Wisconsin turkey was killed, two counties to the southwest.

It is appropriate that the decade ending the pioneer carousal in wheat should likewise have ended the pioneer carousal in pigeon blood. In 1871, within a 50-mile triangle spreading northwestward from my oak, 136 million pigeons are estimated to have nested, and some may have nested in it, for it was then a thrifty sapling 20 feet tall. Pigeon hunters by scores plied their trade with net and gun, club and salt lick, and trainloads of prospective pigeon pie moved southward and eastward toward the cities. It was the last big nesting in Wisconsin, and nearly the last in any state.

This same year 1871 brought other evidence of the march of

empire: the Peshtigo Fire, which cleared a couple of counties of trees and soil, and the Chicago Fire, said to have started from the protesting kick of a cow.

In 1870 the meadow mice had already staged their march of empire; they ate up the young orchards of the young state, and then died. They did not eat my oak, whose bark was already too tough and thick for mice.

It was likewise in 1870 that a market gunner boasted in the *American Sportsman* of killing 6000 ducks in one season near Chicago.

Rest! cries the chief sawyer, and we pause for breath.

* * *

Our saw now cuts the 1860's, when thousands died to settle the question: Is the man-man community lightly to be dismembered? They settled it, but they did not see, nor do we yet see, that the same question applies to the man-land community.

This decade was not without its gropings toward the larger issue. In 1867 Increase A. Lapham induced the State Horticultural Society to offer prizes for forest plantations. In 1866 the last native Wisconsin elk was killed. The saw now severs 1865, the pith-year of our oak. In that year John Muir offered to buy from his brother, who then owned the home farm thirty miles east of my oak, a sanctuary for the wildflowers that had gladdened his youth. His brother declined to part with the land, but he could not suppress the idea: 1865 still stands in Wisconsin history as the birth-year of mercy for things natural, wild, and free.

We have cut the core. Our saw now reverses its orientation in history; we cut backward across the years, and outward toward the far side of the stump. At last there is a tremor in the great trunk; the saw-kerf suddenly widens; the saw is quickly pulled as the sawyers spring backward to safety; all hands cry 'Timber!'; my oak leans, groans, and crashes with earth-shaking thunder, to lie prostrate across the emigrant road that gave it birth.

* * *

Now comes the job of making wood. The maul rings on steel wedges as the sections of trunk are up-ended one by one, only to fall apart in fragrant slabs to be corded by the roadside.

There is an allegory for historians in the diverse functions of saw, wedge, and axe.

The saw works only across the years, which it must deal with one by one, in sequence. From each year the raker teeth pull little chips of fact, which accumulate in little piles, called sawdust by woodsmen and archives by historians; both judge the character of what lies within by the character of the samples thus made visible without. It is not until the transect is completed that the tree falls, and the stump yields a collective view of a century. By its fall the tree attests the unity of the hodge-podge called history.

The wedge, on the other hand, works only in radial splits; such a split yields a collective view of all the years at once, or no view at all, depending on the skill with which the plane of the split is chosen. (If in doubt, let the section season for a year until a crack develops. Many a hastily driven wedge lies rusting in the woods, embedded in unsplittable cross-grain.)

The axe functions only at an angle diagonal to the years, and this only for the peripheral rings of the recent past. Its special function is to lop limbs, for which both saw and wedge are useless.

The three tools are requisite to good oak, and to good history.

*   *   *

These things I ponder as the kettle sings, and the good oak burns to red coals on white ashes. Those ashes, come spring, I will return to the orchard at the foot of the sandhill. They will come back to me again, perhaps as red apples, or perhaps as a spirit of enterprise in some fat October squirrel, who, for reasons unknown to himself, is bent on planting acorns.

The Geese Return

O NE SWALLOW does not make a summer, but one skein of geese, cleaving the murk of a March thaw, is the spring.

A cardinal, whistling spring to a thaw but later finding himself mistaken, can retrieve his error by resuming his winter silence. A chipmunk, emerging for a sunbath but finding a blizzard, has only to go back to bed. But a migrating goose, staking two hundred miles of black night on the chance of finding a hole in the lake, has no easy chance for retreat. His arrival carries the conviction of a prophet who has burned his bridges.

A March morning is only as drab as he who walks in it without a glance skyward, ear cocked for geese. I once knew an educated lady, banded by Phi Beta Kappa, who told me that she had never heard or seen the geese that twice a year proclaim the revolving seasons to her well-insulated roof. Is education possibly a process of trading awareness for things of lesser worth? The goose who trades his is soon a pile of feathers.

The geese that proclaim the seasons to our farm are aware of many things, including the Wisconsin statutes. The southbound November flocks pass over us high and haughty, with scarcely a honk of recognition for their favorite sandbars and sloughs. 'As a crow flies' is crooked compared with their undeviating aim at the nearest big lake twenty miles to the south, where they loaf by day on broad waters and filch corn by night from the freshly cut stubbles. November geese are aware that every marsh and pond bristles from dawn till dark with hopeful guns.

March geese are a different story. Although they have been shot at most of the winter, as attested by their buckshot-battered pinions, they know that the spring truce is now in effect. They wind the oxbows of the river, cutting low over the now gunless points and islands, and gabbling to each sandbar as to a long-lost friend. They weave low over marshes and meadows, greeting each newly melted puddle and pool. Finally, after a few *pro-forma* circlings of our marsh, they set wing and glide silently to the pond, black landing-gear lowered and rumps white against

18

the far hill. Once touching water, our newly arrived guests set up a honking and splashing that shakes the last thought of winter out of the brittle cattails. Our geese are home again!

It is at this moment of each year that I wish I were a muskrat, eye-deep in the marsh.

Once the first geese are in, they honk a clamorous invitation to each migrating flock, and in a few days the marsh is full of them. On our farm we measure the amplitude of our spring by two yardsticks: the number of pines planted, and the number of geese that stop. Our record is 642 geese counted in on 11 April 1946.

As in fall, our spring geese make daily trips to corn, but these are no surreptitious sneakings-out by night; the flocks move noisily to and from corn stubbles through the day. Each departure is preceded by loud gustatory debate, and each return by an even louder one. The returning flocks, once thoroughly at home, omit their *pro-forma* circlings of the marsh. They tumble out of the sky like maple leaves, side-slipping right and left to lose altitude, feet spraddled toward the shouts of welcome below. I suppose the ensuing gabble deals with the merits of the day's dinner. They are now eating the waste corn that the snow blanket has protected over winter from corn-seeking crows, cottontails, meadow mice, and pheasants.

It is a conspicuous fact that the corn stubbles selected by geese for feeding are usually those occupying former prairies. No man knows whether this bias for prairie corn reflects some superior nutritional value, or some ancestral tradition transmitted from generation to generation since the prairie days. Perhaps it reflects the simpler fact that prairie cornfields tend to be large. If I could understand the thunderous debates that precede and follow these daily excursions to corn, I might soon learn the reason for the prairie-bias. But I cannot, and I am well content that it should remain a mystery. What a dull world if we knew all about geese!

In thus watching the daily routine of a spring goose convention, one notices the prevalence of singles—lone geese that do much flying about and much talking. One is apt to impute a disconsolate tone to their honkings, and to jump to the conclusion that they are broken-hearted widowers, or mothers hunting lost children. The seasoned ornithologist knows, however, that such subjective interpretation of bird behavior is risky. I long tried to keep an open mind on the question.

After my students and I had counted for half a dozen years the number of geese comprising a flock, some unexpected light was cast on the meaning of lone geese. It was found by mathematical analysis that flocks of six or multiples of six were far more frequent than chance alone would dictate. In other words, goose flocks are families, or aggregations of families, and lone geese in spring are probably just what our fond imaginings had first suggested. They are bereaved survivors of the winter's shooting, searching in vain for their kin. Now I am free to grieve with and for the lone honkers.

It is not often that cold-potato mathematics thus confirms the sentimental promptings of the bird-lover.

On April nights when it has become warm enough to sit outdoors, we love to listen to the proceedings of the convention in the marsh. There are long periods of silence when one hears only the winnowing of snipe, the hoot of a distant owl, or the nasal clucking of some amorous coot. Then, of a sudden, a strident honk resounds, and in an instant pandemonium echoes. There is a beating of pinions on water, a rushing of dark prows propelled by churning paddles, and a general shouting by the onlookers of a vehement controversy. Finally some deep honker has his last word, and the noise subsides to that half-audible small-talk that seldom ceases among geese. Once again, I would I were a muskrat!

By the time the pasques are in full bloom our goose-convention dwindles, and before May our marsh is once again a mere grassy wetness, enlivened only by redwings and rails.

*   *   *

It is an irony of history that the great powers should have discovered the unity of nations at Cairo in 1943. The geese of the world have had that notion for a longer time, and each March they stake their lives on its essential truth.

In the beginning there was only the unity of the Ice Sheet. Then followed the unity of the March thaw, and the northward hegira of the international geese. Every March since the Pleistocene, the geese have honked unity from China Sea to Siberian

Steppe, from Euphrates to Volga, from Nile to Murmansk, from Lincolnshire to Spitsbergen. Every March since the Pleistocene, the geese have honked unity from Currituck to Labrador, Matamuskeet to Ungava, Horseshoe Lake to Hudson's Bay, Avery Island to Baffin Land, Panhandle to Mackenzie, Sacramento to Yukon.

By this international commerce of geese, the waste corn of Illinois is carried through the clouds to the Arctic tundras, there to combine with the waste sunlight of a nightless June to grow goslings for all the lands between. And in this annual barter of food for light, and winter warmth for summer solitude, the whole continent receives as net profit a wild poem dropped from the murky skies upon the muds of March.

Come High Water

THE SAME logic that causes big rivers always to flow past big cities causes cheap farms sometimes to be marooned by spring floods. Ours is a cheap farm, and sometimes when we visit it in April we get marooned.

Not intentionally, of course, but one can, to a degree, guess from weather reports when the snows up north will melt, and one can estimate how many days it takes for the flood to run the gauntlet of upriver cities. Thus, come Sunday evening, one must go back to town and work, but one can't. How sweetly the spreading waters murmur condolence for the wreckage they have inflicted on Monday morning dates! How deep and chesty the honkings of the geese as they cruise over cornfield after cornfield, each in process of becoming a lake. Every hundred yards some new goose flails the air as he struggles to lead the echelon in its morning survey of this new and watery world.

The enthusiasm of geese for high water is a subtle thing, and might be overlooked by those unfamiliar with goose-gossip, but the enthusiasm of carp is obvious and unmistakable. No sooner has the rising flood wetted the grass roots than here they come, rooting and wallowing with the prodigious zest of pigs turned out to pasture, flashing red tails and yellow bellies, cruising the wagon tracks and cow-paths, and shaking the reeds and bushes in their haste to explore what to them is an expanding universe.

Unlike the geese and the carp, the terrestrial birds and mammals accept high water with philosophical detachment. A cardinal atop a river birch whistles loudly his claim to a territory that, but for the trees, cannot be seen to exist. A ruffed grouse drums from the flooded woods; he must be perched on the high end of his highest drumming log. Meadow-mice paddle ridgeward with the calm assurance of miniature muskrats. From the orchard bounds a deer, evicted from his usual daytime bed in the willow thickets. Everywhere are rabbits, calmly accepting quarters on our hill, which serves, in Noah's absence, for an ark.

The spring flood brings us more than high adventure; it brings likewise an unpredictable miscellany of floatable objects pilfered from upriver farms. An old board stranded on our meadow has, to us, twice the value of the same piece new from the lumberyard. Each old board has its own individual history, always unknown, but always to some degree guessable from the kind of wood, its dimensions, its nails, screws, or paint, its finish or the lack of it, its wear or decay. One can even guess, from the abrasion of its edges and ends on sandbars, how many floods have carried it in years past.

Our lumber pile, recruited entirely from the river, is thus not only a collection of personalities, but an anthology of human strivings in upriver farms and forests. The autobiography of an old board is a kind of literature not yet taught on campuses, but any riverbank farm is a library where he who hammers or saws may read at will. Come high water, there is always an accession of new books.

*   *   *

There are degrees and kinds of solitude. An island in a lake has one kind; but lakes have boats, and there is always the chance that one might land to pay you a visit. A peak in the clouds has another kind; but most peaks have trails, and trails have tourists. I know of no solitude so secure as one guarded by a spring flood; nor do the geese, who have seen more kinds and degrees of aloneness than I have.

So we sit on our hill beside a new-blown pasque, and watch the geese go by. I see our road dipping gently into the waters, and I conclude (with inner glee but exterior detachment) that the question of traffic, in or out, is for this day at least, debatable only among carp.

Draba

WITHIN A few weeks now Draba, the smallest flower that blows, will sprinkle every sandy place with small blooms.

He who hopes for spring with upturned eye never sees so small a thing as Draba. He who despairs of spring with downcast eye steps on it, unknowing. He who searches for spring with his knees in the mud finds it, in abundance.

Draba asks, and gets, but scant allowance of warmth and comfort; it subsists on the leavings of unwanted time and space. Botany books give it two or three lines, but never a plate or portrait. Sand too poor and sun too weak for bigger, better blooms are good enough for Draba. After all it is no spring flower, but only a postscript to a hope.

Draba plucks no heartstrings. Its perfume, if there is any, is lost in the gusty winds. Its color is plain white. Its leaves wear a sensible woolly coat. Nothing eats it; it is too small. No poets sing of it. Some botanist once gave it a Latin name, and then forgot it. Altogether it is of no importance—just a small creature that does a small job quickly and well.

Bur Oak

WHEN SCHOOL children vote on a state bird, flower, or tree, they are not making a decision; they are merely ratifying history. Thus history made bur oak the characteristic tree of southern Wisconsin when the prairie grasses first gained possession of the region. Bur oak is the only tree that can stand up to a prairie fire and live.

Have you ever wondered why a thick crust of corky bark covers the whole tree, even to the smallest twigs? This cork is armor. Bur oaks were the shock troops sent by the invading forest to storm the prairie; fire is what they had to fight. Each April, before the new grasses had covered the prairie with unburnable greenery, fires ran at will over the land, sparing only such old oaks as had grown bark too thick to scorch. Most of these groves of scattered veterans, known to the pioneers as 'oak openings,' consisted of bur oaks.

Engineers did not discover insulation; they copied it from these old soldiers of the prairie war. Botanists can read the story of that war for twenty thousand years. The record consists partly of pollen grains embedded in peats, partly of relic plants interned in the rear of the battle, and there forgotten. The record shows that the forest front at times retreated almost to Lake Superior; at times it advanced far to the south. At one period it advanced so far southward that spruce and other 'rear guard' species grew to and beyond the southern border of Wisconsin; spruce pollen appears at a certain level in all peat bogs of the region. But the average battle line between prairie and forest was about where it is now, and the net outcome of the battle was a draw.

One reason for this was that there were allies that threw their support first to one side, then to the other. Thus rabbits and mice mowed down the prairie herbs in summer, and in winter girdled any oak seedlings that survived the fires. Squirrels planted acorns in fall, and ate them all the rest of the year. June beetles undermined the prairie sod in their grub stage, but defoliated the oaks in their adult stage. But for this geeing and hawing of allies, and hence of the victory, we should not have

today that rich mosaic of prairie and forest soils which looks so decorative on a map.

Jonathan Carver has left us a vivid word-picture of the prairie border in pre-settlement days. On 10 October 1766, he visited Blue Mounds, a group of high hills (now wooded) near the southwestern corner of Dane County. He says:

> I ascended one of the highest of these, and had an extensive view of the country. For many miles nothing was to be seen but lesser mountains, which appeared at a distance like haycocks, they being free from trees. Only a few groves of hickory, and stunted oaks, covered some of the vallies.

In the 1840's a new animal, the settler, intervened in the prairie battles. He didn't mean to, he just plowed enough fields to deprive the prairie of its immemorial ally: fire. Seedling oaks forthwith romped over the grasslands in legions, and what had been the prairie region became a region of woodlot farms. If you doubt this story, go count the rings on any set of stumps on any 'ridge' woodlot in southwest Wisconsin. All the trees except the oldest veterans date back to the 1850's and the 1860's, and this was when fires ceased on the prairie.

John Muir grew up in Marquette County during this period when new woods overrode the old prairies and engulfed the oak openings in thickets of saplings. In his *Boyhood and Youth* he recalls that:

> The uniformly rich soil of the Illinois and Wisconsin prairies produced so close and tall a growth of grasses for fires that no tree could live on it. Had there been no fires, these fine prairies, so marked a feature of the country, would have been covered by the heaviest forest. As soon as the oak openings were settled, and the farmers had prevented running grass-fires, the grubs [roots] grew up into trees and formed tall thickets so dense that it was difficult to walk through them, and every trace of the sunny [oak] 'openings' vanished.

Thus, he who owns a veteran bur oak owns more than a tree. He owns a historical library, and a reserved seat in the theater of evolution. To the discerning eye, his farm is labeled with the badge and symbol of the prairie war.

Sky Dance

Iowned my farm for two years before learning that the sky dance is to be seen over my woods every evening in April and May. Since we discovered it, my family and I have been reluctant to miss even a single performance.

The show begins on the first warm evening in April at exactly 6:50 P.M. The curtain goes up one minute later each day until 1 June, when the time is 7:50. This sliding scale is dictated by vanity, the dancer demanding a romantic light intensity of exactly 0.05 foot-candles. Do not be late, and sit quietly, lest he fly away in a huff.

The stage props, like the opening hour, reflect the temperamental demands of the performer. The stage must be an open amphitheater in woods or brush, and in its center there must be a mossy spot, a streak of sterile sand, a bare outcrop of rock, or a bare roadway. Why the male woodcock should be such a stickler for a bare dance floor puzzled me at first, but I now think it is a matter of legs. The woodcock's legs are short, and his struttings cannot be executed to advantage in dense grass or weeds, nor could his lady see them there. I have more woodcocks than most farmers because I have more mossy sand, too poor to support grass.

Knowing the place and the hour, you seat yourself under a bush to the east of the dance floor and wait, watching against the sunset for the woodcock's arrival. He flies in low from some neighboring thicket, alights on the bare moss, and at once begins the overture; a series of queer throaty *peents* spaced about two seconds apart, and sounding much like the summer call of the nighthawk.

Suddenly the peenting ceases and the bird flutters skyward in a series of wide spirals, emitting a musical twitter. Up and up he goes, the spirals steeper and smaller, the twittering louder and louder, until the performer is only a speck in the sky. Then, without warning, he tumbles like a crippled plane, giving voice in a soft liquid warble that a March bluebird might envy. At a few feet from the ground he levels off and returns to his peenting ground, usually to the exact spot where the performance began, and there resumes his peenting.

It is soon too dark to see the bird on the ground, but you can see his flights against the sky for an hour, which is the usual duration of the show. On moonlit nights, however, it may continue, at intervals, as long as the moon continues to shine.

At daybreak the whole show is repeated. In early April the final curtain falls at 5:15 A.M.; the time advances two minutes a day until June, when the performance closes for the year at 3:15. Why the disparity in sliding scale? Alas, I fear that even romance tires, for it takes only a fifth as much light to stop the sky dance at dawn as suffices to start it at sunset.

*   *   *

It is fortunate, perhaps, that no matter how intently one studies the hundred little dramas of the woods and meadows, one can never learn all of the salient facts about any one of them. What I do not yet know about the sky dance is: where is the lady, and just what part, if any, does she play? I often see two woodcocks

on a peenting ground, and the two sometimes fly together, but they never peent together. Is the second bird the hen, or a rival male?

Another unknown: is the twitter vocal, or is it mechanical? My friend, Bill Feeney, once clapped a net over a peenting bird and removed his outer primary wing feathers; thereafter the bird peented and warbled, but twittered no more. But one such experiment is hardly conclusive.

Another unknown: up to what stage of nesting does the male continue the sky dance? My daughter once saw a bird peenting within twenty yards of a nest containing hatched eggshells, but was this *his* lady's nest? Or is this secretive fellow possibly bigamous without our ever having found it out? These, and many other questions, remain mysteries of the deepening dusk.

The drama of the sky dance is enacted nightly on hundreds of farms, the owners of which sigh for entertainment, but harbor the illusion that it is to be sought in theaters. They live on the land, but not by the land.

The woodcock is a living refutation of the theory that the utility of a game bird is to serve as a target, or to pose gracefully on a slice of toast. No one would rather hunt woodcock in October than I, but since learning of the sky dance I find myself calling one or two birds enough. I must be sure that, come April, there be no dearth of dancers in the sunset sky.

Back from the Argentine

WHEN DANDELIONS have set the mark of May on Wisconsin pastures, it is time to listen for the final proof of spring. Sit down on a tussock, cock your ears at the sky, dial out the bedlam of meadowlarks and redwings, and soon you may hear it: the flight-song of the upland plover, just now back from the Argentine.

If your eyes are strong, you may search the sky and see him, wings aquiver, circling among the woolly clouds. If your eyes are weak, don't try it; just watch the fence posts. Soon a flash of silver will tell you on which post the plover has alighted and folded his long wings. Whoever invented the word 'grace' must have seen the wing-folding of the plover.

There he sits; his whole being says it's your next move to absent yourself from his domain. The county records may allege that you own this pasture, but the plover airily rules out such trivial legalities. He has just flown 4000 miles to reassert the title he got from the Indians, and until the young plovers are a-wing, this pasture is his, and none may trespass without his protest.

Somewhere near by, the hen plover is brooding the four large pointed eggs which will shortly hatch four precocial chicks. From the moment their down is dry, they scamper through the grass like mice on stilts, quite able to elude your clumsy efforts to catch them. At thirty days the chicks are full grown; no other fowl develops with equal speed. By August they have graduated from flying school, and on cool August nights you can hear their whistled signals as they set wing for the pampas, to prove again the age-old unity of the Americas. Hemisphere solidarity is new among statesmen, but not among the feathered navies of the sky.

The upland plover fits easily into the agricultural countryside. He follows the black-and-white buffalo, which now pasture his prairies, and finds them an acceptable substitute for brown ones. He nests in hayfields as well as pastures, but, unlike the clumsy pheasant, does not get caught in hay mowers. Well before the

hay is ready to cut, the young plovers are a-wing and away. In farm country, the plover has only two real enemies: the gully and the drainage ditch. Perhaps we shall one day find that these are our enemies, too.

There was a time in the early 1900's when Wisconsin farms nearly lost their immemorial timepiece, when May pastures greened in silence, and August nights brought no whistled reminder of impending fall. Universal gunpowder, plus the lure of plover-on-toast for post-Victorian banquets, had taken too great a toll. The belated protection of the federal migratory bird laws came just in time.

The Alder Fork—A Fishing Idyl

WE FOUND the main stream so low that the teeter-snipe pattered about in what last year were trout riffles, and so warm that we could duck in its deepest pool without a shout. Even after our cooling swim, waders felt like hot tar paper in the sun.

The evening's fishing proved as disappointing as its auguries. We asked that stream for trout, and it gave us a chub. That night we sat under a mosquito smudge and debated the morrow's plan. Two hundred miles of hot, dusty road we had come, to feel again the impetuous tug of a disillusioned brook or rainbow. There were no trout.

But this, we now remembered, was a stream of parts. High up near the headwaters we had once seen a fork, narrow, deep, and fed by cold springs that gurgled out under its close-hemmed walls of alder. What would a self-respecting trout do in such weather? Just what we did: go up.

In the fresh of the morning, when a hundred whitethroats had forgotten it would ever again be anything but sweet and cool, I climbed down the dewy bank and stepped into the Alder Fork. A trout was rising just upstream. I paid out some line— wishing it would always stay thus soft and dry—and, measuring the distance with a false cast or two, laid down a spent gnat exactly a foot above his last swirl. Forgotten now were the hot miles, the mosquitoes, the ignominious chub. He took it with one great gulp, and shortly I could hear him kicking in the bed of wet alder leaves at the bottom of the creel.

Another, albeit larger, fish had meanwhile risen in the next pool, which lay at the very 'head of navigation,' for at its upper end the alders closed in solid phalanx. One bush, with its brown stem laved in the middle current, shook with a perpetual silent laughter, as if to mock at any fly that gods or men might cast one inch beyond its outermost leaf.

* * *

For the duration of a cigarette I sit on a rock midstream—and watch my trout rise under his guardian bush, while my rod and line hang drying on the alders of the sunny bank. Then—for prudence' sake—a little longer. That pool is too smooth up there. A breeze is stirring and may shortly ruffle it for an instant, and thus make more deadly that perfect cast I shall shortly lay upon its bosom.

It will come—a puff strong enough to shake a brown miller off the laughing alder, and cast it upon the pool.

Ready now! Coil up the dry line and stand midstream, rod in instant readiness. It's coming—a little premonitory shiver in that aspen on the hill lets me get out half a cast, and swish it gently back and forth, ready for the main puff to hit the pool. No more than half a line, mind you! The sun is high now, and any flicking shadow overhead would forewarn my hunker of his impending fate. Now! The last three yards shoot out, the fly falls gracefully at the feet of the laughing alder—he has it! I set hard to hold him out of the jungle beyond. He rushes downstream. In a few minutes he, too, is kicking in the creel.

I sit in happy meditation on my rock, pondering, while my line dries again, upon the ways of trout and men. How like fish we are: ready, nay eager, to seize upon whatever new thing some wind of circumstance shakes down upon the river of time! And how we rue our haste, finding the gilded morsel to contain a hook. Even so, I think there is some virtue in eagerness, whether its object prove true or false. How utterly dull would be a wholly prudent man, or trout, or world! Did I say a while ago that I waited 'for prudence' sake'? That was not so. The only prudence in fishermen is that designed to set the stage for taking yet another, and perhaps a longer, chance.

Time to be at it now—they will soon stop rising. I wade waist deep to head of navigation, poke my head insolently into the shaking alder, and look within. Jungle is right! A coal-black hole above, so canopied in greenness you could not wave a fern, much less a rod, above its rushing depths. And there, almost rubbing his ribs against the dark bank, a great trout rolls lazily over as he sucks down a passing bug.

Not a chance to stalk him, even with the lowly worm. But twenty yards above I see bright sunshine on the water—another opening. Fish a dry fly downstream? It cannot, but it must, be done.

I retreat and climb the bank. Neck deep in jewel-weed and nettles, I detour through the alder thicket to the opening above. With cat-like care not to roil his majesty's bath, I step in, and stand stock-still for five minutes to let things calm down. The while, I strip out, oil, dry, and coil upon my left hand thirty feet of line. I am that far above the portal to the jungle.

Now for the long chance! I blow upon my fly to give it one last fluff, lay it on the stream at my feet, and quickly pay out coil after coil. Then, just as the line straightens out and the fly is sucked into the jungle, I walk quickly downstream, straining my eyes into the dark vault to follow its fortunes. A fleeting glimpse or two as it passes a speck of sunlight shows it still rides clear. It rounds the bend. In no time—long before the roil of my walking has betrayed the ruse—it reaches the black pool. I hear, rather than see, the rush of the great fish; I set hard, and the battle is on.

No prudent man would risk a dollar's worth of fly and leader pulling a trout upstream through the giant toothbrush of alder stems comprising the bend of that creek. But, as I said, no prudent man is a fisherman. By and by, with much cautious unraveling, I got him up into open water, and finally aboard the creel.

I shall now confess to you that none of those three trout had to be beheaded, or folded double, to fit their casket. What was big was not the trout, but the chance. What was full was not my creel, but my memory. Like the whitethroats, I had forgotten it would ever again be aught but morning on the Fork.

Great Possessions

O NE HUNDRED and twenty acres, according to the County Clerk, is the extent of my worldly domain. But the County Clerk is a sleepy fellow, who never looks at his record books before nine o'clock. What they would show at daybreak is the question here at issue.

Books or no books, it is a fact, patent both to my dog and myself, that at daybreak I am the sole owner of all the acres I can walk over. It is not only boundaries that disappear, but also the thought of being bounded. Expanses unknown to deed or map are known to every dawn, and solitude, supposed no longer to exist in my county, extends on every hand as far as the dew can reach.

Like other great landowners, I have tenants. They are negligent about rents, but very punctilious about tenures. Indeed at every daybreak from April to July they proclaim their boundaries to each other, and so acknowledge, at least by inference, their fiefdom to me.

This daily ceremony, contrary to what you might suppose, begins with the utmost decorum. Who originally laid down its protocols I do not know. At 3:30 A.M., with such dignity as I can muster of a July morning, I step from my cabin door, bearing in either hand my emblems of sovereignty, a coffee pot and notebook. I seat myself on a bench, facing the white wake of the morning star. I set the pot beside me. I extract a cup from my shirt front, hoping none will notice its informal mode of transport. I get out my watch, pour coffee, and lay notebook on knee. This is the cue for the proclamations to begin.

At 3:35 the nearest field sparrow avows, in a clear tenor chant, that he holds the jackpine copse north to the riverbank, and south to the old wagon track. One by one all the other field sparrows within earshot recite their respective holdings. There are no disputes, at least at this hour, so I just listen, hoping inwardly that their womenfolk acquiesce in this happy accord over the *status quo ante.*

Before the field sparrows have quite gone the rounds, the

robin in the big elm warbles loudly his claim to the crotch where the icestorm tore off a limb, and all appurtenances pertaining thereto (meaning, in his case, all the angleworms in the not-very-spacious subjacent lawn).

The robin's insistent caroling awakens the oriole, who now tells the world of orioles that the pendant branch of the elm belongs to him, together with all fiber-bearing milkweed stalks near by, all loose strings in the garden, and the exclusive right to flash like a burst of fire from one of these to another.

My watch says 3:50. The indigo bunting on the hill asserts title to the dead oak limb left by the 1936 drought, and to divers near-by bugs and bushes. He does not claim, but I think he implies, the right to out-blue all bluebirds, and all spiderworts that have turned their faces to the dawn.

Next the wren—the one who discovered the knothole in the eave of the cabin—explodes into song. Half a dozen other wrens give voice, and now all is bedlam. Grosbeaks, thrashers, yellow warblers, bluebirds, vireos, towhees, cardinals—all are at it. My solemn list of performers, in their order and time of first song, hesitates, wavers, ceases, for my ear can no longer filter out priorities. Besides, the pot is empty and the sun is about to rise. I must inspect my domain before my title runs out.

We sally forth, the dog and I, at random. He has paid scant respect to all these vocal goings-on, for to him the evidence of tenantry is not song, but scent. Any illiterate bundle of feathers, he says, can make a noise in a tree. Now he is going to translate

for me the olfactory poems that who-knows-what silent creatures have written in the summer night. At the end of each poem sits the author—if we can find him. What we actually find is beyond predicting: a rabbit, suddenly yearning to be elsewhere; a woodcock, fluttering his disclaimer; a cock pheasant, indignant over wetting his feathers in the grass.

Once in a while we turn up a coon or mink, returning late from the night's foray. Sometimes we rout a heron from his unfinished fishing, or surprise a mother wood duck with her convoy of ducklings, headed full-steam for the shelter of the pickerelweeds. Sometimes we see deer sauntering back to the thickets, replete with alfalfa blooms, veronica, and wild lettuce. More often we see only the interweaving darkened lines that lazy hoofs have traced on the silken fabric of the dew.

I can feel the sun now. The bird-chorus has run out of breath. The far clank of cowbells bespeaks a herd ambling to pasture. A tractor roars warning that my neighbor is astir. The world has shrunk to those mean dimensions known to county clerks. We turn toward home, and breakfast.

Prairie Birthday

DURING EVERY week from April to September there are, on the average, ten wild plants coming into first bloom. In June as many as a dozen species may burst their buds on a single day. No man can heed all of these anniversaries; no man can ignore all of them. He who steps unseeing on May dandelions may be hauled up short by August ragweed pollen; he who ignores the ruddy haze of April elms may skid his car on the fallen corollas of June catalpas. Tell me of what plant-birthday a man takes notice, and I shall tell you a good deal about his vocation, his hobbies, his hay fever, and the general level of his ecological education.

* * *

Every July I watch eagerly a certain country graveyard that I pass in driving to and from my farm. It is time for a prairie birthday, and in one corner of this graveyard lives a surviving celebrant of that once important event.

It is an ordinary graveyard, bordered by the usual spruces,

and studded with the usual pink granite or white marble head-stones, each with the usual Sunday bouquet of red or pink geraniums. It is extraordinary only in being triangular instead of square, and in harboring, within the sharp angle of its fence, a pin-point remnant of the native prairie on which the grave-yard was established in the 1840's. Heretofore unreachable by scythe or mower, this yard-square relic of original Wisconsin gives birth, each July, to a man-high stalk of compass plant or cutleaf Silphium, spangled with saucer-sized yellow blooms resembling sunflowers. It is the sole remnant of this plant along this highway, and perhaps the sole remnant in the western half of our county. What a thousand acres of Silphiums looked like when they tickled the bellies of the buffalo is a question never again to be answered, and perhaps not even asked.

This year I found the Silphium in first bloom on 24 July, a week later than usual; during the last six years the average date was 15 July.

When I passed the graveyard again on 3 August, the fence had been removed by a road crew, and the Silphium cut. It is easy now to predict the future; for a few years my Silphium will try in vain to rise above the mowing machine, and then it will die. With it will die the prairie epoch.

The Highway Department says that 100,000 cars pass yearly over this route during the three summer months when the Sil-phium is in bloom. In them must ride at least 100,000 people who have 'taken' what is called history, and perhaps 25,000 who have 'taken' what is called botany. Yet I doubt whether a dozen have seen the Silphium, and of these hardly one will notice its demise. If I were to tell a preacher of the adjoining church that the road crew has been burning history books in his cemetery, under the guise of mowing weeds, he would be amazed and uncomprehending. How could a weed be a book?

This is one little episode in the funeral of the native flora, which in turn is one episode in the funeral of the floras of the world. Mechanized man, oblivious of floras, is proud of his progress in cleaning up the landscape on which, willy-nilly, he must live out his days. It might be wise to prohibit at once all teaching of real botany and real history, lest some future citizen suffer qualms about the floristic price of his good life.

* * *

Thus it comes to pass that farm neighborhoods are good in pro-portion to the poverty of their floras. My own farm was selected for its lack of goodness and its lack of highway; indeed my whole neighborhood lies in a backwash of the River Progress. My road is the original wagon track of the pioneers, innocent of grades or gravel, brushings or bulldozers. My neighbors bring a sigh to the County Agent. Their fencerows go unshaven for years on end. Their marshes are neither dyked nor drained. As between going fishing and going forward, they are prone to prefer fishing. Thus on week ends my floristic standard of living is that of the backwoods, while on week days I subsist as best I can on the flora of the university farms, the university campus, and the adjoining suburbs. For a decade I have kept, for pastime, a record of the wild plant species in first bloom on these two diverse areas:

Species First Blooming in	Suburb and Campus	Backward Farm
April	14	26
May	29	59
June	43	70
July	25	56
August	9	14
September	0	1
Total visual diet	120	226

It is apparent that the backward farmer's eye is nearly twice as well fed as the eye of the university student or businessman. Of course neither sees his flora as yet, so we are confronted by the two alternatives already mentioned: either insure the continued blindness of the populace, or examine the question whether we cannot have both progress and plants.

The shrinkage in the flora is due to a combination of clean-farming, woodlot grazing, and good roads. Each of these neces-sary changes of course requires a larger reduction in the acreage available for wild plants, but none of them requires, or benefits by, the erasure of species from whole farms, townships, or coun-ties. There are idle spots on every farm, and every highway is bordered by an idle strip as long as it is; keep cow, plow, and mower out of these idle spots, and the full native flora, plus dozens of interesting stowaways from foreign parts, could be part of the normal environment of every citizen.

The outstanding conservator of the prairie flora, ironically enough, knows little and cares less about such frivolities: it is the railroad with its fenced right-of-way. Many of these railroad fences were erected before the prairie had been plowed. Within these linear reservations, oblivious of cinders, soot, and annual clean-up fires, the prairie flora still splashes its calendar of colors, from pink shooting-star in May to blue aster in October. I have long wished to confront some hard-boiled railway president with the physical evidence of his soft-heartedness. I have not done so because I haven't met one.

The railroads of course use flame-throwers and chemical sprays to clear the track of weeds, but the cost of such necessary clearance is still too high to extend it much beyond the actual rails. Perhaps further improvements are in the offing.

The erasure of a human subspecies is largely painless—to us— if we know little enough about it. A dead Chinaman is of little import to us whose awareness of things Chinese is bounded by

an occasional dish of chow mein. We grieve only for what we know. The erasure of Silphium from western Dane County is no cause for grief if one knows it only as a name in a botany book.

Silphium first became a personality to me when I tried to dig one up to move to my farm. It was like digging an oak sapling. After half an hour of hot grimy labor the root was still enlarging, like a great vertical sweet-potato. As far as I know, that Silphium root went clear through to bedrock. I got no Silphium, but I learned by what elaborate underground stratagems it contrives to weather the prairie drouths.

I next planted Silphium seeds, which are large, meaty, and taste like sunflower seeds. They came up promptly, but after five years of waiting the seedlings are still juvenile, and have not yet borne a flower-stalk. Perhaps it takes a decade for a Silphium to reach flowering age; how old, then, was my pet plant in the cemetery? It may have been older than the oldest tombstone, which is dated 1850. Perhaps it watched the fugitive Black Hawk retreat from the Madison lakes to the Wisconsin River; it stood on the route of that famous march. Certainly it saw the successive funerals of the local pioneers as they retired, one by one, to their repose beneath the bluestem.

I once saw a power shovel, while digging a roadside ditch, sever the 'sweet-potato' root of a Silphium plant. The root soon sprouted new leaves, and eventually it again produced a flower stalk. This explains why this plant, which never invades new ground, is nevertheless sometimes seen on recently graded roadsides. Once established, it apparently withstands almost any kind of mutilation except continued grazing, mowing, or plowing.

Why does Silphium disappear from grazed areas? I once saw a farmer turn his cows into a virgin prairie meadow previously used only sporadically for mowing wild hay. The cows cropped the Silphium to the ground before any other plant was visibly eaten at all. One can imagine that the buffalo once had the same preference for Silphium, but he brooked no fences to confine his nibblings all summer long to one meadow. In short, the buffalo's pasturing was discontinuous, and therefore tolerable to Silphium.

It is a kind providence that has withheld a sense of history from the thousands of species of plants and animals that have exterminated each other to build the present world. The same kind providence now withholds it from us. Few grieved when the last buffalo left Wisconsin, and few will grieve when the last Silphium follows him to the lush prairies of the never-never land.

The Green Pasture

SOME PAINTINGS become famous because, being durable, they are viewed by successive generations, in each of which are likely to be found a few appreciative eyes.

I know a painting so evanescent that it is seldom viewed at all, except by some wandering deer. It is a river who wields the brush, and it is the same river who, before I can bring my friends to view his work, erases it forever from human view. After that it exists only in my mind's eye.

Like other artists, my river is temperamental; there is no predicting when the mood to paint will come upon him, or how long it will last. But in midsummer, when the great white fleets cruise the sky for day after flawless day, it is worth strolling down to the sandbars just to see whether he has been at work.

The work begins with a broad ribbon of silt brushed thinly on the sand of a receding shore. As this dries slowly in the sun, goldfinches bathe in its pools, and deer, herons, killdeers, raccoons, and turtles cover it with a lacework of tracks. There is no telling, at this stage, whether anything further will happen.

But when I see the silt ribbon turning green with Eleocharis, I watch closely thereafter, for this is the sign that the river is in a painting mood. Almost overnight the Eleocharis becomes a thick turf, so lush and so dense that the meadow mice from the adjoining upland cannot resist the temptation. They move *en masse* to the green pasture, and apparently spend the nights rubbing their ribs in its velvety depths. A maze of neatly tended mouse-trails bespeaks their enthusiasm. The deer walk up and down in it, apparently just for the pleasure of feeling it underfoot. Even a stay-at-home mole has tunneled his way across the dry bar to the Eleocharis ribbon, where he can heave and hump the verdant sod to his heart's content.

At this stage the seedlings of plants too numerous to count and too young to recognize spring to life from the damp warm sand under the green ribbon.

To view the painting, give the river three more weeks of solitude, and then visit the bar on some bright morning just after the sun has melted the daybreak fog. The artist has now laid his colors, and sprayed them with dew. The Eleocharis sod, greener than ever, is now spangled with blue mimulus, pink dragon-head, and the milk-white blooms of Sagittaria. Here and there a cardinal flower thrusts a red spear skyward. At the head of the bar, purple ironweeds and pale pink joe-pyes stand tall against the wall of willows. And if you have come quietly and humbly, as you should to any spot that can be beautiful only once, you may surprise a fox-red deer, standing knee-high in the garden of his delight.

Do not return for a second view of the green pasture, for there is none. Either falling water has dried it out, or rising water has scoured the bar to its original austerity of clean sand. But in your mind you may hang up your picture, and hope that in some other summer the mood to paint may come upon the river.

The Choral Copse

B Y SEPTEMBER, the day breaks with little help from birds. A song sparrow may give a single half-hearted song, a wood-cock may twitter overhead *en route* to his daytime thicket, a barred owl may terminate the night's argument with one last wavering call, but few other birds have anything to say or sing about.

It is on some, but not all, of these misty autumn daybreaks that one may hear the chorus of the quail. The silence is suddenly broken by a dozen contralto voices, no longer able to restrain their praise of the day to come. After a brief minute or two, the music closes as suddenly as it began.

There is a peculiar virtue in the music of elusive birds. Songsters that sing from top-most boughs are easily seen and as easily forgotten; they have the mediocrity of the obvious. What one remembers is the invisible hermit thrush pouring silver chords from impenetrable shadows; the soaring crane trumpeting from behind a cloud; the prairie chicken booming from the mists of nowhere; the quail's Ave Maria in the hush of dawn. No naturalist has even seen the choral act, for the covey is still on its invisible roost in the grass, and any attempt to approach automatically induces silence.

In June it is completely predictable that the robin will give voice when the light intensity reaches 0.01 candle power, and that the bedlam of other singers will follow in predictable sequence. In autumn, on the other hand, the robin is silent, and it is quite unpredictable whether the covey-chorus will occur at all. The disappointment I feel on these mornings of silence perhaps shows that things hoped for have a higher value than things assured. The hope of hearing quail is worth half a dozen risings-in-the-dark.

My farm always has one or more coveys in autumn, but the daybreak chorus is usually distant. I think this is because the coveys prefer to roost as far as possible from the dog, whose interest in quail is even more ardent than my own. One October dawn, however, as I sat sipping coffee by the outdoor fire, a chorus burst into song hardly a stone's throw away. They had roosted under a white-pine copse, possibly to stay dry during the heavy dews.

We felt honored by this daybreak hymn sung almost at our doorstep. Somehow the blue autumnal needles on those pines became thenceforth bluer, and the red carpet of dewberry under those pines became even redder.

Smoky Gold

THERE ARE two kinds of hunting: ordinary hunting, and ruffed-grouse hunting.

There are two places to hunt grouse: ordinary places, and Adams County.

There are two times to hunt in Adams: ordinary times, and when the tamaracks are smoky gold. This is written for those luckless ones who have never stood, gun empty and mouth agape, to watch the golden needles come sifting down, while the feathery rocket that knocked them off sails unscathed into the jackpines.

The tamaracks change from green to yellow when the first frosts have brought woodcock, fox sparrows, and juncos out of the north. Troops of robins are stripping the last white berries from the dogwood thickets, leaving the empty stems as a pink haze against the hill. The creekside alders have shed their leaves, exposing here and there an eyeful of holly. Brambles are aglow, lighting your footsteps grouseward.

The dog knows what is grouseward better than you do. You will do well to follow him closely, reading from the cock of his ears the story the breeze is telling. When at last he stops stock-still, and says with a sideward glance, 'Well, get ready,' the question is, ready for what? A twittering woodcock, or the rising roar of a grouse, or perhaps only a rabbit? In this moment of uncertainty is condensed much of the virtue of grouse hunting. He who must know what to get ready for should go and hunt pheasants.

*   *   *

Hunts differ in flavor, but the reasons are subtle. The sweetest hunts are stolen. To steal a hunt, either go far into the wilderness where no one has been, or else find some undiscovered place under everybody's nose.

Few hunters know that grouse exist in Adams County, for when they drive through it, they see only a waste of jackpines and scrub oaks. This is because the highway intersects a series of west-running creeks, each of which heads in a swamp, but drops to the river through dry sand-barrens. Naturally the northbound highway intersects these swampless barrens, but just above the highway, and behind the screen of dry scrub, every creeklet expands into a broad ribbon of swamp, a sure haven for grouse.

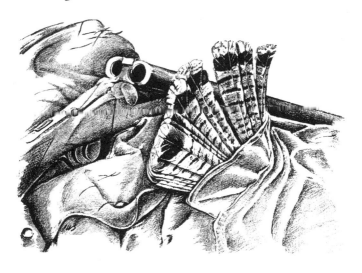

Here, come October, I sit in the solitude of my tamaracks and hear the hunters' cars roaring up the highway, hell-bent for the crowded counties to the north. I chuckle as I picture their dancing speedometers, their strained faces, their eager eyes glued on the northward horizon. At the noise of their passing, a cock grouse drums his defiance. My dog grins as we note his direction. That fellow, we agree, needs some exercise; we shall look him up presently.

The tamaracks grow not only in the swamp, but at the foot of the bordering upland, where springs break forth. Each spring has become choked with moss, which forms a boggy terrace. I call these terraces the hanging gardens, for out of their sodden muck the fringed gentians have lifted blue jewels. Such an October gentian, dusted with tamarack gold, is worth a full stop and a long look, even when the dog signals grouse ahead.

Between each hanging garden and the creekside is a moss-paved deer trail, handy for the hunter to follow, and for the flushed grouse to cross—in a split second. The question is whether the bird and the gun agree on how a second should be split. If they do not, the next deer that passes finds a pair of empty shells to sniff at, but no feathers.

Higher up the creeklet I encounter an abandoned farm. I try to read, from the age of the young jackpines marching across an old field, how long ago the luckless farmer found out that sand plains were meant to grow solitude, not corn. Jackpines tell tall tales to the unwary, for they put on several whorls of branches each year, instead of only one. I find a better chronometer in an elm seedling that now blocks the barn door. Its rings date back to the drouth of 1930. Since that year no man has carried milk out of this barn.

I wonder what this family thought about when their mortgage finally outgrew their crops, and thus gave the signal for their eviction. Many thoughts, like flying grouse, leave no trace of their passing, but some leave clues that outlast the decades. He who, in some unforgotten April, planted this lilac must have thought pleasantly of blooms for all the Aprils to come. She who used this washboard, its corrugations worn thin with many Mondays, may have wished for a cessation of all Mondays, and soon.

Musing on such questions, I become aware of the dog down by the spring, pointing patiently these many minutes. I walk up, apologizing for my inattention. Up twitters a woodcock, batlike, his salmon breast soaked in October sun. Thus goes the hunt.

It's hard on such a day to keep one's mind on grouse, for there are many distractions. I cross a buck track in the sand, and follow in idle curiosity. The track leads straight from one Jersey tea bush to another, with nipped twigs showing why.

This reminds me of my own lunch, but before I get it pulled out of my game pocket, I see a circling hawk, high skyward, needing identification. I wait till he banks and shows his red tail.

I reach again for the lunch, but my eye catches a peeled popple. Here a buck has rubbed off his itchy velvet. How long ago? The exposed wood is already brown; I conclude that horns must therefore be clean by now.

I reach again for the lunch, but am interrupted by an excited yawp from the dog, and a crash of bushes in the swamp. Out springs a buck, flag aloft, horns shining, his coat a sleek blue. Yes, the popple told the truth.

This time I get the lunch all the way out and sit down to eat. A chickadee watches me, and grows confidential about *his* lunch. He doesn't say what he ate, perhaps it was cool turgid ant-eggs, or some other avian equivalent of cold roast grouse.

Lunch over, I regard a phalanx of young tamaracks, their golden lances thrusting skyward. Under each the needles of yesterday fall to earth building a blanket of smoky gold; at the tip of each the bud of tomorrow, preformed, poised, awaits another spring.

Too Early

GETTING UP too early is a vice habitual in horned owls, stars, geese, and freight trains. Some hunters acquire it from geese, and some coffee pots from hunters. It is strange that of all the multitude of creatures who must rise in the morning at some time, only these few should have discovered the most pleasant and least useful time for doing it.

Orion must have been the original mentor of the too-early company, for it is he who signals for too-early rising. It is time when Orion has passed west of the zenith about as far as one should lead a teal.

Early risers feel at ease with each other, perhaps because, unlike those who sleep late, they are given to understatement of their own achievements. Orion, the most widely traveled, says literally nothing. The coffee pot, from its first soft gurgle, underclaims the virtues of what simmers within. The owl, in his trisyllabic commentary, plays down the story of the night's murders. The goose on the bar, rising briefly to a point of order in some inaudible anserine debate, lets fall no hint that he speaks with the authority of all the far hills and the sea.

The freight, I admit, is hardly reticent about his own importance, yet even he has a kind of modesty: his eye is single to his own noisy business, and he never comes roaring into somebody else's camp. I feel a deep security in this single-mindedness of freight trains.

* * *

To arrive too early in the marsh is an adventure in pure listening; the ear roams at will among the noises of the night, without let or hindrance from hand or eye. When you hear a mallard being audibly enthusiastic about his soup, you are free to picture a score guzzling among the duckweeds. When one widgeon squeals, you may postulate a squadron without fear of visual contradiction. And when a flock of bluebills, pitching pondward, tears the dark silk of heaven in one long rending nose-dive, you catch your breath at the sound, but there is nothing to see except stars. This same performance, in daytime, would have to be looked at, shot at, missed, and then hurriedly fitted with an alibi. Nor could daylight add anything to your mind's eye picture of quivering wings, ripping the firmament neatly into halves.

The hour of listening ends when the fowl depart on muted wings for wider safer waters, each flock a blur against the graying east.

Like many another treaty of restraint, the pre-dawn pact lasts only as long as darkness humbles the arrogant. It would seem as if the sun were responsible for the daily retreat of reticence from the world. At any rate, by the time the mists are white over the lowlands, every rooster is bragging *ad lib*, and every corn shock is pretending to be twice as tall as any corn that ever grew. By sun-up every squirrel is exaggerating some fancied indignity to his person, and every jay proclaiming with false emotion about suppositious dangers to society, at this very moment discovered by him. Distant crows are berating a hypothetical owl, just to tell the world how vigilant crows are, and a pheasant cock, musing perhaps on his philanderings of bygone days, beats the air with his wings and tells the world in raucous warning that he owns this marsh and all the hens in it.

Nor are all these illusions of grandeur confined to the birds and beasts. By breakfast time come the honks, horns, shouts, and whistles of the awakened farmyard, and finally, at evening, the drone of an untended radio. Then everybody goes to bed to relearn the lessons of the night.

Red Lanterns

O NE WAY to hunt partridge is to make a plan, based on logic and probabilities, of the terrain to be hunted. This will take you over the ground where the birds ought to be.

Another way is to wander, quite aimlessly, from one red lantern to another. This will likely take you where the birds actually are. The lanterns are blackberry leaves, red in October sun.

Red lanterns have lighted my way on many a pleasant hunt in many a region, but I think that blackberries must first have learned how to glow in the sand counties of central Wisconsin. Along the little boggy streams of these friendly wastes, called poor by those whose own lights barely flicker, the blackberries burn richly red on every sunny day from first frost to the last day of the season. Every woodcock and every partridge has his private solarium under these briars. Most hunters, not knowing this, wear themselves out in the briarless scrub, and, returning home birdless, leave the rest of us in peace.

By 'us' I mean the birds, the stream, the dog, and myself. The stream is a lazy one; he winds through the alders as if he would rather stay here than reach the river. So would I. Every one of his hairpin hesitations means that much more stream-bank where hillside briars adjoin dank beds of frozen ferns and jewelweeds on the boggy bottom. No partridge can long absent himself from such a place, nor can I. Partridge hunting, then, is a creekside stroll, upwind, from one briar patch to another.

The dog, when he approaches the briars, looks around to make sure I am within gunshot. Reassured, he advances with stealthy caution, his wet nose screening a hundred scents for that one scent, the potential presence of which gives life and meaning to the whole landscape. He is the prospector of the air, perpetually searching its strata for olfactory gold. Partridge scent is the gold standard that relates his world to mine.

My dog, by the way, thinks I have much to learn about partridges, and, being a professional naturalist, I agree. He persists in tutoring me, with the calm patience of a professor of logic, in the art of drawing deductions from an educated nose. I delight in seeing him deduce a conclusion, in the form of a point, from data that are obvious to him, but speculative to my unaided eye. Perhaps he hopes his dull pupil will one day learn to smell.

Like other dull pupils, I know when the professor is right, even though I do not know why. I check my gun and walk in. Like any good professor, the dog never laughs when I miss, which is often. He gives me just one look, and proceeds up the stream in quest of another grouse.

Following one of these banks, one walks astride two landscapes, the hillside one hunts from, and the bottom the dog hunts in. There is a special charm in treading soft dry carpets of Lycopodium to flush birds out of the bog, and the first test of a partridge dog is his willingness to do the wet work while you parallel him on the dry bank.

A special problem arises where the belt of alders widens, and the dog disappears from view. Hurry at once to a knoll or point, where you stand stock-still, straining eye and ear to follow the dog. A sudden scattering of whitethroats may reveal his whereabouts. Again you may hear him breaking a twig, or splashing in a wet spot, or plopping into the creek. But when all sound ceases, be ready for instant action, for he is likely on point. Listen now for the premonitory clucks a frightened partridge gives just before flushing. Then follows the hurtling bird, or perhaps two of them, or I have known as many as six, clucking and flushing one by one, each sailing high for his own destination in the uplands. Whether one passes within gunshot is of course a matter of chance, and you can compute the chance if you have time: 360 degrees divided by 30, or whatever segment of the circle your gun covers. Divide again by 3 or 4, which is your chance of missing, and you have the probability of actual feathers in the hunting coat.

The second test of a good partridge dog is whether he reports for orders after such an episode. Sit down and talk it over with him while he pants. Then look for the next red lantern, and proceed with the hunt.

The October breeze brings my dog many scents other than grouse, each of which may lead to its own peculiar episode. When he points with a certain humorous expression of the ears, I know he has found a bedded rabbit. Once a dead-serious point yielded no bird, but still the dog stood frozen; in a tuft of sedge under his very nose was a fat sleeping coon, getting his share of October sun. At least once on each hunt the dog bays a skunk, usually in some denser-than-ordinary thicket of blackberries. Once the dog pointed in midstream: a whir of wings upriver, followed by three musical cries, told me he had interrupted a wood duck's dinner. Not infrequently he finds jacksnipe in heavily pastured alders, and lastly he may put out a deer, bedded for the day on a high streambank flanked by alder bog. Has the deer a poetical weakness for singing waters, or a practical liking for a bed that cannot be approached without making a noise? Judging by the indignant flick of his great white flag it might be either, or both.

Almost anything may happen between one red lantern and another.

*   *   *

At sunset on the last day of the grouse season, every blackberry blows out his light. I do not understand how a mere bush can thus be infallibly informed about the Wisconsin statutes, nor have I ever gone back next day to find out. For the ensuing eleven months the lanterns glow only in recollection. I some-times think that the other months were constituted mainly as a fitting interlude between Octobers, and I suspect that dogs, and perhaps grouse, share the same view.

If I Were the Wind

T HE WIND that makes music in November corn is in a hurry.
The stalks hum, the loose husks whisk skyward in half-
playful swirls, and the wind hurries on.

In the marsh, long windy waves surge across the grassy
sloughs, beat against the far willows. A tree tries to argue, bare
limbs waving, but there is no detaining the wind.

On the sandbar there is only wind, and the river sliding seaward. Every wisp of grass is drawing circles on the sand. I wander over the bar to a driftwood log, where I sit and listen to the
universal roar, and to the tinkle of wavelets on the shore. The
river is lifeless: not a duck, heron, marsh-hawk, or gull but has
sought refuge from wind.

*   *   *

Out of the clouds I hear a faint bark, as of a far-away dog. It is
strange how the world cocks its ears at that sound, wondering.
Soon it is louder: the honk of geese, invisible, but coming on.

The flock emerges from the low clouds, a tattered banner of

birds, dipping and rising, blown up and blown down, blown together and blown apart, but advancing, the wind wrestling lovingly with each winnowing wing. When the flock is a blur in the far sky I hear the last honk, sounding taps for summer.

*   *   *

It is warm behind the driftwood now, for the wind has gone with the geese. So would I—if I were the wind.

Axe-in-Hand

THE LORD giveth, and the Lord taketh away, but He is no longer the only one to do so. When some remote ancestor of ours invented the shovel, he became a giver: he could plant a tree. And when the axe was invented, he became a taker: he could chop it down. Whoever owns land has thus assumed, whether he knows it or not, the divine functions of creating and destroying plants.

Other ancestors, less remote, have since invented other tools, but each of these, upon close scrutiny, proves to be either an elaboration of, or an accessory to, the original pair of basic implements. We classify ourselves into vocations, each of which either wields some particular tool, or sells it, or repairs it, or sharpens it, or dispenses advice on how to do so; by such division of labors we avoid responsibility for the misuse of any tool save our own. But there is one vocation—philosophy—which knows that all men, by what they think about and wish for, in effect wield all tools. It knows that men thus determine, by their manner of thinking and wishing, whether it is worth while to wield any.

* * *

November is, for many reasons, the month for the axe. It is warm enough to grind an axe without freezing, but cold enough to fell a tree in comfort. The leaves are off the hardwoods, so that one can see just how the branches intertwine, and what growth occurred last summer. Without this clear view of treetops, one cannot be sure which tree, if any, needs felling for the good of the land.

I have read many definitions of what is a conservationist, and written not a few myself, but I suspect that the best one is written not with a pen, but with an axe. It is a matter of what a man thinks about while chopping, or while deciding what to chop. A conservationist is one who is humbly aware that with each stroke he is writing his signature on the face of his land. Signatures of course differ, whether written with axe or pen, and this is as it should be.

I find it disconcerting to analyze, *ex post facto*, the reasons

63

behind my own axe-in-hand decisions. I find, first of all, that not all trees are created free and equal. Where a white pine and a red birch are crowding each other, I have an *a priori* bias; I always cut the birch to favor the pine. Why?

Well, first of all, I planted the pine with my shovel, whereas the birch crawled in under the fence and planted itself. My bias is thus to some extent paternal, but this cannot be the whole story, for if the pine were a natural seedling like the birch, I would value it even more. So I must dig deeper for the logic, if any, behind my bias.

The birch is an abundant tree in my township and becoming more so, whereas pine is scarce and becoming scarcer; perhaps my bias is for the underdog. But what would I do if my farm were further north, where pine is abundant and red birch is scarce? I confess I don't know. My farm is here.

The pine will live for a century, the birch for half that; do I fear that my signature will fade? My neighbors have planted no pines but all have many birches; am I snobbish about having a woodlot of distinction? The pine stays green all winter, the birch punches the clock in October; do I favor the tree that, like myself, braves the winter wind? The pine will shelter a grouse but the birch will feed him; do I consider bed more important than board? The pine will ultimately bring ten dollars a thousand, the birch two dollars; have I an eye on the bank? All of these possible reasons for my bias seem to carry some weight, but none of them carries very much.

So I try again, and here perhaps is something; under this pine will ultimately grow a trailing arbutus, an Indian pipe, a pyrola, or a twin flower, whereas under the birch a bottle gentian is about the best to be hoped for. In this pine a pileated woodpecker will ultimately chisel out a nest; in the birch a hairy will have to suffice. In this pine the wind will sing for me in April, at which time the birch is only rattling naked twigs. These possible reasons for my bias carry weight, but why? Does the pine stimulate my imagination and my hopes more deeply than the birch does? If so, is the difference in the trees, or in me?

The only conclusion I have ever reached is that I love all trees, but I am in love with pines.

As I said, November is the month for the axe, and, as in other love affairs, there is skill in the exercise of bias. If the birch stands south of the pine, and is taller, it will shade the pine's leader in the spring, and thus discourage the pine weevil from laying her eggs there. Birch competition is a minor affliction compared with this weevil, whose progeny kill the pine's leader and thus deform the tree. It is interesting to meditate that this insect's preference for squatting in the sun determines not only her own continuity as a species, but also the future figure of my pine, and my own success as a wielder of axe and shovel.

Again, if a drouthy summer follows my removal of the birch's shade, the hotter soil may offset the lesser competition for water, and my pine be none the better for my bias.

Lastly, if the birch's limbs rub the pine's terminal buds during a wind, the pine will surely be deformed, and the birch must either be removed regardless of other considerations, or else it must be pruned of limbs each winter to a height greater than the pine's prospective summer growth.

Such are the pros and cons the wielder of an axe must foresee, compare, and decide upon with the calm assurance that his bias will, on the average, prove to be something more than good intentions.

The wielder of an axe has as many biases as there are species of trees on his farm. In the course of the years he imputes to each species, from his responses to their beauty or utility, and their responses to his labors for or against them, a series of attributes that constitute a character. I am amazed to learn what diverse characters different men impute to one and the same tree.

Thus to me the aspen is in good repute because he glorifies October and he feeds my grouse in winter, but to some of my neighbors he is a mere weed, perhaps because he sprouted so vigorously in the stump lots their grandfathers were attempting to clear. (I cannot sneer at this, for I find myself disliking the elms whose resproutings threaten my pines.)

Again, the tamarack is to me a favorite second only to white pine, perhaps because he is nearly extinct in my township (underdog bias), or because he sprinkles gold on October grouse (gunpowder bias), or because he sours the soil and enables it to grow the loveliest of our orchids, the showy lady's-slipper. On the other hand, foresters have excommunicated the tamarack because he grows too slowly to pay compound interest. In order to clinch this dispute, they also mention that he succumbs periodically to epizootics of saw-fly, but this is fifty years hence for my tamaracks, so I shall let my grandson worry about it. Meanwhile my tamaracks are growing so lustily that my spirits soar with them, skyward.

To me an ancient cottonwood is the greatest of trees because in his youth he shaded the buffalo and wore a halo of pigeons, and I like a young cottonwood because he may some day become ancient. But the farmer's wife (and hence the farmer) despises all cottonwoods because in June the female tree clogs the screens with cotton. The modern dogma is comfort at any cost.

I find my biases more numerous than those of my neighbors because I have individual likings for many species that they lump under one aspersive category: brush. Thus I like the wahoo, partly because deer, rabbits, and mice are so avid to eat his square twigs and green bark and partly because his cerise berries glow so warmly against November snow. I like the red dogwood because he feeds October robins, and the prickly ash because my woodcock take their daily sunbath under the shelter of his thorns. I like the hazel because his October purple feeds my eye, and because his November catkins feed my deer and grouse. I like the bittersweet because my father did, and because the deer, on the 1st of July of each year, begin suddenly to eat the new leaves, and I have learned to predict this event to my guests. I cannot dislike a plant that enables me, a mere professor, to blossom forth annually as a successful seer and prophet.

It is evident that our plant biases are in part traditional. If your grandfather liked hickory nuts, you will like the hickory tree because your father told you to. If, on the other hand, your grandfather burned a log carrying a poison ivy vine and recklessly stood in the smoke, you will dislike the species, no matter with what crimson glories it warms your eyes each fall.

It is also evident that our plant biases reflect not only vocations but avocations, with a delicate allocation of priority as between industry and indolence. The farmer who would rather hunt grouse than milk cows will not dislike hawthorn, no matter if it does invade his pasture. The coon-hunter will not dislike basswood, and I know of quail hunters who bear no grudge against ragweed, despite their annual bout with hayfever. Our biases are indeed a sensitive index to our affections, our tastes, our loyalties, our generosities, and our manner of wasting weekends.

Be that as it may, I am content to waste mine, in November, with axe in hand.

A Mighty Fortress

E VERY FARM woodland, in addition to yielding lumber, fuel, and posts, should provide its owner a liberal education. This crop of wisdom never fails, but it is not always harvested. I here record some of the many lessons I have learned in my own woods.

*   *   *

Soon after I bought the woods a decade ago, I realized that I had bought almost as many tree diseases as I had trees. My woodlot is riddled by all the ailments wood is heir to. I began to wish that Noah, when he loaded up the Ark, had left the tree diseases behind. But it soon became clear that these same diseases made my woodlot a mighty fortress, unequaled in the whole county.

My woods is headquarters for a family of coons; few of my neighbors have any. One Sunday in November, after a new snow, I learned why. The fresh track of a coon-hunter and his hound led up to a half-uprooted maple, under which one of my coons had taken refuge. The frozen snarl of roots and earth was too rocky to chop and too tough to dig; the holes under the roots were too numerous to smoke out. The hunter had quit coonless because a fungus disease had weakened the roots of the maple. The tree, half tipped over by a storm, offers an impregnable fortress for coondom. Without this 'bombproof' shelter, my seed stock of coons would be cleaned out by hunters each year.

My woods houses a dozen ruffed grouse, but during periods of deep snow my grouse shift to my neighbor's woods, where there is better cover. However, I always retain as many grouse as I have oaks wind-thrown by summer storms. These summer windfalls keep their dried leaves, and during snows each such windfall harbors a grouse. The droppings show that each grouse roosts, feeds, and loafs for the duration of the storm within the narrow confines of his leafy camouflage, safe from wind, owl, fox, and hunter. The cured oak leaves not only serve as cover, but, for some curious reason, are relished as food by the grouse.

These oak windfalls are, of course, diseased trees. Without

CHARLES W.
SCHWARTZ

disease, few oaks would break off, and hence few grouse would have down tops to hide in.

Diseased oaks also provide another apparently delectable grouse food: oak galls. A gall is a diseased growth of new twigs that have been stung by a gall-wasp while tender and succulent. In October my grouse are often stuffed with oak galls.

Each year the wild bees load up one of my hollow oaks with combs, and each year trespassing honey-hunters harvest the honey before I do. This is partly because they are more skillful than I am in 'lining up' the bee trees, and partly because they use nets, and hence are able to work before the bees become dormant in fall. But for heart-rots, there would be no hollow oaks to furnish wild bees with oaken hives.

During high years of the cycle, there is a plague of rabbits in my woods. They eat the bark and twigs off almost every kind of tree or bush I am trying to encourage, and ignore almost every kind I should like to have less of. (When the rabbit-hunter plants himself a grove of pines or an orchard, the rabbit somehow ceases to be a game animal and becomes a pest instead.)

The rabbit, despite his omnivorous appetite, is an epicure in some respects. He always prefers a hand-planted pine, maple, apple, or wahoo to a wild one. He also insists that certain salads be preconditioned before he deigns to eat them. Thus he spurns red dogwood until it is attacked by oyster-shell scale, after which the bark becomes a delicacy, to be eagerly devoured by all the rabbits in the neighborhood.

A flock of a dozen chickadees spends the year in my woods. In winter, when we are harvesting diseased or dead trees for our fuel wood, the ring of the axe is dinner gong for the chickadee tribe. They hang in the offing waiting for the tree to fall, offering pert commentary on the slowness of our labor. When the tree at last is down, and the wedges begin to open up its contents, the chickadees draw up their white napkins and fall to. Every slab of dead bark is, to them, a treasury of eggs, larvae, and cocoons. For them every ant-tunneled heartwood bulges with milk and honey. We often stand a fresh split against a nearby tree just to see the greedy chicks mop up the ant-eggs. It lightens our labor to know that they, as well as we, derive aid and comfort from the fragrant riches of newly split oak.

But for diseases and insect pests, there would likely be no

food in these trees, and hence no chickadees to add cheer to my woods in winter.

Many other kinds of wildlife depend on tree diseases. My pileated woodpeckers chisel living pines, to extract fat grubs from the diseased heartwood. My barred owls find surcease from crows and jays in the hollow heart of an old basswood; but for this diseased tree their sundown serenade would probably be silenced. My wood ducks nest in hollow trees; every June brings its brood of downy ducklings to my woodland slough. All squirrels depend, for permanent dens, on a delicately balanced equilibrium between a rotting cavity and the scar tissue with which the tree attempts to close the wound. The squirrels referee the contest by gnawing out the scar tissue when it begins unduly to shrink the amplitude of their front door.

The real jewel of my disease-ridden woodlot is the prothonotary warbler. He nests in an old woodpecker hole, or other small cavity, in a dead snag overhanging water. The flash of his gold-and-blue plumage amid the dank decay of the June woods is in itself proof that dead trees are transmuted into living animals, and vice versa. When you doubt the wisdom of this arrangement, take a look at the prothonotary.

Home Range

THE WILD things that live on my farm are reluctant to tell
me, in so many words, how much of my township is included within their daily or nightly beat. I am curious about
this, for it gives me the ratio between the size of their universe
and the size of mine, and it conveniently begs the much more
important question, who is the more thoroughly acquainted
with the world in which he lives?

Like people, my animals frequently disclose by their actions
what they decline to divulge in words. It is difficult to predict
when and how one of these disclosures will come to light.

*   *   *

The dog, being no hand with an axe, is free to hunt while the
rest of us are making wood. A sudden *yip-yip-yip* gives us notice that a rabbit, flushed from his bed in the grass, is headed
elsewhere in a hurry. He makes a beeline for a woodpile a quarter-mile distant, where he ducks between two corded stacks, a
safe gunshot ahead of his pursuer. The dog, after leaving a few
symbolic toothmarks on the hard oak, gives it up and resumes
his search for some less canny cottontail, and we resume our
chopping.

This little episode tells me that this rabbit is familiar with all
of the ground between his bed in the meadow and his blitz-
cellar under the woodpile. How else the beeline? This rabbit's
home range is at least a quarter-mile in extent.

The chickadees that visit our feeding station are trapped and
banded each winter. Some of our neighbors also feed chickadees, but none band them. By noticing the furthest points from
my feeder at which banded chickadees are seen, we have learned
that the home range of our flock is half a mile across in winter,
but that it includes only areas protected from wind.

In summer, when the flock has dispersed for nesting, banded
birds are seen at greater distances, often mated with unbanded
birds. At this season the chickadees pay no heed to wind, often
being found in open wind-swept places.

The fresh tracks of three deer, clear in yesterday's snow, pass through our woods. I follow the tracks backward and find a cluster of three beds, clear of snow, in the big willow thicket on the sandbar.

I then follow the tracks forward; they lead to my neighbor's cornfield, where the deer have pawed waste corn out of the snow, and also tousled one of the shocks. The tracks then lead back, by another route, to the sandbar. *En route* the deer have pawed at some grass tufts, nuzzling for the tender green sprouts within, and they have also drunk at a spring. My picture of the night's routine is complete. The over-all distance from bed to breakfast is a mile.

Our woods always harbors grouse, but one day last winter, after a deep and soft snow, I could find neither a grouse nor a track of one. I had about concluded that my birds had moved out, when my dog came to a point in the leafy top of an oak blown down last summer. Three grouse flushed out, one by one.

There were no tracks under or near the down top. Obviously these birds had flown in, but from where? Grouse must eat, especially in zero weather, so I examined the droppings for a clue. Among much unrecognizable debris I found bud-scales, and also the tough yellow skins of frozen nightshade berries.

In a thicket of young soft maple I had noticed, in summer, an abundant growth of nightshade. I went there and, after a search, found grouse tracks on a log. The birds had not waded the soft snow; they had walked the logs and picked the berries projecting here and there within their reach. This was a quarter-mile east of the down oak.

That evening, at sunset, I saw a grouse budding in a popple thicket a quarter-mile west. There were no tracks. This completed the story. These birds, for the duration of the soft snow, were covering their home range a-wing, not afoot, and the range was half a mile across.

* * *

Science knows little about home range: how big it is at various seasons, what food and cover it must include, when and how it is defended against trespass, and whether ownership is an individual, family, or group affair. These are the fundamentals of animal economics, or ecology. Every farm is a textbook on animal ecology; woodsmanship is the translation of the book.

Pines above the Snow

A CTS OF creation are ordinarily reserved for gods and poets, but humbler folk may circumvent this restriction if they know how. To plant a pine, for example, one need be neither god nor poet; one need only own a shovel. By virtue of this curious loophole in the rules, any clodhopper may say: Let there be a tree—and there will be one.

If his back be strong and his shovel sharp, there may eventually be ten thousand. And in the seventh year he may lean upon his shovel, and look upon his trees, and find them good.

God passed on his handiwork as early as the seventh day, but I notice He has since been rather noncommittal about its merits. I gather either that He spoke too soon, or that trees stand more looking upon than do fig leaves and firmaments.

* * *

Why is the shovel regarded as a symbol of drudgery? Perhaps because most shovels are dull. Certainly all drudges have dull shovels, but I am uncertain which of these two facts is cause and which effect. I only know that a good file, vigorously wielded, makes my shovel sing as it slices the mellow loam. I am told there is music in the sharp plane, the sharp chisel, and the sharp scalpel, but I hear it best in my shovel; it hums in my wrists as I plant a pine. I suspect that the fellow who tried so hard to strike one clear note upon the harp of time chose too difficult an instrument.

It is well that the planting season comes only in spring, for moderation is best in all things, even shovels. During the other months you may watch the process of becoming a pine.

The pine's new year begins in May, when the terminal bud becomes 'the candle.' Whoever coined that name for the new growth had subtlety in his soul. 'The candle' sounds like a platitudinous reference to obvious facts: the new shoot is waxy, upright, brittle. But he who lives with pines knows that candle has a deeper meaning, for at its tip burns the eternal flame that lights a path into the future. May after May my pines follow their candles skyward, each headed straight for the zenith, and each meaning to get there if only there be years enough before the last trumpet blows. It is a very old pine who at last forgets which of his many candles is the most important, and thus flattens his crown against the sky. You may forget, but no pine of your own planting will do so in your lifetime.

If you are thriftily inclined, you will find pines congenial company, for, unlike the hand-to-mouth hardwoods, they never pay current bills out of current earnings; they live solely on their savings of the year before. In fact every pine carries an open bankbook, in which his cash balance is recorded by 30 June of each year. If, on that date, his completed candle has developed a terminal cluster of ten or twelve buds, it means that he has salted away enough rain and sun for a two-foot or even a three-foot thrust skyward next spring. If there are only four or six buds, his thrust will be a lesser one, but he will nevertheless wear that peculiar air that goes with solvency.

Hard years, of course, come to pines as they do to men, and these are recorded as shorter thrusts, i.e. shorter spaces between the successive whorls of branches. These spaces, then, are an autobiography that he who walks with trees may read at will. In order to date a hard year correctly, you must always subtract one from the year of lesser growth. Thus the 1937 growth was short in all pines; this records the universal drouth of 1936. On the other hand the 1941 growth was long in all pines; perhaps they saw the shadow of things to come, and made a special effort to show the world that pines still know where they are going, even though men do not.

When one pine shows a short year but his neighbors do not, you may safely interpolate some purely local or individual adversity: a fire scar, a gnawing meadowmouse, a windburn, or some local bottleneck in that dark laboratory we call the soil.

*   *   *

There is much small-talk and neighborhood gossip among pines. By paying heed to this chatter, I learn what has transpired during the week when I am absent in town. Thus in March, when the deer frequently browse white pines, the height of the browsings tells me how hungry they are. A deer full of corn is too lazy to nip branches more than four feet above the ground; a really hungry deer rises on his hind legs and nips as high as eight feet. Thus I learn the gastronomic status of the deer without seeing them, and I learn, without visiting his field, whether my neighbor has hauled in his cornshocks.

In May, when the new candle is tender and brittle as an asparagus shoot, a bird alighting on it will often break it off. Every spring I find a few such decapitated trees, each with its wilted candle lying in the grass. It is easy to infer what has happened, but in a decade of watching I have never once *seen* a bird break a candle. It is an object lesson: one need not doubt the unseen.

In June of each year a few white pines suddenly show wilted candles, which shortly thereafter turn brown and die. A pine weevil has bored into the terminal bud cluster and deposited eggs; the grubs, when hatched, bore down along the pith and kill the shoot. Such a leaderless pine is doomed to frustration, for the surviving branches disagree among themselves who is to head the skyward march. They all do, and as a consequence the tree remains a bush.

It is a curious circumstance that only pines in full sunlight are bitten by weevils; shaded pines are ignored. Such are the hidden uses of adversity.

In October my pines tell me, by their rubbed-off bark, when the bucks are beginning to 'feel their oats.' A jackpine about eight feet high, and standing alone, seems especially to incite in a buck the idea that the world needs prodding. Such a tree must perforce turn the other cheek also, and emerges much the worse for wear. The only element of justice in such combats is that the more the tree is punished, the more pitch the buck carries away on his not-so-shiny antlers.

The chit-chat of the woods is sometimes hard to translate. Once in midwinter I found in the droppings under a grouse roost some half-digested structures that I could not identify. They resembled miniature corncobs about half an inch long. I examined samples of every local grouse food I could think of, but without finding any clue to the origin of the 'cobs.' Finally I cut open the terminal bud of a jackpine, and in its core I found the answer. The grouse had eaten the buds, digested the pitch, rubbed off the scales in his gizzard, and left the cob, which was, in effect, the forthcoming candle. One might say that this grouse had been speculating in jackpine 'futures.'

*   *   *

The three species of pine native to Wisconsin (white, red, and jack) differ radically in their opinions about marriageable age. The precocious jackpine sometimes blooms and bears cones a year or two after leaving the nursery, and a few of my 13-year-old jacks already boast of grandchildren. My 13-year-old reds first bloomed this year, but my whites have not yet bloomed; they adhere closely to the Anglo-Saxon doctrine of free, white, and twenty-one.

Were it not for this wide diversity in social outlook, my red squirrels would be much curtailed in their bill-of-fare. Each year in midsummer they start tearing up jackpine cones for the seeds, and no Labor-Day picnic ever scattered more hulls and rinds over the landscape than they do: under each tree the remains of their annual feast lie in piles and heaps. Yet there are always cones to spare, as attested by their progeny popping up among the goldenrods.

Few people know that pines bear flowers, and most of those who do are too prosy to see in this festival of bloom anything more than a routine biological function. All disillusioned folk should spend the second week in May in a pine woods, and such as wear glasses should take along an extra handkerchief. The prodigality of pine pollen should convince anyone of the reckless exuberance of the season, even when the song of the kinglet has failed to do so.

Young white pines usually thrive best in the absence of their parents. I know of whole woodlots in which the younger generation, even when provided with a place in the sun, is dwarfed and spindled by its elders. Again there are woodlots in which no such inhibition obtains. I wish I knew whether such differences lie in tolerance in the young, in the old, or in the soil.

Pines, like people, are choosy about their associates and do not succeed in suppressing their likes and dislikes. Thus there is an affinity between white pines and dewberries, between red pines and flowering spurge, between jackpines and sweet fern. When I plant a white pine in a dewberry patch, I can safely predict that within a year he will develop a husky cluster of buds, and that his new needles will show that bluish bloom which bespeaks health and congenial company. He will outgrow and outbloom his fellows planted on the same day, with the same care, in the same soil, but in the company of grass.

In October I like to walk among these blue plumes, rising straight and stalwart from the red carpet of dewberry leaves. I wonder whether they are aware of their state of well-being. I know only that I am.

Pines have earned the reputation of being 'evergreen' by the same device that governments use to achieve the appearance of perpetuity: overlapping terms of office. By taking on new needles on the new growth of each year, and discarding old needles at longer intervals, they have led the casual onlooker to believe that needles remain forever green.

Each species of pine has its own constitution, which pre-scribes a term of office for needles appropriate to its way of life. Thus the white pine retains its needles for a year and a half; the red and jackpines for two years and a half. Incoming needles take office in June, and outgoing needles write farewell addresses in October. All write the same thing, in the same tawny yellow ink, which by November turns brown. Then the needles fall, and are filed in the duff to enrich the wisdom of the stand. It is this accumulated wisdom that hushes the footsteps of whoever walks under pines.

It is in midwinter that I sometimes glean from my pines something more important than woodlot politics, and the news of the wind and weather. This is especially likely to happen on some gloomy evening when the snow has buried all irrelevant detail, and the hush of elemental sadness lies heavy upon every living thing. Nevertheless, my pines, each with his burden of snow, are standing ramrod-straight, rank upon rank, and in the dusk beyond I sense the presence of hundreds more. At such times I feel a curious transfusion of courage.

To BAND a bird is to hold a ticket in a great lottery. Most of us hold tickets on our own survival, but we buy them from the insurance company, which knows too much to sell us a really sporting chance. It is an exercise in objectivity to hold a ticket on the banded sparrow that falleth, or on the banded chickadee that may some day re-enter your trap, and thus prove that he is still alive.

The tyro gets his thrill from banding new birds; he plays a kind of game against himself, striving to break his previous score for total numbers. But to the old-timer the banding of new birds becomes merely pleasant routine; the real thrill lies in the recapture of some bird banded long ago, some bird whose age, adventures, and previous condition of appetite are perhaps better known to you than to the bird himself.

Thus in our family, the question whether chickadee 65290 would survive for still another winter was, for five years, a sporting question of the first magnitude.

Beginning a decade ago, we have trapped and banded most of the chickadees on our farm each winter. In early winter, the traps yield mostly unbanded birds; these presumably are mostly the young of the year, which, once banded, can thereafter be 'dated.' As the winter wears on, unbanded birds cease to appear in the trap; we then know that the local population consists largely of marked birds. We can tell from the band numbers how many birds are present, and how many of these are survivors from each previous year of banding.

65290 was one of 7 chickadees constituting the 'class of 1937.' When he first entered our trap, he showed no visible evidence of genius. Like his classmates, his valor for suet was greater than his discretion. Like his classmates, he bit my finger while being taken out of the trap. When banded and released he fluttered up to a limb, pecked his new aluminum anklet in mild annoyance, shook his mussed feathers, cursed gently, and hurried away to catch up with the gang. It is doubtful whether he drew any philosophical deductions from his experience (such as 'all is not ants' eggs that glitters'), for he was caught again three times that same winter.

By the second winter our recaptures showed that the class of 7 had shrunk to 3, and by the third winter to 2. By the fifth winter 65290 was the sole survivor of his generation. Signs of genius were still lacking, but of his extraordinary capacity for living, there was now historical proof.

During his sixth winter 65290 failed to reappear, and the verdict of 'missing in action' is now confirmed by his absence during our four subsequent trappings.

At that, of 97 chicks banded during the decade, 65290 was the only one contriving to survive for five winters. Three reached 4 years, 7 reached 3 years, 19 reached 2 years, and 67 disappeared after their first winter. Hence if I were selling insurance to chicks, I could compute the premium with assurance. But this would raise the problem: in what currency would I pay the widows? I suppose in ants' eggs.

I know so little about birds that I can only speculate on why 65290 survived his fellows. Was he more clever in dodging his enemies? What enemies? A chickadee is almost too small to have any. That whimsical fellow called Evolution, having enlarged the dinosaur until he tripped over his own toes, tried shrinking the chickadee until he was just too big to be snapped up by flycatchers as an insect, and just too little to be pursued by hawks and owls as meat. Then he regarded his handiwork and laughed. Everyone laughs at so small a bundle of large enthusiasms.

The sparrow hawk, the screech owl, the shrike, and especially the midget saw-whet owl might find it worth while to kill a chickadee, but I've only once found evidence of actual murder: a screech-owl pellet contained one of my bands. Perhaps these small bandits have a fellow-feeling for midgets.

It seems likely that weather is the only killer so devoid of both humor and dimension as to kill a chickadee. I suspect that in the chickadee Sunday School two mortal sins are taught: thou shalt not venture into windy places in winter, thou shalt not get wet before a blizzard.

I learned the second commandment one drizzly winter dusk while watching a band of chicks going to roost in my woods. The drizzle came out of the south, but I could tell it would turn northwest and bitter cold before morning. The chicks went to bed in a dead oak, the bark of which had peeled and warped into curls, cups, and hollows of various sizes, shapes, and exposures. The bird selecting a roost dry against a south drizzle, but vulnerable to a north one, would surely be frozen by morning. The bird selecting a roost dry from all sides would awaken safe. This, I think, is the kind of wisdom that spells survival in chickdom, and accounts for 65290 and his like.

The chickadee's fear of windy places is easily deduced from his behavior. In winter he ventures away from woods only on calm days, and the distance varies inversely as the breeze. I know several wind-swept woodlots that are chickless all winter, but are freely used at all other seasons. They are wind-swept because cows have browsed out the undergrowth. To the steam-heated banker who mortgages the farmer who needs more cows who need more pasture, wind is a minor nuisance, except perhaps at the Flatiron corner. To the chickadee, winter wind is the boundary of the habitable world. If the chickadee had an office, the maxim over his desk would say: 'Keep calm.'

His behavior at the trap discloses the reason. Turn your trap so that he must enter with even a moderate wind at his tail, and all the king's horses cannot drag him to the bait. Turn it the other way, and your score may be good. Wind from behind blows cold and wet under the feathers, which are his portable roof and air-conditioner. Nuthatches, juncos, tree sparrows, and woodpeckers likewise fear winds from behind, but their heating plants and hence their wind tolerance are larger in the order named. Books on nature seldom mention wind; they are written behind stoves.

I suspect there is a third commandment in chickdom: thou shalt investigate every loud noise. When we start chopping in our woods, the chicks at once appear and stay until the felled tree or riven log has exposed new insect eggs or pupae for their delectation. The discharge of a gun will likewise summon chicks, but with less satisfactory dividends.

What served as their dinner bell before the day of axes, mauls, and guns? Presumably the crash of falling trees. In December 1940, an ice-storm felled an extraordinary number of dead snags and living limbs in our woods. Our chicks scoffed at the trap for a month, being replete with the dividends of the storm.

65290 has long since gone to his reward. I hope that in his new woods, great oaks full of ants' eggs keep falling all day long, with never a wind to ruffle his composure or take the edge off his appetite. And I hope that he still wears my band.

Marshland Elegy

A DAWN wind stirs on the great marsh. With almost imperceptible slowness it rolls a bank of fog across the wide morass. Like the white ghost of a glacier the mists advance, riding over phalanxes of tamarack, sliding across the bog-meadows heavy with dew. A single silence hangs from horizon to horizon.

Out of some far recess of the sky a tinkling of little bells falls soft upon the listening land. Then again silence. Now comes a baying of some sweet-throated hound, soon the clamor of a responding pack. Then a far clear blast of hunting horns, out of the sky into the fog.

High horns, low horns, silence, and finally a pandemonium of trumpets, rattles, croaks, and cries that almost shakes the bog with its nearness, but without yet disclosing whence it comes. At last a glint of sun reveals the approach of a great echelon of birds. On motionless wing they emerge from the lifting mists, sweep a final arc of sky, and settle in clangorous descending spirals to their feeding grounds. A new day has begun on the crane marsh.

*   *   *

A sense of time lies thick and heavy on such a place. Yearly since the ice age it has awakened each spring to the clangor of cranes. The peat layers that comprise the bog are laid down in the basin of an ancient lake. The cranes stand, as it were, upon the sodden pages of their own history. These peats are the compressed remains of the mosses that clogged the pools, of the tamaracks that spread over the moss, of the cranes that bugled over the tamaracks since the retreat of the ice sheet. An endless caravan of generations has built of its own bones this bridge into the future, this habitat where the oncoming host again may live and breed and die.

To what end? Out on the bog a crane, gulping some luckless

frog, springs his ungainly hulk into the air and flails the morning sun with mighty wings. The tamaracks re-echo with his bugled certitude. He seems to know.

* * *

Our ability to perceive quality in nature begins, as in art, with the pretty. It expands through successive stages of the beautiful to values as yet uncaptured by language. The quality of cranes lies, I think, in this higher gamut, as yet beyond the reach of words.

This much, though, can be said: our appreciation of the crane grows with the slow unraveling of earthly history. His tribe, we now know, stems out of the remote Eocene. The other members of the fauna in which he originated are long since entombed within the hills. When we hear his call we hear no mere bird. We hear the trumpet in the orchestra of evolution. He is the symbol of our untamable past, of that incredible sweep of millennia which underlies and conditions the daily affairs of birds and men.

And so they live and have their being—these cranes—not in the constricted present, but in the wider reaches of evolutionary time. Their annual return is the ticking of the geologic clock. Upon the place of their return they confer a peculiar distinction. Amid the endless mediocrity of the commonplace, a crane marsh holds a paleontological patent of nobility, won in the march of aeons, and revocable only by shotgun. The sadness discernible in some marshes arises, perhaps, from their once having harbored cranes. Now they stand humbled, adrift in history.

Some sense of this quality in cranes seems to have been felt by sportsmen and ornithologists of all ages. Upon such quarry as this the Holy Roman Emperor Frederick loosed his gyrfalcons. Upon such quarry as this once swooped the hawks of Kublai Khan. Marco Polo tells us: 'He derives the highest amusement from sporting with gyrfalcons and hawks. At Changanor the Khan has a great Palace surrounded by a fine plain where are found cranes in great numbers. He causes millet and other grains to be sown in order that the birds may not want.'

The ornithologist Bengt Berg, seeing cranes as a boy upon the Swedish heaths, forthwith made them his life work. He followed them to Africa and discovered their winter retreat on the White Nile. He says of his first encounter: 'It was a spectacle which eclipsed the flight of the roc in the Thousand and One Nights.'

*   *   *

When the glacier came down out of the north, crunching hills and gouging valleys, some adventuring rampart of the ice climbed the Baraboo Hills and fell back into the outlet gorge of the Wisconsin River. The swollen waters backed up and formed a lake half as long as the state, bordered on the east by cliffs of ice, and fed by the torrents that fell from melting mountains. The shorelines of this old lake are still visible; its bottom is the bottom of the great marsh.

The lake rose through the centuries, finally spilling over east of the Baraboo range. There it cut a new channel for the river, and thus drained itself. To the residual lagoons came the cranes, bugling the defeat of the retreating winter, summoning the on-creeping host of living things to their collective task of marsh-building. Floating bogs of sphagnum moss clogged the lowered waters, filled them. Sedge and leatherleaf, tamarack and spruce successively advanced over the bog, anchoring it by their root fabric, sucking out its water, making peat. The lagoons disappeared, but not the cranes. To the moss-meadows that replaced the ancient waterways they returned each spring to dance and bugle and rear their gangling sorrel-colored young. These, albeit birds, are not properly called chicks, but *colts*. I cannot explain why. On some dewy June morning watch them gambol over their ancestral pastures at the heels of the roan mare, and you will see for yourself.

One year not long ago a French trapper in buckskins pushed his canoe up one of the moss-clogged creeks that thread the great marsh. At this attempt to invade their miry stronghold the cranes gave vent to loud and ribald laughter. A century or two later Englishmen came in covered wagons. They chopped clearings in the timbered moraines that border the marsh, and in them planted corn and buckwheat. They did not intend, like the Great Khan at Changanor, to feed the cranes. But the cranes do not question the intent of glaciers, emperors, or pioneers. They ate the grain, and when some irate farmer failed to concede their usufruct in his corn, they trumpeted a warning and sailed across the marsh to another farm.

There was no alfalfa in those days, and the hill-farms made poor hay land, especially in dry years. One dry year someone set a fire in the tamaracks. The burn grew up quickly to bluejoint grass, which, when cleared of dead trees, made a dependable hay meadow. After that, each August, men appeared to cut hay. In winter, after the cranes had gone South, they drove wagons over the frozen bogs and hauled the hay to their farms in the hills. Yearly they plied the marsh with fire and axe, and in two short decades hay meadows dotted the whole expanse.

Each August when the haymakers came to pitch their camps, singing and drinking and lashing their teams with whip and tongue, the cranes whinnied to their colts and retreated to the far fastnesses. 'Red shitepokes' the haymakers called them, from the rusty hue which at that season often stains the battleship-gray of crane plumage. After the hay was stacked and the marsh again their own, the cranes returned, to call down out of October skies the migrant flocks from Canada. Together they wheeled over the new-cut stubbles and raided the corn until frosts gave the signal for the winter exodus.

These haymeadow days were the Arcadian age for marsh dwellers. Man and beast, plant and soil lived on and with each other in mutual toleration, to the mutual benefit of all. The marsh might have kept on producing hay and prairie chickens, deer and muskrat, crane-music and cranberries forever.

The new overlords did not understand this. They did not include soil, plants, or birds in their ideas of mutuality. The dividends of such a balanced economy were too modest. They envisaged farms not only around, but *in* the marsh. An epidemic of ditch-digging and land-booming set in. The marsh was gridironed with drainage canals, speckled with new fields and farmsteads.

But crops were poor and beset by frosts, to which the expensive ditches added an aftermath of debt. Farmers moved out. Peat beds dried, shrank, caught fire. Sun-energy out of the Pleistocene shrouded the countryside in acrid smoke. No man raised his voice against the waste, only his nose against the smell. After a dry summer not even the winter snows could extinguish the smoldering marsh. Great pockmarks were burned into field and meadow, the scars reaching down to the sands of the old lake, peat-covered these hundred centuries. Rank weeds sprang out of the ashes, to be followed after a year or two by aspen scrub. The cranes were hard put, their numbers shrinking with the remnants of unburned meadow. For them, the song of the power shovel came near being an elegy. The high priests of progress knew nothing of cranes, and cared less. What is a species more or less among engineers? What good is an undrained marsh anyhow?

For a decade or two crops grew poorer, fires deeper, wood-fields larger, and cranes scarcer, year by year. Only reflooding, it appeared, could keep the peat from burning. Meanwhile cranberry growers had, by plugging drainage ditches, reflooded a few spots and obtained good yields. Distant politicians bugled about marginal land, over-production, unemployment relief, conservation. Economists and planners came to look at the marsh. Surveyors, technicians, CCC's, buzzed about. A counter-epidemic of reflooding set in. Government bought land, re-settled farmers, plugged ditches wholesale. Slowly the bogs are re-wetting. The firepocks become ponds. Grass fires still burn, but they can no longer burn the wetted soil.

All this, once the CCC camps were gone, was good for cranes, but not so the thickets of scrub popple that spread inexorably over the old burns, and still less the maze of new roads that inevitably follow governmental conservation. To build a road is so much simpler than to think of what the country really needs. A roadless marsh is seemingly as worthless to the alphabetical conservationist as an undrained one was to the empire-builders. Solitude, the one natural resource still undowered of alphabets, is so far recognized as valuable only by ornithologists and cranes.

Thus always does history, whether of marsh or market place, end in paradox. The ultimate value in these marshes is wildness, and the crane is wildness incarnate. But all conservation of wildness is self-defeating, for to cherish we must see and fondle, and when enough have seen and fondled, there is no wilderness left to cherish.

*   *   *

Some day, perhaps in the very process of our benefactions, perhaps in the fullness of geologic time, the last crane will trumpet his farewell and spiral skyward from the great marsh. High out of the clouds will fall the sound of hunting horns, the baying of the phantom pack, the tinkle of little bells, and then a silence never to be broken, unless perchance in some far pasture of the Milky Way.

The Sand Counties

EVERY PROFESSION keeps a small herd of epithets, and needs a pasture where they may run at large. Thus economists must find free range somewhere for their pet aspersions, such as submarginality, regression, and institutional rigidity. Within the ample reaches of the Sand Counties these economic terms of reproach find beneficial exercise, free pasturage, and immunity from the gadflies of critical rebuttal.

Soil experts, likewise, would have a hard life without the Sand Counties. Where else would their podzols, gleys, and anaerobics find a living?

Social planners have, of late years, come to use the Sand Counties for a different, albeit somewhat parallel, purpose. The sandy region serves as a pale blank area, of pleasing shape and size, on those polka-dot maps where each dot represents ten bathtubs, or five women's auxiliaries, or one mile of black-top, or a share in a blooded bull. Such maps would become monotonous if stippled uniformly.

In short, the Sand Counties are poor.

Yet in the 1930's, when the alphabetical uplifts galloped like forty horsemen across the Big Flats, exhorting the sand farmers to resettle elsewhere, these benighted folk did not want to go, even when baited with 3 per cent at the federal land bank. I began to wonder why, and finally, to settle the question, I bought myself a sand farm.

Sometimes in June, when I see unearned dividends of dew hung on every lupine, I have doubts about the real poverty of the sands. On solvent farmlands lupines do not even grow, much less collect a daily rainbow of jewels. If they did, the weed-control officer, who seldom sees a dewy dawn, would doubtless insist that they be cut. Do economists know about lupines?

Perhaps the farmers who did not want to move out of the Sand Counties had some deep reason, rooted far back in history, for preferring to stay. I am reminded of this every April when the pasque-flowers bloom on every gravelly ridge. Pasques do not say much, but I infer that their preference harks back to the glacier that put the gravel there. Only gravel ridges are poor enough to offer pasques full elbow-room in April sun. They endure snows, sleets, and bitter winds for the privilege of blooming alone.

There are other plants who seem to ask of this world not riches but room. Such is the little sandwort that throws a white-lace cap over the poorest hilltops just before the lupines splash them with blue. Sandworts simply refuse to live on a good farm, even on a very good farm, complete with rock garden and begonias. And then there is the little Linaria, so small, so slender, and so blue that you don't even see it until it is directly underfoot; who ever saw a Linaria except on a sandblow?

Finally there is Draba, beside whom even Linaria is tall and ample. I have never met an economist who knows Draba, but if I were one I should do all my economic pondering lying prone on the sand, with Draba at nose-length.

There are birds that are found only in the Sand Counties, for reasons sometimes easy, sometimes difficult, to guess. The clay-colored sparrow is there, for the clear reason that he is en-amored of jackpines, and jackpines of sand. The sandhill crane is there, for the clear reason that he is enamored of solitude, and there is none left elsewhere. But why do woodcocks prefer to nest in the sandy regions? Their preference is rooted in no such mundane matter as food, for earthworms are far more abundant on better soils. After years of study, I now think I know the reason. The male woodcock, while doing his peenting prologue to the sky dance, is like a short lady in high heels: he does not show up to advantage in dense tangled ground cover. But on the poorest sand-streak of the poorest pasture or meadow of the Sand Counties, there is, in April at least, no ground cover at all, save only moss, Draba, cardamine, sheep-sorrel, and An-tennaria, all negligible impediments to a bird with short legs. Here the male woodcock can puff and strut and mince, not only without let or hindrance, but in full view of his audience, real or hoped-for. This little circumstance, important for only an hour a day, for only one month of the year, perhaps for only one of the two sexes, and certainly wholly irrelevant to economic stan-dards of living, determines the woodcock's choice of a home.

The economists have not yet tried to resettle woodcocks.

Odyssey

X HAD MARKED time in the limestone ledge since the Paleozoic seas covered the land. Time, to an atom locked in a rock, does not pass.

The break came when a bur-oak root nosed down a crack and began prying and sucking. In the flash of a century the rock decayed, and X was pulled out and up into the world of living things. He helped build a flower, which became an acorn, which fattened a deer, which fed an Indian, all in a single year.

From his berth in the Indian's bones, X joined again in chase and flight, feast and famine, hope and fear. He felt these things as changes in the little chemical pushes and pulls that tug timelessly at every atom. When the Indian took his leave of the prairie, X moldered briefly underground, only to embark on a second trip through the bloodstream of the land.

This time it was a rootlet of bluestem that sucked him up and lodged him in a leaf that rode the green billows of the prairie June, sharing the common task of hoarding sunlight. To this leaf also fell an uncommon task: flicking shadows across a plover's eggs. The ecstatic plover, hovering overhead, poured praises on something perfect: perhaps the eggs, perhaps the shadows, or perhaps the haze of pink phlox that lay on the prairie.

When the departing plovers set wing for the Argentine, all the bluestems waved farewell with tall new tassels. When the first geese came out of the north and all the bluestems glowed wine-red, a forehanded deermouse cut the leaf in which X lay, and buried it in an underground nest, as if to hide a bit of Indian summer from the thieving frosts. But a fox detained the mouse, molds and fungi took the nest apart, and X lay in the soil again, foot-loose and fancy-free.

Next he entered a tuft of side-oats grama, a buffalo, a buffalo chip, and again the soil. Next a spiderwort, a rabbit, and an owl. Thence a tuft of sporobolus.

All routines come to an end. This one ended with a prairie fire, which reduced the prairie plants to smoke, gas, and ashes. Phosphorus and potash atoms stayed in the ash, but the nitrogen atoms were gone with the wind. A spectator might, at this point, have predicted an early end of the biotic drama, for with fires exhausting the nitrogen, the soil might well have lost its plants and blown away.

But the prairie had two strings to its bow. Fires thinned its grasses, but they thickened its stand of leguminous herbs: prairie clover, bush clover, wild bean, vetch, lead-plant, trefoil, and Baptisia, each carrying its own bacteria housed in nodules on its rootlets. Each nodule pumped nitrogen out of the air into the plant, and then ultimately into the soil. Thus the prairie savings bank took in more nitrogen from its legumes than it paid out to its fires. That the prairie is rich is known to the humblest deermouse; why the prairie is rich is a question seldom asked in all the still lapse of ages.

Between each of his excursions through the biota, X lay in the soil and was carried by the rains, inch by inch, downhill. Living plants retarded the wash by impounding atoms; dead plants by locking them to their decayed tissues. Animals ate the plants and carried them briefly uphill or downhill, depending on whether they died or defecated higher or lower than they fed. No animal was aware that the altitude of his death was more important than his manner of dying. Thus a fox caught a gopher in a meadow, carrying X uphill to his bed on the brow of a ledge, where an eagle laid him low. The dying fox sensed the end of his chapter in foxdom, but not the new beginning in the odyssey of an atom.

An Indian eventually inherited the eagle's plumes, and with them propitiated the Fates, whom he assumed had a special interest in Indians. It did not occur to him that they might be busy casting dice against gravity; that mice and men, soils and songs, might be merely ways to retard the march of atoms to the sea.

One year, while X lay in a cottonwood by the river, he was eaten by a beaver, an animal that always feeds higher than he dies. The beaver starved when his pond dried up during a bitter frost. X rode the carcass down the spring freshet, losing more altitude each hour than heretofore in a century. He ended up in the silt of a backwater bayou, where he fed a crayfish, a coon, and then an Indian, who laid him down to his last sleep in a mound on the riverbank. One spring an oxbow caved the bank, and after one short week of freshet X lay again in his ancient prison, the sea.

An atom at large in the biota is too free to know freedom; an atom back in the sea has forgotten it. For every atom lost to the sea, the prairie pulls another out of the decaying rocks. The only certain truth is that its creatures must suck hard, live fast, and die often, lest its losses exceed its gains.

*   *   *

It is the nature of roots to nose into cracks. When Y was thus released from the parent ledge, a new animal had arrived and begun redding up the prairie to fit his own notions of law and order. An oxteam turned the prairie sod, and Y began a succession of dizzy annual trips through a new grass called wheat.

The old prairie lived by the diversity of its plants and animals, all of which were useful because the sum total of their cooperations and competitions achieved continuity. But the wheat farmer was a builder of categories; to him only wheat and oxen were useful. He saw the useless pigeons settle in clouds upon his wheat, and shortly cleared the skies of them. He saw the chinch bugs take over the stealing job, and fumed because here was a useless thing too small to kill. He failed to see the downward wash of over-wheated loam, laid bare in spring against the pelting rains. When soil-wash and chinch bugs finally put an end to wheat farming, Y and his like had already traveled far down the watershed.

When the empire of wheat collapsed, the settler took a leaf from the old prairie book: he impounded his fertility in livestock, he augmented it with nitrogen-pumping alfalfa, and he tapped the lower layers of the loam with deep-rooted corn.

But he used his alfalfa, and every other new weapon against wash, not only to hold his old plowings, but also to exploit new ones which, in turn, needed holding.

So, despite alfalfa, the black loam grew gradually thinner. Erosion engineers built dams and terraces to hold it. Army engineers built levees and wing-dams to flush it from the rivers. The rivers would not flush, but raised their beds instead, thus choking navigation. So the engineers built pools like gigantic beaver ponds, and Y landed in one of these, his trip from rock to river completed in one short century.

On first reaching the pool, Y made several trips through water plants, fish, and waterfowl. But engineers build sewers as well as dams, and down them comes the loot of all the far hills and the sea. The atoms that once grew pasque-flowers to greet the returning plovers now lie inert, confused, imprisoned in oily sludge.

Roots still nose among the rocks. Rains still pelt the fields. Deermice still hide their souvenirs of Indian summer. Old men who helped destroy the pigeons still recount the glory of the fluttering hosts. Black and white buffalo pass in and out of red barns, offering free rides to itinerant atoms.

On a Monument to the Pigeon *

WE HAVE erected a monument to commemorate the funeral of a species. It symbolizes our sorrow. We grieve because no living man will see again the onrushing phalanx of victorious birds, sweeping a path for spring across the March skies, chasing the defeated winter from all the woods and prairies of Wisconsin.

Men still live who, in their youth, remember pigeons. Trees still live who, in their youth, were shaken by a living wind. But a decade hence only the oldest oaks will remember, and at long last only the hills will know.

There will always be pigeons in books and in museums, but these are effigies and images, dead to all hardships and to all delights. Book-pigeons cannot dive out of a cloud to make the deer run for cover, or clap their wings in thunderous applause of mast-laden woods. Book-pigeons cannot breakfast on new-mown wheat in Minnesota, and dine on blueberries in Canada. They know no urge of seasons; they feel no kiss of sun, no lash of wind and weather. They live forever by not living at all.

Our grandfathers were less well-housed, well-fed, well-clothed than we are. The strivings by which they bettered their lot are also those which deprived us of pigeons. Perhaps we now grieve because we are not sure, in our hearts, that we have gained by the exchange. The gadgets of industry bring us more comforts than the pigeons did, but do they add as much to the glory of the spring?

It is a century now since Darwin gave us the first glimpse of the origin of species. We know now what was unknown to all the preceding caravan of generations: that men are only fellow-voyagers with other creatures in the odyssey of evolution. This new knowledge should have given us, by this time, a sense of kinship with fellow-creatures; a wish to live and let live; a sense of wonder over the magnitude and duration of the biotic enterprise.

Above all we should, in the century since Darwin, have come

*The monument to the Passenger Pigeon, placed in Wyalusing State Park, Wisconsin, by the Wisconsin Society for Ornithology. Dedicated 11 May 1947.

to know that man, while now captain of the adventuring ship, is hardly the sole object of its quest, and that his prior assumptions to this effect arose from the simple necessity of whistling in the dark.

These things, I say, should have come to us. I fear they have not come to many.

For one species to mourn the death of another is a new thing under the sun. The Cro-Magnon who slew the last mammoth thought only of steaks. The sportsman who shot the last pigeon thought only of his prowess. The sailor who clubbed the last auk thought of nothing at all. But we, who have lost our pigeons, mourn the loss. Had the funeral been ours, the pigeons would hardly have mourned us. In this fact, rather than in Mr. Du-Pont's nylons or Mr. Vannevar Bush's bombs, lies objective evidence of our superiority over the beasts.

*   *   *

This monument, perched like a duckhawk on this cliff, will scan this wide valley, watching through the days and years. For many a March it will watch the geese go by, telling the river about clearer, colder, lonelier waters on the tundra. For many an April it will see the redbuds come and go, and for many a May the flush of oak-blooms on a thousand hills. Questing wood ducks will search these basswoods for hollow limbs; golden prothonotaries will shake golden pollen from the river willows. Egrets will pose on these sloughs in August; plovers will whistle from September skies. Hickory nuts will plop into October leaves, and hail will rattle in November woods. But no pigeons will pass, for there are no pigeons, save only this flightless one, graven in bronze on this rock. Tourists will read this inscription, but their thoughts will not take wing.

We are told by economic moralists that to mourn the pigeon is mere nostalgia; that if the pigeoners had not done away with him, the farmers would ultimately have been obliged, in self-defense, to do so.

This is one of those peculiar truths that are valid, but not for the reasons alleged.

The pigeon was a biological storm. He was the lightning that played between two opposing potentials of intolerable intensity: the fat of the land and the oxygen of the air. Yearly the feathered tempest roared up, down, and across the continent, sucking up the laden fruits of forest and prairie, burning them in a traveling blast of life. Like any other chain reaction, the pigeon could survive no diminution of his own furious intensity. When the pigeoners subtracted from his numbers, and the pioneers chopped gaps in the continuity of his fuel, his flame guttered out with hardly a sputter or even a wisp of smoke.

Today the oaks still flaunt their burden at the sky, but the feathered lightning is no more. Worm and weevil must now perform slowly and silently the biological task that once drew thunder from the firmament.

The wonder is not that the pigeon went out, but that he ever survived through all the millennia of pre-Babbittian time.

*   *   *

The pigeon loved his land: he lived by the intensity of his desire for clustered grape and bursting beechnut, and by his contempt of miles and seasons. Whatever Wisconsin did not offer him gratis today, he sought and found tomorrow in Michigan, or Labrador, or Tennessee. His love was for present things, and these things were present somewhere; to find them required only the free sky, and the will to ply his wings.

To love what *was* is a new thing under the sun, unknown to most people and to all pigeons. To see America as history, to conceive of destiny as a becoming, to smell a hickory tree through the still lapse of ages—all these things are possible for us, and to achieve them takes only the free sky, and the will to ply our wings. In these things, and not in Mr. Bush's bombs and Mr. DuPont's nylons, lies objective evidence of our superiority over the beasts.

Flambeau

PEOPLE WHO have never canoed a wild river, or who have done so only with a guide in the stern, are apt to assume that novelty, plus healthful exercise, account for the value of the trip. I thought so too, until I met the two college boys on the Flambeau.

Supper dishes washed, we sat on the bank watching a buck dunking for water plants on the far shore. Soon the buck raised his head, cocked his ears upstream, and then bounded for cover.

Around the bend now came the cause of his alarm: two boys in a canoe. Spying us, they edged in to pass the time of day.

'What time is it?' was their first question. They explained that their watches had run down, and for the first time in their lives there was no clock, whistle, or radio to set watches by. For two days they had lived by 'sun-time,' and were getting a thrill out of it. No servant brought them meals: they got their meat out of the river, or went without. No traffic cop whistled them off the hidden rock in the next rapids. No friendly roof kept them dry when they misguessed whether or not to pitch the tent. No guide showed them which camping spots offered a nightlong breeze, and which a nightlong misery of mosquitoes; which firewood made clean coals, and which only smoke.

Before our young adventurers pushed off downstream, we learned that both were slated for the Army upon the conclusion of their trip. Now the *motif* was clear. This trip was their first and last taste of freedom, an interlude between two regimentations: the campus and the barracks. The elemental simplicities of wilderness travel were thrills not only because of their novelty, but because they represented complete freedom to make mistakes. The wilderness gave them their first taste of those rewards and penalties for wise and foolish acts which every woodsman faces daily, but against which civilization has built a thousand buffers. These boys were 'on their own' in this particular sense.

Perhaps every youth needs an occasional wilderness trip, in order to learn the meaning of this particular freedom.

When I was a small boy, my father used to describe all choice camps, fishing waters, and woods as 'nearly as good as the Flambeau.' When I finally launched my own canoe in this legendary stream, I found it up to expectations as a river, but as a wilderness it was on its last legs. New cottages, resorts, and highway bridges were chopping up the wild stretches into shorter and shorter segments. To run down the Flambeau was to be mentally whipsawed between alternating impressions: no sooner had you built up the mental illusion of being in the wilds than you sighted a boat-landing, and soon you were coasting past some cottager's peonies.

Safely past the peonies, a buck bounding up the bank helped us to restore the wilderness flavor, and the next rapids finished the job. But staring at you beside the pool below was a synthetic log cabin, complete with composition roof, 'Bide-A-Wee' signboard, and rustic pergola for afternoon bridge.

Paul Bunyan was too busy a man to think about posterity, but if he had asked to reserve a spot for posterity to see what the old north woods looked like, he likely would have chosen the Flambeau, for here the cream of the white pine grew on the same acres with the cream of the sugar maple, yellow birch, and hemlock. This rich intermixture of pine and hardwoods was and is uncommon. The Flambeau pines, growing on a hardwood soil richer than pines are ordinarily able to occupy, were so large and valuable, and so close to a good log-driving stream, that they were cut at an early day, as evidenced by the decayed condition of their giant stumps. Only defective pines were spared, but there are enough of these alive today to punctuate the skyline of the Flambeau with many a green monument to bygone days.

The hardwood logging came much later; in fact, the last big hardwood company 'pulled steel' on its last logging railroad only a decade ago. All that remains of that company today is a 'land-office' in its ghost town, selling off its cutovers to hopeful settlers. Thus died an epoch in American history: the epoch of cut out and get out.

Like a coyote rummaging in the offal of a deserted camp, the post-logging economy of the Flambeau subsists on the leavings of its own past. 'Gypo' pulpwood cutters nose around in the slashings for the occasional small hemlock overlooked in the main logging. A portable sawmill crew dredges the riverbed for sunken 'deadheads,' many of which drowned during the hell-for-leather log-drives of the glory days. Rows of these mud-stained corpses are drawn up on shore at the old landings—all in perfect condition, and some of great value, for no such pine exists in the north woods today. Post and pole cutters strip the swamps of white cedar; the deer follow them around and strip the felled tops of their foliage. Everybody and everything subsists on leavings.

So complete are all these scavengings that when the modern cottager builds a log cabin, he uses imitation logs sawed out of slab piles in Idaho or Oregon, and hauled to Wisconsin woods in a freight car. The proverbial coals to Newcastle seem a mild irony compared with this.

Yet there remains the river, in a few spots hardly changed since Paul Bunyan's day; at early dawn, before the motor boats awaken, one can still hear it singing in the wilderness. There are a few sections of uncut timber, luckily state-owned. And there is a considerable remnant of wildlife: muskellunge, bass, and sturgeon in the river; mergansers, black ducks, and wood ducks breeding in the sloughs; ospreys, eagles, and ravens cruising overhead. Everywhere are deer, perhaps too many: I counted 52 in two days afloat. A wolf or two still roams the upper Flambeau, and there is a trapper who claims he saw a marten, though no marten skin has come out of the Flambeau since 1900.

Using these remnants of the wilderness as a nucleus, the State Conservation Department began, in 1943, to rebuild a fifty-mile stretch of river as a wild area for the use and enjoyment of young Wisconsin. This wild stretch is set in a matrix of state forest, but there is to be no forestry on the river banks, and as few road crossings as possible. Slowly, patiently, and sometimes expensively the Conservation Department has been buying land, removing cottages, warding off unnecessary roads, and in general pushing the clock back, as far as possible, toward the original wilderness.

The good soil that enabled the Flambeau to grow the best cork pine for Paul Bunyan likewise enabled Rusk County, during recent decades, to sprout a dairy industry. These dairy farmers wanted cheaper electric power than that offered by local power companies, hence they organized a co-operative REA and in 1947 applied for a power dam, which, when built, would clip off the lower reaches of a fifty-mile stretch in process of restoration as canoe-water.

There was a sharp and bitter political fight. The Legislature, sensitive to farmer-pressure but oblivious of wilderness values, not only approved the REA dam, but deprived the Conservation Commission of any future voice in the disposition of power sites. It thus seems likely that the remaining canoe-water on the Flambeau, as well as every other stretch of wild river in the state, will ultimately be harnessed for power.

Perhaps our grandsons, having never seen a wild river, will never miss the chance to set a canoe in singing waters.

Illinois Bus Ride

A FARMER AND his son are out in the yard, pulling a crosscut saw through the innards of an ancient cottonwood. The tree is so large and so old that only a foot of blade is left to pull on.

Time was when that tree was a buoy in the prairie sea. George Rogers Clark may have camped under it; buffalo may have nooned in its shade, switching flies. Every spring it roosted fluttering pigeons. It is the best historical library short of the State College, but once a year it sheds cotton on the farmer's window screens. Of these two facts, only the second is important.

The State College tells farmers that Chinese elms do not clog screens, and hence are preferable to cottonwoods. It likewise pontificates on cherry preserves, Bang's disease, hybrid corn, and beautifying the farm home. The only thing it does not know about farms is where they came from. Its job is to make Illinois safe for soybeans.

I am sitting in a 60-mile-an-hour bus sailing over a highway originally laid out for horse and buggy. The ribbon of concrete has been widened and widened until the field fences threaten to topple into the road cuts. In the narrow thread of sod between the shaved banks and the toppling fences grow the relics of what once was Illinois: the prairie.

No one in the bus sees these relics. A worried farmer, his fertilizer bill projecting from his shirt pocket, looks blankly at the lupines, lespedezas, or Baptisias that originally pumped nitrogen out of the prairie air and into his black loamy acres. He does not distinguish them from the parvenu quack-grass in which they grow. Were I to ask him why his corn makes a hundred bushels, while that of non-prairie states does well to make thirty, he would probably answer that Illinois soil is better. Were I to ask him the name of that white spike of pea-like flowers hugging the fence, he would shake his head. A weed, likely.

A cemetery flashes by, its borders alight with prairie puccoons. There are no puccoons elsewhere; dog-fennels and sowthistles supply the yellow *motif* for the modern landscape. Puccoons converse only with the dead.

Through the open window I hear the heart-stirring whistle of an upland plover; time was when his forebears followed the buffalo as they trudged shoulder-deep through an illimitable garden of forgotten blooms. A boy spies the bird and remarks to his father: there goes a snipe.

*   *   *

The sign says, 'You are entering the Green River Soil Conservation District.' In smaller type is a list of who is cooperating; the letters are too small to be read from a moving bus. It must be a roster of who's who in conservation.

The sign is neatly painted. It stands in a creek-bottom pasture so short you could play golf on it. Near by is the graceful loop of an old dry creek bed. The new creek bed is ditched straight as a ruler; it has been 'uncurled' by the county engineer to hurry the run-off. On the hill in the background are contoured stripcrops; they have been 'curled' by the erosion engineer to retard the run-off. The water must be confused by so much advice.

*   *   *

Everything on this farm spells money in the bank. The farmstead abounds in fresh paint, steel, and concrete. A date on the barn commemorates the founding fathers. The roof bristles with lightning rods, the weathercock is proud with new gilt. Even the pigs look solvent.

The old oaks in the woodlot are without issue. There are no hedges, brush patches, fencerows, or other signs of shiftless husbandry. The cornfield has fat steers, but probably no quail. The fences stand on narrow ribbons of sod; whoever plowed that close to barbed wires must have been saying, 'Waste not, want not.'

In the creek-bottom pasture, flood trash is lodged high in the bushes. The creek banks are raw; chunks of Illinois have sloughed off and moved seaward. Patches of giant ragweed mark where freshets have thrown down the silt they could not carry. Just who is solvent? For how long?

*   *   *

The highway stretches like a taut tape across the corn, oats, and clover fields; the bus ticks off the opulent miles; the passengers talk and talk and talk. About what? About baseball, taxes, sons-in-law, movies, motors, and funerals, but never about the heaving groundswell of Illinois that washes the windows of the speeding bus. Illinois has no genesis, no history, no shoals or deeps, no tides of life and death. To them Illinois is only the sea on which they sail to ports unknown.

Red Legs Kicking

W HEN I call to mind my earliest impressions, I wonder whether the process ordinarily referred to as growing up is not actually a process of growing down; whether experience, so much touted among adults as the thing children lack, is not actually a progressive dilution of the essentials by the trivialities of living. This much at least is sure: my earliest impressions of wildlife and its pursuit retain a vivid sharpness of form, color, and atmosphere that half a century of professional wildlife experience has failed to obliterate or to improve upon.

Like most aspiring hunters, I was given, at an early age, a single-barreled shotgun and permission to hunt rabbits. One winter Saturday, *en route* to my favorite rabbit patch, I noticed that the lake, then covered with ice and snow, had developed a small 'airhole' at a point where a windmill discharged warm water from the shore. All ducks had long since departed southward, but I then and there formulated my first ornithological hypothesis: if there were a duck left in the region, he (or she) would inevitably, sooner or later, drop in at this airhole. I suppressed my appetite for rabbits (then no mean feat), sat down in the cold smartweeds on the frozen mud, and waited.

I waited all afternoon, growing colder with each passing crow, and with each rheumatic groan of the laboring windmill. Finally, at sunset, a lone black duck came out of the west, and without even a preliminary circling of the airhole, set his wings and pitched downward.

I cannot remember the shot; I remember only my unspeakable delight when my first duck hit the snowy ice with a thud and lay there, belly up, red legs kicking.

When my father gave me the shotgun, he said I might hunt partridges with it, but that I might not shoot them from trees. I was old enough, he said, to learn wing-shooting.

My dog was good at treeing partridge, and to forego a sure shot in the tree in favor of a hopeless one at the fleeing bird was my first exercise in ethical codes. Compared with a treed partridge, the devil and his seven kingdoms was a mild temptation.

At the end of my second season of featherless partridge-hunting I was walking, one day, through an aspen thicket when a big partridge rose with a roar at my left, and, towering over the aspens, crossed behind me, hell-bent for the nearest cedar swamp. It was a swinging shot of the sort the partridge-hunter dreams about, and the bird tumbled dead in a shower of feathers and golden leaves.

I could draw a map today of each clump of red bunchberry and each blue aster that adorned the mossy spot where he lay, my first partridge on the wing. I suspect my present affection for bunchberries and asters dates from that moment.

On Top

WHEN I first lived in Arizona, the White Mountain was a horseman's world. Except along a few main routes, it was too rough for wagons. There were no cars. It was too big for foot travel; even sheepherders rode. Thus by elimination, the county-sized plateau known as 'on top' was the exclusive domain of the mounted man: mounted cowman, mounted sheepman, mounted forest officer, mounted trapper, and those unclassified mounted men of unknown origin and uncertain destination always found on frontiers. It is difficult for this generation to understand this aristocracy of space based upon transport.

No such thing existed in the railroad towns two days to the north, where you had your choice of travel by shoe leather, burro, cowhorse, buckboard, freight wagon, caboose, or Pullman. Each of these modes of movement corresponded to a social caste, the members of which spoke a distinctive vernacular, wore distinctive clothes, ate distinctive food, and patronized different saloons. Their only common denominator was a democracy of debt to the general store, and a communal wealth of Arizona dust and Arizona sunshine.

As one proceeded southward across the plains and mesas toward the White Mountain, these castes dropped out one by one as their respective modes of travel became impossible, until finally, 'on top,' the horseman ruled the world.

Henry Ford's revolution has of course abolished all this. Today the plane has given even the sky to Tom, Dick, and Harry.

*   *   *

In winter the top of the mountain was denied even to horsemen, for the snow piled deep on the high meadows, and the little canyons up which the only trails ascended drifted full to the brim. In May every canyon roared with an icy torrent, but soon thereafter you could 'top out'—if your horse had the heart to climb half a day through knee-deep mud.

In the little village at the foot of the mountain there existed, each spring, a tacit competition to be the first rider to invade the high solitudes. Many of us tried it, for reasons we did not stop to analyze. Rumor ran fast. Whoever did it first wore a kind of horseman's halo. He was 'man-of-the-year.'

The mountain spring, storybooks to the contrary notwithstanding, did not come with a rush. Balmy days alternated with bitter winds, even after the sheep had gone up. I have seen few colder sights than a drab gray mountain meadow, sprinkled with complaining ewes and half-frozen lambs, pelted by hail and snow. Even the gay nutcrackers humped their backs to these spring storms.

The mountain in summer had as many moods as there were days and weathers; the dullest rider, as well as his horse, felt these moods to the marrow of his bones.

On a fair morning the mountain invited you to get down and roll in its new grass and flowers (your less inhibited horse did just this if you failed to keep a tight rein). Every living thing sang, chirped, and burgeoned. Massive pines and firs, storm-tossed these many months, soaked up the sun in towering dignity. Tassel-eared squirrels, poker-faced but exuding emotion with voice and tail, told you insistently what you already knew full well: that never had there been so rare a day, or so rich a solitude to spend it in.

An hour later, thunderheads may have blotted out the sun, while your erstwhile paradise cowered under the impending lash of lightning, rain, and hail. Black gloom hung poised, as over a bomb with the fuse lighted. Your horse jumped at every rolling pebble, every crackling twig. When you turned in the saddle to unlash your slicker, he shied, snorted, and trembled as if you were about to unfurl the scroll of an Apocalypse. When I hear anyone say he does not fear lightning, I still remark inwardly: he has never ridden The Mountain in July.

The explosions are fearsome enough, but more so are the smoking slivers of stone that sing past your ear when the bolt crashes into a rimrock. Still more so are the splinters that fly when a bolt explodes a pine. I remember one gleaming white one, 15 feet long, that stabbed deep into the earth at my feet and stood there humming like a tuning fork.

It must be poor life that achieves freedom from fear.

*   *   *

The top of the mountain was a great meadow, half a day's ride across, but do not picture it as a single amphitheater of grass, hedged in by a wall of pines. The edges of that meadow were scrolled, curled, and crenulated with an infinity of bays and coves, points and stringers, peninsulas and parks, each one of which differed from all the rest. No man knew them all, and every day's ride offered a gambler's chance of finding a new one. I say 'new' because one often had the feeling, riding into some flower-spangled cove, that if anyone had ever been here before, he must of necessity have sung a song, or written a poem.

This feeling of having this day discovered the incredible accounts, perhaps, for the profusion of initials, dates, and cattle brands inscribed on the patient bark of aspens at every mountain camp site. In these inscriptions one could, in any day, read the history of *Homo texanus* and his culture, not in the cold categories of anthropology, but in terms of the individual career of some founding father whose initials you recognized as the man whose son bested you at horse-trading, or whose daughter you once danced with. Here, dated in the 'nineties, was his simple initial, without brand, inscribed no doubt when he first arrived alone on the mountain as an itinerant cowpuncher. Next, a decade later, his initial plus brand; by that time he had become a solid citizen with an 'outfit,' acquired by thrift, natural increase, and perhaps a nimble rope. Next, only a few years old, you found his daughter's initial, inscribed by some enamored youth aspiring not only to the lady's hand, but to the economic succession.

The old man was dead now; in his later years his heart had thrilled only to his bank account and to the tally of his flocks and herds, but the aspen revealed that in his youth he too had felt the glory of the mountain spring.

The history of the mountain was written not only in aspen bark, but in its place names. Cow-country place names are lewd, humorous, ironic, or sentimental, but seldom trite. Usually they are subtle enough to draw inquiry from new arrivals, whereby hangs that web of tales which, full spun, constitutes the local folk-lore.

For example, there was 'The Boneyard,' a lovely meadow

where bluebells arched over the half-buried skulls and scattered vertebrae of cows long since dead. Here in the 1880's a foolish cowman, newly arrived from the warm valleys of Texas, had trusted the allurements of the mountain summer and essayed to winter his herd on mountain hay. When the November storms hit, he and his horse had floundered out, but not his cows.

Again, there was 'The Campbell Blue,' a headwater of the Blue River to which an early cowman had brought himself a bride. The lady, tiring of rocks and trees, had yearned for a piano. A piano was duly fetched, a Campbell piano. There was only one mule in the county capable of packing it, and only one packer capable of the almost superhuman task of balancing such a load. But the piano failed to bring contentment; the lady decamped; and when the story was told me, the ranch cabin was already a ruin of sagging logs.

Again there was 'Frijole Cienega,' a marshy meadow walled in by pines, under which stood, in my day, a small log cabin used by any passer-by as an overnight camp. It was the unwritten law for the owner of such real estate to leave flour, lard, and beans, and for the passer-by to replenish such stock as he could. But one luckless traveler, trapped there for a week by storms, had found only beans. This breach of hospitality was sufficiently notable to be handed down to history as a place name.

Finally, there was 'Paradise Ranch,' an obvious platitude when read from a map, but something quite different when you arrived there at the end of a hard ride. It lay tucked away on the far side of a high peak, as any proper paradise should. Through its verdant meadows meandered a singing trout stream. A horse left for a month on this meadow waxed so fat that rain-water gathered in a pool on his back. After my first visit to Paradise Ranch I remarked to myself: what else *could* you call it?

*   *   *

Despite several opportunities to do so, I have never returned to the White Mountain. I prefer not to see what tourists, roads, sawmills, and logging railroads have done for it, or to it. I hear young people, not yet born when I first rode out 'on top,' exclaim about it as a wonderful place. To this, with an unspoken mental reservation, I agree.

Thinking Like a Mountain

A DEEP CHESTY bawl echoes from rimrock to rimrock, rolls down the mountain, and fades into the far blackness of the night. It is an outburst of wild defiant sorrow, and of contempt for all the adversities of the world.

Every living thing (and perhaps many a dead one as well) pays heed to that call. To the deer it is a reminder of the way of all flesh, to the pine a forecast of midnight scuffles and of blood upon the snow, to the coyote a promise of gleanings to come, to the cowman a threat of red ink at the bank, to the hunter a challenge of fang against bullet. Yet behind these obvious and immediate hopes and fears there lies a deeper meaning, known only to the mountain itself. Only the mountain has lived long enough to listen objectively to the howl of a wolf.

Those unable to decipher the hidden meaning know nevertheless that it is there, for it is felt in all wolf country, and distinguishes that country from all other land. It tingles in the spine of all who hear wolves by night, or who scan their tracks by day. Even without sight or sound of wolf, it is implicit in a hundred small events: the midnight whinny of a pack horse, the rattle of rolling rocks, the bound of a fleeing deer, the way shadows lie under the spruces. Only the ineducable tyro can fail to sense the presence or absence of wolves, or the fact that mountains have a secret opinion about them.

My own conviction on this score dates from the day I saw a wolf die. We were eating lunch on a high rimrock, at the foot of which a turbulent river elbowed its way. We saw what we thought was a doe fording the torrent, her breast awash in white water. When she climbed the bank toward us and shook out her tail, we realized our error: it was a wolf. A half-dozen others, evidently grown pups, sprang from the willows and all joined in a welcoming mêlée of wagging tails and playful maulings. What was literally a pile of wolves writhed and tumbled in the center of an open flat at the foot of our rimrock.

In those days we had never heard of passing up a chance to kill a wolf. In a second we were pumping lead into the pack, but with more excitement than accuracy: how to aim a steep downhill shot is always confusing. When our rifles were empty, the old wolf was down, and a pup was dragging a leg into impassable slide-rocks.

We reached the old wolf in time to watch a fierce green fire dying in her eyes. I realized then, and have known ever since, that there was something new to me in those eyes—something known only to her and to the mountain. I was young then, and full of trigger-itch; I thought that because fewer wolves meant more deer, that no wolves would mean hunters' paradise. But after seeing the green fire die, I sensed that neither the wolf nor the mountain agreed with such a view.

* * *

Since then I have lived to see state after state extirpate its wolves. I have watched the face of many a newly wolfless mountain, and seen the south-facing slopes wrinkle with a maze of new deer trails. I have seen every edible bush and seedling browsed, first to anaemic desuetude, and then to death. I have seen every edible tree defoliated to the height of a saddlehorn. Such a mountain looks as if someone had given God a new pruning shears, and forbidden Him all other exercise. In the end the starved bones of the hoped-for deer herd, dead of its own too-much, bleach with the bones of the dead sage, or molder under the high-lined junipers.

I now suspect that just as a deer herd lives in mortal fear of its wolves, do does a mountain live in mortal fear of its deer. And perhaps with better cause, for while a buck pulled down by wolves can be replaced in two or three years, a range pulled down by too many deer may fail of replacement in as many decades.

So also with cows. The cowman who cleans his range of wolves does not realize that he is taking over the wolf's job of trimming the herd to fit the range. He has not learned to think like a mountain. Hence we have dustbowls, and rivers washing the future into the sea.

*   *   *

We all strive for safety, prosperity, comfort, long life, and dull-ness. The deer strives with his supple legs, the cowman with trap and poison, the statesman with pen, the most of us with machines, votes, and dollars, but it all comes to the same thing: peace in our time. A measure of success in this is all well enough, and perhaps is a requisite to objective thinking, but too much safety seems to yield only danger in the long run. Perhaps this is behind Thoreau's dictum: In wildness is the salvation of the world. Perhaps this is the hidden meaning in the howl of the wolf, long known among mountains, but seldom perceived among men.

Escudilla

L IFE IN Arizona was bounded under foot by grama grass, overhead by sky, and on the horizon by Escudilla.

To the north of the mountain you rode on honey-colored plains. Look up anywhere, any time, and you saw Escudilla.

To the east you rode over a confusion of wooded mesas. Each hollow seemed its own small world, soaked in sun, fragrant with juniper, and cozy with the chatter of piñon jays. But top out on a ridge and you at once became a speck in an immensity. On its edge hung Escudilla.

To the south lay the tangled canyons of Blue River, full of whitetails, wild turkeys, and wilder cattle. When you missed a saucy buck waving his goodbye over the skyline, and looked down your sights to wonder why, you looked at a far blue mountain: Escudilla.

To the west billowed the outliers of the Apache National Forest. We cruised timber there, converting the tall pines, forty by forty, into notebook figures representing hypothetical lumber piles. Panting up a canyon, the cruiser felt a curious incongruity between the remoteness of his notebook symbols and the immediacy of sweaty fingers, locust thorns, deer-fly bites, and scolding squirrels. But on the next ridge a cold wind, roaring across a green sea of pines, blew his doubts away. On the far shore hung Escudilla.

The mountain bounded not only our work and our play, but even our attempts to get a good dinner. On winter evenings we often tried to ambush a mallard on the river flats. The wary flocks circled the rosy west, the steel-blue north, and then disappeared into the inky black of Escudilla. If they reappeared on set wings, we had a fat drake for the Dutch oven. If they failed to reappear, it was bacon and beans again.

There was, in fact, only one place from which you did not see Escudilla on the skyline: that was the top of Escudilla itself. Up there you could not see the mountain, but you could feel it. The reason was the big bear.

Old Bigfoot was a robber-baron, and Escudilla was his castle. Each spring, when the warm winds had softened the shadows on the snow, the old grizzly crawled out of his hibernation den in the rock slides and, descending the mountain, bashed in the head of a cow. Eating his fill, he climbed back to his crags, and there summered peaceably on marmots, conies, berries, and roots.

I once saw one of his kills. The cow's skull and neck were pulp, as if she had collided head-on with a fast freight.

No one ever saw the old bear, but in the muddy springs about the base of the cliffs you saw his incredible tracks. Seeing them made the most hard-bitten cowboys aware of bear. Wherever they rode they saw the mountain, and when they saw the mountain they thought of bear. Campfire conversation ran to beef, *bailes*, and bear. Bigfoot claimed for his own only a cow a year, and a few square miles of useless rocks, but his personality pervaded the county.

Those were the days when progress first came to the cow country. Progress had various emissaries.

One was the first transcontinental automobilist. The cowboys understood this breaker of roads; he talked the same breezy bravado as any breaker of bronchos.

They did not understand, but they listened to and looked at, the pretty lady in black velvet who came to enlighten them, in a Boston accent, about woman suffrage.

They marveled, too, at the telephone engineer who strung wires on the junipers and brought instantaneous messages from town. An old man asked whether the wire could bring him a side of bacon.

One spring, progress sent still another emissary, a government trapper, a sort of St. George in overalls, seeking dragons to slay at government expense. Were there, he asked, any destructive animals in need of slaying? Yes, there was the big bear.

The trapper packed his mule and headed for Escudilla.

In a month he was back, his mule staggering under a heavy hide. There was only one barn in town big enough to dry it on. He had tried traps, poison, and all his usual wiles to no avail. Then he had erected a set-gun in a defile through which only the bear could pass, and waited. The last grizzly walked into the string and shot himself.

It was June. The pelt was foul, patchy, and worthless. It seemed to us rather an insult to deny the last grizzly the chance to leave a good pelt as a memorial to his race. All he left was a skull in the National Museum, and a quarrel among scientists over the Latin name of the skull.

It was only after we pondered on these things that we began to wonder who wrote the rules for progress.

* * *

Since the beginning, time had gnawed at the basaltic hulk of Escudilla, wasting, waiting, and building. Time built three things on the old mountain, a venerable aspect, a community of minor animals and plants, and a grizzly.

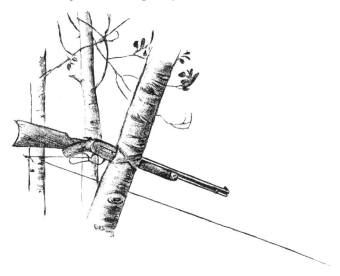

The government trapper who took the grizzly knew he had made Escudilla safe for cows. He did not know he had toppled the spire off an edifice a-building since the morning stars sang together.

The bureau chief who sent the trapper was a biologist versed in the architecture of evolution, but he did not know that spires might be as important as cows. He did not foresee that within two decades the cow country would become tourist country, and as such have greater need of bears than of beefsteaks.

The Congressmen who voted money to clear the ranges of bears were the sons of pioneers. They acclaimed the superior virtues of the frontiersman, but they strove with might and main to make an end of the frontier.

We forest officers, who acquiesced in the extinguishment of the bear, knew a local rancher who had plowed up a dagger engraved with the name of one of Coronado's captains. We spoke harshly of the Spaniards who, in their zeal for gold and converts, had needlessly extinguished the native Indians. It did not occur to us that we, too, were the captains of an invasion too sure of its own righteousness.

Escudilla still hangs on the horizon, but when you see it you no longer think of bear. It's only a mountain now.

Guacamaja

THE PHYSICS of beauty is one department of natural science still in the Dark Ages. Not even the manipulators of bent space have tried to solve its equations. Everybody knows, for example, that the autumn landscape in the north woods is the land, plus a red maple, plus a ruffed grouse. In terms of conventional physics, the grouse represents only a millionth of either the mass or the energy of an acre. Yet subtract the grouse and the whole thing is dead. An enormous amount of some kind of motive power has been lost.

It is easy to say that the loss is all in our mind's eye, but is there any sober ecologist who will agree? He knows full well that there has been an ecological death, the significance of which is inexpressible in terms of contemporary science. A philosopher has called this imponderable essence the *noumenon* of material things. It stands in contradistinction to *phenomenon*, which is ponderable and predictable, even to the tossings and turnings of the remotest star.

The grouse is the noumenon of the north woods, the blue jay of the hickory groves, the whisky-jack of the muskegs, the piñonero of the juniper foothills. Ornithological texts do not record these facts. I suppose they are new to science, however obvious to the discerning scientist. Be that as it may, I here record the discovery of the noumenon of the Sierra Madre: the Thick-billed Parrot.

He is a discovery only because so few have visited his haunts. Once there, only the deaf and blind could fail to perceive his role in the mountain life and landscape. Indeed you have hardly finished breakfast before the chattering flocks leave their roost on the rimrocks and perform a sort of morning drill in the high reaches of the dawn. Like squadrons of cranes they wheel and spiral, loudly debating with each other the question (which also puzzles you) whether this new day which creeps slowly over the canyons is bluer and golder than its predecessors, or less so. The vote being a draw, they repair by separate companies to the high mesas for their breakfast of pine-seed-on-the-half-shell. They have not yet seen you.

But a little later, as you begin the steep ascent out of the canyon, some sharp-eyed parrot, perhaps a mile away, espies this strange creature puffing up the trail where only deer or lion, bear or turkey, is licensed to travel. Breakfast is forgotten. With a whoop and a shout the whole gang is a-wing and coming at you. As they circle overhead you wish fervently for a parrot dictionary. Are they demanding what-the-devil business have you in these parts? Or are they, like an avian chamber-of-commerce, merely making sure you appreciate the glories of their home town, its weather, its citizens, and its glorious future as compared with any and all other times and places whatsoever? It might be either or both. And there flashes through your mind the sad premonition of what will happen when the road is built, and this riotous reception committee first greets the tourist-with-a-gun.

It is soon clear that you are a dull inarticulate fellow, unable to respond by so much as a whistle to the standard amenities of the Sierra morn. And after all, there are more pine cones in the woods than have yet been opened, so let's finish breakfast! This time they may settle upon some tree below the rimrock, giving you the chance to sneak out to the edge and look down. There for the first time you see color: velvet green uniforms with scarlet and yellow epaulets and black helmets, sweeping noisily from pine to pine, but always in formation and always in even numbers. Only once did I see a gang of five, or any other number not comprised of pairs.

I do not know whether the nesting pairs are as noisy as these roistering flocks that greeted me in September. I do know that in September, if there are parrots on the mountain, you will soon know it. As a proper ornithologist, I should doubtless try to describe the call. It superficially resembles that of the piñon jay, but the music of the piñoneros is as soft and nostalgic as the haze hanging in their native canyons, while that of the Guacamaja is louder and full of the salty enthusiasm of high comedy.

In spring, I am told, the pair hunts up a woodpecker hole in some tall dead pine and performs its racial duty in temporary isolation. But what woodpecker excavates a hole large enough?

The Guacamaja (as the natives euphoniously call the parrot) is as big as a pigeon, and hardly to be squeezed into a flicker-loft. Does he, with his own powerful beak, perform the necessary enlargement? Or is he dependent on the holes of the imperial woodpecker, which is said to occur in these parts? To some future ornithological visitor I bequeath the pleasant task of discovering the answer.

The Green Lagoons

IT IS the part of wisdom never to revisit a wilderness, for the more golden the lily, the more certain that someone has gilded it. To return not only spoils a trip, but tarnishes a memory. It is only in the mind that shining adventure remains forever bright. For this reason, I have never gone back to the Delta of the Colorado since my brother and I explored it, by canoe, in 1922.

For all we could tell, the Delta had lain forgotten since Hernando de Alarcón landed there in 1540. When we camped on the estuary which is said to have harbored his ships, we had not for weeks seen a man or a cow, an axe-cut or a fence. Once we crossed an old wagon track, its maker unknown and its errand probably sinister. Once we found a tin can; it was pounced upon as a valuable utensil.

Dawn on the Delta was whistled in by Gambel quail, which roosted in the mesquites overhanging camp. When the sun peeped over the Sierra Madre, it slanted across a hundred miles of lovely desolation, a vast flat bowl of wilderness rimmed by jagged peaks. On the map the Delta was bisected by the river, but in fact the river was nowhere and everywhere, for he could not decide which of a hundred green lagoons offered the most pleasant and least speedy path to the Gulf. So he traveled them all, and so did we. He divided and rejoined, he twisted and turned, he meandered in awesome jungles, he all but ran in circles, he dallied with lovely groves, he got lost and was glad of it, and so were we. For the last word in procrastination, go travel with a river reluctant to lose his freedom in the sea.

'He leadeth me by still waters' was to us only a phrase in a book until we had nosed our canoe through the green lagoons. If David had not written the psalm, we should have felt constrained to write our own. The still waters were of a deep emerald hue, colored by algae, I suppose, but no less green for all that. A verdant wall of mesquite and willow separated the channel from the thorny desert beyond. At each bend we saw egrets standing in the pools ahead, each white statue matched by its white reflection. Fleets of cormorants drove their black prows in quest of skittering mullets; avocets, willets, and yellow-legs

dozed one-legged on the bars; mallards, widgeons, and teal sprang skyward in alarm. As the birds took the air, they accumulated in a small cloud ahead, there to settle, or to break back to our rear. When a troop of egrets settled on a far green willow, they looked like a premature snowstorm.

All this wealth of fowl and fish was not for our delectation alone. Often we came upon a bobcat, flattened to some half-immersed driftwood log, paw poised for mullet. Families of raccoons waded the shallows, munching water beetles. Coyotes watched us from inland knolls, waiting to resume their breakfast of mesquite beans, varied, I suppose, by an occasional crippled shore bird, duck, or quail. At every shallow ford were tracks of burro deer. We always examined these deer trails, hoping to find signs of the despot of the Delta, the great jaguar, *el tigre.*

We saw neither hide nor hair of him, but his personality pervaded the wilderness; no living beast forgot his potential presence, for the price of unwariness was death. No deer rounded a bush, or stopped to nibble pods under a mesquite tree, without a premonitory sniff for *el tigre*. No campfire died without talk of him. No dog curled up for the night, save at his master's feet; he needed no telling that the king of cats still ruled the night; that those massive paws could fell an ox, those jaws shear off bones like a guillotine.

By this time the Delta has probably been made safe for cows, and forever dull for adventuring hunters. Freedom from fear has arrived, but a glory has departed from the green lagoons.

When Kipling smelled the supper smokes of Amritsar, he should have elaborated, for no other poet has sung, or smelled, this green earth's firewoods. Most poets must have subsisted on anthracite.

On the Delta one burns only mesquite, the ultimate in fragrant fuels. Brittle with a hundred frosts and floods, baked by a thousand suns, the gnarled imperishable bones of these ancient trees lie ready-to-hand at every camp, ready to slant blue smoke across the twilight, sing a song of teapots, bake a loaf, brown a kettle of quail, and warm the shins of man and beast. When you have ladled a shovelful of mesquite coals under the Dutch oven, take care not to sit down in that spot before bedtime, lest you rise with a yelp that scares the quail roosting overhead. Mesquite coals have seven lives.

We had cooked with white-oak coals in the corn belt, we had smudged our pots with pine in the north woods, we had browned venison ribs over Arizona juniper, but we had not seen perfection until we roasted a young goose with Delta mesquite.

Those geese deserved the best of brownings, for they had bested us for a week. Every morning we watched the cackling phalanx head inland from the Gulf, shortly to return, replete and silent. What rare provender in what green lagoon was the object of their quest? Again and again we moved camp gooseward, hoping to see them settle, to find their banquet board. One day at about 8 A.M. we saw the phalanx circle, break ranks, sideslip, and fall to earth like maple leaves. Flock after flock followed. At long last we had found their rendezvous.

Next morning at the same hour we lay in wait beside an ordinary-looking slough, its bars covered with yesterday's goosetracks. We were already hungry, for it had been a long tramp from camp. My brother was eating a cold roast quail. The quail was halfway to his mouth when a cackle from the sky froze us to immobility. That quail hung in mid-air while the flock circled at leisure, debated, hesitated, and finally came in. That quail fell in the sand when the guns spoke, and all the geese we could eat lay kicking on the bar.

More came, and settled. The dog lay trembling. We ate quail at leisure, peering through the blind, listening to the small-talk. Those geese were gobbling *gravel.* As one flock filled up and left, another arrived, eager for their delectable stones. Of all the millions of pebbles in the green lagoons, those on this particular bar suited them best. The difference, to a snow goose, was worth forty miles of flying. It was worth a long hike to us.

Most small game on the Delta was too abundant to hunt. At every camp we hung up, in a few minutes' shooting, enough quail for tomorrow's use. Good gastronomy demanded at least one frosty night on the stringer as the necessary interlude between roosting in a mesquite and roasting over mesquite.

All game was of incredible fatness. Every deer laid down so much tallow that the dimple along his backbone would have held a small pail of water, had he allowed us to pour it. He didn't.

The origin of all this opulence was not far to seek. Every mesquite and every tornillo was loaded with pods. The dried-up mud flats bore an annual grass, the grain-like seeds of which could be scooped up by the cupful. There were great patches of a legume resembling coffeeweed; if you walked through these, your pockets filled up with shelled beans.

I remember one patch of wild melons, or *calabasillas,* covering several acres of mudflat. The deer and coons had opened the frozen fruits, exposing the seeds. Doves and quail fluttered over this banquet like fruit-flies over a ripe banana.

We could not, or at least did not, eat what the quail and deer did, but we shared their evident delight in this milk-and-honey wilderness. Their festival mood became our mood; we all reveled in a common abundance and in each other's well-being. I cannot recall feeling, in settled country, a like sensitivity to the mood of the land.

Camp-keeping in the Delta was not all beer and skittles. The problem was water. The lagoons were saline; the river, where we could find it, was too muddy to drink. At each new camp we dug a new well. Most wells, however, yielded only brine from the Gulf. We learned, the hard way, where to dig for sweet water. When in doubt about a new well, we lowered the dog by his hind legs. If he drank freely, it was the signal for us to beach the canoe, kindle the fire, and pitch the tent. Then we sat at peace with the world while the quail sizzled in the Dutch oven, and the sun sank in glory behind the San Pedro Mártir. Later, dishes washed, we rehearsed the day, and listened to the noises of the night.

Never did we plan the morrow, for we had learned that in the wilderness some new and irresistible distraction is sure to turn up each day before breakfast. Like the river, we were free to wander.

To travel by plan in the Delta is no light matter; we were reminded of this whenever we climbed a cottonwood for a wider view. The view was so wide as to discourage prolonged scrutiny, especially toward the northwest, where a white streak at the foot of the Sierra hung in perpetual mirage. This was the great salt desert, on which, in 1829, Sylvester Pattie died of thirst, exhaustion, and mosquitoes. Pattie had a plan: to cross the Delta to California.

Once we had a plan to portage from one green lagoon to a greener one. We knew it was there by the waterfowl hovering over it. The distance was 800 yards through a jungle of *cachinilla*, a tall spear-like shrub which grows in thickets of incredible density. The floods had bent down the spears, which opposed our passage in the manner of a Macedonian phalanx. We discreetly withdrew, persuaded that our lagoon was prettier anyhow.

Getting caught in a maze of *cachinilla* phalanxes was a real danger that no one had mentioned, whereas the danger we had been warned against failed to materialize. When we launched our canoe above the border, there were dire predictions of sudden death. Far huskier craft, we were told, had been overwhelmed by the tidal bore, a wall of water that rages up the river from the Gulf with certain incoming tides. We talked about the bore, we spun elaborate schemes to circumvent it, we even saw it in our dreams, with dolphins riding its crest and an aerial escort of screaming gulls. When we reached the mouth of the river, we hung our canoe in a tree and waited two days, but the bore let us down. It did not come.

The Delta having no place names, we had to devise our own as we went. One lagoon we called the Rillito, and it is here that we saw pearls in the sky. We were lying flat on our backs, soaking up November sun, staring idly at a soaring buzzard overhead. Far beyond him the sky suddenly exhibited a rotating circle of white spots, alternately visible and invisible. A faint bugle note soon told us they were cranes, inspecting their Delta and finding it good. At the time my ornithology was homemade, and I was pleased to think them whooping cranes because they were so white. Doubtless they were sandhill cranes, but it doesn't matter. What matters is that we were sharing our wilderness with the wildest of living fowl. We and they had found a common home in the remote fastnesses of space and time; we were both back in the Pleistocene. Had we been able to, we would have bugled back their greeting. Now, from the far reaches of the years, I see them wheeling still.

*   *   *

All this was far away and long ago. I am told the green lagoons now raise cantaloupes. If so, they should not lack flavor.

Man always kills the thing he loves, and so we the pioneers have killed our wilderness. Some say we had to. Be that as it may, I am glad I shall never be young without wild country to be young in. Of what avail are forty freedoms without a blank spot on the map?

Song of the Gavilan

THE SONG of a river ordinarily means the tune that waters play on rock, root, and rapid.

The Rio Gavilan has such a song. It is a pleasant music, bespeaking dancing riffles and fat rainbows laired under mossy roots of sycamore, oak, and pine. It is also useful, for the tinkle of waters so fills the narrow canyon that deer and turkey, coming down out of the hills to drink, hear no footfall of man or horse. Look sharp as you round the next bend, for it may yield you a shot, and thus save a heart-breaking climb in the high mesas.

This song of the waters is audible to every ear, but there is other music in these hills, by no means audible to all. To hear even a few notes of it you must first live here for a long time, and you must know the speech of hills and rivers. Then on a still night, when the campfire is low and the Pleiades have climbed over rimrocks, sit quietly and listen for a wolf to howl, and think hard of everything you have seen and tried to understand. Then you may hear it—a vast pulsing harmony—its score inscribed on a thousand hills, its notes the lives and deaths of plants and animals, its rhythms spanning the seconds and the centuries.

The life of every river sings its own song, but in most the song is long since marred by the discords of misuse. Overgrazing first mars the plants and then the soil. Rifle, trap, and poison next deplete the larger birds and mammals; then comes a park or forest with roads and tourists. Parks are made to bring the music to the many, but by the time many are attuned to hear it there is little left but noise.

There once were men capable of inhabiting a river without disrupting the harmony of its life. They must have lived in thousands on the Gavilan, for their works are everywhere. Ascend any draw debouching on any canyon and you find yourself climbing little rock terraces or check dams, the crest of one level with the base of the next. Behind each dam is a little plot of soil that was once a field or garden, subirrigated by the showers which fell on the steep adjoining slopes. On the crest of the ridge you may find the stone foundations of a watch tower; here the hillside farmer probably stood guard over his polka-dot acrelets. Household water he must have carried from the river. Of domestic animals he evidently had none. What crops did he raise? How long ago? The only fragment of an answer lies in the 300-year-old pines, oaks, or junipers that now find rootage in his little fields. Evidently it was longer ago than the age of the oldest trees.

The deer love to lie on these little terraces. They afford a level bed, free of rocks, upholstered with oak leaves, and curtained by shrubs. One bound over the dam and the deer is out of sight of an intruder.

One day, by aid of a roaring wind, I crept down upon a buck bedded on a dam. He lay in the shade of a great oak whose roots grasped the ancient masonry. His horns and ears were silhouetted against the golden grama beyond, in which grew the green rosette of a mescal. The whole scene had the balance of a well-laid centerpiece. I overshot, my arrow splintering on the rocks the old Indian had laid. As the buck bounded down the mountain with a goodbye wave of his snowy flag, I realized that he and I were actors in an allegory. Dust to dust, stone age to stone age, but always the eternal chase! It was appropriate that I missed, for when a great oak grows in what is now my garden, I hope there will be bucks to bed in its fallen leaves, and hunters to stalk, and miss, and wonder who built the garden wall.

Some day my buck will get a .30–.30 in his glossy ribs. A clumsy steer will appropriate his bed under the oak, and will munch the golden grama until it is replaced by weeds. Then a freshet will tear out the old dam, and pile its rocks against a tourist road along the river below. Trucks will churn the dust of the old trail on which I saw wolf tracks yesterday.

To the superficial eye the Gavilan is a hard and stony land, full of cruel slopes and cliffs, its trees too gnarled for post or sawlog, its ranges too steep for pasturage. But the old terrace-builders were not deceived; they knew it by experience to be a land of milk and honey. These twisted oaks and junipers bear each year a crop of mast to be had by wildlings for the pawing. The deer, turkeys, and javelinas spend their days, like steers in a cornfield, converting this mast into succulent meat. These golden grasses conceal, under their waving plumes, a subterranean garden of bulbs and tubers, including wild potatoes. Open the crop of a fat little Mearns' quail and you find an herbarium of subsurface

foods scratched from the rocky ground you thought barren.
These foods are the motive power which plants pump through
that great organ called the fauna.

Every region has a human food symbolic of its fatness. The
hills of the Gavilan find their gastronomic epitome in this wise:
Kill a mast-fed buck, not earlier than November, not later than

January. Hang him in a live-oak tree for seven frosts and seven
suns. Then cut out the half-frozen 'straps' from their bed of
tallow under the saddle, and slice them transversely into steaks.
Rub each steak with salt, pepper, and flour. Throw into a Dutch
oven containing deep smoking-hot bear fat and standing on
live-oak coals. Fish out the steaks at the first sign of browning.
Throw a little flour into the fat, then ice-cold water, then milk.
Lay a steak on the summit of a steaming sour-dough biscuit and
drown both in gravy.

This structure is symbolic. The buck lies on his mountain,
and the golden gravy is the sunshine that floods his days, even
unto the end.

Food is the continuum in the Song of the Gavilan. I mean,
of course, not only your food, but food for the oak which feeds

the buck who feeds the cougar who dies under an oak and goes back into acorns for his erstwhile prey. This is one of many food cycles starting from and returning to oaks, for the oak also feeds the jay who feeds the goshawk who named your river, the bear whose grease made your gravy, the quail who taught you a lesson in botany, and the turkey who daily gives you the slip. And the common end of all is to help the headwater trickles of the Gavilan split one more grain of soil off the broad hulk of the Sierra Madre to make another oak.

There are men charged with the duty of examining the construction of the plants, animals, and soils which are the instruments of the great orchestra. These men are called professors. Each selects one instrument and spends his life taking it apart and describing its strings and sounding boards. This process of dismemberment is called research. The place for dismemberment is called a university.

A professor may pluck the strings of his own instrument, but never that of another, and if he listens for music he must never admit it to his fellows or to his students. For all are restrained by an ironbound taboo which decrees that the construction of instruments is the domain of science, while the detection of harmony is the domain of poets.

Professors serve science and science serves progress. It serves progress so well that many of the more intricate instruments are stepped upon and broken in the rush to spread progress to all backward lands. One by one the parts are thus stricken from the song of songs. If the professor is able to classify each instrument before it is broken, he is well content.

Science contributes moral as well as material blessings to the world. Its great moral contribution is objectivity, or the scientific point of view. This means doubting everything except facts; it means hewing to the facts, let the chips fall where they may. One of the facts hewn to by science is that every river needs more people, and all people need more inventions, and hence more science; the good life depends on the indefinite extension of this chain of logic. That the good life on any river may likewise depend on the perception of its music, and the preservation of some music to perceive, is a form of doubt not yet entertained by science.

Science has not yet arrived on the Gavilan, so the otter plays tag in its pools and riffles and chases the fat rainbows from under its mossy banks, with never a thought for the flood that one day will scour the bank into the Pacific, or for the sportsman who will one day dispute his title to the trout. Like the scientist, he has no doubts about his own design for living. He assumes that for him the Gavilan will sing forever.

Cheat Takes Over

J UST AS there is honor among thieves, so there is solidarity and co-operation among plant and animal pests. Where one pest is stopped by natural barriers, another arrives to breach the same wall by a new approach. In the end every region and every resource get their quota of uninvited ecological guests.

Thus the English sparrow, rendered innocuous by the shrinkage in horses, was succeeded by the starling, who thrives in the wake of tractors. The chestnut blight, which had no passport beyond the west boundary of chestnuts, is being followed by the Dutch elm disease, with every chance of spreading to the west boundary of elms. The white-pine blister rust, stopped in its westward march by the treeless plains, effected a new landing via the back door, and is now romping down the Rockies from Idaho toward California.

Ecological stowaways began to arrive with the earliest settlements. The Swedish botanist, Peter Kalm, found most of the European weeds established in New Jersey and New York as early as 1750. They spread as rapidly as the settler's plow could prepare a suitable seedbed.

Others arrived later, from the West, and found thousands of square miles of ready-made seedbed prepared by the trampling hoofs of range livestock. In such cases the spread was often so rapid as to escape recording; one simply woke up one fine spring to find the range dominated by a new weed. A notable instance was the invasion of the intermountain and northwestern foothills by downy chess or cheat grass (*Bromus tectorum*).

Lest you gain too optimistic an impression of this new ingredient of the melting pot, let me say that cheat is not a grass in the sense of forming a live sod. It is an annual weed of the grass family, like foxtail or crabgrass, dying each fall and reseeding that fall or the next spring. In Europe its habitat is the decaying straw of thatched roofs. The Latin word for roof is *tectum*, hence the label 'Brome of the roofs.' A plant that can make a living on the roof of a house can also thrive on this rich but arid roof of the continent.

Today the honey-colored hills that flank the northwestern mountains derive their hue not from the rich and useful bunchgrass and wheatgrass which once covered them, but from the inferior cheat which has replaced these native grasses. The motorist who exclaims about the flowing contours that lead his eye upward to far summits is unaware of this substitution. It does not occur to him that hills, too, cover ruined complexions with ecological face powder.

The cause of the substitution is overgrazing. When the toogreat herds and flocks chewed and trampled the hide off the foothills, something had to cover the raw eroding earth. Cheat did.

Cheat grows in dense stands, and each stem bears a mass of prickly awns which render the mature plant inedible to stock. To appreciate the predicament of a cow trying to eat mature cheat, try walking through it in low shoes. All field workers in cheat country wear high boots. Nylons are here relegated to running boards and concrete sidewalks.

These prickly awns cover the autumn hills with a yellow blanket as inflammable as cotton-wool. It is impossible fully to protect cheat country from fire. As a consequence, the remnants of good browse plants, such as sagebrush and bitterbrush, are being burned back to higher altitudes, where they are less useful as winter forage. The lower fringes of pine timber, needed as winter cover for deer and birds, are likewise being singed back to higher levels.

To a summer tourist, the burning of a few bushes off the foothills may seem a minor loss. He is unaware that, in winter, snow excludes both livestock and game from the higher mountains. Livestock can be fed on valley ranches, but deer and elk must find food in the foothills or starve. The habitable wintering belt is narrow, and the further north one goes, the greater is the disparity between the area of habitable winter range and the area of summer range. Hence these scattering foothill clumps of bitterbrush, sage, and oak, now fast shrinking under the onslaught of cheat fires, are the key to wildlife survival in the whole region. Besides, these scattered bushes often harbor, under their mechanical protection, remnants of native perennial grasses. When the bushes are burned off, these grass remnants succumb to livestock. While the sportsmen and stockmen wrangle over who should move first in easing the burden on the winter range, cheat grass is leaving less and less winter range to wrangle about.

Cheat gives rise to many minor irritations, most of them less important, perhaps, than starving deer or cheat-sores in a cow's mouth, but still worth mentioning. Cheat invades old alfalfa fields and degrades the hay. It blockades newly hatched ducklings from making the vital trek from upland nest to lowland water. It invades the lower fringe of lumber areas, where it chokes out seedling pines and threatens older reproduction with the danger of quick fire.

I experienced a minor irritation myself when I arrived at a 'port of entry' on the northern California border, where my car and baggage were searched by a quarantine officer. He explained politely that California welcomes tourists, but that she must make sure their baggage harbors no plant or animal pests. I asked him what pests. He recited a long list of prospective garden and orchard afflictions, but he did not mention the yellow blanket of cheat, which already extended from his feet to the far hills in every direction.

As is true of the carp, the starling, and the Russian thistle, the cheat-afflicted regions make a virtue of necessity and find the invader useful. Newly sprouted cheat is good forage while it lasts; like as not the lamb chop you ate for lunch was nurtured on cheat during the tender days of spring. Cheat reduces the erosion that would otherwise follow the overgrazing that admitted cheat. (This ecological ring-around-the-rosy merits long thought.)

I listened carefully for clues whether the West has accepted cheat as a necessary evil, to be lived with until kingdom come, or whether it regards cheat as a challenge to rectify its past errors in land-use. I found the hopeless attitude almost universal. There is, as yet, no sense of pride in the husbandry of wild plants and animals, no sense of shame in the proprietorship of a sick landscape. We tilt windmills in behalf of conservation in convention halls and editorial offices, but on the back forty we disclaim even owning a lance.

Clandeboye

EDUCATION, I fear, is learning to see one thing by going blind to another.

One thing most of us have gone blind to is the quality of marshes. I am reminded of this when, as a special favor, I take a visitor to Clandeboye, only to find that, to him, it is merely lonelier to look upon, and stickier to navigate, than other boggy places.

This is strange, for any pelican, duckhawk, godwit, or western grebe is aware that Clandeboye is a marsh apart. Why else do they seek it out in preference to other marshes? Why else do they resent my intrusion within its precincts not as mere trespass, but as some kind of cosmic impropriety?

I think the secret is this: Clandeboye is a marsh apart, not only in space, but in time. Only the uncritical consumers of hand-me-down history suppose that 1941 arrived simultaneously in all marshes. The birds know better. Let a squadron of southbound pelicans but feel a lift of prairie breeze over Clandeboye, and they sense at once that here is a landing in the geological past, a refuge from that most relentless of aggressors, the future. With queer antediluvian grunts they set wing, descending in majestic spirals to the welcoming wastes of a bygone age.

Other refugees are already there, each accepting in his own fashion his respite from the march of time. Forster's terns, like troops of happy children, scream over the mudflats as if the first cold melt from the retreating ice sheet were shivering the spines of their minnowy prey. A file of sandhill cranes bugles defiance of whatever it is that cranes distrust and fear. A flotilla of swans rides the bay in quiet dignity, bemoaning the evanescence of swanly things. From the tip of a storm-wracked cottonwood, where the marsh discharges into the big lake, a peregrine stoops playfully at passing fowl. He is gorged with duck meat, but it amuses him to terrorize the squealing teals. This, too, was his after-dinner sport in the days when Lake Agassiz covered the prairies.

It is easy to classify the attitudes of these wildlings, for each wears his heart on his sleeve. But there is one refugee in Clandeboye whose mind I cannot read, for he tolerates no truck with human intruders. Let other birds spill easy confidence to upstarts in overalls, but not the western grebe! Stalk carefully as I will to the bordering reeds, all I get to see is a flash of silver as he sinks, soundless, into the bay. And then, from behind the reedy curtain of the far shore, he tinkles a little bell, warning all his kind of something. Of what?

I've never been able to guess, for there is some barrier between this bird and all mankind. One of my guests dismissed the grebe by checking off his name in the bird list, and jotting down a syllabic paraphrase of the tinkling bell: '*crick-crick*,' or some such inanity. The man failed to sense that here was something more than a bird-call, that here was a *secret* message, calling not for rendition in counterfeit syllables, but for translation and understanding. Alas, I was, and still am, as helpless to translate it or to understand it as he.

As the spring advances, the bell grows persistent; at dawn and at dusk it tinkles from every open water. I infer that the young grebes are now launched in their watery career, and are receiving parental instruction in the grebe philosophy. But to *see* this schoolroom scene, that is not so easy.

One day I buried myself, prone, in the muck of a muskrat house. While my clothes absorbed local color, my eyes absorbed the lore of the marsh. A hen redhead cruised by with her convoy of ducklings, pink-billed fluffs of greenish-golden down. A Virginia rail nearly brushed my nose. The shadow of a pelican sailed over a pool in which a yellow-leg alighted with warbling whistle; it occurred to me that whereas I *write* a poem by dint of mighty cerebration, the yellow-leg *walks* a better one just by lifting his foot.

A mink slithered up the shore behind me, nose in air, trailing. Marsh wrens made trip after trip to a knot in the bulrushes, whence came the clamor of nestlings. I was starting to doze in the sun when there emerged from the open pool a wild red eye, glaring from the head of a bird. Finding all quiet, the silver body emerged: big as a goose, with the lines of a slim torpedo. Before I was aware of when or whence, a second grebe was there, and on her broad back rode two pearly-silver young, neatly enclosed in a corral of humped-up wings. All rounded a bend before I recovered my breath. And now I heard the bell, clear and derisive, behind the curtain of the reeds.

A sense of history should be the most precious gift of science and of the arts, but I suspect that the grebe, who has neither, knows more history than we do. His dim primordial brain knows nothing of who won the Battle of Hastings, but it seems to sense who won the battle of time. If the race of men were as old as the race of grebes, we might better grasp the import of his call. Think what traditions, prides, disdains, and wisdoms even a few self-conscious generations bring to us! What pride of continuity, then, impels this bird, who was a grebe eons before there was a man.

Be that as it may, the call of the grebe is, by some peculiar authority, the sound that dominates and unifies the marshland chorus. Perhaps, by some immemorial authority, he wields the baton for the whole biota. Who beats the measure for the lake-shore rollers as they build reef after reef for marsh after marsh, as age after age the waters recede to lower levels? Who holds sago and bulrush to their task of sucking sun and air, lest in winter the muskrats starve, and the canes engulf the marsh in lifeless jungle? Who counsels patience to brooding ducks by day, and incites bloodthirst in marauding minks by night? Who exhorts precision for the heron's spear, and speed for the falcon's fist? We assume, because all these creatures perform their diverse tasks without admonition audible to us, that they receive none, that their skills are inborn and their industry automatic, that weariness is unknown to the wild. Perhaps weariness is unknown only to grebes; perhaps it is the grebe who reminds them that if all are to survive, each must ceaselessly feed and fight, breed and die.

The marshlands that once sprawled over the prairie from the Illinois to the Athabasca are shrinking northward. Man cannot live by marsh alone, therefore he must needs live marshless. Progress cannot abide that farmland and marshland, wild and tame, exist in mutual toleration and harmony.

So with dredge and dyke, tile and torch, we sucked the corn-belt dry, and now the wheatbelt. Blue lake becomes green bog, green bog becomes caked mud, caked mud becomes a wheat-field.

Some day my marsh, dyked and pumped, will lie forgotten under the wheat, just as today and yesterday will lie forgotten under the years. Before the last mud-minnow makes his last wiggle in the last pool, the terns will scream goodbye to Clandeboye, the swans will circle skyward in snowy dignity, and the cranes will blow their trumpets in farewell.

PART III: The Upshot

Conservation Esthetic

Barring love and war, few enterprises are undertaken with such abandon, or by such diverse individuals, or with so paradoxical a mixture of appetite and altruism, as that group of avocations known as outdoor recreation. It is, by common consent, a good thing for people to get back to nature. But wherein lies the goodness, and what can be done to encourage its pursuit? On these questions there is confusion of counsel, and only the most uncritical minds are free from doubt.

Recreation became a problem with a name in the days of the elder Roosevelt, when the railroads which had banished the countryside from the city began to carry city-dwellers, *en masse*, to the countryside. It began to be noticed that the greater the exodus, the smaller the per-capita ration of peace, solitude, wildlife, and scenery, and the longer the migration to reach them.

The automobile has spread this once mild and local predicament to the outermost limits of good roads—it has made scarce in the hinterlands something once abundant on the back forty. But that something must nevertheless be found. Like ions shot from the sun, the week-enders radiate from every town, generating heat and friction as they go. A tourist industry purveys bed and board to bait more ions, faster, further. Advertisements on rock and rill confide to all and sundry the whereabouts of new retreats, landscapes, hunting-grounds, and fishing-lakes just beyond those recently overrun. Bureaus build roads into new hinterlands, then buy more hinterlands to absorb the exodus accelerated by the roads. A gadget industry pads the bumps against nature-in-the-raw; woodcraft becomes the art of using gadgets. And now, to cap the pyramid of banalities, the trailer. To him who seeks in the woods and mountains only those things obtainable from travel or golf, the present situation is tolerable. But to him who seeks something more, recreation has become a self-destructive process of seeking but never quite finding, a major frustration of mechanized society.

143

The retreat of the wilderness under the barrage of motorized tourists is no local thing; Hudson Bay, Alaska, Mexico, South Africa are giving way, South America and Siberia are next. Drums along the Mohawk are now honks along the rivers of the world. *Homo sapiens* putters no more under his own vine and fig tree; he has poured into his gas tank the stored motivity of countless creatures aspiring through the ages to wiggle their way to pastures new. Ant-like he swarms the continents.

This is Outdoor Recreation, Latest Model.

Who now is the recreationist, and what does he seek? A few samples will remind us.

Take a look, first, at any duck marsh. A cordon of parked cars surrounds it. Crouched on each point of its reedy margin is some pillar of society, automatic ready, trigger finger itching to break, if need be, every law of commonwealth or commonweal to kill a duck. That he is already overfed in no way dampens his avidity for gathering his meat from God.

Wandering in the near-by woods is another pillar, hunting rare ferns or new warblers. Because his kind of hunting seldom calls for theft or pillage, he disdains the killer. Yet, like as not, in his youth he was one.

At some near-by resort is still another nature-lover—the kind who writes bad verse on birchbark. Everywhere is the unspecialized motorist whose recreation is mileage, who has run the gamut of the National Parks in one summer, and now is headed for Mexico City and points south.

Lastly, there is the professional, striving through countless conservation organizations to give the nature-seeking public what it wants, or to make it want what he has to give.

Why, it may be asked, should such a diversity of folk be bracketed in a single category? Because each, in his own way, is a hunter. And why does each call himself a conservationist? Because the wild things he hunts for have eluded his grasp, and he hopes by some necromancy of laws, appropriations, regional plans, reorganization of departments, or other form of mass-wishing to make them stay put.

Recreation is commonly spoken of as an economic resource. Senate committees tell us, in reverent ciphers, how many millions the public spends in its pursuit. It has indeed an economic aspect—a cottage on a fishing-lake, or even a duck-point on a marsh, may cost as much as the entire adjacent farm.

It has also an ethical aspect. In the scramble for unspoiled places, codes and decalogues evolve. We hear of 'outdoor manners.' We indoctrinate youth. We print definitions of 'What is a sportsman?' and hang a copy on the wall of whosoever will pay a dollar for the propagation of the faith.

It is clear, though, that these economic and ethical manifestations are results, not causes, of the motive force. We seek contacts with nature because we derive pleasure from them. As in opera, economic machinery is employed to create and maintain facilities. As in opera, professionals make a living out of creating and maintaining them, but it would be false to say of either that the basic motive, the *raison d'être*, is economic. The duck-hunter in his blind and the operatic singer on the stage, despite the disparity of their accoutrements, are doing the same thing. Each is reviving, in play, a drama formerly inherent in daily life. Both are, in the last analysis, esthetic exercises.

Public policies for outdoor recreation are controversial. Equally conscientious citizens hold opposite views on what it is and what should be done to conserve its resource-base. Thus the Wilderness Society seeks to exclude roads from the hinterlands, and the Chamber of Commerce to extend them, both in the name of recreation. The game-farmer kills hawks and the bird-lover protects them in the name of shotgun and field-glass hunting respectively. Such factions commonly label each other with short and ugly names, when, in fact, each is considering a different component of the recreational process. These components *differ widely in their characteristics or properties.* A given policy may be true for one but false for another.

It seems timely, therefore, to segregate the components, and to examine the distinctive characteristics or properties of each.

We begin with the simplest and most obvious: the physical objects that the outdoorsman may seek, find, capture, and carry away. In this category are wild crops such as game and fish, and the symbols or tokens of achievement such as heads, hides, photographs, and specimens.

All these things rest upon the idea of *trophy.* The pleasure they give is, or should be, in the seeking as well as in the getting.

The trophy, whether it be a bird's egg, a mess of trout, a basket of mushrooms, the photograph of a bear, the pressed specimen of a wild flower, or a note tucked into the cairn on a mountain peak, is a *certificate*. It attests that its owner has been somewhere and done something—that he has exercised skill, persistence, or discrimination in the age-old feat of overcoming, outwitting, or reducing-to-possession. These connotations which attach to the trophy usually far exceed its physical value.

But trophies differ in their reactions to mass-pursuit. The yield of game and fish can, by means of propagation or management, be increased so as to give each hunter more, or to give more hunters the same amount. During the past decade a profession of wildlife management has sprung into existence. A score of universities teach its techniques, conduct research for bigger and better wild animal crops. However, when carried too far, this stepping-up of yields is subject to a law of diminishing returns. Very intensive management of game or fish lowers the unit value of the trophy by artificializing it.

Consider, for example, a trout raised in a hatchery and newly liberated in an over-fished stream. The stream is no longer capable of natural trout production. Pollution has fouled its waters, or deforestation and trampling have warmed or silted them. No one would claim that this trout has the same value as a wholly wild one caught out of some unmanaged stream in the high Rockies. Its esthetic connotations are inferior, even though its capture may require skill. (Its liver, one authority says, is also so degenerated by hatchery feeding as to forebode an early death.) Yet several over-fished states now depend almost entirely on such man-made trout.

All intergrades of artificiality exist, but as mass-use increases it tends to push the whole gamut of conservation techniques toward the artificial end, and the whole scale of trophy-values downward.

To safeguard this expensive, artificial, and more or less helpless trout, the Conservation Commission feels impelled to kill all herons and terns visiting the hatchery where it was raised, and all mergansers and otters inhabiting the stream in which it is released. The fisherman perhaps feels no loss in this sacrifice of one kind of wild life for another, but the ornithologist is ready to bite off ten-penny nails. Artificialized management has, in effect, bought fishing at the expense of another and perhaps higher recreation; it has paid dividends to one citizen out of capital stock belonging to all. The same kind of biological wildcatting prevails in game management. In Europe, where wild-crop statistics are available for long periods, we even know the 'rate of exchange' of game for predators. Thus, in Saxony one hawk is killed for each seven game birds bagged, and one predator of some kind for each three head of small game.

Damage to plant life usually follows artificialized management of animals—for example, damage to forests by deer. One may see this in north Germany, in northeast Pennsylvania, in the Kaibab, and in dozens of other less publicized regions. In each case over-abundant deer, when deprived of their natural enemies, have made it impossible for deer food plants to survive or reproduce. Beech, maple, and yew in Europe, ground hemlock and white cedar in the eastern states, mountain mahogany and cliff-rose in the West, are deer foods threatened by artificialized deer. The composition of the flora, from wild flowers to forest trees, is gradually impoverished, and the deer in turn are dwarfed by malnutrition. There are no stags in the woods today like those on the walls of feudal castles.

On the English heaths, reproduction of trees is inhibited by rabbits over-protected in the process of cropping partridges and pheasants. On scores of tropical islands both flora and fauna have been destroyed by goats introduced for meat and sport. It would be hard to calculate the mutual injuries by and between mammals deprived of their natural predators, and ranges stripped of their natural food plants. Agricultural crops caught between these upper and nether millstones of ecological mismanagement are saved only at the cost of endless indemnities and barbed wire.

We generalize, then, by saying that mass-use tends to dilute the quality of organic trophies like game and fish, and to induce damage to other resources such as non-game animals, natural vegetation, and farm crops.

The same dilution and damage is not apparent in the yield of 'indirect' trophies, such as photographs. Broadly speaking, a piece of scenery snapped by a dozen tourist cameras daily is not physically impaired thereby, nor does any other resource suffer when the rate increases to a hundred. The camera industry is one of the few innocuous parasites on wild nature.

We have, then, a basic difference in reaction to mass-use as between two categories of physical objects pursued as trophies.

Let us now consider another component of recreation, which is more subtle and complex: the feeling of isolation in nature. That this is acquiring a scarcity-value that is very high to some persons is attested by the wilderness controversy. The proponents of wilderness have achieved a compromise with the road-building bureaus which have the custody of our National Parks and Forests. They have agreed on the formal reservation of roadless areas. Out of every dozen wild areas opened up, one may be officially proclaimed 'wilderness,' and roads built only to its edge. It is then advertised as unique, as indeed it is. Before long its trails are congested, it is being dolled up to make work for CCC's, or an unexpected fire necessitates splitting it in two with a road to haul fire-fighters. Or the congestion induced by advertising may whip up the price of guides and packers, whereupon somebody discovers that the wilderness policy is undemocratic. Or the local Chamber of Commerce, at first quiescent at the novelty of a hinterland officially labeled as 'wild,' tastes its first blood of tourist-money. It then wants more, wilderness or no wilderness.

In short, the very scarcity of wild places, reacting with the *mores* of advertising and promotion, tends to defeat any deliberate effort to prevent their growing still more scarce.

It is clear without further discussion that mass-use involves a direct dilution of the opportunity for solitude; that when we speak of roads, campgrounds, trails, and toilets as 'development' of recreational resources, we speak falsely in respect of this component. Such accommodations for the crowd are not developing (in the sense of adding or creating) anything. On the contrary, they are merely water poured into the already-thin soup.

We now contrast with the isolation-component that very distinct if simple one which we may label 'fresh-air and change of scene.' Mass-use neither destroys nor dilutes this value. The thousandth tourist who clicks the gate of the National Park breathes approximately the same air, and experiences the same contrast with Monday-at-the-office, as does the first. One might even believe that the gregarious assault on the outdoors enhances the contrast. We may say, then, that the fresh-air and change-of-scene component is like the photographic trophy—it withstands mass-use without damage.

We come now to another component: the perception of the natural processes by which the land and the living things upon it have achieved their characteristic forms (evolution) and by which they maintain their existence (ecology). That thing called 'nature study,' despite the shiver it brings to the spines of the elect, constitutes the first embryonic groping of the mass-mind toward perception.

The outstanding characteristic of perception is that it entails no consumption and no dilution of any resource. The swoop of a hawk, for example, is perceived by one as the drama of evolution. To another it is only a threat to the full frying-pan. The drama may thrill a hundred successive witnesses; the threat only one—for he responds with a shotgun.

To promote perception is the only truly creative part of recreational engineering.

This fact is important, and its potential power for bettering 'the good life' only dimly understood. When Daniel Boone first entered into the forests and prairies of 'the dark and bloody ground,' he reduced to his possession the pure essence of 'outdoor America.' He didn't call it that, but what he found is the thing we now seek, and we here deal with things, not names.

Recreation, however, is not the outdoors, but our reaction to it. Daniel Boone's reaction depended not only on the quality of what he saw, but on the quality of the mental eye with which he saw it. Ecological science has wrought a change in the mental eye. It has disclosed origins and functions for what to Boone were only facts. It has disclosed mechanisms for what to Boone were only attributes. We have no yardstick to measure this change, but we may safely say that, as compared with the competent ecologist of the present day, Boone saw only the surface of things. The incredible intricacies of the plant and animal community—the intrinsic beauty of the organism called America, then in the full bloom of her maidenhood—were as invisible and incomprehensible to Daniel Boone as they are today to Mr. Babbitt. The only true development in American recreational resources is the development of the perceptive faculty in Americans. All of the other acts we grace by that name are, at best, attempts to retard or mask the process of dilution.

Let no man jump to the conclusion that Babbitt must take his Ph.D. in ecology before he can 'see' his country. On the contrary, the Ph.D. may become as callous as an undertaker to the mysteries at which he officiates. Like all real treasures of the mind, perception can be split into infinitely small fractions without losing its quality. The weeds in a city lot convey the same lesson as the redwoods; the farmer may see in his cow-pasture what may not be vouchsafed to the scientist adventuring in the South Seas. Perception, in short, cannot be purchased with either learned degrees or dollars; it grows at home as well as abroad, and he who has a little may use it to as good advantage as he who has much. As a search for perception, the recreational stampede is footless and unnecessary.

There is, lastly, a fifth component: the sense of husbandry. It is unknown to the outdoorsman who works for conservation with his vote rather than with his hands. It is realized only when some art of management is applied to land by some person of perception. That is to say, its enjoyment is reserved for landholders too poor to buy their sport, and land administrators with a sharp eye and an ecological mind. The tourist who buys access to his scenery misses it altogether; so also the sportsman who hires the state, or some underling, to be his gamekeeper. The Government, which essays to substitute public for private operation of recreational lands, is unwittingly giving away to its field officers a large share of what it seeks to offer its citizens. We foresters and game managers might logically pay for, instead of being paid for, our job as husbandmen of wild crops.

That a sense of husbandry exercised in the production of crops may be quite as important as the crops themselves is realized to some extent in agriculture, but not in conservation. American sportsmen hold in small esteem the intensive game-cropping of the Scottish moors and the German forests, and in some respects rightly. But they overlook entirely the sense of husbandry developed by the European landholder in the process of cropping. We have no such thing as yet. It is important. When we conclude that we must bait the farmer with subsidies to induce him to raise a forest, or with gate receipts to induce him to raise game, we are merely admitting that the pleasures of husbandry-in-the-wild are as yet unknown both to the farmer and to ourselves.

Scientists have an epigram: ontogeny repeats phylogeny. What they mean is that the development of each individual repeats the evolutionary history of the race. This is true of mental as well as physical things. The trophy-hunter is the caveman reborn. Trophy-hunting is the prerogative of youth, racial or individual, and nothing to apologize for.

The disquieting thing in the modern picture is the trophy-hunter who never grows up, in whom the capacity for isolation, perception, and husbandry is undeveloped, or perhaps lost. He is the motorized ant who swarms the continents before learning to see his own back yard, who consumes but never creates outdoor satisfactions. For him the recreational engineer dilutes the wilderness and artificializes its trophies in the fond belief that he is rendering a public service.

The trophy-recreationist has peculiarities that contribute in subtle ways to his own undoing. To enjoy he must possess, invade, appropriate. Hence the wilderness that he cannot personally see has no value to him. Hence the universal assumption that an unused hinterland is rendering no service to society. To those devoid of imagination, a blank place on the map is a useless waste; to others, the most valuable part. (Is my share in Alaska worthless to me because I shall never go there? Do I need a road to show me the arctic prairies, the goose pastures of the Yukon, the Kodiak bear, the sheep meadows behind McKinley?)

It would appear, in short, that the rudimentary grades of outdoor recreation consume their resource-base; the higher grades, at least to a degree, create their own satisfactions with little or no attrition of land or life. It is the expansion of transport without a corresponding growth of perception that threatens us with qualitative bankruptcy of the recreational process. Recreational development is a job not of building roads into lovely country, but of building receptivity into the still unlovely human mind.

Wildlife in American Culture

THE CULTURE of primitive peoples is often based on wildlife. Thus the plains Indian not only ate buffalo, but buffalo largely determined his architecture, dress, language, arts, and religion.

In civilized peoples the cultural base shifts elsewhere, but the culture nevertheless retains part of its wild roots. I here discuss the value of this wild rootage.

No one can weigh or measure culture, hence I shall waste no time trying to do so. Suffice it to say that by common consent of thinking people, there are cultural values in the sports, customs, and experiences that renew contacts with wild things. I venture the opinion that these values are of three kinds.

First there is value in any experience that reminds us of our distinctive national origins and evolution, i.e. that stimulates awareness of history. Such awareness is 'nationalism' in its best sense. For lack of any other short name, I shall call this, in our case, the 'split-rail value.' For example: a boy scout has tanned a coonskin cap, and goes Daniel-Booneing in the willow thicket below the tracks. He is reenacting American history. He is, to that extent, culturally prepared to face the dark and bloody realities of the present. Again: a farmer boy arrives in the schoolroom reeking of muskrat; he has tended his traps before breakfast. He is reenacting the romance of the fur trade. Ontogeny repeats phylogeny in society as well as in the individual.

Second, there is value in any experience that reminds us of our dependency on the soil-plant-animal-man food chain, and of the fundamental organization of the biota. Civilization has so cluttered this elemental man-earth relation with gadgets and middlemen that awareness of it is growing dim. We fancy that industry supports us, forgetting what supports industry. Time was when education moved toward soil, not away from it. The nursery jingle about bringing home a rabbit skin to wrap the baby bunting in is one of many reminders in folk-lore that man once hunted to feed and clothe his family.

Third, there is value in any experience that exercises those ethical restraints collectively called 'sportsmanship.' Our tools for the pursuit of wildlife improve faster than we do, and sportsmanship is a voluntary limitation in the use of these armaments. It is aimed to augment the role of skill and shrink the role of gadgets in the pursuit of wild things.

A peculiar virtue in wildlife ethics is that the hunter ordinarily has no gallery to applaud or disapprove of his conduct. Whatever his acts, they are dictated by his own conscience, rather than by a mob of onlookers. It is difficult to exaggerate the importance of this fact.

Voluntary adherence to an ethical code elevates the self-respect of the sportsman, but it should not be forgotten that voluntary disregard of the code degenerates and depraves him. For example, a common denominator of all sporting codes is not to waste good meat. Yet it is now a demonstrable fact that Wisconsin deer-hunters, in their pursuit of a legal buck, kill and abandon in the woods at least one doe, fawn, or spike buck for every two legal bucks taken out. In other words, approximately half the hunters shoot any deer until a legal deer is killed. The illegal carcasses are left where they fall. Such deer-hunting is not only without social value, but constitutes actual training for ethical depravity elsewhere.

It seems, then, that split-rail and man-earth experiences have zero or plus values, but that ethical experiences may have minus values as well.

This, then, defines roughly three kinds of cultural nutriment available to our outdoor roots. It does not follow that culture is fed. The extraction of value is never automatic; only a healthy culture can feed and grow. Is culture fed by our present forms of outdoor recreation?

The pioneer period gave birth to two ideas that are the essence of split-rail value in outdoor sports. One is the 'go-light' idea, the other the 'one-bullet-one-buck' idea. The pioneer went light of necessity. He shot with economy and precision because he lacked the transport, the cash, and the weapons requisite for machine-gun tactics. Let it be clear, then, that in their inception, both of these ideas were forced on us; we made a virtue of necessity.

In their later evolution, however, they became a code of sportsmanship, a self-imposed limitation on sport. On them is based a distinctively American tradition of self-reliance, hardihood, woodcraft, and marksmanship. These are intangibles, but they are not abstractions. Theodore Roosevelt was a great sportsman, not because he hung up many trophies, but because he expressed this intangible American tradition in words any schoolboy could understand. A more subtle and accurate expression is found in the early writings of Stewart Edward White. It is not far amiss to say that such men created cultural value by being aware of it, and by creating a pattern for its growth.

Then came the gadgeteer, otherwise known as the sporting-goods dealer. He has draped the American outdoorsman with an infinity of contraptions, all offered as aids to self-reliance, hardihood, woodcraft, or marksmanship, but too often functioning as substitutes for them. Gadgets fill the pockets, they dangle from neck and belt. The overflow fills the auto-trunk, and also the trailer. Each item of outdoor equipment grows lighter and often better, but the aggregate poundage becomes tonnage. The traffic in gadgets adds up to astronomical sums, which are soberly published as representing 'the economic value of wildlife.' But what of cultural values?

As an end-case consider the duck-hunter, sitting in a steel boat behind composition decoys. A put-put motor has brought him to the blind without exercise. Canned heat stands by to warm him in case of a chilling wind. He talks to the passing flocks on a factory caller, in what he hopes are seductive tones; home lessons from a phonograph record have taught him how. The decoys work, despite the caller; a flock circles in. It must be shot at before it circles twice, for the marsh bristles with other sportsmen, similarly accoutred, who might shoot first. He opens up at 70 yards, for his poly-choke is set for infinity, and the advertisements have told him that Super-Z shells, and plenty of them, have a long reach. The flock flares. A couple of cripples scale off to die elsewhere. Is this sportsman absorbing cultural value? Or is he just feeding minks? The next blind opens up at 75 yards; how else is a fellow to get some shooting? This is duck shooting, current model. It is typical of all public grounds, and of many clubs. Where is the go-light idea, the one-bullet tradition?

The answer is not a simple one. Roosevelt did not disdain the modern rifle; White used freely the aluminum pot, the silk tent, dehydrated foods. Somehow they used mechanical aids, in moderation, without being used by them.

I do not pretend to know what is moderation, or where the line is between legitimate and illegitimate gadgets. It seems clear, though, that the origin of gadgets has much to do with their cultural effects. Homemade aids to sport or outdoor life often enhance, rather than destroy, the man-earth drama; he who kills a trout with his own fly has scored two coups, not one. I use many factory-made gadgets myself. Yet there must be some limit beyond which money-bought aids to sport destroy the cultural value of sport.

Not all sports have degenerated to the same extent as duck-hunting. Defenders of the American tradition still exist. Perhaps the bow-and-arrow movement and the revival of falconry mark the beginnings of a reaction. The net trend, however, is clearly toward more and more mechanization, with a corresponding shrinkage in cultural values, especially split-rail values and ethical restraints.

I have the impression that the American sportsman is puzzled; he doesn't understand what is happening to him. Bigger and better gadgets are good for industry, so why not for outdoor recreation? It has not dawned on him that outdoor recreations are essentially primitive, atavistic; that their value is a contrast-value; that excessive mechanization destroys contrasts by moving the factory to the woods or to the marsh.

The sportsman has no leaders to tell him what is wrong. The sporting press no longer represents sport; it has turned billboard for the gadgeteer. Wildlife administrators are too busy producing something to shoot at to worry much about the cultural value of the shooting. Because everybody from Xenophon to Teddy Roosevelt said sport has value, it is assumed that this value must be indestructible.

Among non-gunpowder sports, the impact of mechanization has had diverse effects. The modern field glass, camera, and the aluminum bird-band have certainly *not* deteriorated the cultural value of ornithology. Fishing, but for outboard motors and aluminum canoes, seems less severely mechanized than hunting. On the other hand, motorized transport has nearly destroyed the sport of wilderness travel by leaving only fly-specks of wilderness to travel in.

Fox-hunting with hounds, backwoods style, presents a dramatic instance of partial and perhaps harmless mechanized invasion. This is one of the purest of sports; it has real split-rail flavor; it has man-earth drama of the first water. The fox is deliberately left unshot, hence ethical restraint is also present. But we now follow the chase in Fords! The voice of Bugle Ann mingles with the honk of the flivver! However, no one is likely to invent a mechanical foxhound, or to screw a poly-choke on the hound's nose. No one is likely to teach dog-training by phonograph, or by other painless shortcuts. I think the gadgeteer has reached the end of his tether in dogdom.

It is not quite accurate to ascribe all the ills of sport to the inventor of physical aids-to-sport. The advertiser invents ideas, and ideas are seldom as honest as physical objects, even though they may be equally useless. One such deserves special mention: the 'where-to-go' department. Knowledge of the whereabouts of good hunting or fishing is a very personal form of property. It is like rod, dog, or gun: a thing to be loaned or given as a personal courtesy. But to hawk it in the marketplace of the sports column as an aid to circulation seems to me another matter. To hand it to all and sundry as free public 'service' seems to me distinctly another matter. Even 'conservation' departments now tell Tom, Dick, and Harry where the fish are biting, and where a flock of ducks has ventured to alight for a meal.

All of these organized promiscuities tend to depersonalize one of the essentially personal elements in outdoor sports. I do not know where the line lies between legitimate and illegitimate practice; I am convinced, though, that 'where-to-go' service has broken all bounds of reason.

If the hunting or fishing is good, the 'where-to-go' service suffices to attract the desired excess of sportsmen. But if it is no good, the advertiser must resort to more forcible means. One such is the fishing lottery, in which a few hatchery fish are tagged, and a prize is offered for the fisherman catching the winning number. This curious hybrid between the techniques of science and of the pool hall insures the overfishing of many an already exhausted lake, and brings a glow of civic pride to many a village Chamber of Commerce.

It is idle for the professional wildlife managers to consider themselves aloof from these affairs. The production engineer and the salesman belong to the same company; both are tarred with the same stick.

Wildlife managers are trying to raise game in the wild by manipulating its environment, and thus to convert hunting from exploitation to cropping. If the conversion takes place, how will it affect cultural values? It must be admitted that split-rail flavor and free-for-all exploitation are historically associated. Daniel Boone had scant patience with agricultural cropping, let alone wildlife cropping. Perhaps the stubborn reluctance of the 'one-gallus' sportsman to be converted to the cropping idea is an expression of his split-rail inheritance. Probably cropping is resisted because it is incompatible with one component of the split-rail tradition: free hunting.

Mechanization offers no cultural substitute for the split-rail values it destroys; at least none visible to me. Cropping or management does offer a substitute, which to me has at least equal value: wild husbandry. The experience of managing land for wildlife crops has the same value as any other form of farming; it is a reminder of the man-earth relation. Moreover ethical restraints are involved; thus managing game without resorting to predator-control calls for ethical restraint of a high order. It may be concluded, then, that game cropping shrinks one value (split-rail) but enhances both of the others.

If we regard outdoor sports as a field of conflict between an immensely vigorous process of mechanization and a wholly static tradition, then the outlook for cultural values is indeed dark. But why cannot our concept of sport grow with the same vigor as our list of gadgets? Perhaps the salvation of cultural value lies in seizing the offensive. I, for one, believe that the time is ripe. Sportsmen can determine for themselves the shape of things to come.

The last decade, for example, has disclosed a totally new form of sport, which does not destroy wildlife, which uses gadgets without being used by them, which outflanks the problem of posted land, and which greatly increases the human carrying capacity of a unit area. This sport knows no bag limit, no closed season. It needs teachers, but not wardens. It calls for a new woodcraft of the highest cultural value. The sport I refer to is wildlife research.

Wildlife research started as a professional priestcraft. The more difficult and laborious research problems must doubtless remain in professional hands, but there are plenty of problems suitable for all grades of amateurs. In the field of mechanical invention research has long since spread to amateurs. In the biological field the sport-value of amateur research is just beginning to be realized.

Thus Margaret Morse Nice, an amateur ornithologist, studied song sparrows in her back yard. She has become a world-authority on bird behavior, and has out-thought and outworked many a professional student of social organization in birds. Charles L. Broley, a banker, banded eagles for fun. He discovered a hitherto unknown fact: that some eagles nest in the South in winter, and then go vacationing to the north woods. Norman and Stuart Criddle, wheat ranchers on the Manitoba prairies, studied the fauna and flora of their farm, and became recognized authorities on everything from local botany to wildlife cycles. Elliott S. Barker, a cowman in the New Mexico mountains, has written one of the two best books on that elusive cat: the mountain lion. Do not let anyone tell you that these people made work out of play. They simply realized that the most fun lies in seeing and studying the unknown.

Ornithology, mammalogy, and botany, as now known to most amateurs, are but kindergarten games compared with what is possible for (and open to) amateurs in these fields. One reason for this is that the whole structure of biological education (including education in wildlife) is aimed to perpetuate the professional monopoly on research. To the amateur are allotted only make-believe voyages of discovery, to verify what professional authority already knows. What the youth needs to be told is that a ship is a-building in his own mental dry dock, a ship with freedom of the seas.

In my opinion, the promotion of wildlife research sports is the most important job confronting the profession of wildlife management. Wildlife has still another value, now visible only to a few ecologists, but of potential importance to the whole human enterprise.

We now know that animal populations have behavior patterns of which the individual animal is unaware, but which he nevertheless helps to execute. Thus the rabbit is unaware of cycles, but he is the vehicle for cycles.

We cannot discern these behavior patterns in the individual, or in short periods of time. The most intense scrutiny of an individual rabbit tells us nothing of cycles. The cycle concept springs from a scrutiny of the mass through decades.

This raises the disquieting question: do human populations have behavior patterns of which we are unaware, but which we help to execute? Are mobs and wars, unrests and revolutions, cut of such cloth?

Many historians and philosophers persist in interpreting our mass behaviors as the collective result of individual acts of volition. The whole subject matter of diplomacy assumes that the political group has the properties of an honorable person. On the other hand, some economists see the whole of society as a plaything for processes, our knowledge of which is largely *ex post facto.*

It is reasonable to suppose that our social processes have a higher volitional content than those of the rabbit, but it is also reasonable to suppose that we, as a species, contain population behavior patterns of which nothing is known because circumstance has never evoked them. We may have others the meaning of which we have misread.

This state of doubt about the fundamentals of human population behavior lends exceptional interest, and exceptional value, to the only available analogue: the higher animals. Errington, among others, has pointed out the cultural value of these animal analogues. For centuries this rich library of knowledge has

been inaccessible to us because we did not know where or how to look for it. Ecology is now teaching us to search in animal populations for analogies to our own problems. By learning how some small part of the biota ticks, we can guess how the whole mechanism ticks. The ability to perceive these deeper meanings, and to appraise them critically, is the woodcraft of the future.

To sum up, wildlife once fed us and shaped our culture. It still yields us pleasure for leisure hours, but we try to reap that pleasure by modern machinery and thus destroy part of its value. Reaping it by modern mentality would yield not only pleasure, but wisdom as well.

Wilderness

WILDERNESS IS the raw material out of which man has hammered the artifact called civilization.

Wilderness was never a homogeneous raw material. It was very diverse, and the resulting artifacts are very diverse. These differences in the end-product are known as cultures. The rich diversity of the world's cultures reflects a corresponding diversity in the wilds that gave them birth.

For the first time in the history of the human species, two changes are now impending. One is the exhaustion of wilderness in the more habitable portions of the globe. The other is the world-wide hybridization of cultures through modern transport and industrialization. Neither can be prevented, and perhaps should not be, but the question arises whether, by some slight amelioration of the impending changes, certain values can be preserved that would otherwise be lost.

To the laborer in the sweat of his labor, the raw stuff on his anvil is an adversary to be conquered. So was wilderness an adversary to the pioneer.

But to the laborer in repose, able for the moment to cast a philosophical eye on his world, that same raw stuff is something to be loved and cherished, because it gives definition and meaning to his life. This is a plea for the preservation of some tag-ends of wilderness, as museum pieces, for the edification of those who may one day wish to see, feel, or study the origins of their cultural inheritance.

THE REMNANTS

Many of the diverse wildernesses out of which we have hammered America are already gone; hence in any practical program the unit areas to be preserved must vary greatly in size and in degree of wildness.

No living man will see again the long-grass prairie, where a sea of prairie flowers lapped at the stirrups of the pioneer. We shall do well to find a forty here and there on which the prairie plants can be kept alive as species. There were a hundred such plants, many of exceptional beauty. Most of them are quite unknown to those who have inherited their domain.

But the short-grass prairie, where Cabeza de Vaca saw the horizon under the bellies of the buffalo, is still extant in a few spots of 10,000-acre size, albeit severely chewed up by sheep, cattle, and dry-farmers. If the forty-niners are worth commemorating on the walls of state capitals, is not the scene of their mighty hegira worth commemorating in several national prairie reservations?

Of the coastal prairie there is one block in Florida, and one in Texas, but oil wells, onion fields, and citrus groves are closing in, armed to the teeth with drills and bulldozers. It is last call.

No living man will see again the virgin pineries of the Lake States, or the flatwoods of the coastal plain, or the giant hardwoods; of these, samples of a few acres each will have to suffice. But there are still several blocks of maple-hemlock of thousand-acre size; there are similar blocks of Appalachian hardwoods, of southern hardwood swamp, of cypress swamp, and of Adirondack spruce. Few of these tag-ends are secure from prospective cuttings, and fewer still from prospective tourist roads.

One of the fastest-shrinking categories of wilderness is coastlines. Cottages and tourist roads have all but annihilated wild coasts on both oceans, and Lake Superior is now losing the last large remnant of wild shoreline on the Great Lakes. No single kind of wilderness is more intimately interwoven with history, and none nearer the point of complete disappearance.

In all of North America east of the Rockies, there is only one large area formally reserved as a wilderness: the Quetico-Superior International Park in Minnesota and Ontario. This magnificent block of canoe-country, a mosaic of lakes and rivers, lies mostly in Canada, and can be about as large as Canada chooses to make it, but its integrity is threatened by two recent developments: the growth of fishing resorts served by pontoon-equipped airplanes, and a jurisdictional dispute whether the Minnesota end of the area shall be all National Forest, or partly State Forest. The whole region is in danger of power impoundments, and this regrettable cleavage among proponents of wilderness may end in giving power the whip-hand.

In the Rocky Mountain states, a score of areas in the National Forests, varying in size from a hundred thousand to half a million acres, are withdrawn as wilderness, and closed to roads, hotels, and other inimical uses. In the National Parks the same principle is recognized, but no specific boundaries are delimited. Collectively, these federal areas are the backbone of the wilderness program, but they are not so secure as the paper record might lead one to believe. Local pressures for new tourist roads knock off a chip here and a slab there. There is perennial pressure for extension of roads for forest-fire control, and these, by slow degrees, become public highways. Idle CCC camps presented a widespread temptation to build new and often needless roads. Lumber shortages during the war gave the impetus of military necessity to many road extensions, legitimate and otherwise. At the present moment, ski-tows and ski-hotels are being promoted in many mountain areas, often without regard to their prior designation as wilderness.

One of the most insidious invasions of wilderness is via predator control. It works thus: wolves and lions are cleaned out of a wilderness area in the interest of big-game management. The big-game herds (usually deer or elk) then increase to the point of overbrowsing the range. Hunters must then be encouraged to harvest the surplus, but modern hunters refuse to operate far from a car; hence a road must be built to provide access to the surplus game. Again and again, wilderness areas have been split by this process, but it still continues.

The Rocky Mountain system of wilderness areas covers a wide gamut of forest types, from the juniper breaks of the Southwest to the 'illimitable woods where rolls the Oregon.' It is lacking, however, in desert areas, probably because of that under-aged brand of esthetics which limits the definition of 'scenery' to lakes and pine trees.

In Canada and Alaska there are still large expanses of virgin country

> Where nameless men by nameless rivers wander
> and in strange valleys die strange deaths alone.

A representative series of these areas can, and should, be kept. Many are of negligible or negative value for economic use. It will be contended, of course, that no deliberate planning to this end is necessary; that adequate areas will survive anyhow. All recent history belies so comforting an assumption. Even if wild spots do survive, what of their fauna? The woodland caribou, the several races of mountain sheep, the pure form of woods buffalo, the barren ground grizzly, the freshwater seals, and the whales are even now threatened. Of what use are wild areas destitute of their distinctive faunas? The recently organized Arctic Institute has embarked on the industrialization of the Arctic wastes, with excellent chances of enough success to ruin them as wilderness. It is last call, even in the Far North.

To what extent Canada and Alaska will be able to see and grasp their opportunities is anybody's guess. Pioneers usually scoff at any effort to perpetuate pioneering.

WILDERNESS FOR RECREATION

Physical combat for the means of subsistence was, for unnumbered centuries, an economic fact. When it disappeared as such, a sound instinct led us to preserve it in the form of athletic sports and games.

Physical combat between men and beasts was, in like manner, an economic fact, now preserved as hunting and fishing for sport.

Public wilderness areas are, first of all, a means of perpetuating, in sport form, the more virile and primitive skills in pioneering travel and subsistence.

Some of these skills are of generalized distribution; the details have been adapted to the American scene, but the skill is worldwide. Hunting, fishing, and foot travel by pack are examples.

Two of them, however, are as American as a hickory tree; they have been copied elsewhere, but they were developed to their full perfection only on this continent. One of these is canoe travel, and the other is travel by pack-train. Both are shrinking rapidly. Your Hudson Bay Indian now has a put-put, and your mountaineer a Ford. If I had to make a living by canoe or packhorse, I should likely do likewise, for both are grueling labor. But we who seek wilderness travel for sport are foiled when we are forced to compete with mechanized substitutes. It is footless to execute a portage to the tune of motor launches, or to turn out your bell-mare in the pasture of a summer hotel. It is better to stay home.

Wilderness areas are first of all a series of sanctuaries for the primitive arts of wilderness travel, especially canoeing and packing.

I suppose some will wish to debate whether it is important to keep these primitive arts alive. I shall not debate it. Either you know it in your bones, or you are very, very old.

European hunting and fishing are largely devoid of the thing that wilderness areas might be the means of preserving in this country. Europeans do not camp, cook, or do their own work in the woods if they can avoid doing so. Work chores are delegated to beaters and servants, and a hunt carries the atmosphere of a picnic, rather than of pioneering. The test of skill is confined largely to the actual taking of game or fish.

There are those who decry wilderness sports as 'undemocratic' because the recreational carrying capacity of a wilderness is small, as compared with a golf links or a tourist camp. The basic error in such argument is that it applies the philosophy of mass-production to what is intended to counteract mass-production. The value of recreation is not a matter of ciphers. Recreation is valuable in proportion to the intensity of its experiences, and to the degree to which it *differs from* and *contrasts with* workaday life. By these criteria, mechanized outings are at best a milk-and-water affair.

Mechanized recreation already has seized nine-tenths of the woods and mountains; a decent respect for minorities should dedicate the other tenth to wilderness.

WILDERNESS FOR SCIENCE

The most important characteristic of an organism is that capacity for internal self-renewal known as health.

There are two organisms whose processes of self-renewal have been subjected to human interference and control. One of these is man himself (medicine and public health). The other is land (agriculture and conservation).

The effort to control the health of land has not been very successful. It is now generally understood that when soil loses fertility, or washes away faster than it forms, and when water systems exhibit abnormal floods and shortages, the land is sick.

Other derangements are known as facts, but are not yet thought of as symptoms of land sickness. The disappearance of plants and animal species without visible cause, despite efforts to protect them, and the irruption of others as pests despite efforts to control them, must, in the absence of simpler explanations, be regarded as symptoms of sickness in the land organism. Both are occurring too frequently to be dismissed as normal evolutionary events.

The status of thought on these ailments of the land is reflected in the fact that our treatments for them are still prevailingly local. Thus when a soil loses fertility we pour on fertilizer, or at best alter its tame flora and fauna, without considering the fact that its wild flora and fauna, which built the soil to begin with, may likewise be important to its maintenance. It was recently discovered, for example, that good tobacco crops depend, for some unknown reason, on the preconditioning of the soil by wild ragweed. It does not occur to us that such unexpected chains of dependency may have wide prevalence in nature.

When prairie dogs, ground squirrels, or mice increase to pest levels we poison them, but we do not look beyond the animal to find the cause of the irruption. We assume that animal troubles must have animal causes. The latest scientific evidence points to derangements of the *plant* community as the real seat of rodent irruptions, but few explorations of this clue are being made.

Many forest plantations are producing one-log or two-log trees on soil which originally grew three-log and four-log trees. Why? Thinking foresters know that the cause probably lies not in the tree, but in the micro-flora of the soil, and that it may take more years to restore the soil flora than it took to destroy it.

Many conservation treatments are obviously superficial. Flood-control dams have no relation to the cause of floods. Check dams and terraces do not touch the cause of erosion. Refuges and hatcheries to maintain the supply of game and fish do not explain why the supply fails to maintain itself.

In general, the trend of the evidence indicates that in land, just as in the human body, the symptoms may lie in one organ and the cause in another. The practices we now call conservation are, to a large extent, local alleviations of biotic pain. They are necessary, but they must not be confused with cures. The art of land doctoring is being practiced with vigor, but the science of land health is yet to be born.

A science of land health needs, first of all, a base datum of normality, a picture of how healthy land maintains itself as an organism.

We have two available norms. One is found where land

physiology remains largely normal despite centuries of human occupation. I know of only one such place: northeastern Europe. It is not likely that we shall fail to study it.

The other and most perfect norm is wilderness. Paleontology offers abundant evidence that wilderness maintained itself for immensely long periods; that its component species were rarely lost, neither did they get out of hand; that weather and water built soil as fast or faster than it was carried away. Wilderness, then, assumes unexpected importance as a laboratory for the study of land-health.

One cannot study the physiology of Montana in the Amazon; each biotic province needs its own wilderness for comparative studies of used and unused land. It is of course too late to salvage more than a lopsided system of wilderness study areas, and most of these remnants are far too small to retain their normality in all respects. Even the National Parks, which run up to a million acres each in size, have not been large enough to retain their natural predators, or to exclude animal diseases carried by livestock. Thus the Yellowstone has lost its wolves and cougars, with the result that elk are ruining the flora, particularly on the winter range. At the same time the grizzly bear and the mountain sheep are shrinking, the latter by reason of disease.

While even the largest wilderness areas become partially deranged, it required only a few wild acres for J. E. Weaver to discover why the prairie flora is more drouth-resistant than the agronomic flora which has supplanted it. Weaver found that the prairie species practice 'team work' underground by distributing their root-systems to cover all levels, whereas the species comprising the agronomic rotation overdraw one level and neglect another, thus building up cumulative deficits. An important agronomic principle emerged from Weaver's researches.

Again, it required only a few wild acres for Togrediak to discover why pines on old fields never achieve the size or wind-firmness of pines on uncleared forest soils. In the latter case, the roots follow old root channels, and thus strike deeper.

In many cases we literally do not know how good a performance to expect of healthy land unless we have a wild area for comparison with sick ones. Thus most of the early travelers in the Southwest describe the mountain rivers as originally clear, but a doubt remains, for they may, by accident, have seen them at favorable seasons. Erosion engineers had no base datum until it was discovered that exactly similar rivers in the Sierra Madre of Chihuahua, never grazed or used for fear of Indians, show at their worst a milky hue, not too cloudy for a trout fly. Moss grows to the water's edge on their banks. Most of the corresponding rivers in Arizona and New Mexico are ribbons of boulders, mossless, soil-less, and all but treeless. The preservation and study of the Sierra Madre wilderness, by an international experiment station, as a norm for the cure of sick land on both sides of the border, would be a good-neighbor enterprise well worthy of consideration.

In short all available wild areas, large or small, are likely to have value as norms for land science. Recreation is not their only, or even their principal, utility.

WILDERNESS FOR WILDLIFE

The National Parks do not suffice as a means of perpetuating the larger carnivores; witness the precarious status of the grizzly bear, and the fact that the park system is already wolfless. Neither do they suffice for mountain sheep; most sheep herds are shrinking.

The reasons for this are clear in some cases and obscure in others. The parks are certainly too small for such a far-ranging species as the wolf. Many animal species, for reasons unknown, do not seem to thrive as detached islands of population.

The most feasible way to enlarge the area available for wilderness fauna is for the wilder parts of the National Forests, which usually surround the Parks, to function as parks in respect of threatened species. That they have not so functioned is tragically illustrated in the case of the grizzly bear.

In 1909, when I first saw the West, there were grizzlies in every major mountain mass, but you could travel for months without meeting a conservation officer. Today there is some kind of conservation officer 'behind every bush,' yet as wildlife bureaus grow, our most magnificent mammal retreats steadily toward the Canadian border. Of the 6000 grizzlies officially reported as remaining in areas owned by the United States, 5000 are in Alaska. Only five states have any at all. There seems to be a tacit assumption that if grizzlies survive in Canada and Alaska, that is good enough. It is not good enough for me.

The Alaskan bears are a distinct species. Relegating grizzlies to Alaska is about like relegating happiness to heaven; one may never get there.

Saving the grizzly requires a series of large areas from which roads and livestock are excluded, or in which livestock damage is compensated. Buying out scattered livestock ranches is the only way to create such areas, but despite large authority to buy and exchange lands, the conservation bureaus have accomplished virtually nothing toward this end. The Forest Service has, I am told, established one grizzly range in Montana, but I know of a mountain range in Utah in which the Forest Service actually promoted a sheep industry, despite the fact that it harbored the sole remnant of grizzlies in that state.

Permanent grizzly ranges and permanent wilderness areas are of course two names for one problem. Enthusiasm about either requires a long view of conservation, and a historical perspective. Only those able to see the pageant of evolution can be expected to value its theater, the wilderness, or its outstanding achievement, the grizzly. But if education really educates, there will, in time, be more and more citizens who understand that relics of the old West add meaning and value to the new. Youth yet unborn will pole up the Missouri with Lewis and Clark, or climb the Sierras with James Capen Adams, and each generation in turn will ask: Where is the big white bear? It will be a sorry answer to say he went under while conservationists weren't looking.

DEFENDERS OF WILDERNESS

Wilderness is a resource which can shrink but not grow. Invasions can be arrested or modified in a manner to keep an area usable either for recreation, or for science, or for wildlife, but the creation of new wilderness in the full sense of the word is impossible.

It follows, then, that any wilderness program is a rear-guard action, through which retreats are reduced to a minimum. The Wilderness Society was organized in 1935 'for the one purpose of saving the wilderness remnants in America.'

It does not suffice, however, to have such a society. Unless there be wilderness-minded men scattered through all the conservation bureaus, the society may never learn of new invasions until the time for action has passed. Furthermore a militant minority of wilderness-minded citizens must be on watch throughout the nation, and available for action in a pinch.

In Europe, where wilderness has now retreated to the Carpathians and Siberia, every thinking conservationist bemoans its loss. Even in Britain, which has less room for land-luxuries than almost any other civilized country, there is a vigorous if belated movement for saving a few small spots of semi-wild land.

Ability to see the cultural value of wilderness boils down, in the last analysis, to a question of intellectual humility. The shallow-minded modern who has lost his rootage in the land assumes that he has already discovered what is important; it is such who prate of empires, political or economic, that will last a thousand years. It is only the scholar who appreciates that all history consists of successive excursions from a single starting-point, to which man returns again and again to organize yet another search for a durable scale of values. It is only the scholar who understands why the raw wilderness gives definition and meaning to the human enterprise.

The Land Ethic

WHEN GOD-LIKE Odysseus returned from the wars in Troy, he hanged all on one rope a dozen slave-girls of his household whom he suspected of misbehavior during his absence.

This hanging involved no question of propriety. The girls were property. The disposal of property was then, as now, a matter of expediency, not of right and wrong.

Concepts of right and wrong were not lacking from Odysseus' Greece: witness the fidelity of his wife through the long years before at last his black-prowed galleys clove the wine-dark seas for home. The ethical structure of that day covered wives, but had not yet been extended to human chattels. During the three thousand years which have since elapsed, ethical criteria have been extended to many fields of conduct, with corresponding shrinkages in those judged by expediency only.

THE ETHICAL SEQUENCE

This extension of ethics, so far studied only by philosophers, is actually a process in ecological evolution. Its sequences may be described in ecological as well as in philosophical terms. An ethic, ecologically, is a limitation on freedom of action in the struggle for existence. An ethic, philosophically, is a differentiation of social from anti-social conduct. These are two definitions of one thing. The thing has its origin in the tendency of interdependent individuals or groups to evolve modes of co-operation. The ecologist calls these symbioses. Politics and economics are advanced symbioses in which the original free-for-all competition has been replaced, in part, by co-operative mechanisms with an ethical content.

The complexity of co-operative mechanisms has increased with population density, and with the efficiency of tools. It was simpler, for example, to define the anti-social uses of sticks and stones in the days of the mastodons than of bullets and billboards in the age of motors.

The first ethics dealt with the relation between individuals; the Mosaic Decalogue is an example. Later accretions dealt with the relation between the individual and society. The Golden

Rule tries to integrate the individual to society; democracy to integrate social organization to the individual.

There is as yet no ethic dealing with man's relation to land and to the animals and plants which grow upon it. Land, like Odysseus' slave-girls, is still property. The land-relation is still strictly economic, entailing privileges but not obligations.

The extension of ethics to this third element in human environment is, if I read the evidence correctly, an evolutionary possibility and an ecological necessity. It is the third step in a sequence. The first two have already been taken. Individual thinkers since the days of Ezekiel and Isaiah have asserted that the despoliation of land is not only inexpedient but wrong. Society, however, has not yet affirmed their belief. I regard the present conservation movement as the embryo of such an affirmation.

An ethic may be regarded as a mode of guidance for meeting ecological situations so new or intricate, or involving such deferred reactions, that the path of social expediency is not discernible to the average individual. Animal instincts are modes of guidance for the individual in meeting such situations. Ethics are possibly a kind of community instinct in-the-making.

THE COMMUNITY CONCEPT

All ethics so far evolved rest upon a single premise: that the individual is a member of a community of interdependent parts. His instincts prompt him to compete for his place in that community, but his ethics prompt him also to co-operate (perhaps in order that there may be a place to compete for).

The land ethic simply enlarges the boundaries of the community to include soils, waters, plants, and animals, or collectively: the land.

This sounds simple: do we not already sing our love for and obligation to the land of the free and the home of the brave? Yes, but just what and whom do we love? Certainly not the soil, which we are sending helter-skelter downriver. Certainly not the waters, which we assume have no function except to turn turbines, float barges, and carry off sewage. Certainly not the plants, of which we exterminate whole communities without batting an eye. Certainly not the animals, of which we have already extirpated many of the largest and most beautiful species. A land ethic of course cannot prevent the alteration, management, and use of these 'resources,' but it does affirm their right to continued existence, and, at least in spots, their continued existence in a natural state.

In short, a land ethic changes the role of *Homo sapiens* from conqueror of the land-community to plain member and citizen of it. It implies respect for his fellow-members, and also respect for the community as such.

In human history, we have learned (I hope) that the conqueror role is eventually self-defeating. Why? Because it is implicit in such a role that the conqueror knows, *ex cathedra*, just what makes the community clock tick, and just what and who is valuable, and what and who is worthless, in community life. It always turns out that he knows neither, and this is why his conquests eventually defeat themselves.

In the biotic community, a parallel situation exists. Abraham knew exactly what the land was for: it was to drip milk and honey into Abraham's mouth. At the present moment, the assurance with which we regard this assumption is inverse to the degree of our education.

The ordinary citizen today assumes that science knows what makes the community clock tick; the scientist is equally sure that he does not. He knows that the biotic mechanism is so complex that its workings may never be fully understood.

That man is, in fact, only a member of a biotic team is shown by an ecological interpretation of history. Many historical events, hitherto explained solely in terms of human enterprise, were actually biotic interactions between people and land. The characteristics of the land determined the facts quite as potently as the characteristics of the men who lived on it.

Consider, for example, the settlement of the Mississippi valley. In the years following the Revolution, three groups were contending for its control: the native Indian, the French and English traders, and the American settlers. Historians wonder what would have happened if the English at Detroit had thrown a little more weight into the Indian side of those tipsy scales which decided the outcome of the colonial migration into the cane-lands of Kentucky. It is time now to ponder the fact that the cane-lands, when subjected to the particular mixture of forces represented by the cow, plow, fire, and axe of the pioneer, became bluegrass. What if the plant succession inherent in this dark and bloody ground had, under the impact of these forces, given us some worthless sedge, shrub, or weed? Would Boone and Kenton have held out? Would there have been any overflow into Ohio, Indiana, Illinois, and Missouri? Any Louisiana Purchase? Any transcontinental union of new states? Any Civil War?

Kentucky was one sentence in the drama of history. We are commonly told what the human actors in this drama tried to do, but we are seldom told that their success, or the lack of it, hung in large degree on the reaction of particular soils to the impact of the particular forces exerted by their occupancy. In the case of Kentucky, we do not even know where the bluegrass came from—whether it is a native species, or a stowaway from Europe.

Contrast the cane-lands with what hindsight tells us about the Southwest, where the pioneers were equally brave, resourceful, and persevering. The impact of occupancy here brought no bluegrass, or other plant fitted to withstand the bumps and buffetings of hard use. This region, when grazed by livestock, reverted through a series of more and more worthless grasses, shrubs, and weeds to a condition of unstable equilibrium. Each recession of plant types bred erosion; each increment to erosion bred a further recession of plants. The result today is a progressive and mutual deterioration, not only of plants and soils, but of the animal community subsisting thereon. The early settlers did not expect this: on the ciénegas of New Mexico some even cut ditches to hasten it. So subtle has been its progress that few residents of the region are aware of it. It is quite invisible to the tourist who finds this wrecked landscape colorful and charming (as indeed it is, but it bears scant resemblance to what it was in 1848).

This same landscape was 'developed' once before, but with quite different results. The Pueblo Indians settled the Southwest in pre-Columbian times, but they happened *not* to be equipped with range livestock. Their civilization expired, but not because their land expired.

In India, regions devoid of any sod-forming grass have been settled, apparently without wrecking the land, by the simple expedient of carrying the grass to the cow, rather than vice versa. (Was this the result of some deep wisdom, or was it just good luck? I do not know.)

In short, the plant succession steered the course of history; the pioneer simply demonstrated, for good or ill, what successions inhered in the land. Is history taught in this spirit? It will be, once the concept of land as a community really penetrates our intellectual life.

THE ECOLOGICAL CONSCIENCE

Conservation is a state of harmony between men and land. Despite nearly a century of propaganda, conservation still proceeds at a snail's pace; progress still consists largely of letterhead pieties and convention oratory. On the back forty we still slip two steps backward for each forward stride.

The usual answer to this dilemma is 'more conservation education.' No one will debate this, but is it certain that only the *volume* of education needs stepping up? Is something lacking in the *content* as well?

It is difficult to give a fair summary of its content in brief form, but, as I understand it, the content is substantially this: obey the law, vote right, join some organizations, and practice what conservation is profitable on your own land; the government will do the rest.

Is not this formula too easy to accomplish anything worthwhile? It defines no right or wrong, assigns no obligation, calls for no sacrifice, implies no change in the current philosophy of values. In respect of land-use, it urges only enlightened self-interest. Just how far will such education take us? An example will perhaps yield a partial answer.

By 1930 it had become clear to all except the ecologically blind that southwestern Wisconsin's topsoil was slipping seaward. In 1933 the farmers were told that if they would adopt certain remedial practices for five years, the public would donate CCC labor to install them, plus the necessary machinery and materials. The offer was widely accepted, but the practices were widely forgotten when the five-year contract period was up. The farmers continued only those practices that yielded an immediate and visible economic gain for themselves.

This led to the idea that maybe farmers would learn more quickly if they themselves wrote the rules. Accordingly the Wisconsin Legislature in 1937 passed the Soil Conservation District Law. This said to farmers, in effect: *We, the public, will furnish*

*you free technical service and loan you specialized machinery,
if you will write your own rules for land-use. Each county may
write its own rules, and these will have the force of law.* Nearly
all the counties promptly organized to accept the proffered
help, but after a decade of operation, *no county has yet written
a single rule.* There has been visible progress in such practices as
strip-cropping, pasture renovation, and soil liming, but none in
fencing woodlots against grazing, and none in excluding plow
and cow from steep slopes. The farmers, in short, have selected
those remedial practices which were profitable anyhow, and
ignored those which were profitable to the community, but not
clearly profitable to themselves.

When one asks why no rules have been written, one is told
that the community is not yet ready to support them; education must precede rules. But the education actually in progress
makes no mention of obligations to land over and above those
dictated by self-interest. The net result is that we have more
education but less soil, fewer healthy woods, and as many floods
as in 1937.

The puzzling aspect of such situations is that the existence of
obligations over and above self-interest is taken for granted in
such rural community enterprises as the betterment of roads,
schools, churches, and baseball teams. Their existence is not
taken for granted, nor as yet seriously discussed, in bettering the
behavior of the water that falls on the land, or in the preserving
of the beauty or diversity of the farm landscape. Land-use ethics
are still governed wholly by economic self-interest, just as social
ethics were a century ago.

To sum up: we asked the farmer to do what he conveniently
could to save his soil, and he has done just that, and only that.
The farmer who clears the woods off a 75 per cent slope, turns
his cows into the clearing, and dumps its rainfall, rocks, and
soil into the community creek, is still (if otherwise decent) a
respected member of society. If he puts lime on his fields and
plants his crops on contour, he is still entitled to all the privileges and emoluments of his Soil Conservation District. The
District is a beautiful piece of social machinery, but it is coughing along on two cylinders because we have been too timid,
and too anxious for quick success, to tell the farmer the true
magnitude of his obligations. Obligations have no meaning

without conscience, and the problem we face is the extension of the social conscience from people to land.

No important change in ethics was ever accomplished without an internal change in our intellectual emphasis, loyalties, affections, and convictions. The proof that conservation has not yet touched these foundations of conduct lies in the fact that philosophy and religion have not yet heard of it. In our attempt to make conservation easy, we have made it trivial.

SUBSTITUTES FOR A LAND ETHIC

When the logic of history hungers for bread and we hand out a stone, we are at pains to explain how much the stone resembles bread. I now describe some of the stones which serve in lieu of a land ethic.

One basic weakness in a conservation system based wholly on economic motives is that most members of the land community have no economic value. Wildflowers and songbirds are examples. Of the 22,000 higher plants and animals native to Wisconsin, it is doubtful whether more than 5 per cent can be sold, fed, eaten, or otherwise put to economic use. Yet these creatures are members of the biotic community, and if (as I believe) its stability depends on its integrity, they are entitled to continuance.

When one of these non-economic categories is threatened, and if we happen to love it, we invent subterfuges to give it economic importance. At the beginning of the century songbirds were supposed to be disappearing. Ornithologists jumped to the rescue with some distinctly shaky evidence to the effect that insects would eat us up if birds failed to control them. The evidence had to be economic in order to be valid.

It is painful to read these circumlocutions today. We have no land ethic yet, but we have at least drawn nearer the point of admitting that birds should continue as a matter of biotic right, regardless of the presence or absence of economic advantage to us.

A parallel situation exists in respect of predatory mammals, raptorial birds, and fish-eating birds. Time was when biologists somewhat overworked the evidence that these creatures preserve the health of game by killing weaklings, or that they control rodents for the farmer, or that they prey only on 'worthless'

species. Here again, the evidence had to be economic in order to be valid. It is only in recent years that we hear the more honest argument that predators are members of the community, and that no special interest has the right to exterminate them for the sake of a benefit, real or fancied, to itself. Unfortunately this enlightened view is still in the talk stage. In the field the extermination of predators goes merrily on: witness the impending erasure of the timber wolf by fiat of Congress, the Conservation Bureaus, and many state legislatures.

Some species of trees have been 'read out of the party' by economics-minded foresters because they grow too slowly, or have too low a sale value to pay as timber crops: white cedar, tamarack, cypress, beech, and hemlock are examples. In Europe, where forestry is ecologically more advanced, the noncommercial tree species are recognized as members of the native forest community, to be preserved as such, within reason. Moreover some (like beech) have been found to have a valuable function in building up soil fertility. The interdependence of the forest and its constituent tree species, ground flora, and fauna is taken for granted.

Lack of economic value is sometimes a character not only of

species or groups, but of entire biotic communities: marshes, bogs, dunes, and 'deserts' are examples. Our formula in such cases is to relegate their conservation to government as refuges, monuments, or parks. The difficulty is that these communities are usually interspersed with more valuable private lands; the government cannot possibly own or control such scattered parcels. The net effect is that we have relegated some of them to ultimate extinction over large areas. If the private owner were ecologically minded, he would be proud to be the custodian of a reasonable proportion of such areas, which add diversity and beauty to his farm and to his community.

In some instances, the assumed lack of profit in these 'waste' areas has proved to be wrong, but only after most of them had been done away with. The present scramble to reflood muskrat marshes is a case in point.

There is a clear tendency in American conservation to relegate to government all necessary jobs that private landowners fail to perform. Government ownership, operation, subsidy, or regulation is now widely prevalent in forestry, range management, soil and watershed management, park and wilderness conservation, fisheries management, and migratory bird management, with more to come. Most of this growth in governmental conservation is proper and logical, some of it is inevitable. That I imply no disapproval of it is implicit in the fact that I have spent most of my life working for it. Nevertheless the question arises: What is the ultimate magnitude of the enterprise? Will the tax base carry its eventual ramifications? At what point will governmental conservation, like the mastodon, become handicapped by its own dimensions? The answer, if there is any, seems to be in a land ethic, or some other force which assigns more obligation to the private landowner.

Industrial landowners and users, especially lumbermen and stockmen, are inclined to wail long and loudly about the extension of government ownership and regulation to land, but (with notable exceptions) they show little disposition to develop the only visible alternative: the voluntary practice of conservation on their own lands.

When the private landowner is asked to perform some unprofitable act for the good of the community, he today assents only with outstretched palm. If the act costs him cash this is fair and proper, but when it costs only forethought, open-minded-ness, or time, the issue is at least debatable. The overwhelming growth of land-use subsidies in recent years must be ascribed, in large part, to the government's own agencies for conservation education: the land bureaus, the agricultural colleges, and the extension services. As far as I can detect, no ethical obligation toward land is taught in these institutions.

To sum up: a system of conservation based solely on eco-nomic self-interest is hopelessly lopsided. It tends to ignore, and thus eventually to eliminate, many elements in the land community that lack commercial value, but that are (as far as we know) essential to its healthy functioning. It assumes, falsely, I think, that the economic parts of the biotic clock will function without the uneconomic parts. It tends to relegate to govern-ment many functions eventually too large, too complex, or too widely dispersed to be performed by government.

An ethical obligation on the part of the private owner is the only visible remedy for these situations.

THE LAND PYRAMID

An ethic to supplement and guide the economic relation to land presupposes the existence of some mental image of land as a biotic mechanism. We can be ethical only in relation to something we can see, feel, understand, love, or otherwise have faith in.

The image commonly employed in conservation education is 'the balance of nature.' For reasons too lengthy to detail here, this figure of speech fails to describe accurately what little we know about the land mechanism. A much truer image is the one employed in ecology: the biotic pyramid. I shall first sketch the pyramid as a symbol of land, and later develop some of its implications in terms of land-use.

Plants absorb energy from the sun. This energy flows through a circuit called the biota, which may be represented by a pyra-mid consisting of layers. The bottom layer is the soil. A plant layer rests on the soil, an insect layer on the plants, a bird and rodent layer on the insects, and so on up through various animal groups to the apex layer, which consists of the larger carnivores.

The species of a layer are alike not in where they came from, or in what they look like, but rather in what they eat. Each suc-cessive layer depends on those below it for food and often for other services, and each in turn furnishes food and services to those above. Proceeding upward, each successive layer decreases in numerical abundance. Thus, for every carnivore there are hundreds of his prey, thousands of their prey, millions of insects, uncountable plants. The pyramidal form of the system reflects this numerical progression from apex to base. Man shares an intermediate layer with the bears, raccoons, and squirrels which eat both meat and vegetables.

The lines of dependency for food and other services are called food chains. Thus soil-oak-deer-Indian is a chain that has now been largely converted to soil-corn-cow-farmer. Each species, including ourselves, is a link in many chains. The deer eats a hundred plants other than oak, and the cow a hundred plants other than corn. Both, then, are links in a hundred chains. The pyramid is a tangle of chains so complex as to seem disorderly, yet the stability of the system proves it to be a highly organized structure. Its functioning depends on the co-operation and competition of its diverse parts.

In the beginning, the pyramid of life was low and squat; the food chains short and simple. Evolution has added layer after layer, link after link. Man is one of thousands of accretions to the height and complexity of the pyramid. Science has given us many doubts, but it has given us at least one certainty: the trend of evolution is to elaborate and diversify the biota.

Land, then, is not merely soil; it is a fountain of energy flowing through a circuit of soils, plants, and animals. Food chains are the living channels which conduct energy upward; death and decay return it to the soil. The circuit is not closed; some energy is dissipated in decay, some is added by absorption from the air, some is stored in soils, peats, and long-lived forests; but it is a sustained circuit, like a slowly augmented revolving fund of life. There is always a net loss by downhill wash, but this is normally small and offset by the decay of rocks. It is deposited in the ocean and, in the course of geological time, raised to form new lands and new pyramids.

The velocity and character of the upward flow of energy depend on the complex structure of the plant and animal community, much as the upward flow of sap in a tree depends on its complex cellular organization. Without this complexity, normal circulation would presumably not occur. Structure means the characteristic numbers, as well as the characteristic kinds and functions, of the component species. This interdependence between the complex structure of the land and its smooth functioning as an energy unit is one of its basic attributes.

When a change occurs in one part of the circuit, many other parts must adjust themselves to it. Change does not necessarily obstruct or divert the flow of energy; evolution is a long series of self-induced changes, the net result of which has been to elaborate the flow mechanism and to lengthen the circuit. Evolutionary changes, however, are usually slow and local. Man's invention of tools has enabled him to make changes of unprecedented violence, rapidity, and scope.

One change is in the composition of floras and faunas. The larger predators are lopped off the apex of the pyramid; food chains, for the first time in history, become shorter rather than longer. Domesticated species from other lands are substituted for wild ones, and wild ones are moved to new habitats. In this world-wide pooling of faunas and floras, some species get out of bounds as pests and diseases, others are extinguished. Such effects are seldom intended or foreseen; they represent unpredicted and often untraceable readjustments in the structure. Agricultural science is largely a race between the emergence of new pests and the emergence of new techniques for their control.

Another change touches the flow of energy through plants and animals and its return to the soil. Fertility is the ability of soil to receive, store, and release energy. Agriculture, by overdrafts on the soil, or by too radical a substitution of domestic for native species in the superstructure, may derange the channels of flow or deplete storage. Soils depleted of their storage, or of the organic matter which anchors it, wash away faster than they form. This is erosion.

Waters, like soil, are part of the energy circuit. Industry, by polluting waters or obstructing them with dams, may exclude the plants and animals necessary to keep energy in circulation.

Transportation brings about another basic change: the plants or animals grown in one region are now consumed and returned to the soil in another. Transportation taps the energy stored in rocks, and in the air, and uses it elsewhere; thus we fertilize the garden with nitrogen gleaned by the guano birds from the fishes of seas on the other side of the Equator. Thus the formerly localized and self-contained circuits are pooled on a world-wide scale.

The process of altering the pyramid for human occupation releases stored energy, and this often gives rise, during the pioneering period, to a deceptive exuberance of plant and animal life, both wild and tame. These releases of biotic capital tend to becloud or postpone the penalties of violence.

*   *   *

This thumbnail sketch of land as an energy circuit conveys three basic ideas:

(1) That land is not merely soil.

(2) That the native plants and animals kept the energy circuit open; others may or may not.

(3) That man-made changes are of a different order than evolutionary changes, and have effects more comprehensive than is intended or foreseen.

These ideas, collectively, raise two basic issues: Can the land adjust itself to the new order? Can the desired alterations be accomplished with less violence?

Biotas seem to differ in their capacity to sustain violent conversion. Western Europe, for example, carries a far different pyramid than Caesar found there. Some large animals are lost; swampy forests have become meadows or plow-land; many new plants and animals are introduced, some of which escape as pests; the remaining natives are greatly changed in distribution and abundance. Yet the soil is still there and, with the help of imported nutrients, still fertile; the waters flow normally; the new structure seems to function and to persist. There is no visible stoppage or derangement of the circuit.

Western Europe, then, has a resistant biota. Its inner processes are tough, elastic, resistant to strain. No matter how violent the alterations, the pyramid, so far, has developed some new *modus vivendi* which preserves its habitability for man, and for most of the other natives.

Japan seems to present another instance of radical conversion without disorganization.

Most other civilized regions, and some as yet barely touched by civilization, display various stages of disorganization, varying from initial symptoms to advanced wastage. In Asia Minor and

North Africa diagnosis is confused by climatic changes, which may have been either the cause or the effect of advanced wastage. In the United States the degree of disorganization varies locally; it is worst in the Southwest, the Ozarks, and parts of the South, and least in New England and the Northwest. Better land-uses may still arrest it in the less advanced regions. In parts of Mexico, South America, South Africa, and Australia a violent and accelerating wastage is in progress, but I cannot assess the prospects.

This almost world-wide display of disorganization in the land seems to be similar to disease in an animal, except that it never culminates in complete disorganization or death. The land recovers, but at some reduced level of complexity, and with a reduced carrying capacity for people, plants, and animals. Many biotas currently regarded as 'lands of opportunity' are in fact already subsisting on exploitative agriculture, i.e. they have already exceeded their sustained carrying capacity. Most of South America is overpopulated in this sense.

In arid regions we attempt to offset the process of wastage by reclamation, but it is only too evident that the prospective longevity of reclamation projects is often short. In our own West, the best of them may not last a century.

The combined evidence of history and ecology seems to support one general deduction: the less violent the man-made changes, the greater the probability of successful readjustment in the pyramid. Violence, in turn, varies with human population density; a dense population requires a more violent conversion. In this respect, North America has a better chance for permanence than Europe, if she can contrive to limit her density.

This deduction runs counter to our current philosophy, which assumes that because a small increase in density enriched human life, that an indefinite increase will enrich it indefinitely. Ecology knows of no density relationship that holds for indefinitely wide limits. All gains from density are subject to a law of diminishing returns.

Whatever may be the equation for men and land, it is improbable that we as yet know all its terms. Recent discoveries in mineral and vitamin nutrition reveal unsuspected dependencies in the up-circuit: incredibly minute quantities of certain

substances determine the value of soils to plants, of plants to animals. What of the down-circuit? What of the vanishing species,
the preservation of which we now regard as an esthetic luxury?
They helped build the soil; in what unsuspected ways may they
be essential to its maintenance? Professor Weaver proposes that
we use prairie flowers to reflocculate the wasting soils of the
dust bowl; who knows for what purpose cranes and condors,
otters and grizzlies may some day be used?

LAND HEALTH AND THE A-B CLEAVAGE

A land ethic, then, reflects the existence of an ecological conscience, and this in turn reflects a conviction of individual responsibility for the health of the land. Health is the capacity of
the land for self-renewal. Conservation is our effort to understand and preserve this capacity.

Conservationists are notorious for their dissensions. Superficially these seem to add up to mere confusion, but a more
careful scrutiny reveals a single plane of cleavage common to
many specialized fields. In each field one group (A) regards the
land as soil, and its function as commodity-production; another
group (B) regards the land as a biota, and its function as something broader. How much broader is admittedly in a state of
doubt and confusion.

In my own field, forestry, Group A is quite content to grow
trees like cabbages, with cellulose as the basic forest commodity.
It feels no inhibition against violence; its ideology is agronomic.
Group B, on the other hand, sees forestry as fundamentally different from agronomy because it employs natural species, and
manages a natural environment rather than creating an artificial one. Group B prefers natural reproduction on principle. It
worries on biotic as well as economic grounds about the loss of
species like chestnut, and the threatened loss of the white pines.
It worries about a whole series of secondary forest functions:
wildlife, recreation, watersheds, wilderness areas. To my mind,
Group B feels the stirrings of an ecological conscience.

In the wildlife field, a parallel cleavage exists. For Group A
the basic commodities are sport and meat; the yardsticks of
production are ciphers of take in pheasants and trout. Artificial
propagation is acceptable as a permanent as well as a temporary

recourse—if its unit costs permit. Group B, on the other hand, worries about a whole series of biotic side-issues. What is the cost in predators of producing a game crop? Should we have further recourse to exotics? How can management restore the shrinking species, like prairie grouse, already hopeless as shoot-able game? How can management restore the threatened rari-ties, like trumpeter swan and whooping crane? Can manage-ment principles be extended to wildflowers? Here again it is clear to me that we have the same A-B cleavage as in forestry.

In the larger field of agriculture I am less competent to speak, but there seem to be somewhat parallel cleavages. Scientific agriculture was actively developing before ecology was born, hence a slower penetration of ecological concepts might be expected. Moreover the farmer, by the very nature of his tech-niques, must modify the biota more radically than the forester or the wildlife manager. Nevertheless, there are many discon-tents in agriculture which seem to add up to a new vision of 'biotic farming.'

Perhaps the most important of these is the new evidence that poundage or tonnage is no measure of the food-value of farm crops; the products of fertile soil may be qualitatively as well as quantitatively superior. We can bolster poundage from depleted soils by pouring on imported fertility, but we are not necessar-ily bolstering food-value. The possible ultimate ramifications of this idea are so immense that I must leave their exposition to abler pens.

The discontent that labels itself 'organic farming,' while bear-ing some of the earmarks of a cult, is nevertheless biotic in its direction, particularly in its insistence on the importance of soil flora and fauna.

The ecological fundamentals of agriculture are just as poorly known to the public as in other fields of land-use. For example, few educated people realize that the marvelous advances in technique made during recent decades are improvements in the pump, rather than the well. Acre for acre, they have barely sufficed to offset the sinking level of fertility.

In all of these cleavages, we see repeated the same basic para-doxes: man the conqueror *versus* man the biotic citizen; science the sharpener of his sword *versus* science the searchlight on his universe; land the slave and servant *versus* land the collective organism. Robinson's injunction to Tristram may well be applied, at this juncture, to *Homo sapiens* as a species in geological time:

> Whether you will or not
> You are a King, Tristram, for you are one
> Of the time-tested few that leave the world,
> When they are gone, not the same place it was.
> Mark what you leave.

THE OUTLOOK

It is inconceivable to me that an ethical relation to land can exist without love, respect, and admiration for land, and a high regard for its value. By value, I of course mean something far broader than mere economic value; I mean value in the philosophical sense.

Perhaps the most serious obstacle impeding the evolution of a land ethic is the fact that our educational and economic system is headed away from, rather than toward, an intense consciousness of land. Your true modern is separated from the land by many middlemen, and by innumerable physical gadgets. He has no vital relation to it; to him it is the space between cities on which crops grow. Turn him loose for a day on the land, and if the spot does not happen to be a golf links or a 'scenic' area, he is bored stiff. If crops could be raised by hydroponics instead of farming, it would suit him very well. Synthetic substitutes for wood, leather, wool, and other natural land products suit him better than the originals. In short, land is something he has 'outgrown.'

Almost equally serious as an obstacle to a land ethic is the attitude of the farmer for whom the land is still an adversary, or a taskmaster that keeps him in slavery. Theoretically, the mechanization of farming ought to cut the farmer's chains, but whether it really does is debatable.

One of the requisites for an ecological comprehension of land is an understanding of ecology, and this is by no means co-extensive with 'education'; in fact, much higher education seems deliberately to avoid ecological concepts. An understanding of ecology does not necessarily originate in courses bearing ecological labels; it is quite as likely to be labeled geography,

botany, agronomy, history, or economics. This is as it should be,
but whatever the label, ecological training is scarce.

The case for a land ethic would appear hopeless but for the
minority which is in obvious revolt against these 'modern'
trends.

The 'key-log' which must be moved to release the evolutionary process for an ethic is simply this: quit thinking about
decent land-use as solely an economic problem. Examine each
question in terms of what is ethically and esthetically right, as
well as what is economically expedient. A thing is right when it
tends to preserve the integrity, stability, and beauty of the biotic
community. It is wrong when it tends otherwise.

It of course goes without saying that economic feasibility limits the tether of what can or cannot be done for land. It always
has and it always will. The fallacy the economic determinists
have tied around our collective neck, and which we now need
to cast off, is the belief that economics determines *all* land-use.
This is simply not true. An innumerable host of actions and
attitudes, comprising perhaps the bulk of all land relations, is
determined by the land-user's tastes and predilections, rather
than by his purse. The bulk of all land relations hinges on investments of time, forethought, skill, and faith rather than on
investments of cash. As a land-user thinketh, so is he.

I have purposely presented the land ethic as a product of social
evolution because nothing so important as an ethic is ever
'written.' Only the most superficial student of history supposes
that Moses 'wrote' the Decalogue; it evolved in the minds of a
thinking community, and Moses wrote a tentative summary of
it for a 'seminar.' I say tentative because evolution never stops.

The evolution of a land ethic is an intellectual as well as
emotional process. Conservation is paved with good intentions
which prove to be futile, or even dangerous, because they are
devoid of critical understanding either of the land, or of economic land-use. I think it is a truism that as the ethical frontier
advances from the individual to the community, its intellectual
content increases.

The mechanism of operation is the same for any ethic: social
approbation for right actions: social disapproval for wrong
actions.

By and large, our present problem is one of attitudes and

implements. We are remodeling the Alhambra with a steam-shovel, and we are proud of our yardage. We shall hardly re-linquish the shovel, which after all has many good points, but we are in need of gentler and more objective criteria for its successful use.

OTHER WRITINGS
ON ECOLOGY
AND CONSERVATION

Address before the Albuquerque Rotary Club on Presentation of the Gold Medal of the Permanent Wild Life Protection Fund

Gentlemen:

I want to say first of all that I cannot regard this medal as a personal possession. This medal belongs to the workers of the New Mexico Game Protective Association, and as one of these workers, I am proud to so regard it.

The New Mexico G.P.A. was organized just a year and a half ago. It has barely had time to start its work. There are hundreds of similar organizations all over the country,—many of them eminently successful. Just what is it that has led a national institution like the Permanent Wild Life Protection Fund to single out the New Mexico G.P.A. for this signal honor? What has it done that three states should have patterned their organizations after ours? Why do men like Theodore Roosevelt go out of their way to give the G.P.A. a good word? More curious still—how do people in Russia hear of the New Mexico G.P.A.? It is a fact that just the other day the Association received an inquiry from Kharkow, asking for full information on its organization and methods. This Club, as representative of the progressive citizenship of this State, is, I think, interested in these questions.

The best answer I can offer is that the New Mexico G.P.A. is working toward an exceptionally high ideal by the use of exceptionally practical every-day methods. In this respect it resembles the Rotary Clubs. As per the great philosopher's instructions, *we have hitched our wagon to a star, but we are using just ordinary axle grease to speed it on its stony way.*

Let me illustrate what I mean. The G.P.A. ideal is "to restore to every citizen his inalienable right to know and love the wild things of his native land." We conceive of these wild things as an integral part of our national environment, and are striving to protect, restore, and develop them, not as so many pounds of meat, nor as so many live things to shoot at, but as a tremendous social asset, as a source of democratic and healthful recreation to the millions of today and the tens of millions of tomorrow. But in thus striving we do not preach—too much— of social assets and other philosophical tenets and concepts. We go to the common man and say: "Here, if you want to have anything left for your kid to shoot at, it's time to get busy." He knows what we mean. He sees the ideal—only he doesn't want it talked about. Like all typical Americans, he dreams with the gods but wants to talk and act like a common geezer. I, for one, thank God that this is so.

Again let me illustrate. It is our task to educate the moral nature of each and every one of New Mexico's half million citizens to look upon our beneficial birds and animals, not as so much gun-fodder to satisfy his instinctive love of killing, but as irreplaceable works of art, done in life by the Great Artist. They are to be seen and used and enjoyed to be sure, but never destroyed or wasted. But the process of education is slow, human nature is weak, wild life is disappearing with astounding rapidity, and there are 70,000,000 acres in this State which a handful of wardens must patrol against vandalism. Therefore the vandals who cannot be taught to feel the promptings of decency must be made to feel the hand of the law, and feel it hard. Accordingly, hand in hand with our campaign of education, we have insisted from the start on the merciless prosecution of all willful offenders. To this end the Association demanded, during the last State political campaign, the appointment of an efficient Game Warden, answerable to the public for chastened game hogs, not to the machine for well-mended fences. This demand was considered by some as quite Utopian and unheard-of, and even our friends were betting against us. But the Association made it stick, and we have with us today Mr. Rouault. He is introducing them to the J. P. every day and they are paying their little fines in carload lots. Inasmuch as I did not serve in the campaign which eliminated our State wardenship from politics, I can say with due modesty that it was a unique accomplishment— and sportsmen all over the United States are discussing it with a view to doing likewise. "I have a new idea of New Mexico" writes a total stranger from the East who read of it in our paper. The general who snatched the victory in this case was our president, Miles W. Burford of Silver City. I am sorry he could not respond to your invitation to be here today. He is the man who brings home the bacon when it comes to hunting game hogs. Ever since I have been in New Mexico he has averaged from 20 to 30 convictions a year, and most of the culprits are friends of game protection when he gets through with them. If Miles W. Burford talked as hard as he works, it is my belief that he would be standing here today making this speech.

Gentlemen, I have tried to illustrate what I meant by hitching your wagon to a star, but lubricating it with common axle grease. I believe you have seen my point, because you are practicing the same principle here in this Rotary Club. I need therefore not dwell on it further. I now want to sermonize a little—but not too much—on the condition of the wild life of the State, and bespeak your aid and backing in the work of saving our noblest game animals from immediate extinction.

The average citizen when personally appealed to on behalf of wild life, generally replies that all the game he kills wouldn't amount to pulling a straw out of a ten ton haystack. He implies that therefore he has already done his bit for game conservation. But this answer always reminds me of O. Henry's story about Arkansas feuds. Feuds, says O. Henry, are generally fought out pretty fair and square in the good old state of Arkansas. Your enemy doesn't lie ambushed in a cornfield, and shoot you in the back where your suspenders cross, first because there ain't 'arry cornfields, and second because nobody wears but one suspender. Just so is it true that the average citizen levies only moderate toll on our game supply,— first because there is hardly any game left, and second because what is left is pretty near too scarce to hunt.

I shall not try to describe the individual predicament of each of New Mexico's eight splendid big-game animals. (Incidentally no other state in the Union was endowed by nature with like generosity.) I shall mention just one example, the Mountain Sheep. I choose this most prized of all big game, first because it is our own. (The species of sheep found in our Southwest is found nowhere else in the world, and if we can restore it to our hills, we shall have a natural monopoly.) Second, I choose the sheep because it hovers nearest to the brink of extinction. It is a case of save it now or never.

Coronado was our first publicity agent, and the first thing he mentioned in his diary when he crossed the present border was the "*great herds of wild sheep, with horns the girth of a man's thigh.*" In those days every one of our mountain ranges supported thousands of these magnificent animals. Today there are less than 200 left in the entire State. What wiped out the sheep? The necessary progress of settlement and civilization? Nonsense! Neither settlement nor civilization has ever made and never will make a dent in the vertical acres that are the natural home of the mountain sheep. Those straight up and down rocks are the same now as they were a thousand years before Coronado ever heard of the Gran Quivera. Those rocks are good to raise sheep, and nothing else. To let the sheep become extinct means that those rocks must forever go to waste. Think of it—*a million acres to lie waste a million years!* And as for what has become of the sheep—they have been slaughtered by men and lions—ruthlessly before the advent of game laws, and ruthlessly and willfully every since.

Gentlemen, you can almost see from here ten thousand acres of rocks in the breaks of the Sandias. A stranger just came here and told you what a tremendous asset you had in your local Indian Villages—and you rightly believed him. Would that I had the gift of tongues to come here and tell you what a tremendous asset you have in those rocks,—stocked with mountain sheep!

I could tell you of men who travelled ten thousand miles and spent a fortune for one look at the Argali sheep of Asia. How many men, then, would come here to see your sheep of New Mexico? And how many fortunes would they spend?

I could tell you of your sons who would rise up and call you blessed for your foresight, if you act in time. I could also tell you of sons who may have to shake their heads and wonder why we of today let these splendid creatures slip into oblivion, all because we could see a vision, but would not look.

Gentlemen, the New Mexico Game Protective Association sees two visions. It sees those rocks, and hundreds like them throughout the State, productive of health and pleasure and the good things of life, for all time to come. It also sees those rocks,—a million acres lying waste a million years. It bids you look. It will continue to bid you look. And if I rightly judge the fibre of its men, you will be able to say of each, even as Cervantes said of Don Quixote, that "though he achieved not great things, yet did he die in their pursuit."

Typescript, c. July 1917

Boomerangs

Tassel-eared Gray Squirrels cut off pine boughs. Why! Nobody knows. They evidently have a squirrelish sense of humor.

The pine boughs fall to the ground. Why? Because they can't help it.

An old cow comes along and eats them. Why? For the same reason that humans chew gum—just to be doing something.

The meal of pine boughs is not good for the old cow. In many cases it causes abortion of the calf.

The cowman comes along and is full of wrath. He too has a sense of humor, but in these days an aborted calf is rather a serious joke.

Squirrels play similar jokes on the forester by cutting off millions of immature pine cones, which are the source of the necessary seed crop. Incidentally, this joke is a boomerang to the *foolish squirrels*, who need pine seed to eat. What can be done to chastise the squirrels?

The damage done assumes serious proportions only in localities where the squirrels become abnormally abundant. Why do squirrels become abnormally abundant? *Because of the suicidal butchery of beneficial hawks and owls.*

Across the vast treeless stretches of the San Augustine Plains runs a telephone line and a road. Thousands of migrating hawks alight on the telephone poles to rest. Hundreds of automobiles speed along the road, each apparently armed with a shotgun. And under each telephone pole lie from one to six dead hawks. He who runs may read the story.

Two out of three of these dead hawks are of species that live almost exclusively on prairie-dogs, gophers, squirrels, and other rodents.

Two out of three of these hawk-killing automobiles belong to stockmen who rise in wrath against the rodents.

Talk about foolish SQUIRRELS!

The Pine Cone, April 1918

Wild Lifers vs. Game Farmers
A Plea for Democracy in Sport

IN THE general field of American sportsmanship three things are certain:

1. There has been a general and growing scarcity of game all over the United States.

2. This decrease has not so far been checked on any considerable scale, except in the single case of waterfowl. Waterfowl have shown a perceptible response to the Federal Migratory Bird Law.

3. The annual drain on the game supply will greatly increase after the war. The return of the soldiers, the resumption of a normal amount of recreation by the whole population, and the increase in the number of motor vehicles, good roads, and modern guns, will all make for a greater annual kill.

The three foregoing facts can lead to but one conclusion: we face a dwindling supply and a growing demand for game. What are we going to do about it?

"There is nothing to do about it. The country is settling up and I guess the game must go." This would have been the answer of the average citizen twenty years ago.

"I don't know just how we will go about it, but a fair supply of game must be maintained." This is the answer of the average citizen to-day.

Do we fully appreciate the difference between these two answers? We have not solved the problem, but we have resolved to tackle it. This nationwide determination that "something must be done" is the greatest single achievement of the past generation of sportsmen. It is a big achievement. Extreme pessimists will do well to ponder it carefully.

It remains for this generation to evolve a general plan of action, and then execute it. We are now groping for such a general plan. Countless new departures in game laws, thousands of voluntary organizations devoted to game protection, hundreds of publications theorizing as to ways and means—all these are evidence of the fact that the great American public is seeking an answer to the question, "How shall we perpetuate the game?"

198

What next? This is easy to predict. Out of this maze of gropings will emerge two or more factions, or schools of thought. To these will flock the radicals, the extremists. They will begin forthwith to attack one another's opinions. This fight will be a test of strength, of which the great mass of moderate-minded men will be interested spectators. When one side or the other has developed a preponderance of plausible arguments, of actual demonstrations, and of influence, the moderates will join that side. Its plan will be put into effect—with a toning down of its extreme features, and the incorporation of a few strong points developed by the losing side.

If we may thus predict these probable steps in the evolution of a plan for managing our game, it becomes both interesting and profitable to figure out just what part of the process we are going through at this present time. It is the purpose of this paper (a) to point out that two extreme factions are now emerging; (b) to define their respective claims; and (c) to appraise those claims from a more or less new and, I believe, an important viewpoint. The two factions I will call the "Game Farmers" and the "Wild Lifers." The new viewpoint is that which regards the game not as meat, not as sport, nor yet as a set of zoological specimens, but rather as a source of democratic recreation, a human source, a social asset.

What are the Game Farmers? Since the Hercules Powder Company started to advertise them two years ago, the country has had little opportunity to forget them. In general, the Game Farmers propose to supplement wild game with, or substitute for it, a supply produced under artificially regulated conditions. Radical Game Farmers tend to regard restrictive game laws as eventually hopeless and ineffective.

What are the Wild Lifers? They are the advocates of restrictive game laws; the scarcer the game the more restrictions. Long or even permanent closed seasons on threatened species are a logical corollary of their doctrine. The name, "Wild Lifers," is one recently and sarcastically donated by certain radical Game Farmers.

The easy-going (and sometimes shallow-thinking) moderate is apt to see no real conflict between these two factions. "They are both cranks," he says, "but both partially right. Why not conserve the game as well as we can with laws, and then breed it, too! Let game farming be a supplement to instead of a substitute for game laws, and presto! everything will be lovely."

This is coming to be the view of many moderate-minded men, and the policy of many official state game departments. Will the compromise hold water? This is an important question, to which there is, I believe, no sweeping answer. A comparative analysis and appraisement of the two factions, however, will throw some light on the question.

A first and fundamental distinction between the two is that the game farmer seeks to produce merely something to shoot, while the Wild Lifer seeks to perpetuate, at least, a sample of all wild life, game and non-game. The one caters to the gunner, the other to the whole outdoors-loving public. Inasmuch as the camera man, the sporting naturalist, and other non-gunners are coming to comprise a considerable percentage of the national fraternity of sportsmen, it must be admitted at the start that the Wild Lifer represents, or attempts to represent, the interests of a larger group of citizens than his opponent.

Secondly, the Game Farmer, so far, at least, is purely materialistic as to what his "something to shoot" consists of. If Chinese pheasant is cheaper and easier to raise than the American heath hen, and is equally good game, then, he says, let the heath hen go hang! This may sound like a prejudiced statement, but certainly there is little in his published propaganda of native species as such. On the other hand, the Wild Lifer regards the perpetuation of native species as an end in itself, equal if not greater in importance than the perpetuation of "something to shoot." It may be safely concluded that as to this point the Wild Lifer enjoys the advantage of an ethical as well as of an utilitarian objective.

Thirdly, the Game Farmer makes a great point of "vermin." Natural enemies, he says, destroy more game than guns. On the other hand, many Wild Lifers have been practically silent on this point. This particular point is not one of theory, but of fact, and every keen observer must admit that the Game Farmer is right. Of course, when this point is carried to extremes—as when some Game Farmers argue that as long as vermin remain, restrictive game laws are a useless sacrifice, it becomes an absurdity that will deceive no thinking sportsman.

It may here and now be said that the two extreme points of view on the three foregoing points are by no means beyond reconciliation. The proper care of game does not necessarily imply neglect of non-game. The breeding of "efficient" species does not necessarily imply the neglect of weak native species. The advisability of controlling vermin is plain common sense, which nobody will seriously question. Any reasonable man can and will select and advocate the good point on both sides of the argument. But now we come to the points wherein the "dynamite" lies concealed. To wit:

Game Farming is a business. It must return a profit. Part of the profit comes from marketing all or a part of the game as meat. Game markets, after a twenty-year fight, are closed. The Game Farmer wants them opened—to his products. Some of his publications even hint broadly that they must eventually be opened wide to all game, in order to do away with the restrictions, necessarily cumbersome, incident to making a distinction between the sale of wild game and game artificially raised. The Wild Lifer, on the other hand, regards with apprehension the opening of markets, even to artificially raised game, while the idea of a wide-open market fills him with horror.

Is it possible to reconcile these two points of view? Yes and no. It is conceivable that limited markets—that is, markets for tagged meat raised on licensed game farms—might be indefinitely maintained and even largely expanded, without resulting in serious violation of the laws prohibiting the sale of wild or public game. But the Game Farmer, under such a system (which is in effect the one now being adopted in most states) must forever bear the cost incident to restrictions, such as closed seasons, tagging, licensing, etc. It seems almost axiomatic, however, that a return to wide-open markets would spell the certain doom of wild game, and even edible non-game. The radical game breeder's hints for a wide-open market, therefore, are a wide-open challenge to choose between Game Farming and public game. With a wide-open market, public game could not exist, and game laws would become useless and unnecessary.

There is a second point wherein the doctrine of Game Farming cannot be reconciled with the doctrine of the Wild Lifer. Game Farming, whether conducted by public agencies or private persons, costs money. It cannot succeed unless the hunting is sold for money. It, therefore, inevitably implies the sale or lease of shooting privileges, and in so far as it supplants the present system, it means the end of free hunting. It means that the well-to-do will raise their own game, while the farmers will breed game and sell their shooting to the highest bidder. Even should the farmer not actually produce his game under hens, and even in the case of migratory game, which in the nature of things must remain public, the general spread of Game Farming would soon result in the general spread of commercialized shooting privileges, and the poor man would be left with a few navigable rivers, and the freedom of the seas for his hunting. We may even develop riparian hunting rights!

The writer is aware that even the most extreme proponents of Game Farming have provided, on paper, for the interests of the impecunious sportsman. They tell him of the fine overflow hunting to be picked up outside the poacher-proof fences of game preserves. This is well and good, for those who enjoy the idea of feasting on crumbs, and until the last "outside" coverts have ceased to exist. A wholesale commercialization of shooting privileges, however, would soon leave nothing open but public lands.

We can immediately draw one conclusion from the foregoing discussion of the proposed commercialization of game-meat and hunting privileges, and that is that to grant the wishes of the radical Game Farmers would be tantamount to adopting the European system of game management. A wide-open market, almost universal game farming, commercialized shooting privileges, and some incidental overflow shooting for the poor man—is this not the sum and substance of the European system? It is. And the European system of game management is undemocratic, unsocial, and therefore dangerous. I assume that it is not necessary to argue that the development of any undemocratic system in this country is to be avoided at all costs.

I am well aware that in the foregoing discussion I have avoided two points which add weight to the Game Farmer's argument. Let us consider them separately.

The first is the fact that posting of farm lands, theories of democracy to the contrary notwithstanding, is in some places fast rendering free hunting a thing of the past. This is a fact, not a theory, and we must face it as such. Moreover, with increasing values of lands and livestock, and increasing numbers of care-less hunters, the proportion of posted lands is bound to rapidly increase and will eventually include all intensively developed private holdings.

The second is the fact that even without strictly artificial Game Farming, an abundant supply of wild public game can-not be restored without more or less winter feeding, patrol, vermin-control, maintenance of coverts and food-plants, and other special measures, all of which cost something in money, labor, land or attention. These measures, whether you call them Game Farming or not, cost something and will have the same effect as Game Farming in commercializing hunting privileges.

From the foregoing discussion it seems logical to draw the following conclusions:

1. Free hunting of upland game in intensively developed farming regions will gradually disappear. Farmers will breed and encourage game and lease their hunting privileges to clubs or individuals. (Hunting privileges donated as personal favors are to all intents and purposes commercialized.)

2. Free hunting of migratory waterfowl in intensively devel-oped farming regions will follow the same course, but more slowly. Ducking grounds on private lands will be artificially improved and leased. Ducking grounds on public waters will remain open.

3. Free hunting in poor or forested private lands will dimin-ish, but will probably survive indefinitely. Control of vermin, winter feeding and maintenance of food plants, and other nec-essary semi-artificial measures will remain the duty of public agencies and will become of increasing importance.

4. Free hunting on public lands or waters must and will be preserved and developed at public expense. State forests and parks, national forests and parks, navigable rivers and lakes, and public reservations of all kinds, must, with the exception of necessary game refuges, be left open as the one sure resource of the man who cannot afford to buy his shooting. It is imperative that exclusive privileges be debarred from such lands absolutely, as is now done on the National Forests.

5. Restrictive game laws must continue to be developed and enforced on all lands and all game.

6. Markets must be kept closed to all except tagged and

licensed game artificially produced, and this principle must be guarded as the very keystone of the whole structure of game management.

7. Closed seasons and special public game refuges must be maintained for native species of weak recuperative capacity, and such species must be preserved at public expense.

8. Where conditions are such that free hunting will probably disappear over large areas and there are no public lands or waters left for those who cannot buy their hunting, states and municipalities should start to acquire special public hunting grounds, on which a game supply may be developed at public expense. This suggestion is no more radical than the municipal golf courses and tennis courts proposed ten years ago and now actually available to the public near many cities.

Bulletin of the American Game Protective Association, April 1919

A Turkey Hunt in the Datil National Forest

THERE WERE only four days left of the open season when my hunting partner and I made camp on the evening of November 1 near the forks of Big Pigeon Canyon. Big Pigeon is a long notch cut into the flanks of the San Mateo Mountains, which comprise a part of the Datil National Forest, Socorro County, New Mexico. The Datil Forest, from the sportsman's standpoint, is the cream of the Southwest, and there is no part of the Datil country as interesting to hunt in as the San Mateos. It is a very rough region with a fair amount of water, and endless miles of yellow pine forest interspersed with oak and piñon. Any year that the oak fails to produce acorns it is pretty certain that the piñons will produce nuts, and vice versa, so that the game is nearly always "hog-rolling fat." Winter starvation, in spite of heavy snows, is almost out of the question because of the abundance of mast and of oak and mahogany browse.

My partner and I had designs on the blacktail bucks and festive gobblers which were supposed to inhabit the rough foothills surrounding our camp. After a quail supper (we had bumped into a fine covey on our way out), and a comfortable night, we were up and at it bright and early next morning. The first day was to be devoted to a general reconnaissance of the situation. All day long we scoured the hills on the east side of Big Pigeon, and succeeded in finding a single turkey feather and a couple of deer tracks. We had to admit that evening that the prospects seemed to consist largely of fine weather and scenery. It looked like a wonderful game country,—without game.

Over the oak coals of the campfire we held a council of war. There evidently had been a few deer and turkey around during the summer, but where were they now? It was decided that my partner would spend the next day exploring a higher country in the Beartrap watershed to the north, and I was to go south into the rough breaks of Whitewater and see what I could see.

In the cold, frosty dawn, we set forth. We found hundreds of robins, bluebirds and piñon jays bathing and drinking in the half-frozen waterhole near camp. I never could understand why these little fellows should deliberately choose to get wet, inside and out, so early in the morning. Sharpshinned hawks were always hanging around these water holes, but did not seem to do much execution, because of the handy oak thickets in which the birds could take refuge on short notice. These hardy winter birds seemed to know their business, but we hunters were not so sure that we knew ours, after yesterday's failure to make a strike.

I traveled all morning across a waterless drywash country covered with piñon, pine, and cedar, which a few small tracks showed to be inhabited by white-tail deer. Hunting white-tail in these cedar brakes is about like hunting rabbits in a ragweed patch—it is all hunt and no get. The chance of seeing the quarry is almost negligible. So I kept right on going and about noon topped out on a high ridge overlooking a wild narrow canyon about five hundred feet deep, with a fringe of large oaks and cottonwoods lining the watercourse below. It looked promising. I dropped down a steep hogback along a pretty well-worn cattle trail that indicated water below. When nearly down I heard the familiar alarm note of a robin being chased by a sharp-shin. A water-hole sure enough! Advancing with caution, I soon came up on a beautiful sunny glade, containing fine water, tall gramma grass, and an old deserted cabin—evidently a remnant of the good old days when dogeying, sleepering, and smearing brands were favorite outdoor sports in these remote mountain fastnesses. Those days are over now. The National Forest ranges now carry only graded Herefords worth fifty dollars a head, and the old-time rustler with his nimble branding iron has disappeared with the longhorn steer. The modern cowman fortunate enough to hold a grazing permit on the National Forest, is particular about his neighbors and rides to town in a touring car.

An examination of the watering place showed a few old blacktail tracks, but no turkey sign. However, the whole surroundings felt like game, so I advanced slowly up the creek, examining the cattle trails for tracks and carefully scanning the canyon bottom ahead as the crooks and turns of the water course revealed new views to the eye. Rounding the point of a little bench, I suddenly felt a shock that seemed to freeze my feet to the ground. (I'm sure I felt that turkey in my knees quite as soon as I saw him!) There he was, right over the point of the bench, a big hump-backed gobbler, clipping the seeds off a stalk of wild oats.

I knew there must be more behind the point. My plan was to slip forward a few steps to a little oak tree and get a rest for the first shot. But I couldn't make my knees behave! I freely confess it, they were wobbling—wobbling like a reed shaken in the wind. I can look the biggest blacktail buck in the face without a tremor, but turkey? Never!

However, it didn't last long. I had advanced almost to the oak tree, and could now see at least fifteen birds that looked as big as elephants. They were scratching in the pine needles, and looked to be somewhat over seventy-five yards away. I was almost wholly hidden by the point, and picking every step with all the caution in the world. But you can't fool a turkey. "Put!" and I saw the big gobbler's head go up in the air. This was no time for rests, or other fancy preparations. I threw up the little carbine, drew down on the big bird, and let go. I saw him collapse, and then the fun began! The whole flock stretched their legs and started up the hill on a high trot. The second shot failed to score. At the third shot another fine big bird keeled over just at the edge of the oak thicket which clothed the wall of the canyon. Shot number four was just a formal good-bye as the last bird disappeared into the oaks.

Of course, I went after them. I scrambled up that hill until my heart pounded like a triphammer. I got one more glimpse of a running bird through an opening high up on the hill, but no shot. Exhausted, I slid back down the hill in a great hurry. I was anxious to get back to my two birds. I had seen "dead" turkeys before, and I will say for the benefit of the beginner that they are not really dead till they have a rawhide thong strung through the "hamstring."

My fears were unfounded. Both birds were stone dead, each with a 30-30 soft nose above the butt of the wing. Neither bird had an ounce of flesh torn up—not even the plumage was spoiled. Both were large young birds in prime condition. Subsequent weighing showed that they topped the scaled at 8¾ and 6⅝ pounds respectively. The spreads were 57 and 47 inches. The spread feet (length of track), measured 6 and 5 inches. The crops contained wild oats and very fine grass seed.

Some people shoot steel bullets at turkey. This is a big mistake. I once knocked down three big birds with steel bullets and two of them got up and flew half a mile. I never saw them again.

The same season, while turkey-hunting, I knocked down three big lobo wolves and two of them got away. I am "cured" of steel bullets. Our state law now prohibits their use on big game.

I felt like the king of England when I shouldered those two big birds and started on the long hike to camp. On the way back I had an amusing experience. About sunset, on top of a high ridge, a cottontail jumped up and hopped into some cedars. We needed him in camp, so I started over to shoot his head off. A hawk beat me to it, and chased him back to his back trail. I grabbed at him as he passed, but he hurdled my hand. A few yards further he bumped head on into the two turkeys, which I had thrown down. He somersaulted, recovered, and sailed over the two turkeys in a grand standing high jump, and on his way he delivered a kick to the top turkey with all the *eclat* of a government mule. He dodged under a log, leaving a turkey feather sticking to the bark, and took refuge in a hollow-butted live oak. It seemed to me that he had gone through enough adventures for one day, so I let him alone.

I arrived in camp very late, very tired, very hungry, and very much pleased with things in general. Unfortunately my partner had seen no game. For two more days we scoured the country, but found nothing but some old deer sign. My flock of turkeys did not come back to the same water. I think they were travelers, and my stumbling on to them was sheer luck.

The strongest impression that we carried back with us from our trip was the extreme scarcity of all kinds of game, as compared with what the country actually ought to produce. The San Mateos contain 650 square miles of forest, almost all of it as fine a game country as can be found anywhere. Yet the Forest Service game census figure indicates only about 100 deer; one deer for each six square miles. I think it would be easy for each square mile to carry three deer, or twenty times as many as at present, without interfering in the slightest degree with the production of timber, cattle, or any other forest product. Yet the San Mateos furnish better hunting than the average of New Mexico's 8,300,000 acres of National Forest land.

On our last day in the hills we found one of the "reasons" for the scarcity of deer in New Mexico. In a hidden nook on the sunny side of Big Pigeon Canyon we found the remains of an old Indian meat camp. Around an old brush lean-to were scattered the whitening bones of at least a dozen deer. There were more bones than horns, by which hangs a tale—the usual tale of slaughtered does and fawns. A tumble-down "clothesline" of poles showed where the jerky had been hung out to dry. The horns were all chopped off singly instead of in pairs. What does a meat-hunter care about horns? And the worst of it is that this meat-hunting still goes merrily on, in spite of a scattering of deputy wardens and Forest Officers. The fact of the matter is that poaching Indians are hard to catch. In these days they make only dry camps, away from trails or water. The meat is handled in a separate camp, and the jerky goes forward by dead of night, via the burro route, as the crow flies, to some far pueblo. There is no noise—the hunters even carry a wooden gun-rest so as to waste no ammunition. There is no traveling of beaten trails—the Indian doesn't need them. And even when you find the main camp there is no meat in it, and every Indian is waving a hunting license! Let he who thinks he is a pretty good hand in the woods try to catch an Indian.

But after all the Indian is no worse than the white man. The tenderfoot who lays down a barrage at everything that moves probably cripples as many deer as the Indian eats. The pseudo-sportsman who always comes back with a whole buck (question: what did he eat in camp?) does not set him a very good example. Add to that the meat-hungry trapper or prosecutor, the occasional light-fingered cowhand, and the sheepherder whose employer sometimes tells him to eat deer and save mutton, and it is no wonder that our hunting grounds have been "cleaned."

Right here we have the meat of the whole question—by what device can we prevent the "cleaning" of the hunting grounds? There is no question about the ability of the range to support plenty of deer for everybody. There is no question about the ability of the deer to increase and multiply if we can maintain an adequate breeding stock. How is a breeding stock to be kept up? As long as the whole country is open to hunting it cannot be done. The bung is in the bottom of the barrel, and we need blame only ourselves if the barrel drains dry. But why not put the bung in the side of the barrel? Why not close about twenty or thirty percent of our territory to hunting, and thus insure the maintenance of an irreducible minimum of breeding animals, and thus automatically restock the surrounding territory?

In short we need *Game Refuges*, and here in New Mexico our need is almost desperate. Every year of delay means a ten per cent harder job in repairing the damage. The organized sportsmen of New Mexico have been fighting for game refuges for four years. But Congress does not seem to listen, and our fellow-sportsmen in the East do not seem to care. As far as I know, hardly a finger has been raised to help the West get a refuge bill through Congress since the Hornaday campaign in 1916. The Robinson Game Refuge Bill was introduced in last special session, but apparently received no support. Eastern leaders seemed actually unaware of its existence. Some day eastern sportsmen are going to come out here for their big game hunting; but unless they lend a hand in giving us game refuges, they are going to have little to shoot but scenery.

Of course, it is easy to say that state game refuges are the solution of the problem. But in actual practice in the Southwest state refuges have proven nearly worthless. The state has no paid personnel on the ground, and a refuge unpatrolled had just as well not exist. The federal Forest Service has a paid personnel on the ground, and the Forest Rangers are not only willing but anxious to help. The legislatures almost invariably make state refuges too few and too big and without clear-cut boundaries, and change them at each session. Federal refuges, on the other hand, would be selected by experts and established systematically and permanently.

In New Mexico the sportsmen, though strongly committed to a federal refuge system, actually refused to support a state refuge bill presented before the last legislature because they feared political manipulation. In Arizona thinking sportsmen are complaining that the state refuges, which consist mostly of entire mountain ranges, merely concentrate the hunting on the mountain ranges remaining open. These large refuges, consisting of separate topographic units, have no overflow value. While they preserve the game within their boundaries, to the extent that they are enforced, this benefit is about offset by the intensified drain on open hunting grounds. In short, they are not game refuges at all; they are mere public preserves. The whole state game refuge business, as far as experience indicates in the Southwest, may be dismissed as unsatisfactory.

I hope that the Robinson Bill will be re-introduced before

the regular session of Congress, and that the readers of WILD LIFE will help put it through. The fate of big game on the National Forests—America's last and greatest hunting grounds—hangs in the balance. Let no American sportsman forget that he is a part owner of these forests. They are going to become practically gameless unless something is done, and done quickly. Now is the time to act.

Wild Life, December 1919

The Wilderness and Its Place
in Forest Recreational Policy

WHEN THE National Forests were created the first argument of those opposing a national forest policy was that the forests would remain a wilderness. Gifford Pinchot replied that on the contrary they would be opened up and developed as producing forests, and that such development would, in the long run, itself constitute the best assurance that they would neither remain a wilderness by "bottling up" their resources nor become one through devastation. At this time Pinchot enunciated the doctrine of "highest use," and its criterion, "the greatest good to the greatest number," which is and must remain the guiding principle by which democracies handle their natural resources.

Pinchot's promise of development has been made good. The process must, of course, continue indefinitely. But it has already gone far enough to raise the question of whether the policy of development (construed in the narrower sense of industrial development) should continue to govern in absolutely every instance, or whether the principle of highest use does not itself demand that representative portions of some forests be preserved as wilderness.

That some such question actually exists, both in the minds of some foresters and of part of the public, seems to me to be plainly implied in the recent trend of recreational use policies and in the tone of sporting and outdoor magazines. Recreational plans are leaning toward the segregation of certain areas from certain developments, so that having been led into the wilderness, the people may have some wilderness left to enjoy. Sporting magazines are groping toward some logical reconciliation between getting back to nature and preserving a little nature to get back to. Lamentations over this or that favorite vacation ground being "spoiled by tourists" are becoming more and more frequent. Very evidently we have here the old conflict between preservation and use, long since an issue with respect to timber, water power, and other purely economic resources, but just now coming to be an issue with respect to recreation. It is the fundamental function of foresters to reconcile these conflicts, and to give constructive direction to these issues as they arise. The purpose of this paper is to give definite form to the issue of wilderness conservation, and to suggest certain policies for meeting it, especially as applied to the Southwest.

It is quite possible that the serious discussion of this question will seem a far cry in some unsettled regions, and rank heresy to some minds. Likewise did timber conservation seem a far cry in some regions, and rank heresy to some minds of a generation ago. "The truth is that which prevails in the long run."

Some definitions are probably necessary at the outset. By "wilderness" I mean a continuous stretch of country preserved in its natural state, open to lawful hunting and fishing, big enough to absorb a two weeks' pack trip, and kept devoid of roads, artificial trails, cottages, or other works of man. Several assumptions can be made at once without argument. First, such wilderness areas should occupy only a small fraction of the total National Forest area—probably not to exceed one in each State. Second, only areas naturally difficult of ordinary industrial development should be chosen. Third, each area should be representative of some type of country of distinctive recreational value, or afford some distinctive type of outdoor life, opportunity for which might disappear on other forest lands open to industrial development.

The argument for such wilderness areas is premised wholly on highest recreational use. The recreational desires and needs of the public, whom the forests must serve, vary greatly with the individual. Heretofore we have been inclined to assume that our recreational development policy must be based on the desires and needs of the majority only. The only new thing about the premise in this case is the proposition that inasmuch as we have plenty of room and plenty of time, it is our duty to vary our recreational development policy, in some places, to meet the needs and desires of the minority also. The majority undoubtedly want all the automobile roads, summer hotels, graded trails, and other modern conveniences that we can give them. It is already decided, and wisely, that they shall have these things as rapidly as brains and money can provide them. But a very substantial minority, I think, want just the opposite. It should be decided, as soon as the existence of the demand can be definitely determined, to provide what this minority wants.

In fact, if we can foresee the demand, and make provision for it in advance, it will save much cash and hard feelings. It will be much easier to keep wilderness areas than to create them. In fact, the latter alternative may be dismissed as impossible. Right here is the whole reason for forehandedness in the proposed wilderness area policy.

It is obvious to everyone who knows the National Forests that even with intensive future development, there will be a decreasing but inexhaustible number of small patches of rough country which will remain practically in wilderness condition. It is also generally recognized that these small patches have a high and increasing recreational value. But will they obviate the need for a policy such as here proposed? I think not. These patches are too small, and must grow smaller. They will always be big enough for camping, but they will tend to grow too small for a real wilderness trip. The public demands for camp sites and wilderness trips, respectively, are both legitimate and both strong, but nevertheless distinct. The man who wants a wilderness trip wants not only scenery, hunting, fishing, isolation, etc.—all of which can often be found within a mile of a paved auto highway—but also the horses, packing, riding, daily movement and variety found only in a trip through a big stretch of wild country. It would be pretty lame to forcibly import these features into a country from which the real need for them had disappeared.

It may also be asked whether the National Parks from which, let us hope, industrial development will continue to be excluded, do not fill the public demand here discussed. They do, in part. But hunting is not and should not be allowed within the Parks. Moreover, the Parks are being networked with roads and trails as rapidly as possible. This is right and proper. The Parks merely prove again that the recreational needs and desires of the public vary through a wide range of individual tastes, all of which should be met in due proportion to the number of individuals in each class. There is only one question involved— highest use. And we are beginning to see that highest use is a very varied use, requiring a very varied administration, in the recreational as well as in the industrial field.

An actual example is probably the best way to describe the workings of the proposed wilderness area policy.

The Southwest (meaning New Mexico and Arizona) is a distinct region. The original southwestern wilderness was the scene of several important chapters in our national history. The remainder of it is about as interesting, from about as large a number of angles, as any place on the continent. It has a high and varied recreational value. Under the policy advocated in this paper, a good big sample of it should be preserved. This could easily be done by selecting such an area as the headwaters of the Gila River on the Gila National Forest. This is an area of nearly half a million acres, topographically isolated by mountain ranges and box canyons. It has not yet been penetrated by railroads and to only a very limited extent by roads. On account of the natural obstacles to transportation and the absence of any considerable areas of agricultural land, no net economic loss would result from the policy of withholding further industrial development, except that timber would remain inaccessible and available only for limited local consumption. The entire area is grazed by cattle, but the cattle ranches would be an asset from the recreational standpoint because of the interest which attaches to cattle grazing operations under frontier conditions. The apparent disadvantage thus imposed on the cattlemen might be nearly offset by the obvious advantage of freedom from new settlers, and from the hordes of motorists who will invade this region the minute it is opened up. The entire region is the natural habitat of deer, elk, turkey, grouse, and trout. If preserved in its semi-virgin state, it could absorb a hundred pack trains each year without overcrowding. It is the last typical wilderness in the southwestern mountains. Highest use demands its preservation.

The conservation of recreational resources here advocated has its historic counterpart in the conservation of timber resources lately become a national issue and expressed in the forestry program. Timber conservation began fifteen years ago with the same vague premonitions of impending shortage now discernible in the recreational press. Timber conservation encountered the same general rebuttal of "inexhaustible supplies" which recreational conservation will shortly encounter. After a period of milling and mulling, timber conservation established the principle that timber supplies are capable of qualitative as well as quantitative exhaustion, and that the existence of "inexhaustible" areas of trees did not necessarily insure the supply of bridge timber, naval stores, or pulp. So also will recreational resources be found in more danger of qualitative than quantitative exhaustion. We now recognize that the sprout forests of New England are no answer to the farmer's need for structural lumber, and we admit that the farmer's special needs must be taken care of in proportion to his numbers and importance. So also must we recognize that any number of small patches of uninhabited wood or mountains are no answer to the real sportsman's need for wilderness, and the day will come when we must admit that his special needs likewise must be taken care of in proportion to his numbers and importance. And as in forestry, it will be much easier and cheaper to preserve, by forethought, what he needs, than to create it after it is gone.

Journal of Forestry, November 1921

Blue River

I REINED UP, not sure whether the old cow was dead, or just dying. She had come down out of the drouth-stricken hills to drink, I guess. And now she lay there, quite still, on the hot sandbar. A swarm of brilliant green flies buzzed about her head, and plagued her mouth and eyes. She had craned her neck—the mark was there in the sand—as if for one last look up into the cruel cliffs of Blue River.

I was reflecting on this—especially the ghoulish flies—when it happened. A flash of vermilion—a soft bubbling warble—and a little red bird hovered over the old cow's head, snapping up flies right and left, one after another, for each a cry of ecstasy, in very joy of living. And then with one quick crimson sweep of wing, it disappeared into the green depths of the cottonwood.

Did the old cow see the bird? No. Her dead eyes stared up into the cliffs. Her calf was somewhere up there.

For a while I looked at the old cow, and thought about the little red bird. Then I rode on down Blue River.

Manuscript, June 11, 1922

Goose Music

Twenty years ago the game of golf was commonly regarded in this country as a kind of social ornament, a pretty diversion of the idle rich, but hardly worthy of the curiousity, much less of the serious interest, of men of affairs.

Today scores of cities are building municipal golf courses to make golf available to the rank and file of their citizens.

What has happened? Golf has not changed, and certainly not golfers. The change has been in the public viewpoint. Golf is no longer regarded as an ornamental sport, but as a valuable means of physical, mental (and to the golfer, spiritual) recreation. Golf has become a valuable part of our social economy. Of course it has always been valuable to society, but the twentieth century has been the first to realize the fact.

The same change of viewpoint has occurred toward most other outdoor sports—the frivolities of fifty years ago have become the social necessities of today. But strangely enough, this change is only just beginning to permeate our attitude toward the oldest and most universal of all sports, hunting and fishing.

We have realized dimly, of course, that a day afield was good for the tired business man. We have also realized that the destruction of wild life removed the incentive for days afield. But we have not yet learned to express the value of wild life in terms of social welfare. Some have attempted to justify wild life conservation in terms of meat, others in terms of personal pleasure, others in terms of cash, still others in the interest of science, education, agriculture, art, public health, and even military preparedness. But few have so far clearly realized and expressed the whole truth, namely, that all these things are but factors in a broad social value, and that wild life like golf, is a social asset.

But to those whose hearts are stirred by the sound of whistling wings and quacking mallards, wild life is something even more than this. Golf is an acquired taste, but the instinct which finds delight in the sight and pursuit of game is bred into the very fibre of the race. Golf is a delightful accomplishment, but the love of hunting is almost a physiological character. A man may not care for golf and still be human, but the man who does not like to see, hunt, photograph or otherwise outwit birds or animals is hardly normal. He is super-civilized, and I for one, do not know how to deal with him. Babes do not tremble when they are shown a golf ball, but I should not like to own the boy whose hair does not lift his hat when he sees his first deer. We are dealing, therefore, with something that lies pretty deep. Some can live without opportunity for the exercise and control of the hunting instinct, just as I suppose some can live without work, play, love, business, or other vital adventure. But in these days we regard such deprivations as unsocial. Opportunity for exercise of all the normal instincts has become to be regarded more and more as an inalienable right. The men who are destroying our wild life are alienating one of these rights, and doing a terribly thorough job of it. More than that, they are doing a permanent job of it. When the last corner lot is covered with tenements we can still make a playground by tearing them down, but when the last antelope goes by the boards, not all the playground associations in Christendom can do aught to replace the loss.

One of the anomalies of wild life conservation is that our social asset is being destroyed by the very instinct, for the exercise of which we seek to preserve it. I have often wondered why many Americans, decent at home, are such barbarians afield. I think they must be exaggerated "throwbacks" to the old days when the gentle art of poaching was one of the standard accomplishments of a self-respecting yeoman. If the King still owned all the game, I think I should make a very good poacher myself. I often feel the promptings of breed. I own I would rather kill a mess of mallards shooting with the hoi-polloi just outside the gun club fence, than to kill a backload on the baited preserve. But the King no longer owns the game. It belongs to my friends and neighbors. The gentle art of poaching, therefore, has assumed a new complexion. The poacher is no longer a hero, but a thief. In time he will come to realize this. It is the duty of the forward-looking citizen to speed the day, and of the law to regulate the poacher's conduct meanwhile.

If wild birds and animals are a social asset, how much of an asset are they? It is easy to say that some of us, afflicted with hereditary hunting fever, cannot live satisfactory lives without them. But this does not establish any comparative value, and in these days it is sometimes necessary to choose between necessities. In short, what is a wild goose worth? As compared with other sources of health and pleasure, what is its value in the common denominator of dollars?

Last week I went to hear Sousa's band. It stood me two iron men. They were well spent, but if I had to choose, I would forego the experience for the sight of the big gander that sailed honking into my decoys at daybreak this morning. It was bitter cold and I was all fingers, so I blithely missed him. But miss or no miss I saw him, I heard the wind whistle through his set wings as he came honking out of the gray west, and I felt him so that even now I tingle at the recollection. I doubt not that this very gander has given ten other men two dollars worth of thrills. Therefore I say he is worth at least twenty dollars to the human race.

My notes tell me I have seen a thousand geese this fall. Every one of these in the course of their epic journey from the arctic to the gulf, has on one occasion or another probably served man to the equivalent of twenty dollars. One flock perhaps has thrilled a score of schoolboys, and sent them scurrying home with tales of high adventure. Another, passing overhead of a dark night, has serenaded a whole city with goose music, and awakened who knows what questionings and memories and hopes. A third perhaps has given pause to some farmer at his plough, and brought new thoughts of far lands and journeyings and peoples, where before was only drudgery barren of any thought at all. I am sure those thousand geese are paying human dividends on a value of twenty dollars each. But the resulting $20,000 is only an exchange value, like the sale value of a painting or the copyright of a poem. What about the replacement value? Supposing there were no longer any painting, or poetry, or goose music? It is a black thought to dwell upon, but it must be answered. In dire necessity somebody might write another Iliad, or paint an Angelus, but fashion a goose? "I, the Lord, will answer them. The hand of the Lord hath done this, and the Holy One of Israel created it."

Is it impious to weigh goose music and art in the same scales? I think not, because the true hunter is merely a non-creative artist. Who painted the first picture on a bone in the caves of France? A hunter. Who alone in our modern life so thrills to the sight of living beauty that he will endure hunger and thirst and cold to feed his eye upon it? The hunter. Who wrote the great hunter's poem about the sheer wonder of the wind, the hail, and the snow, the stars, the lightnings, and the clouds, the lion, the deer, and the wild goat, the raven, the hawk, and the eagle, and above all the eulogy of the horse? Job, the greatest dramatic artist since the beginning of the world. Poets sing and hunters scale the mountains primarily for one and the same reason—the thrill to beauty. Critics write and hunters outwit their game primarily for one and the same reason—to reduce that beauty to possession. The differences are largely matters of degree, consciousness, and that sly arbiter of the classification of human activities, language. If then, we can live without goose music, we may as well do away with stars, or sunsets, or Iliads. But the point is that we would be fools to do away with any of them.

What value has wild life from the standpoint of morals and religion? I heard of a boy once who was brought up an atheist. He changed his mind when he saw that there were a hundred odd species of warblers, each bedecked like to the rainbow, and each performing yearly sundry thousands of miles of migration about which scientists wrote wisely but did not understand. No "fortuitous concourse of elements" working blindly through any number of millions of years could quite account for why warblers are so beautiful. No mechanistic theory, even bolstered by mutations, has ever quite answered for the colors of the Caerulean warbler, or the vespers of the woodthrush, or the swansong, or—goose music. I dare say this boy's convictions would be harder to shake than those of many inductive theologians. There are yet many boys to be born, who like Isaiah "may see, and know, and consider, and understand together, that the hand of the Lord hath done this." But where shall they see, and know, and consider? In museums?

What is the effect of hunting and fishing on character, as compared with other outdoor sports? I have already pointed out that the desire lies deeper, that its source is a matter of instinct as well as of competition. A son of a Robinson Crusoe, having never seen a tennis racket, might get along nicely without one, but he would be pretty sure to hunt or fish whether or no he were taught to do so. But this does not establish any superiority as to subjective benefits. Which helps the more to build a man? This question (like the one we used to debate in school about whether boys or girls are the best scholars) might be argued till doomsday. I will not attempt it. But there are two points about hunting which deserve special emphasis. One is that the ethics of sportsmanship are not a fixed code, but must be formulated and practiced by the individual, with no referee but the Almighty. The other is that hunting generally involves the handling of dogs and horses, and the lack of this experience is one of the most serious defects of our gasoline-driven civilization. There was much truth in the old idea that any man ignorant of dogs and horses was not a gentleman. In the West the abuse of horses is still a universal blackball. This rule of thumb was adopted in the cow country long before "character analysis" was invented, and for all we know, may yet outlive it.

But after all it is poor business to prove that one good thing is better than another. The point is that some six or eight millions of Americans like to hunt and fish, that the hunting fever is endemic in the race, that the race is benefitted by any incentive to get out into the open, and is being injured by the destruction of the incentive in this case. To combat this destruction is therefore a social issue.

The difficulty, however, is not so much in proving this principle in the abstract, as in getting people to see and respect its applications. I have seen many a women's club pass resolutions on bird protection, but the "aigrettes" do not come off. I have seen many a law-abiding citizen sit down to a banquet of illegal quail-on-toast, and loudly proclaim his sportsmanship or patriotism. Many of the "best people" at our summer resorts unblushingly buy trout or grouse or venison, and feel delightfully wicked about it, because they see nothing broken but a law. Members of the "Four Hundred" in a middle-western town I know of openly flout the spring-shooting regulations, and their friends accept with warm thanks the ducks thus stolen from their sons. Nightingales tongues were doubtless merely meat to Nero, but it is about time to expect enlightened Americans to know and do better than he.

To conclude: I have congenital hunting fever and three sons. They are little tots and spend their time playing with my decoys and scouring vacant lots with wooden guns. I hope to leave them good health, an education, and possibly even a competence. But what are they going to do with these things if there be no more deer in the hills, and no more quail in the coverts? No more snipe whistling in the meadow, no more piping of widgeons and chattering of teal as darkness covers the marshes; no more whistling of swift wings when the morning star pales in the east! And when the dawn-wind stirs through the ancient cottonwoods, and the gray light steals down from the hills over the old river sliding softly past its wide brown sandbars,—what if there be no more goose-music?

I suppose they will have to play golf.

Manuscript, c. June 1922

Some Fundamentals of Conservation
in the Southwest

T HE FUTURE development of the Southwest must depend largely on the following resources and advantages:

Minerals: Chiefly copper and coal.
Organic: Farms, ranges, forests, waters and water powers.
Climatic: Chiefly health and winter resort possibilities.
Historic: Archaeological and historical interest.
Geographic: On route to California and Mexico.

This discussion is confined to the two first named.

While the last three are of great value, the Southwest should hardly be satisfied to build its future upon them. They are what might be termed "unearned advantages."

Excluding these, it is apparent that all of the remaining economic resources are of such a nature that their permanent usefulness is affected more or less by that idea or method of development broadly called "conservation." It is the purpose of this paper to discuss the extent to which this is true, and the extent to which unskillful or non-conservative methods of exploitation threaten to limit or destroy their permanent usefulness.

A brief statement of some of the salient facts about each of these resources is first necessary as a background.

Minerals: Of 6 of the leading Arizona copper mines, the average life in sight is 22 years. This is a short life. Undoubtedly, our mineral wealth will be expanded from time to time by new processes, better transportation, discovery of additional ore bodies, demand for rare minerals, exploitation of gross minerals such as sulphur and salt, and possible discovery of oil. But the fact remains that with the exception of coal, the mineral wealth of the Southwest, from the standpoint of an economic foundation for society, is exhaustible. Our coal will probably always be handicapped by long hauls and absence of water transport.

Farms & Waters must be considered together. The late drouth ought to have sufficiently redemonstrated that generally speaking, dry farming, as a sole dependence for a livelihood, is a broken reed. The outstanding fact that we can never change is that we have roughly twenty million acres of water producing or mountain area and fifty million acres of area waiting for water. Most of the latter is tillable. But it takes say four feet of water per year to till it, whereas less than two feet falls on the mountains, of which only a very small percent runs off in streams in useable form. Therefore if we impounded all the non-flood run-off and had no evaporation (both impossibilities) we should still have scores of times more land than water to till it. This is partially offset by underground storage of part of the water which does not run off, but nevertheless we still have an overwhelming shortage of water as compared with land. Therefore the term "irrigable land" actually represents a combination of natural resources which is really very rare and accordingly vital to our future. By artificially impounding water we are steadily adding to our irrigated area, but these gains are being offset by erosion losses in the smaller valleys, where water was easily available simply through diversion. Broadly speaking, no net gain is resulting. We are losing the easily irrigable land and "replacing" it by land reclaimed at great expense. The significant fact that is not understood is that this "replacement" is no replacement at all, but rather slicing at one end of our loaf while the other end sloughs away in waste. Some day the slicing and sloughing will meet. Then we shall realize that we needed the whole loaf.

Water Powers. Erosion and silting are likewise deteriorating our water powers, though the silting of a reservoir is not so destructive to its power possibilities as to its use for irrigation. Also the water powers not dependent upon storage are not yet badly damaged. It is obvious, however, that anything which damages the regularity of stream flow and interferes with storage of waters is depreciating the value of our power resources.

Forests. While ___% of our area bears trees, only ____ of this bears sawtimber, of which the present stand is 35 billion feet. Most of this sawtimber land is in the National Forests. The management plans of the Forest Service indicate that if handled under proper methods these sawtimber lands will sustain indefinitely a cut of 300 million feet per year. A larger cut will be possible temporarily because of the excess proportion of mature stands.

New Mexico and Arizona now consume about 450 million feet per year. The salient fact about our forests, therefore, is this: that in the long run the timber yield will only partly suffice to sustain our own agriculture, cities, and mines. While its conservation for these purposes is of course absolutely essential, in order that we may not have to depend on expensive importations. But even with good forestry, the Southwest can not figure on timber export as a future source of wealth.

Ranges: Arizona and New Mexico are carrying about three million sheep and two million cattle. About one-fourth of these are on the National Forests. It would not mean anything to try to state in figures the original carrying capacity of the two States, because much of the virgin range was without water. Great progress has been made in developing water, but there has also taken place a wholesale deterioration in both the quality and quantity of forage. On certain areas of National Forests and privately owned range this deterioration has been checked and the productiveness of the forage partially restored through range improvements and conservative methods of handling stock. The remainder continues to deteriorate under the system of competitive destruction inherited from frontier days but now perpetuated by the archaic land policy of the government and some of the several states. It is safe to state that the condition of our range forage has depreciated 50% and is still going downhill.

This overgrazing of our ranges is chiefly responsible for the erosion which is tearing out our smaller valleys and dumping them into the reservoirs on which our larger valleys are dependent. The significant element in this situation is that cessation of overgrazing will usually not check this erosion.

Summary: All of our organic resources are in a run-down condition. Under existing methods of management our Forests may be expected to improve, but our total possible farm areas are dwindling and our waters and ranges are still deteriorating. In the case of our ranges, deterioration could be easily checked by conservative handling, and the original productiveness regained and restored. But the deterioration of our fundamental resources—land and water—is in the nature of permanent destruction, and the process is cumulative and gaining momentum every year.

EROSION AND ARIDITY

The task of checking the ravages of erosion and restoring our organic resources to a productive condition is so intricate and difficult a problem that we must know something about causes before we can well consider remedies.

Is our Climate Changing? The very first thing to know about causes is whether we are dealing with an "act of God," or merely with the consequences of unwise use by man. If this collapse of stable equilibrium in our soil and its cover is being caused or aggravated by a change in climate, the possible beneficial results of conservation might be very limited. On the other hand, if there is no change of climate going on, the possible results of conservation are limited only by the technical skill which we can train upon the problem and the public backing available to get it applied.

In discussing climatic changes, a clear differentiation between the geological and historical viewpoints is essential. The status of our climate from the geological viewpoint has nothing to do with the question in hand. Any such changes that may be taking place would be too slow to have any bearing on human problems.

Historically speaking, our climate has recently been checked back with considerable accuracy to 1390 A.D. through study of the growth rings of Yellow Pine in Arizona, and to 1220 B.C. through the growth rings of Sequoia in California. These studies, conducted by Douglass and Huntington, demonstrate convincingly that there has been no great increase or decrease in aridity of the Southwest during the last 3,000 years.

Yellow pines recently excavated at Flagstaff show very large growth rings, indicating a wetter climate during some recent geological epoch, but as previously stated, that has a merely academic bearing on our problem.

Ancient Indian ditches and ruins in localities now apparently too dry for either irrigation or dry farming would seem to contradict the conclusion derived from tree rings, but little is known of the age of these relics or the habits of the people who left them. Archaeologists predict that we may soon know more about the age of the cliff culture through possible discoveries connecting it with the now accurately determined chronology of the Maya culture in Central America.

Long straight cedar timbers found in some Southwestern ruins likewise might be taken to indicate a process of desiccation, but other and unknown factors are involved, such as the effect of fire on our forests and the distances from which the timbers were transported.

Changes in the distribution of forest types likewise might be interpreted to throw a little light on the recent tendency of our climate. In the brush forests of southern Arizona there is strong evidence of an uphill recession, such as would accompany desiccation, former woodland now being occupied by brush species and former yellow pine by woodland and brush. At the same time, in the region of the Prescott and Tusayan Forests, there is an indisputable encroachment of juniper downward into former open parks. A similar encroachment of yellow pine is taking place in the Sitgreaves and Apache Forests. Most of these changes, however, can be accounted for through purely local causes such as fire and grazing. This fact, and the fact that any attempt at a climatic theory of causation would result in contradictory conclusions, makes it seem logical to regard these phenomena either as shedding no light on the question of climate, or as possibly somewhat substantiating the conclusion derived from tree-rings.

In general, there thus far appears to be no clear evidence of dessication during any recent unit of time small enough to be considered from an economic standpoint, but at least one line of pretty clear evidence as to the general stability of our climate during the last 3,000 years.

Drouth Cycles and Their Effect. While science has shown that there is no general trend in our climate either for better or for worse, it has shown most conclusively that there are periodic fluctuations which vitally affect our prosperity and the methods of handling our resources. The same tree rings which assure us that Southwestern climate has been stable for 3,000 years, warn us plainly that it has been decidedly unstable from year to year, and that the drouth now so strongly impressed on every mind and pocketbook is not an isolated or an accidental bit of hard luck, but a periodic phenomenon the occurrence of which may be anticipated with almost the same certainty as we anticipate the days and the seasons. It is cause for astonishment that our attitude toward these drouths which wreck whole industries, cause huge wastes of wealth and resources, and even empty the treasures of commonwealths should still be that of the Arkansan toward his roof—in fair weather no need to worry, and in foul weather too wet to work.

The tree rings show, in short, that about every 11 years we have a drouth. Every couple of centuries this 11-year interval lengthens or shortens rather abruptly, running as low as 9 and as high as 14. The drouths vary a little in length and intensity, and usually there is a "double crest" to both the high and low points, i.e., a better or worse year interlarded between the bad or good extremes. But always, and as sure as sunrise, "dust and a bitter wind shall come."

In addition to the 11-year cycle, there is a curious chop or "zig-zag" (2-year cycle), and probably a long low groundswell measured in centuries, but the amplitude of all these is too low to have any great practical present economic significance. The 11-year wave is the one that swamps the boats.

If there be those who doubt whether the tree rings tell a true story, let them be reminded that history supports their testimony. The great flood of the Rio Grande in 1680 is recorded in the trees. The famines of 1680–1690 are there—possibly the drouth that produced them had something to do with the Pueblo Rebellion that sent de Vargas to Santa Fe. The great drouths of 1748, 1780, and 1820–23 are all concurrently reported by trees and historians. And in the last century came the weather records, which likewise concur. Douglass has tied in the 11-year cycle of tree rings with sunspots. Munns has tied in the sunspots with lightning, and Forest fires as recorded in old scars. The chain of evidence as to the existence of the drouth cycle is very complete, and its bearing on economic and conservation problems is obvious. But like much other scientific truth, it may remain "embalmed in books, which are interred in University libraries, and then, long after, worked out by rule of thumb, by practical politicians and business men."

The point is that if every 11 years we may expect a drouth, why not manage our ranges accordingly? This means either stocking them to only their drouth capacity, or arranging to move the stock or feed it when the drouth appears. But instead, we stock them to their normal capacity, and when drouth comes the stock eat up the range, ruin the watershed, ruin the stockman, wreck the banks, get credits from the treasury of the United States, and then die. And the silt of their dying moves on down into our reservoirs to some day dry up the irrigated valleys—the only live thing left.

Equilibrium of Arid Countries. To complete a background for the understanding of natural laws and their operation on our resources it is necessary to consider briefly the so called "balance of nature."

There appears to be a natural law which governs the resistance of nature to human abuse. Broadly speaking, the law is this: the degree of stability varies inversely to the aridity.

Of course, this concept of a "balance of nature" compresses into three words an enormously complex chain of phenomena. But history bears out the law as given. Woolsey* says that decadence has followed deforestation in Palestine, Assyria, Arabia, Greece, Tunisia, Algeria, Italy, Spain, Persia, Sardinia, and Dalmatia. Note that these are all arid or semi-arid. What well-watered country has ever suffered serious permanent damage to all its organic resources from human abuse? None that I know of except China. It might be reasonable to ascribe this one exception to the degree of abuse received. Sheer pressure of millions exerted through uncounted centuries, was simply too much.

A definite causal relation has long been believed to exist between deforestation and decline in productiveness of Nations and their lands. But it strikes me as very curious that a similar causal relation between overgrazing and decadence has never to my knowledge, been positively asserted. All our existing knowledge in forestry indicates very strongly that overgrazing has done far more damage to the Southwest than fires or cuttings, serious as the latter have been. Even the reproduction of Forests has now been found to be impossible under some conditions without the careful regulation of grazing, whereas fire was formerly considered the only enemy.

The relative seriousness of destructive agencies may be illustrated by an example. Take the Sapello watershed, which forms a major part of the GOS range in the Gila National Forest. Old settlers state that when they came to the country, the Sapello was a beautiful trout stream lined with willows. Yet old burned stumps show beyond a doubt that great fires burned in the watershed of the Sapello for at least a century previous to settlement. These fires spoiled the timber, but they did not spoil the land. Since then we have kept the fires out, but livestock has come in. And now the watercourse of the Sapello is a pile of boulders. In short, a century of fires without grazing did not spoil the Sapello, but a decade of grazing without fires ruined it, as far as the watercourses are concerned.

*"Studies in French Forestry" by T.S. Woolsey, _____, 192__.

Now the remarkable thing about the Sapello is that it has not been overgrazed. The GOS range is pointed to with pride as a shining example of range conservation. The lesson is that under our peculiar Southwestern conditions, any grazing at all, no matter how moderate, is liable to overgraze and ruin the watercourses. And the wholesale tearing out of watercourses is sufficient to silt our irrigation reservoirs, whether or no it is followed by wholesale erosion of the range itself.

Of course this one example does not prove that grazing is the outstanding factor in upsetting the equilibrium of the Southwest. It is rapidly becoming the opinion of conservationists, however, that such is the case, and the erosion-control works of some kind are the price we will have to pay if we wish to utilize our ranges without ruining our agriculture.

Examples of Destruction: The effect of unwise range use on the range industry, or of unwise cutting upon the lumber industry, or of unwise farming on the land, are all too obvious to require illustration. What we need to appreciate is how abuses in one of these industries in one place may unwittingly injure another industry in another place.

A census of 30 typical agricultural mountain valleys in the National Forests of the Southwest shows 4 ruined, 8 partly ruined, 15 started to erode, and only 3 undamaged. Of the 27 valleys damaged, every case may be ascribed to grazing or overgrazing, supplemented more or less by clearing of cover from streambanks, fire, and starting of washes along roads or trails.

A detailed survey of one mountain valley (Blue River, Arizona) shows 3500 acres of farm land washed out, population reduced two thirds, and half a million paid for a road over the hills because there was no longer any place to put a road in the valley. This entire loss may be ascribed to overgrazing of creek bottoms and unnecessary clearing of banks.

A special study of one cattle ranch showed that the loss of 60 acres of farm land through erosion imposed a permanent tax of $6 per head on the cost of production. This was a herd of 860 head.

Data on reservoirs shows that Elephant Butte and Roosevelt Lake must probably be raised prematurely because of silting. One of the big Pecos dams (Lake MacMillan) is said to have silted up 60% in 15 years. A detailed report on the Zuni

Reservoir,* which may be considered typical of a smaller class, shows that its life will be 21 years, 12 of which have passed. Silting is forcing the amortization of this half-million dollar investment at the rate of $7 per irrigated acre per year. Raising the dam is necessary to extend its life. In all these cases the silting seems to have been faster than was calculated, and is tending to force the amortization of the investments during alarmingly short periods. Inexpensive desilting methods have not yet been devised. What will be left of the Southwest if silting cuts down our already meagre facilities for storage of an already meagre waterflow?

Here are some typical flood figures: Cave Creek, which flooded Phoenix in 1921, destroyed $150,000 in property and forced construction of a dam costing $500,000. The Pueblo flood of 1921 cost $17,000,000. A little flood in Taos Canyon in 19__ destroyed a new road costing $15,000. Every year it costs $40,000 to clear the diversion plants below Elephant Butte of silt from side-washes. These are merely random examples. Undoubtedly we always had floods, but all the evidence indicates that they usually spent themselves without damage while our watercourses were protected by plenty of vegetation, and such damage as occurred was quickly healed up by the roots remaining in the ground.

Summary: Our organic resources are not only in a run-down condition, but in our climate, bear a delicately balanced interrelation to each other. Any upsetting of this balance causes a progressive deterioration that may not only be felt hundreds of miles away, but may continue after the original disturbance is removed and affect populations and resources wholly unconnected with the original cause. Erosion eats into our hills like a contagion, and floods bring down the loosened soil upon our valleys like a scourge. Water, soil, animals, and plants—the very fabric of prosperity, react to destroy each other and us. Science can and must unravel those reactions, and government must enforce the findings of science. This is the economic bearing of conservation on the future of the Southwest.

*Silt Problem of the Zuni Reservoir, H. F. Robinson, Amer. Soc. C. E., Vol. 83, p. 868, 1920.

Thus far we have considered the problem of conservation of land purely as an economic issue. A false front of exclusively economic determinism is so habitual to Americans in discussing public questions that one must speak in the language of compound interest to get a hearing. In my opinion, however, one can not round out a real understanding of the situation in the Southwest without likewise considering its moral aspects.

In past and more outspoken days conservation was put in terms of decency rather than dollars. Who can not feel the moral scorn and contempt for poor craftsmanship in the voice of Ezekiel when he asks: *Seemeth it a small thing unto you to have fed upon good pasture, but ye must tread down with your feet the residue of your pasture? And to have drunk of the clear waters, but ye must foul the residue with your feet?*

In these two sentences may be found an epitome of the moral question involved. Ezekiel seems to scorn waste, pollution, and unnecessary damage as something unworthy—as something damaging not only to the reputation of the waster, but to the self-respect of the craft and the society of which he is a member. We might even draw from his words a broader concept—that the privilege of possessing the earth entails the responsibility of passing it on, the better for our use, not only to immediate posterity, but to the Unknown Future, the nature of which is not given us to know. It is possible that Ezekiel respected the soil, not only as a craftsman respects his material, but as a moral being respects a living thing.

Many of the world's most penetrating minds have regarded our so-called "inanimate nature" as a living thing, and probably many of us who have neither the time nor the ability to reason out conclusions on such matters by logical processes, have felt intuitively that there existed between man and earth a closer and deeper relation than would necessarily follow the mechanistic conception of the earth as our physical provider and abiding place.

Of course in discussing such matters we are beset on all sides with the pitfalls of language. The very words "living thing" have an inherited and arbitrary meaning derived not from reality, but from human perceptions of human affairs. But we must use them, for better or for worse.

A good expression of this conception of an organized animate nature is given by the Russian philosopher Ouspensky, who presents the following analogy:

> Were we to observe, from the inside, one cubic centimetre of the human body, knowing nothing of the existence of the entire body and of man himself, then the phenomena going on in this little cube of flesh would seem like elemental phenomena in inanimate nature.

He then states that it is at least not impossible to regard the earth's parts—soil, mountains, rivers, atmosphere, etc.,—as organs, or parts of organs, of a coordinated whole, each part with a definite function. And if we could see this whole, as a whole, through a great period of time, we might perceive not only organs with coordinated functions, but possibly also that process of consumption and replacement which in biology we call the metabolism, or growth. In such case we would have all the visible attributes of a living thing, which we do not now realize to be such because it is too big, and its life processes too slow. And there would also follow that invisible attribute—a soul, or consciousness—which not only Ouspensky, but many philosophers of all ages, ascribe to all living things and aggregations thereof, including the "dead" earth.

There is not much discrepancy, except in language, between this conception of a living earth, and the conception of a dead earth, with enormously slow, intricate, and inter-related functions among its parts, as given us by physics, chemistry, and geology. The essential thing for present purposes is that both admit the interdependent functions of the elements. But "anything indivisible is a living being" says Ouspensky. Possibly, in our intuitive perceptions, which may be truer than our science and less impeded by words than our philosophies, we realize the indivisibility of the earth—its soil, mountains, rivers, forests, climate, plants, and animals, and respect it collectively not only as a useful servant but as a living being, vastly less alive than ourselves in degree, but vastly greater than ourselves in time and space—a being that was old when the morning stars sang together, and when the last of us has been gathered unto his fathers, that will still be young.

Philosophy, then, suggests one reason why we can not

destroy the earth with moral impunity; namely, that the "dead" earth is an organism possessing a certain kind and degree of life, which we intuitively respect as such. Possibly, to most men of affairs, this reason is too intangible to either accept or reject as a guide to human conduct. But philosophy also offers another and more easily debatable question; was the earth made for man's use, or has man merely the privilege of temporarily possessing an earth made for other and inscrutable purposes? The question of what he can properly do with it must necessarily be affected by this question.

Most religions, in so far as I know, are premised squarely on the assumption that man is the end and purpose of creation, and that not only the dead earth, but all creatures thereon, exist solely for his use. The mechanistic or scientific philosophy does not start with this as a premise, but ends with it as a conclusion, and hence may be placed in the same category for the purpose in hand. This high opinion of his own importance in the universe Jeannette Marks stigmatizes as "the great human impertinence." John Muir, in defense of rattlesnakes, protests: "—as if nothing that does not obviously make for the benefit of man had any right to exist; as if our ways were God's ways." But the noblest expression of this anthropomorphism is Bryant's "Thanatopsis"

> —The hills
> Rock-ribbed and ancient as the sun,—the vales
> Stretching in pensive quietness between;
> The venerable woods—rivers that move
> In majesty, and the complaining brooks
> That make the meadows green, and, poured round all
> Old ocean's gray and melancholy waste,—
> *Are but the solemn decorations all*
> *Of the great tomb of man.*

Since most of mankind today profess either one of the anthropomorphic religions or the scientific school of thought which is likewise anthropomorphic, I will not dispute the point. It just occurs to me, however, in answer to the scientists, that God started his show a good many million years before he had any men for audience—a sad waste of both actors and music—and in answer to both, that it is just barely possible that God himself likes to hear birds sing and see flowers grow. But here again we encounter the insufficiency of words as symbols for realities.

Granting that the earth is for man—there is still a question: what man? Did not the cliff dwellers who tilled and irrigated these our valleys think that they were pinnacle of creation—that these valleys were made for them? Undoubtedly. And then the Pueblos? Yes. And then the Spaniards? Not only thought so, but said so. And now we Americans? Ours beyond a doubt! (How happy a definition is that one of Hadley's which states, "Truth is that which prevails in the long run"!)

Five races—five cultures—have flourished here. We may truthfully say of our four predecessors that they left the earth alive, undamaged. It is possibly a proper question for us to consider what the sixth shall say about us? If we are logically anthropomorphic, yes. We and

> —all that tread
> The globe are but a handful to the tribes
> That slumber in its bosom. Take the wings
> Of morning; pierce the Barcan wilderness
> Or lose thyself in the continuous woods
> Where rolls the Oregon, and hears no sound
> Save his own dashings—yet the dead are there,
> And millions in those solitudes, since first
> The flight of years began, have laid them down
> In their last sleep.

And so, in time, shall we. And if there be, indeed, a special nobility inherent in the human race—a special cosmic value, distinctive from and superior to all other life—by what token shall it be manifest?

By a society decently respectful of its own and all other life, capable of inhabiting the earth without defiling it? Or by a society like that of John Burroughs' potato-bug, which exterminated the potato, and thereby exterminated itself? As one or the other shall we be judged in "the derisive silence of eternity."

Typescript, c. March 1923

A Criticism of the Booster Spirit

WHEN THE historians of the future write the story of our generation, the growth and spread of the Booster spirit will, I think, rank as one of the outstanding phenomena of the twentieth century.

Boosterism is not as yet firmly established in any country but our own. Perhaps it will not be. But it is an undeniable fact that it touches the daily lives of a hundred million Americans, and dominates the lives of some of them. This alone establishes it as one of the great political and economic forces of our time.

Boosterism is hard to gather up within the confines of a definition. From the viewpoint of a Booster, it might be called the application to civics of the truism that faith will move mountains. From the viewpoint of the critical observer, it might be defined by paraphrasing Decatur: "My _____! May she always be right! But right or wrong, my _____!" Directions: insert in the blank the name of any lodge, ward, corporation, luncheon club, city, county, or state which you own, or which owns you, and Boost!

Boosterism is new, at least in its abuses. Civic or group loyalty, in the more solid sense, is of course as old as morality and civilization, but the (to me) unholy wedlock between the moral principle of loyalty and the technique of billboard advertising is a recent and not altogether pleasing addition to the things that are under the sun.

The uses of Boosterism need no defense from me. The organizer of the Chamber of Commerce extols them adequately when he awakens the civic consciousness of our town for forty per cent of the gate receipts. The only thing about Boosterism that is not expounded to us daily is its abuses and fallacies. These I will attempt to describe.

The philosophy of boost is premised on certain tenets, which are proclaimed every little while by menu cards, convention badges, billboards, windshields and civic orators, but which do not appear to have yet been collected in a creed. To write such a creed is not an appropriate task for an unbeliever. Possibly I entirely misapprehend the matter, but this is as I understand it:

1. To be big and grow bigger is the end and aim of cities and citizens. To be small when young is excusable, but to stay small is failure.

2. The way to grow big is to advertise advantages and ignore defects, thereby abolishing them. Self-criticism is akin to treason.

3. Growth by labor, frugality, or natural increase is slow and old-fashioned. Growth in population is attained by decoying it from some other town or state. Growth in wealth is attained by attracting tourists or capital from elsewhere, or extracting appropriations from public treasuries.

4. Earned increment may indicate industry, but unearned increment proves vision and brains.

5. Unanimity is the only defensible attitude toward public questions. Minority opinions merely complicate the situation.

6. Taxes are crushing enterprise, and must be reduced, but our appropriations are entirely inadequate.

7. Bribing conventions and setting stool-pigeons for tourists are signs of friendly rivalry between cities.

8. The up-and-comingness of a town varies directly as the congestion of its billboards, luncheon clubs, and traffic, and inversely as its parking space.

9. Educational institutions, libraries, and parks are valuable business assets. They attract strangers.

10. Skilled craftsmen may move to our town if they want to, but we *must* have oil men and motor tourists, for they are the salt of the earth.

This may not be all of it, but it is enough. Let us examine in detail whether and why these propositions are true.

First, what, concretely, is our ambition as a city? "100,000 by 1930"— we have blazoned it forth like an army with banners. This is well and good—a city has as much "right" to resolve to attain a phenomenal growth in population as a citizen has to resolve to have 15 children, if not more so. And how are we going to get the 100,000? By advertising our climate, by craft and strategy in manipulating the location of institutions, and by increasing tourist traffic. There is nothing necessarily wrong about any of these things. But none of them are creative effort in any real sense. Supposing every city likewise resolved to live and grow by its wits instead of by creating values? (Most of them are, and maybe that is what is wrong with the country.)

Moreover, just why do we wish to grow by unearned increment instead of an earned increment derived from our own basic resources? Does it ever occur to the booster that we have fifty million acres of range in this state injured or ruined by overgrazing, that could be made into a source of wealth and prosperity beside which his tourists and sanatoria are mere bubbles? That we have a potential agriculture in this valley, crippled by seepage and threatened by silting, that is declining by neglect while he is playing with conventions and brass bands? That the lack of public interest in these real resources is causing them to deteriorate instead of develop?

Moreover, just why are we so much more intense about decoying newcomers to New Mexico than we are about securing better education, better recreational facilities, better public health service, and cleaner government for the citizens already here? Did anybody ever see a boosters' program that dealt with any of these internal betterments with even a fraction of the earnestness and ingenuity which it devotes to log-rolling for doubtful appropriations or entertaining motorists?

Can anyone deny that the vast fund of time, brains, and money now devoted to making our city big would actually make it better if diverted to betterment instead of bigness?

Moreover are we sure that if we effected these internal betterments for our own citizens, that we would have to bribe, threaten and cajole new people and new institutions to come here? I am afraid we could not keep them away.

In boosting, as in the Inquisition, the end justifies the means. Just now the boosters are lashing the latent patriotism of the Nation to build by public subscription a huge memorial sanatorium to the War Mothers of America—in Albuquerque. The sweep and daring of the idea is as splendid as its avowed motive is sordid and miserable. Would you want the Marble Manufacturer to conceive the splendid idea of passing the hat among your friends, in order that he might build, for cost plus ten per cent, a monument to *your* mother? What is the difference? Will this splendid, monstrous scheme find favor where stand the crosses, row on row, in Flanders fields? But, say the boosters, while the scheme is selfish for Albuquerque, it will give expression to unselfish and lofty motives throughout the Nation. Indeed! Was the Statue of Liberty thus conceived? Did the Westminster Chamber of Commerce boost the Abbey? And why not charge a fee of admission to the battleground at Gettysburg? Perhaps we shall accomplish this thing, and its greatness, like the grass, will grow and bury the inglorious memory of its inception.

> Pile the bodies high at Austerlitz and Waterloo
> Shovel them under and let me work—
> I am the grass, I cover all.

As Machiavelli, our preceptor since the Great War, once said: "Our experience has been that those who have done great things have held good faith of little account."

The booster is intensely provincial. A year ago he demanded a National Park for New Mexico. He did not know where or how, but he knew jolly well why: A National Park would be a tourist-getter of the first water, and tourists are to be desired above all things. They come, they see, they spend, and they are even known to come back.

Now a National Park is nothing more or less than the given word of the United States government that the place so designated is superlative among natural wonders. Had New Mexico places worthy of this high guarantee? If so, were they so situated as to comprise a unit that could be encompassed by a boundary which would say "Here it is"? If not, was there any danger of our government being induced to certify as superlative something that was not so? The booster should worry! Could the (his) government deny that any state outclassed New Mexico in natural wonders? Could the (his) government deny that the other children had been served pie and he had not? The government came pretty near giving its querulous child a bottle of water to hush it up.

As with the given word of the United States, so with its pocketbook. The boosters of Santa Fe and Las Vegas conceived a scenic highway across the Sangre de Cristo Range. To recreate and inspire their own citizens? No indeed, to fetch tourists. It was "the wonderland of the Americas," and like all wonderlands except that of the refreshing Alice, it far excelled Switzerland, with which the boosters are always entirely familiar. What would this scenic highway cost? "A mere detail, that—find out later—all we know is that it would cost too much for us to build. It's about time the government did something for northern New Mexico anyhow." Could the government, in justice to existing needs for roads elsewhere, afford to appropriate? "We are not representing 'elsewhere'—we are building up our city." Should the "wonderland" continue under the Agricultural Department as a National Forest? "It will continue under the department that helps us get the money. If your department won't, there are plenty of others that will."

Thus is the pork barrel filled—and emptied. Thus do we attain "less government in business, and more business in government." Thus are the burdens of taxation reduced. Thus do we build cities and attain prosperity. Thus also does little Willie kick and squeal when his father denies his unseasonable demand for a new bicycle.

The booster's yardstick is the dollar, and if he recognizes any other standard of value, or any other agency of accomplishment, he makes it a point of pride not to admit it. Even works of charity are bought and sold, like cabbages or gasoline. Do we want to do something for the Boy Scouts? We levy a subscription, hire an architect, and build them a cabin in the mountains (which the Scouts ought to have built themselves), and proceed to forget the Scout movement. We can not see that what we should give toward such causes is usually not much money, but a little human interest.

A few months ago somebody discovered that the Bursum Bill raised the question of possible disintegration of the Pueblo Indian communes. A booster editor, commenting on the situation, cooly pointed out that the tourist-getting value of the Indians depended on their distinctive culture, which should *therefore* be preserved until our industrial development made it no longer possible to do so. This was, I hope, the ultimate impertinence of boosterism in the Southwest. That the Indian culture and ours should have been placed in competition for the possession of this country was inevitable, but the cool assumption that this last little fragment must necessarily disappear in order that an infinitesimal percentage of soot, bricks, and dollars may be added to our own, betrays a fundamental disrespect for the Creator, who made not only boosters, but mankind, in his image.

The booster seems almost proud of the ugliness and destruction that accompany industrialism. That some of this is inevitable and necessary I am the first to admit. That it can not be mitigated I emphatically deny. Is there any real economic necessity for the army of billboards that marches across the peaceful landscapes of the Rio Grande Valley, flaunting its ribald banners in the face of the eternal hills, and shouting at every turn of the road what is the best brand of chewing gum, tires, or tobacco? And to top off this indignity, there is even a billboard erected by a Business Woman's Club, proclaiming the virtues of our city! "Et tu, Brute?"

Whence cometh this noise? Is it a business necessity? On the contrary, it is one of those competitive business evils that merely cost money and benefit nobody. A zone for billboards at the entrance to the city, advising travellers of the kind and location of its services, would be justifiable. But a gauntlet of billboards fifty miles long is not only bad business, but miserably bad taste.

Is there any sound economic reason why our comely public buildings can not be grouped around a public plaza, instead of cramped into scattered lots where they will shortly be elbowed by such a maze of butcher shops and five-and-ten-cent stores as to be visible only from an airplane? No reason, except that boosters and politicians do not know and will not learn the modern devices of public finance like the "Excess Condemnation Plan," which would give us a plaza without additional cost. In all this needless ugliness the booster is not so much ruthless as clumsy. A hundred percenter in making the flag fly and the eagle scream, he is awkward in self-government. Worshipping commerce, he is slow to regulate its own abuses.

The typical booster is entirely out of contact with the most fundamental of his boasted resources, the soil. Ask the average one how many bushels an acre of corn produces in our valley and he doesn't know, but he will quote you yards of statistics on what the tourist spends in our town. Ask him what is wrong with the livestock industry and he will answer drouth, or foreign competition, or other accessories-after-the-fact. He doesn't know that the fundamental reason is lack of a stable land tenure to produce grass, and that his own unintelligent and irresponsible politics is in turn responsible for this. Knowing nothing of the soil, he does not have the confidence of those who till the soil, and accordingly his spasmodic efforts at drainage or other betterments come to naught. Happily, there are exceptions to this. Banks and boosters, in places, are doing a splendid and successful work in rebuilding the agriculture of the south, where the boll-weevil wrecked the cotton crop and the boosters had to do something or move out.

Growing away from the soil has spiritual as well as economic consequences which sometimes lead one to doubt whether the booster's hundred per cent Americanism attaches itself to the country, or only to the living which we by hook or crook extract from it. Recently our boosters "discovered" the Sandias. Since Coronado came, and before, they have offered cool shades and peace to the inhabitants of this valley, but suddenly we realize that they are there, and that they are beautiful. Do we rejoice that our citizens shall henceforth enjoy them? Not so. "I love thy rocks and rills, thy woods and templed hills"—as tourist bait.

The booster is covetous of trifles, blissfully devoid of public policy, intolerant of minorities, ruthless, unscrupulous, provincial, and extravagant of the government's purse as he is generous of his own, but he is not proud. Cleaning the boots of tourists, conventions, prospective investors, and other dispensers of "prosperity" is congenial labor, performed with an obsequiousness worthy of a head-waiter, and with as good an eye for gratuities. "Ich Dien, but please like our town." Conventions present their demands for civic hospitality in the same categorical imperative as an ultimatum to the Turks, and the boosters receive it with a polite humility that a Turk could never emulate. The ordinary relations of guest and host, premised on mutual consideration and self respect, are displaced by a brazen self-interest that survives nowhere else but in diplomacy and international relations. Auto tourists demand "service," under pain of blackballing the town, and they get it. New enterprises demand a "bonus," under pain of locating elsewhere. It is a hopeful sign that this "bonus" system is rapidly falling into disrepute.

It is characteristic of the "small boy" psychology of the booster that he recognizes no kind of civic service save his own. I once heard a subscription committee vehemently berate a dentist for his refusal to sign on the dotted line. They charged him with ignoring his civic obligations. As a matter of fact, the highly skilled and utterly conscientious professional services of that particular dentist had done more for the town, even measured by its own materialistic standards, than the new Chamber of Commerce which the committee purported to represent. He had lived the precept of Carlyle, who said "The latest gospel in this world is, Know thy work and do it."

Likewise characteristic of the small boy is the booster tendency toward mutual admiration societies. The solemn altruism and lofty ethical codes of our four-and-twenty varieties of luncheon clubs are not—as many outsiders aver—an hypocrisy, forgotten in the daily practice of their members. On the contrary, these codes are a uniform, like the plumes and swords of fraternal orders, and worn for a like purpose—the lifting up of the individual out of the treadmill of industry. Whether we know it or not, we all need and seek this lifting up.

And even boosters are lifted. The full measure of devotion often given to booster movements commands respect and admiration, regardless of the present fallacies of the cause. Look back on the birth of political and religious liberty, and the more recent birth of internationalism, and see how each is full of fallacies and extremes ranging from the tragic to the ludicrous. But sincerity is never ludicrous. Let us critics, therefore beware, in ridiculing the fallacies of this new thing "lest we laugh in the wrong place, and thus commit impiety when we think we are achieving wit."

One more admission of the possibility that true vitality and greatness underlies the booster idea. I once knew a doctor, who on the completion of his medical studies, returned to his home town to practice. He soon saw that the place was too small for him. "I realized," he says, "that I would either have to move to the kind of a town I needed, or else make over my home town into that kind of a place. I decided to make over my home town." And he did. He did it through a Chamber of Commerce.

The sweep and daring, the utter simplicity and directness of

such occasional manifestations of the booster spirit give the lie
to any easy assumption that it is all froth and noise. Somewhere,
somehow, it contains the germ of a better order of things. Even
in our town there are symptoms of it.

Every day on my way to my office I pass a booster billboard
which exhorts me as follows: "Cities do not happen—BE A
BUILDER—Support your Chamber of Commerce." Splendid
truths, the first two. I detest billboards, but this one interests
me. Be a builder! There is a real ring in those words. I look over
at the towering beauty of "The Franciscan," and am proud.

> What vigor raised those spires; what joyful hand
> Put strength into those arches, gave the free
> Rock this immense and grotesque dignity,
> Making the structure greater than it planned!
> What laughter shook the builders as they scanned
> Those grinning gargoyles, and a jubilee
> Spirit enlarged the workers' energy;
> While, laid with love, each stone was made to stand!

The boosters built this lovely thing. I recall the travail of civic
spirit, the fight with civic sloth and inertia, which converted the
dream to reality. I recall the contest between the mediocrity
which wanted "plain commercial architecture" and the vision
which saw a building reflecting the history and traditions of the
Southwest. The vision won. Out of this immense, vigorous,
unlovely thing called Boosterism, provincial as a carpet-bagger,
ruthless as the Juggernaut, intolerant as a Prussian, boisterous
as Huckleberry Finn, but courageous as the Vikings grew "The
Franciscan." Is it too much to hope that this force, harnessed
to a finer ideal, may some day accomplish good as well as big
things? That our future standard of civic values may even exclude quantity, obtained at the expense of quality, as not worth
while? When this is accomplished shall we vindicate the truth
that "the virtue of a living democracy consists not in its ability
to avoid mistakes, but in its ability to profit by them."

Typescript, November 6, 1923

Pioneers and Gullies

PIONEERING A new country is hard labor. It has absorbed the best brawn and brains of the Nordic race since before the dawn of history. Anthropologists tell us that we, the Nordics, have a racial genius for pioneering, surpassing all other races in ability to reduce the wilderness to possession.

But if we saw a Nordic settler perspiring profusely to put a new field under irrigation while a flood was eating away his older field for lack of a few protective works, we should call that settler an inefficient pioneer. Yet that is exactly what we seem to be doing in trying to develop the Southwest. The only difference is that while one individual is putting the new field under irrigation, another individual is losing the older field from floods, and a third is causing the floods through misuse of his range. This scattering of cause and effect and of loss and gain among different owners or industries may give the individual his alibi, but it changes not one whit the inefficiency of our joint enterprise in "developing" the country. We, the community, are saving at the spigot and wasting at the bunghole, and it is time we realized it and mended our ways.

While our Government and our capitalists are laboring to bring new land under irrigation by the construction of huge and expensive works, floods are tearing away, in small parcels, here and there, an aggregate of old land, much of it already irrigated, which is comparable to the new land in area and value. The opening of these great reclamation projects we celebrate by oratory and monuments, but the loss of our existing farms we dismiss as an act of God—like the storm or the earthquake, inevitable. But it is not an act of God; on the contrary, it is the direct result of our own misuse of the country we are trying to improve.

Proof? A survey of 30 small agricultural valleys in the mountain sections of Arizona and New Mexico shows 12 wholly or partly ruined, 9 with erosion started, and 9 with little or no erosion. Roughly, we are losing nearly half of these mountain valleys.

The total irrigable acreage of U.S. Reclamation Projects in the two states is 430,000 acres. The loss to date in the 30 mountain valleys is 10,000 acres. Doubling this for the additional losses in small creeks not covered by the survey, but within the mountain area, would give 20,000 acres. The mountain area surveyed is one-seventh of the total area of the two States, and does not include such valleys as the Gila and San Juan where the really big losses have occurred. The Pueblo flood alone is known to have torn out 2500 acres. Olmstead* says the Gila destroyed 2500 acres in 1915 in Graham county alone, and is threatening 30,000 acres of farm land in this county. I feel safe in stating that erosion has destroyed agricultural land running into six figures in the two states.

Let us consider just one of these eroded valleys in detail. Blue river, in the White mountains, originally flowed through about 4000 acres of cultivated land. This land supported about 45 ranches and 300 people. Floods tore out the land, and today 400 acres remain cultivable, supporting about 20 ranches and 90 people. The land lost would now be worth $150 per acre, or $540,000. This loss, as cash, would pay for a tidy little reclamation project. It would have warranted an expenditure of $100 per acre for protective works. But after all, a cash value can not express the actual loss. Not only were 34 established homes destroyed, but the land carried away was a "key" resource, necessary for the proper utilization of the range, timber, and recreational values on half a million acres of adjacent mountains. There is no other land in the region suitable for homes, stock-ranches, mills, roads, and schools. Let us get the full significance of this by examining each item in detail.

Take, for instance, the adjacent range. On this lost farm land the stockmen lived and had their alfalfa, grain fields, gardens and orchards. With no fields, all feed for saddle and work horses and weak range stock must be either dispensed with or packed in 60 miles from the railroad at great cost. This may make the difference between a profitable and an unprofitable stock-raising operation. In one case where detailed figures were worked out, it was found that the loss of 60 acres of farming land to a stockman running 850 cattle caused a loss of 24% in gross income and increased his cost of production $6.50 per head.

*"Flood Control on the Gila River," Frank H. Olmstead, U.S. Geological Survey, 1917.

Moreover a stock ranch deprived of its garden patch, orchard, milk cows, and poultry is no fit place to establish a home and raise a family. Regardless of the profit of the business, it is an unsocial institution.

But this is not all. The destruction of the bottom lands destroyed the only feasible location for the road necessary to connect the ranches with each other, with schools and with the outside world, and to enable timber and minerals to be hauled out to market. Floods have left no place for a road. Children must now ride to school on horseback, and during floods they can not even do that. The Government and the counties are now actually spending half a million dollars on a road through this country, but it can not tap what remains of the Blue River community because it is unsafe to put a road on a sandbar. It must clamber high over the rocks and hills, at huge expense.

We, the community, have "developed" Blue River by overgrazing the range, washing out half a million in land, taking the profits out of the livestock industry, cutting the ranch homes by two-thirds, destroying conditions necessary for keeping families in the other third, leaving the timber without an outlet to the place where it is needed, and now we are spending half a million to build a road round this place of desolation which we have created. And to "replace" this smiling valley which Nature gave us free, we are spending another half a million to reclaim an equal acreage of desert some other place.

Just what is the nature of this process by which overgrazing of the range destroys the valleys necessary to make the range industry profitable? In past years most engineers and conservationists have believed that moderate grazing did not produce erosion. History and experience have shown, however, that this theory must be applied with caution. In scantily watered country, to graze the range at all often means to overgraze the watercourses and bottom lands. Some concentration of stock at these points is difficult to avoid, even under careful management. When a bad flood encountered a virgin watercourse full of vigorous trees, willows, vines, weeds and grass, it may have scoured it pretty severely, but the living roots remained to spring up and recover the land and cause the next more moderate flood to heal the scars instead of enlarging them. But when floods encounter a watercourse through bare fields, timber grazed clear of all undergrowth, and earth-scars like roads, trails, and ditches built parallel with the stream, the gouges left by one flood are liable to be enlarged by the next flood; an unprotected channel is excavated; the trees merely act as levers to pry off the undermined banks, the process of oxbowing cuts first one side of the bottom and then the other, eating into the very base of the hills; side-gullies running back from the deepened creek-channel cut at right angles into the remaining bottoms and benches, draining the natural *cienagas* and hay meadows and changing the grasses to a less resistant forage type, and in the long run our "improved" valley becomes a desolation of sandbars, rockpiles and driftwood, a sad monument to the unintelligence and misspent energy of us, the pioneers.

This is what I mean when I say that in the Southwest it is doubtful whether we are creating more useful land with the labor of our hands than we are unintentionally destroying with the trampling of our feet. But why is it that Nature is so quick to punish unintelligent "development" in the Southwest?

Every region seems to have a different resistance to every kind of use or abuse by man. The degree and nature of this resistance seem to be determined by climate. The more arid the climate, the less the resistance of the region to abuse. In Europe, with its wet climate, many centuries of use and abuse by man have altered but not destroyed the land, vegetation, and animal life. Britain, New England, Canada, the South, the Middle West and the Northwest are broadly in the same category.

Palestine and Asia Minor, on the other hand, have a semi-arid climate. Scores of centuries of use and abuse by man have to a large extent destroyed the vegetation, animal life and even the soil itself. The Bible is full of evidence that the mountains of the Holy Land in the time of the Prophets supported real forests; the range was abundant and excellent; many living streams found their source in the higher lands. Great forest fires swept the mountains unchecked. Grazing was the principal industry and doubtless the range was at least locally overgrazed, just as is happening today in the Southwest. The forests have long since disappeared, and the mountains are too bare to support a forest fire.

Vanished forests can be replaced by huge expenditures, but

no country has ever replaced lost agricultural land on a big scale. The Incas came the nearest to it in the terraces which they built with soil packed in on their backs. We will not have the patience to do that. We have no way to restore the soil to lands that have washed away. Soil is the fundamental resource, and its loss the most serious of all losses.

Soil is not the only resource which shows a lower resistance to use and abuse in arid countries. Forests grow more slowly and are exceedingly difficult to reproduce after cutting. Desirable forage under excessive use loses its vitality and reverts to weeds. Game shows less resistance to hunting than in wet regions. All of these factors interact in a very complex manner with each other and with soil conditions, necessitating the fullest and most skillful coöperation among the various professions in charge of conservation work.

Coming back to soil: Erosion of soil is always accompanied by disturbance or damage to the usable water supply. In valleys like the Mimbres, the Sapello and the Blue, what were once trout streams have been entirely covered up by debris. While the water may be still there, it is buried. In streams like the Galisteo and Puerco, the channel has so deepened that water can not be diverted into the ditches which once supported orchards and farms. And finally let us not forget that most of the land destroyed on our watersheds is being dumped as silt into our great irrigation reservoirs, gradually reducing their storage capacity. After they are full of mud, then what?

In these early and hopeful days, the loss of land by erosion can always be temporarily made good by reclaiming new lands. The destruction of easy and cheap road routes can be met by rebuilding the road on the hills. The filling of dams can be staved off by building them higher or building new ones. But mark this well: the total possible acreage of tillable irrigable land, the total possible acre-feet of accessible water and the total storage capacity of dam-sites—these three things set the limits of the total possible future development of the Southwest. The virgin supply of each was limited; the subsequent losses, no matter with what energy we "replace" them, are steadily lowering the limits already set. To a degree we are facing the question of whether we are here to "skin" the Southwest and then get out, or whether we are here to found a permanent civilized community with room to grow and improve. We can not long continue to accept our losses without admitting that the former, rather than the latter, is by way of becoming the real result of our occupancy.

So far little has been said about remedies, which are, of course, the thing really worth talking about. It has been asserted that erosion is the result of overgrazing, and that some local overgrazing is difficult to avoid, even on ranges that are not overstocked. But nobody advocates that we cease grazing.

The situation does not call for a taboo upon grazing, but rather constitutes a challenge to the craftsmanship of our stockmen and the technical skill of grazing experts in devising controls that will work, and to the courage of our administrators in enforcing those controls in a manner fair both to the conflicting interests and to the community.

The stockmen must recognize that the privilege of grazing use carries with it the obligation to minimize and control its effects by more skilful and conservative methods. The day will come when the ownership of land will carry with it the obligation to so use and protect it with respect to erosion that it is not a menace to other landowners and the public. Just as it is illegal for one landowner to menace the public peace or health by maintaining disorderly or unsanitary conditions on his land, so will it become illegal for him to menace the public streams, reservoirs, irrigation projects, or the lands of his neighbors by allowing erosion to take place. But it is cheaper to prevent erosion than to cure it, and the cost of such prevention must some day be passed on uniformly by all landowners to all consumers of their products.

But enforced responsibility of landowners is of the future. What are the prevention methods that can be used *now* by those owners sufficiently progressive, or sufficiently menaced by impending loss, to do so?

A diagnosis of the process of destruction gives the most reliable pointers as to the best process of prevention and cure. First and foremost, a vigorous growth of grass on the watershed, and more especially on the watercourses, is essential. The science of range management has made great strides in the last decade in developing conservative methods of range use. Some of them were described in the October, 1923 issue of *Sunset.* It is coming to be generally admitted by stockmen that they are more profitable than the old destructive methods. Why, then, are they not in general use?

Because under present conditions it does not pay the average stockman to use them. In the National forests a genuine and frequently successful effort has been made to prevent overgrazing by careful regulation, but on the public range outside of the forests no control of any kind is exercised. First come, first served. This lack of regulation causes each stockman to try to get as much stock as possible on the range at the earliest possible moment, resulting in continuous and disastrous overgrazing. Further procrastination in effecting a public-domain policy is unthinkable. It matters a great deal more that some decisive policy be adopted than that such policy be ideally correct. The prospects are that the stockmen are about to agree on a Federal leasing bill. It will be the tenth principal attempt at legislation since 1900. Why not pass it?

So much for the first step in watershed conservation—the prevention of erosion by maintaining the grass cover on the range in general. It is by all odds the most important step. But there are other steps necessary. For instance, in the Southwest there has been a striking coincidence between the inception of erosion and the eating out of the native willows by stock. Willows formerly grew in most of our cañons and river bottoms. They are a palatable winter feed and soon disappear. There is no doubt that the grazing out of the willows has been the direct cause of streambank erosion in hundreds of cases.

It is very hard to maintain grass and willows on watercourses used by stock. The natural concentration of stock, especially in winter and spring, destroys them. Therefore many bottoms will have to be fenced, and merely lightly grazed as reserve pastures, and the willows artificially restored by planting cuttings on the banks of the stream. Experiments in such work indicate that banks can be willowed, cuttings two feet apart, for less than fifty cents per one hundred feet. The usefulness of such pastures can be regarded as offsetting the cost of the fencing. Of course the fences must be so located as to leave sufficient water-gaps and to provide for road routes.

Fencing will be practicable only in the wider cañons. Willowing will be practicable only on fenced lightly grazed pastures or agricultural fields. For watercourses that can not be fenced, some plant to replace the native willows but resistant to grazing either through having thorns or being non-palatable, will have to be found. The machinery of the Department of Agriculture has been set to work to find such a plant through its plant exploration service.

Farming lands can often be economically protected from bank-cutting by inexpensive works. Felling trees into the channel at strategic places and chaining the end of the trunk to its own stump is a method that makes the flood divert itself, rather than to divert it by the sheer strength of expensive walls and dams. Willows can often be advantageously planted under the protection of such felled tree-tops. Riprapping with woven wire fencing strung parallel with the bank on green spring-set cottonwood posts, which grow and form trees, is a cheap and good method.

Often it is necessary for landowners along a creek to work out a unified plan, else there is danger that the diligence of one owner will result merely in passing the trouble down the creek to his neighbors. Here is a fine opportunity for leadership and technical advice by county agents, Forest officers, and similar officials. It is unfortunate that our agricultural colleges have not seized their opportunity to develop erosion-control technique for the benefit of stockmen and farmers.

In addition to preventing erosion by conserving a grass cover on the range, and controlling it by protecting stream banks, there remains the huge problem of gully-control on the watershed as a whole. Many lands are being so cut up by gullies as to drain and dry the soil and thus change the type of forage. Many a fine glade, park, *valle, canada* or hay meadow has a gully gradually eating along its whole length, where a few minutes of throwing logs, stones, and brush into the head of the gully would prevent its further spread. There is a best way even in plugging a gully, and this best way deserves the careful study of engineers. Where an acre of grazing land worth $2.00 or of a hay meadow worth $40.00 can be saved by plugging a gully at a cost in time of 25¢, it is disregarding the public welfare and the principles of sound private business not to plug it.

Natural resources are interdependent, and in semi-arid countries are often set in a hair-trigger equilibrium which is quickly upset by uncontrolled use. As a consequence, uncontrolled use of one local resource may menace the economic system of whole regions. Therefore, to protect the public interest, certain resources must remain in public ownership, and ultimately the use of all resources will have to be put under public regulation, regardless of ownership. This is the fundamental reason why the Nation retains ownership of the mountain forests and one of the reasons why the Nation builds and regulates reclamation projects. But while partial provision has been made, through the Forest Service and Reclamation Service, to conserve the forests and the water supply, no provision has been made to conserve that fundamental resource, land.

The first step to remedy this omission is to reform the conditions of land tenure, especially on the unreserved public domain, so that the livestock industry can practice the conservation methods which the science of range management has already worked out.

The second step is for all agencies concerned, under the leadership of agricultural colleges, to develop and demonstrate the cheapest and best methods of artificial erosion control, and urge all landowners to utilize them. This will enable owners to control some of the losses of land that will otherwise continue unchecked.

The third step, which must come later, is to put all land in the region threatened by erosion under Government inspection as to the adequacy of erosion control, and to force all owners to conserve their lands to the extent that is found reasonable and practicable. If they fail to do so, the Government must install the necessary controls and assess the landowner with the cost.

The greater the delay in the first two steps, the more urgent and drastic becomes the third.

Sunset Magazine, May 1924

Grass, Brush, Timber, and Fire in Southern Arizona

ONE OF the first things which a forester hears when he begins to travel among the cow-camps of the southern Arizona foothills is the story of how the brush has "taken the country." At first he is inclined to classify this with the legend, prevalent among the old timers of some of the northern states, about the hard winters that occurred years ago. The belief in the encroachment of brush, however, is often remarkably circumstantial. A cow-man will tell about how in the 1880's on a certain mesa he could see his cattle several miles, whereas now on the same mesa he can not even find them in a day's hunt. The legend of brush encroachment must be taken seriously.

Along with it goes an almost universal story about the great number of cattle which the southern Arizona foothills carried in the old days. The old timers say that there is not one cow now where there used to be 10, 20, 30, and so on. This again might be dismissed but for the figures cited as to the branding of old cattle outfits, of which the location and area of range are readily determinable. This story likewise must be taken seriously.

In some quarters the forester will find a naive belief that the two stories represent cause and effect, that by putting more cattle on the range the old days of prosperity for the range industry might somehow be restored.

The country in which the forester finds these prevalent beliefs consists of rough foothills corresponding in elevation to the woodland type. Above lie the forests of western yellow pine. Below lie the semi-desert ranges characteristic of the southern Arizona plains. The area we are dealing with is large, comprising the greater part of the Prescott, Tonto, Coronado, and Crook National Forests as well as much range outside the Forests. The brush that has "taken the country" comprises dozens of species, in which various oaks, manzanita, mountain mahogany and ceanothus predominate. Here and there alligator junipers of very large size occur. Along the creek bottoms the brush becomes a hardwood forest.

Five facts are so conspicuous in this foothill region as to immediately arrest the attention of a forester.

(1) Widespread abnormal erosion. This is universal along watercourses with sheet erosion in certain formations, especially granite.

(2) Universal fire scars on all the junipers, oaks, or other trees old enough to bear them.

(3) Old juniper stumps, often leveled to the ground, evidently by fire.

(4) Much juniper reproduction merging to pine reproduction in the upper limits of the type.

(5) Great thrift and size in the junipers or other woodland species which have survived fire.

A closer examination reveals the following additional facts:

First, the reproduction is remarkably even aged. A few ring counts immediately establish the significant fact that none of it is over 40 years old. It is therefore contemporaneous with settlement; this region having been settled and completely stocked with cattle in the 1880's.

Second, the reproduction is encroaching on the parks. These parks, in spite of heavy grazing, still contain some grass. It would appear, therefore, that this reproduction has something to do with grass.

Third, one frequently sees manzanita, young juniper or young pines growing within a foot or two of badly fire-scarred juniper trees. These growths being very susceptible to fire damage, they could obviously not have survived the fires which produced the scars. Ring counts show that these growths are less than 40 years old. One is forced to the conclusion that there have been no widespread fires during the last 40 years.

Fourth, a close examination of the erosion indicates that it, too, dates back about 40 years and is therefore contemporaneous with settlement, removal of grass, and cessation of fires.

These observations coordinate themselves in the following theory of what has happened: Previous to the settlement of the country, fires started by lightning and Indians kept the brush thin, kept the juniper and other woodland species decimated, and gave the grass the upper hand with respect to possession of the soil. In spite of the periodic fires, this grass prevented erosion. Then came the settlers with their great herds of livestock. These ranges had never been grazed and they grazed them to death, thus removing the grass and automatically checking the possibility of widespread fires. The removal of the grass relieved the brush species of root competition and of fire damage and thereby caused them to spread and "take the country." The removal of grass-root competition and of fire damage brought in the reproduction. In brief, the climax type is and always has been woodland. The thick grass and thin brush of pre-settlement days represented a temporary type. The substitution of grazing for fire brought on a transition of thin grass and thick brush. This transition type is now reverting to the climax type—woodland.

There may be other theories which would coordinate these observable phenomena, but if there are such theories nobody has propounded them, and I have been unable to formulate them.

One of the most interesting checks of the foregoing theory is the behavior of species like manzanita and piñon. These species are notoriously susceptible to fire damage at all ages. Take manzanita: One finds innumerable localities where manzanita thickets are being suppressed and obliterated by pine or juniper reproduction. The particular manzanita characteristic of the region (*Arctostaphylos pungens*) is propagated by brush fires, seedling (not coppice) reproduction taking the ground whenever a fire has killed the other brush species or reduced them to coppice. It is easy to think back to the days when these manzanita thickets, now being killed, were first established by a fire in what was then grass and brush. Cattle next removed the grass. Pine and juniper then reproduced due to the absence of grass and fire, and are now overtopping the manzanita. Take piñon: It is naturally a component of the climax woodland type but mature piñons are hardly to be found in the region; just a specimen here and there sufficient to perpetuate the species which has evidently been decimated through centuries of fires. Nevertheless today there is a large proportion of piñon in the woodland reproduction which is coming in under some of the Prescott brushfields.

Another interesting check is found in the present movement of type boundaries. Yellow pine is reproducing down hill into the woodland type. Juniper is reproducing down hill into the semi-desert type. This down-hill movement of type lines is so conspicuous and so universal as to establish beyond a doubt that the virgin condition previous to settlement represented a temporary type due to some kind of damage, and completely refutes the possible assumption that the virgin conditions were climax and the present tendency is away from rather than toward a climax.

A third interesting check is found in the parks. In general there are two alternative hypotheses for Southwestern parks—the one assuming chemical or physical soil conditions unfavorable to forests and the other assuming the exclusion of forests by damage. When the occasional forest tree found in any park is scrubby, it indicates in general defective soil conditions. When the occasional forest tree shows vigor and thrift, it indicates that the park was established by damage and that the soil is suitable. Nothing could be more conspicuous than the vigor and thrift of the ancient junipers scattered through the parks of the southern Arizona foothills. We may safely assume that these parks were not caused by defective soil conditions. That they were caused by grass fires is evidenced by the survival of grass species in spite of the extra heavy grazing which occurs in them and by the universal fire scars that prevail on the old junipers in them. The fact that they are now reproducing to juniper clinches the argument.

A fourth check bears on the hypothesis that the virgin grass was heavy enough to carry severe fires. The check consists in the occurrence of "islands" where topography has prevented grazing. One will find small benches high on the face of precipitous cliffs which, in spite of poor and dry soil, bear an amazing stand of grasses simply because they have never been grazed. One even finds huge blocks of stone at the base of cliffs where a little soil has gathered on the top of the block and a thrifty stand of grasses survives simply because livestock could not get at it.

The most impressive check of all is the occurrence of junipers evidently killed by a single fire from 50 years to many centuries ago, on areas where there is now neither brush nor grass and where the junipers were so scattered (as evidenced by their remains) that it is absolutely necessary to assume a connecting medium. If the connecting medium had been brush it could hardly have been totally wiped out because neither fire nor grazing exterminates a brushfield. It is necessary to assume that the connecting medium consists of grass. It is significant that the above described phenomenon occurs mostly on granitic formations where it is easy to think that a heavy stand of grass might have been exterminated by even moderate grazing due to the loose nature of the soil.

Assuming that all the foregoing theory is correct, let us now consider what it teaches us about erosion. Why has erosion been enormously augmented during the last 40 years? Why has not the encroachment of brush checked the erosion which was induced by the removal of grass? Why did not the fires of pre-settlement days cause as much erosion as the grazing of post-settlement days?

It is obvious at the start that these questions can not be answered without rejecting some of our traditional theories of erosion. The substance of these traditional theories and the extent to which they must be amended before they can be applied to the Southwest, I have discussed elsewhere.* It will be well to repeat, however, that the acceptance of my theory as to the ecology of these brushfields carries with it the acceptance of the fact that at least in this region grass is a much more effective conserver of watersheds than foresters were at first willing to admit, and that grazing is the prime factor in destroying watershed values. In rough topography grazing always means some degree of localized overgrazing, and localized overgrazing means earth-scars. All recent experimentation indicates that earth-scars are the big causative agent of erosion. An excellent example is cited by Bates, who shows that the logging road built to denude Area B at Wagon Wheel Gap has caused more siltage than the denudation itself. Another conspicuous example is on the GOS cattle range in the Gila Forest, where earth-scars due to concentration of cattle along the water-courses have caused an entire trout stream to be buried by detritus, in spite of the fact that conservative range management has preserved the remainder of the watershed in an excellent condition.

Let us now consider the bearing of this theory on Forest administration. We have learned that during the pre-settlement period of no grazing and severe fires, erosion was not abnormally

---

*A Plea for Recognition of Artificial Works in Forest Erosion Control Policy, Journal of Forestry, March, 1921.

Pioneers and Gullies, Sunset Magazine, May, 1924.

Watershed Handbook, Southwestern District, issued December, 1923.

active. We have learned that during the post-settlement period of no fires and severe grazing, erosion became exceedingly active. Has our administrative policy applied these facts?

It has not. Until very recently we have administered the southern Arizona Forests on the assumption that while over-grazing was bad for erosion, fire was worse, and that therefore we must keep the brush hazard grazed down to the extent necessary to prevent serious fires.

In making this assumption we have accepted the traditional theory as to the place of fire and forests in erosion, and rejected the plain story written on the face of Nature. He who runs may read that it was not until fires ceased and grazing began that abnormal erosion occurred. We have likewise rejected the story written in our own fire statistics, which shows that on the Tonto Forest only about ⅓ of 1% of the hazard area burns over each year, and that it would therefore take 300 years for fire to cover the forest once. Even if the more conservative grazing policy which now prevails should largely enhance the present brush hazard by restoring a little grass, neither the potential danger of fire damage nor the potential cost of fire control could compare with the existing watershed damage. Moreover the reduction of the brush hazard by grazing is to a large degree impossible. This brush that has "taken the country" consists of many species, varying greatly in palatability. Heavy grazing of the palatable species would simply result in the unpalatable species closing in, and our hazard would still be there.

There is one point with respect to which both past policy and present policy are correct, and that is the paramount value of watersheds. The old policy simply erred in its diagnoses of how to conserve the watershed. The range industry on the Tonto Forest represents a present capital value of around three millions. Since this is about one third of the total Roosevelt Reservoir drainage we may assume roughly that the range industry affecting the Reservoir is worth nine millions. The Roosevelt Dam and the irrigation works of the Salt River Valley represent a cash expense by the Government of around twelve millions. The agriculture lands dependent upon this irrigation system are worth about fifty millions, not counting dependent industries. Grazing interests worth nine millions, therefore, must be balanced against agricultural interests worth sixty-two millions. To the extent that there is a conflict between the existence of the range industry and the permanence of reclamation, there can be no doubt that the range industry must give way.

In discussing administrative policy, I have tried to make three points clear: First, 15 years of Forest administration were based on an incorrect interpretation of ecological facts and were, therefore, in part misdirected. Second, this error of interpretation has now been recognized and administrative policy corrected accordingly. Third, while there can be no doubt about the enormous value of European traditions to American forestry, this error illustrates that there can also be no doubt about the great danger of European traditions to American forestry; this error also illustrates that there can be no doubt about the great danger of European traditions uncritically accepted and applied, especially in such complex fields as erosion.

The present situation in the southern Arizona brushfields may be summed up administratively as follows:

(1) There has been great damage to the watershed resources.

(2) There has been great benefit to the timber resources.

(3) There has been great damage to the range resources.

Whether the benefit to timber could have been obtained with lesser damage to watersheds and ranges is an academic question dealing with bygones and need not be discussed. Our present job is to conserve the benefit to timber and minimize the damage to watershed and range in so far as technical skill and good administration can do it. Wholesale exclusion of grazing is neither skill nor administration, and should be used only as a last resort. The problem which faces us constitutes a challenge to our technical competency as foresters—a challenge we have hardly as yet answered, much less actually attempted to meet. We are dealing right now with a fraction of a cycle involving centuries. We can not obstruct or reverse the cycle, but we can bend it; in what degree remains to be shown.

There are some interesting sidelights which enter into the foregoing discussions but which could not there be covered in detail. One of them is the extreme age of the junipers and juniper stumps. In one case I found a 36" alligator juniper with over half its basal cross-section eaten out by fire. On each edge of this huge scar were four overlapping healings. The last healing on each edge of the scar counted forty rings. Within 24" of the scar were two yellow pines of 20" diameter just emerging from the blackjack stage. Each must have been 130 years old. Neither showed any scars, but upon chopping into the side adjacent to the juniper, each was found to contain a buried fire-scald in the fortieth ring. It was perfectly evident that these 130-year pines had grown in the interval between the fires which consumed half the basal cross-section of the juniper, and the subsequent fires which resulted in the latest series of four healings. The fires which really ate into the juniper would most certainly have killed any pine standing only 24" distant. The conclusion is that the juniper attained its present diameter more than 130 years ago. The size of the main scar certainly indicates a long series of repetitions of scarring, drying and burning at the base of the juniper. The time necessary to attain a 36" diameter is in itself a matter of centuries. Consider now that other junipers killed by fire 40 years ago were found to still retain ¼" twigs, and then try to interpret in terms of centuries the meaning of the innumerable stumps of juniper (the wood is almost immune to decay) which dot the surface of the Arizona foothills. Who can doubt that we have in these junipers a graphic record of forest history extending back behind and beyond the Christian era? Who can doubt that this article discloses merely the main broad outlines of the story?

The following instance also tells us something about the intervals at which fires occurred. I mentioned a juniper with a big scar and four successive healings of which the last counted forty rings. The last was considerably the thickest. In a general way I would say that the previous fires probably occurred at intervals of approximately a decade. Ten years is plenty of time for a lusty growth of grass to come back and accumulate the fuel for another fire. This would reconcile my general theory with the known fact that fires injure most species of grass, it being entirely thinkable for the grass to recover from any such injury during a ten-year interval.

The foregoing likewise strengthens the supposition that root competition with grass rather than fire, was the salient factor in keeping down the brush during pre-settlement days. Brush species which coppice with as much vigor as those of the Arizona brushfields could stage quite a comeback during a ten-year surcease of fire if they were not inhibited by an additional competitor like grass roots.

Whether grass competition or fire was the principal deter-rent of timber reproduction is hard to answer because the two factors were always paired, never isolated. Probably either one would have inhibited extensive reproduction. In northern Ari-zona there are great areas where removal of grass by grazing has caused spectacular encroachment of juniper on park areas. But here again both grass competition and fire evidently caused the original park, and both were removed before reproduction came in.

It is very interesting to compare what has happened in the woodland type with what has happened in the semi-desert type immediately below it. Here also old timers testify to a radical encroachment of brush species like mesquite and cat's-claw. They insist, however, that while this semi-desert type originally contained much grass, it never contained enough grass to carry fire. There are no signs of old fires. The encroachment of brush in this type can therefore be ascribed only to the removal of grass competition.

There are many loose masonry walls of Indian origin in the headwaters of drainages both in the woodland and semi-desert types. These have been fondly called "erosion-control works" by some enthusiastic forest officers, but it is perfectly evident that they were built as agriculture terraces, and that their func-tion in erosion control was accidental. It is significant that any number of these terraces now contain heavy brush and even timber. Since they are prehistoric, the Indians could not have had metals, and therefore could not have easily cleared them of timber or brush. Therefore their sites must have been either barren or grassy when the Indians built them. This conforms with the belief that brush has encroached in both the woodland and semi-desert ranges.

In the brush fields of California the drift of administrative policy is toward heavy grazing as a means of reducing fire haz-ard. If the ecology of these California brushfields is similar to the ecology of the Arizona brushfields, it would appear obvious that either my Arizona theory or the California grazing policy is wrong. The point is that there is no similarity. The rainfall of the California brushfields is nearly twice that of the Arizona brushfields. Its seasonal distribution is different, and from what I can learn there is a great deal more duff and more herbs and other inflammable material under the California brush. It would appear, therefore, that the California tendency toward heavier grazing and the tendency in the Southwestern District toward much lighter grazing are not inconsistent because the two regions are not comparable.

The radical encroachment of brush in southern Arizona has had some interesting effects on game. There is one mountain range on the Tonto where the brush has become so thick as to almost prohibit travel, and where a thrifty stock of black bears have established themselves. The old hunters assure me that there were no black bears in these mountains when the country was first settled. It is likewise a significant fact that the wild turkey has been exterminated throughout most of the Arizona brushfields, whereas it has merely been decimated further north. It seems possible that turkeys require a certain proportion of open space in order to thrive. Plenty of open spaces originally existed, but the recent encroachment of brush has abolished them, and possibly thus made the birds fall an easier prey to predatory animals.

The cumulative abnormal erosion which has occurred coincident with the encroachment of brush and the decimation of grass naturally has its worst effect in the siltage of reservoirs. The data kept by Southwestern reclamation interests on siltage of reservoirs is regrettably inadequate, but it is sufficient to indicate one salient fact, viz., that the greater part of the loosened material is at the present time in transit toward the reservoir, rather than already dumped into it. Blockading this detritus in transit is therefore just as important as desilting the storage sites. The methods of blockading it will obviously be a combination of mechanical and vegetative obstructions, and with these foresters should be particularly qualified to deal. This fact further accentuates the responsibility of the Forest Service, and indicates that the watershed work of the future belongs quite as much to the forester as to the hydrographer and engineer.

Journal of Forestry, October 1924

The River of the Mother of God

I AM CONSCIOUS of a considerable personal debt to the continent of South America.

It has given me, for instance, rubber for motor tires, which have carried me to lonely places on the face of Mother Earth where all her ways are pleasantness, and all her paths are peace.

It has given me coffee, and to brew it, many a memorable campfire with the dawn-wind rustling in autumnal trees.

It has given me rare woods, pleasant fruits, leather, medicines, nitrates to make my garden bloom, and books about strange beasts and ancient peoples. I am not unmindful of my obligation for these things. But more than all of these, it has given me the River of the Mother of God.

The river has been in my mind so long that I cannot recall just when or how I first heard of it. All that I remember is that long ago a Spanish Captain, wandering in some far Andean height, sent back word that he had found where a mighty river falls into the trackless Amazonian forest, and disappears. He had named it *El Rio del Madre de Dios.* The Spanish Captain never came back. Like the river, he disappeared. But ever since some maps of South America have shown a short heavy line running eastward beyond the Andes, a river without beginning and without end, and labelled it the River of the Mother of God.

That short heavy line flung down upon the blank vastness of tropical wilderness has always seemed the perfect symbol of The Unknown Places of the earth. And its name, resonant of the clank of silver armor and the cruel progress of the Cross, yet carrying a hush of reverence and a murmur of the prows of galleons on the seven seas, has always seemed the symbol of Conquest,—the Conquest that has reduced those unknown Places, one by one, until now there are none left.

And when I read that MacMillan has planted the Radio among the Eskimos of the furthest polar seas, and that Everest is all but climbed, and that Russia is founding fisheries in Wrangel Land, I know the time is not far off when there will no more be a short line on the map, without beginning and without end; no mighty river to fall from far Andean heights into the Amazonian wilderness, and disappear. Motor boats will sputter through those trackless forests, the clank of steam hoists will be heard in the Mountain of the Sun, and there will be phonographs and chewing gum upon the River of the Mother of God.

No doubt it was "for this the earth lay preparing quintillions of years, for this the revolving centuries truly and steadily rolled." But it marks a new epoch in the history of mankind, an epoch in which Unknown Places disappear as a dominant fact in human life.

Ever since paleolithic man became conscious that his own home hunting ground was only part of a greater world, Unknown Places have been a seemingly fixed fact in human environment, and usually a major influence in human lives. Sumerian tribes, venturing the Unknown Places, found the valley of the Euphrates and an imperial destiny. Phoenician sailors, venturing the unknown seas, found Carthage and Cornwall and established commerce upon the earth. Hanno, Ulysses, Eric, Columbus—history is but a succession of adventures into the Unknown. For unnumbered centuries the test of men and nations has been whether they "chose rather to live miserably in this realm, pestered with inhabitants, or to venture forth, as becometh men, into those remote lands."

And now, speaking geographically, the end of the Unknown is at hand. This fact in our environment, seemingly as fixed as the wind and the sunset, has at last reached the vanishing point. Is it to be expected that it shall be lost from human experience without something likewise being lost from human character?

I think not. In fact, there is an instinctive human reaction against the loss of fundamental environmental influences, of which history records many examples. The chase, for instance, was a fundamental fact in the life of all nomadic tribes. Again and again, when these tribes conquered and took possession of agricultural regions, where they settled down and became civilized and had no further need of hunting, they nevertheless continued it as a sport, and as such it persists to this day, with ten million devotees in America alone.

It is this same reaction against the loss of adventure into the unknown which causes the hundreds of thousands to sally forth each year upon little expeditions, afoot, by pack train, or by canoe, into the odd bits of wilderness which commerce and "development" have regretfully and temporarily left us here and there. Modest adventurers to be sure, compared with Hanno, or Lewis and Clark. But so is the sportsman, with his setter dog in pursuit of partridges, a modest adventurer compared with his Neolithic ancestor in single combat with the Auroch bull. The point is that along with the necessity for expression of racial instincts there happily goes that capacity for illusion which enables little boys to fish happily in wash-tubs. That capacity is a precious thing, if not overworked.

But there is a basic difference between the adventures of the chase and the adventures of wilderness travel. Production of game for the chase can, with proper skill, be superimposed upon agriculture and forestry and can thus be indefinitely perpetuated. But the wilderness cannot be superimposed upon anything. The wilderness and economics are, in every ordinary sense, mutually exclusive. If the wilderness is to be perpetuated at all, it must be in areas exclusively dedicated to that purpose.

We come now to the question: Is it possible to preserve the element of Unknown Places in our national life? Is it practicable to do so, without undue loss in economic values? I say "yes" to both questions. But we must act vigorously and quickly, before the remaining bits of wilderness have disappeared.

Like parks and playgrounds and other "useless" things, any system of wilderness areas would have to be owned and held for public use by the Government. The fortunate thing is that the Government already owns enough of them, scattered here and there in the poorer and rougher parts of the National Forests and National Parks, to make a very good start. The one thing needful is for the Government to draw a line around each one and say: "This is wilderness, and wilderness it shall remain. A place where Americans may venture forth, as becometh men, into remote lands."

Such a policy would not subtract even a fraction of one per cent from our economic wealth, but would preserve a fraction of what has, since first the flight of years began, been wealth to the human spirit.

There is a current advertisement of Wells' Outline of History which says "The unforgivable sin is standing still. In all Nature, to cease to grow is to perish." I suppose this pretty accurately summarizes the rebuttal which the Economic American would make to the proposal of a national system of wilderness playgrounds. But what is standing still? And what constitutes growth? The Economic American has shown very plainly that he thinks growth is the number of ciphers added yearly to the national population and the national bank-roll. But the Gigantosaurus tried out that definition of growth for several million years. He was a quantitative economist of the first water. He added two ciphers to his stature, and a staggering row of them to his numbers. But he perished, the blind victim of natural and "economic" laws. They made him, and they destroyed him.

There has been just one really new thing since the Gigantosaurus. That new thing is Man, the first creature in all the immensities of time and space whose evolution is self-directed. The first creature, in any spiritual sense, to create his own environment. Is it not in that fact, rather than in mere ciphers of dollars or population, that we have grown?

The question of wilderness playgrounds is a question in self-control of environment. If we had not exercised that control in other ways, we would already be in process of destruction by our own ciphers. Wilderness playgrounds simply represent a new need for exercising it in a new direction. Have we grown enough to realize this before it is too late?

I say "too late" because wilderness is the one thing we can not build to order. When our ciphers result in slums, we can tear down enough of them to re-establish parks and playgrounds. When they choke traffic, we can tear down enough of them to build highways and subways. But when our ciphers have choked out the last vestige of the Unknown Places, we cannot build new ones. To artificially create wilderness areas would overwork the capacity for illusion of even little boys with wash-tubs.

Just what is it that is choking out our last vestiges of wilderness? Is it real economic need for farmlands? Go out and see them—they contain no farmlands worthy of the name. Is it real economic need for timber? They contain timber to be sure, much of it better to look at than to saw, but until we start growing timber on the eighty million acres of fire-gutted wastes created by our "economic" system we have small call to begrudge what timber they contain. The thing that is choking out the wilderness is not true economics at all, but rather that Frankenstein which our boosters have builded, the "Good Roads Movement."

This movement, entirely sound and beneficial in its inception, has been boosted until it resembles a gold-rush, with about the same regard for ethics and good craftsmanship. The spilled treasuries of Nature and of the Government seem to incite about the same kind of stampede in the human mind.

In this case the yellow lure is the Motor Tourist. Like Mammon, he must now be spelled with a capital, and as with Mammon, we grovel at his feet, and he rules us with the insolence characteristic of a new god. We offer up our groves and our greenswards for him to camp upon, and he litters them with cans and with rubbish. We hand him our wild life and our wild flowers, and humbly continue the gesture after there are none left to hand. But of all offerings, foolish roads are to him the most pleasing sacrifice.

(Since they are mostly to be paid for by a distant treasury or by a distant posterity, they are likewise pleasing to us.)

And of all foolish roads, the most pleasing is the one that "opens up" some last little vestige of virgin wilderness. With the unholy zeal of fanatics we hunt them out and pile them upon his altar, while from the throats of a thousand luncheon clubs and Chambers of Commerce and Greater Gopher Prairie Associations rises the solemn chant "There is No God but Gasoline and Motor is his Prophet!"

The more benignant aspects of the Great God Motor and the really sound elements of the Good Roads Movement need no defense from me. They are cried from every housetop, and we all know them. What I am trying to picture is the tragic absurdity of trying to whip the March of Empire into a gallop.

Very specifically, I am pointing out that in this headlong stampede for speed and ciphers we are crushing the last remnants of something that ought to be preserved for the spiritual and physical welfare of future Americans, even at the cost of acquiring a few less millions of wealth or population in the long run. Something that has helped build the race for such innumerable centuries that we may logically suppose it will help preserve it in the centuries to come.

Failing this, it seems to me we fail in the ultimate test of our vaunted superiority—the self-control of environment. We fall back into the biological category of the potato bug which exterminated the potato, and thereby exterminated itself.

Typescript, c. December 1924

Conserving the Covered Wagon

ONE EVENING I was talking to a settler in one of those irrigated valleys that stretch like a green ribbon across the colorful wastes of southern Arizona. He was showing me his farm, and he was proud of it. Broad acres of alfalfa bloom, fields of ripening grain, and a dip and a sweep of laden orchards redolent of milk and honey, all created with the labor of his own hands. Over in one corner I noticed a little patch of the original desert, an island of sandy hillocks, sprawling mesquite trees, with a giant cactus stark against the sky, and musical with the sunset whistle of quail. "Why don't you clear and level that too, and complete your farm?" I asked, secretly fearing he intended to do so.

"Oh, that's for my boys—a sample of what I made the farm out of," he replied quietly. There was no further explanation. I might comprehend his idea, or think him a fool, as I chose.

I chose to think him a very wise man—wise beyond his kind and his generation. That little patch of untamed desert enormously increased the significance of his achievement, and conversely, his achievement enormously increased the significance of the little patch. He was handing down to his sons not only a piece of real estate, but a Romance written upon the oldest of all books, the land. The Romance of The March of Empire.

It set me to thinking. Our fathers set great store by this Winning of the West, but what do we know about it? Many of us have never seen what it was won from. And how much less will the next generation know? If we think we are going to learn by cruising round the mountains in a Ford, we are largely deceiving ourselves. There is a vast difference between the days of the "Free Tourist Campground—Wood and Water Furnished," and the Covered Wagon Days.

> "We pitched our tents where the buffalo feed,
>   Unheard of streams were our flagons;
>   And we sowed our sons like the apple seed
>   In the trail of the prairie wagons."

Yes—sowed them so thick that tens of thousands are killed each year trying to keep out of the way of each other's motors.

Is this thickness necessarily a blessing to the sons? Perhaps. But not an unmixed blessing. For those who are so inclined, we might at least preserve a sample of the Covered Wagon Life. For after all, the measure of civilization is in its contrasts. A modern city is a national asset, not because the citizen has planted his iron heel on the breast of nature, but because of the different kinds of man his control over nature has enabled him to be. Saturday morning he stands like a god, directing the wheels of industry that have dominion over the earth. Saturday afternoon he is playing golf on a kindly greensward. Saturday evening he may till a homely garden or he may turn a button and direct the mysteries of the firmament to bring him the words and songs and deeds of all the nations. And if, once in a while, he has the opportunity to flee the city, throw a diamond hitch upon a pack-mule, and disappear into the wilderness of the Covered Wagon Days, he is just that much more civilized than he would be without the opportunity. It makes him one more kind of a man—a pioneer.

We do not realize how many Americans have an instinctive craving for the wilderness life, or how valuable to the Nation has been their opportunity of exercising that instinct, because up to this time the opportunity has been automatically supplied. Little patches of Covered Wagon wilderness have persisted at the very doors of our cities. But now these little parches are being wiped out at a rate which takes one's breath away. And the thing that is wiping them out is the motor car and the motor highway. It is of these, their uses and their abuses, that I would speak.

Motor cars and highways are of course the very instruments which have restored to millions of city dwellers their contact with the land and with nature. For this reason and to this extent they are a benefaction to mankind. But even a benefaction can be carried too far. It was one of Shakespeare's characters who said:

> "For Virtue, grown into a pleurisy
> Dies of its own too-much."

To my mind the Good Roads Movement has become a Good Roads Mania; it has grown into a pleurisy. We are building good roads to give the rancher access to the city, which is good, and to give the city dweller access to recreation in the forests and mountains, which is good, but we now, out of sheer momentum, are thrusting more and ever more roads into every little remaining patch of wilderness, which in many cases is sheer stupidity. For by so doing we are cutting off, irrevocably and forever, our national contact with the Covered Wagon days.

Pick up any outdoor magazine and the chances are that on the first page you will find an article describing the adventures of some well-to-do sportsman who has been to Alaska, or British Columbia, or Africa, or Siberia in search of wilderness and the life and hardy sports that go with it. He has pushed to the Back of Beyond, and he tells of it with infinite zest. It has been his Big Adventure. Why? Because he brought home the tusk of the elephant or the hide of a brown bear? No, fundamentally no. Rather because he has proved himself to be still another kind of man than his friends gave him credit for. He has been, if only for one fleeting month, a pioneer, and met the test. He has justified the Blood of the Conquerors.

But have these well-to-do travelers in foreign wilds a monopoly on the Covered Wagon blood? Here is the point of the whole matter. They have not. In every village and in every city suburb and in every skyscraper are dozens of the self-same blood. But they lack the opportunity. It is the opportunity, not the desire, on which the well-to-do are coming to have a monopoly. And the reason is the gradually increasing destruction of the nearby wilderness by good roads. The American of moderate means can not go to Alaska, or Africa, or British Columbia. He must seek his big adventure in the nearby wilderness, or go without it.

Ten years ago, for instance, there were five big regions in the National Forests of Arizona and New Mexico where the Covered Wagon blood could disport at will. In any one of them a man could pack up a mule and disappear into the tall uncut for a month without ever crossing his back track. Today there is just one of the five left. The Forest Service, the largest custodian of land in either State, has naturally and rightly joined with the good roads movement, and today has built or is helping to build good roads right through the vitals of four of these five big regions. As wilderness, they are gone, and gone forever. So far so good. But shall the Forest Service now do the same with the fifth and last?

Round this last little remnant of the original Southwest lies

an economic empire without any wilderness playground or the
faintest chance of acquiring one. Texas, Oklahoma, and the rich
valleys and mines of Arizona and New Mexico already support
millions of Americans. The high mountains of the National
Forests are their natural and necessary recreation grounds.
The greater part of these mountain areas is already irrevocably
dedicated to the motorized forms of recreation. Is it unreasonable or visionary to ask the Forest Service to preserve the one
remaining portion of unmotorized wilderness for those who
prefer that sort of place?

Would it be unreasonable or visionary to ask the Government to set aside similar remnants of wilderness here and there
throughout the National Forests and National Parks? Say one
such area, if possible, in each State?

As a matter of fact, the officials of the Forest Service are al-
ready considering doing just that. Colonel William B. Greeley,
Chief Forester, in addressing a meeting of the American Game
Protective Association, put it this way:

> "We all recognize what the forest background of the
> United States has meant to this country—how it has given
> stamina and resourcefulness and mental and physical vigor
> to every oncoming generation of Americans. We must pre-
> serve something of that forest background for the future.
> It seems to me that in the National Forests, while we are
> building roads, as we must; while we are developing areas
> for the utilization of timber, as we must; while we are
> opening up extensive regions for the camper, the summer
> vacationist, and the masses of people who have the God-
> given right to enjoy these areas—we should keep here and
> there as part of the picture some bit of wilderness frontier,
> some hinterland of mountain and upland lake that the
> roads and automobiles will have to pass by.
>
> "The law laid down for the guidance of the Forest Ser-
> vice was that these public properties must be administered
> for the greatest good of the greatest number in the long
> run. When Secretary Wilson laid down that rule, prob-
> ably he was thinking more of timber and water and for-
> age than anything else, but today the same rule applies
> just as clearly as it did in the time of Roosevelt in 1905. I

think we can all agree that the greatest good of the greatest number of American citizens in the long run does
require that in their own National Forests there should
be preserved some bits of unspoiled wilderness where the
young America of the future can take to the outdoors in
the right way."

But let no man think that because a few foresters have ten-
tatively formulated a wilderness policy, that the preservation
of a system of wilderness remnants is assured in the National
Forests. Do not forget that the good roads mania, and all forms
of unthinking Boosterism that go with it, constitute a steam
roller the like of which has seldom been seen in the history
of mankind. No steam roller can overwhelm a good idea or
a righteous policy, but it might very readily flatten out, one
by one, the remaining opportunities for applying this particular policy. After these remnants are gone, a correct wilderness
policy would be useless.

What I mean is this: The Forest Service will naturally select
for wilderness playgrounds the roughest areas and those poorest
from the economic standpoint. But it will be physically impossible to find any area which does not embrace some economic
values. Sooner or later some private interest will wish to develop
these values, at which time those who are thinking in terms of
the national development in the broad sense and those who are
thinking of local development in the narrow sense will come to
grips. And forthwith the private interests will invoke the aid of
the steam roller. They always do. And unless the wilderness idea
represents the mandate of an organized, fighting and voting
body of far-seeing Americans, the steam roller will win.

At the present moment, the most needed move is to secure
recognition of the need for a Wilderness Area Policy from the
National Conference on Outdoor Recreation, set up by President Coolidge for the express purpose of coördinating the
many conflicting recreational interests which have arisen in recent years. If the spirit of the Covered Wagon really persists, as
I firmly believe it does, its devotees must speak now, or forever
hold their peace.

Sunset Magazine, March 1925

The Pig in the Parlor

IN THE May 11 SERVICE BULLETIN there is an item from D–6 which says in effect that the "wild-life enthusiasts" need not fret about the invasion of wilderness areas by roads, because in Germany there is a mile of dirt road for every 105 acres of forest, and a mile of hard road for every 220 acres of forest. Germany, it says, spends up to 35 cents per acre per year for forest roads, and because we have not attained such beatitude we need not worry yet about overdoing the road game.

In short, the wilderness area idea is assumed to be an anti-road idea. The assumption is incorrect. It is just exactly as incorrect as Editor Abbott's assumption that recreational development is anti-forestry. My plea is that the wilderness idea be not condemned, especially by foresters, without first acquiring at least a rudimentary understanding of what it is all about.

I do not know of a single "enthusiast" for wilderness areas who denies the need for more forest roads. It is not a question of how many roads, but a question of distribution of roads. The wilderness idea simply affirms that a well-balanced plan for the highest use of National Forests will exclude roads from certain areas so that the unmotorized forms of public recreation will not be left high and dry, just as summer homes are excluded from certain areas so that the camper will not be left high and dry. The only difference is that where a public camp ground requires a forty, a public wilderness area requires a few townships.

Roads and wilderness are merely a case of the pig in the parlor. We now recognize that the pig is all right—for bacon, which we all eat. But there no doubt was a time, soon after the discovery that many pigs meant much bacon, when our ancestors assumed that because the pig was so useful an institution he should be welcomed at all times and places. And I suppose that the first "enthusiast" who raised the question of limiting his distribution was construed to be uneconomic, visionary, and anti-pig.

Service Bulletin (U.S. Forest Service), June 8, 1925

Wilderness as a Form of Land Use

FROM THE earliest times one of the principal criteria of civilization has been the ability to conquer the wilderness and convert it to economic use. To deny the validity of this criterion would be to deny history. But because the conquest of wilderness has produced beneficial reactions on social, political, and economic development, we have set up, more or less unconsciously, the converse assumption that the ultimate social, political, and economic development will be produced by conquering the wilderness entirely—that is, by eliminating it from our environment.

My purpose is to challenge the validity of such an assumption and to show how it is inconsistent with certain cultural ideas which we regard as most distinctly American.

Our system of land use is full of phenomena which are sound as tendencies but become unsound as ultimates. It is sound for a city to grow but unsound for it to cover its entire site with buildings. It was sound to cut down our forests but unsound to run out of wood. It was sound to expand our agriculture, but unsound to allow the momentum of that expansion to result in the present overproduction. To multiply examples of an obvious truth would be tedious. The question, in brief, is whether the benefits of wilderness-conquest will extend to ultimate wilderness-elimination.

The question is new because in America the point of elimination has only recently appeared upon the horizon of foreseeable events. During our four centuries of wilderness-conquest the possibility of disappearance has been too remote to register in the national consciousness. Hence we have no mental language in which to discuss the matter. We must first set up some ideas and definitions.

WHAT IS A WILDERNESS AREA?

The term wilderness, as here used, means a wild, roadless area where those who are so inclined may enjoy primitive modes of travel and subsistence, such as exploration trips by pack-train or canoe.

The first idea is that wilderness is a resource, not only in the physical sense of the raw materials it contains, but also in the sense of a distinctive environment which may, if rightly used, yield certain social values. Such a conception ought not to be difficult, because we have lately learned to think of other forms of land use in the same way. We no longer think of a municipal golf links, for instance, as merely soil and grass.

The second idea is that the value of wilderness varies enormously with location. As with other resources, it is impossible to dissociate value from location. There are wilderness areas in Siberia which are probably very similar in character to parts of our Lake states, but their value to us is negligible, compared with what the value of a similar area in the Lake states would be, just as the value of a golf links would be negligible if located so as to be out of reach of golfers.

The third idea is that wilderness, in the sense of an environment as distinguished from a quantity of physical materials, lies somewhere between the class of non-reproducible resources like minerals, and the reproducible resources like forests. It does not disappear proportionately to use, as minerals do, because we can conceive of a wild area which, if properly administered, could be traveled indefinitely and still be as good as ever. On the other hand, wilderness certainly cannot be built at will, like a city park or a tennis court. If we should tear down improvements already made in order to build a wilderness, not only would the cost be prohibitive, but the result would probably be highly dissatisfying. Neither can a wilderness be grown like timber, because it is something more than trees. The practical point is that if we want wilderness, we must foresee our want and preserve the proper areas against the encroachment of inimical uses.

Fourth, wilderness exists in all degrees, from the little accidental wild spot at the head of a ravine in a Corn Belt woodlot to vast expanses of virgin country—

> *"Where nameless men by nameless rivers wander*
> *And in strange valleys die strange deaths alone."*

What degree of wilderness, then, are we discussing? The answer is, *all degrees.* Wilderness is a relative condition. As a form of land use it cannot be a rigid entity of unchanging content, exclusive of all other forms. On the contrary, it must be a flexible thing, accommodating itself to other forms and blending with them in that highly localized give-and-take scheme of land-planning which employs the criterion of "highest use." By skilfully adjusting one use to another, the land planner builds a balanced whole without undue sacrifice of any function, and thus attains a maximum net utility of land.

Just as the application of the park idea in civic planning varies in degree from the provision of a public bench on a street corner to the establishment of a municipal forest playground as large as the city itself, so should the application of the wilderness idea vary in degree from the wild, roadless spot of a few acres left in the rougher parts of public forest devoted to timber-growing, to wild, roadless regions approaching in size a whole national forest or a whole national park. For it is not to be supposed that a public wilderness area is a new kind of public land reservation, distinct from public forests and public parks. It is rather a new kind of land-dedication within our system of public forests and parks, to be duly correlated with dedications to the other uses which that system is already obligated to accommodate.

Lastly, to round out our definitions, let us exclude from practical consideration any degree of wilderness so absolute as to forbid reasonable protection. It would be idle to discuss wilderness areas if they are to be left subject to destruction by forest fires, or wide open to abuse. Experience has demonstrated, however, that a very modest and unobtrusive framework of trails, telephone line and lookout stations will suffice for protective purposes. Such improvements do not destroy the wild flavor of the area, and are necessary if it is to be kept in usable condition.

WILDERNESS AREAS IN
A BALANCED LAND SYSTEM

What kind of case, then, can be made for wilderness as a form of land use?

To preserve any land in a wild condition is, of course, a reversal of economic tendency, but that fact alone should not condemn the proposal. A study of the history of land utilization shows that good use is largely a matter of good balance—of wise adjustment between opposing tendencies. The modern movements toward diversified crops and live stock on the farm, conservation of eroding soils, forestry, range management, game management public parks—all these are attempts to balance opposing tendencies that have swung out of counterpoise.

One noteworthy thing about good balance is the nature of the opposing tendencies. In its more utilitarian aspect, as seen in modern agriculture, the needed adjustment is between economic uses. But in the public park movement the adjustment is between an economic use, on the one hand, and a purely social use on the other. Yet, after a century of actual experience, even the most rigid economic determinists have ceased to challenge the wisdom of a reasonable reversal of economic tendency in favor of public parks.

I submit that the wilderness is a parallel case. The parallelism is not yet generally recognized because we do not yet conceive of the wilderness environment as a resource. The accessible supply has heretofore been unlimited, like the supply of air-power, or tide-power, or sunsets, and we do not recognize anything as a resource until the demand becomes commensurable with the supply.

Now after three centuries of overabundance, and before we have even realized that we are dealing with a non-reproducible resource, we have come to the end of our pioneer environment and are about to push its remnants into the Pacific. For three centuries that environment has determined the character of our development; it may, in fact, be said that, coupled with the character of our racial stocks, it is the very stuff America is made of. Shall we now exterminate this thing that made us American?

Ouspensky says that, biologically speaking, the determining characteristic of rational beings is that their evolution is self-directed. John Burroughs cites the opposite example of the potato bug, which, blindly obedient to the law of increase, exterminates the potato and thereby exterminates itself. Which are we?

WHAT THE WILDERNESS HAS CONTRIBUTED TO AMERICAN CULTURE

Our wilderness environment cannot, of course, be preserved on any considerable scale as an economic fact. But, like many other receding economic facts, it can be preserved for the ends of sport. But what is the justification of sport, as the word is here used?

Physical combat between men, for instance, for unnumbered centuries was an economic fact. When it disappeared as such, a sound instinct led us to preserve it in the form of athletic sports and games. Physical combat between men and beasts since first the flight of years began was an economic fact, but when it disappeared as such, the instinct of the race led us to hunt and fish for sport. The transition of these tests of skill from an economic to a social basis has in no way destroyed their efficacy as human experiences—in fact, the change may be regarded in some respects as an improvement.

Football requires the same kind of back-bone as battle but avoids its moral and physical retrogressions. Hunting for sport in its highest form is an improvement on hunting for food in that there has been added, to the test of skill, an ethical code which the hunter formulates for himself and must often execute without the moral support of bystanders.

In these cases the surviving sport is actually an improvement on the receding economic fact. Public wilderness areas are essentially a means for allowing the more virile and primitive forms of outdoor recreation to survive the receding economic fact of pioneering. These forms should survive because they likewise are an improvement on pioneering itself.

There is little question that many of the attributes most distinctive of America and Americans are the impress of the wilderness and the life that accompanied it. If we have any such thing as an American culture (and I think we have), its distinguishing marks are a certain vigorous individualism combined with ability to organize, a certain intellectual curiosity bent to practical ends, a lack of subservience to stiff social forms, and an intolerance of drones, all of which are the distinctive characteristics of successful pioneers. These, if anything, are the indigenous part of our Americanism, the qualities that set it apart as a new rather than an imitative contribution to civilization. Many observers see these qualities not only bred into our people, but built into our institutions. Is it not a bit beside the point for us to be so solicitous about preserving those institutions without giving so much as a thought to preserving the environment which produced them and which may now be one of our effective means of keeping them alive?

WILDERNESS LOCATIONS

But the proposal to establish wilderness areas is idle unless acted on before the wilderness has disappeared. Just what is the present status of wilderness remnants in the United States?

Large areas of half a million acres and upward are disappearing very rapidly, not so much by reason of economic need, as by extension of motor roads. Smaller areas are still relatively abundant in the mountainous parts of the country, and will so continue for a long time.

The disappearance of large areas is illustrated by the following instance: In 1910 there were six roadless regions in Arizona and New Mexico, ranging in size from half a million to a million acres, where the finest type of mountain wilderness pack trips could be enjoyed. Today roads have eliminated all but one area of about half a million acres.

In California there were seven large areas ten years ago, but today there are only two left unmotorized.

In the Lake states no large unmotorized playgrounds remain. The motor launch, as well as the motor road, is rapidly wiping out the remnants of canoe country.

In the Northwest large roadless areas are still relatively numerous. The land-plans of the Forest Service call for exclusion of roads from several areas of moderate size.

Unless the present attempts to preserve such areas are greatly strengthened and extended, however, it may be predicted with certainty that, except in the Northwest, all of the large areas already in public ownership will be invaded by motors in another decade.

In selecting areas for retention as wilderness, the vital factor of location must be more decisively recognized. A few areas in the national forests of Idaho or Montana are better than none, but, after all, they will be of limited usefulness to the citizen of Chicago or New Orleans who has a great desire but a small purse and a short vacation. Wild areas in the poor lands of the Ozarks and the Lake states would be within his reach. For the great urban populations concentrated on the Atlantic seaboards, wild areas in both ends of the Appalachians would be especially valuable.

Are the remaining large wilderness areas disappearing so

rapidly because they contain agricultural lands suitable for settlement? No; most of them are entirely devoid of either existing or potential agriculture. Is it because they contain timber which should be cut? It is true that some of them do contain valuable timber, and in a few cases this fact is leading to a legitimate extension of logging operations; but in most of the remaining wilderness the timber is either too thin and scattered for exploitation, or else the topography is too difficult for the timber alone to carry the cost of roads or railroads. In view of the general belief that lumber is being overproduced in relation to the growing scarcity of stumpage, and will probably so continue for several decades, the sacrifice of wilderness for timber can hardly be justified on grounds of necessity.

Generally speaking, it is not timber, and certainly not agriculture, which is causing the decimation of wilderness areas, but rather the desire to attract tourists. The accumulated momentum of the good-roads movement constitutes a mighty force, which, skilfully manipulated by every little mountain village possessed of a chamber of commerce and a desire to become a metropolis, is bringing about the extension of motor roads into every remaining bit of wild country, whether or not there is economic justification for the extension.

Our remaining wild lands are wild because they are poor. But this poverty does not deter the booster from building expensive roads through them as bait for motor tourists.

I am not without admiration for this spirit of enterprise in backwoods villages, nor am I attempting a censorious pose toward the subsidization of their ambitions from the public treasuries; nor yet am I asserting that the resulting roads are devoid of any economic utility. I do maintain, (1) that such extensions of our road systems into the wilderness are seldom yielding a return sufficient to amortize the public investment; (2) that even where they do yield such a return, their construction is not necessarily in the public interest, any more than obtaining an economic return from the last vacant lot in a parkless city would be in the public interest. On the contrary, the public interest demands the careful planning of a system of wilderness areas and the permanent reversal of the ordinary economic process within their borders.

To be sure, to the extent that the motor-tourist business

is the cause of invasion of these wilderness playgrounds, one kind of recreational use is merely substituted for another. But this substitution is a vitally serious matter from the point of view of good balance. It is just as unwise to devote 100% of the recreational resources of our public parks and forests to motorists as it would be to devote 100% of our city parks to merry-go-rounds. It would be just as unreasonable to ask the aged to indorse a park with only swings and trapezes, or the children a park with only benches, or the motorists a park with only bridle-paths, as to ask the wilderness recreationist to indorse a universal priority for motor roads. Yet that is what our land plans—or rather lack of them—are now doing; and so sacred is our dogma of "development" that there is no effective protest. The inexor-able molding of the individual American to a standardized pattern in his economic activities makes all the more undesirable this unnecessary standardization of his recreational tastes.

PRACTICAL ASPECTS OF ESTABLISHING WILDERNESS AREAS

Public wilderness playgrounds differ from all other public areas in that both their establishment and maintenance would entail very low costs. The wilderness is the one kind of public land that requires no improvements. To be sure, a simple system of fire protection and administrative patrol would be required, but the cost would not exceed two or three cents per acre per year. Even that would not usually be a new cost, since the greater part of the needed areas are already under administration in the rougher parts of the national forests and parks. The action needed is the permanent differentiation of a suitable system of wild areas within our national park and forest system.

In regions such as the Lake states, where the public domain has largely disappeared, lands would have to be purchased; but that will have to be done, in any event, to round out our park and forest system. In such cases a lesser degree of wilderness may have to suffice, the only ordinary utilities practicable to exclude being cottages, hotels, roads, and motor boats.

The retention of certain wild areas in both national forests and national parks will introduce a healthy variety into the wilderness idea itself, the forest areas serving as public hunting grounds, the park areas as public wild-life sanctuaries, and both kinds as public playgrounds in which the wilderness environments and modes of travel may be preserved and enjoyed.

THE CULTURAL VALUE OF WILDERNESS

Are these things worth preserving? This is the vital question. I cannot give an unbiased answer. I can only picture the day that is almost upon us when canoe travel will consist in paddling in the noisy wake of a motor launch and portaging through the back yard of a summer cottage. When that day comes, canoe travel will be dead, and dead, too, will be a part of our Americanism. Joliet and La Salle will be words in a book, Champlain will be a blue spot on a map, and canoes will be merely things of wood and canvas, with a connotation of white duck pants and bathing "beauties."

The day is almost upon us when a pack-train must wind its way up a graveled highway and turn out its bell-mare in the pasture of a summer hotel. When that day comes the pack-train will be dead, the diamond hitch will be merely rope, and Kit Carson and Jim Bridger will be names in a history lesson. Rendezvous will be French for "date," and Forty-Nine will be the number preceding fifty. And thenceforth the march of empire will be a matter of gasoline and four-wheel brakes.

European outdoor recreation is largely devoid of the thing that wilderness areas would be the means of preserving in this country. Europeans do not camp, cook, or pack in the woods for pleasure. They hunt and fish when they can afford it, but their hunting and fishing is merely hunting and fishing, staged in a setting of ready-made hunting lodges, elaborate fare, and hired beaters. The whole thing carries the atmosphere of a picnic rather than that of a pack trip. The test of skill is confined almost entirely to the act of killing, itself. Its value as a human experience is reduced accordingly.

There is a strong movement in this country to preserve the distinctive democracy of our field sports by preserving free hunting and fishing, as distinguished from the European condition of commercialized hunting and fishing privileges. Public shooting grounds and organized cooperative relations between sportsmen and landowners are the means proposed for keeping these sports within reach of the American of moderate means. Free hunting and fishing is a most worthy objective, but it deals with only one of the two distinctive characteristics of American sport. The other characteristic is that our test of skill is primarily the act of living in the open, and only secondarily the act of killing game. It is to preserve this primary characteristic that public wilderness playgrounds are necessary.

Herbert Hoover aptly says that there is no point in increasing the average American's leisure by perfecting the organization of industry, if the expansion of industry is allowed to destroy the recreational resources on which leisure may be beneficially employed. Surely the wilderness is one of the most valuable of these resources, and surely the building of unproductive roads in the wrong places at public expense is one of the least valuable of industries. If we are unable to steer the Juggernaut of our own prosperity, then surely there is an impotence in our vaunted Americanism that augurs ill for our future. The self-directed evolution of rational beings does not apply to us until we become collectively, as well as individually, rational and self-directing.

Wilderness as a form of land-use is, of course, premised on a qualitative conception of progress. It is premised on the assumption that enlarging the range of individual experience is as important as enlarging the number of individuals; that the expansion of commerce is a means, not an end; that the environment of the American pioneers had values of its own, and was not merely a punishment which they endured in order that we might ride in motors. It is premised on the assumption that the rocks and rills and templed hills of this America are something more than economic materials, and should not be dedicated exclusively to economic use.

The vanguard of American thought on the use of land has already recognized all this, in theory. Are we too poor in spirit, in pocket, or in idle acres to recognize it likewise in fact?

Journal of Land & Public Utility Economics, October 1925

Mr. Thompson's Wilderness

IN THE May 14 Bulletin Mr. Manly Thompson of D–4 demolishes the wilderness policy. He does it so effectively that I am led to wonder whether the resulting corpse was alive to begin with. Some of its original attributes, as discerned by Mr. Thompson, make me think not.

First and most important, Mr. Thompson discovers that wilderness areas are at bottom semi-private preserves, to be kept for the benefit of the few who have the time and money to travel in them.

This imputation of an unholy alliance with Wealth can best be checked by observing the users of our going areas, such as the Superior or the Gila.

I have seen fellows who looked wealthy, preceded by a safari of guides, puffing over the trails of each, but they didn't look as if they owned the wilderness.

I have also seen fellows who I know were wealthy on our Forest Highways, but nobody has yet condemned our good roads policy on these grounds.

Secondly, Mr. Thompson wonders whether a self-respecting wilderness enthusiast would really want to play in a wilderness marked out and protected by a paternal government.

It all depends on what is self-respect. Would a self-respecting athlete play at a game rather than wait for a real battle? Would a self-respecting boy fish in a wash-tub? Maybe,—if he has to. The capacity for illusion may not be self-respect; enthusiasm for half-loaves may be bogus; but the world continues habitable by reason of these failings.

But these matters are all details. They are not the issue. The issue is whether any human undertaking as vast as the National Forests can be run on a single objective idea, executed by an invariable formula. The formula in question is: Land + forestry = boards. We need to use it more than we do. But can we run the National Forests by it alone?

Many big moves have gone on the rocks trying to do the like. Ours will survive to the extent that we realize that it, or any other phase of the social order, is necessarily an intelligent compromise between conflicting principles, as distinguished

287

from the complete dominance of the one most recently re-discovered.

Whether we like it or no, National Forest policy is outgrowing the question of boards. We are confronted by issues in sociology as well as silviculture,—we are asked to show by our deeds whether we think human minorities are worth bothering about; whether we regard the current ideals of the majority as ultimate truth or as a phase of social evolution; whether we weigh the value of any human need (like recreation) wholly by quantitative measurements; whether we too have forgotten that economic prosperity is a means, not an end.

These issues do not often come up in running a real estate office or selling shoes. They always come up in founding a State or an industry, or in pioneering any great and new departure in human affairs. The National Forests are such. The wilderness idea is a small but significant outgrowth of the idea of National Forests. Its importance is that of a test case. The decision, in my opinion, will indicate whether the U.S. Forest Service is tending to become a federal bureau which executes the laws, or a national enterprise which makes history.

To Mr. Thompson and to any forester of like mind I would say what Voltaire said to his scoffing friend: "It is the duty of a man like you to have preferences, but not exclusions."

Service Bulletin (U.S. Forest Service), June 6, 1928

The American Game Policy in a Nutshell

SEVERAL CENTURIES ago a group of doctors got into an argument over the question of whether or no the blood circulates. They banged the table long and mightily, proving to each other it must be so, and that it couldn't be so. When they were nearly worn out, one of them had the brilliant idea of trying an experiment to find out whether it were so or not. Thereupon the argument ended, and the doctors had time to tend their patients.

We conservationists are the doctors of our game supply. We have many ideas as to what needs to be done, and these ideas quite naturally conflict. We are in danger of pounding the table about them, instead of going out on the land and giving them a trial. The only really new thing which this game policy suggests is that we quit arguing over abstract ideas, and instead go out and try them.

The idea of settling mooted questions by experiment is often ridiculously simple as a matter of hindsight, but it is not so simple as a matter of foresight. It seems like a waste of time, and a dangerous example, to give the other fellow's ideas a trial when we know to begin with that they are wrong. Nevertheless there is really grave danger that if we do not make these concessions, nothing at all will be tried, and there will be no progress.

Game conservation is at this moment in a particularly difficult stage of its development. The set of ideas which served to string out the remnants of the virgin game supply, and to which many of us feel an intense personal loyalty, seem to have reached the limit of their effectiveness. Something new must be done. Nearly all of us are agreed what it is, but there are differences of opinion about who should do it, what methods should be used, and who should pay for it, and how. The differences of opinion are not so numerous, however, as to render it at all impracticable to try all of them. This game policy simply enumerates some of these differences, and urges that they be subject to the test of experience.

The committee which drafted the tentative document for discussion at the Seventeenth Annual Game Conference included almost as many diverse opinions as any other group of sportsmen. I think that we taught each other a good deal about how not to be unduly afraid of the other fellow's proposition. If it is bad, a trial will demonstrate that fact much more quickly than pounding the table. If it is good, the same is true.

The writing of this policy, and its hoped-for adoption, is hardly a beginning of what needs to be done. There remains the much bigger job of organizing and executing the local demonstrations which the policy advocates. This is where the real skill and leadership will be required. The kind of demonstration I have reference to is illustrated by the one now under way in Ingham County, Michigan. It seeks to develop a system of game management executed by organized farmers and supported by organized sportsmen, and to see whether such a system can actually produce game by paying the farmer for labor and materials rather than for shooting privileges. We have argued this question for a decade, but I dare say that the Michigan experiment will convince more people what the answer is than another decade of debate.

A vote for the adoption of this policy is, in my opinion, a vote for the idea of experimentation, rather than a vote for any one of the particular systems to be experimented with. It must be freely admitted, however, that a vote for this policy is an admission that things are not as they should be, and that radical changes are in order. If there be any one who thinks that game conservation is "progressing splendidly," let him vote no.

A vote for this policy is also an admission that sportsmen are not the only group concerned with game conservation. If there be any one who thinks that we can solve the game problem without going into full and equal partnership with the land-owner and the protectionist, let him vote no.

If there are any hidden meanings in the policy, they are not intended to be there, and the purpose of the discussions is to bring them out into the daylight.

I want to thank the members of the committee for the hard and often tedious work which they have contributed during the last two years, and for the complete absence of haggling over petty detail which has characterized their negotiations.

There will, of course, be opposition to the policy. This is as it should be. If the opposition can point out enough fallacies and errors to warrant rejection, well and good. I will only add this: that to reject the policy without undertaking to formulate a better one will be akin to suicide.

I have four reasons behind this statement.

The game stock, for one thing, is losing by delay. We are still losing stock, range, and even species.

Second, this drought allowed grazing and fire to shrink our covers on intensively used land as much in one year as in five ordinary years. Some mechanism for reversing the continued loss of our richest game ranges must get under way.

Third, the agricultural depression represents a priceless opportunity to plant the idea of game as a secondary farm crop, wholly free from any foreseeable overproduction.

Fourth, we sportsmen are on the carpet. Many other groups are watching us, some with interest, others with something nearing exasperation. I am afraid the farmers, without whom we can do nothing, are among these. Our present position is a defensive one. Our critics are no more reasonable than we are, but they tend to have the public ear. Our whole situation demands a positive program; an offensive strategy. Shouting outworn formulas only makes matters worse. We need a game policy.

Transactions of the 17th American Game Conference, December 1–2, 1930

Game and Wild Life Conservation

THIS IS a reply to Mr. T. T. McCabe's well written and persuasive *exposé* of two recent manifestations of the sportsman's movement: my "Game Survey of the North Central States," and the several publications issued by "More Game Birds in America." Both are, I take it, inclusively condemned as "a framework of pernicious doctrines, too often speciously glossed over."

Mr. McCabe's attitude raises what seems to me a fundamental issue. I hope that it may provoke some badly needed cerebration among both protectionists and sportsmen, and especially among those intergrades like myself, who share the aspirations of both.

There are many sportsmen who laugh at any attempt to embody the protectionist point-of-view in any game program. "Whatever you do the protectionists will be against it." Mr. McCabe's paper furnishes scant comfort to those of us who have been holding out against this attitude, because we see in it the indefinite continuation of the present deadlock, from which the sharpest pens gain much glory, but the game gains nothing except a further chance to disappear.

"More Game Birds" on the one hand, and the "Game Survey" (as further developed in the "American Game Policy") on the other, represent the opposite wings of the sportsman's camp. From their very inception they agreed to disagree on the very issues with respect to which Mr. McCabe presumably finds them both "pernicious," namely: predator control, exotics, degree of commercialization, and artificial propagation. This divergence, great enough to seem fundamental to two groups of hardened sportsmen, would, I had hoped, be perceptible to readers of the *Condor*.

I do not imply that Mr. McCabe should agree with either "More Game Birds" or myself on these moot questions. I ask, though, whether it is good for conservation for him to dismiss both, with one breath, as equally subversive of what he considers sound policy. (I think this is not too strong a statement, since Mr. McCabe says "these proposals are an offer . . . to the

292

nation, for its game birds," to which he would reply, "Not for sale.")

Of course, no disagreement is ever as simple as it looks on paper. A partial explanation of this one lies, I think, in the fact that Mr. McCabe's game policy, whether he realizes it or not, consists of a system of *personal wishes* which might be realized if America consisted of 120 million ornithologists, whereas mine is a system of *proposed public actions* designed to fit the unpleasant fact that America consists largely of business men, farmers, and "Rotarians," busily playing the national game of economic expansion. Most of them admit that birds, trees, and flowers are nice to have around, but few of them would admit that the present "depression" in waterfowl is more important than the one in banks, or that the status of the blue goose has more bearing on the cultural future of America than the price of U. S. Steel.

Now if Mr. McCabe and I had the courage to challenge this universal priority for things material and things economic, we might consistently hoist the banner "Not For Sale" and die heroically under the heels of the mob. But have we not already compromised ourselves? I realize that every time I turn on an electric light, or ride on a Pullman, or pocket the unearned increment on a stock, or a bond, or a piece of real estate, I am "selling out" to the enemies of conservation. When I submit these thoughts to a printing press, I am helping cut down the woods. When I pour cream in my coffee, I am helping to drain a marsh for cows to graze, and to exterminate the birds of Brazil. When I go birding or hunting in my Ford, I am devastating an oil field, and re-electing an imperialist to get me rubber. Nay more: when I father more than two children I am creating an insatiable need for more printing presses, more cows, more coffee, more oil, and more rubber, to supply which more birds, more trees, and more flowers will either be killed, or what is just as destructive, evicted from their several environments.

What to do? I see only two courses open to the likes of us. One is to go live on locusts in the wilderness, if there is any wilderness left. The other is surreptitiously to set up within the economic Juggernaut certain new cogs and wheels whereby the residual love of nature, inherent even in "Rotarians," may be made to recreate at least a fraction of those values which their love of "progress" is destroying. A briefer way to put it is: if we want Mr. Babbitt to rebuild outdoor America, we must let him use the same tools wherewith he destroyed it. He knows no other.

I by no means imply that Mr. McCabe should agree with this view. I do imply that to accept the economic order which is destroying wild life disqualifies us from rejecting any and all economic tools for its restoration, on the grounds that such tools are impure and unholy.

With what other than economic tools, for instance, can we cope with progressive eviction of game (and most other wild life) from our rich agricultural lands by clean farming and drainage? Does anyone still believe that restrictive game laws alone will halt the wave of destruction which sweeps majestically across the continent, regardless of closed seasons, paper refuges, bird-books-for-school-children, game farms, Izaak Walton Leagues, Audubon Societies, or the other feeble palliatives which we protectionists and sportsmen, jointly or separately, have so far erected as barriers in its path? Does Mr. McCabe know a way to induce the average farmer to leave the birds some food and cover without paying him for it? To raise the fund for such payment without in some way taxing sportsmen?

I have tried to build a mechanism whereby the sportsmen and the Ammunition Industry could contribute financially to the solution of this problem, without dictating the answer themselves. The mechanism consists of a series of game fellowships, set up in the agricultural colleges, to examine the question of whether slick-and-clean agriculture is really economic, and if not, to advise farmers how they can, by leaving a little cover and food, raise a game crop, and market the surplus by sale of shooting privileges to sportsmen. This mechanism is, I take it, specious. Have the protectionists a better one to offer?

Another mechanism which I have tried to build is the committee of sportsmen and protectionists charged with setting forth a new wild life policy. Has Mr. McCabe read it?

These things I have done, and I make no apology for them. Even if they should ultimately succeed, they will not restore the good old days of free hunting of wholly natural wild life (which I loved as well as Mr. McCabe), but they may restore something. That something will be more native to America, and available on more democratic terms, than "More Game Birds" pheasants, even though it be less so than Mr. McCabe's dreams of days gone by.

Let me admit that my cogs and wheels are designed to perpetuate wild life to shoot, as well as wild life to look at. This is because I believe that hunting takes rank with agriculture and nature study as one of three fundamentally valuable human contacts with the soil. Secondly, because hunting revenue offers the only available "coin of the realm" for buying from Mr. Babbitt the environmental modifications necessary to offset the inroads of industry.

I admit the possibility that I am wrong about hunting. The total cessation of it would certainly conserve some forms of wild life in some places. Any ecologist must, however, admit that the resulting distribution and assortment of species would be very irregular and arbitrary, and quite unrelated to human needs. The richest lands would be totally devoid of game because of lack of cover, and the poorer lands nearly so because of the lack of food. The intermediate zones might have a great deal of game. Each species would shrink to those localities where economic accident offered the requisite assortment of environmental requirements. That same condition—namely the fortuitous (as distinguished from purposeful) make-up of wild life environments—shares, with overshooting, the credit for our present deplorable situation.

The protectionists will, at this point, remind me of the possibilities of inviolate sanctuaries, publicly owned, in which habitable environments are perpetuated at public expense. Let us by all means have as many as possible. But will Mr. Babbitt vote the necessary funds for the huge expansion in sanctuaries which we need? He hasn't so far. It is "blood money" which has bought a large part of what we have. Moreover, sanctuaries propose to salvage only a few samples of wild life. I, for one, demand more. I demand of Mr. Babbitt that game and wildlife be one of the normal products of every farm, and the enjoyment of it a part of the normal environment of every boy, whether he live next door to a public sanctuary or elsewhere.

Mr. McCabe taxes me with omitting any mention of game production on public lands, where the one-gallus hunter will have free access to it. I can only infer that he has not read the

American Game Policy. Has any group ever proposed a larger public land program, and called for more wildlife production thereon? The Policy admits, to be sure, the unpleasant fact that lands must be cheap in order to be public. It advocates the paid-hunting system only for those lands too expensive for the public to own.

Finally Mr. McCabe taxes me with too much interest in exotics. Modesty forbids me to refute this charge in detail. I have persuaded two states to go out of the pheasant business, and several others to limit it to half their area. I devised the "glaciation hypothesis" which seems to exclude pheasants from about a third of the United States. On the other hand, I have recommended the continuation of pheasants and Hungarians in certain regions where economic changes have so radically altered the environment as to make the restoration of native game prohibitive in cost. Just what native species would Mr. McCabe recommend for east-central Wisconsin, or for northern Iowa, or for farm land in Massachusetts?

Let it by no chance be inferred that because I speak as a sportsman I defend the whole history of the sportsman's movement. Hindsight shows that history contains any number of blunders, much bad ecology, and not a few actions which must be construed as either stubbornness or hypocrisy. For every one of these, one could point out a counterpart in the history of the protectionists, only there has been no "Emergency Committee" with either the means or the desire to compile and advertise them. Fifteen years ago, for instance, the protectionists closed the prairie chicken in Iowa, and then sat calmly by while plow and cow pushed the species almost to the brink of oblivion. Was this a blunder? Yes—but what of it? Is there any human aspiration which ever scored a victory without losing to some extent its capacity for self-criticism? The worthiness of any cause is not measured by its clean record, but by its readiness to see the blots when they are pointed out, and to change its mind. Is there not some way in which our two factions can point out each other's sophistries and blunders, without losing sight of our common love for what Mr. Babbitt is trampling under foot? Must the past mistakes of each group automatically condemn every future effort of either to correct them?

To me, the most hopeful sign in the sportsman's movement

is that several little groups have publicly avowed that the old program is a failure. Each is struggling to devise a new formula. I am conceited enough to believe that the formula my little group is trying to put together comes as near meeting the ugly realities of economics on the one hand, and the ideals of the protectionists on the other, as any yet devised. Mr. McCabe's paper will neither help nor hinder its future acceptance or rejection among sportsmen, but it may hinder its thoughtful consideration by the protectionist camp, and thus prevent what I had devoutly hoped for: their active participation in its development, modification and growth.

Lest this be construed as an idle boast, let me point out that as chairman of the Game Policy Committee, I asked the A. O. U. to appoint a representative to sit on or with the Committee, and to pull the reins whenever the Committee got into proposals subversive of the protectionists' point of view. He has not yet pulled. I hereby invite Mr. McCabe to sit with him.

In short, I beg for a little selectivity in weighing the new departures proposed by the other fellow. I also pray for the day when some little group of protectionists will publicly avow that their old formula of restriction is not the whole Alpha-to-Omega of conservation. With both sides in doubt as to the infallibility of their own past dogmas, we might actually hang together long enough to save some wild life. At present, we are getting good and ready to hang separately.

The Condor, March–April 1932

A History of Ideas in Game Management
(from *Game Management*)

GAME MANAGEMENT IS the art of making land produce sustained annual crops of wild game for recreational use.

Its nature is best understood by comparing it with the other land-cropping arts, and by viewing its present ideas and practices against a background of their own history. This chapter compares game management with other forms of agriculture, and sketches its evolution in space and time.

Comparisons. Like the other agricultural arts, game management produces a crop by controlling the environmental factors which hold down the natural increase, or productivity, of the seed stock.

The various arts differ greatly, however, in the degree of control which they attempt to exert, and in the nature of the seed stocks which they grow.

Game management and forestry employ natural species. The bobwhite quail produced by management, and the mature white pine produced by silviculture, are indistinguishable in both form and behavior from their aboriginal progenitors. Compare these now with the products of horticulture, agronomy, and animal husbandry. Who would recognize, without being told, the identity in origin of the Yellow Dent corn and the lowly teosinthe; of a Hereford steer and a wild ox; of a Grimes Golden and the wild apple of Eden?

Game management and forestry grow natural species in an environment not greatly altered for the purpose in hand, relying on partial control of a few factors to enhance the yield above what unguided nature would produce. Their controls are barely visible; an observer, unless he were an expert, could see no difference between managed and unmanaged terrain. Hence their success depends more on the exercise of skill in the selection of the right factors and the right controls, than on heavy investments of labor or materials.

The other forms of agriculture, on the other hand, more or less completely rebuild the environment by cultivation, so that the crop competes with nothing but itself, and must usually be replanted each year. Most domesticated plants and animals are incapable of survival in the wild state, much less of perpetuating themselves as wild populations.

Game farming is an intensified form of game management which propagates wild species in confinement, usually for later release as wild seed stock, or as a supplement to the wild crop.

In game, as in forestry and agriculture, there is no sharp line between the practice which merely exploits a natural supply, and the practice which harvests a crop produced by management. Any practice may be considered as entitled to be called game management if it controls one or more factors with a view to maintaining or enhancing the yield.

The definition of game management which opens this chapter specifies *wild* game *for recreational use*. The purpose of attaching these specifications is to introduce, at the outset, a qualitative as well as a quantitative criterion of what constitutes successful practice. The production of tame game for use as meat is animal husbandry. Its harvesting is hardly recreation. A later chapter on esthetics asserts that the recreational value of game is inverse to the artificiality of its origin, and hence in a broad way to the degree of control exercised in its production.

There are all degrees of control. What degree represents the best compromise between quantity and quality is a perplexing problem in esthetics and social engineering. It seems reasonable to accept some moderate degree of control, rather than to lose species, or to suffer the restriction of sport to those financially able to follow the wholly wild game of the shrinking frontier into other lands. A discussion of these questions will follow in Chapter XVI.

History shows that game management nearly always has its beginnings in the control of the hunting factor. Other controls are added later. The sequence seems to be about as follows:

1. Restriction of hunting.
2. Predator control.
3. Reservation of game lands (as parks, forests, refuges, etc.).
4. Artificial replenishment (restocking and game farming).
5. Environmental controls (control of food, cover, special factors, and disease).

North America has reached the stage where controls of the fifth class are becoming necessary. The present game conservation movement is groping toward the realization of this fact.

Evolution in Europe and Asia. The practice of some degree of game management dates back to the beginnings of human history. Taverner (1930) has pointed out that laws for the regulation of hunting have their origin in the tribal taboos which grew up in the early stages of social evolution. The tribes observing taboos which were biologically effective in preserving the game supply were more likely to survive and prosper, he believes, than the tribes which did not. In short, hunting customs, like plant and animal species, were evolved by a process of selection, in which survival was determined by successful competition. Game laws grew out of these hunting customs.

The first written restriction on the taking of game is probably that contained in the Mosaic Law. In the Book of the Covenant, in which are detailed "the statutes and the judgments which ye shall observe . . . in the land which the Lord . . . hath given thee to possess," Moses decrees:

> "If a bird's nest chance to be before thee in the way, in any tree or on the ground, with young ones or eggs, and the dam sitting upon the young, or upon the eggs, thou shalt not take the dam with the young: thou shalt in any wise let the dam go, but the young thou mayest take unto thyself; that it may be well with thee, and that thou mayest prolong thy days." (Deuteronomy 22:6.)

The plainly implied intent is conservation of the "dam" or hen as breeding stock. The phraseology is as circumstantial and repetitive as the act of any modern legislature, save only for the discreet omission of what shall be done with eggs. However, even modern "Committees on Fish and Game" have been known to be ambiguous.

The Mosaic game law was evidently an advance beyond that of his Egyptian taskmasters, whose spirited depiction of hunting scenes shows them to have been keen sportsmen (Pratt, 1923), but whose records reveal no worries over the conservation of sport.

The Greeks and Romans had game laws, but the objective was not the conservation of sport. Solon forbade the Athenians to hunt, because they "gave themselves up to the chase, to the neglect of the mechanical arts." Not all of the Greek leaders, however, were so strait-laced. Xenophon, in an oft-quoted passage, asserts:

> "Men who love sport will reap therefrom no small advantage . . . it is an excellent training for war. . . . Such men, if required to make a trying march . . . will not break down; . . . they will be able to sleep on a hard bed and keep good watch over the post entrusted to them. In advance against the enemy they will . . . obey their orders, for it is thus wild animals are taken. . . . They will have learned steadfastness; . . . they will be able to save themselves . . . in marshy, precipitous, or otherwise dangerous ground, for from experience they will be quite at home in it. Men like these . . . have rallied and fought against the victorious enemy . . . and have beaten them by their courage and endurance."

Thus, as between Solon and Xenophon, we have the first emergence of that still mooted question: Is sport an asset to society?

The Roman emperor Justinian recognized the right of an owner of land to forbid another from killing game on his property, but the issue was one of trespass, not conservation. We find no game management in the Græco-Roman culture.

Curiously enough the first clear record of a well-rounded system of game management for conservation purposes is found not in Europe, but in the Mongol Empire. Marco Polo, in the narrative of his travels across Asia, thus describes the game laws of Kublai, "The Great Khan" (A.D. 1259–1294):

> "There is an order which prohibits every person throughout all the countries subject to the Great Khan, from daring to kill hares, roebucks, fallow deer, stags, or other animals of that kind, or any large birds, between the months of March and October. This is that they may increase and multiply; and as the breach of this order is attended with punishment, game of every description increases prodigiously."

The phrase, "this is that they may increase and multiply," leaves no doubt as to the intent of Kublai's edicts.

Kublai's technique had already evolved beyond mere control of hunting. Near the city of Changanoor in Cathay, Marco Polo found on the Khan's preserves great food patches and a complete system of winter feeding and cover control. He relates that:

> "At this place . . . there is also a fine plain, where is found in great numbers, cranes, pheasants, partridges, and other birds. He [the Khan] derives the highest degree of amusement from sporting with gerfalcons and hawks, the game being here in vast abundance.
>
> "Near to this city is a valley frequented by great numbers of partridges and quails, for whose food the Great Khan causes millet, and other grains suitable to such birds, to be sown along the sides of it every season, and gives strict command that no person shall dare to reap the seed; in order that the birds may not be in want of nourishment. Many keepers, likewise, are stationed there for the preservation of the game, that it may not be taken or destroyed, as well as for the purpose of throwing the millet to the birds during the winter. So accustomed are they to this feeding, that upon the grain being scattered and the man's whistling, they immediately assemble from every quarter. The Great Khan also directs that a number of small buildings be prepared for their shelter during the night; and, in consequence of these attentions, he always finds abundant sport when he visits this country; and even in the winter, at which season, on account of the severity of the cold, he does not reside there, he has camel-loads of the birds sent to him, wherever his court may happen to be at the time."

This is the earliest known instance of food and cover control combined with restrictions on hunting. Its completeness implies a long previous course of evolution. Although now six centuries old, it sets a pace in management technique which our most modern state would be hard pressed to follow. Kublai's ideas of democracy in sport are of course another matter. They would need some revision.

Game management in feudal Europe, a century after the days of Kublai Khan's food patches, had not yet learned to control either food or cover. It had, however, developed the regulation of hunting (in the interests of the ruling class) to a high degree—so high that the rebellion of the "one gallus" yeomanry, as personified by Robin Hood, ultimately constituted one of the forces which overthrew the feudal system. These hunting controls began as customs rather than laws. A minute and circumstantial account of such customs is given by Edward, second Duke of York, Master of Game to his cousin. Henry IV, in his *litel symple book, Master of Game*, written between 1406 and 1413. (Incidentally this same Edward appears as villain in Shakespeare's *Richard II*. He met his death as a leader of the English vanguard at Agincourt in 1415.)

Edward clearly shows that custom, not law, more or less definitely delimited open and closed seasons for big game. Thus the hart or red-deer season opened at St. John's tide (June 24) and ended on Holyrood Day (September 14). This was the period when the hart was "in grease," *i.e.*, was fattest and best fit for meat. The season evidently ended with the rut, when the meat became strong. The idea of conservation was apparently absent or subordinate.

Written laws establishing closed seasons for conservation purposes go back, in England, at least to Henry VIII, who decreed protection for waterfowl and their eggs from May 31 to August 31. James I added pheasants and partridges. Non-game birds were apparently not protected until 1831.

Hunting custom in Edward's time decreed something equivalent to the modern buck law. A "warrantable hart" was defined as a "hart of ten" (points). Lesser stags (staggards), yearlings (bullocks), fawns (calves), and does (hinds), were either not killed at all, or only during the great drives in which the King participated. All of these lesser sex and age classes collectively constituted "rascal," or unwarrantable deer.

A distinction was drawn between "dry" and "wet" hinds—the former being warrantable, but only during the *winter* (September 14 until Lent), rather than during the hart season of summer and fall.

Hunting custom definitely limited permissible methods and equipments. Edward points out that "beyond the sea" (France) deer were taken "with hounds, with grey hounds, and with nets and with cords, and with other harness, with pits and with shot (bows) and with other gins (traps). . . . *But in England they are not slain except with hounds or with shot.*"

It is not clear whether the English taboo on "other gins" was a game conservation measure or a class distinction. Whichever it was, there rings in Edward's "But in England" that same clear note of the sportsman's disdain for improper methods which still adorns many a hunting tale.

By the time of Henry VII the limitation of equipments had gained definite legal form. Herons could not be taken except by hawk or long bow. Limitation of hours began with Elizabeth's prohibition of night hunting of pheasants. The gradual restriction of equipments and abusive practices progressed in England to the prohibition of pole-traps in 1904, and of bird lime in 1925.

Did management in feudal England control any factor other than hunting? Edward leaves us in doubt. He says that wolves, foxes, wildcats, etc., were hunted as vermin, but there is no clear statement whether vermin-control was for game management purposes, or merely for sport, or for the protection of livestock. Otters, it is clear, were hunted for the protection of fish. Edward points out that:

"No fish can escape them. . . . They do great harm, especially in ponds and in stanks, for a couple of otters . . . shall well destroy the fish of a great pond or great stank, and *therefore men hunt them.*"

Public bounties as a means of controlling predators came into use much later. *Game and Gun* (February, 1931) points out that Henry VIII placed a bounty on crows, choughs, and rooks. He assessed the bill against the local landowners. Elizabeth, however, empowered church wardens to levy a tax on land, and with the funds thus procured to pay public bounties not only on these birds, but also on pie, stare, martyn hawk, fursekyte, moldkyte, buzzard, shag, cormorant, ringtail, irin, rave, kingfisher, bullfinch, fitchew, polecat, weasel, stoat, wildcat, or other "ravening birds and vermin." Evidently fishermen and orchardists had caught the contagious idea that vermin were responsible for their short crops. Thus do proscription lists tend to grow during the prebiological stages of management. Later, with the advent of biological research, they invariably tend to shrink.

To revert to Edward and the fifteenth century: Were there any controls of cover and food in those days? Apparently not. Numerous hunting parks or forests, though, had long since been established. The idea of setting aside areas for the benefit of privileged hunters goes back into the remote past, and apparently grew by slow degrees into the idea of setting aside areas for the benefit of the game, and finally into the idea of protecting all landowners against trespass, so that each would have an incentive to manage his own game. Trespass penalties of almost savage severity mark the beginning of the process. Penalties only heavy enough to sustain the landowner's incentive mark its later stages. *Public* reservations for conservation purposes appear at a very late stage.

English hunting reservations for the privileged, as described by Malcolm and Maxwell (1910) and Johnson (1819) were first formally recognized in a "charter of the forest" granted by Canute the Dane in 1062. William the Conqueror and his successors "did daily increase those oppressions by making more new forests in the lands of their subjects, to their great impoverishment" until "the greatest part of the kingdom was then converted into forests."

These hunting reservations were of two kinds. A "forest" was the exclusive prerogative of royalty, and was governed by special forest laws. A forest consisted of:

> "A circuit of woody grounds and pastures, known in its
> bounds as privileged for the peaceable being and abiding of wild beasts and fowls of forest, chase, and warren, to be under the king's protection for his princely
> delight, bounded with irremovable marks and meres . . .
> replenished with beasts of venery and chase, and great
> coverts of vert for succour of said beasts; for preservation
> thereof there are particular laws, privileges, and officers
> belonging there unto."

A "chase" was a similar tract but might be held by a subject, and was protected only by the common law.

As early as 1229 the number of royal "forests" began to be curtailed, while by 1617 most of them had dissolved.

Henry VII (1485–1509) was the first English king to recognize that the common landowner might wisely be granted protection from trespass. He forbade the taking of pheasants and partridges on other people's land without the permission of the owner. James I (1603–1625) extended this to all shooting on all land. Here was the first "owner's permission" trespass law.

The Roman emperor, Justinian, had recognized the same legal principle centuries before, but with him it was a matter of landowner's rights, not a matter of incentive for game production. These English enactments, however, clearly imply that the welfare of game was one of their objectives.

When our modern state legislators in solemn conclave debate whether such "owner's permission" trespass laws are necessary, do they realize that they are coping with no new question, but rather one which came up in Roman times, and was settled in England three centuries ago?

James I apparently first applied the reservation idea for the benefit of the game, as distinguished from that of the hunter. An act passed in his reign decreed that "hail shot in hand guns" (to wit: a shotgun) might not be discharged within 600 paces of a heronry. Here was, in effect, a publicly established breeding refuge.

Henry VIII had long before, in 1536, closed an area near his Westminster Palace, in what is now metropolitan London, to shooting of pheasants, herons, and partridges. Whether this was just a little shooting preserve for his own use, or whether it was a real refuge, is not disclosed. The same doubt pertains to many a minor "refuge" today.

The first breeding refuge for non-game birds was decreed by Parliament in 1869.

Artificial rearing of game for restocking coverts may have begun as early as 1523, when the account book for Henry VIII's privy purse shows that on December 22 he paid a small sum to the "french preste the *fesaunt breeder* for to buy him a goune." It is clear enough that this "french preste" was the keeper of the royal pheasantries, but Maxwell points out that these may have been maintained for aviary or culinary, rather than restocking, purposes. Maxwell says, "It is less than a century since the practice of rearing pheasants became at all well known in this country."

Artificial propagation of mallard ducks, Maxwell points out, dates back to 1631. A letter of that date, accompanying a delivery of 200 eggs, leaves little doubt that propagation was resorted to for purposes of sport (hawking) and on a considerable scale.

We may note in passing that the first mention of artificial propagation coincides in date with the first revival of the Mosaic prohibition of robbing wild nests. Henry VIII set up severe penalties for the possession of wild eggs (Johnson, p. 314). "Bootleg" eggs are still the bane of the English gamekeeper.

Deliberate controls of cover and food in Europe can be assigned no definite date of beginning. Negative controls, *i.e.*, prohibiting destructive practice, began long before positive controls, *i.e.*, the building up of damaged land. Thus William and Mary in about 1604 prohibited the burning of nesting cover in spring (Johnson, p. 294), but I can find no clear instance of systematic cover improvement previous to the beginning of heather control on the Scotch grouse moors, which *The Grouse in Health and Disease* (1911) and Maxwell both say occurred between 1850 and 1873. (The former authority will hereafter be cited as *The Grouse Report.*) Prohibition followed long after by restoration appears to be a fixed sequence of human thought and action on conservation affairs.

Cover control to facilitate shooting is clearly earlier, at least on the continent, than cover control to enlarge the game crop. Malmesbury mentions well-developed "remises" on Hungarian estates in 1799 and 1800, also grain-baiting of wild boars to decoy them within range of blinds. While convenience in shooting was the main idea in these remises, the idea of controlling vegetation to enhance the game crop was evidently not wholly absent. Malmesbury mentions "a small remise *sown* with broom and high grass," in which he and his party killed 96 partridges and 16 hares. Possibly all these remises were to some degree "sown" or "hand made." He describes one as "an English mile long, and about half as wide—covered with high grass, clumped with copse wood, fern, and broom—so that the game lay well." There is possibly an objective inference in the word "clumped." Incidentally he mentions that 1200 head of pheasants, partridges, and hares had been killed in this remise the year before, whereas on the day he hunted it "only" 408 head were killed. The former figure, if his dimensions were right, means an annual yield of four head of small game per acre.

European game management today seeks to control all of the factors determining wild populations. Many American sportsmen have the mistaken impression that European game management relies largely on artificial propagation. Artificial rearing, to be sure, is widely used for pheasants, but in eastern Europe, and probably also elsewhere, wild management or "environmental controls" are used exclusively for all species, including pheasants, with entire success. Maxwell says that even in England a few landowners produce their pheasants entirely by wild management. Artificial propagation is never used for British grouse, and to only a small extent for gray partridge.

Although management in Europe came first and biology afterward, there is plenty of evidence that biological guidance is now increasingly sought as a means of making management more effective, and fairer to non-game species of wild life. The Grouse Report represents the first comprehensive attempt to apply science to the control of the disease factor. While the disease cycle still periodically decimates the British grouse, recovery has been speeded up to such an extent that only a third of the years fall below 50 per cent of normal in yield.

Evolution in America. The history of American management is until recently almost wholly a history of hunting controls. The sequence and direction of their development, from the Revolution up to 1911, is set forth in Palmer's admirable *Chronology and Index* (1912). Palmer points out that at the time of the Revolution, 12 of the 13 colonies had enacted closed seasons on certain species, while several had also prohibited certain destructive equipments and methods, and the export and sale of deerskins. The first closure for a term of years was placed on Massachusetts deer in 1718. The beginning of a warden system appeared in Massachusetts and New Hampshire about 1850. The first protection for non-game birds appeared in Connecticut and New Jersey in 1850.

The enactment of state game laws followed close on the heels of the retreating frontier, reaching the Pacific in California in 1852. By 1880 all of the states had game laws. The first bag limit (25 prairie chickens per day) appeared in Iowa in 1878; the first rest day in Maryland in 1872. Market hunting was first tabooed by Arkansas in 1875.

A hunting license was first required by New York in 1864; a non-resident license by New Jersey in 1864.

Federal supervision of interstate game began with the Lacey Act, which in 1900 prohibited interstate commerce in illegal game. It was followed by our present migratory bird bills, which were introduced in 1904 and 1908, but not passed until 1913. These bills, having been questioned on grounds of constitutionality, were finally anchored to the Constitution by the Canadian treaty of 1916.

This partial review of the sequence of American ideas deals, it will be observed, wholly with *restrictions* on when, what, and how one might hunt, and with the organization and financing of enforcement agencies.

We have next to trace the sequence of development in America of the complementary idea of *production* or cropping of game, either by artificial propagation or by environmental controls.

It has no fixed date or point of origin.

The first American plantings of exotics, as traced by Phillips (1928) took place about 1790, when one Richard Bache, a son-in-law of Benjamin Franklin, planted Hungarian partridges on his New Jersey estate. These early plantings were doubtless motivated not so much by a shortage of native game as by a residual affection for the wild life of "the old country," or else by that queer desire to possess something new which all flesh is heir to.

The first state game farm would be a defensible point of origin for the production or cropping idea. This, according to Palmer, was established in Illinois in 1905.

The first refuge would be another logical point. The word "refuge" as a device used in game management did not come into use until about 1910, but the group of ideas now associated with that word was in practice much earlier. The whole modern mechanism of a refuge for ducks, including a strand of wire for a boundary, feed placed inside, and a sunset rule on the surrounding ground, was in effect on Weber's Pond, in the Horicon Marsh, Wisconsin, in 1891. Jack Miner (1923, p. 58) started his now famous waterfowl refuge at Kingsville,

Ontario, in 1907, and Allen Green his refuge at Oakville, Iowa, in the same year. Pennsylvania established her first state refuge for upland game in 1905.

The first national park closed to hunting (Yellowstone, 1894) or the first national game reservation (Wichita, 1905) or bird reservation (in Canada, Last Mountain Lake, 1887; in the United States, Pelican Island, 1903) might also be selected as marking the American origin of environmental controls for wild life. Refuges, parks, and reservations, however, may more truly be considered as half-way points between the restrictive idea and the idea of environmental controls. Another half-way idea is that of limiting the kill to the annual increase. The first public attempt to apply this principle, doubtless borrowed either from foresters or stockmen, was Wyoming's issue of "limited licenses" for moose about 1915.

The first public control of food supply by artificial food patches occurred on the Pennsylvania refuges in 1917. By 1920 state food patches were being installed on a considerable scale.

The first public control of a game disease epidemic was the stamping out of hoof-and-mouth disease by the Bureau of Animal Industry after its outbreak in the deer herd of the Stanislaus National Forest of California in 1924.

The first public predator control for game purposes is so thoroughly fused with livestock predator control that no dates can be set. Bounties on predators go back indefinitely. Appropriations for government trapping date from 1915.

The first large-scale private practice of game management, in the sense of a rounded-out system of control of all actionable factors, based on a preceding scientific life-history investigation, was instituted by Herbert L. Stoddard on the South-Georgia Quail Preserves during the period 1924–1928.

The large-scale practice of public game management on publicly owned shooting grounds began on the National Forests at an indeterminate date (since 1910), and in Pennsylvania about 1919.

In short, during the last two or three decades, restrictive legislation has been gradually reinforced by the growth of the idea of production through environmental controls. The production idea is as yet still in its infancy.

This evolution of technique from custom toward law, and from restriction toward production, does not of itself suffice for an understanding of the game movement in America today. Of even greater importance is the evolution of the objectives toward which the technique is applied, and the evolution of scientific tools for its improvement.

The Conservation Idea. European game management for centuries had one simple and precise objective: the improvement of hunting for and by the private landholder.

In America the dominant idea until about 1905 was to *perpetuate*, rather than to improve or create, hunting. The thought was that restriction of hunting could "string out" the remnants of the virgin supply, and make them last a longer time. Hunting was thought of and written about as *something which must eventually disappear*, not as something which might be produced at will.

Our game laws under the restrictive idea were essentially a device for *dividing up* a dwindling treasure which nature, rather than man, had produced. Naturally enough, the policy of division strongly reflected the democratic ideas underlying our political system. Here was something new under the sun: a game system based on an equally distributed citizenship, rather than, as in Europe, on an unequally distributed landownership.

But the passing years made it more and more apparent that this novel system, however admirable in theory, had in practice failed to halt the accelerating decline in game supply. Public-spirited sportsmen groped earnestly for new formulas. The direction of their search was to develop more perfectly the restrictive idea. Better law enforcement and prohibition of market hunting were decided to be the way out.

The game literature of the closing century is saturated with these two ideas. They became personal dogma and public law. "Game protection" became a "Cause." The game hog and the market hunter were duly pilloried in press and banquet hall, and to some extent in field and wood, but the game supply continued to wane.

Came then Theodore Roosevelt, with the idea of "conservation through wise use." Wild life, forests, ranges, and water-power were conceived by him to be *renewable organic* resources, which might last forever if they were *harvested scientifically, and not faster than they reproduced.*

"Conservation" had until then been a lowly word, sleeping obscurely in the back of the dictionary. The public had never heard it. It carried no particular connotation of woods or waters. Overnight it became the label of a national issue.

The Roosevelt doctrine of conservation determined the subsequent history of American game management in three basic respects:

1. It recognized all these "outdoor" resources as one integral whole.

2. It recognized their "conservation through wise use" as a public responsibility, and their private ownership as a public trust.

3. It recognized science as a tool for discharging that responsibility.

It left cloudy, however, the question of what kinds of game could best be renewed under public initiative, and what kinds by public encouragement and regulation of private initiative. In big game, Roosevelt correctly forecast a combination of private preserves and public shooting grounds. He wrote in 1909:

"Game preservation may be of two kinds. In one the individual landed proprietor, or a group of such individuals, erect and maintain a private game preserve, the game being their property just as much as domestic animals. Such preserves often fill a useful purpose, and if managed intelligently and with a sense of public spirit and due regard for the interests and feelings of others, may do much good, even in the most democratic community. But wherever the population is sufficiently advanced in intelligence and character, a far preferable and more democratic way of preserving the game is by a system of public preserves, of protected nurseries and breeding grounds, while the laws define the conditions under which all alike may shoot the game and the restrictions under which all alike must enjoy the privilege. It is in this way that the wild creatures of the forest and the mountain can best and most permanently be preserved."

The small-game question was left in uncertain status. Subsequent evolution, however, is gradually answering the whole question. The trend is toward recognizing land-value and mobility as the criteria of public vs. private game management. Migratory birds (mobile, and often occupying cheap lands) became a national charge in 1916. The present moment is seeing the emergence of the idea that forest game (mobile, and on cheap land) can be largely a public charge, whereas farm game (non-mobile, and usually occupying expensive land) can only be managed by private initiative under public regulation (American Game Policy of 1930).

Science as a Tool. Roosevelt's idea of science as a tool for conservation seems a truism to us now, but it was new in 1910. It may be well for the reader to be reminded of the human history interwoven with its growth.

The early naturalists of the two centuries preceding the birth of "Conservation" regarded a species as one of the phenomena of nature which needed to be discovered, catalogued, and described. They realized, and marvelled, that

> "For it the Earth lay preparing quintillions of years
>   Without one single animal or plant.
>   For it the revolving centuries truly and steadily rolled."

"Gentlemen, look at this wonder," they said, as they held up a new discovery. Then they set about to catalogue it, comfortably assuming that only the same blind forces which had caused it to be there, could, in the fullness of time, cause it to perish from the earth.

But it soon became evident that a species did not continue or discontinue its existence, like a planet or a geological stratum or a sunset, regardless of what the scientist thought or did about it.

This "civilization" which at one moment held it up, saying, "Gentlemen, look at this wonder," might next throw it down and destroy it with all the nonchalance of a glacial epoch.

The naturalist's first response to the realization of this anomaly was to heave a sigh and hasten the completion of his cataloguing, lest by chance some species disappear before receiving the baptism of a Latin name. In some instances, like that of the Arizona elk, this actually happened.

With the Rooseveltian era, however, came the Crusader for conservation, a new kind of naturalist who refused to stomach this anomaly. He insisted that our conquest of nature carried with it a moral responsibility for the perpetuation of the threatened forms of wild life. This avowal was a forward step of inestimable importance. In fact, to any one for whom wild things are something more than a pleasant diversion, it constitutes one of the milestones in moral evolution.

Game management is merely an attempt to deal with the corollary question: How shall we conserve wild life without evicting ourselves?

The Crusaders wrote many volumes, but these told us why rather than how wild life and civilization should be adjusted to each other. These men were mostly biologists, but strangely enough their technique was not biological. It was, rather, an intensification of the pre-existing idea of protective legislation, which experience has now shown does not alone suffice, even when enforced. It retards, but does not reverse, the forces of destruction.

Our sporting literature fell in line with the Crusaders, but pioneered no extensions of their ideas. It consisted for a long time of mildly pleasant hunting yarns, sometimes of literary merit, which hoped with varying degrees of fervency that there would be some game left for our sons, and recommended with varying degrees of skill more laws to retard the day of reckoning. One periodical, *The Game Breeder*, broke away at an early date and pioneered the idea of game production through private initiative, but it leaned toward artificialized game-farming technique, and toward open markets to reinforce the private production incentive. These two corollaries, particularly the latter, beclouded the intrinsic merit of the central idea. This periodical must, however, be credited with the origin of the private initiative idea in America. Its program had the outstanding merit of realism and of constructive discontent with pious phrases.

So far we have the scientist, but not his science, employed as an instrument of game conservation. I do not know who first used science creatively as a tool to produce wild game crops in America. Roosevelt had it in mind as a guide for game

regulatory measures, and of course knew of its use for environmental controls in forestry. The idea was doubtless conceived
by some one long before it was first successfully applied by the
Biological Survey to quail management in Georgia.

The early attempts to apply biology to the management of
game as a wild crop soon disclosed the fact that science had
accumulated more knowledge of how to distinguish one species from another than of the habits, requirements, and inter-
relationships of living populations. Until recently science could
tell us, so to speak, more about the length of a duck's bill than
about its food, or the status of the waterfowl resource, or the
factors determining its productivity. It is now become more
realistic. Scientists see that before the factors of productivity
can be economically manipulated, they must first be discovered
and understood; that it is the task of science not only to furnish
biological facts, but also to build on them a new technique by
which the altruistic idea of conservation can be made a practical reality.

These, briefly, are the mental paths which led to the present
American idea of game management. The fact that hindsight
shows them a bit crooked should not detract due credit from
the pioneers who broke the way. There is no end to this path—
our present notions will as surely be outdated as those which
we here outdate. We seem due at this moment for a worthwhile
advance. Both scientists and sportsmen now see that effective
conservation requires, in addition to public sentiment and laws,
a deliberate and purposeful manipulation of the environment—
the same kind of manipulation as is employed in forestry. They
are also beginning to see that in game, as in forestry, this manipulation can be accomplished only by the landowner, and that
the private landowner must be given some kind of an incentive
for undertaking it.

There are still those who shy at this prospect of a man-made
game crop as at something artificial and therefore repugnant.
This attitude shows good taste but poor insight. Every head of
wild life still alive in this country is already artificialized, in that
its existence is conditioned by economic forces. Game management merely proposes that their impact shall not remain wholly

fortuitous. The hope of the future lies not in curbing the influence of human occupancy—it is already too late for that—but in creating a better understanding of the extent of that influence and a new ethic for its governance. Bailey (1915) says:

> "We are at pains to stress the importance of conduct; very well: conduct toward the earth is an essential part of it. . . . To make the earth productive and to keep it clean and to bear a reverent regard for its products is the special prerogative of good agriculture."

Game Management, 1933

The Virgin Southwest

THE MAJOR premise of civilization is that the attainments of one generation shall be available to the next.

Some social sciences, by their very nature, cast doubt upon the validity of this premise. Archeology, for example, describes an endless caravan of societies, now dead, for whom it did not hold true. On the other hand the art of government is concerned with countering such doubts, not wholly, I take it, out of altruistic regard for the unborn, but rather out of an imperative need for confidence among the living. The changing "tempo" of the generations, so convincingly described by Ortega in "The Revolt of the Masses," consists, perhaps, of fluctuations in their social confidence. Be that as it may, any matter which challenges the validity of the major premise is, ipso facto, a matter of concern to all thoughtful men.

It is only recently that the biological sciences have had new occasion to challenge it, in their discovery of an abnormal erosion-rate in some of our best soils. The rate is rapid elsewhere, but in the Southwest and the adjoining semi-arid regions it is nothing short of alarming. At the mouth of one Utah canyon, for example, erosive deposits display seasonal color-layers, from which a chronology similar to that of tree-rings has been built. It shows more movement of soil since the introduction of livestock to the watershed fifty years ago than had previously occurred since the recession of the glacial epoch.

"Discovery" is a slow process. It is almost a generation since certain ecologists, range-managers, foresters, and engineers saw and described the present southwestern situation, but it is only a year or two since the social consequences of its continuance were given credence by the lay public. Even statesmen now show signs of being aware that the best soils are slipping, sliding, toward the sea, and that the basic cause of this abnormal movement is the devegetation of the range through overgrazing by domestic livestock.

I think, though, that the thoughtful citizen still entertains a mental reservation,—he regards this thing as important, if true. This is only natural, since he is unable to weigh personally the technical evidence; he must take the ecologist's word for it. The fact of abnormal erosion, however, can be established on historical as well as ecological evidence. This paper aims to present such evidence as gathered from a single document: the journal of James Ohio Pattie, who trapped beaver in this region almost a generation before the Santa Fe Trail opened it to wholesale economic exploitation. Certain other material of miscellaneous origin, and certain personal observations, are interjected to give relief to the Pattie narrative.

Pattie was a young Missourian of the Boone and Kenton tradition, with an eye for game, grass, and timber. He travelled down the Rio Grande and the Gila, trapping beavers, in 1824. In 1825 (?) he came back up the Grand Canyon of the Colorado.

On the journey from Santa Fe to San Felipe, Pattie speaks of "a handsome plain, covered with herds of domestic animals." Continuing down the Upper Rio Grande Valley to Socorro, he "traversed the same beautiful plain country," on which grazed "the same multitude of domestic animals." There must have been heavy grass, not only along the river but *on the mesas* adjoining mesas today; many of them have become bare sand dunes.

Pattie remarks that the valley floor was not cultivated except at San Felipe and above Socorro. At these points the valley is narrow and the river has a steep gradient. They would be the easiest places to divert irrigation water from an *unsilted river channel*, because the flatter the gradient of a stream, the more work is required to build intake ditches up its banks.

While the main valley was used for grazing, the farming, according to Pattie, was mostly conducted in side streams like the Puerco. Today the reverse is true. The main valley is all farmed, except where seepage (due to silting) makes it too wet, while the side streams are fit only for grazing, because erosion has gutted all the irrigable land.

Cozzens says that in 1859(?) the channel of the Puerco was only 12 to 15 feet deep where it crosses the road from Isleta to Acoma and Zuni. Abert says that in 1846 it was only 10 or 12 feet deep at a point a few miles higher up. Today, at these same spots, the channel of the Puerco is a miniature Grand Canyon carved in clay. I recollect it as over a hundred yards wide and thirty feet deep.

Pattie remarks that at Socorro the valley was thinly timbered, but covered with willow and cottonwood brush in which "great numbers of bear, deer, and turkey" found refuge. One infers there was little large timber anywhere along the upper river. Today the ancient cottonwoods that line its irrigation ditches are its principal ornament. Most of these cottonwoods *are rooted in the ridges of silt* that have resulted from the annual cleaning of the ditch channels; in fact the older ditches *have raised themselves from five to ten feet above the valley floor* by gradual siltage.

What do these seemingly disjointed facts tell us about the virgin Southwest?

They tell us that in Pattie's day the Rio Grande drained a stable watershed, devoid of abnormal erosion. Even the sand dunes adjoining the river carried a heavy growth of grass. By reason of this grass, prairie fires swept across the valley and kept it devoid of large timber. The river channel, now so filled with silt that it is actually higher than the valley floor, was then so far below the floor that irrigation was difficult, except at the points where steep gradients facilitated the building of intakes. In short we now have scant grass, much erosion, and a river so choked with silt that it bogs its own bottoms with seepage and poisons their fertility with alkali. In Pattie's day there was grass everywhere, little erosion, a normal river, and bottomlands of sweet well-drained soil.

Pattie's testimony is really superfluous; there is hardly an acre that does not tell its own story to those who understand the speech of hills and rivers. The Galisteo, which winds across Pattie's "handsome plain" has since been lived upon. We see the skeletons of ancient fruit trees, toppling one by one into the parched arroyo, which year by year gnaws away the loam of what was once a farm.

That farm was irrigated once,—one can trace the old ditches winding across the remnants of bottomland. If irrigated, there must have been a stream. There is no stream now, only a trickle in the sand.

The stream banks must have been shallow and gentle, else the water could not have been led upon the land. They are not shallow now. The channel is a flood-torn chasm.

If there were ditches, there must have been wide stretches of level friendly soil to irrigate. That soil has been dumped as silt into the main river; one farm washed away to curse another in the making, somewhere below.

Pattie's handsome plain is still green, at times, but it is the kind of green which could deceive only a tourist. It is not the greenness of grass, it is the greenness of tumbleweeds and snakeweed and pinque,—worthless substitutes which a denuded nature has invoked to cover her nakedness. On this same Galisteo Doniphan, in 1846, found "grass and water abundant and of good quality."

It might be argued by some that the farming which once occupied valleys like the Galisteo started the erosion which has since destroyed them. That this is not true is attested by valleys which were farmed before Coronado came, but did not erode until livestock was introduced. The San Jose is a case in point.

Everybody observes the lava cliffs which line its valley, black from centuries of oxidation in the sun. At their base runs a horizontal band of gray and red. It is like the tell-tale whiteness of a school-boy's face which shows, by contrast, where he has been washed. These cliffs have been washed—by erosion. The gray and red band is the measure of the soil which floods have torn away from the as yet unblackened rock—more farms gutted out to clog rivers and fill reservoirs, somewhere below.

Nothing has changed in the watershed of the San Jose except *grass*. Coronado and those who came after him brought sheep and goats and cattle to the Indians, and the subsequent overgrazing of the whole watershed is what upset its equilibrium. Throughout the Southwest the worst erosion is in the regions of the oldest settlements, because it is there that overgrazing has been most severe through the longest time.

On the north flank of Mt. Taylor is dramatic proof of the when and why of erosion. Winding up and down across the treeless foothills, threading in and out of crest and hollow, is an old earth-scar, overgrown with chemise and snakeweed, but nevertheless clearly traceable for miles, like the track of some great serpent. It is the Santa Fe Trail.

Wherever it crosses a hump the old roadbed is worn two and three foot deep into the soil. The grades followed, and the manner of winding around rocks and obstacles, are exactly the same as one would select in driving a heavy wagon over the same route today, with this significant exception: at the bottom of every hollow is now a steep-banked arroyo which no wagon could possibly cross. There are more of these arroyos than an army of engineers could bridge in months. There can be no two ways to read the history written on these hills. The story is as plain as a street blocked by many deep ditches. If you knew the street had been used in 1849, you would know the ditches had been dug since.

How long since? In the bottom of the arroyos which cross the old trail are chemise bushes and sometimes scraggly junipers, sprung from the juniper forests higher up the mountain. Cut off the oldest and count back the annual rings of wood. They too will tell you 1850. Overgrazing started these arroyos, and in all probability it was overgrazing by the livestock which accompanied the immigrant trains, which thus destroyed this, their own wagon road. This probability is strengthened by the fact that the erosion is oldest and worst near the water-holes at which the Forty-Niners camped and grazed their thousands of animals.

Let us now rejoin Pattie on his trip down the Rio Grande. He left the river near what is now San Marcial and crossed southwesterly to the copper mines at Santa Rita del Cobre. From Santa Rita he went to the head of the Gila River to trap beavers. He caught "trout" where the river emerges from the mountains, probably near the present settlement of Cliffs. (If these were really trout, rather than "bony-tails," then the trout extended fifteen miles farther downstream than they do now.) The first night of trapping at this point yielded 30 beavers. But the important thing is not so much the abundance of beaver, as the fact that these hardy trappers "*were much fatigued by the difficulty of getting through the high grass which covered the heavily timbered bottom.*"

Today, at this spot, and for miles above and below, the river is flanked by naked bars of sand and cobblestones, and the bottoms, except where fenced, are as bare of grass, as naked of timber, as the top of a billiard table.

Ascending the box of the Gila, Pattie describes "a thick tangle of grapevines and underbrush" through which he crawled, sometimes on hands and knees. At the forks of the river (now the XSX cattle ranch), the banks were still "very brushy, and frequented by numbers of bears." Here too, there is not little brush and many cobble bars.

Chop down the oldest of the young sycamores and alders

that have found rootage on the cobble bars which have replaced Pattie's bottoms, and you will find that few are older than the cow-business, which invaded these hills in the early eighties.

A year later Pattie followed down the Gila to its junction with the Colorado. There on February 26, 1825, he tells in a single sentence more of what has befallen the Southwest than could be compressed into a volume today. This is the sentence: "At twelve we started up the Red River (Rio Colorado), which is between two and three hundred yards wide, a deep bold stream, *and the water at this point is entirely clear.*"

The Colorado today discharges 12,000 acre feet of silt per year, enough to cover half a township with a foot of mud. Clear water in the Colorado is unknown.

Again Pattie, this time at the mouth of the Little Colorado above the Grand Canyon: "On the fifteenth (April) we returned to the banks of the Red River, *which is here a clear beautiful stream.*"

Pattie's finding clear water in February might be explained away on the grounds that headwater snows were still intact, but his report of clear water in both February and April, with no intimation of any opposite condition during the interim journey along its course, indicates to me that our present Colorado resembles Pattie's only in location and name. The present river is never clear,—not only that but it is carrying the richest soils of Arizona into the Gulf of California, which has become in very fact "the vermillion sea."

The foregoing comparisons of what Pattie saw and what we see today are merely random examples of what has happened, in some degree, to almost every watershed in the Southwest. On many of the National Forests and on a few well-managed private ranches the damage is partial and confined mainly to loss of bottomlands. Near many old settlements the damage is complete, erosion having exposed enough rocks to substitute what might be called a mechanical equilibrium for the vegetative one which once existed. In most places the damage is still in process, and the process is cumulative.

It has been necessary to offer proof of these changes because most people do not know that any change has taken place, and some who do know deny that overgrazing is the primary cause. They persist in believing either that abnormal erosion was always there, or that it is somehow an act of God instead of an act of goats, sheep, and cows.

In trying to picture the meaning of the term overgrazing, it is important that the reader divest his mind of the assumption that overgrazing constitutes a uniformly distributed excess of consumption over growth. More often than not the excessive utilization of one plant or type of ground is accompanied by the underutilization of another. For this reason the very diversity of the country has contributed to its undoing. If a mountain cow on a cold winter day has the choice of basking in the warm sun of a hardwood bottom, or of climbing upon the wind-swept mesa, or scrambling among the rocky slopes between the two, she will choose the bottom. In fact, she may browse the last bottomland willow to death before the bunch grass on the slopes is even touched. It seems as if the greater the diversity of types, the less uniform their utilization and the quicker the inception of damage.

The reader must grasp the fact that overgrazing is more than mere lack of visible forage. It is rather a lack of vigorous roots of desirable forage plants. An area is overgrazed to the extent its palatable plants are thinned out or weakened in growing power. It takes more than a few good rains, or a temporary removal of livestock, to cure this thinning or weakening of palatable plants. In some cases it may take years of skillful range management to effect a cure; in others erosion has so drained and leached the soil that restoration is a matter of decades; again it has removed the soil entirely. In the latter event restoration involves geological periods of time, and thus for human purposes must be dismissed as impossible.

There was once a widespread impression that forest fires, as well as overgrazing, were an important cause of watershed damage. Recent evidence in other regions supports this belief, but not here. On the contrary, observations on their sequence and relative importance in the Arizona brushfields, indicates that when the cattle came the grass went, the fires diminished, and erosion began.

The rivers on which we have built storage reservoirs or power dams deposit their deltas not only in the sea, but behind the dams. We build these to store water, and mortgage our irrigated valleys and our industries to pay for them, but every year they store a little less water and a little more mud. Reclamation, which should be for all time, thus becomes in part the source of a merely temporary prosperity.

The rivers which get their silt from the hills use it to scour the valleys which they once fertilized. Thus the Gila Valley, a garden since the Indian days, stretching almost across the breadth of Arizona, has lost 6000 acres of natural agricultural land since Pattie trapped beaver there, and may lose 33,000 acres more before the damage is complete. During the same period artificial reclamation has watered only 46,000 acres in the Gila drainage. Yet we think of reclamation as a net addition to the wealth of the arid west. In the Southwest it is more accurate to regard it, in part, as a mere offset to our own clumsy destruction of the natural bottoms which required no expensive dams and reservoirs, and which the Indians cultivated before irrigation bonds had a name, and before the voice of the booster was heard in the land.

We can say this: That what we call "development" is not a uni-directional process, especially in a semi-arid country. To develop this land we have used engines that we could not control, and have started actions and reactions far different from those intended. Some of these are proving beneficial; most of them harmful. This land is too complex—the simple processes of "the mass-mind" armed with modern tools. To live in real harmony with such a country seems to require either a degree of public regulation we will not tolerate, or a degree of private enlightenment we do not possess.

But of course we must continue to live with it according to our lights. Two things hold promise of improving those lights. One is to apply science to land-use. The other is to cultivate a love of country a little less spangled with stars, and a little more imbued with that respect for mother-earth the lack of which is, to me, the outstanding attribute of the machine age.

Typescript, May 6, 1933

The Conservation Ethic

W**HEN GOD-LIKE** Odysseus returned from the wars in Troy, he hanged all on one rope some dozen slave-girls of his household whom he suspected of misbehavior during his absence.

This hanging involved no question of propriety, much less of justice. The girls were property. The disposal of property was then, as now, a matter of expediency, not of right and wrong.

Criteria of right and wrong were not lacking from Odysseus' Greece: witness the fidelity of his wife through the long years before at last his black-prowed galleys clove the wine-dark seas for home. The ethical structure of that day covered wives, but had not yet been extended to human chattels. During the three thousand years which have since elapsed, ethical criteria have been extended to many fields of conduct, with corresponding shrinkages in those judged by expediency only.

This extension of ethics, so far studied only by philosophers, is actually a process in ecological evolution. Its sequences may be described in biological as well as philosophical terms. An ethic, biologically, is a limitation on freedom of action in the struggle for existence. An ethic, philosophically, is a differentiation of social from anti-social conduct. These are two definitions of one thing. The thing has its origin in the tendency of interdependent individuals or societies to evolve modes of coöperation. The biologist calls these symbioses. Man elaborated certain advanced symbioses called politics and economics. Like their simpler biological antecedents, they enable individuals or groups to exploit each other in an orderly way. Their first yardstick was expediency.

The complexity of coöperative mechanisms increased with population density, and with the efficiency of tools. It was simpler, for example, to define the anti-social uses of sticks and stones in the days of the mastodons than of bullets and billboards in the age of motors.

At a certain stage of complexity, the human community found expediency-yardsticks no longer sufficient. One by one it has evolved and superimposed upon them a set of ethical yardsticks. The first ethics dealt with the relationship between individuals. The Mosaic Decalogue is an example. Later accretions dealt with the relationship between the individual and society. Christianity tries to integrate the individual to society, Democracy to integrate social organization to the individual.

There is as yet no ethic dealing with man's relationship to land and to the non-human animals and plants which grow upon it. Land, like Odysseus' slave-girls, is still property. The land-relation is still strictly economic, entailing privileges but not obligations.

The extension of ethics to this third element in human environment is, if we read evolution correctly, an ecological possibility. It is the third step in a sequence. The first two have already been taken. Civilized man exhibits in his own mind evidence that the third is needed. For example, his sense of right and wrong may be aroused quite as strongly by the desecration of a nearby woodlot as by a famine in China, a near pogrom in Germany, or the murder of the slave-girls in ancient Greece. Individual thinkers since the days of Ezekiel and Isaiah have asserted that the despoliation of land is not only inexpedient but wrong. Society, however, has not yet affirmed their belief. I regard the present conservation movement as the embryo of such an affirmation. I here discuss why this is, or should be, so.

Some scientists will dismiss this matter forthwith, on the ground that ecology has no relation to right and wrong. To such I reply that science, if not philosophy, should by now have made us cautious about dismissals. An ethic may be regarded as a mode of guidance for meeting ecological situations so new or intricate, or involving such deferred reactions, that the path of social expediency is not discernible to the average individual. Animal instincts are just this. Ethics are possibly a kind of advanced social instinct in-the-making.

Whatever the merits of this analogy, no ecologist can deny that our land-relation involves penalties and rewards which the individual does not see, and needs modes of guidance which do not yet exist. Call these what you will, science cannot escape its part in forming them.

ECOLOGY—ITS RÔLE IN HISTORY

A harmonious relation to land is more intricate, and of more consequence to civilization, than the historians of its progress seem to realize. Civilization is not, as they often assume, the enslavement of a stable and constant earth. It is a state of *mutual and interdependent coöperation* between human animals, other animals, plants, and soils, which may be disrupted at any moment by the failure of any of them. Land-despoliation has evicted nations, and can on occasion do it again. As long as six virgin continents awaited the plow, this was perhaps no tragic matter,—eviction from one piece of soil could be recouped by despoiling another. But there are now wars and rumors of wars which foretell the impending saturation of the earth's best soils and climates. It thus becomes a matter of some importance, at least to ourselves, that our dominion, once gained, be self-perpetuating rather than self-destructive.

This instability of our land-relation calls for example. I will sketch a single aspect of it: the plant succession as a factor in history.

In the years following the Revolution, three groups were contending for control of the Mississippi valley: the native Indians, the French and English traders, and American settlers. Historians wonder what would have happened if the English at Detroit had thrown a little more weight into the Indian side of those tipsy scales which decided the outcome of the Colonial migration into the cane-lands of Kentucky. Yet who ever wondered why the cane-lands, when subjected to the particular mixture of forces represented by the cow, plow, fire, and axe of the pioneer, became bluegrass? What if the plant succession inherent in this "dark and bloody ground" had, under the impact of these forces, given us some worthless sedge, shrub, or weed? Would Boone and Kenton have held out? Would there have been any overflow into Ohio? Any Louisiana Purchase? Any transcontinental union of new states? Any Civil War? Any machine age? Any depression? The subsequent drama of American history, here and elsewhere, hung in large degree on the reaction of particular soils to the impact of particular forces exerted by a particular kind and degree of human occupation. No statesman-biologist selected those forces, nor foresaw their effects. That chain of events which on the Fourth of July we call our National Destiny hung on a "fortuitous concourse of elements," the interplay of which we now dimly decipher *by hindsight only.*

Contrast Kentucky with what hindsight tells us about the

Southwest. The impact of occupancy here brought no blue-grass, nor other plant fitted to withstand the bumps and buffetings of misuse. Most of these soils, when grazed, reverted through a successive series of more and more worthless grasses, shrubs, and weeds to a condition of unstable equilibrium. Each recession of plant types bred erosion; each increment to erosion bred a further recession of plants. The result today is a progressive and mutual deterioration, not only of plants and soils, but of the animal community subsisting thereon. The early settlers did not expect this, on the cienegas of central New Mexico some even cut artificial gullies to hasten it. So subtle has been its progress that few people know anything about it. It is not discussed at polite tea-tables or go-getting luncheon clubs, but only in the arid halls of science.

All civilization seem to have been conditioned upon whether the plant succession, under the impact of occupancy, gave a stable and habitable assortment of vegetative types, or an unstable and uninhabitable assortment. The swampy forests of Caesar's Gaul were utterly changed by human use—for the better. Moses' land of milk and honey was utterly changed—for the worse. Both changes are the unpremeditated resultant of the impact between ecological and economic forces. We now decipher these reactions retrospectively. What could possibly be more important than to foresee and control them?

We of the machine age admire ourselves for our mechanical ingenuity; we harness cars to the solar energy impounded in carboniferous forests; we fly in mechanical birds; we make the ether carry our words or even our pictures. But are these not in one sense mere parlor tricks compared with our utter ineptitude in keeping land fit to live upon? Our engineering has attained the pearly gates of a near-millennium, but our applied biology still lives in nomad's tents of the stone age. If our system of land-use happens to be self-perpetuating, we stay. If it happens to be self-destructive we move, like Abraham, to pastures new.

Do I overdraw this paradox? I think not. Consider the transcontinental airmail which plies the skyways of the Southwest—a symbol of its final conquest. What does it see? A score of mountain valleys which were green gems of fertility when first described by Coronado, Espejo, Pattie, Abert, Sitgreaves, and Cozzens. What are they now? Sandbars, wastes of cobbles and burroweed, a path for torrents. Rivers which Pattie says were clear, now muddy sewers for the wasting fertility of an empire. A "Public Domain," once a velvet carpet of rich buffalo-grass and grama, now an illimitable waste of rattlesnake-bush and tumble-weed, too impoverished to be accepted as a gift by the states within which it lies. Why? Because the ecology of this South-west happened to be set on a hair-trigger. Because cows eat brush when the grass is gone, and thus postpone the penalties of over-utilization. Because certain grasses, when grazed too closely to bear seed-stalks, are weakened and give way to inferior grasses, and these to inferior shrubs, and these to weeds, and these to naked earth. Because rain which spatters upon veg-etated soil stays clear and sinks, while rain which spatters upon devegetated soil seals its interstices with colloidal mud and hence must run away as floods, cutting the heart out of country as it goes. Are these phenomena any more difficult to foresee than the paths of stars which science deciphers without the error of a single second? Which is the more important to the permanence and welfare of civilization?

I do not here berate the astronomer for his precocity, but rather the ecologist for his lack of it. The days of his cloistered sequestration are over:

> "Whether you will or not,
>   You are a king, Tristram, for you are one
>   Of the time-tested few that leave the world,
>   When they are gone, not the same place it was.
>   Mark what you leave."

Unforseen ecological reactions not only make or break his-tory in a few exceptional enterprises—they condition, circum-scribe, delimit, and warp all enterprises, both economic and cultural, that pertain to land. In the cornbelt, after grazing and plowing out all the cover in the interests of "clean farming," we grew tearful about wild-life, and spent several decades pass-ing laws for its restoration. We were like Canute command-ing the tide. Only recently has research made it clear that the implements for restoration lie not in the legislature, but in the farmer's toolshed. Barbed wire and brains are doing what laws alone failed to do.

In other instances we take credit for shaking down apples

which were, in all probability, ecological windfalls. In the Lake States and the Northeast lumbering, pulping, and fire accidentally created some scores of millions of acres of new second-growth. At the proper stage we find these thickets full of deer. For this we naively thank the wisdom of our game laws.

In short, the reaction of land to occupancy determines the nature and duration of civilization. In arid climates the land may be destroyed. In all climates the plant succession determines what economic activities can be supported. Their nature and intensity in turn determine not only the domestic but also the wild plant and animal life, the scenery, and the whole face of nature. We inherit the earth, but within the limits of the soil and the plant succession we also *rebuild* the earth,—without plan, without knowledge of its properties, and without understanding of the increasingly coarse and powerful tools which science has placed at our disposal. We are remodelling the Alhambra with a steam-shovel.

ECOLOGY AND ECONOMICS

The conservation movement is, at the very least, an assertion that these interactions between man and land are too important to be left to chance, even that sacred variety of chance known as economic law.

We have three possible controls: Legislation, self-interest, and ethics. Before we can know where and how they will work, we must first understand the reactions. Such understanding arises only from research. At the present moment research, inadequate as it is, has nevertheless piled up a large store of facts which our land using industries are unwilling, or (they claim) unable, to apply. Why? A review of three sample fields will be attempted.

Soil science has so far relied on self-interest as the motive for conservation. The landholder is told that it pays to conserve his soil and its fertility. On good farms this economic formula has improved land-practice, but on poorer soils vast abuses still proceed unchecked. Public acquisition of submarginal soils is being urged as a remedy for their misuse. It has been applied to some extent, but it often comes too late to check erosion, and can hardly hope more than to ameliorate a phenomenon involving in some degree *every square foot* on the continent.

Legislative compulsion might work on the best soils where it is least needed, but it seems hopeless on poor soils where the existing economic set-up hardly permits even uncontrolled private enterprise to make a profit. We must face the fact that, by and large, no defensible relationship between man and the soil of his nativity is as yet in sight.

Forestry exhibits another tragedy—or comedy—of *Homo sapiens*, astride the runaway Juggernaut of his own building, trying to be decent to his environment. A new profession was trained in the confident expectation that the shrinkage in virgin timber would, as a matter of self-interest, bring an expansion of timber-cropping. Foresters are cropping timber on certain parcels of poor land which happen to be public, but on the great bulk of private holdings they have accomplished little. Economics won't let them. Why? He would be bold indeed who claimed to know the whole answer, but these parts of it seem agreed upon: modern transport prevents profitable tree-cropping in cut-out regions until virgin stands in all others are first exhausted; substitutes for lumber have undermined confidence in the future need for it; carrying charges on stumpage reserves are so high as to force perennial liquidation, overproduction, depressed prices, and an appalling wastage of unmarketable grades which must be cut to get the higher grades; the mind of the forest owner lacks the point-of-view underlying sustained yield; the low wage-standards on which European forestry rests do not obtain in America.

A few tentative gropings toward industrial forestry were visible before 1929, but these have been mostly swept away by the depression, with the net result that forty years of "campaigning" have left us only such actual tree-cropping as is underwritten by public treasuries. Only a blind man could see in this the beginnings of an orderly and harmonious use of the forest resource.

There are those who would remedy this failure by legislative compulsion of private owners. Can a landholder be successfully compelled to raise any crop, let alone a complex long-time crop like a forest, on land the private possession of which is, for the moment at least, a liability? Compulsion would merely hasten that avalanche of tax-delinquent land-titles now being dumped into the public lap.

Another and larger group seeks a remedy in more public ownership. Doubtless we need it—we are getting it whether we need it or not—but how far can it go? We cannot dodge the fact that the forest problem, like the soil problem, *is coextensive with the map of the United States.* How far can we tax other lands and industries to maintain forest lands and industries artificially? How confidently can we set out to run a hundred-yard dash with a twenty foot rope tying our ankle to the starting point? Well, we are bravely "getting set," anyhow.

The trend in wild-life conservation is possibly more encouraging than in either soils or forests. It has suddenly become apparent that farmers, out of self-interest, can be induced to crop game. Game crops are in demand, staple crops are not. For farm-species, therefore, the immediate future is relatively bright. Forest game has profited to some extent by the accidental establishment of new habitat following the decline of forest industries. Migratory game, on the other hand, has lost heavily through drainage and over-shooting; its future is black because motives of self-interest do not apply to the private cropping of birds so mobile that they "belong" to everybody, and hence to nobody. Only governments have interests coextensive with their annual movements, and the divided counsels of conservationists give governments ample alibi for doing little. Governments could crop migratory birds because their marshy habitat is cheap and concentrated, but we get only an annual crop of new hearings on how to divide the fast-dwindling remnant.

These three fields of conservation, while but fractions of the whole, suffice to illustrate the welter of conflicting forces, facts, and opinions which so far comprise the result of the effort to harmonize our machine civilization with the land whence comes its sustenance. We have accomplished little, but we should have learned much. What?

I can see clearly only two things:

First, that the economic cards are stacked against some of the most important reforms in land-use.

Second, that the scheme to circumvent this obstacle by public ownership, while highly desirable and good as far as it goes, can never go far enough. Many will take issue on this, but the issue is between two conflicting conceptions of the end towards which we are working.

One regards conservation as a kind of sacrificial offering, made for us vicariously by bureaus, on lands nobody wants for other purposes, in propitiation for the atrocities which still prevail everywhere else. We have made a real start on this kind of conservation, and we can carry it as far as the tax-string on our leg will reach. Obviously, though it conserves our self-respect better than our land. Many excellent people accept it, either because they despair of anything better, or because they fail to see the *universality of the reactions needing control.* That is to say their ecological education is not yet sufficient.

The other concept supports the public program, but regards it as merely extension, teaching, demonstration, an initial nucleus, a means to an end, but not the end itself. The real end is a *universal symbiosis with land,* economic and esthetic, public and private. To this school of thought public ownership is a patch but not a program.

Are we, then, limited to patchwork until such time as Mr. Babbitt has taken his Ph.D. in ecology and esthetics? Or do the new economic formulae offer a short-cut to harmony with our environment?

THE ECONOMIC ISMS

As nearly as I can see, all the new isms—Socialism, Communism, Fascism, and especially the late but not lamented Technocracy —outdo even Capitalism itself in their preoccupation with one thing: The distribution of more machine-made commodities to more people. They all proceed on the theory that if we can all keep warm and full, and all own a Ford and a radio, the good life will follow. Their programs differ only in ways to mobilize machines to this end. Though they despise each other, they are all, in respect of this objective, as identically alike as peas in a pod. They are competitive apostles of a single creed: *salvation by machinery.*

We are here concerned, not with their proposals for adjusting men and machinery to goods, but rather with their lack of any vital proposal for adjusting men and machines to land. To conservationists they offer only the old familiar palliatives: Public ownership and private compulsion. If these are insufficient now, by what magic are they to become sufficient after we change our collective label?

Let us apply economic reasoning to a sample problem and see where it takes us. As already pointed out, there is a huge area which the economist calls submarginal, because it has a minus value for exploitation. In its once-virgin condition, however, it could be "skinned" at a profit. It has been, and as a result erosion is washing it away. What shall we do about it?

By all the accepted tenets of current economics and science we ought to say "let her wash." Why? Because staple land-crops are overproduced, our population curve is flattening out, science is still raising the yields from better lands, we are spending millions from the public treasury to retire unneeded acreage, and here is nature offering to do the same thing free of charge; why not let her do it? This, I say, is economic reasoning. *Yet no man has so spoken*. I cannot help reading a meaning into this fact. To me it means that the average citizen shares in some degree the intuitive and instantaneous contempt with which the conservationist would regard such an attitude. We can, it seems, stomach the burning or plowing-under of over-produced cotton, coffee, or corn, but the destruction of mother-earth, however "submarginal," touches something deeper, some subeconomic stratum of the human intelligence wherein lies that something—perhaps the essence of civilization—which Wilson called "the decent opinion of mankind."

THE CONSERVATION MOVEMENT

We are confronted, then, by a contradiction. To build a better motor we tap the uttermost powers of the human brain; to build a better countryside we throw dice. Political systems take no cognizance of this disparity, offer no sufficient remedy. There is, however, a dormant but widespread consciousness that the destruction of land, and of the living things upon it, is wrong. A new minority have espoused an idea called conservation which tends to assert this as a positive principle. Does it contain seeds which are likely to grow?

Its own devotees, I confess, often give apparent grounds for skepticism. We have, as an extreme example, the cult of the barbless hook, which acquires self-esteem by a self-imposed limitation of armaments in catching fish. The limitation is commendable, but the illusion that it has something to do with

salvation is as naive as some of the primitive taboos and morti-
fications which still adhere to religious sects. Such excrescences
seem to indicate the whereabouts of a moral problem, however
irrelevant they be in either defining or solving it.

Then there is the conservation-booster, who of late has been
rewriting the conservation ticket in terms of "tourist-bait." He
exhorts us to "conserve outdoor Wisconsin" because if we don't
the motorist-on-vacation will streak through to Michigan, leaving us only a cloud of dust. Is Mr. Babbitt trumping up hard-
boiled reasons to serve as a screen for doing what he thinks is
right? His tenacity suggests that he is after something more
than tourists. Have he and other thousands of "conservation
workers" labored through all these barren decades fired by a
dream of augmenting the sales of sandwiches and gasoline? I
think not. Some of these people have hitched their wagon to a
star—and that is something.

Any wagon so hitched offers the discerning politician a quick
ride to glory. His agility in hopping up and seizing the reins
adds little dignity to the cause, but it does add the testimony
of his political nose to an important question: is this conservation something people really want? The political objective,
to be sure, is often some trivial tinkering with the laws, some
useless appropriation, or some pasting of pretty labels on ugly
realities. How often, though, does any political action portray
the real depth of the idea behind it? For political consumption a new thought must always be reduced to a posture or a
phrase. It has happened before that great ideas were heralded
by growing-pains in the body politic, semi-comic to those onlookers not yet infected by them. The insignificance of what
we conservationists, in our political capacity, say and do, does
not detract from the significance of our persistent desire to do
something. To turn this desire into productive channels is the
task of time, and ecology.

The recent trend in wild life conservation shows the direction
in which ideas are evolving. At the inception of the movement
fifty years ago, its underlying thesis was to save species from
extermination. The means to this end were a series of restrictive enactments. The duty of the individual was to cherish and
extend these enactments, and to see that his neighbor obeyed

them. The whole structure was negative and prohibitory. It assumed land to be a constant in the ecological equation. Gunpowder and blood-lust were the variables needing control.

There is now being superimposed on this a positive and affirmatory ideology, the thesis of which is to prevent the deterioration of environment. The means to this end is research. The duty of the individual is to apply its findings to land, and to encourage his neighbor to do likewise. The soil and the plant succession are recognized as the basic variables which determine plant and animal life, both wild and domesticated, and likewise the quality and quantity of human satisfactions to be derived. Gun-powder is relegated to the status of a tool for harvesting one of these satisfactions. Blood-lust is a source of motive-power, like sex in social organization. Only one constant is assumed, and that is common to both equations: the love of nature.

This new idea is so far regarded as merely a new and promising means to better hunting and fishing, but its potential uses are much larger. To explain this, let us go back to the basic thesis—the preservation of fauna and flora.

Why do species become extinct? Because they first become rare. Why do they become rare? Because of shrinkage in the particular environments which their particular adaptations enable them to inhabit. Can such shrinkage be controlled? Yes, once the specifications are known. How known? Through ecological research. How controlled? By modifying the environment with those same tools and skills already used in agriculture and forestry.

Given, then, the knowledge and the desire, this idea of controlled wild culture or "management" can be applied not only to quail and trout, but to *any living thing* from bloodroots to Bell's vireos. Within the limits imposed by the plant succession, the soil, the size of the property, and the gamut of the seasons, the landholder can "raise" any wild plant, fish, bird, or mammal he wants to. A rare bird or flower need remain no rarer than the people willing to venture their skill in *building it a habitat.* Nor need we visualize this as a new diversion for the idle rich. The average dolled-up estate merely proves what we will some day learn to acknowledge: that bread and beauty grow best together. Their harmonious integration can make farming not only a business but an art; the land not only a food-factory but an instrument for self-expression, on which each can play music of his own choosing.

It is well to ponder the sweep of this thing. It offers us nothing less than a renaissance—a new creative stage—in the oldest, and potentially the most universal, of all the fine arts. "Landscaping," for ages dissociated from economic land-use, has suffered that dwarfing and distortion which always attends the relegation of esthetic or spiritual functions to parks and parlors. Hence it is hard for us to visualize a creative art of land-beauty which is the prerogative, not of esthetic priests but of dirt farmers, which deals not with plants but with biota, and which wields not only spade and pruning shears, but also draws rein on those invisible forces which determine the presence or absence of plants and animals. Yet such is this thing which lies to hand, if we want it. In it are the seeds of change, including, perhaps, a rebirth of that social dignity which ought to inhere in land-ownership, but which, for the moment, has passed to inferior professions, and which the current processes of land-skinning hardly deserve. In it, too, are perhaps the seeds of a new fellowship in land, a new solidarity in all men privileged to plow, a realization of Whitman's dream to "*plant companion-ship as thick as trees along all the rivers of America.*" What bitter parody of such companionship, and trees, and rivers, is offered to this our generation!

I will not belabor the pipe-dream. It is no prediction, but merely an assertion that the idea of controlled environment contains colors and brushes wherewith society may some day paint a new and possibly a better picture of itself. Granted a community in which the combined beauty and utility of land determines the social status of its owner, and we will see a speedy dissolution of the economic obstacles which now beset conservation. Economic laws may be permanent, but their im-pact reflects what people want, which in turn reflects what they know and what they are. The economic set-up at any one mo-ment is in some measure the result, as well as the cause, of the then prevailing standard of living. Such standards change. For example: some people discriminate against manufactured goods produced by child-labor or other anti-social processes. They have learned some of the abuses of machinery, and are willing to use their custom as a leverage for betterment. Social pressures have also been exerted to modify ecological processes which happened to be simple enough for people to understand;—witness the very effective boycott of bird-skins for millinery ornament. We need postulate only a little further advance in ecological education to visualize the application of like pressures to other conservation problems.

For example: the lumberman who is now unable to practice forestry because the public is turning to synthetic boards may then be able to sell man-grown lumber "to keep the mountains green." Again: certain wools are produced by gutting the public domain; couldn't their competitors, who lead their sheep in greener pastures, so label their product? Must we view forever the irony of educating our sons with paper, the offal of which pollutes the rivers which they need quite as badly as books? Would not many people pay an extra penny for a "clean" newspaper? Government may some day busy itself with the legitimacy of labels used by land-industries to distinguish conservation products, rather than with the attempt to operate their lands for them.

I neither predict nor advocate these particular pressures—their wisdom or unwisdom is beyond my knowledge. I do assert that these abuses are just as real, and their correction every whit as urgent, as was the killing of egrets for hats. *They differ only in the number of links composing the ecological chain of cause and effect.* In egrets there were one or two links, which the mass-mind saw, believed, and acted upon. In these others there are many links; people do not see them, nor believe us who do. The ultimate issue, in conservation as in other social problems, is whether the mass-mind *wants to* extend its powers of comprehending the world in which it lives, or, granted the desire, *has the capacity to do so.* Ortega, in his "Revolt of the Masses," has pointed to the first question with devastating lucidity. The geneticists are gradually, with trepidations, coming to grips with the second. I do not know the answer to either. I simply affirm that a sufficiently enlightened society, by changing its wants and tolerances, can change the economic factors bearing on land. It can be said of nations, as of individuals: "as a man thinketh, so is he."

It may seem idle to project such imaginary elaborations of

culture at a time when millions lack even the means of physical existence. Some may feel for it the same honest horror as
the Senator from Michigan who lately arraigned Congress for
protecting migratory birds at a time when fellow-humans lacked
bread. The trouble with such deadly parallels is we can never be
sure which is cause and which is effect. It is not inconceivable
that the wave phenomena which have lately upset everything
from banks to crime-rates might be less troublesome if the
human medium in which they run *readjusted its tensions.* The
stampede is an attribute of animals interested solely in grass.

Journal of Forestry, October 1933

Conservation Economics

THE MOON, they say, was born when some mighty planet, zooming aimlessly through the firmament, happened to pass so near the earth as to lift off a piece of its substance and hurl it forth into space as a new and separate entity in the galaxy of heavenly bodies.

Conservation, I think, was "born" in somewhat this same manner in the year A.D. 1933. A mighty force, consisting of the pent-up desires and frustrated dreams of two generations of conservationists, passed near the national money-bags whilst opened wide for post-depression relief. Something large and heavy was lifted off and hurled forth into the galaxy of the alphabets. It is still moving too fast for us to be sure how big it is, or what cosmic forces draw rein on its career. My purpose is to discuss the new arrival and his prospects in life.

We must first of all understand the sequence of events which generated the lifting force. For the last half-century there has grown up a widespread conviction that our whip-hand over nature is no unmixed blessing. We have gained an easier living, but in the process of getting it we are losing two things of possibly equal value: (1) The permanence of the resources whence comes our bread and butter; (2) the opportunity of personal contact with natural beauty.

Conservation is the effort to so use the whip that these two losses will be minimized.

Its history in America may be compressed into two sentences: We tried to get conservation by buying land, by subsidizing desirable changes in land use, and by passing restrictive laws. The last method largely failed; the other two have produced some small samples of success.

The "New Deal" expenditures are the natural consequence of this experience. Public ownership or subsidy having given us the only taste of conservation we have ever enjoyed, the public money-bags being open, and private land being a drug on the market, we have suddenly decided to buy us a real mouthful, if not indeed, a square meal.

Is this good logic? Will we get a square meal? These are the questions of the hour.

GEOGRAPHY

The monumental Copeland Report on forestry, and some lesser labors in other fields, have recently shed much light on these questions, but it seems to me that we can further illuminate them by considering the simple geography of the phenomena which conservation seeks to control. Forests, erosion, and game each have certain characteristics and certain limitations affecting their dispersion over the land. Can these be made to fit the geographical peculiarities of public ownership? For instance:

1. Public lands are necessarily of limited dispersion.
2. The ratio of public to private land cannot exceed what the private tax-base plus operating revenues if any, will carry.
3. The minimum unit of public land must be large enough to carry a custodian.

Let us examine the geography of game in the light of these limitations. Wild game has an inherent intolerance of concentration. Few enthusiasts are aware of this simple but important fact. The most skillful culture cannot build a wild stand heavier than a bird per acre, or a deer per 20 acres. Take upland birds as an example. The safe limit of annual kill is one-third the population, hence under ideal conditions it takes 3 acres to put a bird in the hunting coat. Under the non-Utopian realities of actual practice it will likely take at least 6 acres. Perhaps half of Wisconsin is suitable to be cropped for birds. On this half the state could bag 3 million birds yearly, or 15 for each hunter now licensed. This is ample, but it assumes *all suitable land* to be cropped. By no stretch of the imagination could the public own all suitable land. Moreover, if it did, the land would no longer be farmed, whereupon its productive capacity for game would sink to a much lower figure. If the public owned and cropped a tenth of the state—3 million acres—it could produce only 5 birds for each hunter now licensed. What, now, is left for the unlicensed thousands who have leisure but no place to spend it, and for the non-residents who are the answer to the booster's prayer?

We can, to be sure, get heavier yields by artificial propagation, but the cost would be prohibitive and the esthetic quality of the product distinctly lower. It also happens that waterfowl differ from other game. They have no intolerance of concentration.

Large-scale public ownership of marshlands, therefore, is feasible. It is also necessary, because the interstate movements of waterfowl render the incentive for their private production partially inoperative. Hence waterfowl stand as an exception to the rule.

It is clear, however, that the inherent dispersion of the phenomena dealt with in game management makes public game production a mere supplement to production on private lands. Game must grow as a by-product of other land uses. "Sport for all" is obtainable only by using all the land. Public game cropping as a sole dependence is excluded by the very nature of the game itself.

Consider, now, the geography of forests. Forestry is unique in that timber products can be grown in one place and used in another. This is not true of game or fish or erosion control, or scenery, or wildflowers, or birdsongs. Forestry is unique also in this respect: Consumption of timber products is not increasing. Hence it is probably feasible to relegate the timber-growing function to public lands. It is not, to be sure, a desirable solution of the forest problem, because the secondary functions of erosion control, wild life production, and recreation decline as dispersion decreases. Wood waste goes up as dispersion goes down. The social disciplines which private landowners might derive from timber-growing certainly are partly lost when the job is done vicariously by public agents. Until 1933, both foresters and lumbermen clung tenaciously to the theory that there must be both private and public forestry, despite the near-failure of all efforts to bring private practice into existence. Since 1933, however, there has been a virtual stampede for public ownership. Even Article X of the Lumber Code seems to be bending in the direction of a preparation for public acquisition of cutovers.

What, now, is the geography of soil erosion and floods? What is the dispersion of the phenomena which determine the regimen of the Mississippi?—which determine whether the topsoil on farms shall stay where it is, or be dumped into the Gulf of Mexico? Unless science has utterly deluded itself, the answer is at variance with the recent trend of land policy. With as much certainty as we know whether swallows hibernate in mud, and whether the elements are fire, water, and air, we know that the dispersion of potential erosion is as universal as the dispersion of cultivation, grazing, slope, and rain. How, then, shall we control it by purchasing a few headwaters and riverbanks and converting them into public forests? These spots are, I admit, usually the most vulnerable, and their public afforestation will, I admit, retard the degeneration of our soil and water resources, but will it assure the physical integrity of America in A.D. 2000, or even A.D. 1950? Most assuredly not. It is a geographic axiom that there is no such assurance except in the *conservative use of every acre on every watershed in America*, whether it be farm or forest, public or private. In the West are dozens of irrigation projects "protected" by a headwater-patch of national forest, each subjoined by a watershed on which overgrazing, fire, and dry-farming have run riot. Most of these "protected" reservoirs began to choke with silt before the ink was dry on their bonds. This disease of erosion is a leprosy of the land, hardly to be cured by slapping a mustard plaster on the first sore. The only cure is the universal reformation of land-use, and the longer we dabble with palliatives, the more gigantic grows the job of restoration.

Let us now examine the geography of that subtle, complex, and (barring agriculture) most important of all the uses of land: recreation. Recreation is a perpetual battlefield because it is a single word denoting as many diverse things as there are diverse people. One can discuss it only in personal terms. A sawlog can be scaled, and a covey of quail is 15 birds, but there is no unit of either volume or value wherewith diverse persons can impersonally measure or compare recreational use. Those who have opinions about it must admit, like Whitman, that

> "Whatever the sounding, whatever the sea or the sail,
>   Man brings all things to the test of himself."

The salient geographic character of outdoor recreation, to my mind, is that recreational use is self-destructive. The more people are concentrated on a given area, the less is the chance of their finding what they seek. This is not true of the uncritical mob, but I see no more reason for running a national or state park to please the mob than a public art gallery or a public university. A slum is a slum, whether in the Bowery or on the Yellowstone. Dispersion, then, is the first principle of recreational planning. Dispersion of outdoor playgrounds has the equally important attribute of enhancing their accessibility.

It is inconceivable to me that the "leisure for all" revealed to us in Mr. Hoover's dream can be spent mainly, or even in large part, on public recreation grounds. Already the public grounds are so congested that the solitary recreationists must either invade such of their roadless hinterlands as may have temporarily escaped the CWA, or avoid them altogether. The expanding demand for recreation must in some way be spread over both public and private lands, or else, like Shakespeare's virtue, it will "die of its own too-much."

Let it be clear that I do not challenge the purchase of public lands for conservation. For the first time in history we are buying on a scale commensurate with the size of the problem. I do challenge the growing assumption that bigger buying is a substitute for private conservation practice. Bigger buying, I fear, is serving as an escape-mechanism,—it masks our failure to solve the harder problem. The geographic cards are stacked against its ultimate success. In the long run it is exactly as effective as buying half an umbrella.

INTEGRATION

It has always been admitted that the several kinds of conservation should be integrated with each other, and with other economic land uses. The theory is that one and the same oak will grow sawlogs, bind soil against erosion, retard floods, drop acorns to game, furnish shelter for song birds, and cast shade for picnics; that one and the same acre can and should serve forestry, watersheds, wild life, and recreation simultaneously. It required the open money-bags of 1933, however, to demonstrate what a disparity still exists between this paper ideal and the actual performance of a field-foreman turned loose with a crew and a circular of instructions on how to do some one particular kind of conservation work. There was, for example, the road crew cutting a grade along a clay bank so as permanently to roil the troutstream which another crew was improving with dams and shelters; the silvicultural crew felling the "wolf trees" and border shrubbery needed for game food; the roadside-cleanup crew burning all the down oak fuel wood available to the fireplaces being built by the recreation-ground crew; the planting crew setting pines all over the only open clover-patch available to the deer and partridges; the fire-line crew burning up all the hollow snags on a wild-life refuge, or worse yet, felling the gnarled veterans which were about the only scenic thing along a "scenic road." In short, the ecological and esthetic limitations of "scientific" technology were revealed in all their nakedness.

Such crossed wires were frequent, even in the CCC camps where crews were directed by brainy young technicians, many of them fresh from conservation schools, but each schooled only in his particular "specialty." What atrocities prevailed in the more ephemeral organizations like the CWA, he who runs may read. The instructive part of this experience is not that cub foreman should lack omniscience in integrating conservation, but that the high-ups (of which I was one) *did not anticipate* these conflicts of interest, sometimes did not see them when they occurred, and were ill-prepared to adjust them when seen. The plain lesson is that to be a practitioner of conservation on a piece of land takes more brains, and a wider range of sympathy, forethought, and experience, than to be a specialized forester, game manager, range manager, or erosion expert in a college or a conservation bureau. Integration is easy on paper, but a lot more important and more difficult in the field than any of us foresaw. None of us had ever had enough volume and variety of field labor simultaneously at work to be fully aware of either its pitfalls or its possibilities. If the *accouchement* of conservation in 1933 bore no other fruits, this sobering experience would alone be worth its pains and cost.

If trained technicians on public lands find it no small task to integrate the diverse public interests in land-use, what shall we say of the private landowner, scrambling for a hard-earned living, who has not even been told what these public interests are?

LEGISLATION

It is a conspicuous fact that almost all our present laws and appropriations are single-track measures dealing with a single aspect of land-use. During the summer of 1933, it became an equally conspicuous fact that when applied to the soil these measures frequently clash, or at best, fail to dovetail with each other.

Take, for example, a hypothetical Wisconsin farm, and count the geeings and hawings which result from having a dozen drivers for a single horse.

First we have the AAA paying the farmer a bonus for taking

land out of corn or tobacco. Is the farmer encouraged to re-organize his layout of fields so as to divert this idle acreage permanently to game, forestry, or erosion control? No—that is not the business of the AAA. On the contrary, he is free to clear new woods, or push his pastures further up the hill, to the actual detriment of forestry, game, and erosion.

Again we have the CCC, building free check-dams in the farmer's gullies, and doing a splendid job of it. But does the CCC stipulate that he must pull his cows down off the steep slopes, and so revise his farming that new gullies will not form? To a very limited extent, and only in the most flagrant cases. The single-track approach is virtually precluded from revising other land uses so as to give permanence to the benefits it confers.

Again we have the Forest Crop Law, offering a tax rebate to those who practice forestry. Does the timber owner who makes his woods produce not only timber but also game, erosion-control, fur, or wildflowers, gain any preferred status thereby? Not at all, despite the fact that he may benefit the public ten times as much as he who practices forestry only, and despite the fact that the legislature which passed the law, and the conservation commission which administers it, are equally interested in these "side-issues."

This hypothetical farm may be in a fire-protection district which receives federal aid from the Clarke-McNary Law. The district may qualify as to fire, but be a public menace as to wild life, or recreation. These things, however, cannot sway the inspector who passes on compliance with fire-control standards. He must listen only to the rigid single-track definition of conservation embalmed in his particular single-track statute.

These bewilderments, of course, extend far beyond the conservation field. The public game farm restocks the coverts which the public highway crew has just burned up or cut down. Congress is about to tax duck hunters to restore the marshes which its own agents have caused to be drained. The Agricultural Colleges preach fences for the public grazing ranges,—the Interior Department prohibits them. Not all of these reversals are preventable—hindsight is better than foresight, and always will be; sincere public servants disagree on what is sound public policy, and always will. The list, however, is sufficiently impressive to raise these basic questions:

(a) Does the rigid statutory single-track definition of conservation attain even its own limited object? History so far answers: seldom.

(b) Can the private landowner be expected to integrate these uncoördinated definitions into a single system of land use? Not, I think, if government experts find it difficult to do so.

(c) When the taxpayer learns what poor teamwork exists between the various conservation dollars, will he be satisfied to roll more of them down the same old rut? I doubt it.

(d) If single-track subsidy or compulsion will not work, and if the alternative of public acquisition is not a solution, then what is the solution?

ECONOMICS

In attempting to throw light on this question, we must first examine briefly the time-honored supposition that conservation is profitable, and that the profit-incentive is sufficient to motivate its practice.

Forestry and erosion-control are often profitable *if started before deterioration sets in*,—seldom if started later. Advanced erosion is always unprofitable to control if regarded from the local viewpoint, but if one adds the cost of handling the floods and silting caused by the dislocated soil, it is cheaper to cure it at its source, even though the cost may exceed the value of the land.

Game management is profitable if some major crop carries the land and if the environment need not be rebuilt,—seldom if the game alone must carry the land, or if the land is ruined.

Recreation and allied esthetic uses seldom offer direct income. They can usually be considered profitable only by the general public, and after crediting intangibles.

It is apparent even from this brief survey that:

1. Direct profits are operative only in spots.
2. Advanced deterioration usually precludes profits.
3. No balanced program can be built on profit alone. Public intervention is necessary.
4. Prevention, whatever the cost, is usually cheaper than cure.
5. Incentives are more promising than penalties, because penalties are *ex post facto*.

The wholesale public expenditures for 1933 indicate that from now on, whenever a private landowner so uses his land as to injure the public interest, *the public will eventually pay the bill*, either by buying him out, or by donating the repairs, or both. Hence the prevention of damage to the soil, or to the living things upon it, has become a first principle of public finance. Abuse is no longer merely a question of depleting a capital asset, *but of actually creating a cash liability against the taxpayer*. I hope the reader will ponder this well. It is a new frame for our picture which nullifies many pre-existing grooves of thought.

The thing to be prevented is destructive private land-use of any and all kinds. The thing to be encouraged is the use of private land in such a way as to combine the public and the private interest to the greatest possible degree. If we are going to spend large sums of public money anyhow, why not use it to subsidize desirable combinations in land use, instead of to cure, by purchase, prohibition, or repair, the headache arising from bad ones?

I realize fully that such a question qualifies me for the asylum for political and economic dreamers. Yet I submit that the proposal is actually less radical politically, and possibly cheaper in economic cost, than the stampede for public ownership in which our most respectable conservatives have now joined.

Let me illustrate. Last summer I participated in the building of hundreds of erosion check-dams, each string of dams costing a sum the interest on which is greater than the taxes from the land they protect. These dams were "cures," necessary ones. But how about prevention of land uses creating more gullies needing more dams? If the farmer or stockman had, in the first place, been offered a differential tax of, let us say, 25 per cent in favor of conservative use, perhaps no dams need ever have been built. The economic saving would have been 75 per cent. Politically, is it any more radical to offer careless farmers a differential tax than to offer them free dams?

The CCC camps are planting forests on many burned-over acres at a cost as yet unannounced, but it is certainly not less than the commercial cost of $5–$10 per acre. Would the dollar or half-dollar interest on this "cure," offered as a differential tax, have prevented the lumberman who originally cut the timber from allowing the fire to run? If the present forest tax laws do not offer sufficient inducement to prevent a repetition of the tragedy, is it not logical to consider "raising the ante," or even remitting taxes altogether, on such forest properties as safeguard the public interest? Is it necessarily cheaper or better to wait and buy the charred remains as a public forest?

Our game departments are artificially restocking grazed-out or burned-over coverts year after year at $2.50 per bird, and often to no effect. How about paying the same sum to the farmer, in the form of differential taxes or shooting fees, for fencing cover spots, for feeding, and for posting the land? I know a thousand places where $2.50 worth of fence or feed will produce not one, but *ten* birds per year, ad infinitum. It would require $2,500, plus an annual bill for custodian service, to get the same results by public land purchase.

Let me at this point also plead for what may be called the "suppressed minorities" of conservation. The landowner whose boundaries happen to include an eagle's nest, or a heron rookery, or a patch of lady-slippers, or a remnant of native prairie sod, or an historical oak, or a string of Indian mounds—such a landowner is the custodian of a public interest, to an equal or sometimes greater degree than one growing a forest, or one fighting a gully. We already have such a welter of single-track statutes that new and separate prohibitions or subsidies for each of these "minority interests" would be hard to enact, and still harder to enforce or administer. Perhaps this impasse offers a clue to the whole broad problem of conservation policy. It suggests the need for some comprehensive fusion of interests, some sweeping simplification of conservation law, which sets up for each parcel of land a single criterion of land-use: "Has the public interest in *all* its resources been protected?" which motivates that criterion by a single incentive, such as the differential tax, and which delegates the function of judging compliance to some single and highly trained administrative field-inspector, subject to review by the courts. Such a man would have to be a composite tax assessor, county agent, and conservation ecologist. Such a man is hard to build, but easier, I think, than to build a law specifying in cold print the hundreds of alternative ways of handling the land resources of even a single farm.

It would perhaps be unnecessary for the law itself to define the public interest, nor for the inspector to adhere to a rigid unchanging definition through a long period of years. Such an elastic regulation of private compliance with public interest is already in successful operation in the Industrial Safety Service established by the Wisconsin Industrial Commission Act (Revised Statutes, Chap. 101).

I have administered land too long to have any illusion, or to wish to create one, that this idea of preventive subsidy is as simple as it sounds, but I doubt if it would be as complicated as the cures on which we are now embarked. Differential taxes, I realize, must reach far enough back into national finance to forestall the mere local shifting of the tax burden, and must be based on some workable criterion of good vs. bad land use. How to define it? Who to define it? Are differential taxes the best, or even a possible vehicle? I don't know. I do know that it would be hard to find a less workable criterion of that composite thing called conservation than the single-track statutes we now employ. Some of them may be tolerable as a definition of the single land-use with which each deals, but as criteria of the combination of conflicting or coöperating uses which constitute the actual land problem, they seem hopeless.

I am no economist, and no jurist. It seems clear, however, even to a layman that previous to 1933 the entire search for economic mechanisms was confined within the pre-existing limits sanctioned in our political and economic law and custom. It suddenly appears that those limits are too narrow.

Is this, after all, surprising? Our legal and economic structure was evolved on a terrain (central and western Europe) inherently more resistant to abuse than any other part of the earth's surface, and at a time when our engines for subjugating the soil were still too weak to ruin it. We have transplanted that structure to a new terrain, at least half of which is set on a hair-trigger of ecological balance. We have invented engines of unprecedented coarseness and power, and placed them freely in the hands of ignorant men. I do not regret this social experiment,—it is creation's most daring attempt to mitigate the rigors of tooth-and-claw evolution—but I assert we should be surprised, not that the pre-existing structure needs widening, but that it will serve at all.

One of the symptoms of inadequacy in our now existing structure is the perennial stalemate over the public domain.

How can we keep it without a huge expansion of federal machinery? How can we give it away without the certainty of misuse? There is indeed scant choice between the horns of this dilemma. But would there be a dilemma if there were such a thing as *contingent* possession, or else a differential tax exerting a constant positive pressure in favor of good use?

This paper forecasts that conservation will ultimately boil down to rewarding the private landowner who conserves the public interest. It asserts the new premise that if he fails to do so, his neighbors must ultimately pay the bill. It pleads that our jurists and economists anticipate the need for workable vehicles to carry that reward. It challenges the efficacy of single-track land laws, and the economy of buying wrecks instead of preventing them. It advances all these things, not with any illusion that they are truth, but out of a profound conviction that the public is at last ready to do something about the land problem, and that we are offering it twenty competing answers instead of one. Perhaps the cerebration induced by a blanket challenge may still enable us to grasp our opportunity.

Journal of Forestry, May 1934

The Arboretum and the University

For twenty centuries and longer, all civilized thought has rested upon one basic premise: that it is the destiny of man to exploit and enslave the earth.

The biblical injunction to "go forth and multiply" is merely one of many dogmas which imply this attitude of philosophical imperialism.

During the past few decades, however, a new science called ecology has been unobtrusively spreading a film of doubt over this heretofore unchallenged "world view." Ecology tells us that no animal—not even man—can be regarded as independent of his environment. Plants, animals, men, and soil are a community of interdependent parts, an organism. No organism can survive the decadence of a member. Mr. Babbitt is no more a separate entity than is his left arm, or a single cell of his biceps. Neither are those aggregations of men and earth which we call Madison, or Wisconsin, or America. It may flatter our ego to be called the sons of man, but it would be nearer the truth to call ourselves the brothers of our fields and forests.

The incredible engines wherewith we now hasten our world-conquest have, of course, not heard of these ecological quibblings; neither, perhaps, have the incredible engineers. These engines are double-edged swords. They can be used for ecological coöperation. They are being used for ecological destruction on a scale almost geological in magnitude. In Wisconsin, for example, the northern half of the state has been rendered partially uninhabitable for the next two generations by man-made fire, while the southwestern quarter has been deteriorated for the next century by man-made erosion. In central Wisconsin a single fire in 1930 burned the soil off the better part of two counties.

It can be stated as a sober fact that the iron-heel attitude has already reduced by half the ability of Wisconsin to support a coöperative community of men, animals, and plants during the next century. Moreover, it has saddled us with a repair bill, the magnitude of which we are just beginning to appreciate.

If some foreign invader attempted such loot, the whole nation would resist to the last man and the last dollar. But as long as

we loot ourselves, we charge the indignity to "rugged individualism," and try to forget it. But we cannot quite. There is a
feeble minority called conservationists, who are indignant about
something. They are just beginning to realize that their task
involves the reorganization of society, rather than the passage
of some fish and game laws.

What has all this to do with the Arboretum? Simply this: If
civilization consists of coöperation with plants, animals, soil and
men, then a university which attempts to define that coöperation must have, for the use of its faculty and students, places
which show what the land was, what it is, and what it ought to
be. This Arboretum may be regarded as a place where, in the
course of time, we will build up an exhibit of what was, as well
as an exhibit of what ought to be. It is with this dim vision of
its future destiny that we have dedicated the greater part of the
Arboretum to a reconstruction of original Wisconsin, rather
than to a "collection" of imported trees.

The iron-heel mentality is, of course, indifferent to what Wisconsin was. This is exactly the reason why the University cannot
be. I am here to say that the invention of a harmonious relationship between men and land is a more exacting task than the invention of machines, and that its accomplishment is impossible
without a visual knowledge of the land's history. Take the grass
marsh here under our view: From the recession of the glacier
until the days of the fur trade, it was a tamarack bog—stems and
stumps are still imbedded there. In its successive layers of peat
are embalmed both the pollens which record the vegetation of
the bog and the surrounding countryside, and also the bones
of its animals. During some drouth, man-caused fires burned
off the tamarack, which gave place first to grass and brush, and
then, under continual burning and grazing, to straight grass.
This is the history and status of a thousand other marshes.
What will happen if the decomposed surface peat is all burned
off? At what stage of the retrogression from forest to meadow
is the marsh of greatest use to the animal community? How is
that desirable stage to be attained and maintained? What is the
role of drainage? These questions are of national importance.
They determine the future habitability of the earth, materially
and spiritually. They are just as important as whether to join the
League of Nations—it is only our iron-heel inheritance which

makes the comparison ludicrous. The scientist does not know the answer—he has been too busy inventing machines. The time has come for science to busy itself with the earth itself. The first step is to reconstruct a sample of what we had to start with. That, in a nutshell, is the Arboretum.

Land Pathology

THE PROPERTIES of animal and plant populations are now to some extent known. Their interactions with environment are becoming predictable. Ecological predictions are made with such certainty as to be used daily in farm, factory, and hospital.

The properties of human populations and their interactions with land are still imperfectly understood. Predictions of behavior are made, but with much uncertainty, and hence are seldom used. Economists, conservationists, and planners are just beginning to become aware that there is a basic ecology involved.

Philosophers have long since claimed that society is an organism, but with few exceptions they have failed to understand that the organism includes the land which is its medium. The properties of human populations, which are the joint domain of sociologist, economist, and statesman, are all conditioned by land.

We may never put society and its land into a test tube, but some of their interactions are discernible by ordinary observation. This paper attempts to define and discuss those which pertain to land conservation.

Conservation is a protest against destructive land use. It seeks to preserve both the utility and beauty of the landscape. It now invokes the aid of science as a means to this end. Science has never before been asked to write a prescription for an esthetic ailment of the body politic. The effort may benefit scientists as well as laymen and land.

Conservationists are sharply divided into groups, interested respectively in soil fertility, soil erosion, forests, parks, ranges, water flows, game, fish, fur, non-game animals, landscape, wild flowers, etc.

These divergent foci of interest clearly arise from individual limitations of taste, knowledge, and experience. They also reflect the age-old conflict between utility and beauty. Some believe the two can be integrated, on the same land, to mutual advantage. Others believe their opposing claims must be fought out and settled by exclusive dedication of each parcel of land to either the one use or the other.

This paper proceeds on two assumptions. The first is that

there is only one soil, one flora, one fauna, one people, and hence only one conservation problem. Each acre should produce what it is good for and no two are alike. Hence a certain acre may serve one, or several, or all of the conservation groups.

The second is that economic and esthetic land uses can and must be integrated, usually on the same acre. To segregate them wastes land, and is unsound social philosophy. The ultimate issue is whether good taste and technical skill can both exist in the same landowner. This is a challenge to agricultural education.

When we examine the history of interactions between society and land, there emerge at once a series of observational deductions. We cannot check their accuracy by controlled experiments, but they may at that be more dependable than deductions drawn by historians and statesmen who commonly know nothing of ecology in the lower organisms. These are:

(1) Before the machine age, destructive interactions between society and land tended to right themselves by automatic adjustments similar to those now seen to exist in animal communities. These include population cycles, emigration, starvation, interpredation, etc.

(2) The early phases of machine civilization occurred on land especially resistant to abuse. Northwestern Europe, for example, seems to possess extraordinary recuperative capacity, i.e. capacity, when disturbed, to establish new and stable equilibria between soil, plants, and animals.

(3) Destructive interactions probably contributed to the decay of some early societies even before the machine age. Semi-arid climates such as the eastern Mediterranean, and continental climates such as the Chinese interior, are possibly especially susceptible to upsets of equilibrium. All this, however, is conjectural, due to the possible masking effect of climatic change.

(4) America presents the first instance of a society, heavily equipped with machines, invading a terrain in large part set on a hair-trigger. The accelerating velocity of destructive interactions is unmistakable and probably unprecedented. Recuperative mechanisms either do not exist, or have not had time to get under way. The mechanism

of these interactions in such resources as soil, forests, ranges, and wild life has been traced, at least in its grosser aspects, and found to be strongly inter-connected.

(5) Not all the destruction is wrought directly by machines. The machines release natural forces, such as fire, erosion, floods, and disease, and give them an unnatural play, devoid of checks and balances. Machines also, in one way or another, nullify the checks and balances on domestic animals.

These five assertions may perhaps have weathered enough history to be called deductions. Of equal interest, however, is a further series of opinions based on very recent events. These are:

(6) Remedial practices are being worked out but are not being applied except on public land or at public expense. This presents no sufficient solution because of the universal geographic dispersion of the destructive processes. Public action cannot become universal without breaking down the tax-base which supports it.

(7) The present legal and economic structure, having been evolved on a more resistant terrain (Europe) and before the machine age, contains no suitable ready-made mechanisms for protecting the public interest in private land. It evolved at a time when the public had no interest in land except to help tame it.

(8) The unprecedented velocity of land-subjugation in America involved much hardship, which in turn created traditions which ignore esthetic land uses. The subsequent growth of cities has permitted a re-birth of esthetic culture, but in landless people who have no opportunity to apply it to the soil. The large volume and low utility of conservation legislation may be attributed largely to this maladjustment; also the dissentious character of the conservation movement.

(9) Rural education has been preoccupied with the transplantation of machinery and city culture to the rural community, latterly in the face of economic conditions so adverse as to evict the occupants of submarginal soils.

The net result has been to intensify destructive forces on the abandoned land, and to further defer any rebirth of land esthetics in landowners.

With this background, we may now pose the question: What can the social and physical sciences, as now mobilized in this or other universities, do toward hastening the needed adjustment between society as now equipped, and land-use as now practiced?

We may, perhaps, first narrow the field by one exclusion. For the moment, at least, it would seem safe to conclude that all those remedies which hinge upon public purchase, or the extension of existing types of law or administration need no particular stimulation. Their momentum is already great.

We may also conjecture, from recent history, that it will require the injection of some new and potent forces to effect any real change.

In my opinion, there are two possible forces which might operate *de novo*, and which universities might possibly create by research. One is the formulation of mechanisms for protecting the public interest in private land. The other is the revival of land esthetics in rural culture.

The further refinement of remedial practices is equally important, but need not here be emphasized because it already has some momentum.

Out of these three forces may eventually emerge a land ethic more potent than the sum of the three, but the breeding of ethics is as yet beyond our powers. All science can do is to safeguard the environment in which ethical mutations might take place.

The possible ethic, and the philosophical basis for predicting its emergence, has been discussed in several recent publications.*† Land esthetics lies outside the scope of this paper. A preliminary discussion of vehicles for public influence on private land-use has been published,‡ but will here be restated from a different angle.

*De Beaux, Oscar. 1932. *Biological Ethics.* Italian Mail & Tribune, Florence.
†Leopold, Aldo. 1933. *The Conservation Ethic.* Jour. Forestry, Vol. XXXI, No. 6, October, pp. 634–643.
‡_____. 1934. *Conservation Economics.* Jour. Forestry, Vol. XXXII, No. 5, May, pp. 537–544.

A convenient way to open up the subject is to review the sequence of ideas and experiences which led to the present situation.

It was at first assumed that the profit motive would impel landowners to conserve. This expectation is so far frustrated, and we can now see at least three reasons why.

One is that in the presence of excess land, it was cheaper, or at least appeared cheaper, to exploit new land than to conserve old.

Another is that the profit motive operates only during the early stages of land deterioration. It would often pay the individual owner to reclaim slightly damaged land, but in this early stage he does not yet know it is damaged. By the time he sees the damage, it is beyond his means to cure it. It has become a community damage, and thus a charge against the public treasury.

Another is that the competition of synthetic materials, usually of mineral origin, has destroyed confidence in the future of such products as lumber.

When private conservation for profit failed to materialize, legislative compulsion was advanced as an alternative. By this time, however, science had shown good land-use to require much positive skill as well as negative abstention. Compulsion was never tried on any scale.

The recent Lumber Code was a self-imposed compulsion of great promise, but is now thrown out by the Courts. It collided in some of its implications with certain older doctrines of great and massive stability.

Confronted by this succession of obstacles, conservation has now turned to government ownership and subsidy as the way out. The fallacy inherent in this policy has already been pointed out: There is nothing to prevent *all* our vulnerable land from eventually running through the same sequence of private deterioration followed by public repairs.

The system contains the seeds of its own eventual breakdown. It lacks some way to prevent the beginnings of the landslide— some mechanism for checking deterioration while costs are still low. This critical point lies *ipso facto* on private holdings; the government holds only the wrecks. It would cost the government less to prevent these wrecks than repair them. But how prevent them? A vehicle for rewarding good private practices, and penalizing bad ones, is a possible answer, and also the only visible way to prevent the public repairs policy from dying, like the dinosaur, of its own bigness.

Incidentally, such a vehicle could also be used to encourage the conservation of landscape beauty. There never has been even any initial assumption as to how else this could be done. A few parcels of outstanding scenery are immured as parks, but under the onslaughts of mass transportation their possible function as "outdoor universities" is being impaired by the very human need which impelled their creation. Parks are over-crowded hospitals trying to cope with an epidemic of esthetic rickets; the remedy lies not in hospitals, but in daily dietaries. The vast bulk of land beauty and land life, dispersed as it is over a thousand hills, continues to waste away under the same forces as are undermining land utility. The private owner who today undertakes to conserve beauty on his land, does so in defiance of all man-made economic forces from taxes down—or up. There is much beauty left—animate and inanimate—but its existence, and hence its continuity, is almost wholly a matter of accident.

I plead, in short, for positive and substantial public encour-agement, economic and moral, for the landowner who con-serves the public values—economic or esthetic—of which he is the custodian. The search for practicable vehicles to carry that encouragement is a research problem, and I think a soluble one. A solution apparently calls for a synthesis of biological, legal, and economic skills, or, if you will, a social application of the physical sciences of the sort now sought by this university's "Science Inquiry."

I might say, defensively, that such a vehicle would not nec-essarily imply regimentation of private land-use. The private owner would still decide what to use his land for; the public would decide merely whether the net result is good or bad for its stake in his holdings.

Those charged with the search for such a vehicle must first seek to intellectually encompass the whole situation. It may mean something far more profound than I have foreseen. Any remedy may imply corollary commitments and changes.

One of these I can see plainly. Every American has tattooed on his left breast the basic premise that manifestations of economic energy are inherently beneficent. Yet there is one which to me seems malignant, not inherently, but because a good thing has outrun its limits of goodness. We learn, in ecology at least, that all truths hold only within limits. Here is a good thing—the improvement in economic tools. It has exceeded the speed, or degree, within which it was good. Equipped with this excess of tools, society has developed an unstable adjustment to its environment, from which both must eventually suffer damage or even ruin. Regarding society and land collectively as an organism, that organism has suddenly developed pathological symptoms, i.e. self-accelerating rather than self-compensating departures from normal functioning. The tools cannot be dropped, hence the brains which created them, and which are now mostly dedicated to creating still more, must be at least in part diverted to controlling those already in hand. Granted that science can invent more and more tools, which might be capable of squeezing a living even out of a ruined countryside, yet who wants to be a cell in that kind of a body politic? I for one do not.

Typescript, April 15, 1935

Coon Valley:
An Adventure in Cooperative Conservation

THERE ARE two ways to apply conservation to land. One is to superimpose some particular practice upon the pre-existing system of land-use, without regard to how it fits or what it does to or for other interests involved.

The other is to reorganize and gear up the farming, forestry, game cropping, erosion control, scenery, or whatever values may be involved so that they collectively comprise a harmonious balanced system of land-use.

Each of our conservation factions has heretofore been so glad to get any action at all on its own special interest that it has been anything but solicitous about what happened to the others. This kind of progress is probably better than none, but it savors too much of the planless exploitation it is intended to supersede.

Lack of mutual cooperation among conservation groups is reflected in laws and appropriations. Whoever gets there first writes the legislative ticket to his own particular destination. We have somehow forgotten that all this unorganized avalanche of laws and dollars must be put in order before it can permanently benefit the land, and that this onerous job, which is evidently too difficult for legislators and propagandists, is being wished upon the farmer and upon the administrator of public properties. The farmer is still trying to make out what it is that the many-voiced public wants him to do. The administrator, who is seldom trained in more than one of the dozen special fields of skill comprising conservation, is growing gray trying to shoulder his new and incredibly varied burdens. The stage, in short, is all set for somebody to show that each of the various public interests in land is better off when all cooperate than when all compete with each other. This principle of integration of land uses has been already carried out to some extent on public properties like the National Forests. But only a fraction of the land, and the poorest fraction at that, is or can ever become public property. The crux of the land problem is to show that integrated use is possible on private farms, and that such integration is mutually advantageous to both the owner and the public.

362

Such was the intellectual scenery when in 1933 there appeared upon the stage of public affairs a new federal bureau, the United States Soil Erosion Service. Erosion-control is one of those new professions whose personnel has been recruited by the fortuitous interplay of events. Previous to 1933 its work had been to define and propagate an idea, rather than to execute a task. Public responsibility had never laid its crushing weight on their collective shoulders. Hence the sudden creation of a bureau, with large sums of easy money at its disposal, presented the probability that some one group would prescribe its particular control technique as the panacea for all the ills of the soil. There was, for example, a group that would save land by building concrete check-dams in gullies, another by terracing fields, another by planting alfalfa or clover, another by planting slopes in alternating strips following the contour, another by curbing cows and sheep, another by planting trees.

It is to the lasting credit of the new bureau that it immediately decided to use not one, but all, of these remedial methods. It also perceived from the outset that sound soil conservation implied not merely erosion control, but also the integration of all land crops. Hence, after selecting certain demonstration areas on which to concentrate its work, it offered to each farmer on each area the cooperation of the government in installing on his farm a reorganized system of land-use, in which not only soil conservation and agriculture, but also forestry, game, fish, fur, flood-control, scenery, songbirds, or any other pertinent interest were to be duly integrated. It will probably take another decade before the public appreciates either the novelty of such an attitude by a bureau, or the courage needed to undertake so complex and difficult a task.

The first demonstration area to get under way was the Coon Valley watershed, near LaCrosse, in west-central Wisconsin. This paper attempts a thumbnail sketch of what is being done on the Coon Valley Erosion Project. Coon Valley is one of the innumerable little units of the Mississippi Valley which collectively fill the national dinner pail. Its particular contribution is butterfat, tobacco, and scenery.

When the cows which make the butter were first turned out upon the hills which comprise the scenery, everything was all right because there were more hills than cows, and because the soil still retained the humus which the wilderness vegetation through the centuries had built up. The trout streams ran clear, deep, narrow, and full. They seldom overflowed. This is proven by the fact that the first settlers stacked their hay on the creek-banks, a procedure now quite unthinkable. The deep loam of even the steepest fields and pastures showed never a gully, being able to take on any rain as it came, and turn it either upward into crops, or downward into perennial springs. It was a land to please everyone, be he an empire-builder or a poet.

But pastoral poems had no place in the competitive indus-trialization of pre-war America, least of all in Coon Valley with its thrifty and ambitious Norse farmers. More cows, more silos to feed them, then machines to milk them, and then more pasture to graze them—this is the epic cycle which tells in one sentence the history of the modern Wisconsin dairy farm. More pasture was obtainable only on the steep upper slopes, which were timber to begin with, and should have remained so. But pasture they now are, and gone is the humus of the old prairie which until recently enabled the upland ridges to take on the rains as they came.

Result: Every rain pours off the ridges as from a roof. The ravines of the grazed slopes are the gutters. In their pastured condition they cannot resist the abrasion of the silt-laden tor-rents. Great gashing gullies are torn out of the hillside. Each gully dumps its load of hillside rocks upon the fields of the creek bottom, and its muddy waters into the already swollen streams. Coon Valley, in short, is one of the thousand farm communities which, through the abuse of its originally rich soil, has not only filled the national dinner pail, but has created the Mississippi flood problem, the navigation problem, the overproduction problem, and the problem of its own future continuity.

The Coon Valley Erosion Project is an attempt to combat these national evils at their source. The "nine-foot channel" and endless building of dykes, levees, dams and harbors on the lower river, are attempts to put a halter on the same bull after he has gone wild.

The Soil Erosion Service says to each individual farmer in Coon Valley: "The government wants to prove that your farm can be brought back. We will furnish you free labor, wire, seed, lime, and planting stock, if you will help us reorganize your

cropping system. You are to give the new system a 5-year trial."
A total of 315 farmers, or nearly half of all the farms in the watershed, have already formally accepted the offer. Hence we now
see foregathered at Coon Valley a staff of technicians to figure
out what should be done; a C.C.C. camp to perform labor; a
nursery, a seed warehouse, a lime quarry, and other needed
equipments; a series of contracts with farmers, which, collectively, comprise a "regional plan" for the stabilization of the
watershed and of the agricultural community which it supports.

The plan, in a nutshell, proposes to remove all cows and
crops from the steep slopes, and to use these slopes for timber
and wildlife only. More intensive cultivation of the flat lands is
to make up for the retirement of the eroding hillsides. Gently
sloping fields are to be terraced or strip-cropped. These changes,
plus contour farming, good crop rotations, and the repair of
eroding gullies and stream banks, constitute the technique of
soil restoration.

The steep slopes now to be used for timber and game have
heretofore been largely in pasture. The first visible evidence of
the new order on a Coon Valley farm is a C.C.C. crew string-
ing a new fence along the contour which marks the beginning
of forty per cent gradients. This new fence commonly cuts off
the upper half of the pasture. Part of this upper half still bears
timber, the rest is open sod. The timbered part has been grazed
clear of undergrowth, but with protection this will come back
to brush and young timber and make range for ruffed grouse.
The open part is being planted, largely to conifers—white pine,
Norway pine, and Norway spruce for north slopes, Scotch pine
for south slopes. The dry south slopes present a special problem. In pre-settlement days they carried hazel, sumac, and bluestem rather than timber, the grass furnishing the medium for
quick hot fires. Will these hot dry soils, even under protection,
allow the planted Scotch pine to thrive? I doubt it. Only the
north slopes and coves will develop commercial timber, but all
the fenced land can at least be counted upon to produce game
and soil cover and cordwood.

Creek banks and gullies, as well as steep slopes, are being
fenced and planted. Despite their much smaller aggregate area,
these bank plantings will probably add more to the game carrying capacity of the average farm than will the larger solid blocks

of plantings on slopes. This prediction is based on their superior dispersion, their higher proportion of deciduous species, and their richer soils.

The bank plantings have showed up a curious hiatus in our silvicultural knowledge. We have learned so much about the growth of the noble conifers that we employ higher mathematics to express the profundity of our information, but at Coon Valley there have arisen, unanswered, such sobering elementary questions as this: What species of willow grow from cuttings? When and how are cuttings made, stored, and planted? Under what conditions will sprouting willow logs take root? What shrubs combine thorns, shade tolerance, grazing resistance, capacity to grow from cuttings, and the production of fruits edible by wild life? What are the comparative soil-binding properties of various shrub and tree roots? What shrubs and trees allow an understory of grass to grow, thus affording both shallow and deep rootage? How do native shrubs or grasses compare with cultivated grasses for rootbinding terrace outlets? What silvicultural treatment favors an ironwood understory to furnish buds for grouse? Can white birch for budding be planted on south slopes? Under what conditions do oak sprouts retain leaves for winter game cover?

Forestry and fencing are not the alpha and omega of Coon Valley technique. In odd spots of good land near each of the new game coverts, the observer will see a newly enclosed spot of a half-acre each. Each of these little enclosures is thickly planted to sorghum, kaffir, millet, proso, sunflower. These are the food patches to forestall winter starvation in wild life. The seed and fence were furnished by the government, the cultivation and care by the farmer. There were 337 such patches grown in 1934—the largest food patch system in the United States, save only that found on the Georgia Quail Preserves. There is already friendly rivalry among many farmers as to who has the best food patch, or the most birds using it. This feeding system is, I think, accountable for the fact that the population of quail in 1934–35 was double that of 1933–34, and the pheasant population was quadrupled. Such a feeding system, extended over all the farms of Wisconsin, would, I think, double the crop of farm game in a single year.

This whole effort to rebuild and stabilize a countryside is not without its disappointments and mistakes. A December blizzard flattened out most of the food-patches and forced recourse to hopper feeders. The willow cuttings planted on stream banks proved to be the wrong species and refused to grow. Some farmers, by wrong plowing, mutilated the new terraces just built in their fields. The 1934 drouth killed a large part of the plantings of forest and game cover.

What matter, though, these temporary growing pains when one can cast his eyes upon the hills and see hard-boiled farmers who have spent their lives destroying land now carrying water by hand to their new plantations? American lumbermen may have become so steeped in economic determinism as actually to lack the personal desire to grow trees, but not Coon Valley farmers! Their solicitude for the little evergreens is sometimes almost touching. It is interesting to note, however, that no such pride or tenderness is evoked by their new plantings of native hardwoods. What explains this difference in attitude? Does it arise from a latent sentiment for the conifers of the Scandinavian homeland? Or does it merely reflect that universal urge to capture and domesticate the exotic which found its first American expression in the romance of Pocahontas, and its last in the Americanization of the ringnecked pheasant?

Most large undertakings display, even on casual inspection, certain policies or practices which are diagnostic of the mental attitude behind the whole venture. From these one can often draw deeper inferences than from whole volumes of statistics. A diagnostic policy of the Coon Valley staff is its steadfast refusal to straighten streams. To those who know the speech of hills and rivers, straightening a stream is like shipping vagrants—a very successful method of passing trouble from one place to the next. It solves nothing in any collective sense.

Not all the sights of Coon Valley are to be seen by day. No less distinctive is the nightly "bull session" of the technical staff. One may hear a forester expounding to an engineer the basic theory of how organic matter in the soil decreases the per cent of run-off; an economist holds forth on tax rebates as a means to get farmers to install their own erosion control. Underneath the facetious conservation one detects a vein of thought—an attitude toward the common enterprise—which is strangely reminiscent of the early days of the Forest Service. Then, too, a staff of technicians, all under thirty, was faced by a common task so large and so long as to stir the imagination of all but dullards. I suspect that the Soil Erosion Service, perhaps unwittingly, has recreated a spiritual entity which many older conservationists have thought long since dead.

American Forests, May 1935

Why the Wilderness Society?

PERHAPS IT is a truth, one day to be recognized, that no idea is significant except in the presence of its opposite.

This country has been swinging the hammer of development so long and so hard that it has forgotten the anvil of wilderness which gave value and significance to its labors. The momentum of our blows is so unprecedented that the remaining remnant of wilderness will be pounded into road-dust long before we find out its values.

Under these circumstances it is fitting that those who perceive one or more of these values should band together for purposes of mutual education and common defense.

I say mutual education because I doubt whether anyone who does not sense these values of his own accord can be genuinely convinced that they exist. The record of administrators who have absorbed the custodianship of formally proclaimed "wilderness areas" bears out this doubt. The process of splitting seems often to go merrily on at almost the same rate as before. Possibly the Society can help retard this tendency toward demolition of existing wilderness areas, as well as push the establishment of new ones.

There is particular need for a Society now because of the pressure of public spending for work relief. Wilderness remnants are tempting fodder for those administrators who possess an infinite labor supply but a very finite ability to picture the real needs of his country.

The recreational value of wilderness has been set forth so ably by Marshall, Koch, and others that it hardly needs elaboration at this time. I suspect, however, that the scientific values are still scantily appreciated, even by members of the Society. These scientific values have been set forth in print, but only in the studiously "cold potato" language of the ecological scientist. Actually the scientific need is both urgent and dramatic.

The long and short of the matter is that all land-use technologies—agriculture, forestry, watersheds, erosion, game, and range management—are encountering unexpected and baffling obstacles which show clearly that despite the superficial advances in technique, *we do not yet understand and cannot yet control* the long-time interrelations of animals, plants, and mother earth. Some of these problems, such as "soil sickness" in forestry, will merely retard a part of the technical advance in that field. Others, notably some of the deeper aspects of range management and erosion control, foreshadow the possible permanent loss of whole geographic regions.

Let me give just one example: Weaver at Nebraska finds that prairie soils lose their granulation and their water-equilibrium when too long occupied by exotic crops. Apparently native prairie plants are necessary to restore that biotic stability which we call conservation. It is possible that dust storms, erosion, floods, agricultural distress, and depletion of range in the plains region all hark back fundamentally to degranulation. Perhaps degranulation also plays a part in these same phenomena elsewhere.

Here then is a new discovery which may illuminate basic questions of national policy. On it may hinge the future habitability of a third of the continent. But how shall it be followed up if there be no prairie flora left to compare with cultivated flora? And who cares a hang about preserving prairie flora except those who see the values of the wilderness?

The Wilderness Society is, philosophically, a disclaimer of the biotic arrogance of *Homo americanus*. It is one of the focal points of a new attitude—an intelligent humility toward man's place in nature.

The Living Wilderness, September 1935

Wilderness
("To an American conservationist . . .")

To an American conservationist, one of the most insistent impressions received from travel in Germany is the lack of wildness in the German landscape.

Forests are there—interminable miles of them, spires of spruce on the skyline, glowering thickets in ravines, and many a quick glimpse "where the yellow pines are marching straight and stalwart up the hillside where they gather on the crest." Game is there—the skulking roebuck or even a scurrying *rudel* of red-deer is to be seen any evening, even from a train-window. Streams and lakes are there, cleaner of cans and old tires than our own, and no worse beset with hotels and "bide-a-wee" cottages. But yet, to the critical eye, there is something lacking that should not be lacking in a country which actually practices, in such abundant measure, all of the things we in America preach in the name of "conservation." What is it?

Let me admit to begin with the obvious difference in population density, and hence in population pressure, on the economic mechanisms of land-use. I knew of that difference before coming over, and think I have made allowance for it. Let it further be clear that I did not hope to find in Germany anything resembling the great "wilderness areas" which we dream and talk about, and sometimes briefly set aside, in our National Forests and Parks. Such monuments to wildness are an esthetic luxury which Germany, with its timber deficit and the evident land-hunger of its teeming millions, cannot afford. I speak rather of a certain quality which should be but is not found in the ordinary landscape of producing forests and inhabited farms; a quality which still in some measure persists in some of the equivalent landscapes of America, and which we I think tacitly assume will be enhanced by rather than lost in the hoped-for practice of conservation. I speak specifically to the question of whether and under what limitations that assumption is correct.

It may be well to first inquire whether the Germans themselves, who know and love their rocks and rills with an intensity long patent to all the world, admit any such esthetic deficit in their countryside. "Yes" and "no" are of course worthless as criteria of such a question. I offer in evidence, first, the existence of a very vigorous esthetic discontent, in the form of a "Naturschutz" (nature-protection) movement, the equivalent of which preceded the emergence of the wilderness idea in America. This impulse to save wild remnants is always, I think, the forerunner of the more important and complex task of mixing a degree of wildness with utility. I also submit that the Germans are still reading Cooper's "Leatherstocking" and Parkman's "Oregon Trail," and still flock to the wild-west movies. And when I asked a forester with a philosophical bent why people did not flock to his forest to camp out, as in America, he shrugged his shoulders and remarked that perhaps the tree-rows stood too close together for convenient tenting! All of which, of course, does not answer the question. Or does it?

And this calls to mind what is perhaps the first element in the German deficit: their former passion for unnecessary outdoor geometry. There is a lag in the affairs of men,—the ideas which were seemingly buried with the cold hard minds of the early-industrial era rise up out of the earth today for us to live with. Most German forests, for example, though laid out over a hundred years ago, would do credit to any cubist. The trees are not only in rows and all of a kind, but often the various age-blocks are parallelograms, which only an early discovery of the ill-effects of wind saved from being rectangles. The age-blocks may be in ascending series—1, 2, 3—like the proverbial stepladder family. The boundary between wood and field tends to be sharp, straight, and absolute, unbroken by those charming little indecisions in the form of draw, coulee, and stump-lot, which, especially in our "shiftless" farming regions, bind wood and field into an harmonious whole. The Germans are now making a determined effort to get away from cubistic forestry—experience has revealed that in about the third successive crop of conifers in "pure" stands the microscopic flora of the soil becomes upset and the trees quit growing, but it will be another generation before the new policy emerges in landscape form.

Not so easily, though, will come any respite from what the geometrical mind has done to the German rivers. If there were only room for them, it would be a splendid idea to collect all the highway engineers in the world, and also their intellectual kith and kin the Corps of Army Engineers, and settle them for life upon the perfect curves and tangents of some "improved" German river. I am aware, of course, that there are weighty commercial reasons for the canalization of the larger rivers, but I also saw many a creek and rivulet laid out straight as a dead snake, and with masonry banks to boot. I am depressed by such indignities, and I have black misgivings over the swarm of new bureaus now out to improve the American countryside. It is, I think, an historical fact that no American bureau equipped with money men and machines ever refused *on principle* to straighten a river, save only one—the Soil Conservation Service.

Another more subtle (and to the average traveller, imperceptible) element in the deficit of wildness is the near-extirpation of birds and animals of prey. I think it was Stewart Edward White who said that the existence of one grizzly conferred a flavor to a whole county. From the German hills that flavor has vanished—a victim to the misguided zeal of the game-keeper and the herdsman. Even the ordinary hawks are nearly gone—in four months travel I counted only ___. And the great owl or "Uhu"—without whose vocal austerity the winter night becomes a mere blackness—persists only in the farthest marches of East Prussia. Before our American sportsmen and game keepers and stockmen have finished their self-appointed task of extirpating our American predators, I hope that we may begin to realize a truth already written bold and clear on the German landscape: that success in most over-artificialized land-uses is bought at the expense of the public interest. The game-keeper buys an unnatural abundance of pheasants at the expense of the public's hawks and owls. The fish-culturist buys an unnatural abundance of fish at the expense of the public's herons, mergansers, and terns. The forester buys an unnatural increment of wood at the expense of the soil, and in that wood maintains an unnatural abundance of deer at the expense of all palatable shrubs and herbs.

This effect of too-many-deer on the ground-flora of the forest deserves special mention because it is an illusive burglary of esthetic wealth, the more dangerous because unintentional and unseen. Forest undergrowth consists of many species, some palatable to deer, others not. When too dense a deer population is built up, and there are no natural predators to trim it down, the palatable plants are grazed out, whereupon the deer must

be artificially fed by the game-keeper, whereupon next year's
pressure on the palatable species is still further increased, etc.
ad infinitum. The end result is the extirpation of the palatable
plants,—that is to say an unnatural simplicity and monotony
in the vegetation of the forest floor, which is still further aggravated by the too-dense shade cast by the artificially crowded
trees, and by the soil-sickness already mentioned as arising from
pure conifers. One is put in mind of Shakespeare's warning that
"virtue, grown into a pleurisy, dies of its own too-much." Be
that as it may, the forest landscape is deprived of a certain exuberance which arises from a rich variety of plants fighting with
each other for a place in the sun. It is almost as if the geological clock had been set back to those dim ages when there were
only pines and ferns. I never realized before that the melodies
of nature are music only when played against the undertones of
evolutionary history. In the German forest—that forest which
inspired the *Erlkönig*—one now hears only a dismal fugue out
of the timeless reaches of the carboniferous.

Manuscript, c. December 1935

Wilderness
("The two great cultural advances . . .")

THE TWO great cultural advances of the past century were the Darwinian theory and the development of geology. The one explained how and the other where we live. Compared with such ideas, the whole gamut of mechanical and chemical invention pales into a mere matter of current ways and means.

Just as important, however, as the origin of plants, animals, and soil is the question of how they operate as a community. Darwin lacked time to unravel any more than the beginnings of an answer. That task has fallen to the new science of ecology, which is daily uncovering a web of interdependencies so intricate as to amaze—were he here—even Darwin himself, who, of all men, should have the least cause to tremble before the veil.

One of the anomalies of modern ecology is that it is the creation of two groups, each of which seems barely aware of the existence of the other. The one studies the human community almost as if it were a separate entity, and calls its findings sociology, economics, and history. The other studies the plant and animal community, comfortably relegates the hodge-podge of politics to "the liberal arts." The inevitable fusion of these two lines of thought will, perhaps, constitute the outstanding advance of the present century.

Manuscript, c. December 1935

Threatened Species:
A Proposal to the Wildlife Conference for an Inventory of the Needs of Near-Extinct Birds and Animals

THE VOLUME of effort expended on wildlife conservation shows a large and sudden increase. This effort originates from diverse sources, and flows through diverse channels toward diverse ends. There is a widespread realization that it lacks coordination and focus.

Government is attempting to secure coordination and focus through reorganization of departments, laws, and appropriations. Citizen groups are attempting the same thing through reorganization of associations and private funds.

But the easiest and most obvious means to coordination has been overlooked: explicit definition of the immediate needs of particular species in particular places. For example: Scores of millions are being spent for land purchase, C.C.C. labor, fences, roads, trails, planting, predator control, erosion control, poisoning, investigations, water developments, silviculture, irrigation, nurseries, wilderness areas, power dams, and refuges, within the natural range of the grizzly bear.

Few would question the assertion that to perpetuate the grizzly as a part of our national fauna is a prime duty of the conservation movement. Few would question the assertion that any one of these undertakings, at any time and place, may vitally affect the restoration of the grizzly, and make it either easy or impossible of accomplishment. Yet no one has made a list of the specific needs of the grizzly, in each and every spot where he survives, and in each and every spot where he might be reintroduced, so that conservation projects in or near that spot may be judged in the light of whether they *help* or *hinder* the perpetuation of the noblest of American mammals.

On the contrary, our plans, departments, bureaus, associations, and movements are all focused on abstract categories such as recreation, forestry, parks, nature education, wildlife research, more game, fire control, marsh restoration. Nobody cares anything for these except as means toward ends. What ends? There are of course many ends which cannot and many others which need not be precisely defined at this time. But it admits of no doubt that the immediate needs of threatened members of our fauna and flora must be defined now or not at all.

Until they are defined and made public, we cannot blame public agencies, or even private ones, for misdirected effort, crossed wires, or lost opportunities. It must not be forgotten that the abstract categories we have set up as conservation objectives may serve as alibis for blunders, as well as ends for worthy work. I cite in evidence the C.C.C. crew which chopped down one of the few remaining eagle's nests in northern Wisconsin, in the name of "timber stand improvement." To be sure, the tree was dead, and according to the rules, constituted a fire risk.

Most species of shootable non-migratory game have at least a fighting chance of being saved through the process of purposeful manipulation of laws and environment called management. However great the blunders, delays, and confusion in getting management of game species under way, it remains true that powerful motives of local self-interest are at work in their behalf. European countries, through the operation of these motives, have saved their resident game. It is an ecological probability that we will evolve ways to do so.

The same cannot be said, however, of those species of wilderness game which do not adapt themselves to economic land-use, or of migratory birds which are owned in common, or of non-game forms classed as predators, or of rare plant associations which must compete with economic plants and livestock, or in general of all wild native forms which fly at large or have only an esthetic and scientific value to man. These, then, are the special and immediate concern of this inventory. Like game, these forms depend for their perpetuation on protection and a favorable environment. They need "management"—the perpetuation of good habitat—just as game does, but the ordinary motives for providing it are lacking. They are the threatened element in outdoor America,—the crux of conservation policy. The new organizations which have now assumed the name "wildlife" instead of "game," and which aspire to implement the wildlife movement, are I think obligated to focus a substantial part of their effort on these threatened forms.

This is a proposal, not only for an inventory of threatened forms in each of their respective places of survival, but an inventory of the information, techniques, and devices applicable to each species in each place, and of local human agencies capable of applying them. Much information exists, but it is scattered in many minds and documents. Many agencies are or would be willing to use it, if it were laid under their noses. If for a given problem no information exists, or no agency exists, that in itself is useful inventory.

For example, certain ornithologists have discovered a remnant of the Ivory-billed Woodpecker—a bird inextricably interwoven with our pioneer tradition—the very spirit of that "dark and bloody ground" which has become the locus of the national culture. It is known that the Ivory-bill requires as its habitat large stretches of virgin hardwood. The present remnant lives in such a forest, owned and held by an industry as reserve stumpage. Cutting may begin, and the Ivory-bill may be done for at any moment. The Park Service has or can get funds to buy virgin forests, but it does not know of the Ivory-bill or its predicament. It is absorbed in the intricate problem of accommodating the public which is mobbing its parks. When it buys a new park, it is likely to do so in some "scenic" spot, with the general objective of making room for more visitors, rather than with the specific objective of perpetuating some definite thing to visit. Its wildlife program is befogged with the abstract concept of inviolate sanctuary. Is it not time to establish particular parks or their equivalent for particular "natural wonders" like the Ivory-bill?

You may say, of course, that one rare bird is no park project—that the Biological Survey should buy a refuge, or the Forest Service a National Forest, to take care of the situation. Whereupon the question bounces back: the Survey has only duck money; the Forest Service would have to cut the timber. But is there anything to prevent the three possible agencies concerned from getting together and agreeing whose job this is, and while they are at it, a thousand other jobs of like character? And how much each would cost? And just what needs to be done in each case? And can anyone doubt that the public, through Congress, would support such a program? Well—this is what I mean by an inventory and plan.

Some sample lists of the items which need to be covered are

wilderness and other game species, such as grizzly bear, desert and bighorn sheep, caribou, Minnesota remnants of spruce partridge, masked bobwhite, Sonora deer, peccary, sagehen; predator and allied species, such as the wolf, fisher, otter, wolverine and condor; migratory birds, including the trumpeter swan, curlews, sandhill crane, Brewster's warbler; plant associations, such as prairie floras, bog floras, Alpine and swamp floras.

In addition to these forms, which are rare everywhere, there is the equally important problem of preserving the attenuated edges of species common at their respective centres. The turkey in Colorado, or the ruffed grouse in Missouri, or the antelope in Nebraska, are rare species within the meaning of this document. That there are grizzlies in Alaska is no excuse for letting the species disappear from New Mexico.

It is important that the inventory represent not merely a protest of those privileged to think, but an agreement of those empowered to act. This means that the inventory should be made by a joint committee of the conservation bureaus, plus representatives of the Wildlife Conference as representing the states and the associations. The plan for each species should be a joint commitment of what is to be done and who is to do it. The bureaus, with their avalanche of appropriations, ought to be able to loan the necessary expert personnel for such a committee, without extra cost. To sift out any possible imputation of bureaucratic, financial, or clique interest, the inter-bureau committee should feed its findings to the public through a suitable group in the National Research Council, and subject to the Council's approval. The necessary incidental funds for a secretary, for expense of gathering testimony and maps, and for publications might well come from the Wildlife Institute, or from one of the scientific foundations.

There is one cog lacking in the hoped-for machine: a means to get some kind of responsible care of remnants of wildlife remote from any bureau or its field officers. Funds can hardly be found to set up special paid personnel for each such detached remnant. It is of course proved long ago that closed seasons and refuge posters without personnel are of no avail. Here is where associations with their far-flung chapters, state officers or departments, or even private individuals can come to the rescue. One of the tragedies of contemporary conservation is the isolated individual or group who complains of having no job. The lack is not of jobs, but of eyes to see them.

The inventory should be the conservationist's eye. Every remnant should be definitely entrusted to a custodian—ranger, warden, game manager, chapter, ornithologist, farmer, stock-man, lumberjack. Every conservation meeting—national, state, or local—should occupy itself with hearing their annual reports. Every field inspector should contact their custodians—he might often learn as well as teach. I am satisfied that thousands of enthusiastic conservationists would be proud of such a public trust, and many would execute it with fidelity and intelligence.

I can see in this set-up more conservation than could be bought with millions of new dollars, more coordination of bureaus than Congress can get by new organization charts, more genuine contacts between factions than will ever occur in the war of the inkpots, more research than would accrue from many gifts, and more public education than would accrue from an army of orators and organizers. It is, in effect, a vehicle for putting Jay Darling's concept of "ancestral ranges" into action on a quicker and wider scale than could be done by appropriations alone.

American Forests, March 1936

Naturschutz in Germany

I WAS quizzing a high official of the German game administration about Pheasant management. He listened politely to
my questions, but his mind would not "stay put." His thoughts
were elsewhere. He had just returned to Germany from a stag-
hunt in the Carpathians and he was "all in a glow" about it.
He wanted to talk Carpathians, not Pheasants. So I switched
the subject.

Had he killed a stag? No. He had declined half a dozen invitations to shoot the finest stags in Germany, had gone to
Rumania instead, and killed nothing. But such tracks as he had
seen! And by what a narrow squeak he had missed a shot at a
truly wild stag in those truly wild mountains! What's more, he
had heard a wolf howl! He had seen a bear track! Eagles—flying
about camp every day. Horned Owls, serenading his lonely tent
every night. A lynx, too, had left his footprint by the spring. All
this in a virgin forest, as yet untouched by the forester's axe, and
full of blackberry jungles and wild feed!

"Thus, and not otherwise, do hillmen desire their hills."

I suppose it is difficult for the American reader, who, through
no fault of his own, can still hear a Horned Owl if he wishes,
to understand this nostalgia of the German for wildness, as
distinguished from mere forests or mere game. We Americans,
in most states at least, have not yet experienced a bearless, wolfless, Eagleless, catless woods. We yearn for more deer and more
pines, and we shall probably get them. But do we realize that
to get them, as the Germans have, at the expense of their wild
environment and their wild enemies, is to get very little indeed?

I recite this as a kind of frame for my sketch of the Naturschutz movement, which is embarked on a very positive and
aggressive program of wild-life restoration in Germany. A traveling fellowship from the Carl Schurz Foundation made it possible for me, during the past summer, to gather the information
here presented.

RARE SPECIES

The most pressing job in both Germany and America is to
prevent the extermination of rare species. I here present the

score of the two countries in conserving the larger birds and mammals. In interpreting this, bear in mind that our job is much the easier, our human population being just a tenth as dense.

The *Great Bustard* (*Grosser Trappe*) corresponds in size, wildness, and appearance to our Wild Turkey, the difference being that he inhabits fields instead of woods. He is holding up well, especially in Brandenburg; a recent census shows 2000 Bustards within fifty miles of Berlin. While legally classed as shootable game, very few Bustards are actually shot. If we had 2000 genuinely Wild Turkeys in and near the District of Columbia (which, of course, we have not), we might claim equal performance.

Despite centuries of shooting, and spring shooting at that, the *Auerhahn* or Capercailzie is still found in all large German forests of suitable composition. However, only males are killed, and the total bag from each forest is very carefully regulated to fit the reproductive capacity of the local breeding stock. The Auerhahn is so deeply entrenched in German tradition that one gags at comparing him with any non-German bird, but he is like our Sage-cock in being a very large, highly specialized Grouse. Since our Sage-cock is shrinking rapidly under the onslaught of both grazing and guns, while the Auerhahn is shrinking only slowly, if at all, we will have to yield the conservation score to Germany.

"The German rivers—confined in their strait-jackets of masonry—will bear for centuries the scars of that epidemic of geometry which blighted the German mind in the 1800's."

The *Birkhahn* is strikingly similar to our Sharp-tailed Grouse in size, habits, and habitat. He differs mainly in his black color. Both Birkhahn and Sharp-tail are, with local exceptions, shrinking by reason of drainage, grazing, or reforestation of their habitats. Both countries lose in this instance.

The *Haselhuhn* is the counterpart of our Spruce Partridge, except that he inhabits hardwood underbrush instead of spruce swamps. Both species are shrinking rapidly, the former under too mush forestry, the latter under too little. Both countries lose in this case.

The *Black Stork* is not the traditional stork of the village housetop, but rather a woods-nesting species corresponding roughly to our Egrets. He is rare and shrinking; our Egrets decidedly expanding. The European Egret is gone from Germany. We can chalk ourselves a mark here, and break the chalk if we feel like it.

The *Hockerschwan*, one of the three European Swans, still breeds in numbers in both Mecklenberg and East Prussia, whereas, our only breeding Swan has been lost save for one small remnant. I think the Germans have the edge in this case.

The four *Eagles* once breeding in Germany are either pushed out or back to the Alps. We are, of course, doing our best to lose our two Eagles but have not yet had time. We score on a fumble.

The *Gray Crane*, corresponding to our Sandhill Crane,

The Great Uhu, or European Horned Owl, is being reintroduced into the German forests, after having been nearly exterminated in the interests of more game. The Germans now realize that "to get more game at the expense of its wild environment and wild enemies is to get very little indeed." (View taken at the government "owl-farm" at the Schorfheide, where Owlets from East Prussia are raised to maturity for later distribution as breeding stock.)

breeds in numbers at the Schorfheide, within an hour of Berlin, and in several other spots. Our only remaining breeding Cranes are in the Lake States and Florida-Georgia. Cranes are shrinking in both countries through drainage and highways. If we build a road through the Okeefinokee Crane-range, we certainly deserve to lose this play. If not, we might, after the Resettlement Administration has completed its purchase of Crane-ranges in the Lake States, claim an even score.

The *Wisent*, or European bison, is at such a low ebb that the German remnant, preserved at the Schorfheide, has been cross-bred with our buffalo in an effort to bring it back. This is equivalent to the proposal, never carried out, to cross the Heath Hen with the Prairie Chicken. The intent is to gradually weed out the buffalo characters by selective culling. Our buffalo obviously is in better case.

The *Elch* (moose) is still shootable game in Germany, but is rather narrowly localized, mostly in East Prussia. A strong effort is being made to establish a new herd at the Schorfheide, but

Great Bustard, or Trappe. A recent census shows 2000 Bustards in Brandenburg, near Berlin. "If we had 2000 genuinely Wild Turkeys in and near the District of Columbia, we might claim equal performance."

the severe overgrazing of this range by deer makes this an uphill job. Great areas of pine are being artificially underplanted with hardwoods to make moose-feed. The German moose problem really corresponds, in point of difficulty, not to our moose, but rather to our straggling remnant of caribou in Minnesota. Until the Resettlement Administration recently took up the job of consolidating a range, this, our sole remaining herd of caribou, had been notoriously neglected for years by all parties concerned. If we admit this comparison, we must chalk up a mark for Germany.

(I cannot here forbear to interject a remark made to me some years ago by a state game warden of Minnesota, in response to my question: "What luck are you having in building up your caribou?" "We don't bother with them much," he replied. "They are too scarce to hunt, and they stay so far back from the roads that we can't show them to tourists, so, after all, what good are they?")

The *Chamoix* is still managed as huntable game in the German Alps. Except where run out of his winter range by the growing horde of ski-parties, he is doing well; compared with our shrinking Bighorns, very well; compared with our mountain goat, as well. We may score this, to vary the monotony, even up.

Bears are exterminated in Germany. The last bear was killed in Westphalia in 1752 and in Bohemia in 1856. In such cramped quarters, it may have been impossible for Germany to perpetuate her bears. It seems incongruous, though, for us to accept the better score for bear conservation when our Government has just finished eradicating the grizzly from all but a few of our National Forests.

Otter and *Marten* are still widely distributed, the latter particularly furnishing a regular annual fur crop. There are certainly more otters and martens harvested each year in Germany than remain alive in the United States. German *Beaver*, on the other hand, are reduced to one colony, whereas our beaver are thriving. In respect of the three furbearers collectively, we may possibly claim a drawn score.

Summing up these 13 larger birds and mammals of the rare or threatened class, and making no allowance for the German handicap in human population density, we have:

    5 drawn scores
    4 better survivals in Germany
    <u>4</u> better survivals in the United States
   13

I did not attempt any study of the conservation of rare plants. In general, the rare forest plants of Germany have suffered severely under the pressure of too many deer and too much spruce, while the rare marsh plants have largely succumbed to drainage. Germany had no prairie, and hence has no prairie flora to worry about.

An analysis of the German deer problem will appear as a separate paper in the *Journal of Forestry*.

PREDATOR CONTROL

The status of and attitude toward predators is, of course, a sensitive index to the power and quality of the Naturschutz movement in any country. Germany is today experiencing the same conflict as we are between the game keeper, with his traditional beliefs in rigid control, and the ornithologist, with his striving toward an ecological interpretation of predation.

Each of the two countries has two kinds of sportsmen, those who reason with the eye and believe the only good Hawk is a dead one, and those who reason with the mind and perceive that the vulnerability of game to predators may be determined by forces other than the shot gun or pole-trap. Each has two kinds of ornithologists, those who recite "more good than harm" statistics, and those who see in predation a complex mechanism as yet little understood, but probably definitely related to and necessary for a healthy biota. Each has two kinds of game-management—the kind which builds up such an unnaturally high game density that vulnerability to predators is inevitable, and the kind which prides itself on a natural (and usually quite invulnerable) game-stand. Finally, cutting across each of these classes, is the mental category which asserts that predators, like game, have a positive value as a form of natural beauty, and, on the other hand, the category which brands the recognition of all values, save only that of gun-fodder, as chicken-hearted sentimentality.

The human line-ups are thus substantially identical, but I

think that research in the ecology of predation is farther advanced in America, while officialdom in Germany leans more toward the ecological view. The reason for this official leaning lies partly, at least, in the fact that Naturschutz, as an expression of nationalism, is one of the very explicit tenets of the ruling party. Our political parties espouse "conservation" in general terms, but they carefully avoid commitment on its internal contradictions. Hence when occasion arises to split a wilderness with a road, or sacrifice a salmon stream to power dams, they may do so without embarrassment.

While the dispersion of attitudes in Germany is similar to ours, the status of predators is worse. This is to be expected, in view of the denser human population and the longer period during which intensive game-keeping has been practiced. Some predatory species, such as weasel and iltis, are resistant to abuse; these continue common in Germany, even after centuries of ruthless control. Others, like raptors, are nonresistant. During three months' travel in Germany, I saw only 45 Hawks, and no Owls. The Hawk tally follows:

	Buteo-like	Falcon-like	Accipitrine	Unknown	Total
August 15–30	7	4	1	2	14
September	10	4	7		21
October	6	2		1	9
November 1–15	1				1
	—	—	—	—	—
	24	10	8	3	45

This represents 50 days afield, an average count of about a Hawk per day. The travel distance varied from local foot-trips up to long rides in open cars.

Mrs. Nice* in 1933 counted 53 Hawks in 37 days' driving across the United States, an average of 1.4 Hawks per day, but her count was made in midsummer, whereas my count included the September migration, with its influx of Scandinavian and

*Nice, M. M. "A Hawk Census from Arizona to Massachusetts." Wilson Bulletin, Vol. XLVI, No. 2, June, 1934, pp. 93–95.

Finnish birds. Eliminating September, my German count is 0.4 Hawks per day, as against Mrs. Nice's American count of 1.4 per day.

It occurred to me that the German habit of keeping records of game and predators killed on particular areas presented an opportunity to arrive at what might be called the "predator-cost" of game-keeping operations. Records proved easy to get, but *comparable* records not so easy. It proved to be impossible to iron out all variables (see footnote), but below are the data, such as they are.

PREDATOR-COST PER HEAD OF GAME KILLED*

Estate	In	Area Acres	Period	1 Total small game	2 Total predators	3 Ratio	4 Total game birds	5 Total Hawks	6 Ratio
A	Saxony	5000	1911–1933	13,448	4081	3.3	4126	586	7.0
B	Mecklenburg	?	1880–1926	6302	1036 (mammals and Crows only)	4.6	939	x	x
C	Mecklenburg	?	1876–1925	1450	1064	1.4	70	(345 Hawks and Crows)	x
D	Lettland State Forests	3,750,000?	1922–1929	(118,799)	(245,577)	(0.5)	?	?	?
E	Silesia	2800	1924–1934	12,197	883	13.8	8127	(237 Hawks and Crows)	x
F	Silesia	150,000?	1934	58,066	3498	18.6	35,980	245	147.0

*Variables in table: Col. 1 excludes water-fowl and big game in all cases except D. Col. 2 includes dogs, cats, and Crows, as well as predatory mammals and raptors, except that raptors are missing from B, and in D squirrels and bears are included. Col. 4 includes the bag of birds only (*i.e.*, it excludes rabbits and hares). Col. 5 is Hawks only except in C and E, where Crows and Magpies are included.

In general, we may say that it is the practice in Germany to kill one predator for each 2–15 head of small game bagged, or one Hawk for each 7 or more game-birds bagged. This is the "predator-cost" of game-keeping as conceived by keepers. How much this might be reduced by ecologically-minded game-managers remains to be seen.

Much as Germany has lost through indiscriminate predator-control in the past, the present attitude is by no means one of crying over spilt milk. A very definite predator-restoration policy

A 17-month Bull Elch (German moose). For the purpose of establishing a new herd in the Schorf-heide, hundreds of acres of pine woods are being under-planted to oak, ash, and other hardwoods good for browse.

has been begun. Thus the great "Uhu," which is the counter-part of our Horned Owl, is being replanted in the Schorfheide National Park, and I understand in several of the national for-ests. It had been exterminated except in East Prussia.

Nests of Eagles and rare Hawks are, as a rule, zealously guarded as "held in trust" for the nation—on one estate even Goshawk nests are treasured. I can personally attest that this estate had a good stand of Pheasants and Partridges. I would, of course, expect trouble if Goshawk nests were allowed to be-come really numerous, but that is another question. It is not the regretful trimming down of a too-abundant raptor, but rather the zestful eradication of any and all raptors, and the implied assumption that only game has value, which discredits the game movement in any country.

BIRDS VS. FORESTRY

In America nearly all ornithologists are advocates of forestry, and at least an occasional forester is an ornithologist. It may come as a shock to both when I say that, in Germany, over-artificialized forestry is now recognized as having unknowingly inflicted a near-disaster on forest bird-life. We are here accus-tomed to regard wild-life conservation and forest conservation as parallel and interdependent objectives, and, of course, this is still true. The German experience, however, indicates that it is true *only when the system of forestry is of the right kind.* In other words, we must convert an indiscriminate into a discriminate enthusiasm.

The trouble in Germany all arose from planting spruce and pine in pure unmixed stands over great areas. In Saxony, for example, one forest which contained 2 per cent of spruce in 1822, had, by artificial planting, been converted into 73 per cent spruce in 1932.

Space does not here permit explaining why this was done, or what penalties forestry itself has suffered therefrom. These questions are being treated in a separate paper. The present point is that the native bird fauna cannot thrive, or even survive, in a forest so utterly unlike the natural forest.

This is of great import to America. Our forestry is still so new that we can select the right kind if we want to. We have many regions where fire has reduced the per cent of conifers far below the natural level, and where wild life would benefit greatly from moderate conifer plantings. The German experience, however, is a plain warning that forestry willy-nilly involves more public interests than just timber supply, and that those interests may be injured or aided by the forester, depending on the broad-mindedness, skill, and foresight he brings to his job.

Many Germans are aware of the birdlessness of pure spruce and pure pine, and a few have actually begun to measure the extent and nature of the damage. A brilliant example of such research has recently been published by Vietinghoff,* who owns and lives upon an estate, Neschwitz, mostly pine forest, which has been in his family since 1763, and which he is now converting from pure pine to mixed pine and hardwoods, with the double objective of improving both wild life and timber.

The fact that he derives his livelihood from the timber, and only pleasure from the wild life, adds a unique authority to his findings. We landless American foresters in public employ are, after all, talking about what *somebody else* ought to do.

Vietinghoff finds that there are 40 species of birds which could (and in former times did) breed in the pine type of his

*Vietinghoff-Riesch, Frhr. v. "Die neve Bestrebungen des Forstlichen Natur-schutzes in Deutschland, mit besonderer Berücksichtigung des Vogelschutzes." Weltforstwirtschaft Bd. II Heft 4/6, Berlin, 1935.

"Once in a while a dead tree is left standing for Woodpeckers— a negligence unthinkable in former years."

region (east Saxony). Of these, 19 nest in holes and 21 in the open. These figures represent the inherent richness and composition of the ornithological community.

Of this potential 40 species, several—notably the Black Stork—have already been exterminated.

The optimum surviving sample area shows 18 species, 7 hole-breeders and 11 open. Artificialization of the forest, in short, has cut its bird fauna at least in half, and distorted the composition adversely to the hole-breeders (as would be expected where dead, down, and hollow trees have been anathema to foresters).

The density of this optimum surviving sample was 0.95 pairs per acre (well under most American breeding censuses).

Another very old (150-year) pine forest had about the same density (1.0 pairs per acre) but a normal composition, due, no doubt, to more holes.

Contrasted with these optima, a typical clear cutting replanted artificially to pine (the kind heretofore standard in Germany forestry) supports 3 species, all open breeders, with a density too thin to measure.

After 5 years this rises to 5 species with a density of 0.4 pairs per acre.

After 15 years it may rise to 10 species with a density of 0.7 pairs.

Not until the fortieth year do the hole-breeders begin to

appear at all, and their normal ratio is not approached until 100 years, by which time the tree harvest is ripe for the axe, whereupon the hole-breeders are again expropriated.

It is apparent, then, that under the old-style German silviculture the bird fauna of the pine forest suffers a strong impoverishment in both variety and density, and also such a distortion of composition as to be tantamount to the exclusion of hole-breeders.

All of the foregoing refers to forests without artificial nest-boxes. By means of such boxes, a nearly normal variety and density of bird species has been maintained, not only at Neschwitz, but in many other German forests. Vietinghoff has elaborated and refined the nest-box technique originally developed by von Berlepsch, with whose translated writings* many Americans are already familiar.

The Naturschutz movement, however, aims at something far higher than such synthetic substitutes. Vietinghoff regards his own contributions to artificial nesting as nothing better than a stop-gap to bridge the period of transition from artificial to natural forest. "Parallel with the building of artificial nesting-sites," he asserts, "*there must develop the objective of making them superfluous by restoring to the forest its right to be fruitful in a natural way.*"

Now a shock for bird-lovers: The erection of bird-boxes, while increasing the variety and density of birds, by no means insures an artificial forest against insect epidemics. It merely opposes a regimented bird population to a regimented insect food-supply. Both are unbalanced, both internally and in relation to each other. The insect problem, Vietinghoff believes, is insoluble except by a return to natural ecological safeguards. The ideal set up by Vietinghoff[†] for German forestry is a complete and natural flora and fauna "from the bacteria in the soil to the Eagle in the air."

---

*Heismann M. "How to Attract and Protect Wild Birds." Witherby & Co., London, 1908.

[†] Since this was written, Vietinghoff has been appointed as Professor of Naturschutz in the Tharandt Forest School of the University of Dresden. His job will be to work out by research the ecological questions raised by the Naturschutz movement.

THE LANDSCAPE

It is a far cry, of course, from this ideal to the actual landscape of Germany. There is no Eagle in the air, and the flora and fauna are far from natural. No man can doubt, though, either the intensity or the power of the German revulsion against over-artificial land-use. In some respects the landscape already expresses that revulsion. There are no billboards. The roads and trails disfigure the countryside less than ours. The retreat of the conifers has begun—clumps of beech and oak dot the sombre green of the heretofore ubiquitous spruces. Once in a while a dead tree is left standing—a negligence unthinkable in former years.

Not all of the mistakes of the engineering era, however, can be retrieved, even with time. The German marshes are gone. The German heaths are fast going. And the German rivers—confined in their strait-jackets of masonry—will bear for centuries the scars of that epidemic of geometry which blighted the German mind in the 1800's. Some of these distortions of nature were necessary, but not many. As in America, the landscape is a human document written upon the page of geological history. In a truly mathematical sense, it is an integrated expression of all the virtues, foibles, and fallacies of its successive generations of human occupants.

Bird-Lore, March–April 1936

Conservationist in Mexico

THE PREDATORY Apache of our Southwest was early rounded up and confined in reservations, whereas across the line in Mexico he was, until his recent near-extinction, allowed to run at large. Therefore our southwestern mountains are now badly gutted by erosion, whereas the Sierra Madre range across the line still retains the virgin stability of its soils and all the natural beauty that goes with that enviable condition.

This seemingly disconnected reasoning will appear absurd only to those who still believe that the world is composed of a number of things, the inter-relationships of which are obvious or nearly so.

As a matter of fact, the statement is substantially accurate. This article aims to explain why and to philosophize on the irony of it. For it is ironical that Chihuahua, with a history and a terrain so strikingly similar to southern New Mexico and Arizona, should present so lovely a picture of ecological health, whereas our own states, plastered as they are with National Forests, National Parks and all the other trappings of conservation, are so badly damaged that only tourists and others ecologically color-blind, can look upon them without a feeling of sadness and regret.

Let me hasten to add that this enviable contrast holds good only for the mountains. The low country on both sides of the line has been equally abused and spoiled. The Sierras escaped because of the mutual fear and hatred between Apaches and Mexicans. So great was the fear of Indians that the Sierras were never settled, hence never grazed, hence never eroded. This holds true up to Pancho Villa's revolution of 1916. During the revolution bandits performed the same ecological function as Indians. Since then, depression and unstable land policies have served to keep the mountains green.

It is this chain of historical accidents which enables the American conservationist to go to Chihuahua today and feast his eyes on what his own mountains were like before the Juggernaut. To my mind these live oak-dotted hills fat with side oats grama, these pine-clad mesas spangled with flowers, these lazy trout streams burbling along under great sycamores and cottonwoods, come near to being the cream of creation. But on our side of the line the grama is mostly gone, the mesas are spangled with snakeweed, the trout streams are now cobble-bars.

Somehow the watercourse is to dry country what the face is to human beauty. Mutilate it and the whole is gone. The rest of the organism may survive and even do useful work. The econo-mist, the engineer, or the forester may feel there has been no great loss and adduce statistics of production to prove it. But there are those who know, nevertheless, that a great wrong has been committed—perhaps the greatest of all wrongs, and the sadder because both unintentional and irretrievable.

The Chihuahua Sierras burn over every few years. There are no ill effects, except that the pines are a bit farther apart than ours, reproduction is scarcer, there is less juniper, and there is much less brush, including mountain mahogany—the cream of the browse feed. But the watersheds are intact, whereas our own watersheds, sedulously protected from fire, but merci-lessly grazed before the forests were created, and much too hard since, are a wreck. If there be those who do not yet know they are a wreck, let them read Will C. Barnes' history of the San Simon Valley of Arizona in the October issue of AMERICAN FORESTS.

The Chihuahua Sierras have been grazed only near the Mor-mon colonies. The Mormons were not afraid of Apaches and they sprinkled many a mountain valley with their brick ranch houses. Near the colony I visited—Colonia Pacheco—overgrazing and erosion have not progressed as far as they had in the White Mountains of Arizona in 1910. But the colonies are microscopic when compared with the bulk of the mountain area, which from my observation is for the most part ungrazed.

Very recently the Mexican "Resettlement Administration" has scattered landless voters over many a non-irrigable moun-tain valley, to dry-farm if the Lord sent rain and to get along somehow in any event. The only improvement over our own Act of June 11, 1906, is that the scattering is done only where there is enough land for a community and that the settlers have no guns.

These forest homesteaders are "deadening" the pines, scratching corn into the thin soil and day-herding their goats on the nearest hillside, a type of agriculture intermediate between an Appalachian hill-farm, a Philippine caigin, and a New Mexico "Small Holding Claim." I recognize the land pressure which forces the adoption of such a policy, but I also recognize the inevitable ruin which will follow. One can tell when nearing one of these settlements by the thinning sod, the thickening weeds, the browsed-off willows, and the oaks skinned for tanbark. Just so were our own dry canyons sent to their death.

But these resettlements are also as yet microscopic when compared with the bulk of the mountain area. They occur only near roads, and roads are as yet poor and far between. Engineers would call the mountains roadless.

In Arizona and New Mexico there are in general two kinds of deer range, the overstocked and the nearly empty. Most of the herds are very thin, but every few years some new spot flares up with a sudden overpopulation of deer. The Kaibab was the first of these, but there has been a new one every year or two for a decade. Often, before the heavy wheels of legislative adjustment can turn, the range is severely injured. Most laymen have no comprehension of what a serious thing it is to overtax a browse range, especially in an arid climate. Recovery is a matter of decades, rather than of years. Some ranges wash away before they can recover.

Deer irruptions are by no means confined to the Southwest. They are breaking out from Georgia to Wisconsin, and from California to Pennsylvania. Why? Have deer always fluctuated from scarcity to overabundance? History would hardly so indicate.

In Chihuahua one can glean, by comparison, a hint of what may be the matter with our deer. Whitetail deer are abundant in the Sierras, but not excessive. So are wild turkeys. In nine days of hard hunting, two of us saw 187 deer, fifty of them bucks of two or more prongs. Deer irruptions are unknown. Mountain lions and wolves are still common. I doubt whether the lion-deer ratio is much different from that of Coronado's time. There are no coyotes in the mountains, whereas with us there is universal complaint from Alaska to New Mexico that the coyote has invaded the high country to wreak havoc on both game and livestock.

I submit for conservationists to ponder the question of whether the wolves have not kept the coyotes out? And whether the presence of a normal complement of predators is not, at least in part, accountable for the absence of irruption? If so, would not our rougher mountains be better off and might we not have more normalcy in our deer herds, if we let the wolves and lions come back in reasonable numbers?

At the very least, the Sierras present to us an example of an abundant game population thriving in the midst of its natural enemies. Let those who habitually ascribe all game scarcity to predators or who prescribe predator control as the first and inevitable step in all game management, take that to heart.

On the dry tops of the highest mesas, in the bottoms of the roughest and wildest canyons, anywhere in fact where a short watershed is intercepted by a ledge, dyke, or other favorable spot for impounding soil, the traveler in the Sierras finds loose-masonry dams constructed by the hand of man. There are hundreds of them.

How old are they? Who built them? What for? The first two questions find a ready answer. Not infrequently a 200-year-old pine is found growing behind the dam, its root-collar flush with the surface of the impounded soil. Obviously the dam is older than the tree. Unless Coronado and his captains had an unsuspected weakness for laying rock, and also more time and manpower than their journals indicate, these dams were built by prehistoric Indians.

In one case I saw the rocks of the dam clutched tightly in the roots of a great tree. Nobody stuck them there to fool tourists. Moreover there are dams in spots no white man has ever looked upon.

What were the dams for? This question is not so easy to answer. Some local residents say "erosion control." It might be conceivable that the Indians built dams to protect their more valuable soils—say in irrigated valleys—against erosion. But many of the dams I am describing are found around the edges of high mesas a thousand feet above the nearest permanent water. If such a spot ever showed erosion, the natural thing would be to seek a new spot, rather than to laboriously check a gully with rocks.

One is forced back to the theory that these dams were built to create little fields or food patches. The purpose was to impound soil where it would be irrigated by the runoff from slight rainfalls. The choice of locations strongly substantiates this belief. Short watersheds composed mostly of bare rock were especially favored, provided there was a ledge or dyke or narrow place offering secure footing for the dam. In such spots the lightest rain produced runoff and irrigated the field, whereas the heaviest rain could not gather headway enough to tear out the dam.

What crops were raised in these little fields? This, to me, is a perplexing question. Their small size and the wide dispersion seems to preclude constant patrol against game, while the absence of metal tools seems to preclude game-proof fencing. Surely there were deer, turkey, and bears enough in those days to wreck any crop of plants palatable to them. The clue must lie in plants palatable to Indians but not to animals. Corn, it appears, is not molested by game until the ears form, but after that I fail to see how it could get by. Squash and melons would have the same weakness. Beans would seemingly be vulnerable at all times. Potatoes, peppers, and tobacco might possibly qualify as game-proof. I wonder if the archaeologists have considered game damage in reconstructing their picture of prehistoric Indian agriculture?

Everybody in Mexico has heard of the new motor road to Mexico City and is hoping for one like it to his village. The tourist-promotion policy of the present government is well known. It appears then that funds alone will limit the rate at which the Sierra Madre is opened up. The policy of settling the landless in the mountain valleys will, if it persists, add further velocity to the road-building process and it will scatter livestock, as well as hunters and tourists, over the mountain country. The end result will be bad, unless Mexico does a better job than we have done in the regulation of grazing.

I sometimes wonder whether semi-arid mountains can be grazed at all without ultimate deterioration. I know of no arid region which has ever survived grazing through long periods of time, although I have seen individual ranches which seemed to hold out for shorter periods. The trouble is that where water is unevenly distributed and feed varies in quality, grazing usually means overgrazing.

With the extension of roads, recreation so-called will of course repeat the now familiar process of losing in quality as it gains in quantity of human service. Mexican citizens protest that they are going strong on National Parks and Forests. They are particularly proud of the International Park at Big Bend. They do not realize that these devices, laudable and necessary as they are, have not exempted us from the inexorable process of losing quality to gain quantity.

Mexico's experience with American hunters is an illuminating example of the limitations inherent in conservation formulae. It is no secret that until recently many visiting American hunters made pigs of themselves. Neither is it any secret that they were often aided and abetted in so doing by commercial guides. Mexico in self-defense has adopted the formula of clapping on a high license fee, and of limiting non-resident hunting to members of bonded "clubs." The theory is to call the bond for any misbehavior.

But how does the formula actually work? The bonded hunter is careful enough to stay within the law, but after such outlays he is, I think, equally careful to take all the law allows. In other words, he helps himself pretty generously and the drain on the game is probably not much less than it was in the lawless days.

I point to no moral except that we seem ultimately always thrown back on individual ethics as the basis of conservation policy. It is hard to make a man, by pressure of law or money, do a thing which does not spring naturally from his own personal sense of right and wrong.

Our own Southwest was pretty badly misused before the idea of conservation was born. As a result, our own conservation program for the region has been in a sense a post-mortem cure. There are, however, two magnificent semi-arid regions in which settlement came later than the conservation idea. One is South Africa and the other is the Mexican mountains. Hence both are of world-wide interest as laboratories in which conservation can be given a full and fair test. Can they arrest and control the wasteful and predatory nature of what we call "development"? The self-defeating nature of mass-use of outdoor resources? Or are these evils inherent in industrial civilization? The next few decades will probably bring us the answer.

Perhaps a clear answer to these complex questions of policy is too much to hope for, but in any event the Sierra Madre offers us the chance to describe, and define, in actual ecological measurements, the lineaments and physiology of an unspoiled mountain landscape. What is the mechanism of a natural forest? A natural watershed? A natural deer herd? A natural turkey range? On our side of the line we have few or no natural samples left to measure. I can see here the opportunity for a great international research enterprise which will explain our own history and enlighten the joint task of profiting by its mistakes.

American Forests, March 1937

Conservation Blueprints

THE CONSERVATION movement in America is about to pass one of the milestones in its career: the creation of a federal Department of Conservation.

I have watched this idea grow since it was first broached by Commissioner Alexander, of Louisiana, a score of years ago. Leadership in its promotion has been assumed by many men almost humorously diverse in character, but all alike in two respects: all were seeking a political career in conservation, and all knew a little—but not too much—about the subject.

This is significant because, in order to have much faith in such a scheme, one must not know too much. To repose confidence in a shifting of official blueprints requires deep enthusiasm and shallow understanding.

The situation reminds me of a Forest Supervisor, who, on being transferred to a new forest, directed all the desks in the headquarter office to be shifted. He was vaguely dissatisfied with his staff, and thought that by rearranging their desks he might rearrange their performance. It did not occur to him that his staff perhaps needed weeding instead of shifting, or that a shift of ideas might do more good than a shift of seats.

Those who now complain the loudest about Secretary Ickes' impending reorganization scheme are, ironically enough, those whose accumulated thoughts and acts have made it possible. It all goes back to the fundamental question: What is a bureau? We have one and all assumed that a bureau is a law, an appropriation, an overhead, and a group of physical acts of government; a piece of land bought, a road built, a fire put out, a can of fish dumped, a flock of sheep given (or denied) a grazing permit, a sawlog sold, a new duck regulation promulgated.

If we grant the premise that conservation is the sum of these physical acts of government, then it becomes difficult to refute the proposal that they might be better coordinated if executed by a single cabinet head. When we grant this premise we classify conservation as essentially an engineering enterprise—biological engineering, if you wish—but nevertheless engineering, and as such properly assignable to an engineering and public works Department. Once we grant this premise, we also give President

Roosevelt a chance to ascribe all opposition to a desire to have Secretary Wallace, rather than Secretary Ickes, at the helm of the ship.

In my view the premise is false and superficial. These physical acts of government are the manifestations of a public desire for conservation, but not the substance of the thing itself. Conservation might make splendid headway if they did not exist; it might languish even though the whole treasury were emptied to build bigger and better forests, parks, hatcheries, and check-dams.

The real substance of conservation lies not in the physical projects of government, but in the mental processes of citizens. The road in park or forest is not the thing; what matters is where and for what the park-visitor or forest-user wants roads. The acreage bought for public parks or forests is not the thing; what matters is whether private landowners regard their forests and their landscapes as a public trust. The fire put out by a CCC crew is not the thing; what matters is whether people are careless with fire in the woods. The can of fish dumped is not the thing; what matters is the attitude of the fisherman toward the public resource he is privileged to harvest. The sheep grazing permit is not the thing; what matters is whether the sheepman knows or cares that he is helping to build the Great American Desert. The sawlog sold is not the thing; what matters is whether the citizen who buys a board or a newspaper knows or cares where it comes from, knows or cares whether it is the product of exploitation or land-cropping. The regulation on ducks is not the thing; what matters is whether the duck hunter is ashamed or proud to bequeath to his sons a duckless, marshless continent, and if ashamed, whether this in any wise affects his trigger-finger. Lastly and most important, the check-dam in a farmer's gully is not the thing; what matters is whether a social stigma attaches to the ownership of a gullied farm; whether the farmer realizes that to leave behind a fertile, stable, and beautiful farmstead is in these days a greater and more difficult achievement than to endow a hospital or found an industry.

All the acts of government, in short, are of slight importance to conservation except as they affect the acts and thoughts of citizens. A bigger conservation bureau is not necessarily a better one. Perfect coordination among bureaus is not necessarily progress; citizens may learn more from bureau quarrels than bureau regimentation. In fact, bureaus do not matter except as they mobilize brains to influence people. It has happened again and again that the smallest bureau has the biggest thoughts. One of the plainest lessons from the New Deal boom in bureaus is that accomplishment is *not* proportional to size, appropriations, or authority, nor is it much affected by organization blueprints. If we can deduce any rule at all, it is this: accomplishment is proportional to how long and how earnestly a bureau has wrestled with its problem of leadership in public thought. Some bureaus—the Forest Service, for example—have, in my view, made some headway *despite* the load of new dollars and new physical chores given them by the New Deal. The headway comes not from the new dollars, but from the intellectual traditions built up during preceding decades of financial poverty.

When Mr. Ickes sets himself up as the Secretary of Conservation, he seeks a heavy responsibility. Why not have a Secretary of Economics? A Secretary of Ethics and Morality? All are alike in that all transact not only all government departments, but all acts of all citizens. Conservation, in short, is an aspect of the national philosophy, not a group of governmental "projects." I can see just one important thing that might be accomplished by the new plan: such an exaggeration of the bureaucratic concept of progress that the average citizen may come at last to realize that the "Secretary of Conservation" is not Mr. Ickes, but himself.

This is not a plea for the status quo ante. The past helmsmanship of Agriculture leaves much to be desired, and the past quarrels between foresters and park men are tiresome indeed. But is a change of captains any remedy? Is there any remedy except a new popular concept of what both are for?

Incidentally, it is doubtful whether the Secretaryship of Conservation will accomplish even that coordination of superficial engineering chores which its proponents hope for. Everybody who knows the ropes knows that the mere re-grouping of bureaus cuts off about as many desirable affiliations as it creates. Thus the proposed re-grouping under Interior cuts off forestry from farming, and wildlife from farming. This is the price it pays for putting forestry and parks together. Re-grouping of any sort is toying with superficialities. It may or may not be advisable, but in no case is it fundamental. Real reorganization can come only by building better landowners. Who is captain at Washington is of little consequence, but a change of captains at this juncture is dangerous because it will inevitably prolong the fallacy that move No. 1 is at Washington rather than at home.

American Forests, December 1937

Engineering and Conservation

T HE PUBLIC mind is a mirror into which every vocation reflects its image. That image may flatter its subject, or the
contrary, depending upon accumulated public impressions of
the group and how its members live, think, and work.

A decade ago the public image of labor was a rather pleasing
one. Since the advent of CIO it has become much harder to
look at.

In the writings of Alexander Hamilton and Thomas Jefferson
we find the word "industrialist" used as a term of high honor.
Today one uses the term guardedly.

The banker's picture has of late suffered an unflattering distortion, culminating in the newspaper epithet "bankster" in
the early 1930s.

Not long ago the railroads had cloven hooves; now what
with rate reductions, streamliners, and 35-cent dinners they have
acquired merit and may soon sprout wings.

It is clear that, in general, the underdog tends to be upper-
most in public favor. Conversely, when a profession becomes
important or powerful, it has need to look to its laurels.

The engineer, from Kitchener to Herbert Hoover, enjoyed
a public image of ever-increasing comeliness. The reasons are
too well known to need comment. At the present moment,
however, the word "engineer" in the minds of some conservationists is associated with an attitude toward natural resources
which they dislike. It evokes in them a mental image of marshes
needlessly drained, of rivers expensively channelized to revive an
expiring navigation, of floods aggravated by stream straightening and by constricting levees, of irrigation reservoirs silted before the maturity of their bonds, and of a veritable mycelium of
roads at least a part of which are built regardless of cost or need.

This tendency to challenge the engineer is admittedly confined to that small group preoccupied with the biological aspects of public policy. As a member of this group I here attempt
to shed some light on their reactions. That these reactions are
just and fair I cannot certify, but the avowal that they exist may
be a useful first step toward clearing the issue.

We may perhaps strike at the root of the matter by this

generalization: the engineer believes, and has taught the public to believe, that a constructed mechanism is inherently preferable to a natural one. The conservationist believes the contrary.

All generalizations are inaccurate, including this one. A few cases may help clarify the intended meaning.

Consider the Columbia River dams. As between abundant power and abundant salmon, priority automatically went to power. The dams were started before the probable destruction of the salmon resource was seriously debated. It made no difference that the need for power was questionable, the fate of the salmon was nearly certain. By an axiom long in the making, the man-made resource must be superior to the natural one. I do not know whether the engineers built the axiom or the axiom built the engineers. The result is the same.

The Mississippi dams involve a more subtle issue. That the great river is sick all will agree. Treatment can be applied either to the channel where the symptoms are most conspicuous, or to the deranged watershed which gives rise to the symptoms. The engineers started to bandage the channel with steel and concrete before giving ear to the question of what ails the organism as a whole. The case of course involves many other issues which I do not here discuss. I point out merely the seeming assumption that skillful structures can solve our water problems, and (by implication) exempt us from the penalties of bungling land use.

The history of irrigation reservoirs in the West presents a similar question. In many instances the silting life of a storage basin was assumed during the promotion stage to be perpetual. During the construction stage it would be scaled down to a century, and during the pay-up stage it would finally appear as a generation. Isolated errors in predicting the life of reservoirs would be natural enough, but their repetition through forty years of experience forces the observer to conclude that the profession as a whole is not yet conscious of that organic disintegration which has afflicted nearly all semi-arid watersheds since their occupation by livestock. (There are brilliant individual exceptions to this rule. Olmstead's report on the Gila River is one such.)

When some inventor comes out with a new alloy the engineers lose no time making a path to his door. But discoveries outside the engineering field may have an equal bearing on the responsibilities of the engineering profession. Take, for example, Lowdermilk's formulation, in terms of physical chemistry, of the basic mechanism by which plants influence runoff. This reorients the old controversy about the influence of forests and presents a challenging opportunity for joint research by soil chemists, engineers, and botanists. But who is doing such research? I here criticise all three parties for inaction.

Again, take Weaver's discovery that the composition of the plant community determines the ability of soils to retain their granulation, and hence their stability. If finally verified, this new principle may necessitate the revision of our entire system of thought on flood control and erosion control. I do not hear it discussed among engineers (nor, for that matter, among economists, business men, or statesmen).

The cases I have cited all involve big and complex issues of national importance. Consider now, for contrast, a small and local one. In the sand counties of central Wisconsin are many defunct drainage districts. In 1933 the government began to buy out the surviving farmers and convert the area into a wildlife reservation. Travel in the area had always followed "sandtracks." There were hundreds of miles of these tracks; unimproved but passable routes winding picturesquely through the jack pines and scrub oaks.

I believe it is an engineering fact that in sand a semi-sodded track is the best possible road short of a surfaced turnpike. But the engineers could not resist the temptation of soft yardage, abundant CCCs, and government gas. Today the area is geometrically gridironed with graded sandpiles, expensively inferior to the old tracks. It looks as if some new glacier had acquired the knack of laying down eskers with a transit. The drainage of this region was, by hindsight, a mistake, but now in our effort to give it back to the birds, we must give it one last mutilating gouge with power tools.

This same propensity for carving soft landscapes perhaps accounts for the recent drainage of nearly the whole Atlantic tidal marsh from Maine to Alabama. This was done with relief labor, in the name of mosquito control, over the protests of wildlife interests. These marshes are the wintering ground of many species of migratory waterfowl and the breeding ground of others. The effectiveness of such drainage as a mosquito control measure is at least debatable. Biological methods of mosquito control are known but were not tried. The project was not led by engineers and is chargeable to engineering only in the sense that it shows what the mechanical idea of landscaping can do when combined with too much haste, too much government money, a resort-owner's chamber of commerce, and the prevalent unconsciousness of biological equilibria. I suspect that the real impulse behind the whole venture is the local realtor's solicitude for silk stockings on his beaches.

I mention last what to me seems the least discussed but most regrettable instance of short-sighted engineering—the wholesale straightening of small rivers and creeks. This is done to hasten the runoff of local flood waters, and of course aggravates the piling up of flood peaks in major streams. It is, on its face, a process of pushing trouble downstream, of seeking benefit for the locality at the expense of the community. In justice the stream-straightener should indemnify the public for damage; in practice I fear the public may at times subsidize him with relief labor.

I know of at least one engineering group which has foresworn stream-straightening—the Soil Conservation Service. I salute them.

The interplay of engineering and ecological evils is an insidious thing. I know a locality in western Dane County where erosion is gradually destroying the upland cornfields. The farmers must have corn; their only recourse is the marshy creek bottoms. These, however, are subject to flashy floods. To raise corn on the bottoms the floods will have to be prodded downstream by straightening, which in turn will aggravate the flashy runoff and augment erosion. Thus the cycle of misuse.

Incidentally these marshy bottoms contain the only wildlife cover and are now good pasture. The cover will disappear with straightening, and the pasture will have to move back to the eroded uplands.

These cases collectively imply, but I will now specifically admit, certain qualifications which, in justice, I must attach to my criticism of the engineer.

First of all, let me admit that in some cases the biological professions seem just as remiss as the engineering group.

Secondly, let me admit that the engineer is to me a symbol

for a state of the public mind, as well as a professional man who has made mistakes. The cited instances of error are chargeable to voters and politicians as well as engineers. The Columbia dams, the Mississippi dams, the irrigation reservoirs, the needless roads and the mosquito drainage were backed by strong local booster and even pork-barrel interests. Every professional man must, within limits, execute the jobs people are willing to pay for. But every profession in the long run writes its own ticket. It does so through the emergence of leaders who can afford to be skeptical out loud and in public—professors, for example. What I here decry is not so much the prevalence of public error in the use of engineering tools as the scarcity of engineering criticism of such misuse. Perhaps that criticism exists *in camera*, but it does not reach the interested layman.

I admit, too, that the engineer is not the only focus for biological discontent. The chemist scattering new comforts with one hand and new pollutions with the other, evokes in us the same disquiet. Both professions exemplify priority for the synthetic over the natural, a certain atrophy of esthetic discrimination, a yearning for prosperity and comfort at any cost. I do not claim that we, the disaffected, disdain the prosperity and the comforts. Our only contribution is the idea that the cost is large, unnecessarily large.

With these qualifying admissions I now summarize my criticism: The engineer has respect for mechanical wisdom because he created it. He has disrespect for ecological wisdom, not because he is contemptuous of it, but because he is unaware of it. We have, in short, two professions whose responsibilities for land use overlap much, but whose respective zones of awareness overlap only a little. What can we say about their future relationship? About the direction of possible adjustments?

All history shows this: that civilization is not the progressive elaboration of a single idea, but the successive dominance of a series of ideas. Greece, Rome, the Renaissance, the industrial age, each had a new and largely distinct zone of awareness. The people of each lived not in a better, nor a worse, but in a new and different intellectual field. Progress, if there be any, is the slender hoard of fragments retained from the whole intellectual succession.

Engineering is clearly the dominant idea of the industrial age.

What I have here called ecology is perhaps one of the contenders for a new order. In any case our problem boils down to increasing the overlap of awareness between the two.

This may prove less difficult than appears on the surface, for the ecologist is in many ways an engineer. The biotic mechanism is too complex to enable him to predict its reactions; therefore he advocates what an engineer would in like case: go slow, cut and try.

He feels an engineer's admiration for this complexity which defies science, and an engineer's aversion for discarding any of its parts. The real difference lies in the ecologist's conviction that to govern the animate world it must be led rather than coerced. To me this is engineering wisdom; the reason the engineer does not display it is unawareness of the animate world.

The tools which the engineer has given the public are so crude and powerful that they invite coercive use. It is not likely that the public will lay them down. The only alternative is the pooling of engineering and ecological skills for wiser use of those tools. Is this pooling under way? Perhaps. We now see engineers and ecologists jointly attacking the soil erosion problem, but only after the resource reached an advanced stage of deterioration. Need we always await the willy-nilly pressure of wrecked resources before professional cooperation begins?

We end, I think, at what might be called the standard paradox of the twentieth century: our tools are better than we are, and grow better faster than we do. They suffice to crack the atom, to command the tides. But they do not suffice for the oldest task in human history: to live on a piece of land without spoiling it.

Typescript, April 11, 1938

Natural History, the Forgotten Science

O NE SATURDAY night a few weeks ago two middle-aged farmers set the alarm clock for a dark hour of what proved to be a snowy, blowy Sunday. Milking over, they jumped into a pick-up and sped for the sand counties of central Wisconsin, a region productive of tax deeds, tamaracks, and wild hay. In the evening they returned with a truck full of young tamarack trees and a heart full of high adventure. The last tree was planted in the home marsh by lantern-light. There was still the milking.

In Wisconsin "man bites dog" is stale news compared with "farmer plants tamarack." Our farmers have been grubbing, burning, draining and chopping tamarack since 1840. In the region where these farmers live the tree is exterminated. Why then should they want to replace it? Because after twenty years they hope to re-introduce sphagnum moss under the grove, and then ladyslippers, pitcher plants, and the other nearly-extinct wildflowers of the aboriginal Wisconsin bogs.

No extension bureau had offered these farmers any prize for this utterly quixotic undertaking. Certainly no hope of gain motivated it. How then can one interpret its meaning? I call it Revolt—revolt against the tedium of the merely economic attitude toward land. We assume that because we had to subjugate the land to live on it, that therefore the best farm is the one most completely tamed. These two farmers had learned from experience that the wholly tamed farm offers not only a slender livelihood but a constricted life. They had caught the idea that there is pleasure to be had in raising wild crops as well as tame ones. They propose to devote a little spot of marsh to growing native wildflowers. Perhaps they wish for their land what we all wish for our children—not only a chance to make a living, but also a chance to express and develop a rich and varied assortment of inherent capabilities, both wild and tame. What better expresses land than the plants which originally grew on it?

I am here then to talk about the pleasure to be had in wild things, about natural history studies as a combination sport and science.

History has not conspired to make my task an easy one. We naturalists have much to live down. There was a time when ladies and gentlemen wandered afield not so much to learn how the world is put together as to gather subject matter for tea-time conversation. This was the era of dickey-bird ornithology, of botany expressed in bad verse, of ejaculatory vapors such as "ain't nature grand." But if you will scan the amateur ornithological or botanical journals of today you will see that a new attitude is abroad. I shall not try to define it, but rather to describe to you some people who exemplify it. In selecting these people I shall include only amateurs—that is to say, I exclude all who receive either pay or university credit for their natural history work.

I know an industrial chemist who spends his spare time in reconstructing the history of the passenger pigeon and its dramatic demise as a member of our fauna. The pigeon became extinct before this chemist was born, but he has dug up more knowledge of pigeons than any contemporary possessed. How? By reading every newspaper ever printed in our state, as well as contemporary diaries, letters, and books. I estimate that he has read 100,000 documents in his search for pigeon data. This gigantic labor, which would kill any man undertaking it as a task, fills him with the keen delight of a hunter scouring the hills for scarce deer, of an archeologist digging up Egypt for a scarab. And of course such an undertaking requires more than digging. After the scarab is found its interpretation requires the highest skill—a skill not to be learned from others, but rather created by the digger as he digs. Here, then, is a man who has found adventure, exploration, science and sport, all in the backyard of current history where millions of lesser men find only boredom.

Another exploration—this time literally of a back yard, is a study of the Song Sparrow conducted by an Ohio housewife. This commonest of birds had been scientifically labelled, pigeonholed a hundred years ago, and forthwith forgotten. Our Ohio amateur had the notion that in birds, as in people, there are things to be known over and above name, sex, and clothes. She began trapping the song sparrows in her garden, marking each with a celluloid anklet, and being thus able to identify each individual by its colored marker, to observe and record their migrations, feedings, fightings, singings, matings, nestings and deaths; in short, to decipher the inner workings of the sparrow community. In ten years she knew more about sparrow society, sparrow politics, sparrow economics, and sparrow psychology than anyone had ever learned about any bird. Science beat a path to her door. She has published the first volume of a monograph on her backyard researches. Ornithologists of all nations seek her counsel.

These two amateurs happen to have achieved fame, but no thought of fame motivated their original work. Fame came *ex post facto*. It is not fame, however, that I am talking about. They achieved personal satisfactions which are more important than fame, and hundreds of other amateurs are achieving these satisfactions. I now ask: What is our educational system doing to encourage personal amateur scholarship in the natural history field?

We can perhaps seek an answer to this question by dropping in on a typical class in a typical zoology department. We find there students memorizing the names of the bumps on the bones of a cat. It is important, of course, to study bones, otherwise we should never comprehend the evolutionary process by which animals came into existence. But why memorize the bumps? We are told that this is part of biological discipline. I ask, though, whether a comprehension of the living animal and how it holds its place in the sun is not an equally important part. Unfortunately the living animal is virtually omitted from the present system of zoological education. In my own university, for example, we offer no course in ornithology or mammalogy.

Botanical education is in like case, except perhaps that the displacement of interest in the living flora has been not quite so extreme.

The reason for this eviction of outdoor studies from the schools goes back into history. Laboratory biology came into existence at about the time when amateur natural history was of the dickey-bird variety, and when professional natural history consisted of labelling species, and amassing facts about food habits without interpreting them. In short, a growing and vital laboratory technique was at that time placed in competition with a stagnated outdoor technique. It was quite natural that laboratory biology soon came to be regarded as the superior form of science. As it grew it crowded natural history out of the educational picture.

The present educational marathon in memorizing the geography of bones is the aftermath of this perfectly logical process of competition. It has, of course, other justifications: medical students need it. Zoology teachers need it. But I contend that the average citizen does not need it as badly as he needs some understanding of the living world.

In the interim, field studies have developed techniques and ideas quite as scientific as those of the laboratory. The amateur student is no longer confined to pleasant ambles in the country resulting merely in lists of species, lists of migration dates, and lists of rarities. Bird banding, feather-marking, censusing, and experimental manipulations of behavior and environment are techniques available to all, and they are quantitative science. The amateur can, if he has imagination and persistence, select and solve actual scientific natural history problems as virgin as the stratosphere. My two amateurs are cases in point.

The modern view is not to regard laboratory and field as competitive, but rather as complementary studies. Curricula, however, do not yet reflect this new situation. It takes money to enlarge curricula, hence the average college student who inclines toward natural history avocations is rebuffed rather than encouraged by his university. Instead of being taught to see his native countryside with appreciation and intelligence, he is taught to carve cats. Let him be taught both if this is possible, but if one must be omitted let it be the latter.

To visualize more clearly the lop-sidedness and sterility of biological education as a means of building citizens, let's go afield with some typical Phi Beta Kappa student and ask him some questions. We can safely assume he knows how angiosperms and cats are put together, but let us test his comprehension of how Missouri is put together.

We are driving down a country road in northern Missouri. Here is a farmstead. Look at the trees in the yard and the soil in the field and tell us whether the original settler carved his farm out of prairie or woods. Did he eat prairie chicken or wild turkey for his Thanksgiving? What plants grew here originally which do not grow here now? Why did they disappear? What did the prairie plants have to do with creating the corn-yielding capacity of this soil? Why does this soil erode now but not then?

Again, suppose we are touring the Ozarks. Here is an abandoned field in which the ragweed is sparse and short. Does this tell us anything about why the mortgage was foreclosed? About how long ago? Would this field be a good place to look for quail? Does short ragweed have any connection with the human story behind yonder graveyard? If all the ragweed in this watershed were short, would that tell us anything about the future of floods in the stream? About the future prospects for bass or trout?

I fear that our Phi Beta Kappa biologist would consider these questions insane, but they are not. Any amateur naturalist with a seeing eye should be able to speculate intelligently on all of them, and have a lot of fun doing it. You will see, too, that modern natural history deals only incidentally with the identity of plants and animals, and only incidentally with their habits and behaviors. It deals principally with their relations to each other, their relation to the soil and water in which they grow, and their relations to the human beings who sing about "my country" but see little or nothing of its inner workings. This new science of relationships is called ecology, but what we call it matters nothing. The question is, does the educated citizen know he is only a cog in an ecological mechanism? That if he will work with that mechanism his mental wealth and his material wealth can expand indefinitely. But that if he refuses to work with it, it will ultimately grind him to dust. If education does not teach us these things, then what is education for?

You here in Missouri are just reorganizing your conservation department. You are hearing about teaching conservation in the schools. The implication is that something is to be added to the curriculum. I submit conservation is no new excrescence on an already bulky curriculum. It seems to me that if all teaching does not deal with our relations to the land, it is not teaching at all.

Conservationists have, I fear, adopted the pedagogical method of the prophets: we mutter darkly about impending doom if people don't mend their ways. The doom is impending, all right; no one can be an ecologist, even an amateur one, without seeing it. But do people mend their ways for fear of calamity? I doubt it. They are more likely to do it out of pure curiosity and interest. We shall be ready, I think, to practice conservation when "farmer plants tamarack" is no longer news.

Typescript, April 26, 1938

A Survey of Conservation

CONSERVATION IS a bird which flies faster than the shot we aim at it.

I can remember the day when I was sure that reforming the Game Commission would give us conservation. A group of us worked like Trojans cleaning house at the Capitol. When we got through we found we had just started. We learned that you can't conserve game by itself; to rebuild the game resource you must first rebuild the game range, and this means rebuilding the people who use it, and all of the things they use it for. The job we aspired to perform with a dozen volunteers is now baffling a hundred professionals. The job we thought would take five years will barely be started in fifty.

Our target, then, is a receding one. The task grows greater year by year, but so does its importance. We begin by seeking a few trees or birds; to get them we must build a new relationship between men and land.

Conservation is a state of harmony between men and land.

By land is meant all of the things on, over, or in the earth.

Harmony with land is like harmony with a friend; you cannot cherish his right hand and chop off his left. That is to say, you cannot love game and hate predators; you cannot conserve the waters and waste the ranges; you cannot build the forest and mine the farm. The land is one organism. Its parts, like our own parts, compete with each other and cooperate with each other. The competitions are as much a part of the inner workings as the cooperations. You can regulate them—cautiously—but not abolish them.

The outstanding scientific discovery of the twentieth century is not television, nor radio, but rather the complexity of the land-organism. Only those who know most about it can appreciate how little we know about it. The last word in ignorance is the man who says of an animal or plant: "What good is it?" If the land mechanism as a whole is good, then every part is good, whether we understand it or not. If the biota, in the course of aeons, has built something we like but do not understand,

416

then who but a fool would discard seemingly useless parts? To keep every cog and wheel is the first precaution of intelligent tinkering.

Have we learned this first principle of conservation: to preserve all the parts of the land mechanism? No, because even the scientist does not yet recognize all of them.

In Germany there is a mountain called the Spessart. Its south slope bears the most magnificent oaks in the world. American cabinet-makers, when they want the last word in quality, use Spessart oak. The north slope, which should be the better, bears an indifferent stand of Scotch pine. Why? Both slopes are part of the same state forest; both have been managed with equally scrupulous care for two centuries. Why the difference?

Kick up the litter under the oaks and you will see that the leaves rot almost as fast as they fall. Under the pines, though, the needles pile up as a thick duff; decay is much slower. Why? Because in the Middle Ages the south slope was preserved as a deer forest by a hunting bishop; the north slope was pastured, plowed and cut by settlers, just as we do with our woodlots in Wisconsin and Iowa today. Only after this period of abuse was the north slope replanted to pines. During this period of abuse something happened to the microscopic flora and fauna of the soil. The number of species was greatly reduced, i.e., the digestive apparatus of the soil lost some of its parts. Two centuries of conservation have not sufficed to restore these losses. It required the modern microscope, and a century of research in soil science, to discover the existence of these "small cogs and wheels" which determine harmony or disharmony between men and land in the Spessart.

American conservation is, I fear, still concerned mostly with show-pieces. We have not yet learned to think in terms of small cogs and wheels. Look at our own back yard: at the prairies of Iowa and southern Wisconsin. What is the most valuable part of the prairie? The fat black soil, the chernozem. Who built the chernozem? Some say the glaciers, but there is black loam far beyond the limits of the ice. The black prairie was built by the prairie plants, a hundred distinctive species of grasses, herbs, and shrubs; by the prairie fungi, insects, and bacteria; by the prairie mammals and birds, all interlocked in one humming community of cooperation and competitions, one biota. This biota, through twenty thousand years of living and dying, burning and growing, preying and fleeing, freezing and thawing, built that dark and bloody ground we call prairie.

Our grandfathers did not, could not, know the origin of their prairie empire. They killed off the prairie fauna and drove the flora to a last refuge on railroad embankments and roadsides. To our engineers this flora is merely weeds and brush; they ply it with grader and mower, with CCC and WPA. Through processes of plant succession predictable by any botanist, the prairie garden becomes a refuge for quack grass. After the garden is gone, the highway department employs landscapers to dot the quack with elms, and with artistic clumps of Scotch pine, Japanese barberry, and *Spiraea vanhouttei*. Conservation committees, en route to some important convention, whiz by and applaud this zeal for roadside beauty.

Some day we may need this prairie flora not only to look at, but to rebuild the wasting soil of prairie farms. Many species may then be missing. We have our hearts in the right place, but we do not yet recognize the small cogs and wheels.

In our attempts to save the bigger cogs and wheels, we are still pretty naive. A little repentance just before a species goes over the brink is enough to make us feel virtuous. When the species is gone we have a good cry and repeat the performance.

The recent extermination of the grizzly from most of the western stock-raising states is a case in point. Yes, we still have grizzlies in the Yellowstone. But the species is ridden by imported parasites; the rifles wait on every refuge boundary; new dude ranches and new roads constantly shrink the remaining range; every year sees fewer grizzlies on fewer ranges in fewer states. We console ourselves with the comfortable fallacy that a single museum-piece will do, ignoring the clear dictum of history that a species must be saved *in many places* if it is to be saved at all.

The ivory-billed woodpecker, the California condor, and the desert sheep are the next candidates for rescue. The rescues will not be effective until we discard the idea that one sample will do; until we insist on living with our flora and fauna in as many places as possible.

We need knowledge—public awareness—of the small cogs and wheels, but sometimes I think there is something we need even worse. It is the thing which "Forest and Stream," on its editorial masthead, once called "a refined taste in natural objects." Have we made any headway in developing "a refined taste in natural objects"?

In the northern parts of the lake states we have a few wolves left. Each state offers a bounty on wolves. In addition, it may invoke the expert services of the U.S. Biological Survey in wolf-control. Yet both the Biological Survey and the several conservation commissions complain of an increasing number of localities where there are too many deer for the available feed. Foresters complain of periodic damage from too many rabbits. Why, then, continue the public policy of wolf-extermination? We debate such questions in terms of economics and biology. The mammalogists assert the wolf is the natural check on too many deer. The sportsmen reply they will take care of excess deer. Another decade of argument and there will be no wolves to argue about. One conservation inkpot cancels another until the resource is gone. Why? Because the basic question has not been debated at all. The basic question hinges on "a refined taste in natural objects." Is a wolfless north woods any north woods at all?

The hawk and owl question seems to me a parallel one. When you band a hundred hawks in fall, twenty are shot and the bands returned during the subsequent year. No four-egged bird on earth can withstand such a kill. Our raptors are on the toboggan.

Science has been trying for a generation to classify hawks and owls into "good" and "bad" species, the good being those which do more economic good than harm. It seems to me a mistake to call the issue on economic grounds, even sound ones. The basic issue transcends economics. The basic question is whether a hawkless owlless countryside is a livable countryside for Americans with eyes to see and ears to hear. Hawks and owls are a part of the land mechanism. Shall we discard them because they compete with game and poultry? Can we assume that these competitions, which we perceive, are more important than the cooperations which we do not perceive?

The fish predator question is likewise parallel. I worked this summer for a club which owns (and cherishes) a delectable trout stream, set in a matrix of virgin forest. There are thirty thousand acres of the stuff that dreams are made of. But look more closely and you fail to see what "a refined taste in natural objects" demands of such a setting. Only once in a great while does a kingfisher rattle his praise of rushing water. Only here and there does an otter-slide on the bank tell the story of pups rollicking in the night. At sunset you may or may not see a heron; the rookery has been shot out. This club is in the throes of a genuine educational process. One faction wants simply more trout; another wants trout plus all the trimmings, and has employed a fish ecologist to find ways and means. Superficially the issue again is "good" and "bad" predators, but basically the issue is deeper. Any club privileged to own such a piece of land is morally obligated to keep all its parts, even though it means a few less trout in the creel.

In the lake states we are proud of our forest nurseries, and of the progress we are making in replanting what was once the north woods. But look in these nurseries and you will find no white cedar, no tamarack. Why no cedar? It grows too slowly, the deer eat it, the alders choke it. The prospect of a cedarless north woods does not depress our foresters; cedar has, in effect, been purged on grounds of economic inefficiency. For the same reason beech has been purged from the future forests of the Southeast. To these voluntary expungements of species from our future flora, we must add the involuntary ones arising from the importation of diseases: chestnut, persimmon, white pine. Is it sound economics to regard any plant as a separate entity, to proscribe or encourage it on the grounds of its individual performance? What will be the effect on animal life, on the soil, and on the health of the forest as an organism? Is there not an esthetic as well as an economic issue? Is there, at bottom, any real distinction between esthetics and economics? Why did New York State vote "no" on the constitutional amendment to turn over the Adirondack forest preserve to economic forestry? I do not know the answers, but I can see in each of these questions another receding target for conservation.

I have a bird dog named Gus. When Gus can't find pheasants he works up an enthusiasm for Sora rails and meadowlarks. This whipped-up zeal for unsatisfactory substitutes masks his failure to find the real thing. It assuages his inner frustration.

We conservationists are like that. We set out a generation ago to convince the American landowner to control fire, to grow forests, to manage wildlife. He did not respond very well. We have virtually no forestry, and mighty little range management, game management, wildflower management, pollution control, or erosion control being practiced voluntarily by private land-owners. In many instances the abuse of private land is worse than it was to begin with. If you don't believe that, watch the strawstacks burn on the Canadian prairies; watch the fertile mud flowing down the Rio Grande; watch the gullies climb the hillsides in the Palouse, in the Ozarks, in the riverbreaks of southern Iowa and western Wisconsin.

To assuage our inner frustration over this failure, we have found us a meadowlark. I don't know which dog first caught the scent; I do know that it happened in 1933, and that every dog on the field whipped into an enthusiastic backing-point. I did myself. The meadowlark was the idea that if the private landowner won't practice conservation, let's build a bureau to do it for him.

Like the meadowlark, this substitute has its good points. It smells like success. It is satisfactory on poor land which bureaus can buy and cover with CCCs. The trouble is that it contains no device for preventing good private land from becoming poor public land. There is danger in the assuagement of honest frustration; it helps us forget we have not yet found a pheasant.

I'm afraid the meadowlark is not going to remind us. He is flattered by his sudden importance.

Why is it that conservation is so rarely practiced by those who must extract a living from the land? It is said to boil down, in the last analysis, to economic obstacles. Take forestry as an example: the lumberman says he will crop his timber when stumpage values rise high enough, and when wood substitutes quit under-selling him. He said this decades ago. In the interim, stumpage values have gone down, not up; substitutes have increased, not decreased. Forest devastation goes on as before. I admit the reality of this predicament. I suspect that the forces inherent in unguided economic evolution are not all beneficent. Like the forces inside our own bodies, they may become malignant, pathogenic. I believe that many of the economic forces inside the modern body-politic are pathogenic in respect of harmony with land.

What to do? Right now there is a revival of the old idea of legislative compulsion. I fear it's another meadowlark. I think we should seek some organic remedy—something that works from the inside of the economic structure.

We have learned to use our votes and our dollars for conservation. Must we perhaps use our purchasing power also? If exploitation-lumber and forestry-lumber were each labelled as such, would we prefer to buy the conservation product? If the wheat threshed from burning strawstacks could be labelled as such, would we have the courage to ask for conservation-wheat, and pay for it? If pollution paper could be distinguished from clean paper, would we pay the extra penny? Over-grazing beef vs. range-management beef? Corn from chernozem, not subsoil? Butter from pasture slopes under twenty per cent? Celery from ditchless marshes? Broiled whitefish from five-inch nets? Oranges from unpoisoned groves? A trip to Europe on liners which do not dump their bilgewater? Gasoline from capped wells?

The trouble is that we have developed, along with our skill in the exploitation of land, a prodigious skill in false advertising. I do not want to be told by advertisers what is a conservation product. The only alternative is a consumer-discrimination unthinkably perfect, or else a new batch of bureaus to certify "this product is clean." The one we can't hope for, the other we don't want. Thus does conservation in a democracy grow ever bigger, ever further.

Not all the straws which denote the wind are cause for sadness. There are several which hearten me. In a single decade conservation has become a profession and a career for hundreds of young "technicians." Ill-trained, many of them; intellectually tethered by bureaucratic superiors, most of them; but in dead earnest, nearly all of them. I look at these youngsters and believe they are hungry to learn new cogs and wheels, eager to build a better taste in natural objects. They are the first generation of leaders in conservation which ever learned to say "I don't know." After all one can't be too discouraged about an idea which hundreds of young men believe in and live for.

Another hopeful sign: Conservation research, in a single decade, has blown its seeds across three continents. Nearly every university from Oxford to Oregon State has established new research or new teaching in some field of conservation. Barriers of language do not prevent the confluence of ideas; Finland, Scandinavia, Germany and Russia are turning out work remarkably similar to our own.

Once poor as a church mouse, American conservation research now dispenses "federal aid" of several kinds in many ciphers.

These new foci of cerebration are developing not only new facts, which I hope is important, but also a new land philosophy, which I know is important. Our first crop of conservation prophets followed the evangelical pattern; their teachings generated much heat but little light. An entirely new group of thinkers is now emerging. It consists of men who first made a reputation in science, and now seek to interpret the land mechanism in terms which any scientist can approve and any layman understand; men like Paul Sears, Robert Cushman Murphy, Charles Elton, Fraser Darling. Is it possible that science, once seeking only easier ways to live off the land, is now to seek better ways to live with it?

We shall never achieve harmony with land, any more than we shall achieve justice or liberty for people. In these higher aspirations the important thing is not to achieve, but to strive. It is only in mechanical enterprises that we can expect that early or complete fruition of effort which we call "success."

The problem, then, is how to bring about a striving for harmony with land among a people many of whom have forgotten there is any such thing as land, among whom education and culture have become almost synonymous with landlessness. This is the problem of "conservation education."

When we say "striving," we admit at the outset that the thing we need must grow from within. No striving for an idea was ever injected wholly from without.

When we say "striving," I think we imply an effort of the mind as well as a disturbance of the emotions. It is inconceivable to me that we can adjust ourselves to complexities of the land-mechanism without an intense curiosity to understand its workings and an habitual personal study of those workings. The urge to comprehend must precede the urge to reform.

When we say "striving," we likewise disqualify at least in part the two vehicles which conservation propagandists have most often used: fear and indignation. He who, by a lifetime of observation and reflection, has learned much about our maladjustments with land is entitled to fear, and would be something less than honest if he were not indignant. But for teaching the fresh mind, these are outmoded tools. They belong to history.

My own gropings come to a dead end when I try to appraise the profit motive. For a full generation the American conservation movement has been substituting the profit motive for the fear motive, yet it has failed to motivate. We can all see profit in conservation practice, but the profit accrues to society rather than to the individual. This, of course, explains the trend, at this moment, to wish the whole job on the government.

When one considers the prodigious achievement of the profit motive in wrecking land, one hesitates to reject it as a vehicle for restoring land. I incline to believe we have overestimated the scope of the profit motive. Is it profitable for the individual to build a beautiful home? To give his children a higher education? No, it is seldom profitable, yet we do both. These are, in fact, ethical and esthetic premises which underlie the economic system. Once accepted, economic forces tend to align the smaller details of social organization into harmony with them.

No such ethical and esthetic premise yet exists for the condition of the land these children must live in. Our children are our signature to the roster of history; our land is merely the place our money was made. There is as yet no social stigma in the possession of a gullied farm, a wrecked forest, or a polluted stream, provided the dividends sufficed to send the youngsters to college. Whatever ails the land, the government will fix it.

I think we have here the root of the problem. What conservation education must build is an ethical underpinning for land economies and a universal curiosity to understand the land-mechanism. Conservation may then follow.

Typescript, c. 1938

The Farmer as a Conservationist

CONSERVATION MEANS harmony between men and land.
When land does well for its owner, and the owner does well by his land; when both end up better by reason of their partnership, we have conservation. When one or the other grows poorer, we do not.

Few acres in North America have escaped impoverishment through human use. If someone were to map the continent for gains and losses in soil fertility, waterflow, flora, and fauna, it would be difficult to find spots where less than three of these four basic resources have retrograded; easy to find spots where all four are poorer than when we took them over from the Indians.

As for the owners, it would be a fair assertion to say that land depletion has broken as many as it has enriched.

It is customary to fudge the record by regarding the depletion of flora and fauna as inevitable, and hence leaving them out of the account. The fertile productive farm is regarded as a success, even though it has lost most of its native plants and animals. Conservation protests such a biased accounting. It was necessary, to be sure, to eliminate a few species, and to change radically the distribution of many. But it remains a fact that the average American township has lost a score of plants and animals through indifference for every one it has lost through necessity.

What is the nature of the process by which men destroy land? What kind of events made it possible for that much-quoted old-timer to say: "You can't tell me about farming; I've worn out three farms already and this is my fourth"?

Most thinkers have pictured a process of gradual exhaustion. Land, they say, is like a bank account: if you draw more than the interest, the principal dwindles. When Van Hise said "Conservation is wise use," he meant, I think, restrained use.

Certainly conservation means restraint, but there is something else that needs to be said. It seems to me that many land resources, when they are used, get out of order and disappear or deteriorate before anyone has a chance to exhaust them.

Look, for example, at the eroding farms of the cornbelt.

425

When our grandfathers first broke this land, did it melt away with every rain that happened to fall on a thawed frost-pan? Or in a furrow not exactly on contour? It did not; the newly broken soil was tough, resistant, elastic to strain. Soil treatments which were safe in 1840 would be suicidal in 1940. Fertility in 1840 did not go down river faster than up into crops. Something has got out of order. We might almost say that the soil bank is tottering, and this is more important than whether we have overdrawn or underdrawn our interest.

Look at the northern forests: did we build barns out of all the pineries which once covered the lake states? No. As soon as we had opened some big slashings we made a path for fires to invade the woods. Fires cut off growth and reproduction. They outran the lumberman and they mopped up behind him, destroying not only the timber but also the soil and the seed. If we could have kept the soil and the seed, we should be harvesting a new crop of pines now, regardless of whether the virgin crop was cut too fast or too slow. The real damage was not so much the overcutting, it was the run on the soil-timber bank.

A still clearer example is found in farm woodlots. By pasturing their woodlots, and thus preventing all new growth, cornbelt farmers are gradually eliminating woods from the farm landscape. The wildflowers and wildlife are of course lost long before the woodlot itself disappears. Overdrawing the interest from the woodlot bank is perhaps serious, but it is a bagatelle compared with destroying the capacity of the woodlot to yield interest. Here again we see awkward use, rather than over-use, disordering the resource.

In wildlife the losses from the disordering of natural mechanisms have, I suspect, far exceeded the losses from exhaustion. Consider the thing we call "the cycle," which deprives the northern states of all kinds of grouse and rabbits about seven years out of every ten. Were grouse and rabbits always and everywhere cyclic? I used to think so, but I now doubt it. I suspect that cycles are a disorder of animal populations, in some way spread by awkward land-use. We don't know how, because we do not yet know what a cycle is. In the far north cycles are probably natural and inherent, for we find them in the untouched wilderness, but down here I suspect they are not inherent. I suspect they are spreading, both in geographic sweep and in number of species affected.

Consider the growing dependence of fishing waters on artificial restocking. A big part of this loss of toughness inheres in the disordering of waters by erosion and pollution. Hundreds of southerly trout streams which once produced natural brook trout are stepping down the ladder of productivity to artificial brown trout, and finally to carp. As the fish resource dwindles, the flood and erosion losses grow. Both are expressions of a single deterioration. Both are not so much the exhaustion of a resource as the sickening of a resource.

Consider deer. Here we have no exhaustion; perhaps there are too many deer. But every woodsman knows that deer in many places are exterminating the plants on which they depend for winter food. Some of these, such as white cedar, are important forest trees. Deer did not always destroy their range. Something is out of kilter. Perhaps it was a mistake to clean out the wolves; perhaps natural enemies acted as a kind of thermostat to close the "draft" on the deer supply. I know of deer herds in Mexico which never get out of kilter with their range; there are wolves and cougars there, and always plenty of deer but never too many. There is substantial balance between those deer and their range, just as there was substantial balance between the buffalo and the prairie.

Conservation, then, is keeping the resource in working order, as well as preventing over-use. Resources may get out of order before they are exhausted, sometimes while they are still abundant. Conservation, therefore, is a positive exercise of skill and insight, not merely a negative exercise of abstinence or caution.

What is meant by skill and insight?

This is the age of engineers. For proof of this I look not so much to Boulder Dams or China Clippers as to the farmer boy tending his tractor or building his own radio. In a surprising number of men there burns a curiosity about machines and a loving care in their construction, maintenance, and use. This bent for mechanisms, even though clothed in greasy overalls, is often the pure fire of intellect. It is the earmark of our times.

Everyone knows this, but what few realize is that an equal bent for the mechanisms of nature is a possible earmark of some future generation.

No one dreamed, a hundred years ago, that metal, air, petroleum, and electricity could coordinate as an engine. Few realize today that soil, water, plants, and animals are an engine, subject, like any other, to derangement. Our present skill in the care of mechanical engines did not arise from fear lest they fail to do their work. Rather was it born of curiosity and pride of understanding. Prudence never kindled a fire in the human mind; I have no hope for conservation born of fear. The 4-H boy who becomes curious about why red pines need more acid than white is closer to conservation than he who writes a prize essay on the dangers of timber famine.

This necessity for skill, for a lively and vital curiosity about the workings of the biological engine, can teach us something about the probable success of farm conservation policies. We seem to be trying two policies, education and subsidy. The compulsory teaching of conservation in schools, the 4-H conservation projects, and school forests are examples of education. The woodlot tax law, state game and tree nurseries, the crop control program, and the soil conservation program are examples of subsidy.

I offer this opinion: these public aids to better private land use will accomplish their purpose only as the farmer matches them with this thing which I have called skill. Only he who has planted a pine grove with his own hands, or built a terrace, or tried to raise a better crop of birds can appreciate how easy it is to fail; how futile it is passively to follow a recipe without understanding the mechanisms behind it. Subsidies and propaganda may evoke the farmer's acquiescence, but only enthusiasm and affection will evoke his skill. It takes something more than a little "bait" to succeed in conservation. Can our schools, by teaching, create this something? I hope so, but I doubt it, unless the child brings also something he gets at home. That is to say, the vicarious teaching of conservation is just one more kind of intellectual orphanage; a stop-gap at best.

Thus we have traversed a circle. We want this new thing, we have asked the schools and the government to help us catch it, but we have tracked it back to its den under the farmer's doorstep.

I feel sure that there is truth in these conclusions about the human qualities requisite to better land use. I am less sure about many puzzling questions of conservation economics.

Can a farmer afford to devote land to woods, marsh, pond, windbreaks? These are semi-economic land uses,—that is, they have utility but they also yield non-economic benefits.

Can a farmer afford to devote land to fencerows for the birds, to snag-trees for the coons and flying squirrels? Here the utility shrinks to what the chemist calls "a trace."

Can a farmer afford to devote land to fencerows for a patch of ladyslippers, a remnant of prairie, or just scenery? Here the utility shrinks to zero.

Yet conservation is any or all of these things.

Many labored arguments are in print proving that conservation pays economic dividends. I can add nothing to these arguments. It seems to me, though, that something has gone unsaid. It seems to me that the pattern of the rural landscape, like the configuration of our own bodies, has in it (or should have in it) a certain wholeness. No one censures a man who loses his leg in an accident, or who was born with only four fingers, but we should look askance at a man who amputated a natural part on the grounds that some other is more profitable. The comparison is exaggerated; we had to amputate many marshes, ponds and woods to make the land habitable, but to remove any natural feature from representation in the rural landscape seems to me a defacement which the calm verdict of history will not approve, either as good conservation, good taste, or good farming.

Consider a single natural feature: the farm pond. Our god-father the Ice-king, who was in on the christening of Wisconsin, dug hundreds of them for us. We have drained ninety and nine. If you don't believe it, look on the original surveyor's plot of your township; in 1840 he probably mapped water in dozens of spots where in 1940 you may be praying for rain. I have an undrained pond on my farm. You should see the farm families flock to it of a Sunday, everybody from old grandfather to the new pup, each bent on the particular aquatic sport, from water lilies to bluegills, suited to his (or her) age and waistline. Many of these farm families once had ponds of their own. If some drainage promoter had not sold them tiles, or a share in a steam shovel, or some other dream of sudden affluence, many of them would still have their own water lilies, their own bluegills, their own swimming hole, their own redwings to hover over a buttonbush and proclaim the spring.

If this were Germany, or Denmark, with many people and little land, it might be idle to dream about land-use luxuries for every farm family that needs them. But we have excess plowland; our conviction of this is so unanimous that we spend a billion out of the public chest to retire the surplus from cultivation. In the face of such an excess, can any reasonable man claim that economics prevents us from getting a life, as well as a livelihood, from our acres?

Sometimes I think that ideas, like men, can become dictators. We Americans have so far escaped regimentation by our rulers, but have we escaped regimentation by our own ideas? I doubt if there exists today a more complete regimentation of the human mind than that accomplished by our self-imposed doctrine of ruthless utilitarianism. The saving grace of democracy is that we fastened this yoke on our own necks, and we can cast it off when we want to, without severing the neck. Conservation is perhaps one of the many squirmings which foreshadow this act of self-liberation.

The principle of wholeness in the farm landscape involves, I think, something more than indulgence in land-use luxuries. Try to send your mind up in an airplane; try to see the *trend* of our tinkerings with fields and forests, waters and soils. We have gone in for governmental conservation on a huge scale. Government is slowly but surely pushing the cutovers back into forest; the peat and sand districts back into marsh and scrub. This, I think, is as it should be. But the cow in the woodlot, ably assisted by the ax, the depression, the June beetle, and the drouth, is just as surely making southern Wisconsin a treeless agricultural steppe. There was a time when the cessation of prairie fires added trees to southern Wisconsin faster than the settlers subtracted them. That time is now past. In another generation many southern counties will look, as far as trees are concerned, like the Ukraine, or the Canadian wheatlands. A similar tendency to create *monotypes*, to block up huge regions to a single land-use, is visible in many other states. It is the result of delegating conservation to government. Government cannot own and operate small parcels of land, and it cannot own and operate good land at all.

Stated in acres or in board feet, the crowding of all the timber into one place may be a forestry program, but is it conservation? How shall we use forests to protect vulnerable hillsides and riverbanks from erosion when the bulk of the timber is up north on the sands where there is no erosion? To shelter wildlife when all the food is in one county and all the cover in another?

To break the wind when the forest country has no wind, the farm country nothing but wind? For recreation when it takes a week, rather than an hour, to get under a pine tree? Doesn't conservation imply a certain interspersion of land-uses, a certain pepper-and-salt pattern in the warp and woof of the land-use fabric? If so, can government alone do the weaving? I think not.

It is the individual farmer who must weave the greater part of the rug on which America stands. Shall he weave into it only the sober yarns which warm the feet, or also some of the colors which warm the eye and the heart? Granted that there may be a question which returns him the most profit as an individual, can there be *any* question which is best for his community? This raises the question: is the individual farmer capable of dedicating private land to uses which profit the community, even though they may not so clearly profit him? We may be over-hasty in assuming that he is not.

I am thinking, for example, of the windbreaks, the evergreen snow-fences, hundreds of which are peeping up this winter out of the drifted snows of the sandy counties. Part of these plantings are subsidized by highway funds, but in many others the only subsidy is the nursery stock. Here then is a dedication of private land to a community purpose, a private labor for a public gain. These windbreaks do little good until many land-owners install them; much good after they dot the whole countryside. But this "much good" is an undivided surplus, payable not in dollars, but rather in fertility, peace, comfort, in the sense of something alive and growing. It pleases me that farmers should do this new thing. It foreshadows conservation. It may be remarked, in passing, that this planting of windbreaks is a direct reversal of the attitude which uprooted the hedges, and thus the wildlife, from the entire cornbelt. Both moves were fathered by the agricultural colleges. Have the colleges changed their mind? Or is an osage windbreak governed by a different kind of economics than a red pine windbreak?

There is still another kind of community planting where the thing to be planted is not trees but thoughts. To describe it, I want to plant some thoughts about a bush. It is called bog-birch.

I select it because it is such a mousy, unobtrusive, inconspicuous, uninteresting little bush. You may have it in your marsh but have never noticed it. It bears no flower that you would recognize as such, no fruit which bird or beast could eat. It doesn't grow into a tree which you could use. It does no harm, no good, it doesn't even turn color in fall. Altogether it is the perfect nonentity in bushes; the complete biological bore.

But is it? Once I was following the tracks of some starving deer. The tracks led from one bog-birch to another; the browsed tips showed that the deer were living on it, to the exclusion of scores of other kinds of bushes. Once in a blizzard I saw a flock of sharptail grouse, unable to find their usual grain or weed seeds, eating bog-birch buds. They were fat.

Last summer the botanists of the University Arboretum came to me in alarm. The brush, they said, was shading out the white ladyslippers in the Arboretum marsh. Would I ask the CCC crews to clear it? When I examined the ground, I found the offending brush was bog-birch. I cut the sample shown on the left of the drawing. Notice that up to two years ago rabbits had mowed it down each year. In 1936 and 1937 the rabbits had spared it, hence it grew up and shaded the ladyslippers. Why? Because of the cycle; there were no rabbits in 1936 and 1937. This past winter of 1938 the rabbits mowed off the bog-birch, as shown on the right of the drawing.

It appears, then, that our little nonentity, the bog-birch, is important after all. It spells life or death to deer, grouse, rabbits, ladyslippers. If, as some think, cycles are caused by sunspots, the bog-birch might even be regarded a sort of envoy for the solar system, dealing out appeasement to the rabbit, in the course of which a suppressed orchid finds its place in the sun.

The bog-birch is one of hundreds of creatures which the farmer looks at, or steps on, every day. There are 350 birds, ninety mammals, 150 fishes, seventy reptiles and amphibians, and a vastly greater number of plants and insects native to Wisconsin. Each state has a similar diversity of wild things.

Disregarding all those species too small or too obscure to be visible to the layman, there are still perhaps 500 whose lives we might know, but don't. I have translated one little scene out of the life-drama of one species. Each of the 500 has its own drama. The stage is the farm. The farmer walks among the players in all his daily tasks, but he seldom sees any drama, because he does not understand their language. Neither do I, save for a few lines here and there. Would it add anything to farm life if the farmer learned more of that language?

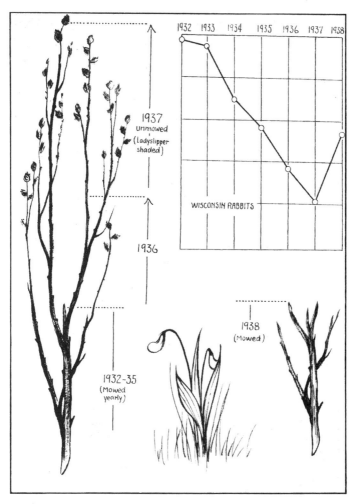

The Story of a Cycle
A mousy, unobtrusive little bush, the bog-birch, plays an important role
in the ups and downs of plant and animal life. Here is illustrated how it
spells life or death to deer, grouse, rabbits, and ladyslippers in Wisconsin.
In 1932 to 1935 rabbits were abundant and ate down the
bog-birches each winter, giving the ladyslippers the sun. During 1936 and
1937 the cycle decimated the rabbits and the bog-birches grew high and
shaded out the ladyslippers. In 1938 the rabbits recovered, mowed down
the birches and the ladyslippers regained their place in the sun.

One of the self-imposed yokes we are casting off is the false idea that farm life is dull. What is the meaning of John Steuart Curry, Grant Wood, Thomas Benton? They are showing us drama in the red barn, the stark silo, the team heaving over the hill, the country store, black against the sunset. All I am saying is that there is also drama in every bush, if you can see it. When enough men know this, we need fear no indifference to the welfare of bushes, or birds, or soil, or trees. We shall then have no need of the word conservation, for we shall have the thing itself.

The landscape of any farm is the owner's portrait of himself.

Conservation implies self-expression in that landscape, rather than blind compliance with economic dogma. What kinds of self-expression will one day be possible in the landscape of a cornbelt farm? What will conservation look like when transplanted from the convention hall to the fields and woods?

Begin with the creek: it will be unstraightened. The future farmer would no more mutilate his creek than his own face. If he has inherited a straightened creek, it will be "explained" to visitors, like a pock-mark or a wooden leg.

The creek banks are wooded and ungrazed. In the woods, young straight timber-bearing trees predominate, but there is also a sprinkling of hollow-limbed veterans left for the owls and squirrels, and of down logs left for the coons and fur-bearers. On the edge of the woods are a few wide-spreading hickories and walnuts for nutting. Many things are expected of this creek and its woods: cordwood, posts, and sawlogs; flood-control, fishing and swimming; nuts and wildflowers; fur and feather. Should it fail to yield an owl-hoot or a mess of quail on demand, or a bunch of sweet william or a coon-hunt in season, the matter will be cause for injured pride and family scrutiny, like a check marked "no funds."

Visitors when taken to the woods often ask, "Don't the owls eat your chickens?" Our farmer knows this is coming. For answer, he walks over to a leafy white oak and picks up one of the pellets dropped by the roosting owls. He shows the visitor how to tear apart the matted felt of mouse and rabbit fur, how to find inside the whitened skulls and teeth of the bird's prey. "See any chickens?" he asks. Then he explains that his owls are valuable to him, not only for killing mice, but for excluding other owls which *might* eat chickens. His owls get a few quail and many rabbits, but these, he thinks, can be spared.

The fields and pastures of this farm, like its sons and daughters, are a mixture of wild and tame attributes, all built on a foundation of good health. The health of the fields is their fertility. On the parlor wall, where the embroidered "God Bless Our Home" used to hang in exploitation days, hangs a chart of the farm's soil analyses. The farmer is proud that all his soil graphs point upward, that he has no check dams or terraces, and needs none. He speaks sympathetically of his neighbor who has the misfortune of harboring a gully, and who was forced to call in the CCC. The neighbor's check dams are a regrettable badge of awkward conduct, like a crutch.

Separating the fields are fencerows which represent a happy balance between gain in wildlife and loss in plow-land. The fencerows are not cleaned yearly, neither are they allowed to grow indefinitely. In addition to bird song and scenery, quail and pheasants, they yield prairie flowers, wild grapes, raspberries, plums, hazelnuts, and here and there a hickory beyond the reach of the woodlot squirrels. It is a point of pride to use electric fences only for temporary enclosures.

Around the farmstead are historic oaks which are cherished with both pride and skill. That the June beetles once got one is remembered as a slip in pasture management, not to be repeated. The farmer has opinions about the age of his oaks, and their relation to local history. It is a matter of neighborhood debate whose oaks are most clearly relics of oak-opening days, whether the healed scar on the base of one tree is the result of a prairie fire or a pioneer's trash pile.

Martin house and feeding station, wildflower bed and old orchard go with the farmstead as a matter of course. The old orchard yields some apples but mostly birds. The bird list for the farm is 161 species. One neighbor claims 165, but there is reason to suspect he is fudging. He drained his pond; how could he possibly have 165?

His pond is our farmer's special badge of distinction. Stock is allowed to water at one end only; the rest of the shore is fenced off for the ducks, rails, redwings, gallinules, and muskrats. Last spring, by judicious baiting and decoys, two hundred ducks were induced to rest there a full month. In August, yellow-legs use the bare mud of the water-gap. In September the pond yields an armful of waterlilies. In the winter there is skating for the youngsters, and a neat dozen of rat-pelts for the boys' pin-money. The farmer remembers a contractor who once tried to talk drainage. Pondless farms, he says, were the fashion in those days; even the Agricultural College fell for the idea of making land by wasting water. But in the drouths of the thirties, when the wells went dry, everybody learned that water, like roads and schools, is community property. You can't hurry water down the creek without hurting the creek, the neighbors, and yourself.

The roadside fronting the farm is regarded as a refuge for the prairie flora; the educational museum where the soils and plants of pre-settlement days are preserved. When the professors from the college want a sample of virgin prairie soil, they know they can get it here. To keep this roadside in prairie, it is cleaned annually, always by burning, never by mowing or cutting. The farmer tells a funny story of a highway engineer who once started to grade the cutbanks all the way back to the fence. It developed that the poor engineer, despite his college education, had never learned the difference between a silphium and a sunflower. He knew his sines and cosines, but he had never heard of the plant succession. He couldn't understand that to tear out all of the prairie sod would convert the whole roadside into an eyesore of quack and thistle.

In the clover field fronting the road is a huge glacial erratic of pink granite. Every year, when the geology teacher brings her class out to look at it, our farmer tells how once, on a vacation trip, he matched a chip of the boulder to its parent ledge, two hundred miles to the north. This starts him on a little oration on glaciers; how the ice gave him not only the rock, but also the pond, and the gravel pit where the kingfisher and the bank swallows nest. He tells how a powder salesman once asked for permission to blow up the old rock "as a demonstration in modern methods." He does not have to explain his little joke to the children.

He is a reminiscent fellow, this farmer. Get him wound up and you will hear many a curious tidbit of rural history. He will tell you of the mad decade when they taught economics in the local kindergarten, but the college president couldn't tell a bluebird from a blue cohosh. Everybody worried about getting his share; nobody worried about doing his bit. One farm washed down the river, to be dredged out of the Mississippi at another farmer's expense. Tame crops were over-produced, but nobody had room for wild crops. "It's a wonder this farm came out of it without a concrete creek and a Chinese elm on the lawn." This is his whimsical way of describing the early fumblings for "conservation."

American Forests, June 1939

A Biotic View of Land

IN PIONEERING times wild plants and animals were tolerated, ignored, or fought, the attitude depending on the utility of the species.

Conservation introduced the idea that the more useful wild species could be managed as crops, but the less useful ones were ignored and the predaceous ones fought, just as in pioneering days. Conservation lowered the threshold of toleration for wildlife, but utility was still the criterion of policy, and utility attached to species rather than to any collective total of wild things. Species were known to compete with each other and to cooperate with each other, but the cooperations and competitions were regarded as separate and distinct; utility as susceptible of quantitative evaluation by research. For proof of this we need look no further than the bony framework of any campus or capitol: department of economic entomology, division of economic mammalogy, chief of food habits research, professor of economic ornithology. These agencies were set up to tell us whether the red-tailed hawk, the gray gopher, the lady beetle, and the meadowlark are useful, harmless, or injurious to man.

Ecology is a new fusion point for all the natural sciences. It has been built up partly by ecologists, but partly also by the collective efforts of the men charged with the economic evaluation of species. The emergence of ecology has placed the economic biologist in a peculiar dilemma: with one hand he points out the accumulated findings of his search for utility, or lack of utility, in this or that species; with the other he lifts the veil from a biota so complex, so conditioned by interwoven cooperations and competitions, that no man can say where utility begins or ends. No species can be "rated" without the tongue in the cheek; the old categories of "useful" and "harmful" have validity only as conditioned by time, place, and circumstance. The only sure conclusion is that the biota as a whole is useful, and biota includes not only plants and animals, but soils and waters as well.

In short, economic biology assumed that the biotic function and economic utility of a species was partly known and the rest could shortly be found out. That assumption no longer holds good; the process of finding out added new questions faster than new answers. The function of species is largely inscrutable, and may remain so.

When the human mind deals with any concept too large to be easily visualized, it substitutes some familiar object which seems to have similar properties. The "balance of nature" is a mental image for land and life which grew up before and during the transition to ecological thought. It is commonly employed in describing the biota to laymen, but ecologists among each other accept it only with reservations, and its acceptance by laymen seems to depend more on convenience than on conviction. Thus "nature lovers" accept it, but sportsmen and farmers are skeptical ("the balance was upset long ago; the only way to restore it is to give the country back to the Indians"). There is more than a suspicion that the dispute over predation determines these attitudes, rather than vice versa.

To the lay mind, balance of nature probably conveys an actual image of the familiar weighing scale. There may even be danger that the layman imputes to the biota properties which exist only on the grocer's counter.

To the ecological mind, balance of nature has merits and also defects. Its merits are that it conceives of a collective total, that it imputes some utility to all species, and that it implies oscillations when balance is disturbed. Its defects are that there is only one point at which balance occurs, and that balance is normally static.

If we must use a mental image for land instead of thinking about it directly, why not employ the image commonly used in ecology, namely the biotic pyramid? With certain additions hereinafter developed it presents a truer picture of the biota. With a truer picture of the biota, the scientist might take his tongue out of his cheek, the layman might be less insistent on utility as a prerequisite for conservation, more hospitable to the "useless" cohabitants of the earth, more tolerant of values over and above profit, food, sport, or tourist-bait. Moreover, we might get better advice from economists and philosophers if we gave them a truer picture of the biotic mechanism.

I will first sketch the pyramid as a symbol of land, and later develop some of its implications in terms of land use.

Plants absorb energy from the sun. This energy flows through a circuit called the biota. It may be represented by the layers of a pyramid (Fig. I). The bottom layer is the soil. A plant layer rests on the soil, an insect later on the plants, and so on up through various groups of fish, reptiles, birds, and mammals. At the top are predators.

The species of a layer are alike not in where they came from, nor in what they look like, but rather in what they eat. Each successive layer depends on those below for food and often for other services, and each in turn furnishes food and services to those above. Each successive layer decreases in abundance; for every predator there are hundreds of his prey, thousands of their prey, millions of insects, uncountable plants.

The lines of dependency for food and other services are called food chains. Each species, including ourselves, is a link in many food chains. Thus the bobwhite quail eats a thousand kinds of plants and animals, i.e., he is a link in a thousand chains. The pyramid is a tangle of chains so complex as to seem disorderly, but when carefully examined the tangle is seen to be a highly organized structure. Its functioning depends on the cooperation and competition of all its diverse links.

In the beginning, the pyramid of life was low and squat; the food chains short and simple. Evolution has added layer after layer, link after link. Man is one of thousands of accretions to

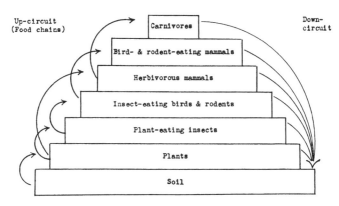

Fig. I.—Biotic pyramid, showing plant and animal community as an energy circuit.

the height and complexity of the pyramid. Science has given us many doubts, but it has given us at least one certainty; the trend of evolution is to elaborate the biota.

Land, then, is not merely soil; it is a fountain of energy flowing through a circuit of soils, plants, and animals. Food chains are the living channels which conduct energy upward; death and decay return it to the soil. The circuit is not closed; some energy is dissipated in decay, some is added by absorption, some is stored in soils, peats, and forests, but it is a sustained circuit, like a slowly augmented revolving fund of life.

The upward flow of energy depends on the complex structure of the plant and animal community, much as the upward flow of sap in a tree depends on its complex cellular organization. Without this complexity normal circulation would not occur. Structure means the characteristic numbers, as well as the characteristic kinds and functions of the species.

This interdependence between the complex structure of land and its smooth functioning as an energy circuit is one of its basic attributes.

When a change occurs in one part of the circuit, many other parts must adjust themselves to it. Change does not necessarily obstruct the flow of energy; evolution is a long series of self-induced changes, the net result of which has been probably to accelerate the flow; certainly to lengthen the circuit.

Evolutionary changes, however, are usually slow and local. Man's invention of tools has enabled him to make changes of unprecedented violence, rapidity, and scope.

One change is in the composition of floras and faunas. The larger predators are lopped off the cap of the pyramid; food chains, for the first time in history, are made shorter rather than longer. Domesticated species are substituted for wild ones, and wild ones moved to new habitats. In this world-wide pooling of faunas and floras, some species get out of bounds as pests and diseases, others are extinguished. Such effects are seldom intended or foreseen; they represent unpredicted and often untraceable readjustments in the structure. Agricultural science is largely a race between the emergence of new pests and the emergence of new techniques for their control.

Another change affects the flow of energy through plants and animals, and its return to the soil. Fertility is the ability of soil to receive, store, and return energy. Agriculture, by overdrafts on the soil, or by too radical a substitution of domestic for native species in the superstructure, may clog the channels of flow or deplete storage. Soils depleted of their stores wash away faster than they form. This is erosion.

Waters, like soils, are part of the energy circuit. Industry, by polluting waters, excludes the plants and animals necessary to keep energy in circulation.

Transportation brings about another basic change: the plants or animals grown in one region are consumed and return to the soil in another. Thus the formerly localized and self-contained circuits are pooled on a world-wide scale.

The process of altering the pyramid for human occupation releases stored energy, and this often gives rise, during the pioneering period, to a deceptive exuberance of plant and animal life, both wild and tame. These releases of biotic capital tend to becloud or delay the penalties of violence.

This thumbnail sketch of land as an energy circuit conveys three ideas more or less lacking from the balance of nature concept:

(1) That land is not merely soil.

(2) That the native plants and animals kept the energy circuit open; others may or may not.

(3) That man-made changes are of a different order than evolutionary changes, and have effects more comprehensive than is intended or foreseen.

These ideas, collectively, raise two basic issues: Can the land adjust itself to the new order? Can violence be reduced?

Biotas seem to differ in their capacity to sustain violence. Western Europe, for example, carries a far different pyramid than Caesar found there. Some large animals are lost; many new plants and animals are introduced, some of which escape as pests; the remaining natives are greatly changed in distribution and abundance. Yet the soil is still fertile, the waters flow normally, the new structure seems to function and to persist. There is no visible stoppage of the circuit.

Western Europe, then, has a resistant biota. Its processes are tough, elastic, resistant to strain. No matter how violent the alterations, the pyramid, so far, has developed some new *modus vivendi* which preserves its habitability for man and for most of the other natives.

The semiarid parts of both Asia and America display a different reaction. In many spots there is no longer any soil fit to support a complex pyramid, or to absorb the energy returning from such as remains. A cumulative process of wastage has set in. This wastage in the biotic organism is similar to disease in an animal, except that it does not culminate in absolute death. The organism recovers, but at a low level of complexity and human habitability. We attempt to offset the wastage by reclamation, but where the regimen of soils and waters is disturbed it is only too evident that the prospective longevity of reclamation projects is short.

The combined evidence of history and ecology seems to support one general deduction: the less violent the man-made changes, the greater the probability of successful readjustment in the pyramid. Violence, in turn, would seem to vary with human population density; a dense population requires a more violent conversion of land. In this respect, America has a better chance for nonviolent human dominance than Europe.

It is worth noting that this deduction runs counter to pioneering philosophy, which assumes that because a small increase in density enriched human life, that an indefinite increase will enrich it indefinitely. Ecology knows of no density relationship which holds within wide limits, and sociology seems to be finding evidence that this one is subject to a law of diminishing returns.

Whatever may be the equation for men and land, it is improbable that we as yet know all its terms. The recent discoveries in mineral and vitamin nutrition reveal unsuspected dependencies in the up-circuit; incredibly minute quantities of certain substances determine the value of soils to plants, of plants to animals. What of the down-circuit? What of the vanishing species, the preservation of which we now regard as an aesthetic luxury? They helped build the soil; in what unsuspected ways may they be essential to its maintenance? Professor Weaver proposes that we use prairie flowers to reflocculate the wasting soils of the dust bowl; who knows for what purpose cranes and condors, otters and grizzlies may some day be used?

Can the violence be reduced? I think that it can be, and that
most of the present dissensions among conservationists may
be regarded as the first gropings toward a nonviolent land use.

For example, the fight over predator control is no mere conflict of interest between field-glass hunters and gun-hunters.
It is a fight between those who see utility and beauty only in
pheasants or trout. It grows clearer year by year that violent
reductions in raptorial and carnivorous species as a means of
raising game and fish are necessary only where highly artificial
(i.e., violent) methods of management are used. Wild-raised
game does not require hawkless coverts, and the biotically educated sportsman gets no pleasure from them.

Forestry is a turmoil of naturalistic movements.

Thus the Germans, who taught the world to plant trees like
cabbages, have scrapped their own teachings and gone back
to mixed woods of native species, selectively cut and naturally
reproduced (*Dauerwald*). The "cabbage brand" of silviculture,
at first seemingly profitable, was found by experience to carry
unforeseen biotic penalties: insect epidemics, soil sickness, declining yields, foodless deer, impoverished flora, distorted bird
populations. In their new Dauerwald the hard-headed Germans
are now propagating owls, woodpeckers, titmice, goshawks, and
other useless wildlife.

In America, the protests against radical "timber stand improvement" by the C.C.C. and against the purging of beech,
white cedar, and tamarack from silvicultural plans are on all
fours with Dauerwald as a return to nonviolent forestry. So
is the growing skepticism about the ultimate utility of exotic
plantations. So is the growing alarm about the epidemic of new
Kaibabs, the growing realization that only wolves and lions can
insure the forest against destruction by deer and insure the deer
against self-destruction.

We have a whole group of discontents about the sacrifice of
rare species: condors and grizzlies, prairie flora and bog flora.
These, on their face, are protests against biotic violence. Some
have gone beyond the protest stage: witness the Audubon researches for methods of restoring the ivory-billed woodpecker
and the desert bighorn; the researches at Vassar and Wisconsin
for methods of managing wildflowers.

The wilderness movement, the Ecological Society's campaign

for natural areas, the German *Naturschutz*, and the international committees for wildlife protection all seek to preserve samples of original biota as standards against which to measure the effects of violence.

Agriculture, the most important land use, shows the least evidence of discontent with pioneering concepts. Conservation, among agricultural thinkers, still means conservation of the soil, rather than of the biota including the soil. The farmer must by the nature of his operations modify the biota more radically than the forester or the wildlife manager; he must change the ratios in the pyramid and exclude the larger predators and herbivores. This much difference is unavoidable. Nevertheless it remains true that the exclusions are always more radical than necessary; that the substitution of tame for wild plants and the annual renewal of the plant succession creates a rich habitat for wildlife which has never been consciously utilized except for game management and forestry. Modern "clean farming," despite its name, sends a large portion of its energy into wild plants; a glance at the aftermath of any stubble will prove this. But the animal pyramid is so simplified that this energy is not carried upward; it either spills back directly into the soil, or at best passes through insects, rodents, and small birds. The recent evidence that rodents increase on abused soils (animal weed theory) shows, I think, a simple dearth of higher animal layers, an unnatural downward deflection of the energy circuit at the rodent layer. Biotic farming (if I may coin such a term) would consciously carry this energy to higher levels before returning it to the soil. To this end it would employ all native wild species not actually incompatible with tame ones. These species would include not merely game, but rather the largest possible diversity of flora and fauna.

Biotic farming, in short, would include wild plants and animals with tame ones as expressions of fertility. To accomplish such a revolution in the landscape, there must of course be a corresponding revolution in the landholder. The farmer who now seeks merely to preserve the soil must take account of the superstructure as well; a good farm must be one where the wild fauna and flora has lost acreage without losing its existence.

It is easy, of course, to wish for better kinds of conservation, but what good does it do when on private lands we have very little of any kind? This is the basic puzzle for which I have no solution.

It seems possible, though, that prevailing failure of economic self-interest as a motive for better private land use has some connection with the failure of the social and natural sciences to agree with each other, and with the landholder, on a common concept of land. This may not be it, but ecology, as the fusion point of sciences and all the land uses, seems to me the place to look.

Journal of Forestry, September 1939

Lakes in Relation to Terrestrial Life Patterns

Mechanized man, having rebuilt the landscape, is now rebuilding the waters. The sober citizen who would never submit his watch or his motor to amateur tamperings freely submits his lakes to drainings, fillings, dredgings, pollutions, stabilizations, mosquito control, algae control, swimmer's itch control, and the planting of any fish able to swim. So also with rivers. We constrict them with levees and dams, and then flush them with dredgings, channelizations, and the floods and silt of bad farming.

The willingness of the public to accept and pay for these contradictory tamperings with the natural order arises, I think, from at least three fallacies in thought. First, each of these tamperings is regarded as a separate project because it is carried out by a separate bureau or profession, and as expertly executed because its proponents are trained, each in his own narrow field. The public does not know that bureaus and professions may cancel one another, and that expertness may cancel understanding. Second, any constructed mechanism is assumed to be superior to a natural one. Steel and concrete have wrought much good, therefore anything built with them must be good. Third, we perceive organic behavior only in those organisms which we have built. We know that engines and governments are organisms; that tampering with a part may affect the whole. We do not yet know that this is true of soils and water.

Thus men too wise to tolerate hasty tinkerings with our political constitution accept without a qualm the most radical amendments to our biotic constitution.

FOOD CIRCUITS IN SOIL AND WATER

Soil and water are not two organic systems, but one. Both are organs of a single landscape; a derangement in either affects the health of both. We acknowledge this interaction between water and land after erosion or pollution makes them sick, but we lack a "language" for describing their normal interactions. Such a language must deal, for one thing, with their exchanges of nutrient materials.

All land represents a downhill flow of nutrients from the hills to the sea. This flow has a rolling motion. Plants and animals suck nutrients out of the soil and air and pump them upward through the food chains; the gravity of death spills them back into the soil and air. Mineral nutrients, between their successive trips through this circuit, tend to be washed downhill. Lakes retard this downhill wash, and so do soils. Without the impounding action of soils and lakes, plants and animals would have to follow their salts to the coast line.

The rate of retardation depends, for one thing, on the length and the termini of the food chains. A nutrient salt impounded in an oak may take a century to pass through an acorn, a squirrel, a redtail, and parasite before it re-enters the soil for another upward roll. The same particle may take only a year to pass through a corn plant and a fieldmouse to the soil. Again it may pass through a grass, a cow, a pig, and a member of the Townsend Club, emerging not into the soil, but into a sewer and thence into a lake. Civilization shortens food chains, and routes them into lakes and rivers instead of fields and pastures.

The rate of retardation depends also on the fertility of soils. Fertile soils wash slowly. They support long chains if we let them do so. Food circuits are intricately adjusted to maintain normal rates of retardation. A normal soil balances its intake from the decomposition of rocks against its loss from downhill wash. We now know, to our cost, the disturbing effects of too low a rate: erosion. A normal water balances its intake from the soil against its outwash to the sea. Pollution is an excess of intake arising from erosion, or from routing land wastes to water. Underfed soils thus mean overfed waters. Healthy land, by balancing the internal economy of each, balances the one against the other.

The food balance between soils and waters is accomplished not only by circuitous routes of flow, but also by eddies and back-currents. That is to say, some animals pump food back uphill. These local reversals of the downhill flow have not, to my knowledge, been described or measured. They may be important to science, and to land health, or conservation.

MOVEMENTS FROM WATER TO LAND
AND FROM LAND TO WATER

Back-currents are likely to be clearly visible in areas inhabited by some animal requiring a larger supply of a particular nutrient than the soil supplies. The red deer on the Scottish highlands is a case in point. Here nutrients are scarce because the soil is derived from sterile rocks. The red deer's yearly production of new antlers calls for more calcium and phosphorus than his highland range can supply. Where and how does he get them?

Fraser Darling (1) records the facts which I have arranged in Fig. 1 as a calcium-phosphorus food chain. The deer gets a little, but not enough, of these horn-building salts from the native herbs and grasses. His supply increases when fires concentrate in ashes the dilute supplies stored in the heather. Hence game-keepers practice rotation burning on the moors. To make good his deficiency in horn-building salts, the deer taps the aquatic food chain of the lakes and tarns, where rich supplies are concentrated in aquatic animals. He eats frogs immobilized by frost (1, 2). As his relative, the reindeer, is reported to do, he may eat duck eggs (4) and dead fish (5). By acquiring such unusual or "depraved" food habits, the deer requisitions from lakes what his terrestrial range fails to provide.

That the stored salts are what the red deer is after is shown by certain other extraordinary food habits which help balance his calcium-phosphorus economy. He eats the velvet from his own horns; the bones of dead deer left by hunters; his own cast antlers or those of other deer; the rabbit or vole which has extracted salts from these same materials and then chanced to die (1, 2). Direct ingestion of lemmings and mice by wild reindeer has been recorded (5) and may also be practiced by the red deer.

The ingestion of aquatic animals by deer is an uphill movement of nutrients; a back-current of the downhill stream. Food which has already "passed" the terrestrial deer but lies temporarily impounded in lakes is pulled back into the terrestrial circuit. On the other hand, the ingestion by deer of velvet, horns, bones, and dead rodents is not a back-current, but rather a short circuit in the usual roll of the food chain. The salts contained in these body parts would normally re-enter the soil and become (in part) available to the deer as plants, but by shorting this normal circuit he recovers them in less time and with less waste.

The quantity of minerals involved in these movements is small, but even small quantities may, on poor soils, be of critical importance. Range managers now realize that the continued "deportation" of phosphorus and calcium in the bones of cattle and sheep may eventually impoverish grazing ranges (7). Darling hints that deportation in sheep may have helped to impoverish the Scottish moors.

Many animals other than red deer tap aquatic food chains and restore food to terrestrial circuits. Many also move food in the opposite direction. The net retardation, or preponderance of uphill transport, varies from zero upward. The length of uphill transport also varies from short to long distances. Thus river ducks, geese, gulls, terns, rails, bitterns, frogs, snakes, and muskrats eat in or at the edge of water and die or defecate inland, but they likewise eat inland and die or defecate in water. There is no clear preponderance of uphill transport. The first three range far inland, the others not far. Eagles, crows, swallows, bears, deer, caribou, and moose carry food both to and from water, but they probably move more food uphill than downhill, and to a considerable distance inland. River-spawning salmon which die inland perform a large and long uphill transport. Guano birds, penguins, herons, otters, minks, skunks, bats, and certain water-hatching, land-dying insects perform a preponderance of uphill transport, but only to a short distance inland.

Probably no other food chain concentrates so much food on so small an area as that ending in guano birds (6). The whole aquatic garden of the south Pacific ships its produce, via the upwelling Humboldt current, to the coastal guanays, which deposit it on their rainless island rookeries as guano. Here then is a bottleneck where the oceanic food circuit achieves a "voltage" of extraordinary intensity. The guano deposits, however, lie so near the shore and in so dry a climate that until they are moved further inland by man they have little effect on terrestrial circuits. Antarctic penguins likewise carry oceanic foods inland, but their deposits are refrigerated and eventually slide back into the sea. As against the long list of higher animals which transport food in a prevalently uphill direction, I can think of only two, man and the beaver, which get most of their food on land and deposit most of it in the water. Marsh-roosting blackbirds also do this, but only in autumn.

Most animals merely circulate food within the terrestrial or aquatic circuit which is their habitat. Thus the diving ducks, except when caught by some land predator, feed from and die

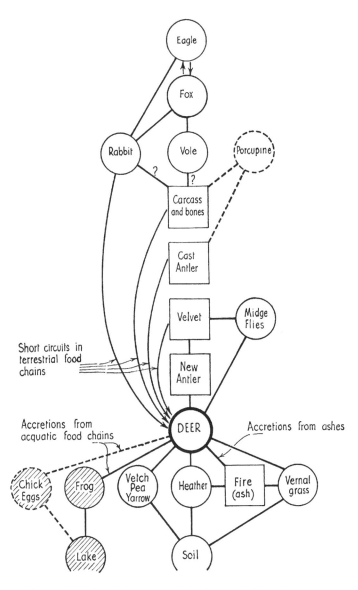

Fig. 1.— *Calcium-phosphorus food chain of red deer, after Fraser Darling (solid lines), with additions for other deer, after other authors (dotted lines).*

into the aquatic circuits. Gallinaceous birds, except when shot by a hunter with modern conveniences, feed from and die into the terrestrial circuits.

LONG-DISTANCE TRANSPLANTATIONS

Migratory birds and fish move food to a distance from its point of origin. Until man began to ship foods and fertilizer, the only long-distance movers were water, air, and migratory animals. Migratory birds must move a considerable volume of food, with more than transitory effects. Thus Hawkins (3) points out that the plant community under passenger pigeon roosts was distinguishable for decades after the pigeons were gone.

Transplantations by migratory animals have no clear orientation uphill or downhill.

SUMMARY AND DISCUSSION

Soil health and water health are not two problems, but one. There is a circulatory system of food substances common to both, as well as a circulatory system within each. The downhill flow is carried by gravity, the uphill flow by animals.

There is a deficit in uphill transport, which is met by the decomposition of rocks. Long food chains, by retarding downhill flow, reduce this deficit. It is further reduced by storage in soils and lakes. The continuity and stability of inland communities probably depend on this retardation and storage.

These movements of food substances seem to constitute, collectively, the nutritional system of the biotic organism. It may be surmised, by analogy with individual plants and animals, that it has qualitative as well as quantitative aspects. The recent history of biology is largely a disclosure of the importance of qualitative nutrition within plants and animals, and within land and water communities. Is it also important as between land and water? Does the wild goose, reconnoitering the farmer's cornfield, bring something more than wild music from the lake, take something more than waste corn from his field?

Such questions are, for the moment, beyond the boundaries of precise knowledge, but not beyond the boundaries of intelligent speculation. We can at least foresee that the prevalent mutilations of soil and water systems, and wholesale simplification of native faunas and floras, may have unpredictable repercussions. Neither agriculturists nor aquaculturists have so far shown any consciousness of this possibility. A prudent technology should alter the natural order as little as possible.

REFERENCES

1. DARLING, F. F. 1937. A Herd of Red Deer. Oxford University Press, London.
2. ———1939. A Naturalist on Rona. Clarendon Press, Oxford.
3. HAWKINS, ARTHUR S. 1940. A wildlife history of Faville Grove, Wisconsin. Trans. Wis. Acad. Sci., 32:40.
4. LEOPOLD, ALDO. 1933. Game Management. Scribner's, New York.
5. MURIE, OLAUS J. 1935. Alaska-Yukon Caribou. U.S. Biol. Survey, North Amer. Fauna Series, no. 54.
6. MURPHY, ROBERT C. 1936. Oceanic Birds of South America, pp. 286–295. American Museum of Natural History, New York.
7. U. S. FOREST SERVICE. 1936. The Western Range, p. 407. Doc. 199, 74 Congr., 2 Sess.

A Symposium on Hydrobiology, 1941

Wilderness As a Land Laboratory

THE RECREATIONAL value of wilderness has been often and ably presented, but its scientific value is as yet but dimly understood. This is an attempt to set forth the need of wilderness as a base-datum for problems of land-health.

The most important characteristic of organism is that capacity for internal self-renewal known as health.

There are two organisms in which the unconscious automatic processes of self-renewal have been supplemented by conscious interference and control. One of these is man himself (medicine and public health). The other is land (agriculture and conservation).

The effort to control the health of land has not been very successful. It is now generally understood that when soil loses fertility, or washes away faster than it forms, and when water systems exhibit abnormal floods and shortages, the land is sick.

Other evidences are generally known as facts, but not as symptoms of land-sickness. The disappearance of plant and animal species without visible causes despite efforts to protect them, and the irruption of others as pests, despite efforts to control them, must, in the absence of simpler explanations, be regarded as symptoms of derangement in the land-organism. Both are occurring too frequently to be dismissed as normal evolutionary changes.

The status of thought on these ailments of the land is reflected in the fact that our treatments for them are still prevailingly local.

Thus when a soil loses fertility we pour on fertilizer, or at best alter its tame flora and fauna, without considering the fact that its wild flora and fauna, which build the soil to begin with, may likewise be important to its maintenance. It was recently discovered, for example, that good tobacco crops depend, for some unknown reason, on the pre-conditioning of the soil by wild ragweed. It does not occur to us that such unexpected chains of dependency may have wide prevalence in nature.

When prairie dogs, ground squirrels, or mice increase to pest levels we poison them, but we do not look beyond the animal to find the cause of the irruption. We assume that animal troubles must have animal causes. The latest scientific evidence points to derangements of the *plant* community as the real seat of rodent irruptions, but few or no explorations of this clue are being made.

Many forest plantations are producing one-log or two-log trees on soil which originally grew three-log and four-log trees. Why? Advanced foresters know that the cause probably lies not in the tree, but in the micro-flora of the soil, and that it may take more years to restore the soil flora than it took to destroy it.

Many conservation treatments are obviously superficial. Flood control dams have no relation to the cause of floods. Check dams and terraces do not touch the cause of erosion. Refuges and propagating plants to maintain animals do not explain why the animal fails to maintain itself.

In general, the trend of the evidence indicates that in land, just as in the human body, the symptom may lie in one organ and the cause in another. The practices we now call conservation are, to a large extent, local alleviations of biotic pain. They are necessary, but they must not be confused with cures. The art of land-doctoring is being practiced with vigor, but the science of land-health is a job for the future.

A science of land health needs, first of all, a base-datum of normality, a picture of how healthy land maintains itself as an organism.

We have two available norms. One is found where land physiology remains largely normal despite centuries of human occupation. I know of only one such place: northeastern Europe. It is not likely that we shall fail to study it.

The other and most perfect norm is wilderness. Paleontology offers abundant evidence that wilderness maintained itself for immensely long periods; that its component species were rarely lost, neither did they get out of hand; that weather and water built soil as fast or faster than it was carried away. Wilderness, then, assumes unexpected importance as a land-laboratory.

One cannot study the physiology of Montana in the Amazon; each biotic province needs its own wilderness for comparative studies of used and unused land. It is of course too late to salvage more than a lop-sided system of wilderness remnants, and most of these remnants are far too small to retain their normality. The latest report* from Yellowstone Park, for example, states that cougars and wolves are gone. Grizzlies and mountain sheep are probably going. The irruption of elk following the loss of carnivores has damaged the plant community in a manner comparable to sheep grazing. "Hoofed locusts" are not necessarily tame.

I know of only one wilderness south of the Canadian boundary which retains its full flora and fauna (save only the wild Indian) and which has only one intruded species (the wild horse). It lies on the summit of the Sierra Madre in Chihuahua. Its preservation and study, as a norm for the sick lands on both sides of the border, would be a good neighborly act well worthy of international consideration.

All wilderness areas, no matter how small or imperfect, have a large value to land-science. The important thing is to realize that recreation is not their only or even their principal utility. In fact, the boundary between recreation and science, like the boundaries between park and forest, animal and plant, tame and wild, exists only in the imperfections of the human mind.

The Living Wilderness, July 1941

---

*Murie, Adolph. Ecology of the coyote in the Yellowstone. Fauna Series no. 4 of the National Parks of the United States.

Yet Come June

EMPIRES SPREAD over the continents, destroying the soils, the floras and faunas, and each other. Yet the trees grow.

Philosophies spread over the empires, teaching the good life with tank and bomb. Machines crawl over the empires, hauling goods. Goods are plowed under, or burned. Goods are hawked over the ether, and along lanes where Whitman smelled locust blossoms morning and evening. Quarrels over goods are planted thick as trees along all the rivers of America. The offal of goods floats down the rivers, settles in the swimming holes. Fish choked with goods float belly-up in the shallows. Dykes to grow goods dry up the waterfowl. Dams to make goods block the salmon runs, but not the barges carrying goods. Railroads carrying goods race the barges. Trucks carrying goods race the railroads. Cars carrying consumers of goods race the trucks. Yet the trees grow.

A folklore of goods fills the curricula. Farmers learn the farm is a factory. Chemists and physicists harness power, biology harnesses plants and animals, all for goods. Politics is the redistribution of goods. Literature and the arts portray the drama of the haves and have-nots. Research is not to decipher the universe, but to step up production. Yet the trees grow.

The rains which fall on the just and the unjust wash silt from the factory-farms. The brooks that make the meadows green feed silt to the rivers. The vales, lying in pensive quietness between, feed silt to the brooks. The hills, rock-ribbed and ancient as the sun, feed silt to the vales. Yet the trees grow.

Manuscript, December 23, 1941

457

The Round River: A Parable of Conservation

O NE OF the marvels of early Wisconsin was the Round River, a river which flowed into itself, and thus sped around and around in a never-ending circuit. Paul Bunyan discovered it, and the Bunyan saga tells how he floated many a log down its restless waters.

No one has suspected Paul of speaking in parables, yet in this instance he did. Wisconsin not only *had* a round river, Wisconsin *is* one. The current is the stream of energy which flows out of the soil into plants, thence into animals, thence back into the soil in a never-ending circuit of life. "Dust unto dust" is a desiccated version of the Round River concept.

We of the genus *Homo* ride the logs which float down the Round River, and by a little judicious "burling" we have learned to guide their direction and speed. This feat entitles us to the specific appellation *sapiens*. The technique of burling is called economics, the remembering of old routes is called history, the selection of new ones is called statesmanship, the conversation about oncoming riffles and rapids is called politics. Some of the crew aspire to burl not only their own logs, but the whole flotilla as well. This collective bargaining with nature is called national planning.

In our educational system, the biotic continuum is seldom pictured to us as a stream. From our tenderest years we are fed with facts about the soils, floras, and faunas which comprise the channel of Round River (biology), about their tissues and substances (chemistry), about their origins in time (geology and evolution), about the technique of exploiting them (agriculture and engineering). But the concept of a current with drouths and freshets, backwaters and bars, is left to inference. To learn the hydrology of the biotic stream we must think at right angles to evolution and examine the collective behavior of biotic materials. This calls for a reversal of specialization; instead of learning more and more about less and less, we must learn more and more about the whole biotic landscape.

Ecology is a "new science" which attempts this feat of thinking in a plane perpendicular to Darwin. Ecology is an infant just learning to talk, and like other infants, is engrossed with its own coinage of big words. Its working days lie in the future. Ecology is destined to become the lore of Round River, a belated attempt to convert our collective knowledge of biotic materials into a collective wisdom of biotic navigation. This, in the last analysis, is conservation.

The biotic stream is capable of flowing in long or short circuits, rapidly or slowly, uniformly or in spurts, in declining or ascending volume. No one understands these variations, but they probably depend on the composition and arrangement of the soils, faunas, and floras which are the conductors or channels of flow.

A rock decays and forms soil. In the soil grows an oak, which bears an acorn, which feeds a squirrel, which feeds an Indian, who ultimately lays him down to his last sleep in the great tomb of man—to grow another oak:

$$\text{rock} \to \text{soil} \to \text{oak} \to \text{acorn} \to \text{squirrel} \to \text{Indian}$$

Ecology calls this sequence of stages in the transmission of energy a food chain, but it can be more accurately envisioned as a pipe-line. It is a fixed route or channel, established by evolution. Each joint in the pipe is adapted to receive from the preceding joint and transmit to the succeeding joint.

The pipeline leaks at every joint. Not all the rock forms soil. Squirrels do not get all the acorns, nor do Indians get all the squirrels; some die and decay and return directly to the soil. Due to this spillage en route, only part of the energy in any local biota reaches its terminus. This loss of volume may be depicted thus:

$$\text{rock} \to \text{soil} \to \text{oak} \to \text{acorn} \to \text{squirrel} \to \text{Indian}$$

In addition to losses from spillage, energy is side-tracked into branches. Thus the squirrel drops a crumb of his acorn, which feeds a quail, which feeds a horned owl, which feeds a parasite. Thus we see that the pipeline branches like a tree. The owl eats not only quail, but also rabbit, which is a link in still another line:

$$\text{rock} \to \text{soil} \leftrightarrow \text{sumac} \leftrightarrow \text{rabbit} \leftrightarrow \text{tularemia}$$

Thus we see each animal and each plant is the "intersection" of many pipelines; the whole system is cross-connected.

Nor is food the only important thing transmitted from one species to another. The oak grows not only acorns; it grows fuel for the Indian, browse for deer, hollow dens for raccoons, salad for June beetles, shade for ferns and bloodroots. It fashions domiciles for gall wasps, it cradles the tanager's nest; its fallen leaves insulate the soil from frost, its unfallen leaves screen the owl from the crow and the partridge from the fox, and all the while its roots are splitting rocks to make more soil to make more oaks. We see, then, that chains of plants and animals are not merely "food chains," but chains of dependency for a maze of services and competitions, of piracies and cooperations. This maze is complex; no efficiency engineer could blueprint the biotic organization of a single acre. It has grown more complex with time. Paleontology discloses aboriginal chains at first short and simple, growing longer and more complicated with each revolving century of evolution. Round River, then, in geological time, grows ever wider, deeper, and longer.

For the biotic community to survive, its internal processes must balance, else its member-species would disappear. That particular communities *do* survive for long periods is well known: Wisconsin, for example, in 1840 had substantially the same soil, fauna, and flora as at the end of the ice age, i.e. 20,000 years ago. We know this because the bones of its animals and the pollens of its plants are preserved in the peat bogs. The successive strata of peats, with their differing abundance of pollens, even record the weather; thus around 5000 B.C. an abundance of ragweed pollen indicates either a series of drouths, or a great stamping of buffalo, or severe fires on the prairie. These recurring exigencies did not prevent the survival of the 350 kinds of birds, 90 mammals, 150 fishes, 70 reptiles, or the thousands of insects and plants. That all these should survive as an internally balanced community for 200 centuries shows an astonishing stability in the original biota. Science cannot explain the mechanisms of stability, but even a layman can see two of its effects: (1) Fertility, when extracted from rocks, circulated through such elaborate food chains that it accumulated as fast or faster than it washed away. (2) This geological accumulation of fertility paralleled the diversification of flora and fauna; stability and diversity were apparently inter-dependent.

————

We have dealt, so far, with the characteristics of Round River in the pre-Bunyan eras. What now of that *enfant terrible*, Paul, and we, his heirs and assigns? What are we doing to the river, and what is the river doing to us? Are we burling our log of state with skill, or only with energy?

We have radically modified the biotic stream; we had to. Food chains now begin with corn and alfalfa instead of oaks and bluestem, flow through cows, hogs, and poultry instead of into elk, deer and grouse, thence into farmers, flappers, and freshmen instead of Indians. That the flow is voluminous you can determine by consulting the telephone directory, or the AAA. Its total volume per unit time is probably much greater than in the pre-Bunyan eras, but curiously enough science has never measured this.

Tame animals and plants have no tenacity as links in the new food chain; they are maintained, artificially, by the labor of farmers, aided by tractors and horses, and abetted by a new kind of animal: the Professor of Agriculture. Paul Bunyan's burling was self-taught; now we have a "pro" standing on the bank giving free instruction.

Each substitution of a tame plant or animal for a wild one, or an artificial waterway for a natural one, is accompanied by a readjustment in the circulating system of the land. We do not understand or foresee these readjustments, we are unconscious of them unless the end effect is bad. Whether it be Franklin Roosevelt rebuilding Florida for a ship canal, or Farmer Jones rebuilding a Wisconsin meadow for cow pasture, we are too busy with new tinkerings to think of end effects. That so many are painless attests the youth and elasticity of the land-organism.

Now to appraise the new order in terms of the two criteria: (1) Does it maintain fertility? (2) Does it maintain a diverse fauna and flora? Soils in the first stages of exploitation display a burst of plant and animal life. The abundant crops which evoked thanksgiving in the pioneers is well known, but there was also a burst of wild plants and animals. A score of imported food-bearing weeds had been added to the native flora, the soil was still rich, and landscape had been diversified by patches of plowland and pasture. The abundance of wildlife reported by the pioneers was in part the response to this diversity.

Such high metabolism is characteristic of new-found lands.

It may represent normal circulation, or it may represent the combustion of stored fertility, i.e., biotic fever. One cannot distinguish the fever from normality by asking the biota to bite a thermometer. It can only be told *ex post facto* by the effect on the soil. What was the effect? The answer is written in gullies on a thousand fields and CCC camps on a thousand hills. Crop yields per acre have remained about stationary, i.e., the vast technological improvements in farming have only offset the wastage in soil. In some regions like the dust bowl, the biotic stream has already shrunk below the point of navigability, and Paul's heirs have moved to California to ferment the grapes of wrath.

As for diversity, what remains of our native fauna and flora remains only because agriculture has not gotten around to destroying it. The present ideal of agriculture is clean-farming; clean-farming means a food chain aimed solely at economic profit and purged of all non-conforming links, a sort of *Pax Germana* of the agricultural world. Diversity, on the other hand, means a food chain aimed to harmonize the wild and the tame in the joint interest of stability, productivity and beauty.

Clean farming, to be sure, aspires, to rebuild the soil, but it employs to this end only imported plants, animals, and fertilizers. It sees no need for the native flora and fauna which built the soil in the first place. Can stability be synthesized out of imported plants and animals? Is fertility which comes in sacks sufficient? These are the questions at issue.

No living man really knows. Testifying for the workability of clean farming is northeastern Europe, where a degree of biotic stability has been retained (except in humans) despite the wholesale artificialization of the landscape.

Testifying for its non-workability are all the other lands where it has ever been tried, including our own, and the tacit evidence of evolution, in which diversity and stability are so closely intertwined as to seem two names for one fact.

Typescript, c. 1941

The Grizzly—A Problem in Land Planning

IN 1909, when I first saw the west, there were grizzlies in every major mountain mass, but you could travel for months without meeting a salaried conservation officer.

Today there is some kind of a conservation officer "behind every bush." We have half a dozen bureaus interested in wildlife; many of them own wild lands. Some receive appropriations for wildlife. Most have discretionary authority to buy and exchange land for consolidation of public holdings. Yet as wildlife bureaus grow, the most magnificent mammal still at large on their lands shrinks steadily toward the Canadian border.

The table shows the official statistics since 1924. While the total number of U.S. grizzlies hovers around 1000 head, an alarming shrinkage in distribution has taken place. Two states have just lost their grizzlies: Oregon and Utah. Four have so few that it's "last call": Arizona, New Mexico, Colorado, and Washington. Only three have substantial remnants: Montana, Wyoming, Idaho. Only two National Parks have any, and it is common knowledge that the park remnants are not doing well. Gabrielson, in his new book, *Wildlife Conservation*, speaks of "the near extinction within the United States of the grizzly bear," but offers no comments or plans.

The status of the official mind in respect of the grizzly is even more alarming than the grizzly census. There seems to be a tacit assumption that if grizzlies survive in Canada and Alaska, that is good enough. It is not good enough for me. The big Alaskan bears are specifically distinct. Moreover, relegating grizzlies to Alaska is about like relegating happiness to heaven; one may never get there.

Saving the grizzly depends almost wholly on land-planning. What is needed is a series of large areas, preferably scattered over half a dozen states, from which roads and livestock are excluded, or in which livestock damage is compensated for so as to do away with the need for eliminating bears. Remission of grazing fees might be one simple way to compensate for bear losses. Buying out scattered ranches is likely the best way in most cases.

463

Grizzly protection is admittedly a subject poisonous to stock-men, but only because there has never been any segregation of stock range from bear range. This is the job land-planners have failed to notice. I am asking why. Why can't land-use planning make room for at least a few grizzly ranges within the United States?

I have heard recently of one grizzly range set aside in Montana by the Forest Service. I salute the Missoula office of the Bureau. On the other hand, I know of one state where the Forest Service has recently promoted sheep grazing in its only remaining grizzly range. In its last two reports this state reported its grizzlies as gone. It required no prophet to foresee this outcome.

The difficulties of segregating stock range from bear range vary from zero to insuperable, and the longer the delay the fewer the easy chances for permanent grizzly ranges. With the extension of roads and grazing equities easy chances become hard, and hard ones become impossible. Thus does time work to "justify" official apathy.

That an official apathy exists is a conclusion forced on us by history. Why does it exist? I don't know. It is easy, of course, for us to sit in a hotel and pass indignant resolutions about subjects like this. It is less easy to live out in the sticks and retain a national point of view on questions of this sort. Administrators, I fear, tend to do their wildlifing in the interest of deer and elk, of which we have a glut in most regions, but which furnish the gunfodder on which public sentiment feeds. The grizzly as gunfodder is negligible. But I insist that posterity will not smile on the loss of the grizzly. The buffalo and the pigeon used good land and competed with important economic activities. The grizzly uses the poorest land we own; the creation of a dozen grizzly ranges would make no perceptible dent in the economic output of the west.

Permanent grizzly ranges and permanent wilderness areas are of course two aspects of one problem. To enthuse about either requires a long view of conservation, and an historical perspective. Only those able to see the pageant of evolution can be expected to value its theatre, the wilderness, or its outstanding achievement: the grizzly. But if education really educates, there will, in time, be more and more citizens who understand that relics of the old West add meaning and value to the new. Youth yet unborn will pole up the Missouri with Lewis and Clark, or climb the Sierras with James Capen Adams, and each generation in turn will ask: where is the big white bear? It will be a sorry answer to say he went under while conservationists weren't looking.

STATUS OF GRIZZLY BEAR, 1924–1940

Year	1924	1927	1930	1937	1938	1939	1940
(A) NATIONAL FORESTS OF U.S.							
Arizona		20	9		1	1	
Colorado	27	19	17	9	26	10	5
Idaho.	74	142	110	58	55	44	38
Montana	458	433	526	435	440	470	480
New Mexico . . .		21	18	4	3	2	2
Oregon		1					
Utah		13	1		2		
Washington	22	98	17	5	9	9	6
Wyoming.	62	133	172	160	155	167	210
	643	880	870	671	691	703	741
(B) NATIONAL PARKS							
Montana				118	126	100	122
Wyoming.				300	280	310	330
				418	406	410	452
(C) INDIAN RESERVATIONS							
Montana							61
Wyoming.					3	3	3
Arizona						6	
New Mexico						40	
					3	49	64
(D) OTHER LANDS							
New Mexico							1
Idaho.				20	20		
Montana					1		
				20	21		1
Total in United States				1109	1121	1162	1258

Outdoor America, April 1942

The Role of Wildlife in a Liberal Education

MOST OF the wildlife education so far attempted is that designed to teach professionals how to do their job. I here discuss another kind: that aimed to teach citizens the function of wildlife in the land organism.

The two kinds contrast sharply in their war status. Perhaps the output of professionals is now excessive, even if there were no war. On the other hand, wildlife teaching for laymen has the same war status as any other branch of science or of the arts; to suspend teaching it is to suspend culture. Culture is our understanding of the land and its life; wildlife is an essential fraction of both.

The bulk of our funds and brains are invested in professional education. In my opinion it is time to "swap ends" to curtail sharply the output of professionals, and to throw the manpower and dollars thus released into a serious attempt to tell the whole campus, and thus eventually the whole community, what wildlife conservation is all about.

To see our predicament clearly, we must see its history.

When wildlife education started a decade ago, three strong forces impelled us to our present course.

One was the obvious preference for preparing men to earn a salary rather than to live a life.

The second was the depression. The pump-priming policy sucked at the conservation schools like a waterspout. Anyone bearing a sheepskin, wet or dry, could soar into the clouds as a paid expert.

The third was expediency. It is easier to teach wildlife to a professional student in 3 years than to a lay student in a semester or two. Once a professional enrolls he must listen, be the teaching good, bad, or indifferent. On the other hand the lay student elects wildlife courses; if the teaching is not vital, he can elect something else.

To what extent are these three pulls still pulling?

Depression is dead. Expediency is no argument. The question, then, boils down to future jobs. Bureaus are now laying plans for another post-war pump-priming era, but it is a mystery to me where we are to find either the cash or the credit for a repetition of 1933. I do not anticipate a post-war boom in "wildlifers." If I am right, and the market for professionals continues poor, then the deans and the presidents and the donors of wildlife funds will have the option of either shrinking the present schools, or switching their emphasis from professional to liberal teaching.

It is not likely that this switch can be made successfully if postponed until the eleventh hour. The time to start is now.

Fortunately the process of conversion does not call for a complete abandonment of professional output. All-campus teaching cannot be vital without research, and research is not possible without assistants, experimental areas, and definite local projects. This residuum of research can be made to produce a small high-grade annual crop of professionals at the same time that it feeds the all-campus teaching effort with vital local facts and questions.

In my own unit, I began this conversion 3 years ago, when the present overproduction of professionals first became visible. The response from the campus-at-large has been gratifying. I would recommend the change to others, even if there were no war to force the issue.

Liberal education in wildlife is not merely a dilute dosage of technical education. It calls for somewhat different teaching materials and sometimes even different teachers. The objective is to teach the student to see the land, to understand what he sees, and enjoy what he understands. I say land rather than wildlife, because wildlife cannot be understood without understanding the landscape as a whole. Such teaching could well be called land ecology rather than wildlife, and could serve very broad educational purposes.

Perhaps the most important of these purposes is to teach the student how to put the sciences together in order to use them. All the sciences and arts are taught as if they were separate. They are separate only in the classroom. Step out on the campus and they are immediately fused. Land ecology is putting sciences and arts together for the purpose of understanding our environment.

An illustration of what I mean appears in Figure 1, which traces some of the lines of dependency (or food chains, so called) in an ordinary community. These lines are the arteries of a living thing—the land. In them circulates food drawn from the soil, pumped by a million acts of cooperation and competition among animals and plants. That the land lives is implicit in its survival through eons of time.

Who is the land? We are, but no less the meanest flower that blows. Land ecology discards at the outset the fallacious notion that the wild community is one thing, the human community another.

What are the sciences? Only categories for thinking. Sciences can be taught separately, but they can't be used separately, either for seeing land or doing anything with it. It was a surprise to me to find this was "news" to many well-trained but highly specialized graduate students.

What is art? Only the drama of the land's workings.

With such a synthesis as a starting point, the tenets of conservation formulate themselves almost before the teacher can suggest them. Basic to all conservation is the concept of land-health; the sustained self-renewal of the community. It is at once self-evident from such an over-all view of the community that land-health is more important than surpluses or shortages in any particular land-product. The "famine concept" of conservation is valid mainly for inorganic resources, yet most teachers still apply it to all resources.

There is no need to persuade the student of land ecology that machines to dominate the land are useful only while there is a healthy land to use them on, and that land-health is possibly dependent on land-membership, that is that a flora and fauna too severely simplified or modified may not tick as well as the original. He can see for himself that there is no such thing as good or bad species; a species may get out of hand, but to terminate its membership in the land by human fiat is the last word in anthropomorphic arrogance.

Finally, the student can deduce, if he thinks hard enough, the peculiar nature of human economics. What we call economic laws are merely the impact of our changing wants on the land which supplies them. When that impact becomes destructive of our own tenure in the land, as is so conspicuously the case today, then the thing to examine is the validity of the wants themselves.

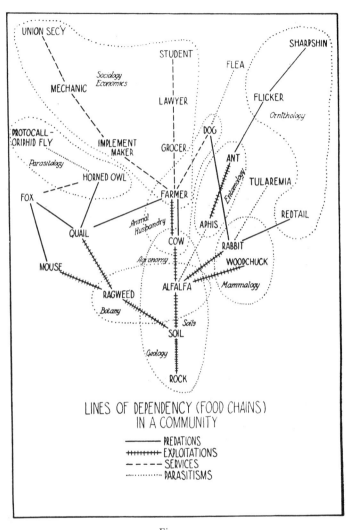

LINES OF DEPENDENCY (FOOD CHAINS)
IN A COMMUNITY

——————— PREDATIONS
++++++++ EXPLOITATIONS
– – – – – SERVICES
·············· PARASITISMS

Figure 1.

I have been sketching the end points, rather than the beginnings, of instruction in land ecology. To reach those end points, the teacher must of course construct a bridge of hard-headed factual materials drawn not only from natural history, but from all land-sciences. This of course raises the question: why is it our job to synthesize and orient; why doesn't agriculture, or geography, or some other bigger and more important discipline do it for us?

My answer is: it is not our job, but it is our opportunity. If this opportunity is real, it is fair to ask: why hasn't it been seen and seized long ago? Why haven't the bigger and more important disciplines synthesized an ecological land concept? I am not sure of the answer, but I think I can see why in zoology and botany. Their pattern of teaching was set by the emergence of the theory of evolution. Some professors are still adding new findings to the evolutionary structure, but in the mind of the average student evolution quits growing, that is dies, when he receives his diploma. There is little opportunity for him to add to his classroom knowledge. Ecology, on the other hand, can lead to lifelong opportunities for study and even experimentation. Therefore, for purposes of a liberal education, ecology is superior to evolution as a window from which to view the world.

Transactions of the 7th North American Wildlife Conference,
April 8–10, 1942

The Last Stand

SOMETIME IN 1943 or 1944 an axe will bite into the snowy sapwood of a giant maple. On the other side of the same tree a crosscut saw will talk softly, spewing sweet sawdust into the snow with each repetitious syllable. Then the giant will lean, groan, and crash to earth: the last merchantable tree of the last merchantable forty of the last virgin hardwood forest of any size in the Lake States.

With this tree will fall the end of an epoch.

There will be an end of cheap, abundant, high-quality sugar maple and yellow birch for floors and furniture. We shall make shift with inferior stuff, or with synthetic substitutes.

There will be an end of cathedral aisles to echo the hermit thrush, or to awe the intruder. There will be an end of hardwood wilderness large enough for a few days' skiing or hiking without crossing a road. The forest primeval, in this region, will henceforward be a figure of speech.

There will be an end of the pious hope that America has learned from her mistakes in private forest exploitation. Each error, it appears, must continue to its bitter end; conservation must wait until there is little or nothing to conserve.

Finally, there will be an end of the best schoolroom for foresters to learn what remains to be learned about hardwood forestry: the mature hardwood forest. We know little, and we understand only part of what we know.

This last stand of the northern hardwoods is in the Porcupine Mountain region of the Upper Peninsula of Michigan. Fifty years ago northern hardwoods covered seven million acres in the Lake States. Five years ago the main remnant in the Porcupine region still comprised 170,000 acres. By 1941 this had shrunk to 140,000 acres. Last winter's cuttings were extra large due to war demand. At the present rate of cutting, only stands too rocky or poor to repay the operator have much chance to outlive the next two years. After that fires are likely to polish up the slashings, leaving a nice pile of brushy rocks as a monument to our generation.

There are, of course, odd bits of uncut hardwoods left elsewhere. The largest bit (10,000 acres) is owned by a private club, and is kept to look at. It is ironical that this club may in the end outscore the combined efforts of the Congress of the United States, the U.S. Forest Service, the sovereign state of Michigan, and the mighty lumber industry as a conserver of virgin forest.

The sugar maple is as American as the rail fence or the Kentucky rifle. Generations have been rocked in maple cradles, clothed from maple spinning wheels, and fed with maple-sweetened cakes served on maple tables before maple fires. Yet the demise of the maple forest brings us less regret than the demise of an old tire. Like the shrew who burrows in maple woods, we take our environment for granted while it lasts. Unlike the shrew, we make shift with substitutes. The poorest is the European "Norway maple," a colorless fast-growing tree persistently used by misguided suburbanites to kill lawns. Wisconsin has used Norway maples to shade its capitol. No governor and no citizen has protested this affront to the peace and dignity of the state.

Maple boards, like maple shade, take time to grow. We have lots of prospective maple lumber in second-growth stands. It is doubtful whether these regrowths will ever achieve the quality or volume of the original stands, first because we shall lack the patience to wait for them to mature; secondly because the maple forest is one of the most highly organized communities on earth; hence the slashing likely inures its future capacity to produce.

Few laymen realize that the penalties of violence to a forest may far outlast its visible evidence. I know a hardwood forest called the Spessart, covering a mountain on the north flank of the Alps. Half of it has sustained cuttings since 1605, but was never slashed. The other half was slashed during the 1600's, but has been under intensive forestry during the last 150 years. Despite this rigid protection, the old slashing now produces only mediocre pine, while the unslashed portion grows the finest cabinet oak in the world; one of those oaks fetches a higher price than a whole acre of the old slashings. On the old slashings the litter accumulates without rotting, stumps and limbs disappear slowly, natural reproduction is slow. On the unslashed portion little disappears as it falls, stumps and limbs rot at once, natural reproduction is automatic. Foresters attribute the inferior performance of the old slashing to its depleted microflora, meaning that underground community of bacteria, molds, fungi, insects, and burrowing mammals which constitute half the environment of a tree.

The existence of the term microflora implies, to the layman, that science knows all the citizens of the underground community, and is able to push them around at will. As a matter of fact, science knows little more than that the community exists, and that it is important. In a few simple communities like alfalfa, science knows how to add certain bacteria to make the plants grow. In a complex forest, science knows only that it is best to let well enough alone.

But industry doesn't know this. I fear that the present mistreatment of the northern hardwoods may be pondered more seriously in 2042 than in 1942. Industries wince with pain when fixers and planners lay violent hands on their highly organized economic community, yet these same industries fix their forests to death with never a flicker of recognition that the same principle is involved. In neither case do we understand all the intricacies of internal adjustment. Communities are like clocks, they tick best while possessed of all their cogs and wheels.

While the northern hardwood forest, like the Spessart, is injured by violence, it is known to stand up under gentle intelligent use to an extraordinary degree. You can cut a third of the volume of a 200-year-old stand and come back every 20 years and take as much again. The reason inheres in the extreme shade-tolerance of the sugar maple and its associated species. Under each mature veteran stand a dozen striplings, full-height and ready to lay on wood the year after the felled veteran bequeaths to them his place in the sun. This method of quick turnover utilization is called selective logging. Its technology has been fully explored by the research branch of the Forest Service. It differs from slash logging in that the mature trees are cut periodically instead of simultaneously, and the striplings are left to grow instead of to burn in the next fire.

How has industry, with its ear ever cocked for new technology, received this innovation? The answer is written on the face of the hills. Industry, with the notable exception of a half-dozen companies, is slashing as usual. The reason given is that most mills are so nearly cut out anyhow that they cannot await the deferred returns of selective logging; they prefer to die quickly in their accustomed shower of sawdust, rather than to live forever on a reduced annual budget of boards.

One is apt to make the error of assuming that a corporation possesses the attributes of a prudent person. It may not. It is a new species of animal, created by mutation, with a morphology of its own and a behavior pattern which will unfold with time. One can only say that its behavior pattern as an owner of forests is so far not very prudent.

Years ago, when the green robe of the Porcupines still spread over much of upper Michigan, bills were introduced in Congress to buy the area as a National Forest. At that time, the proceeds from selective logging would have paid for the land, and left the growing forest to boot. Nothing was done.

Today, when the green robe of the Porcupines has shrunk to the dimensions of a barely respectable necktie, bills are still before Congress. I suppose Congress hesitates to buy, fearing catcalls from patriotic constituents who assume that all internal problems can wait. Most of them doubtless can and should, but not this one. The war will surely outlast this remnant of forest.

I doubt whether public acquisition, as a means of assuring the national timber supply, is a satisfactory substitute for forestry practice by private owners. The job is too big. When government takes over a small area for decent use, it aims to educate by example, but I fear it also generates a false assurance that things are on the mend. In any event the Porcupine necktie is now too small to be of any consequence as a source of timber. But the Porcupine necktie is more than timber; it is a symbol. It portrays a chapter in national history which we should not be allowed to forget. When we abolish the last sample of the Great Uncut, we are, in a sense, burning books. I am convinced that most Americans of the new generation have no idea what a decent forest looks like. The only way to tell them is to show them. To preserve a remnant of decent forest for public education is surely a proper function of government, regardless of one's views on the moot question of large-scale timber production. Moreover, the Porcupines offer the only steep topography available to the public in the snow-belt of the Lake States; they have a future as a ski area, provided they are not further denuded. The necktie is worth keeping for this purpose alone.

I would like to see the Porcupine region acquired and preserved as an act of national contrition, as the visible reminder of an unsolved problem, as a token of things hoped for. To this end it had best be kept roadless, axeless, hotelless, and open only to ski or foot travel. The mere existence of such a token-forest might hasten the day when the green robe again spreads over the Lake States, and when the cutting and using of mature timber becomes an act of normal land-cropping, rather than an act of land-pillage.

Outdoor America, May–June 1942

Land-Use and Democracy

CONSERVATION EDUCATION appeared, before December 7, to be making considerable headway.

Now, against a background of war, its looks like a milk-and-water affair. War has defined the issue: we must prove that democracy can use its land decently. At our present rate of progress we *might* arrive at decent land-use a century or two hence. That is too little and too late.

Conservation education, in facing up to its task, reminds me of my dog when he faces another dog too big for him. Instead of dealing with the dog, he deals with a tree bearing his trademark. Thus he assuages his ego without exposing himself to danger.

Just so we deal with bureaus, policies, laws, and programs, which are the *symbols* of our problem, instead of with resources, products, and land-users, which *are* the problem. Thus we assuage our ego without exposing ourselves to contact with reality.

The symbols of conservation have become complex and confusing, but its essential reality has the devastating simplicity of the needle's eye. If we don't like the way landowner X is using the natural resources of which he is owner, why do we buy his products? Why do we invest in his securities? Why do we accord him the same social standing as landowner Y, who makes an honest attempt to use his land as if he were its trustee? Why do we tell our government to reform Mr. X, instead of doing it ourselves? The answer must be either that we do not know the limits of what government can do, or that we don't care deeply enough to risk personal action or danger.

When the Audubon Society killed the millinery feather trade in 1913, what was its real weapon, the prohibitory law or the refusal of intelligent women to buy wild bird plumage? The answer is plain. The law was merely the symbol of a conviction in the mind of a minority. That conviction was so strong and unequivocal that it was willing to risk direct action, danger of ridicule, and even danger of mistakes to achieve the common good.

I have no illusion that all of the products of land-abuse are as easy to identify, or as easy to do without, as a wild bird-skin on a hat. I do assert that many products of land-abuse can be identified as such, and can be discriminated against, given the conviction that it is worth the trouble. Conversely, the products of good land-use can often be singled out and favored.

Back now to education: who is to be educated? By tacit consent it is the *coming generation*; we have only to teach them why and how to act. Here is the dog again, addressing the symbol, walking around the problem instead of facing-up to it.

"Children are like grown-ups: they understand what others *do* better than what others are *saying*. Unless the grown-up world shows itself willing to practice conservation, that practice will be hard for the younger generation to adopt." With these two sentences, Paul Sears demolishes the "let posterity do it" school of education.

There is lacking only a simple formula by which we, and posterity, may act to make America a permanent institution instead of a trial balloon. The formula is: learn how to tell good land-use from bad. Use your own land accordingly, and refuse aid and comfort to those who do not.

Isn't this more to the point than merely voting, petitioning, and writing checks for bigger and better bureaus, in order that our responsibilities may be laid in bigger and better laps?

Such an approach may be implemented with cases that present an intellectual gradient suitable for all ages and all degrees of land-use education. No one person, young or old, need feel any obligation to act beyond his own personal range of vision.

For example, a case visible to all who ride and read: does a good American shave with soaps that plaster rock and rill with signs, hiding bad manners behind a barrage of puns? Can the legislature abate this nuisance while the voter rewards its impudence with his custom?

Again, a little less obvious: does a good American accept gifts of stolen goods, or credit scores made by cheating? To wit: ducks bought from the pusher, or refrigerated beyond the legal date? Venison hung up by the guide? Wildflowers pilfered without consent? Can society prevent by law what it condones by social usage?

A little harder: Does one buy Christmas trees that should have been left to grow? How does one tell trees representing legitimate thinnings from trees representing exploitation and robbery? Both are for sale; neither is labeled. Could they be?

Up a step: Dairy X buys milk from steep eroding pastures, which spill floods on the neighbors, and ruin streams. It also buys milk from careful farmers, and mixes the two, so that conservation milk is indistinguishable from exploitation milk. What should the conscientious buyer do? What can the careful farmer do? Could farmers form pools to regulate their own pasture practices, as they now regulate butterfat and bacteria?

Still harder: Lumberman X claims to practice forestry. His boards are necessarily knottier than those offered by lumberman Y, who is still skinning the illimitable (?) woods where rolls the Oregon, and hears no sound save his own dashings. Which board do you buy? Should you buy the honest board, even at a higher price?

Simple, but really tough: Should one accept pay for doing the decent thing to land, as most landowners do when the AAA pays them for lowering their ratio of corn and cotton to legumes and grass? If this is defensible for a year, is it for a decade?

Again: Newspaper X buys its paper from a sulphite mill which turns its wastes into the river that moves in majesty. All other mills do the same, and all other newspapers. Each editorial on conservation sends its additional spurt of offal into the public waters. Your cousin draws his paycheck from the mill, and your brother draws his from the newspaper. "There ought to be a law"; in fact there is a law, but it is not enforced; it can't be. An extra penny for each newspaper would pay the cost of reclaiming the offal, and thus break the whole vicious circle. Whose penny is going to break it? How? When? Has this anything to do with the struggle between democracy and fascism?

Finally: Nearly all American wheat is the product of exploitation. Behind your breakfast toast is the burning strawstack, feeding the air with nitrogen belonging in the soil. Behind your birthday cake is the eroding Palouse, the over-wheated prairies, feeding the rivers with silt for army engineers to push around with dredge and shovel, at your expense; for irrigation engineers to fill their dams with, at the expense of the future. Behind each loaf of (inedible) baker's bread is the "ever normal" granary, the roar of the combine, the swish of the gang-plow, ravaging the land they were built to feed, because it is cheaper to raise wheat by exploitation than by honest farming. It wouldn't be cheaper if exploitation wheat lacked a market. You are the market, but transportation has robbed you of all power to discriminate. If you want conservation wheat, you will have to raise it yourself.

These are samples of the easy, the possible, the difficult, and the insoluble realities of conservation, presented as problems for the citizen. Education, so far, presents them only as problems for his agents.

When the ecologist sees any given force at work in the animal community, he can safely predict that it will operate only up to the length of its tether, after which some other force will take over.

Conservation is our attempt to put human ecology on a permanent footing. Milk-and-water education has convinced people that such an attempt should be made, and they have told their government to act for them. Some other force must now persuade them to act for themselves.

Money-minded people think they are acting when they pay taxes. This hallucination, during the "defense" period, nearly cost us the war. It will cost us our natural resources if we persist in it.

To analyze the problem of action, the first thing to grasp is that government, no matter how good, can only do certain things. Government can't raise crops, maintain small scattered structures, administer small scattered areas, or bring to bear on small local matters that combination of solicitude, foresight, and skill which we call husbandry. Husbandry watches no clock, knows no season of cessation, and for the most part is paid for in love, not dollars. Husbandry of somebody else's land is a contradiction in terms. Husbandry is the heart of conservation.

The second thing to grasp is that when we lay conservation in the lap of the government, it will always do the things it can, even though they are not the things that most need doing.

The present over-emphasis on game farms, fish hatcheries, nurseries and artificial reforestation, importation of exotic species, predator control, and rodent control is here in point. These are things government can do. Each has an alternative, more or less developed, along naturalistic lines, *i.e.*, management or guidance of natural processes. Research shows these alternatives to be, in general, superior. But they involve husbandry, which government can do only on its own lands. Government lands are a minor fraction of our land area. Therefore government neglects the superior things that need doing, and does the inferior things that it can do. It then imputes to these things an importance and an efficacy they do not merit, thus distorting the growth of public intelligence.

This whole twisted confusion stems from the painless path, from milk-and-water education, from prolonging our reliance on vicarious conservation.

The end result is that ideas once wholly beneficial begin to boomerang on the user, a clear sign, to the ecologist, that some new adjustment is in order. A case in point is the idea of sanctuary. Sanctuaries and refuges have done enormous good; we would have kept few rare species without them; but for them shootable water-fowl would surely have disappeared. Yet on every hand are signs that we expect too much of them. Most public forests are now shrinking or abolishing their refuges because excess deer and elk, in the absence of natural predators, have become a scourge to the forest and to themselves. Some national parks are being eaten up, and have no recourse except to shoot or to shrink; a pair of sharp horns for any park man to sit on. Many notably successful sanctuaries are now ringed by commercial shooting "clubs"; there is a grave question whether the birds would not be better off without both the sanctuary and the clubs. When administration is in the hands of politicians who care more for votes than for birds, there is not even a question.

Why these kickbacks? The answer, I fear, is that sanctuaries are one of the things government can do, but the growth of private ethics and naturalistic management needed to go with them is beyond the powers of government.

It seems to me that sanctuaries are akin to monasticism in the dark ages. The world was so wicked it was better to have islands of decency than none at all. Hence decent citizens retired to monasteries and convents. Once established, these islands became an alibi for lack of private reform. People said: "We pay the bills for all this virtue. Let goodness stay where it belongs, and not pester practical folks who have to run the world." The present attitude of some duck-hunters offers a close parallel. The more monasteries or sanctuaries, the grimmer the incongruity between inside and outside.

We need more sanctuaries, but some of them will boomerang

until they serve a better public. This is particularly true of deer and elk sanctuaries which are too big, duck or goose sanctuaries choked in a noose of limit-shooting clubs, or any sanctuary deprived of its natural predators.

One of the curious evidences that "conservation programs" are losing their grip is that they have seldom resorted to self-government as a cure for land abuse. "We who are about to die," unless democracy can mend its land-use, have not tried democracy as a possible answer to our problem.

I do not here refer to such superficial devices as advisory boards, who offer their wisdom to others, or such predatory devices as pressure groups, who exist to seize what they can. I refer rather to social and economic units who turn the light of self-scrutiny on themselves.

NRA was perhaps a start toward responsible self-scrutiny in industry, but the Supreme Court snapped the rising grouse before he ever got above the alders.

The present Soil Conservation Districts are perhaps a start to-ward self-scrutiny in farming, but they dare not use their powers for lack of voter-support. These districts are self-governing farm communities which have set themselves up as legal entities. In many states the district is authorized to write land-use regula-tions with the force of law. So far they dare not. But if farmers once asked: "Why don't we tackle our own erosion-control? I'll pull my cows off the hill if you will," the machinery for action is at hand.

Farmers do not yet ask such rash questions. Why? Probably because they have been led to believe that CCC camps, AAA checks, 4-H clubs, extension, meetings, speeches, and other subsidies and uplifts will do the trick. Those who really know land know this is not true; these milk-and-water measures have indeed retarded the rate of soil-loss, but they have not reversed it. Thus we see that the painless path not only fails to lead us to conservation, but sometimes actually retards the growth of critical intelligence on the whereabouts of alternative routes.

No new device in human affairs is ever an unmixed bless-ing. The idea here proposed: hitching conservation directly to the producer-consumer relation, instead of to the government, entails some serious risks. It would present the professional advertiser with an opportunity for euphemized deception and equivocation vastly larger than cigarettes. The more complex the product or process, the wider the field for the trained hood-winker.

This brings us to the real and indispensable functions of government in conservation. Government is the tester of fact vs. fiction, the umpire of bogus vs. genuine, the sponsor of research, the guardian of technical standards, and, I hasten to add, the proper custodian of land which, for one reason or another, is not suited to private husbandry. These functions will become real and important as soon as conservation begins to grow from the bottom up, instead of from the top down, as is now the case.

Conservation is a state of health in the land-organism. Health expresses the cooperation of the interdependent parts: soil, water, plants, animals, and people. It implies collective self-renewal and collective self-maintenance.

When any one part lives by depleting another, the state of health is gone. As far as we know, the state of health depends on the retention in each part of the full gamut of species and materials comprising its evolutionary equipment.

Culture is a state of awareness of the land's collective functioning. A culture premised on the destructive dominance of a single species can have but short duration.

Audubon, September–October 1942

The Prairie: The Forgotten Flora

O N SEPT. 3, 1763, a decade before the Revolution, Captain Jonathan Carver left Mackinac for the wilds of "Ouisconsin." He wanted to prove that the French explorers, while they had covered a lot of ground, had not kept their eyes open. He, an Englishman, was going to show them how to make and record observations.

To this little circumstance we probably owe the explicit descriptions our state recorded in Carver's Journal.*

Proceeding to Green Bay and up the Fox, he arrived at Fond du Lac, and on Sept. 20 continued his ascent of the river toward "the carrying place," or Portage. (His disdain of everything French apparently included place-names.)

"About twelve miles before I reached the carrying place, I observed several small mountains which extended quite to it."

These, I suppose, were the moraines north of Portage.
  Carver remarks of the Fox as it approaches Portage:

"I cannot recollect anything else that is remarkable in this river, except that it is so serpentine for five miles as to gain (only) one quarter of a mile."

Mrs. Kinzie later noted the same circumvolution.

"The Carrying Place between the Fox and the Ouisconsin Rivers is in breadth not more than a mile and three quarters, though in some maps it is so delineated as to appear to be ten miles."

Carver here digresses to suggest that French geographers twist or omit their rivers, and even run them uphill, in order to mislead the English. Having demolished the incompetents, he returns to Portage:

*Carver, Capt. Jonathan. *Three Years Travels Through the Interior Parts of North America*. Key and Simpson, Philadelphia, 1796. 360pp.

"Near one half of the way, between the rivers, is a morass overgrown with a kind of long grass" (doubtless the
marsh between Portage and the Agency House). "*The
rest of it is a plain with some few oak and pine trees growing thereon.*"

Here, then, is an assertion, by a competent Englishman (no
less), that the original landscape surrounding the Agency House
was prairie, bearing only scattered oaks and pines.

Mrs. Kinzie,* arriving at Portage in 1831, confirms Carver's
description in many passages of "Waubun," but she adds that a
"thickly wooded ridge" lay to the north. This, I suppose, was
one of the moraines.

The wide prevalence of prairie in the region is attested by
Carver's description of the view from Blue Mounds:

"For miles nothing was to be seen but lesser mountains,
which appeared at a distance like hay cocks, they being
free from trees. Only a few groves of hickory, and stunted
oaks, covered some of the vallies."

What is prairie?

There is irony in this question. Half of southern Wisconsin was once prairie. Now that we must fight to maintain our
national existence, one might presuppose a universal interest
in the raw materials of and on which states were built. Yet I
have never encountered, in any school or college textbook, an
adequate description of prairie. Prairie, to most Americans, is a
flat place once dotted with covered wagons.

Prairie was, in fact, a community of plants and animals so
organized as to build, through the centuries, the rich soil which
now feeds us.

The plants included not only grasses, but also herbs and
shrubs, to a total of 50 or 75 species. This plant community
was adapted, with extraordinary precision, to the vagaries of
drouth, fire, grazing mammals, and Indians. The more the Indians burned it, the more legumes it grew, the more nitrogen

*Kinzie, Mrs. John H. *Waubun*. Banta Publishing Co., Menasha, 1930.

they pulled out of the air, and the richer it got. So, even among plants, we encounter the uses of adversity.

Many prairie plants bear flowers of singular beauty, and nearly all colored in fall like a maple in the woods.

Some of the prairie plants are now nearly extinct; many have become uncommon; none retain their original dominance (save only rag weed, which was adapted to ground torn up by buffalo, and now finds ground torn up by Mr. McCormick to be just as good). Most of the prairie flora has disappeared from view, partly by reason of plow and cow, and partly by reason of competitive Asiatic and European weeds and grasses. None of the grasses now dominant in southern Wisconsin is native. Roadsides, the natural refuge for prairie, are becoming more and more untenable for anything save sweet clover, quack, and blue grass.

This old flora, like an old book, should be preserved for its historical associations. We can hardly understand our history without knowing what was here before we were.

The practical question is: where, and by whom, shall the prairie flora be given a roothold on some odd bits of its former domain? The university is giving it some hundred acres of the Arboretum. An equally suitable place is the Agency House property at Portage.

We have here restored at great pains, the architecture and furniture of an 1830 household, and then set it in a landscape monopolized by stowaways from Asia. It is only what we don't know about plants that prevents such an incongruity from hurting us.

A roothold for prairie is not to be achieved by wishing it; aggressors are hard to dislodge, particularly quack. There are many of prairie species, requiring a considerable range of cultural methods. These methods were unknown a decade ago; they are now being worked out, at the Arboretum and elsewhere. While the re-establishment of prairie requires much skill and some expense, its maintenance fortunately requires nothing but an occasional burn.

Stock of a dozen plants still exists on the unplowed parts

of the Agency property: turkey-foot bluestem, little bluestem, prairie clover, lupine, spider wort, lead plant, flowering spurge, puccoon, indigo-plant, lespediza, *Anemone cylindrica*, blazing-star. Seeds of many more are to be had for the gathering, if one knows where to look.

I urge that a prairie be reestablished as the necessary and logical environment for the Agency House.

Typescript, November 6, 1942

What Is a Weed?

To live in harmony with plants is, or should be, the ideal of good agriculture. To call every plant a weed which cannot be fed to livestock or people is, I fear, the actual practice of agricultural colleges. I am led to this baleful conclusion by a recent perusal of "The Weed Flora of Iowa," one of the authoritative works on the identification and control of weed pests.*

"Weeds do an enormous damage to the crops of Iowa" is the opening sentence of the book. Granted. "The need of a volume dealing with weeds . . . has long been felt by the public schools." I hope this is true. But among the weeds with which the public schools feel need of dealing are the following:

> Black-eyed Susan (*Rudbeckia hirta*) "succumbs readily to cultivation."
> A model weed!

> Partridge pea (*Cassia chamaecrista*) "grows on clay banks and sandy fields," where it may be "readily destroyed by cutting."

The inference is that even clay banks must be kept clean of useless blooms. Nothing is said of the outstanding value of this plant as a wildlife food, or of its nitrogen-fixing function.

> Flowering spurge (*Euphorbia corollata*) is "common in gravelly soils" and "difficult to exterminate. To eradicate this plant the ground should be given a shallow plowing and the root-stocks exposed to the sun."

Nothing is said of the wisdom of plowing gravelly soils at all, or of the fact that this spurge belonged to the prairie flora, and is one of the few common relics of Iowa's prairie years. Presumably the public schools are not interested in this.

> Prairie goldenrod (*Solidago regida*), which "though often a very troublesome weed in pastures, is easily killed by cultivation."

*"The Weed Flora of Iowa," 1926 Bulletin no. 4, Iowa Geological Survey, 715 pp.

The locality troubled by this uncommon and lovely golden-rod is indeed exceptional. The University of Wisconsin Arboretum, in order to provide its botany classes with a few specimens to look at, had to propagate this relic of the prairie flora in a nursery. On my own farm it was extinct, so I hand-planted two specimens, and take pride in the fact that they have reproduced half a dozen new clumps.

> Horsemint (*Monarda mollis*). "This weed is easily exter-minated by cultivation," and "should not be allowed to produce seeds."

During an Iowa July, human courage, likewise, might easily be exterminated but for the heartening color-masses and fra-grance of this common (and as far as I know) harmless survivor of the prairie days.

> Ironweed (*Vernonia baldwinii*) is "frequently a trouble-some weed, but it is usually not difficult to exterminate in cultivated fields."

It would be difficult to exterminate from my mind the August landscape in which I took my first hunting trip, trailing after my father. The dried-up cowtracks in the black muck of an Iowa bottomland looked to me like small chasms, and the purple-topped ironweeds like tall trees. Presumably there are still school children who might have the same impressions, despite indoctrination by agricultural authority.

> Peppermint (*Mentha piperita*). "This plant is frequently found along brooks. The effectual means of killing it is to clear the ground of the root-stocks by digging."

One is moved to ask whether, in Iowa, nothing useless has the right to grow along brooks. Indeed why not abolish the brook, which wastes many acres of otherwise useful farmland.

> Water pepper (*Polygonum hydropiper*) "not very trouble-some . . . except in low places. Fields that are badly in-fested should be plowed and drained."

No one can deny that this is a weed, albeit a pretty one. But even after drainage, would not some annual, and perhaps a

more troublesome one, follow every plowing? Has Iowa repealed the plant succession?

It is also of interest to note that the Iowa wildlife research
unit finds *Polygonum hydropiper* to be

Wild rose (*Rosa pratincola*). "This weed often persists,"
as a relic of the original prairie flora, "in grain fields of
northern Iowa. Thorough cultivation for a few seasons
will, however, usually destroy the weed."

No comment.

Blue vervain (*Verbena hastata*) and Hoary vervain (*V.
stricta*). The vervains, admittedly weedy, are "easily destroyed by cultivation" and are "frequent in pastures," but
nothing is said about why they are frequent.

The obvious reasons are soil depletion and overgrazing. To
tell this plain ecological fact to farmers and schoolchildren
would seem proper in an authoritative volume on weed-control.

Chicory (*Cichorium intybus*) "is not often seen in good
farming districts except as a wayside weed. Individual
plants may be destroyed by close cutting and applying
salt to the root in hot dry weather."

Schoolchildren might also be reminded that during hot dry
weather this tough immigrant is the only member of the botanical melting-pot courageous enough to decorate with ethereal
blue the worst mistakes of realtors and engineers.

If the spirit and attitude of "The Weed Flora of Iowa" were
peculiar to one book or one state, I would hardly feel impelled
to challenge it. This publication is, however, only one sample
of a powerful propaganda, conducted by many farming states,
often with the aid of federal subsidy, and including not only publications but also weed laws and specialized extension workers.
That such a propaganda is necessary to protect agriculture is,
I think, obvious to all who have ever contended with a serious

plant pest. What I challenge is not the propaganda, but the false premises which seem to be common to this and all other efforts to combat plant or animal pests.

The first false premise is that every wild species occasionally harmful to agriculture is, by reason of that fact, to be blacklisted for general persecution. It is ironical that agricultural science is now finding that some of the "worst" weed species perform useful or even indispensable functions. Thus the hated ragweed and the seemingly worthless horseweed are found to prepare the soil, by some still mysterious alchemy, for high-quality high-yield tobacco crops. Preliminary fallowing with these weeds is now recommended to farmers.*

The second false premise is the emphasis on weed-control, as against weed-prevention. It is obvious that most weed problems arise from overgrazing, soil exhaustion, and needless disturbance of more advanced successional stages, and that prevention of these misuses is the core of the problem. Yet they are seldom mentioned in weed literature.

These same false premises characterize public predator-control. Because too many cougars or wolves were incompatible with livestock, it was assumed that no wolves or cougars would be ideal for livestock. But the scourge of deer and elk which followed their removal on many ranges has simply transferred the role of pest from carnivore to herbivore. Thus we forget that no species is inherently a pest, and any species may become one.

The same false premises characterize rodent-control. Overgrazing is probably the basic cause of some or most outbreaks of range rodents, the rodents thriving on the weeds which replace the weakened grasses. This relationship is still conjectural, and it is significant that no rodent-control agency has, to my knowledge, started any research to verify or refute it. Still if it is true, we may poison rodents till doomsday without effecting a cure. The only cure is range-restoration.

The same false premises beset the hawk and owl question. Originally rated as all "bad," their early defenders sought to remedy the situation by reclassifying part of them as "good."

*Lunn W. M., D. E. Brown, J. E. McMurtrey, Jr., and W. W. Garner (1939). "Tobacco following bare and natural weed fallow and pure stands of certain weeds," *Jour. Agric. Research*, vol. 59, no. 11, pp. 829–846.

Hawk-haters, and gunners with a trigger-itch, have had lots of fun throwing this fallacy back in our faces. We should have been better off to assert, in the first place, that good and bad are attributes of numbers, not of species; that hawks and owls are members of the native fauna and as such are entitled to share the land with us; that no man has the moral right to kill them except when sustaining injury.

It seems to me that both agriculture and conservation are in the process of inner conflict. Each has an ecological school of land-use, and what I may call an "iron heel" school. If it be a fact that the former is the truer, then both have a common problem of constructing an ecological land-practice. Thus, and not otherwise, will one cease to contradict the other. Thus, and not otherwise, will either prosper in the long run.

Typescript, August 2, 1943

Post-War Prospects

THE IMPENDING industrialization of the world, now foreseen by everyone, means that many conservation problems
heretofore local will shortly become global.

No one has yet asked whether the industrial communities
which we intend to plant in the new and naked lands are more
valuable, or less valuable, than the indigenous fauna and flora
which they, to a large extent, displace and disrupt. Such a question requires a degree of objectivity not yet achieved, either by
mice or by men.

We have, though, gone half way. The conservation movement is asking whether the impact of industry on the biota
cannot be made more gentle, more intelligent, less wasteful.

One defect in conservation is that it is so far an *ex post facto*
effort. When we have nearly finished disrupting a fauna and
flora, we develop a nostalgic regret about it, and a wish to save
the remnants. Why not do the regretting and saving in advance?

There is little evidence, in the cases now pending, of any such
advance planning.

Take the Alaskan Highway, a military necessity, but also a
dismemberment of the last large wilderness in North America.
I hear my neighbors anticipating a motor trip over the highway, but they do not foresee its probable effect on the grizzly,
the mountain sheep and the caribou. They do not foresee that
the present highway, which splits the wilderness in half, will
soon be followed by stub highways which split it into quarters,
sixteenths, etc. They do not realize that air-highways to new
mining camps already traverse the land of little sticks; that air-
borne trappers are using poison to harvest fur on the tundras.
They are unaware of what all Arctic history hammers home: that
outdoor ethics evaporate under the midnight sun.

Again, take the impending industrialization of South America
and Mexico. Power machinery and guns have heretofore been
scarce and localized in these countries. Will our good neighbors
use these new toys any more wisely than we did?

Siberia is being industrialized with dramatic speed. No one
knows the details, for the Russians hold their cards close to

their chests. If plan-wise conservation is possible anywhere in the world, it should be possible in Siberia among the pioneers of planning. Siberia has a rich resident fauna, and in addition has long been a reservoir for replenishing the migratory wildlife of Europe, especially waterfowl. What the Siberians do with their newly acquired guns, plows, cows, drainage machinery and roads will be felt from the Arctic Circle to the Nile.

Within the United States, wildlife problems seem to grow as fast or faster than solutions.

We have been able to bring back the waterfowl part way because both ends of their migration route were in good shape; all that the birds had to do was to run the gauntlet between. The gauntlet is now lengthening. Sportsmen from my home town now go to Churchill for goose shooting, to The Pas for ducks. Oil wells, already present in the winter home of the blue goose, now look hopefully at the Everglades. Mexico wants tourists, and will surely get them, both with and without guns. International treaties speak with less authority than oil wells and chilled shot.

Our internal problems were heretofore problems of scarcity. The last decade has now added new problems of excess. Excess deer and elk are eating up many national forests, national parks and other forest and range lands. There is little evidence that the public is learning to foresee and *prevent* these outbreaks, as distinguished from attempting to cure them. When the time for cure arrives, the damage to the habitat is already completed.

There is a prevalent assumption that conservation education is making headway, albeit slowly. It is assumed that if we reach good people with good educational materials, that good results will follow. I wonder if this does not over-simplify the problem.

The other day I noticed, on the front lawn of a successful doctor, a mountain ash tree in process of strangulation by a wire which had been wrapped around it years ago. The doctor passes within three feet of this tree four times a day. He either has not seen the wire, or he has no concept of a tree as a living thing, or he attaches no value to the tree, or he fears that a rusty wire might soil his gloves. This doctor would instantly detect, and act upon, any human body similarly threatened, nor would he spare gloves in doing so. My guess is that he, as an "economic man," has outgrown any consciousness of land, plants, or animals, except perhaps during the hunting season, when he shows brief interest in game birds. The quality of this interest is on a par with his interest in golf balls. Both are objects to be pursued for sport, and then forgotten.

The concept of mountain ash as a cog in the biotic mechanism of his native state is, I fear, nonexistent in his mind. He has no mental picture of mountain ash as winter color, as a full dinner pail for the returning robins, as a scent of blossoms on a May evening. Such concepts lie outside the boundary of his area of consciousness. His area of consciousness, and everybody else's since the world began, is moving. The prevailing direction is *away* from the land. Can education change this? I wish I knew.

While the post-war prospect is for the most part a gloomy one, it is not wholly devoid of encouraging omens.

In my view the most encouraging is the recent discovery that the fertility of the soil determines the nutritional value of the plants grown on it. We have heretofore assumed that it determined only the size of the crop.

At first glance this may seem irrelevant to conservation. Actually, it may prove to be revolutionary. It means that hereafter every plant, including every agricultural product grown for food, will have a qualitative as well as a quantitative value. "A bushel of wheat" will no longer define anything. It must also be specified what vitamins, minerals and other determiners of nutritive value that particular bushel offers. Wheat grown on healthy soil carries the potentiality of healthy animals and healthy people: wheat grown on abused soil is something less than wheat.

This new concept affects conservation in many ways. First, it knocks the props out from under the prevalent assumption that our relation to land is wholly economic.

Secondly, it may ultimately explain many successes and failures in bird and mammal conservation which are now recognized as facts, but for which no reasons are known. The grouse and rabbit cycle, for example, has been suspected of being a nutritional phenomenon. This lends new color to the suspicion.

Thirdly, and most important, it places on the landowner a new obligation to conserve the soil, and one less easily evaded than the old and familiar obligation to posterity. He who erodes his field now erodes the health of his children and his neighbors. It is ironical that chemistry, the most materialistic of sciences, has thus unwittingly synthesized a conscience for land-use.

Audubon, January–February 1944

Conservation: In Whole or in Part?

THERE ARE two kinds of conservationist, and two systems of thought on the subject.

One kind feels a primary interest in some one aspect of land (such as soil, forestry, game, or fish) with an incidental interest in the land as a whole.

The other feels a primary interest in the land as a whole, with incidental interest in its component resources.

The two approaches lead to quite different conclusions as to what constitutes conservative land-use, and how such use is to be achieved.

The first approach is overwhelmingly prevalent. The second approach has not, to my knowledge, been clearly described. This paper aims to sketch the concept of land-as-a-whole.

LAND-HEALTH

Conservation is a state of health in the land.

The land consists of soil, water, plants, and animals, but health is more than a sufficiency of these components. It is a state of vigorous self-renewal in each of them, and in all collectively. Such collective functioning of interdependent parts for the maintenance of the whole is characteristic of an organism. In this sense land is an organism, and conservation deals with its functional integrity, or health.

This is almost, but not quite, the same as the familiar "renewable resource" concept. The latter tells us that a particular resource may be healthy or sick, but not that the sickness of one may undermine the health of all.

Conservation is usually thought of as dealing with the *supply* of resources. This "famine concept" is inadequate, for a deficit in the supply in any given resource does not necessarily denote lack of health, while a failure of function always does, no matter how ample the supply. Thus erosion, a malfunction of soil and water, is more serious than "timber famine," because it deteriorates the entire land community permanently, rather than one resource temporarily.

ATTITUDES

Mass man is unconscious of land-health for three reasons.

First he was, until recently, unable to injure it. He lacked the tools.

Secondly, European civilization developed on a landscape extraordinarily resistant to disorganization, i.e. one which endures very rough usage and severe modification without derangement of function. Thus the oak forests of England became closely grazed sheep downs without losing their soil. The fauna and flora shifted, but did not disintegrate.*

Thirdly, science could not, until recently, distinguish fact from fancy in the reaction of land to human use. Thus the Mediterranean countries were permanently deteriorated by overgrazing and erosion before their inhabitants knew what was happening, or why.

As a result of these three historical accidents, the European races acquired machines for dominating land before they had evolved the social inhibitions requisite for their safe use.

In short, the power to injure land-health grew faster than the consciousness that it can be injured.

Land, to the average citizen, is still something to be tamed, rather than something to be understood, loved, and lived with. Resources are still regarded as separate entities, indeed, as commodities, rather than as our cohabitants in the land-community.

DIVERSITY AND STABILITY UP TO 1840

The Wisconsin land was stable, i.e. it retained its health, for a long period before 1840. The pollens imbedded in peat bogs show that the native plants comprising the prairie, the hardwood forest, and the coniferous forest are about the same now as they were at the end of the glacial period, 20,000 years ago. Since that time these major plant communities were pushed alternately northward and southward several times by long climatic cycles, but their membership and organization remained intact. Thus, in one northward push the prairie once reached nearly to Lake Superior; in one southward push the Canadian forest reached to Indiana.

*Farrow, E. P. 1925. Plant life on East Anglian heaths. Cambridge University Press.

The bones of animals show that the fauna shifted with the flora, but its composition or membership likewise remained intact. The soils not only remained intact, but actually gained in depth and fertility with wind-deposits of loessial soils. With this came a gain in the volume of plant and animal life.

The native Wisconsin community which thus proved its ability to renew itself for 200 centuries was very diverse. It included 350 species of birds, 90 mammals, 174 fishes, 72 amphibians and reptiles, roughly 20,000 insects, about 1500 higher plants, and an unknown but very great number of lower plants and lower animals.

All these creatures were functional members of the land, and their collective activities constituted its inner workings from the glacial epoch to 1840.

These "inner workings" of the community included, as everyone knows, a high proportion of tooth and claw competition, varying in degree from mere jostling to murder. It is hard for the layman, who sees plants and animals in perpetual conflict with each other, to conceive of them as cooperating parts of an organism. Yet the fact remains that throughout geological time up to 1840, the extinction of one species by another occurred more rarely than the creation of new species by evolution, and that occurred very rarely indeed, for we have little evidence of new species appearing during the period of recorded history. The net trend of the original community was thus toward more and more diversity of native forms, and more and more complex relations between them. Stability or health was associated with, and perhaps caused by, this diversity and complexity.

DIVERSITY AND STABILITY SINCE 1840

Since 1840 some members of the native community have been removed. Familiar examples include the buffalo, wild turkey, passenger pigeon, Carolina paroquet, wolverene, marten, and fisher.

Others have been added. These include not only imported birds and mammals like English sparrow, starling, pheasant, Norway rat, and house mouse, but also many wild plants (most weeds are European or Asiatic), many insects good and bad, and many diseases. Domesticated plants, mammals and birds have also been added, and constitute the bulk of the new community.

In one measured sample in Columbia County the domestic plus imported wild birds and mammals constitute 99 per cent of the weight of the total present bird and mammal community.*

Most of the native species which persist have undergone changes in numerical status or distribution, or both, since 1840. The prairie flora and fauna occupied the best soils, and hence were supplanted early. Later pressures severely curtailed and modified the marsh, bog, forest, and aquatic floras and faunas. Everybody knows of these changes, hence they need not be described.

LOSSES AND GAINS

It is necessary to state at this point that this paper is not a nostalgic rehearsal of the glories of primeval Wisconsin. It is an attempt to approach objectively a case of land-illness which nobody understands. The changes we have made in the Wisconsin land are not all inherently or necessarily wasteful. Many of them have enriched and expanded certain elements in the native fauna and flora whilst shrinking others. There is no doubt at all that the introduction of agriculture has increased the numbers, if not the diversity, of many native animals and some native plants. A sketch of these changes has been published.[†]

SYMPTOMS OF ILLNESS

Coincident with this period of man-made change in the land community, many symptoms of impaired land-health have become apparent. Most of these are familiar individually, but they are seldom viewed collectively, or as possibly related to each other and to the land as a whole.

Of the various symptoms of illness, soil erosion and abnormal floods are by far the most important. Most critical observers agree that both are getting worse. Much is known of the superficial causes of both, but little of the underlying "physiology" of soil and water.

Less familiar are some of the qualitative deteriorations in land

*Prairie du Sac Area, Columbia County, unpublished manuscript.
[†]Committee on Wildlife Conservation (Aldo Leopold, Chmn.; L. J. Cole, N. C. Fassett, C. A. Herrick, Chancey Juday, and George Wagner) Report. The University and conservation of Wisconsin wildlife. Bull. of the Univ. of Wis., Science Inquiry Publication III, Madison, Feb. 1937, 39 pp.

crops. In farm crops, it appears that better varieties and better
cultural methods have just about offset the decline in the productivity of the soil. The reason seems to be plain loss of fertility. It has been discovered recently that decline in soil fertility
reduces not only the gross yields of crops, but the nutritional
value of the crops, and the welfare of animals which eat them.*

The qualitative deterioration of crops applies to trees as well
as to agronomic plants. We used to grow 4-log pines; now we
do well to grow 2-log pines on the same sites. What, besides
fire, has happened to soil? Similar deteriorations have occurred
in Europe,† and are by no means understood.

All too familiar are those symptoms of land-illness caused by
the importation of exotic diseases and pests. There is no mystery about such pains and ailments as the white pine blister rust,
chestnut blight, gypsy moth, the corn borer, Dutch elm disease,
the Norway rat, the starling, the house mouse, the Canada
thistle, and the creeping jenny or German carp. Their ultimate
effect on the land, however, presents many unsolved problems,
including the damage done by control operations.

Less familiar are the many instances in which native plants
and animals, heretofore presumably "well-behaved" citizens of
the land community, have assumed all the attributes of pests.
The white grub, the cankerworm, the meadowmouse, the fire
blight of oaks, and the spruce bud-worm are cases in point.

One of the very recent instances of pest behavior by a heretofore "well-behaved" member of the native community is the
irruption of deer in Wisconsin and many other states.‡ While
the superficial "causes" of this phenomenon are well known to
be a coincidence of lumbering, law enforcement, fire-control,
predator-control, and selective harvesting through buck laws,
nevertheless it remains a deep mystery why equivalent coinci-
dences never (as far as we know) produced irruptions of hoofed
mammals previous to human interference. In all probability
some as yet unknown causes lie behind the more superficial
ones; possibly fluctuations in the vitamin content of foods.

*Albrecht, W. A. 1943. Soil and livestock. The Land, 2(4):298–305. And other
papers by the same author.
† Leopold, Aldo. 1936. Deer and Dauerwald in Germany. Jour. Forestry,
XXXIV(4,5):366–375, 460–466.
‡ Leopold, Aldo. 1943. Deer irruptions. Wis. Cons. Bull., VIII(8):1–11.

New plant and animal diseases are now appearing so rapidly that we do not yet know whether they represent some native organism "gone outlaw," or some newly imported pest. Thus the new pine disease, now obliterating plantations of Norway and Jack pine in Oconto and nearby counties, has an unclassified causative agent of unknown origin.

Native members of the community sometimes simply disappear without visible cause, and often despite protective efforts. Prairie chickens, spruce grouse, and certain wildflowers probably belong in this class. Imported species may likewise disappear: the Hungarian partridge seems to be on the decline in Wisconsin, after an initial success, without visible cause.

Finally we have unexplained changes in the population behavior of plants and animals; these behaviors are often of considerable economic importance. Thus there is more than a presumption that population cycles have tended to become more violent in all hares and rabbits, in all grouse, and in foxes. Cyclic population behavior has perhaps spread to pheasants and bobwhite quail.

The conservationist who is interested in land as a whole is compelled to view these symptoms collectively, and as probable maladjustments of the land community. Some of them are understood superficially, but hardly any are understood deeply enough to warrant the assertion that they are separate phenomena, unrelated to each other and to the whole. In point of time, nearly all of them are probably new, and fall within the post-1840 period of violent change in the land community. Are they causally related to the period of change, or did the two coincide by accident?

To assert a causal relation would imply that we understand the mechanism. As a matter of fact, the land mechanism is too complex to be understood, and probably always will be. We are forced to make the best guess we can from circumstantial evidence. The circumstantial evidence is that stability and diversity in the native community were associated for 20,000 years, and presumably depended on each other. Both are now partly lost, presumably because the original community has been partly lost and greatly altered. Presumably the greater the losses and alterations, the greater the risk of impairments and disorganizations.

This leads to the "rule of thumb" which is the basic premise of ecological conservation: the land should retain as much of its original membership as is compatible with human land-use. The land must of course be modified, but it should be modified as gently and as little as possible.

This difference between gentleand restrained, as compared with violent and unrestrained, modification of the land is the difference between organic and mustard-plaster therapeutics in the field of land-health.

There are reasons for gentle land-use over and above the presumed risk to the health of the land. Sauer* has pointed out that the domesticated plants and animals which we use now are not necessarily those we will need a century hence. To the extent that the native community is extinguished, the genetical source of new domesticated plants and animals is destroyed.

This general concept of land-health as an attribute of the original native community as a whole, and of land-illness as probably related to violent changes and consequent disorganization, may be called, for short, the "unity concept."

UNITY AND LAND-USE

If the components of land have a collective as well as a separate welfare, then conservation must deal with them collectively as well as separately. Land-use cannot be good if it conserves one component and injures another. Thus a farmer who conserves his soil but drains his marsh, grazes his woodlot, and extinguishes the native fauna and flora is not practicing conservation in the ecological sense. He is merely conserving one component of land at the expense of another.

The conservation department which seeks to build up game birds by extinguishing non-game predators, or to retain excessive deer populations at the expense of the forest, is doing the same thing.

The engineer who constructs dams to conserve water, develop power, or control floods is not practicing conservation if the actual regimen of water which results, either above or below the dam, destroys more values than it creates. I know of no single impoundment of water in which all of the land values

*Sauer, Carl O. 1938. Theme of plant and animal destruction in economic history. Jour. Farm Economics, XX(4):765–775.

affected were weighed in advance. (Unfortunately it must be stated in the same breath, that ecologists competent to weigh all of them do not yet exist.)

Lop-sided conservation is encouraged by the fact that most Bureaus and Departments are charged with the custody of a single resource, rather than with the custody of the land as a whole. Even when their official titles denote a broader mandate, their actual interests and skills are commonly much narrower. The term "land" now brackets a larger span of knowledge than one human mind can compass.

Ironically enough it is the farmer who is, by implication at least, left to unify, as best he can, the conflicts and overlaps of bureaudom. Separatism in bureaus is probably a necessary evil, but this is not the case in agricultural colleges. If the arguments of this paper are valid, the agricultural colleges have a far deeper responsibility for unification of land-use practice than they, or the public, have so far realized.

I will sketch later some of the practical applications of the land-unity concept to land-use and land-users.

UNITY AND ECONOMICS

Some components of the land community are inherently of economic importance (soil, forests, water) while others cannot possibly be, except in a very indirect sense (wildflowers, song-birds, scenery, wilderness areas).

Some components are of economic importance to the community, but of dubious profit to the individual owner (most marshes, most cover on streambanks and steep slopes, most windbreaks).

Some are profitable for the individual to retain if they are still in a productive state, but of dubious profit if they have to be created de novo, or if they have to be rebuilt after being damaged (woodlots).

It follows that if conservation on private lands is to be motivated solely by profit, no unified conservation is even remotely possible. Community welfare, a sense of unity in the land, and a sense of personal pride in such unity, must in some degree move the private owner, as well as the public. Conservation cannot possibly "pay" except when the meaning is restricted to components that happen to be profitable. Conservation often pays in the sense that the profitable components can carry the unprofitable ones, just as in any industrial enterprise, a unified purpose involves carrying profitable and unprofitable component enterprises, each necessary to the functioning of the whole.

The fallacious assumption that each separate act of conservation can or must be profitable before its practice can be recommended to farmers is possibly responsible for the meagre fruits of forty years of education, extension, and public demonstration in the conservation field. It is undoubtedly responsible for many dubious claims of profit which are commonly made, or implied, in presenting the subject to the public. It is presumably axiomatic that any "program" saddled with over-claims will backfire in the long run.

Sound conservation propaganda must present land health, as well as land products, as the objective of "good" land-use. It must present good land-use primarily as an obligation to the community. Many constituent parts of it are indeed profitable, and where this is the case, the fact can and should be emphasized. But many constituent parts of it are not, and failure to assert this at once subverts education to the intellectual level of a cheap "sales" campaign, in which only virtues are mentioned.

No one need harbor any illusion that the farmer will immediately undertake the unprofitable components of "good" land-use. But it is probably not illusory to assume that fractional truth is no truth, and that one-resource conservation programs are inherently fractional.

ACTS VS. SKILLS; LAW VS. EDUCATION

Conservative land-use consists of a system of acts, motivated by a desire, and executed with skill.

Laws and policies must deal almost exclusively with acts, because desires and skills are intangible, and cannot be defined in law, nor created by law. Acts without desire or skill are likely to be futile. Thus, during the CCC epoch many Wisconsin farmers were induced, by subsidy, to perform the acts of soil conservation, but those who lacked desire and skill dropped the acts as soon as the subsidy was withdrawn.

This limitation of conservation law and policy is inherent and unavoidable. It can be offset only by education, which is not precluded from dealing with desires and skills.

Whether education can create these desires and skills is an open question. Certainly it can not do so in time to avoid a much further disorganization of land health than now exists. This paper does not claim to assess the chances for success of the unity concept. It claims only to assess the basic logic of the conservation program.

FARM PRACTICE

Some of the attitudes toward farm land implied in the unity concept have already been set forth in popular form.* Summarized in terms of education, these implications add up rather simply to this: the farmer should know the original as well as the introduced components of his land, and take a pride in retaining at least a sample of all of them. In addition to healthy soil, crops, and livestock, he should know and feel a pride in a healthy sample of marsh, woodlot, pond, stream, bog, or roadside prairie. In addition to being a conscious citizen of his political, social, and economic community, he should be a conscious citizen of his watershed, his migratory bird flyway, his biotic zone. Wild crops as well as tame crops should be a part of his scheme of farm management. He should hate no native animal or plant, but only excess or extinction in any one of them.

Cash outlays for unprofitable components of land are of course not to be expected, but outlays of thought, and to a reasonable extent of spare time, should be given with pride, just as they are now given to equivalent enterprises in human health and civic welfare.

SUMMARY

Conservation means land-health as well as resource-supply. Land-health is the capacity for self-renewal in the soils, waters, plants, and animals that collectively comprise the land.

Stable health was associated geologically with the full native community which existed up to 1840. Impairments are coincident with subsequent changes in membership and distribution. The "inner workings" of land are not understood, but a causal relation between impairments and degree of change is

*Leopold, Aldo. 1941. Wildlife conservation on the farm. Wis. Agriculturist and Farmer Bulletin, Racine, Wis., 24 pp.

probable. This leads to the rule-of-thumb that changes should be as gentle and as restrained as compatible with human needs.

Land-use is good only when it considers all of the components of land, but its human organization often tends to conserve one at the expense of others.

Some components of land can be conserved profitably, but others not. All are profitable to the community in the long run. Unified conservation must therefore be motivated primarily as an obligation to the community, rather than as an opportunity for profit.

Acts of conservation without the requisite desires and skills are futile. To create these desires and skills, and the community motive, is the task of education.

                                        Typescript, November 1, 1944

The Outlook for Farm Wildlife

TWENTY YEARS have passed since Herbert Stoddard, in Georgia, started the first management of wildlife based on research.

During those two decades management has become a profession with expanding personnel, techniques, research service, and funds. The colored pins of management activity puncture the map of almost every state.

Behind this rosy picture of progress, however, lie three fundamental weaknesses:

1. Wildlife habitat in fertile regions is being destroyed faster than it is being rebuilt.

2. Many imported and also native species exhibit pest behavior. A general disorganization of the wildlife community seems to be taking place.

3. Private initiative in wildlife management has grown very slowly.

In this appraisal of the outlook, I deal principally with the first two items in their bearing on farm wildlife.

Gains and losses in habitat.—Wildlife in any settled country is a resultant of gains and losses in habitat. Stability, or equilibrium between gains and losses, is practically nonexistent. The weakness in the present situation may be roughly described as follows: On worn-out soils we are gaining cover but losing food, at least in the qualitative sense. On fertile soils we are losing cover, hence the food which exists is largely unavailable.

Where cover and food still occur together on fertile soils, they often represent negligence or delay, rather than design.

There is a confusing element in the situation, for habitat in the process of going out often yields well.

For example, on the fertile soils of southern Wisconsin, the strongholds of our remaining wildlife are the wood lot, the fencerow, the marsh, the creek, and the cornshock. The wood lot is in process of conversion to pasture; the fencerow is in process of abolition; the remaining marsh is in process of drainage; the creeks are getting so flashy that there is a tendency to channelize them. The cornshock has long been en route to the silo, and the corn borer is speeding up the move.

Using pheasant as an example, such a landscape often yields well while in process of passing out. The marsh, grazed, or drained or both, serves well enough for cover up to a certain point, while the manure spreader substitutes for cornshocks up to a certain point. The rapid shift in the status of plant successions may in itself stimulate productivity.

The situation is complicated further by a "transmigration" of land use. Originally uplands were plowed and lowlands pastured. Now the uplands have eroded so badly that corn yields are unsatisfactory, hence corn must move to the lowlands while pasture must move to the uplands. In order that corn may move to the lowlands, they must be either tilled, drained, or channelized. This, of course, tends to destroy the remaining marsh and natural stream.

The upshot is a good "interim" crop which has a poor future. I don't know how widely a similar situation prevails outside my own state, but I suspect that the basic pattern, with local variations, is widely prevalent.

Runaway populations.—Wildlife is never destroyed except as the soil itself is destroyed; it is simply converted from one form to another. You cannot prevent soil from growing plants, nor can you prevent plants from feeding animals. The only question is: What kind of plants? What kind of animals? How many?

Ever since the settlement of the country, there has been a tendency for certain plants and animals to get out-of-hand. These runaway populations include weeds, pests, and disease organisms. Usually these runaways have been foreigners (like the carp, Norway rat, Canada thistle, chestnut blight, and white pine blister rust) but native species (like the June beetle and various range rodents) are clearly also capable of pest behavior.

Up to the time of the chestnut blight, these runaways did not threaten wildlife directly on any serious scale, but they now do, and it is now clear that the pest problem is developing several new and dangerous angles:

1. World-wide transport is carrying new "stowaways" to new habitats on an ascending scale. (Example: *Anopheles gambiae* to Brazil, bubonic plague to western states.)

2. Modern chemistry is developing controls which may be as dangerous as the pests themselves. (Example: DDT.)

3. Additional native species, heretofore law-abiding citizens of the flora and fauna, are exhibiting pest behavior. (Example: excess deer and elk.)

These three new angles must be considered together to appreciate their full import. Mildly dangerous pests like ordinary mosquitoes evoked control measures which severely damaged wildlife; desperately dangerous pests will evoke corresponding control measures, and when these collide with wildlife interests, our squeak of pain will not even be heard.

Moreover, wildlife itself is threatened directly by pests. Sometimes they hit so fast and hard that the funeral is over before the origin of the malady is known. Thus in Wisconsin, we have a new disease known as burn blight, the cause of which is still unknown. It threatens to destroy young Norway pine and jack pine, especially plantations. Oak wilt, the cause of which was only recently discovered, is steadily reducing red and black oaks. Our white pine is already blighted except on artificially-controlled areas. Bud-worm is in the spruce. Hickory can't grow because of a weevil which bites the terminal bud. Deer have wiped out most white cedar and hemlock reproduction. Sawfly has again raided the tamaracks. June beetles began years ago to whittle down the bur and white oaks, and continue to do so. Bag worm is moving up from the south and west and may get our red cedars. Dutch elm disease is headed west from Ohio. What kind of a wood lot or forest fauna can we support if every important tree species has to be sprayed in order to live?

Shrubs are not quite so hard hit, but the shrub flora has its troubles. On the University of Wisconsin Arboretum, an area dedicated to the rebuilding of the original native landscape, the Siberian honeysuckle is calmly usurping the understory of all woods, and threatens to engulf even the marshes.

In Wisconsin wood lots it is becoming very difficult to get oak reproduction even when we fence out the cows. The cottontails won't let a young oak get by. One can't interest the farmer in a wood lot which reproduces only weed trees.

Of the dozen pests mentioned on this page, four are imported, seven are runaway native species, and one is of unknown origin. Of the 12, 6 have become pests in the last few years.

Farm crops and livestock exhibit a parallel list of pests, of which the worst now rampant in my region is the corn borer. The corn borer can be controlled by fall plowing, but what that will do to cornbelt wildlife is something I dislike to think about.

It all makes a pattern. Runaway populations are piling up in numbers and severity. In the effort to rescue one value, we trample another. Wild plants and animals suffer worst because we can't spend much cash on controls or preventives. Everything we lose will be replaced by something else, almost invariably inferior. As Charles Elton* has said: "The biological cost of modern transport is high."

In short, we face not only an unfavorable balance between loss and gain in habitat, but an accelerating disorganization of those unknown controls which stabilize the flora and fauna, and which, in conjunction with stable soil and a normal regimen of water, constitute land-health.

The human background.—Behind both of these trends in the physical status of the landscape lies an unresolved contest between two opposing philosophies of farm life. I suppose these have to be labeled for handy reference, although I distrust labels:

1. *The farm is a food-factory*, and the criterion of its success is salable products.

2. *The farm is a place to live*. The criterion of success is a harmonious balance between plants, animals, and people; between the domestic and the wild; between utility and beauty.

Wildlife has no place in the food-factory farm, except as the accidental relic of pioneer days. The trend of the landscape is toward a monotype, in which only the least exacting wildlife species can exist.

On the other hand, wildlife is an integral part of the farm-as-a-place-to-live. While it must be subordinated to economic needs, there is a deliberate effort to keep as rich a flora and fauna as possible, because it is "nice to have around."

It was inevitable and no doubt desirable that the tremendous momentum of industrialization should have spread to farm life. It is clear to me, however, that it has overshot the mark, in the sense that it is generating new insecurities, economic and ecological, in place of those it was meant to abolish. In its extreme

*Journal of Animal Ecology, 1944, 13:1:87–88.

form, it is humanly desolate and economically unstable. These extremes will some day die of their own too-much, not because they are bad for wildlife, but because they are bad for farmers.

When that day comes, the farmer will be asking us how to enrich the wildlife of his community. Stranger things have happened. Meanwhile we must do the best we can on the ecological leavings.

Transactions of the 10th North American Wildlife Conference,
February 8, 1945

The Land-Health Concept and Conservation

AUGUSTE COMTE, and later Herbert Spencer, pointed out that there is a natural sequence in the development of the sciences, and that this sequence represents a gradient from the simple toward the complex. Spencer's sequence was physics—chemistry—biology—psychology—sociology.

According to this sequence, ecology, the sociology of the biota, will be the last science to achieve the stage of predictable reactions. This expectation presents a peculiar dilemma, because there is urgent need of predictable ecology at this moment. The reason is that our new physical and chemical tools are so powerful and so widely used that they threaten to disrupt the capacity for self-renewal in the biota. This capacity I will call land-health.

The symptoms of disorganization, or land-sickness, are well known. They include abnormal erosion, abnormal intensity of floods, decline of yields in crops and forests, decline of carrying capacity in pastures and ranges, outbreak of some species as pests and the disappearance of others without visible cause, a general tendency toward the shortening of species lists and of food chains, and a world-wide dominance of plant and animal weeds. With hardly a single exception, these phenomena of disorganization are only superficially understood.

George P. Marsh, in *The Earth as Modified by Human Action* (1874), was one of the first to sense that soil, water, plants, and animals are organized collectively in such a way as to present the possibility of disorganization. His case histories describe many degrees of biotic sickness in many geographic regions. They are probably the ultimate source of the biotic ideas now known as conservation.

One might offer an ironic definition of conservation as follows: Conservation is a series of ecological predictions made by laymen because ecologists have failed to offer any.

Need I stop to prove this? The names of Theodore Roosevelt, Gifford Pinchot, William T. Hornaday, Hugh H. Bennett, and Jay N. Darling seem to spring out of recent American history with an emphatic reply. This paper is, in substance, a plea for ecological prediction by ecologists, whether or no the time is ripe. If we wait for our turn in the Spencerian sequence, there will not be enough healthy land left even to define health. We are, in short, land-doctors forced by circumstance to reverse the logical order of our service to society. No matter how imperfect our present ability, it is likely to contribute something to social wisdom which would otherwise be lacking.

CONDITIONS REQUISITE FOR LAND-HEALTH

I have no illusion that the thousands of ecological questions raised by modern land-use can all be assessed by ecologists. What I mean by "prediction" is a shrewd guess on just one basic question: What are the probable conditions requisite for the perpetuation of biotic self-renewal or land-health? This would define a goal for conservationists to strive toward. They now have no basic goal bracketing all component groups. Each group has its own goal, and it is common knowledge that these conflict and nullify each other to a large degree.

I will record my own guess first in a figure of speech. The biotic clock may continue ticking if we:

1. Cease throwing away its parts.
2. Handle it gently.
3. Recognize that its importance transcends economics.
4. Don't let too many people tinker with it.

THE INTEGRITY OF THE PARTS

Paleontology teaches us that most land was stable, at least in terms of time-scales applicable to human affairs, up to the point at which fauna, flora, soil, or waters were radically modified for human use. Disorganization seldom preceded the wholesale conversion of land with modern tools. It is necessary to suppose, therefore, that a high degree of interdependence exists between the capacity for self-renewal and the integrity of the native communities.

To cite a case: evolution made few changes in the species lists of Europe and America since the last glaciation, nor have the soil or water systems changed materially. Communities were pushed around by climatic cycles, but they did not disappear, and their membership remained intact. The big changes in fauna, flora, soil, and water have all occurred in the last few centuries. We must assume, therefore, that some causal connection exists between the integrity of the native communities and their ability for self-renewal. To assume otherwise is to assume that we understand the biotic mechanisms. The absurdity of such an assumption hardly needs comment, especially to ecologists.

There are, of course, practical limits of both time and space which curtail the degree to which the species list can be retained in settled regions. No one debates the removal of the buffalo or the pigeon from the cornbelt. But we are today extinguishing many species, or relegating them to National Parks, on grounds that are ecologically false. Thus the timber wolf, already extinguished over most of the West, is at the point of being extinguished in the Lake States, with official sanction and in fact subsidy, because he eats deer. The assumption is that rifles can trim the deer herd, but the fact is that in Wisconsin and Michigan at least, the deer herd is trimming us. Not only are deer nullifying the reforestation program, but they are tending to eliminate at least three tree species from the future forest: white cedar, hemlock, and yew. The proportion of white pine is being lowered in many localities. The effect of excess deer on lesser vegetation, on other animals, and ultimately on soil, is not known, but it may be large. It has been suggested that the snowshoe hare, under the impact of overbrowsing by deer, ceases to exhibit cyclic population behavior, and that the ruffed grouse is injuriously affected through depletion of its food and cover plants.

Here then is a chain reaction of unknown length threatening the integrity of the fauna and flora over great areas, and arising from a single error in prediction: that human predation by rifle is the biotic equivalent of wolf-predation.

This is one of hundreds of land-use errors, made by laymen-administrators in the name of conservation, and all based on the assumption that we are at liberty to prune the species-list of members considered "useless," harmful, or unprofitable.

That we must alter the distribution and abundance of species before we understand the consequences of doing so is taken for granted. These modifications are reversible, and hence not very dangerous. But extirpation is never reversible. It is already too late to restore the wolf to the western deer ranges because the indigenous races are extinct.

Closely related to the needless pruning of species lists is the question of their needless enlargement by the importation of exotics. Space forbids my covering this. I will only say that the idea of preference for natives hardly exists in fish management, agronomy, and horticulture, and has only a tenuous hold in game management, forestry, and range management. Soil management is just discovering that there is a soil fauna and a soil flora.

VIOLENCE IN LAND-USE

All land must be converted, either in its plant successions, topography, or water relations, before it can support an industrial economy. My guess here is that the less violent these conversions, the more likely they are to be durable, and the less likely they are to exhibit unforeseen repercussions.

A veritable epidemic of violence prevails at the present moment in the field of water management. Flood-control dams, hydroelectric dams, channelization and dyking of rivers, watershed authorities, drainages, lake outlet controls, and impoundments are running riot, all in the name of development and conservation. I am not wise enough to know which of these conversions are ecologically sound, but the most superficial observer can see that:

1. Most of them deal with symptoms, not with organic causes.
2. Their promoters are innocent of (or oblivious to) the principle that violence is risky.
3. Many of them involve irreversible changes in the organization of the biota.
4. Collectively, their use of economic arguments is naive. In one case, economic advantage is held to supersede all opposing considerations; in the next "intangible" benefit is held to supersede all economics.
5. In all of them, control of nature by concrete and steel is held to be inherently superior to natural or biotic controls.
6. In all of them, the economic products of violence are held to be more valuable than natural products.

The philosophy of violence extends far beyond water management. The reckless use of new poisons in agronomy, horticulture, wildlife control, fish management, forestry, and soil fumigation is well known. Poisons for public health are no novelty. Poisons to offset pollution in lakes and rivers are no novelty. Again I am not wise enough to say which of these violent treatments are sound, but it is obvious that the same doubts arise: they deal with symptoms; their promoters are innocent of probable repercussions; they involve many irreversible changes; because they are quicker than biotic controls, they are assumed to be superior to them.

ESTHETICS

The biota is beautiful collectively and in all its parts, but only a few of its parts are useful in the sense of yielding a profit to the private landowner. Healthy land is the only permanently profitable land, but if the biota must be whole to be healthy, and if most of its parts yield no saleable products, then we cannot justify ecological conservation on economic grounds alone. To attempt to do so is sure to yield a lopsided, and probably unhealthy, biotic organization.

Herein lies the tragedy of modern land-use education. We have spent several generations teaching the farmer that he is not obligated to do anything on or to his land that is not profitable to him as an individual. We can thank his neglect and inertia, and perhaps the hollow sound of our own voice, for the survival of such useless plants and animals, and such natural soils and waters, as remain alive today.

We have rationalized this fallacy by relegating the conservation of the merely beautiful to the state. We can thank this subterfuge for our national parks, forests, and a sprinkling of wilderness areas, but we can also thank it for a million farmers who year-by-year grow richer at the bank, poorer in soil, and bankrupt in spiritual relationship to things of the land.

The divorcement of things practical from things beautiful, and the relegation of either to specialized groups or institutions, has always been lethal to social progress, and now it threatens the land-base on which the social structure rests. The fallacy has its roots in an imperfect view of growth. All sciences, arts, and philosophies are converging lines; what seems separate today is fused tomorrow. Tomorrow we shall find out that no land unnecessarily mutilated is useful (if, indeed, it is still there). The true problem of agriculture, and all other land-use, is to achieve both utility and beauty, and thus permanence. A farmer has the same obligation to help, within reason, to preserve the biotic integrity of his community as he has, within reason, to preserve the culture which rests on it. As a member of the community, he is the ultimate beneficiary of both.

HUMAN DENSITY

The trend of animal ecology shows, with increasing clarity, that all animal behavior-patterns, as well as most environmental and social relationships, are conditioned and controlled by density. It seems improbable that man is any exception to this rule.

It is almost trite to say that the ecological state called civilization became possible at a certain minimum density-threshold. It seems equally probable that above a certain maximum density its benefits begin to cancel out, and its mechanisms become unstable. Improvements in organization may raise that maximum, but they can hardly abolish it.

I have studied animal populations for twenty years, and I have yet to find a species devoid of maximum density controls. In some species the control mechanism inheres within the species, and operates by eviction and resultant vulnerability to predation (quail, muskrat). In others the control is external (deer), and consists of predation, or starvation if that fails. In all species one is impressed by one common character: If one means of reduction fails, another takes over.

It is possible to interpret the impending disorganization of land as taking over the reducing job after we foiled the normal mechanism by industrialization, medicine, and other devices. There is a striking parallelism between the present worldwide strife, and the social status of an overpopulated muskrat marsh just prior to catastrophe.

In any event it is unthinkable that we shall stabilize our land without a corresponding stabilization of our own density. It is notorious that many of the "undeveloped" regions are already overpopulated.

CONCLUSION

These then are my personal guesses as to the conditions requisite for land-health. Some of them step beyond "science" in the narrow sense, because everything really important steps beyond it. I do not claim that my guesses are objective. They are admittedly wishful. Objectivity is possible only in matters too small to be important, or in matters too large to do anything about.

Manuscript, December 21, 1946

Scarcity Values in Conservation

NOSTALGIA FOR the good old days when everything was abundant is almost universal among conservationists. Comparison between the then and the now furnishes the pattern for most of our books, talks, and dreams. We lament the lost thunder of galloping buffalo, the sky-darkening clouds of pigeons and waterfowl, the flowing sea of prairie, the velvet silence of the virgin woods. Yet nothing is clearer than this: our grandfathers, who had the opportunity to see these things, did not value them, as personal experience, as highly as we think we would have.

There are two possible explanations. Appreciation may have been enhanced by the intervening gains in education, or we may be incapable of appreciating anything until it has grown scarce.

The first explanation flatters us, the second does not, as we usually admit the one and ignore the other. This paper attempts to shed light on both, for both undoubtedly play important roles in conservation thought.

Wilderness, by common consent, has value as a human experience. The consent became conscious, however, only when the last remnants of wilderness in this country were about to disappear under the onslaught of good roads. Daniel Boone valued the wilderness mainly as an outlet for his personal prowess in destroying it. Nothing can be clearer than the fact that scarcity has created a part of the value which we now attach to the wilderness.

Did education also create a part? Perhaps in the case of a few ecologists and evolutionists who happen to be also woodsmen, but these men are scarce. The average proponent of wilderness areas in the National Forests and Parks has little more appreciation of ecology and evolution than Daniel Boone did. His biological education, if any, dealt with the anatomy and physiology of frogs, not with the anatomy and physiology of biotas. He appreciates wilderness because it is an outlet for his personal prowess in wilderness recreation. He differs from Boone in only two respects: his gadgets fill a pack train rather than a pocket, and he has the notion that if he sets no fires, leaves no cans, and obeys the game laws, that he can come back and do it all again. That is to say his mind has grasped the idea of *repeated use* of wild lands, or (as a forester would say) *sustained yield* of wilderness values.

It would be idle to belittle the potency of this idea of repeated use, yet I think we have jumped from it to one further idea which needs belittling. I refer to the all but universal assumption that the more people use a wilderness area, the more benefit society reaps from its establishment.

As a matter of practical administration this doctrine that wilderness must be used by many in order to be useful to many will one day defeat the whole system of wilderness conservation. An earnest young technician writes, in substance: If you show the trumpeter swans to the public they can't breed; if you don't show them they have no value. A zealous game official said to me: the caribou are too scarce to hunt, and the bogs prevent showing them to tourists, so what good are they? A conscientious forest supervisor said: the elk and deer are getting too thick in the wilderness area; few hunters will go in after them; what can we do but build the roads needed to let the hunters in? When I mildly suggested that amnesty for wolves and lions might dispense with the road, my remark seemed irrelevant. What value is a game herd, the presence of which benefits only wolves and lions?

In politics, a few advanced thinkers in a few advanced countries have developed a respect for minorities. A rare viewpoint, creed, or culture is perhaps not wholly unlike a rare kind of country, bird, or mammal in its possible contribution to the good life. Certainly both have the common denominator of possible extinguishment.

Just why do we respect political minorities, and accord them a value worth preserving? Perhaps the answer would shed light on the value of ecological "minorities" such as wild country or threatened species of wildlife.

Manuscript, c. 1946

Deadening

THE OLD oak had been girdled and was dead.

There are degrees of death in abandoned farms. Some old houses cock an eye at you as if to say "Somebody will move in. Wait and see."

But this farm was different. Girdling old oak to squeeze one last crop out of the barnyard has the same finality as burning furniture to keep warm.

Manuscript, c. 1946

Wherefore Wildlife Ecology?

A T THE beginning of this course I did not try to define its object, because any attempt at definition would at that time have consisted of meaningless words. I shall now confide in you what the course is driving at.

The object is to teach you how to read land. Land is soil, water, plants and animals. Each of these "organs" of land has meaning as a separate entity, just as fingers, toes, and teeth have. But each has a much larger meaning as the component parts of the organism. No one can understand an animal by learning only its parts, yet when we attempt to say that an animal is "useful," "ugly," or "cruel" we are failing to see it as part of the land. We do not make the error of calling a carburetor "greedy." We see it as part of a functioning motor.

Much can be learned about land with amateur equipment, provided one learns how to think in scientific terms. Hence I am asking you to read the best professional literature, but in the field to use only the eyes, ears, and notebook which everybody carries. The lectures try to connect the two.

What I hope to teach is perhaps ecological research as an outdoor "sport." Yet "sport" is hardly accurate, because in sport one tries to do well what thousands have done better. In ecology one tries to do well what few have ever done at all, at least not in one's home region. The thing I am teaching, then, is amateur exploration, research for fun, in the field of land.

I have an ulterior motive, as everyone has. I am interested in the thing called "conservation." For this I have two reasons: (1) without it, our economy will ultimately fall apart; (2) without it many plants, animals, and places of entrancing interest to me as an explorer will cease to exist. I do not like to think of economic bankruptcy, nor do I see much object in continuing the human enterprise in a habitat stripped of what interests me most.

That there is some basic fallacy in present-day conservation is shown by our response to it. Instead of living it, we turn it over to bureaus. Even the landowner, who has the best opportunity to practice it, thinks of it as something for government to worry about.

I think I know what the fallacy is. It is the assumption, clearly borrowed from modern science, that the human relation to land is only economic. It is, or should be, esthetic as well. In this respect our present culture, and especially our science, is false, ignoble, and self-destructive.

If the individual has a warm personal understanding of land, he will perceive of his own accord that it is something more than a breadbasket. He will see land as a community of which he is only a member, albeit now the dominant one. He will see the beauty, as well as the utility, of the whole, and know the two cannot be separated. We love (and make intelligent use of) what we have learned to understand.

Hence this course. I am trying to teach you that this alphabet of "natural objects" (soils and rivers, birds and beasts) spells out a story, which he who runs may read—if he knows how. Once you learn to read the land, I have no fear of what you will do to it, or with it. And I know many pleasant things it will do to you.

Manuscript, c. Spring 1947

The Ecological Conscience

EVERYONE OUGHT to be dissatisfied with the slow spread of conservation to the land. Our "progress" still consists largely of letterhead pieties and convention oratory. The only progress that counts is that on the actual landscape of the back forty, and here we are still slipping two steps backward for each forward stride.

The usual answer to this dilemma is "more conservation education." My answer is yes by all means, but are we sure that only the *volume* of educational effort needs stepping up? Is something lacking in its *content* as well? I think there is, and I here attempt to define it.

The basic defect is this: we have not asked the citizen to assume any real responsibility. We have told him that if he will vote right, obey the law, join some organizations, and practice what conservation is profitable on his own land, that everything will be lovely; the government will do the rest.

This formula is too easy to accomplish anything worthwhile. It calls for no effort or sacrifice; no change in our philosophy of values. It entails little that any decent and intelligent person would not have done, of his own accord, under the late but not lamented Babbitian code.

No important change in human conduct is ever accomplished without an internal change in our intellectual emphases, our loyalties, our affections, and our convictions. The proof that conservation has not yet touched these foundations of conduct lies in the fact that philosophy, ethics, and religion have not yet heard of it.

I need a short name for what is lacking; I call it the ecological conscience. Ecology is the science of communities, and the ecological conscience is therefore the ethics of community life. I will define it further in terms of four case histories, which I think show the futility of trying to improve the face of the land without improving ourselves. I select these cases from my own state, because I am there surer of my facts.

About 1930 it became clear to all except the ecologically blind that Wisconsin's topsoil was slipping seaward. The farmers were told in 1933 that if they would adopt certain remedial practices for five years, the public would donate CCC labor to install them, plus the necessary machinery and materials. The offer was widely accepted, but the practices were widely forgotten when the five-year contract period was up. The farmers continued only those practices that yielded an immediate and visible economic gain for themselves.

This partial failure of land-use rules written by the government led to the idea that maybe farmers would learn more quickly if they themselves wrote the rules. Hence, in 1937, the Wisconsin Legislature passed the Soil Conservation District Law. This said to the farmers, in effect: "We, the public, will furnish you free technical service and loan you specialized machinery, if you will write your own rules for land-use. Each county may write its own rules, and these will have the force of law." Nearly all the counties promptly organized to accept the proferred help, but after a decade of operation, *no county has yet written a single rule*. There has been visible progress in such practices as strip-cropping, pasture renovation, and soil liming, but none in fencing woodlots or excluding plow and cow from steep slopes. The farmers, in short, selected out those remedial practices which were profitable anyhow, and ignored those which were profitable to the community, but not clearly profitable to themselves. The net result is that the natural acceleration in rate of soil-loss has been somewhat retarded, but we nevertheless have less soil than we had in 1937.

I hasten to add that no one has ever told farmers that in land-use the good of the community may entail obligations over and above those dictated by self-interest. The existence of such obligations is accepted in bettering rural roads, schools, churches, and baseball teams, but not in bettering the behavior of the water that falls on the land, nor in preserving the beauty or diversity of the farm landscape. Land-use ethics are still governed wholly by economic self-interest, just as social ethics were a century ago.

To sum up: we have asked the farmer to do what he conveniently could to save his soil, and he has done just that, and only that. The exclusion of cows from woods and steep slopes is not convenient, and is not done. Moreover some things are being done that are at least dubious as conservation practices: for example marshy stream bottoms are being drained to relieve the pressure on worn-out uplands. The upshot is that woods, marshes, and natural streams, together with their respective faunas and floras, are headed toward ultimate elimination from southern Wisconsin.

All in all we have built a beautiful piece of social machinery—the Soil Conservation District—which is coughing along on two cylinders because we have been too timid, and too anxious for quick success, to tell the farmer the true magnitude of his obligations. Obligations have no meaning without conscience, and the problem we face is the extension of the social conscience from people to land.

PAUL BUNYAN'S DEER

The Wisconsin lumberjack came very near accomplishing, in reality, the prodigious feats of woods-destruction attributed to Paul Bunyan. Following Paul's departure for points west, there followed an event little heralded in song and story, but quite as dramatic as the original destruction of the pineries: there sprang up, almost over night, an empire of brushfields.

Paul Bunyan had tired easily of salt pork and corned beef, hence he had taken good care to see that the deer of the original pineries found their way regularly to the stewpot. Moreover there were wolves in Paul's day, and the wolves had performed any necessary pruning of the deer heard which Paul had overlooked. But by the time the brushfields sprang into being, the wolves had been wiped out and the state had passed a buck-law and established refuges. The stage was set for an irruption of deer.

The deer took to the brushfields like yeast tossed into the sourdough pot. By 1940 the woods were foaming with them, so to speak. We Conservation Commissioners took credit for this miracle of creation; actually we did little but officiate at the birth. Anyhow, it was a herd to make one's mouth water. A tourist from Chicago could drive out in the evening and see fifty deer, or even more.

This immense deer herd was eating brush, and eating well. What was this brush? It consisted of temporary short-lived sun-loving trees and bushes which act as a nurse crop for the future forest. The forest comes up under the brush, just as alfalfa or clover comes up under oats or rye. In the normal succession, the brush is eventually overtopped by the forest tree seedlings, and we have the start of a new forest.

In anticipation of this well known process, the state, the counties, the U.S. Forest Service, the pulp mills, and even some lumber mills staked out "forests" consisting, for the moment, of brush. Large investments of time, thought, cash, CCC labor, WPA labor, and legislation were made in the expectation that Nature would repeat her normal cycle. The state embarked on a tax subsidy, called the Forest Crop Law, to encourage land-owners to hang on to their brushfields until they were replaced by forest.

But we failed to reckon with the deer, and with deer hunters and resort owners. In 1942 we had a hard winter and many deer starved. It then became evident that the original "nurse-trees" had grown out of reach of deer, and that the herd was eating the oncoming forest. The remedy seemed to be to reduce the herd by legalizing killing of does. It was evident that if we didn't reduce the herd, starvation would, and we would eventually lose both the deer and the forest. But for five consecutive years the deer hunters and resort owners, plus the politicians interested in their votes, have defeated all attempts at herd-reduction.

I will not tire you with all the red herrings, subterfuges, eva-sions, and expedients which these people have used to befog this simple issue. There is even a newspaper dedicated solely to defaming the proponents of herd-reduction. These people call themselves conservationists, and in one sense they are, for in the past we have pinned that label on anyone who loves wildlife, however blindly. These conservationists, for the sake of maintaining an abnormal and unnatural deer herd for a few more years, are willing to sacrifice the future forest, and also the ultimate welfare of the herd itself.

The motives behind this "conservation" are a wish to prolong easy deer hunting, and a wish to show numerous deer to tour-ists. These perfectly understandable wishes are rationalized by protestations of chivalry to does and fawns. As an unexpected aftermath of this situation, there has been a large increase of illegal killing, and of abandonment of illegal carcasses in the woods. Thus herd-control, of a sort, is taking place outside the law. But the food-producing capacity of the forest has been overstrained for a decade, and the next hard winter will bring catastrophic starvation. After that we shall have very few deer, and these will be runty from malnutrition. Our forest will be a moth-eaten remnant consisting largely of inferior species of trees.

The basic fallacy in this kind of "conservation" is that it seeks to conserve one resource by destroying another. These "conservationists" are unable to see the land as a whole. They are unable to think in terms of community rather than group welfare, and in terms of the long as well as the short view. They are conserving what is important to them in the immediate future, and they are angry when told that this conflicts with what is important to the state as a whole in the long run.

There is an important lesson here: the flat refusal of the average adult to learn anything new, i.e., to study, To understand the deer problem requires some knowledge of what deer eat, of what they do not eat, and of how a forest grows. The average deer hunter is sadly lacking in such knowledge, and when anyone tries to explain the matter, he is branded forthwith as a long-haired theorist. This anger-reaction against new and unpleasant facts is of course a standard psychiatric indicator of the closed mind.

We speak glibly of conservation education, but what do we mean by it? If we mean indoctrination, then let us be reminded that it is just as easy to indoctrinate with fallacies as with facts. If we mean to teach the capacity for independent judgment, then I am appalled by the magnitude of the task. The task is large mainly because of this refusal of adults to learn anything new.

The ecological conscience, then, is an affair of the mind as well as the heart. It implies a capacity to study and learn, as well as to emote about the problems of conservation.

JEFFERSON DAVIS' PINES

I have a farm in one of the sand-counties of central Wisconsin. I bought it because I wanted a place to plant pines. One reason for selecting my particular farm was that it adjoined the only remaining stand of mature pines in the County.

This pine grove is an historical landmark. It is the spot (or very near the spot) where, in 1828, a young Lieutenant named Jefferson Davis cut the pine logs to build Fort Winnebago. He floated them down the Wisconsin River to the fort. In the ensuing century a thousand other rafts of pine logs floated past this grove, to build that empire of red barns now called the Middle West.

This grove is also an ecological landmark. It is the nearest spot where a city-worn refugee from the south can hear the wind sing in tall timber. It harbors one of the best remnants of deer, ruffed grouse, and pileated woodpeckers in southern Wisconsin.

My neighbor, who owns the grove, has treated it rather decently through the years. When his son got married, the grove furnished lumber for the new house, and it could spare such light cuttings. But when war prices of lumber soared skyward, the temptation to slash became too strong. Today the grove lies prostrate, and its long logs are feeding a hungry saw.

By all the accepted rules of forestry, my neighbor was justified in slashing the grove. The stand was even-aged, mature, and invaded by heart-rot. Yet any schoolboy would know, in his heart, that there is something wrong about erasing the last remnant of pine timber from a county. When a farmer owns a rarity he should feel some obligation as its custodian, and a community should feel some obligation to help him carry the economic cost of custodianship. Yet our present land-use conscience is silent on such questions.

THE FLAMBEAU RAID

The Flambeau was a river so lovely to look upon, and so richly endowed with forests and wildlife, that even the hard-bitten fur traders of the freebooting 1700's enthused about it as the choicest part of the great north woods.

The freebooting 1800's expressed the same admiration, but in somewhat different terms. By 1930 the Flambeau retained only one 50-mile stretch of river not yet harnessed for power, and only a few sections of original timber not yet cut for lumber or pulp.

During the 1930's the Wisconsin Conservation Department started to build a state forest on the Flambeau, using these remnants of wild woods and wild river as starting points. This was to be no ordinary state forest producing only logs and tourist camps; its primary object was to preserve and restore the remnant of canoe-water. Year by year the Commission bought land, removed cottages, fended off unnecessary roads, and in general started the long slow job of re-creating a stretch of wild river for the use and enjoyment of young Wisconsin.

The good soil which enabled the Flambeau to grow the best cork pine for Paul Bunyan likewise enabled Rusk County, during recent decades, to sprout a dairy industry. These dairy farmers wanted cheaper electric power than that offered by local power companies. Hence they organized a cooperative REA and applied for a power dam which, when built, will clip off the lower reaches of canoe-water which the Conservation Commission wanted to keep for recreational use.

There was a bitter political fight, in the course of which the Commission not only withdrew its opposition to the REA dam, but the Legislature, by statute, repealed the authority of the Conservation Commission and made County Commissioners the ultimate arbiters of conflict between power values and recreational values. I think I need not dwell on the irony of this statute. It seals the fate of all wild rivers remaining in the state, including the Flambeau. It says, in effect, that in deciding the use of rivers, the local economic interest shall have blanket priority over statewide recreational interests, with County Commissioners as the umpire.

The Flambeau case illustrates the dangers that lurk in the semi-honest doctrine that conservation is only good economics. The defenders of the Flambeau tried to prove that the river in its wild state would produce more fish and tourists than the impounded river would produce butterfat, but this is not true. We should have claimed that a little gain in butterfat is less important to the state than a large loss in opportunity for a distinctive form of outdoor recreation.

We lost the Flambeau as a logical consequence of the fallacy that conservation can be achieved easily. It cannot. Parts of every well-rounded conservation program entail sacrifice, usually local, but none-the-less real. The farmers' raid on our last wild river is just like any other raid on any other public wealth; the only defense is a widespread public awareness of the values at stake. There was none.

THE UPSHOT

I have described here a fraction of that huge aggregate of problems and opportunities which we call conservation. This aggregate of case-histories shows one common need: an ecological conscience.

The practice of conservation must spring from a conviction of what is ethically and esthetically right, as well as what is economically expedient. A thing is right only when it tends to preserve the integrity, stability, and beauty of the community, and the community includes the soil, waters, fauna, and flora, as well as people.

It cannot be right, in the ecological sense, for a farmer to drain the last marsh, graze the last woods, or slash the last grove in his community, because in doing so he evicts a fauna, a flora, and a landscape whose membership in the community is older than his own, and is equally entitled to respect.

It cannot be right, in the ecological sense, for a farmer to channelize his creek or pasture his steep slopes, because in doing so he passes flood trouble to his neighbors below, just as his neighbors above have passed it to him. In cities we do not get rid of nuisances by throwing them across the fence onto the neighbor's lawn, but in water-management we still do just that.

It cannot be right, in the ecological sense, for the deer hunter to maintain his sport by browsing out the forest, or for the bird-hunter to maintain his by decimating the hawks and owls, or for the fisherman to maintain his by decimating the herons, kingfishers, terns, and otters. Such tactics seek to achieve one kind of conservation by destroying another, and thus they subvert the integrity and stability of the community.

If we grant the premise that an ecological conscience is possible and needed, then its first tenet must be this: economic provocation is no longer a satisfactory excuse for unsocial land-use (or, to use somewhat stronger words, for ecological atrocities). This, however, is a negative statement. I would rather assert positively that decent land-use should be accorded social rewards proportionate to its social importance.

I have no illusions about the speed of accuracy with which an ecological conscience can become functional. It has required 19 centuries to define decent man-to-man conduct and the process is only half done; it may take as long to evolve a code of decency for man-to-land conduct. In such matters we should not worry too much about anything except the direction in which we travel. The direction is clear, and the first step is to *throw your weight around* on matters of right and wrong in land-use. Cease being intimidated by the argument that a right action is impossible because it does not yield maximum profits, or that a wrong action is to be condoned because it pays. That philosophy is dead in human relations, and its funeral in land-relations is overdue.

Bulletin of the Garden Club of America, June 1947

The Deer Swath

ONE HOT afternoon in August I sat under the elm, idling, when I saw a deer pass across a small opening a quarter-mile east. A deer trail crosses our farm, and at this point any deer travelling is briefly visible from the shack.

I then realized that half an hour before I had moved my chair to the best spot for watching the deer trail; that I had done this habitually for years, without being clearly conscious of it. This led to the thought that by cutting some brush, I could widen the zone of visibility. Before night the swath was cleared, and within the month I detected several deer which otherwise would likely have passed unseen.

The new deer swath was pointed out to a series of weekend guests for the purpose of watching their later reactions to it. It was soon clear that most of them forgot it quickly, while others watched it, as I did, whenever chance allowed. The upshot was the realization that there are four categories of outdoorsmen: deer hunters, duck hunters, bird hunters, and non-hunters. These categories have nothing to do with sex or age, or accoutrements; they represent four diverse habits of the human eye. The deer hunter habitually watches the next bend; the duck hunter watches the skyline; the bird hunter watches the dog; the non-hunter does not watch.

When the deer hunter sits down he sits where he can see ahead, and with his back to something. The duck hunter sits where he can see overhead, and behind something. The non-hunter sits where he is comfortable. None of these watch the dog. The bird hunter watches only the dog, and always knows where the dog is, whether or no visible at the moment. The dog's nose is his eye. Many hunters who carry a shotgun in season have never learned to watch the dog, or to interpret his reactions to scent.

There are good outdoorsmen who do not conform to these categories. There is the ornithologist who hunts by ear, and uses the eye only to follow up on what his ear has detected. There is the botanist who hunts by eye, but at much closer range; he is a marvel at finding plants, but seldom sees birds or mammals. There is the forester who sees only trees, and the insects and fungi which prey upon trees; he is oblivious to all else. And finally there is the sportsman who sees only game, and regards all else as of little interest or value.

There is one elusive mode of hunting which I cannot associate exclusively with any of these groups: the search for scats, tracks, feathers, dens, roostings, rubbings, dustings, diggings, feedings, fightings, or preyings collectively known to woodsmen as "reading sign." This skill is rare, and too often seems to be inverse to book-learning.

The counterpart of animal sign-reading exists in the plant field, but skill is equally rare in occurrence, and elusive in distribution. To prove this I cite the African explorer who detected the former scratchings of a lion on the bark of a tree, twenty feet up. The scratching, he said, had been made when the tree was young.

That biological jack-of-all trades called ecologist tries to be and do all of these things. Needless to say, he does not succeed; the best he can do is to alternate his modes of hunting. I find that while hunting plants, I can give only indifferent attention to animals, and vice versa. The ecologist has the choice of setting forth with glass, gun, axe, trowel, or shovel, and adjusting his eye and mind to the tools at hand.

The common denominator of all hunters is the realization that there is always something to hunt. The world teems with creatures, processes, and events which are trying to elude you; there is always a deer, and always a swath down which he can be seen. Every ground is a hunting ground, whether it lies between you and the curbstone, or in those illimitable woods where rolls the Oregon. The final test of the hunter is whether he is keen to go hunting in a vacant lot.

Typescript, February 29, 1948

SELECTED JOURNALS

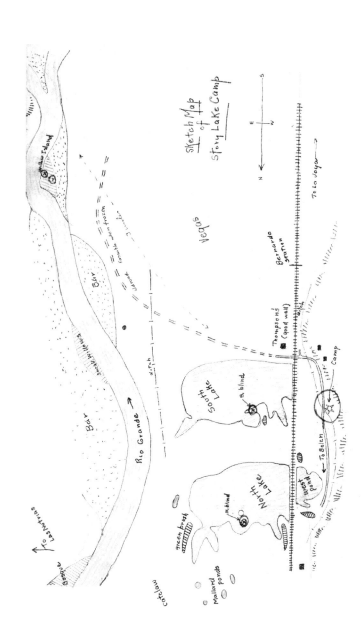

Sketch Map
of
Story Lake Camp

"Gettin' Ganders on the Rio"

Bernardo Camp,
December 16–22, 1920.

Dec. 16   Left Albuquerque 9 A.M., arrived Bernardo Lakes 3 P.M. after stops at Los Lunas and Belen and bad sand between Sabinal and Bernardo. Had to use tarp and hire cowpuncher with saddle-horse to get through.

Found 50 ducks sitting on West Pond and could see the white flash of sprig and widgeons as we pitched camp in the dry bed of an acequia. Built adobe stove and made everything shipshape—then set off to get something for supper. Carl stayed at West Pond while I went down to S. Lake. Each got a nice gadwall before sunset. 30 snow-geese went down the river. Prospects look fine.

For supper tried to boil rice in pond water—even Flick couldn't eat it—but gadwall breasts with bread and gravy made a feast just the same.

Solid comfort with stove in tent—works fine. Hay beds, seasoned pear wood to burn (from an old abandoned orchard), and all kinds of luxuries.

Carl's gadwall had streaks and spots over entire breast, like a hen mallard.

Dec. 17   Carl and Starker stayed in blind on South Lake while I explored river. Knocked down two mallards—got the drake by letting him swim into my bank, but followed the hen 3 miles to Willow Island without being able to get her. Quite a gathering of geese below island; found a dug blind on a point and nearly got a close shot at a big bunch. Several gulls flying over river.

At noon came back and found Carl and Starker had a widgeon and two bluebill, also a jacksnipe. Walking in at noon flushed a big covey of quail out of a mesquite bush within 60 yards of camp. We got five and had a fine stew for supper.

In evening shot near camp—very few ducks came in—Carl got a drake and I got a widgeon.

Chauvin and party camped near road this P.M. and came over in the evening to spin yarns.

Dec. 18   Spread 59"; length from tip bill to end tail 38½"; track 4" wide, 5½" long with dewclaw; bill 2¼"; triangle 1¾" base and 2" high, vertical leg in back; head from base bill horizontally 3¾", 2¾" deep at the back of the triangle; black on neck from base of jaw 5½". 3" gray; body length breast to tip tail 22", body depth 8". Weight 8.75# after 4 days; probably 9# fresh.

This is the goose that got too close to Carl out on Willow Island and came down with a great thump within a few feet of where Starker was lying in the bushes.

There was a fine flight of geese in the morning and more

or less ducks all day, but we couldn't hit them. A big flock of snow-geese were sitting in the North Lake in the morning and passed twice during the day.

A great gathering of blue herons on the bar below us—saw 15 in the air at one time. Also saw gulls, both brown ones and adult white ones.

Carl says: "We got our gander but haven't yet put the 'S' on it."

Dec. 19   Carl and Starker snoozed while I sneaked down to the blind, set the decoys, and killed a hen sprig, a big full-plumaged gadwall, and two butterballs. Came back and found Carl shaving, so I had to follow suit. Then went out after quail, found four coveys of 12 to 15 birds each and we each got five. Carl got four bunnies and I got two—they are very plentiful. In the evening Carl and Starker picked up 1 gadwall, 2 widgeons, 2 spoonies, 1 butterball. I explored the north shore of the North Lake and missed three fine shots at a gadwall, getting one widgeon. Tonight the shooting and the tumult dies as the Sunday hunters depart.

Dec. 20   Watch out of whack and made a bad guess as to rising hour—had to go back for a nap after breakfast. Proper time to get up in December is just before the sword of Orion sinks in the west.

Heavy wind and snowstorm. Carl went to the North Lake

with part of the decoys and picked up a widgeon, a ruddy, and a butterball. At noon came back and after dinner went quail hunting. Found three coveys, all very small except one which contained 20 birds. Carl got 9 birds and 4 rabbits; I got 4 and 1 rabbit. Last covey would not lie until a hawk passed over, after which they laid tight. I lost 2 cripples. Coming back found 4 birds feeding in Chauvin's old camp site; he had predicted they would do this.

Instead of going out for the evening shoot, we compounded a special banquet. Menu: Fried rabbit, mashed potatoes, buttered toast, rice pudding, and black postum. Some feed.

Tomorrow we go back to Willow Island to match wits and luck with the honkers.

Dec. 21   To the Willow Bar—enormous flock of geese on bar as we approached. Cold, cloudy, windy day. Carl chased up a big flock of widgeons from bar north of island. They passed down the river out of range save for one bird, who thought he would stay with the decoys. He did.

Got so cold we all moved out of the pits into the willow thicket where we built a "stand-up" blind with a fire in it. Soon the widgeons came back up the river and we dropped one.

Next an old drake mallard came floating down the main channel with the floating ice. I sneaked out to the shore and folded him up with the second barrel.

Carl walked down and jumped six geese off a bar which came up the river nicely, only thirty yards high, but too far to the east. He then crossed the river and walked way up on the Las Nutrias side and chased them back. They came along only twenty yards high but passed away west of the dry channel behind the island. So we had to go home without the "S" on the gander.

Tomorrow we make one last round up on the ducks.

Dec. 22 Up by daylight, but another car of hunters had arrived during the night, and chased out the few ducks in the lake before we got out. Carl went to the South Lake but didn't get a shot. I went to North Lake—nothing there—but after a long search found three mallards on a little frozen hole. Made a very elaborate sneak up to easy forty yards—and then missed with both barrels.

On way back to camp—in order not to come in skunked— skirted the foothill for a few hundred yards and kicked out a quail and a bunny and got both.

Broke camp and got started about 11:30, hiring a team to pull us through the sand to Sabinal. Just below Sabinal jumped a fine covey along the road—followed them up and got four apiece. Later found another covey near Jarales but they were regular race-horses and we didn't do them any damage.

Arrived home about 4:30 P.M. with a load of game that would make a man stagger, and appetites in proportion.

The Delta Colorado
being an account of a
VOYAGE OF DISCOVERY by
Carl & Aldo Leopold—Gentlemen-Adventurers
into the
Mythical Straits of Annian, the
Jungles of the Rio del Pescador, &
The Environs of the Vermillion Sea

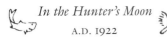

In the Hunter's Moon
A.D. 1922

*"Many voyages have been pretended, yet
hitherto never any thoroughly accomplished
by our nation, of exact discovery into the
bowels of those main, ample, & vast
countries" —Sir Humphrey Gilbert*

Oct. 25—Wednesday After arriving in Yuma at midnight Tuesday, we were up at daylight and found the river flowing under a bridge only a stone's throw from the hotel. It looked like plenty of water.

Called at Reclamation Service Headquarters, where I met Mr. Ray Priest, Assistant Project Manager. He had just been to the mouth of the river in a skiff with a traveller named Freeman, who had come down from the very headwaters. They had encountered 3 days' hard tracking in the Pescadero country and Yuma had been about to send out a rescue party. Priest said not to try it. Mr. Berry of the Customs said the same.

Called on Col. B. F. Fly who very kindly devoted his whole day to seeing us off. After buying our chuck and getting a haircut, we left at 3 P.M. for San Luis in a W–D Ford truck belonging to Will Lowe. The canoe loaded on diagonally worked very well. An interesting ride through the rich Yuma Valley landed us at the International Boundary about 5 P.M. Here Col. Fly introduced us to Major Y. Gomez Yarrias, a government engineer, Alexandre Sortillon, our host for the night and driver for tomorrow, Major Arienza, the newly elected Comisario of San Luis, and Lieut. Lopez the commander of the garrison. It being agreed that we were harmless hunters and not the conspirators of a new revolution, we all repaired to the saloon and had some real beer. Col. Fly then returned to Yuma, while we spent a very interesting evening at Sortillon's, discussing the country with Major Gomez and hearing always of the terrible tide-rips and the impracticability of venturing into them with our canoe. It was finally decided to leave the canoe temporarily at San Luis while we spent a week or so at the head of the Rillito after deer.

Among the evening callers at the Sortillon's was Sr. Corvola, a finance inspector on a "delicate mission," the Comisario's office and records having been burned just a day or two previous to the recent election. Also Sr. Limon, a government wireless operator.

Slept on the floor of Sortillon's restaurant, and awoke bright and early for the eventful

Oct. 26—Thursday Left about 10 A.M. in Sortillon's Ford for Rillito, where we arrived about 1 P.M. and unloaded on the bank of a pretty little slough, dismissing Sortillon with instructions to

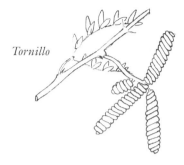

Tornillo

come back in a week. Even as we drove up to slough a beautiful snowy heron flushed from the reedy bank, and several cormorants were fishing in a wide place below camp. Flick flushed a covey of quail.

We built an Apache style "rancheria" for shade and after completing camp took a walk up the Rillito. Carl got one quail and we found an unbelievable number of cat and coyote tracks in the sandbars and on the banks of the stream. As we got back to camp a very large coyote was drinking just below at the head of the little lake—we nearly got a shot at him. That night we could hear geese passing—they would set up a great cackling when they saw our fire. Quite a coyote chorus during the night.

Oct. 27—Friday   At daylight I killed a huge* drake mallard flying up the stream. Explored upstream and got our first lesson in arrowweed thickets. They are barren deserts, full of unkillable

---

*Weighed 1 bucket plus 2 cups water plus pocket knife = 3# 3 oz.

but dog-killing rabbits, and the ease of travel is from difficult to impossible. A couple of miles above camp we came on a very pretty lagoon, from which 3* widgeon flushed. Carl got them all. Here also were the tracks of a huge buck and a doe. A great flock of wavies came exploring up the Rillito about 10 o'clock and went on back again—presumably to El Doctor. From the hill on the mesa near this lagoon we could see the whole delta and even the mirage-like mud flats at Santa Clara. A howling wilderness is the only name for it.

In the evening we set out a couple of traps above camp and tried the mullet, which were jumping in great numbers. No luck. Roast duck and sourdough biscuit tonight—but the noodles we spoiled by trying to boil them in the salty water from our "well."

At noon we had a swim and wash day, likewise barber-shop. Water fine but cold.

Oct. 28—Saturday Explored south. Deer tracks more numerous, including quite a few very small ones which may be fawns or maybe little whitetails. Rillito has many long pools, on which were snowy herons, night & great blue herons, cormorants, grebes, coots, and kingfishers. Also a few spoonbills. One flock of wavies came exploring upstream, and we heard another flock out on the mesa. More experience with arrowweed jungles.

There are a few cattle here which seem to eat cane.

The quail killed yesterday had a crop full of berries which we today identified as mistletoe. It grows on tornillo and mesquite.

About 2 P.M. heard an auto on the road. Carl went up. The

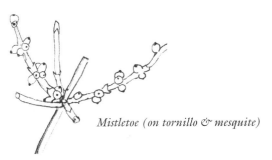

Mistletoe (on tornillo & mesquite)

* Weighed 1 bucket plus 3 cups water plus pocket knife ÷ 3 = 1# 6 oz. each.

two men in it didn't want to talk. They had the back seat full of wet looking crates.

This evening we fished, Carl rigging a throw line. Got a big carp*—probably 2#—that fought at least as hard as a bass, several smaller carp, and a small mullet. Rabbit belly proved a better bait than pork fat.

At evening a team passed. A big burly Mexicano, 4 big mules, and probably a ton of "hooch." You could smell it tambien. This proved to be Dominguez of La Bolsa. He camped at the "agua dulce" north of our camp and we fed him up on noodles and sourdough biscuits and then plied him in poor Spanish anent deer and geese.

Oct. 29—Sunday   A cold night. Some impertinent coon took our fish. The upper coyote trap had a drowned buzzard in it— the proverbial wet hen was handsome in comparison.

South along the mesa, quail hunting and prospecting. Got 2 birds, both full of tornillo hulls. A Gambel quail track is 2" long x 1½" wide toe to toe. There are 5 feathers in his plume.

On climbing one of the dunes or "montes" we found a huge bay of low country south of camp. Cut across to it. No deer tracks there or along the edge coming back. The deer must use the other montes east of camp.

* Sheepshead

Back at noon. After dinner a flock of avocets came over. Carl got three. They are the most delicately beautiful of all waterbirds. Carl also killed one of the stout-billed waders, with a white rump.

Description Length 15" Wing 12" Bill 2⅜" stout. Feet gray, slightly webbed. Rump white, primaries with a white bar, upper parts heron-gray, back barred, chin white, belly white, rest of under parts gray, under wing coverts nearly black, weight less than avocet (willet).

Rest of afternoon we fished, catching many small mullet. Put them in a sandbar pool. Sunday dinner we had before dark by way of celebration—quail & mashed potatoes and a very successful batch of sourdough bread of which Carolo was the author—his first attempt.

Oct. 30—Monday As we were eating breakfast I knocked down a big mallard and Carolo two widgeons. Many geese flew up over the mesa and clamored mightily around the upper lagoon. We first went up to look at the traps. The first one was gone, and a clawed up bank told us why. We were rather blankly wondering whether the light stake had come off when we heard a rustling back in the arrowweed. Breaking our way through the dense growth, one to each side of the noise, Carl sang out "Coyote!" and at the same time the coyote made a run for it. He made pretty good progress and we were afraid he might pull out. So Carl put a .32 bullet behind his ear and we carried our

catch back to the Rillito. It was a very pretty young female in fine fur, but when we hung her up for skinning we found the fur was loose. So we had to content ourselves with the brush. So far it was a pretty large morning.

Then took a hike to the "Montes" north of camp but found no deer sign. When we got back at noon a blue heron was in our fish pen, and left with great reluctance and protestation.

The flats north of camp have many snail shells—evidently carried by high water.

Fished in the evening. Decided that our so-called "carp" were sheepshead, as the mouth is not pointed downward, but forward, and they lack the carp's "whiskers."

Mullet

Had sheepshead and mullet for supper, but found both were so soft and soapy as to be non-edible.

The geese made a great to-do up the Rillito. Carl said it sounded like a daughter getting home from college.

Gathered up our traps preparatory to moving to the Punta de Mesa tomorrow, where there are said to be "muchos venados."

Agua dulce for Flick

Oct. 31—Tuesday Francisco, a vaquero for Jesus of the Rancho Salada, arrived with his "carrillo" and a team of buckskin mules about 9 A.M. We loaded up and arrived at the Punta about noon, telling Francisco to come back Thursday.

Took a walk up the Colorado Viejo and set a trap with the carcass of a mallard. At the foot of the Punta are a series of pools, full of herons, lined with waving willows of the most delicate green, and the water, bearing the reflections of the willows, is of a brilliant verdigris hue. A weird and impressive place. No deer tracks. Killed 4 quail. Their crops contained a few tornillo hulls and whole grasshoppers, and a huge amount of minute hard lozenge-shaped shiny bronze-black seed, together with their hulls. I think this must be (arrowweed) pigweed seed. These contain a white kernel.

A very pleasant camp on the mesa in a clump of mesquite trees. Had the mallard for supper, with whole rice. (At the Rillito camp a coyote had got away with our trap—pulled the stake.)

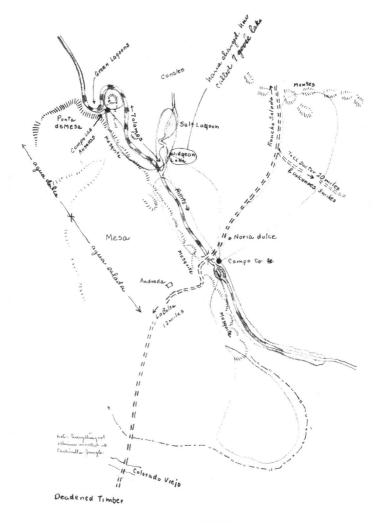

Green Lagoons

Canales

Have changed. now
collect ? goose lake

Montes

Punta
de Mesa

Salt Lagoon

Rancho Salada

Talones

Campo Las
Animas

Widgeon
Lake

Mesquite

To El Doctor 20 miles

agua dulce

B volcanoes 3 miles

Rillito

Mesa

Noria dulce

agua salada

Mesquite

Campo Co ?

Andrada

Mesquite

La Bolsa
12 miles

Mesquite

not: Everything not
otherwise marked is
Cachinilla Jungle.

Colorado Viejo

Deadened Timber

Sketch map of Rillito

Nov. 1—Wednesday Down the Rillito. Found some deer tracks, mostly old, and sweet water. Killed 3 more quail. No deer tracks in the Montes along the mesa. A great clamor of geese below us, but we arrived just in time to see 7 bunches strung out back for El Doctor. These had been using Widgeon Lake, which is on one of the "canales" and is salt, not sweet. Evidently then the geese do not come there for fresh water. Probably they come for gravel, of which there is plenty though we can recall none below.

Above Widgeon Lake is a big salt lake on which were cormorant, spoonbill, ruddies, avocets, yellowlegs, widgeons, 1 willet (?), 1 jacksnipe, and two kinds of sandpipers in flocks, one very tiny, the other about the size of jacksnipe. There were no goose tracks. Also saw coots, grebes, vermillion flycatcher, kingfisher, & black phoebe, and a small white gull with red bill and dark wing tips (royal tern?).

Coming back we sighted a huge "chimney" of cranes wheeling high in the sky over the Punta. When they got the glint of the sun they showed *pure white* and looked like a huge skyrocket bursting into white sparks. Gradually they worked east and when over us suddenly formed into a series of "V"s and started for El Doctor. Carl counted 130 when they were in this formation. They still showed *white* and looked like great draped strings of pearls against the blue. At no time did they make a sound. I cannot see how sandhill cranes could show so white. Could they have been whooping cranes?

Killed another quail in camp, and packed up for a before-daylight hike to Widgeon Lake after geese.

Field sketch showing formation

Nov. 2—Thursday (Goose Day) Up at 4 A.M. and hiking across the mesa by 5 A.M. Left our stuff packed with a note for Francisco to haul it back to Coyote Camp. Very interesting making our way in the dark, especially breaking through the cane and cachanilla to the Rillito. Got to the goose bar well before sun-up but nothing there except ducks. About seven Carl started up to Salt Lake to see if they were there. He had barely left when a big white flock swung in over the mesa and headed for the blind on set wings. They came over about 30 yards high. By shooting sideways into the line it would have rained geese, but I didn't want to chase any cripples. So I took the two end ones overhead and killed both stone dead. By now Carl was back and we were starting a war dance when another bunch hove in sight. Carl took the gun. They got in the sun on him but he got one dead. Immediately came another bunch, out of which Carl made a pretty double. Then another, and I made a double. This made seven, which was enough. We were hungry, so went up to the lighting place and hid under a tornillo where we were demolishing cold roast quail and sourdough biscuits when a single came in and lit within what we afterward paced at 18 yards. We suspended lunch, motions, and almost breathing for five minutes while we watched him—all except Flick—who couldn't make his eyes behave, in spite of my hand on his collar. Finally the single got nervous and left, but here came 11 more and lit within 25 yards. We watched them a long time. All these geese keep up a continual hum of small talk not audible at a distance. We plainly saw them go after the coarse sand immediately after settling down. Their wing coverts drape down over their primaries like heron plumes. Some always have their heads up. When they begin shaking their heads they are getting ready to go. At this time they line up in pairs facing the wind, so that they spring up in formation.

The seven made a he-load packing them down to Coyote Camp. On the way we saw sign, probably coyote but possibly coon, containing a mass of the hard wings of *Dytiscus* beetles, hair, and tornillo beans. At Coyote Camp we had a swim and then Alex Sortillon and Francisco arrived. In the afternoon we ran down to see La Bolsa. The tide was in. It didn't look bad for canoe work. They say sharks come up this far. On the way back we saw four huge black frigate birds flying east. Also saw a peculiar buzzard that must have been a *Caracara*. Goose roasted in the dutch oven tonight. Saw a coyote near camp in the moonlight. Weighed up the geese. They broke the scales but weighed about 5¼# each. One of the brick-tinged young ones was so tender that the skin pulled off with the breast feathers.

Nov. 3—Friday   To El Doctor with Sortillon. Arrived about 10 A.M. There were lots of teal, blue and green wing, of which Carl killed 3. Three geese came over rather high. I shot behind with the first barrel but dropped one dead with the second. The big spring pours up right in the cattails—and is warm but fine and sweet. A huge wheeling flock of sandhill cranes passed by going south. After lunch a flock of about 100 geese lit in the lagoon in front of us. Posted Alex for a pass shot while we went around and flushed. He hit 2 but both got away.

The mirage effects here are remarkable. It looks as if the whole world were a goose swamp but everything in the way of water over ½ mile distant is likely to prove non-existent, as well as the beautiful alamos that stand on its shores and the lines of fowl that seem to be sitting on its sandbars. Alex says that wells sunk here rise with the tide, and that there is one place where on puncturing the mud with a stick a column of water as high as a man spouts out.

We left rather reluctantly and arrived below San Luis at dark, where Alex dropped us on a fine grassy bank of the Rillito while he went in to bring down the canoe in the morning.

Nov. 4—Saturday   We celebrated wash-day and shaved off some very long beards. Repacked the outfit for boat work. Alex arrived with the boat about 9 A.M. Stowed cargo and embarked on the Rillito. Found lots of exercise, in the form of two bridges and three beaver dams, two of which we had to portage; also

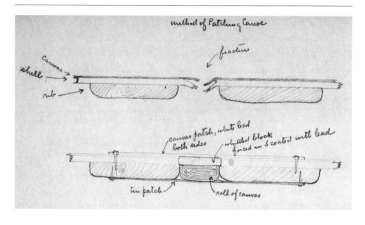

many log jams and fallen trees which we had to cut out. Going over one of the latter we pulled a tenderfoot trick in letting the canoe down on the stub of a limb. This poked a clean hole an inch in diameter right through her bottom, so we had to haul up and become a dry dock crew. With a piece of tin from a tin can, a piece of canvas, and white lead we contrived a patch which never leaked a drop.

Some interesting scenery, much willow cotton, many herons, but few ducks. At sunset a Cocopa boy riding bareback came out on the bank while we were making another portage around a willow thicket. He swore in English before he saw us but could sabe neither English or Spanish when we asked him how far to the Hidalgo ranch.

Earlier in the afternoon we stepped ashore at an Indian clearing and found some fine melons. At sunset we passed a skunk on the bank. While I cooked supper Carl stepped out and killed a couple of quail and a dove. Night was very cold.

Nov. 5—Sunday Started about 10 A.M. after letting some clothes dry. Better going today although we had to portage around one log jam and chopping our way through several others and a dozen windfalls. Very pretty travelling along the Rillito, with frequent grassy banks and handsome white barked cottonwoods. Saw many herons and hawks and horned owls, also many coon and beaver tracks, but no deer. Shortly after lunch we reached the Hidalgo ranch but the old man was not at home. His rather attractive daughter was very polite but could tell us nothing about the country, and her beau, who was on deck in very neat cowpuncher clothes, could but wouldn't. Camped above the ranch and Carl went on a quail hunt. Got 2 and half a dozen doves. I fished and caught many small catfish but none big enough to clean. Set a coon trap baited with a live catfish in a wet cowtrack, also quail cleanings. Then joined Carl. We saw—or rather heard—an enormous covey in a patch of tall weeds, but they were hard to work and easy to miss.

The doves killed today were full of wild melon seed.

Had a fine supper of teal, dove, quail & mashed potatoes and CSL brand sourdough biscuits. A fine camp.

Rillito at Junction Oxen Levy

November 6—Monday   CSL: *Ten o'clock saw us headed some-where southwest—canoe baggage and personnel aboard Señor Hidalgo's spring wagon. It was rough dusty going except along the Rillito which we soon left, taking a course across semi desert almost treeless delta plain. Lunched at one in the edge of a pigweed patch. Aldo got four quail with four shells.*

Steady travel all afternoon. We passed Laronia's cow camp in a beautiful grassy bosque and at four stopped at another camp to ask information. There were hundreds of quail and many doves. We added six quail to our larder. With only a mile to the river, but no road, we decided to try and make it before sundown. It was tough work for the team, thru heavy arrowweed and many small flood-water gullies. But with big bosque ahead and the air full of cormorants and ducks our hopes were high until we encountered a small muddy slough. A prospect developed no way to get ahead, it was almost dark so we camped down in the smoothest available spot. Hidalgo's yarns provided the evening's entertainment.

November 7—Tuesday   Quail roosted in the mesquite bush within six feet of our lean-to, flying out as we got up for an early start. Aldo got breakfast while I prospected north along the slough. Located a big lagoon and as I walked back toward camp, surprised a bobcat on the open mud bank. Got in two 30-30 shots before the cat made cover. Flick trailed a few yards and barked. It took a 32 to finish the job. The cat hung from shoulder to heel. Aldo skinned her out.

We finally got into the river and found it a beautiful large stream—banks overgrown with drooping willows. Considerable beaver and some deer tracks. Made permanent camp about a mile up stream in a mesquite orchard. Quail are everywhere but this is venado country so we are keeping quiet. A paddle up river before supper netted an appetite. The quail would not be enticed by our candle lantern.

Nov. 8—Wednesday   Took a paseo by canoe, getting off shortly after sunup. At the point where the Lagoon joins the river occurred the famous game of Pussy-wants-a-corner. Carl, who had the bow, sighted a big bob fishing on the small island which forms the point. We promptly got in between the island and shore and had the old bob cornered in a willow thicket. Carl went ashore with the shotgun and stood guard while I backed out the boat to drive her out. It was too easy. She came out between us, hell bent for election. We didn't wake up till she had made a fifteen foot jump across the little channel, when I bid her god-speed with an ineffectual shot into the jungle. It was inconceivable that this cat could get away from us. But she did.

On down the river (*what* river Lord only knows—it may be the Santa Clara, the Pescadero, or the Bee) Carl sighted another cat in a willow thicket. He made a quick shot and partly knocked her down but she kept going. Went ashore and tried to trail her up but no luck.

Carl bringing home the bobcat

Mallard Bay

About 2 miles below camp the river began to break up and we soon encountered a complete log jam stopping all further progress. I used to talk pretty brave about wiggling through the Labyrinth of the Colorado, of which this is probably the head. But we learned something on the Rillito. Neither of us had any desire to travel through that log jam.

Coming back we caught a wet cormorant by diving him down. He put up quite a fight with his hooked bill. Set him out for live bait at one of the cat sets. Also set 2 beaver traps.

In the evening, we explored up stream, finding great fields of hemp and arrowweed but deer tracks scarce. Built a quail trap out of dead arrowweed as we did not want to shoot around camp and needed meat.

Every evening a great flight of cormorants comes in to the lagoon from the north, and every morning they go out. Around camp, in camp, and in fact all over are incredible numbers of quail. Also many doves. A few ducks fly over the lagoon.

This night a beaver kept slapping the river right by camp. Sounded like a large heavy boulder plomping into the water. We have a grass bed and sleep with great comfort.

Nov. 9—Thursday   Up before sun and eastward up the lagoon. Great droves of herons and cormorants accumulated before us like a round-up. Much fine mesquite and grass country on the banks, and very little current. About four or five miles up we found many fine big mallards. Lagoon broke up into several live and several dead channels, the former very swift, and navigable only with difficulty. Found very few deer tracks.

After lunch and a nap we decided to lay in some meat, so I killed a greenhead and Carl got 13 quail. Found that in walking through the wild hemp one can gather quite a lot of beans by simply holding the hands cupped and letting them rain in from overhead. Killed a couple of coots for trap bait. Killed a duckhawk chasing a heron.

On the way back we were suddenly aware that a great caterwauling going on in the jungle to our left was not the usual croaking and fighting of herons and fowl, but rather a real genuine back-alley cat fight, with claws, whiskers, and all the trimmings. We quickly headed for the racket but the wind was dead against us, and when the fight got fairly in our lea it suddenly ceased. We caught a glimpse of one of the parties to the controversy sneaking off under the shadows, but not enough to shoot at.

Our live bait had gotten loose, and will henceforth trail a piece of blue bacon string over the boundless green miles of the Delta. We rebaited with coot. Saw an egret just below camp; also a few white herons and many buzzards. Carl took a still hunt on the point before supper and found much fresh deer sign.

Nov. 10—Friday   Organized a deer drive. I sat on the lane near camp while Carl still-hunted the east side of the point. There he sat while I hunted out the west side. This took till noon but no deer, although they made fresh tracks within 20 yards of camp last night. At the point I found a Mexican black hawk in one of the traps we had baited with a coot. Hawks and buzzards are so plentiful that one cannot leave any bait exposed.

Carl caught a large mullet on his throw-line this noon.

We each saw a cat this morning, but neither shot for fear of spoiling the deer hunt. Carl had a dead-sure chance at his. One can often locate cats by the scolding of the quail, which are so

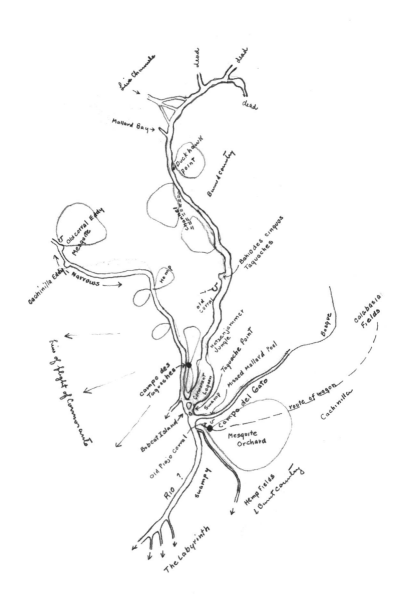

Big alamos at The Narrows

Looking for a hole through the cachinilla

nearly everywhere that one can follow anybody or anything through the woods by the quail scolding and flushing.

CSL: *We took an evening hunt below Campo del Gato. Found numerous tracks in a big mesquite park. Carl missed a coyote which almost ran into him. The cormorants were roosting in the willows as we came home.*

Nov. 11—Saturday   We paddled up the river all morning against a strong current. Found an old corral and killed a mess of quail after lunch. Aldo got four with the 30-30 shooting 32's. Saw another flock of cranes wheeling eastward over the lagoon.

The river becomes swift and narrow about 2 miles above camp, and lined with down willows.

Hunted the point again this evening. Carl thought he found where fawns had been playing on a hard mud slough since our last hunt yesterday morning. I stood on a pass and tried to count the cormorant flocks coming in, but gave it up. There must be several thousand. They roost in the trees, but unless their perch is very high above the water they hit the water first in order to get the benefit of their feet in taking flight. When disturbed at night it is doubtful if they can again take to trees. If not they may spend the night on the water, and this may

Waiting

*Sloughbed with hemp
in background*

account for the few flightless individuals one always finds on
the Lagoon and on the river.

We reset one of the traps for cat just above camp, baiting with
the remains of the mallard and quail.

Nov. 12—Sunday First made the round of the traps, which
we had not visited yesterday. The beaver trap was sprung but
empty. We reset it in a different place. The bobcat trap contained a small coon. He looked very wet and lonesome, but his
hide looked fair so we skinned him out and reset. He had been
in a day and the glands under the pit of his caught foreleg had
swollen and inflamed. Cased his hide and made another deer
hunt of the Del Gato mesquite orchard. The wind changed on
us and the mesquite country soon changed to hemp. We saw

ravens sitting near where Carl hit the coyote Nov 10. I have no doubt he is about there dead, but we couldn't find him.

Coming back we saw 7 mallards light in the little channel where Carl killed his cat. Made a sneak and I missed a big greenhead with both barrels. But I got a hen with a third shell. She flushed late and tried to follow the others. Flick retrieved her promptly from the arrowweed.

Carl saw the cranes again this morning—a huge flock. He says they are white with black wingtips.

Paddling home we again heard a loud splashing under a patch of cane bank near the creek. I'm pretty sure it's a beaver who airs and suns himself under there. Or maybe a coon.

Campo Taquache

In evening went north on the east bank and killed 14 quail for carne seco. Smoked them over mesquite coals that evening. Quite a little deer sign up there. Quail, noodles, and cornbread for supper, with raisin preserves. A big mesquite fire to celebrate our last evening in camp, and made plans for one last try at the deer.

Nov. 13—Monday   Up extra early and started up the Lagoon, after looking at our traps, one of which contained a dead buzzard. A fine bunch of mallards on the Lagoon but we didn't dare shoot. A little above the old corral Carl sighted a whole bunch of animals on shore under a patch of cane and mesquite. We hoped they were cats but as we stole up in the canoe we saw they were a whole family of coons.

I took the shotgun and killed one dead with the first barrel and thought I killed the big one with the second. The big one had disappeared, however, so we put Flick on her trail and he soon barked about a hundred yards up the bank in a dense mesquite thicket full of deep mud. We rushed up and found the big crippled one treed under a pile of dead brush. Shot her in the nose with the shotgun and then went back to pile up the unexpected results of our "deer" hunt and look them over. They were big and fat and in better fur than the previous one.

Went on up the Lagoon and made a hunt on the north bank but found very few tracks. As usual, great numbers of* quail and doves. Then we drifted down the Lagoon eating some lunch and went ashore on the point to skin out coons and incidentally watch for mallards, which had been passing regularly. They continued to pass, but always saw us and the snow-white coons, they being so covered with fat as to look like a big lump of lard. The young one skinned out a lot easier than the old one. The latter was a female—former a male.

Back to camp, regretfully taking up the traps as we went. Carl had another mullet on his throw-line. Lost his pipe in the Lagoon shooting at some teal. Packed up the outfit, including the grass bed, and took our final paddle down the river to the Campo del Gato, where we were just setting up for the night when Hidalgo arrived with his team, as per appointment. Roast

*Carl saw a sharp-shin carrying a quail.

mallard dinner to celebrate our last night in camp. At evening heard a whistling in the swamp which Hidalgo said was a beaver. At bedtime heard geese passing below us going east. These were the only geese we saw or heard in this region.

Nov. 14—Tuesday   Up extra early and breakfast over by sun up. Did not replenish the sourdough—the empty kettle a sad symbol of bright days gone by. Hit the cachanilla while the morning sun sculptured old Sierra Mayor into changing shapes and shadows. Fine fresh breeze from the north.

In the calabasa fields the myriad quail were out feeding and whistling in welcome of warm sunlight. Walked along beside the wagon and killed a last fine mess of 14 birds.

White herons sat on the lagoons to the north as we passed. Saw 5 pelicans passing as we crossed the big chemise flats. Killed a sharp-shin. Made Hidalgo's by noon and were his guests for luncheon. The wind blew gusts of sand through the wattled walls of his dining hall as we ate tamales and drank coffee. The pet pig, Flick, 2 dogs, 5 children, and a black mare stood guard by the door, watchful for the crumbs of the master's table, and sortied into the hall when the crumbs failed to materialize. A little white-toothed dusky-faced boy haunted Flick's side trying to feed him watermelon, and repeating over and over again some kind of assurance that sandias were fine food for dogs. A little sick girl, wrapped in a shabby overcoat, sat in a dim corner and watched us with great soft eyes. And all the while our host poured coffee and recounted with large gesture and gusto brave tales of the days when he was a free-lance vaquero seeking fortune and adventure on the Arizona frontier. Of adventure he found great store—of fortune many a fair beginning. Meanwhile the wind blew gusts of sand, the little boy chanted to Flick of watermelons, and the little girl looked with great eyes upon us. Finally the coffee pot went dry, and we started.

Arrived at San Luis before sundown, and hopped a ride on a load of beef hides into Yuma, where we arrived about 8 P.M. A bath, a call on our good friend Col. Fly, and we caught a midnight train for home.

"Choosing rather to live miserably within this realm pestered with inhabitants than to adventure forth, as becometh men, into those remote lands" —Sir Humphrey Gilbert

GAME FEEDS

Deer

Mesquite beans	Many tracks circling bean-bearing trees.
Willow shoots	Along Rillito below Punta.
(Screwbeans)	Reported.
(Chemise)	Reported.
? Carissa (Bamboo cane)	May have been cattle. Cane browsed by them.

Coons

Dytiscus beetles	Seen in sign which seemed to be coon
Screwbeans	sign. Might possibly have been
Calabasa seeds	coyote.
(Fish)	
(Grain)	

Coyote

? Rabbit	All sign contained fur.

Beaver

Willow	All cuttings were willow. Not enough cottonwood to form feed.

Quail

Watergrass seed	Both in the hulls and dry. In most crops.
Pigweed seed	Minute bronze-black.
Screwbeans	Including hulls.
Grasshoppers	Taken whole.
Mistletoe berries	Many live on these where no water-grass or pigweed.
Hemp beans	Found in 1 crop.
(Mesquite beans)	
(Calabasa seeds)	Found only in dove crops.
Mesquite leaves	1 crop. Leaves were red mature foliage. Roughage?

Doves

Watergrass seed	
(Pigweed seed)	
(Hemp seed)	Always around hemp patches.
Calabasa seed	1 crop full of these.

BIRDS SEEN ON THE COLORADO DELTA

Water Birds Misc.
Great Blue Heron
Snowy Heron
Night Heron
American Bittern
Frigate Bird
Gull (sp.?)
Cormorant (Farallone?)
Coot
Grebe (sp.?)
Vestpocket Sandpiper (sp.?)
_____ Sandpiper (sp.?)
Sora Rail
Killdeer
Tern (Royal?)
Egret
Spotted Sandpiper
White Pelican
Sandhill Crane
Whooping Crane

Game Birds
Gambel Quail
Mourning Dove
Snow Goose
Mallard
Widgeon
Greenwing Teal
Bluewing Teal
Pintail
Avocet
Summer Yellowleg
Jacksnipe
Willet
Ruddy Duck
Spoonbill
Redhead
Merganser (Hooded?)

Birds of Prey
Mex. Black Hawk
Sharp-shin Hawk
Cooper Hawk
Redtail Hawk
Caracara
Raven (sp.?)
Crow
Turkey Buzzard
Redshoulder Hawk
Duckhawk
Marsh Hawk
Roadrunner
Sparrowhawk
Bald Eagle (?)
Golden Eagle
Horned Owl
Prairie Owl

Small Birds
Black Phoebe
Vermillion Flyc.
Robin
Kinglet (sp.?)
Flicker
Wren (sp.?)
Phainopepla
Cardinal
Thresher (sp.?)
Swallows (sp.?)
Kingfisher
Mexican Ground Dove
Brown Towhee
Song Sparrow
Chipping Sparrow
Shrike
Brewer Blackbird
Junco

MISCELLANEOUS CAMP NOTES

FUEL WOODS

Mesquite is the finest coaling wood in the U.S. It burns slowly and steadily with a small pale flame. The coals are hard as anthracite and very durable. Green pieces with enough heartwood burn well mixed with dead. Detached pieces afire at one end will burn completely up, independently. When very old the wood is brittle.

Tornillo makes a hot fire but is only fair for coals.

Willow Round pieces coal better than split. Charred pieces coal better than uncharred. Coals are soft and not durable. Beaver cuttings just barely dry are best. Not comparable to mesquite. Smoke is acrid and disagreeable.

––––––––––––––––

COOKING

1 handful of bran or cornmeal is all that 2 cups of flour will stand for sourdough without sacrifice of rising qualities. Bran bread needs extra shortening to prevent toughness.

50–50 or slightly more is the proper amount of meal for cornbread.

Apples and other fruit swell up prunes better than they will independently.

To eat cold as well as hot knead dough as solid as possible. This reduces shrinkage on cooling. Real wet sourdough in solid loaf will not cook at all, except as hotcakes and in muffin tins.

"Pass the bread please"

Agua dulce	Fresh water	Other water "salada"
Gobernadora	Greasewood	On edges of mesa
Canutillo	Green Rabbit Brush	
Chivo Cimarron	Mt. Sheep	Hidalgo says "borregas c."
Biboros cornitos	Sidewinder	Horned Rattlesnake
Tecolote	Owl	
Guajolote	Turkey	
Gato des Montes	Bobcat	
Cachora	Lizard	
Marea	Tide	Max. 21' in Gulf. Bay of Fundy 30'
La Bolsa	Pocket	
Castor	Beaver	
Taquache	Coon (Sortillon)	Hidalgo says "Batate." T. = possum
Topo	Gopher	
Sorio	Skunk	
Fivia	Wild Hemp	In great fields on overflows
Medano	Sand Dune	
Bocya	tracks	
Socete	mud	
Sucate	grass	Watergrass, needlegrass, sedges, Galleta, Sacaton
Cachanilla	Arrowweed	Almost everywhere
Bahio	low place	
Batamote	Gila willow	Very scarce
Gatuna	Devil's Galleta	What we call "furze"
Carissa	Bamboo Cane	In small patches on banks

Posa	Waterhole	
Calabasias	Wild Melon	Said to be eaten by deer
Bledo	Pigweed	Fine quail feed & cover
Jaria	Gray willow	Very scarce
Saus	Tree willow	The principal tree of the bosques
Pescado volador	Mullet	"Leaping fish"
Pato buceo	Cormorant	"Diving duck"
Tesotas	Catclaw	
Lievre	Jackrabbit	
Cadillo	Cockleburr	Generally with Pigweed

Canada, 1924

June 11, 1924   'Twas Wednesday noon when we set sail from Winton, Minnesota, going up Fall Lake in an old launch, thence by truck over an old logging grade 4 miles into the S.W. arm of Basswood Lake. Here we loaded up our two 16' Racine canoes and struck N.E. for the international boundary. About 5:00 P.M. we got to the Canadian Ranger Station (Quetico Provincial Park), bought our licenses of Ranger Seeley, and headed north about a mile and pitched camp. Starker's fishing fever was running high, so we paddled out to a little island and caught two pickerel for supper.

Our camp was under a fine stand of Norway pine, where hermit-thrushes were singing. It is already apparent that the pine timber on the Canadian side is all uncut and not much burned, while on the American side there is not a pine left. The numerous islands are fortunately all covered with fine mature pines.

Roast pickerel for supper. When we went to bed at nine it wasn't yet dark.

June 12   Gave up trying to stay in bed until about 4:30 A.M. Eating breakfast a black mallard and several small mergansers passed by. Headed north toward Canadian Point, where in a wide part of the lake we found a big bunch of loons, the banks of pine timber echoing their calls. Starker trolled and caught a big pickerel with a parasitic worm projecting from his side. In spite of this he was fat. Put him back of course. About 10 A.M. reached the Basswood River and soon got to the first falls, portaging around them and finding our outfit good to carry but not quite down to where we could make it in one trip. Had some lunch and Carl and Fritz caught two fine wall-eyed pike, in addition to pickerel which we let go. Several red-breasted mergansers passed over. Then we portaged another falls, but the next rapid we ran (with great éclat). Then we portaged the lower falls, at the foot of which Fritz added another wall-eye and Starker caught a pickerel. About 3 P.M. we camped on the portage of still another very pretty fall which is probably the end of the river and the beginning of Crooked Lake. There is considerable style to this camp, which is on a grassy knoll overlooking the fall, with an International Boundary Monument for a tent-peg.

575

Boiled wall-eyed pike with mustard sauce for supper. After supper we fed an Indian who chanced along in a birchbark canoe, and then went fishing. Carl flirted with a huge pike at the foot of the falls, but couldn't hook him. Fritz caught another wall-eye but put him back. After threatening rain it cleared up with a beautiful sunset. Fished again—Starker caught a wall-eye all on his own—he is learning to throw a spoon—and Carl caught the granddaddy of the white-eyed tribe, a beautiful big four pounder. This was on one of the jointed plugs. Everybody caught pike. Turned in at 9:00 after 17½ hours. Even then it wasn't fully dark.

June 13 Got underway about seven. Rounding a point near the painted cliffs Fritz and Starker saw two does. Carl and I came up and snapped at one of them which broke and ran at 40 yards. The scenery is extraordinary. Went up a blind bay by mistake and found a muskeg with moose tracks. They had evidently come down for the lily with a rosette of red leaves on the bottom. Moose tracks were visible in the lake bottom as well as on the shore.

Soon we came to a narrows with a current literally full of big pike—we caught several and let them go.

No sooner had we started on than I sighted two deer on a grassy shore. Carl and I made the sneak. They seemed to see us at a quarter mile but resumed feeding and playing like a pair of puppies, striking with their front feet and dodging sidewise. They too were after the red lilies, fragments of which were floating in the water. We had the wind and light both in our favor and got up to not more than 30 yards, snapping two films.

We nooned on a fine point of solid rock, open to the breeze, with deep pitchoffs full of big pike, and big shiners all along the shoreline. Fritz caught a 7¾ pounder, and Starker a smaller one and a wall-eye. Many grouse were drumming here. A pair of tree swallows had a nest in a woodpecker hole in an old jack pine. The hole was alive with big red ants. How its young would survive the ants I can't imagine.

Continuing through Crooked Lake I caught a big wall-eye of 5¼#, which we kept for supper. Camped on a little rock island with only half a dozen trees and no mosquitoes. Tried a fish mulligan consisting of the planked wall-eye cut into big boneless cubes, ham, potatoes, mixed dehydrated vegetables, rice, and noodles. It was a huge success. We had the broth first (thus avoiding any need for a hot drink) and the rest afterward. It was so good we christened it Island Mulligan and the camp Mulligan Island.

After supper Fritz and Starker went back to a narrows with a strong current where we had seen many wall-eyes, while Carl and I went trolling for trout. We were soon diverted, however, by a persistent bawling across the lake, which we took to be either a bear cub (which bawls very like a calf) or a calf moose. We landed and found a lake with a little muskeg full of moose tracks, beds, trails, and piles of sign. By this time the bawling had stopped, the wind being quartering against us. We lifted the canoe over and found we were on an arm connecting with the channel where the boys were fishing. They had landed a huge pike and were playing another one, at a place where the pike had run a school of shiners up into the shore rocks and had them surrounded. The minnows were dashing frantically while the pike slashed right and left in the shallows. One could hook a pike at nearly every cast. Fritz had de-barbed a spoon so as to facilitate getting them off for release. Everybody caught pike (and a few wall-eyes) till the mosquitoes and approaching dark sent us to camp, towing the two big ones to have their pictures taken tomorrow.

We distinctly heard grouse drumming at 9:30 P.M., after dark. The moon was nearly full. Hermit thrushes were also singing.

June 14 Up a little later this morning and got started about seven. Trolled for trout a while but caught nothing but little pickerel. Continued west through the channels of Crooked Lake. A party of Indians, headed for La Croix, passed us. Arrived at Curtain Falls for lunch. Two miles before we got there we could hear the roar, and a quarter mile away one could feel the moist cool air full of spray vapor. They are really quite a show.

A pileated woodpecker flew across the channel near the falls. We had heard them previously drumming in the woods.

At the falls we had a pow-pow and decided to strike off north into the wilder country rather than continue along the Indian route along Shortiss Island. We went down the first bay, where we mistakenly supposed the portage to be, and discovered a little hidden lake on which was an eagle. Moose, deer, and bear tracks, all fresh were on the sand beach at its outlet.

On a bare rock in this bay we found a nest of three young herring gulls. The old ones flew overhead and tried to lead us away. The young took to the water as we approached. We ran one down and caught it—a pretty downy chick, white with black dots. It did not dive, but swam well. However the down plumage soaked up water rather rapidly.

We now tried the second bay and found the portage. A big buck, whose fresh tracks we found in the sand, snorted and

stampeded up the hill as we landed. Saw two grouse, moose, and deer tracks on the portage. Crossed an unnamed lake and then portaged into Roland Lake. It was immediately apparent that we had here the green water of the real north country, rather than the brown water of Crooked and Basswood. We camped on a beautiful rock point full of reindeer moss and backed by pines. Hermit thrushes serenaded us at supper, and a loon called from a far bay. Starker, as usual, started to fish, and from the canoe landing hooked what we supposed (from his spots) to be a small pickerel, but he fought as no pickerel ever did. On landing him we found him to be a beautifully spotted lake trout. This was on a barbless spoon—which we shall use hereafter. Starker got two more trout. We have had two big ambitions—seeing moose and catching trout, and have now solved the trout problem.

After supper Fritz stumbled upon a hen mallard setting eight eggs right in the pine forest. The number of adventures awaiting us in this blessed country seems without end. Watching the gray twilight setting upon our lake we could truly say that "all our ways are pleasantries and all our paths are peace."

June 15   Fried lake trout for breakfast were positively the sweetest fish ever eaten.

All the trout on stringers were dead. Have never yet found a way to keep trout alive, short of a tight pen in the water.

A fine chorus of white-throated sparrows when the sun came

up. "Ah poor Canada! Canada!" Thank the Lord for country as poor as this.

Laundering, sewing, and wetrocking bee around camp. Then we explored the lake and found tomorrow's portage into Trout Lake. Trolled to the sand beach where we found fresh moose tracks and had a fine but brief swim, the water being cold. Coming back to camp we photographed the mallard nest. The nest consisted of a hollow pushed into the dry litter under the overhanging branches of a little spruce. It had a perfect circle of a rim consisting of the gray down of the hen. The behavior of the hen was entirely different when approached from the water instead of the land—from the land she played cripple, whereas from the water she sprang directly into the air and hardly quacked. Only 8 eggs and nest full.

While boiling tea for lunch Starker caught another trout. After a nap all around we engaged in the very serious occupation of catching perch minnows to be used as bait for the evening fishing. Later I made Starker a bow of white cedar. In the evening we caught a few trout, one of which we had for supper. It was a female and had pink flesh, whereas the previous ones had white flesh. There are minnows and crawfish in these fish, indicating shore feeding. A large proportion are caught on first casts, indicating that they get used to a spoon and no longer

get excited about it. The first three minnows also drew bites, but later minnows wouldn't work.

Carl and I learned something while casting in a bay behind camp. The water was covered with willow cotton, which gummed up the line and the ferrules so as to make casting nearly impossible.

At dark a solitary loon serenaded us with his lonesome call, which Fritz imitates very well. This call seems to prevail at night, while the laughing call is used during the day. Carl remembers the laughing call at night, however, on the trip we made to Drummond Island with Dad about 1905.

The Lord did well when he fitted the loon and his music into this lonesome land.

June 16 Underway by seven and over the portage into Trout Lake. A stiff S.W. wind gave us a little tussle getting across into the Islands. From here we skirted the lee shores on an exploration trip into the S.W. arm, where in a fine sand-beach bay we noticed all the cedars were defoliated up to a 6 foot "high water mark." We landed to investigate and decided it was undoubtedly a winter "deer yard," the occasional spruces not being trimmed up. The cedars on the shoreline overhanging the water had undoubtedly been browsed off from the ice.

We now rigged a couple of shirt-tail sails, put the canoes side

by side, and returned up the lake "four sheets in the wind," trolling as we went. Right now we hooked a big fish which proved to be a four pound trout. He was hooked severely, so we kept him for supper. We then attached the little barbless spoon and at once hooked a small trout, indicating that the size of the lure has a good deal to do with the size of the fish.

Lunched on a little dream of an island consisting of a single tree on a single rock. Looked like rain, so we decided not to push on to Darkey Lake. Got up the tent and hustled in some wood from across the channel just in time before she came down in sheets, whereupon we holed up and made some—

RAINY DAY OBSERVATIONS

Carl: The nice thing about this country is that there is no cut lumber on the shorelines. We haven't seen a sawed board since we left Basswood Lake.

Fritz: We don't know where we're going but we always get there. Following lakeshore on the big lakes there is seldom more than one way to go and a man always knows what's at the end of it. Up here there are twenty ways and every one different.

Starker: There are no Indians or tourists to bother us. We've seen one last-year's camp since we left Curtain Falls.

New Leech   First seen in Roland Lake. Olive green with orange lines on each side and a row of orange dots along the dorsal line.

Lichens   Our rock island is covered with gray lichens, which in dry weather flatten out and expose only their "rubberized" upper surfaces, thus allowing a minimum of evaporation. The minute a drop of water strikes them, this surface turns olive green and the outer edges curl up, exposing the rough absorptive under-surface to the rain. Their individual plants must attain great age, since we have passed numerous places where initials have persisted for years by being scraped into the lichen covers of rocks.

Toward evening it cleared beautifully and we all went fishing. Caught several small ones and then came back for supper (Trout Chowder and very good.) After supper about sundown we noticed trout wallowing on the surface and gave them a try. Fritz hooked a whale which we played hard for 36 minutes. The fish sounded with extreme persistence. Finally Fritz brought him in and the barbless spoon fell out of his mouth as he hit the bottom of the boat. He weighed six pounds and was 28¾" long. Tied him up overnight and next morning took his picture before letting him go. He was a wonderful fish and one of the hardest fighters imaginable.

The loons called and whitethroats sang as we were playing him, and before we brought him home the full moon hung in the East and we had to read the scales by the fire.

June 17   Packed up and underway by a little after seven. It was a clear sparkling day with a stiff north breeze. We found the portage into Darkey Lake very steep and full of fallen fire-killed pine. On the second trip we bumped right into a pair of partridges with at least ten or a dozen chicks, of which we caught two to take a photo. The old hen had a number of calls, one a hiss like a bull snake, to defy the enemy. Another a cluck like a hen to reassure the brood to sit tight. Another a meow like a catbird, evidently meaning alarm. Also an alarm chirp like a Gambel quail. I'm not sure the hen gave all these calls—both

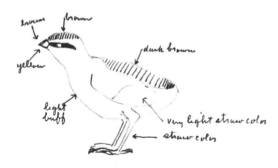

she and the cock were on deck all the time, trying to save the day. The chicks had a peep just like any chick. They were in the down—I would guess less than a week old. The colors were about as in the drawing.

Looked for the Indian paintings supposed to be found on the

cliffs in the lower part of Darkey Lake but couldn't find them. The water we find is intermediate—not so green as Trout Lake and not so brown as Crooked Lake. It has an outlet, and we found later contains pike, perch, wall-eyes, trout, and, unfortunately, carp.

Explored the northwest arm down to the outlet, hoping to find bass. We are sure we saw some small ones. At the outlet we found big three and four pound carp in great numbers. Had a lot of fun gigging or snagging them with a spoon. I also tried a bow and arrow and later a spear with a nail lashed to the point. The spear worked right now—the very first shot I got a big one right through the back. These carp were active, hard, and nicely colored, and were spawning. When the spawn dropped from hooked fish, great numbers of minnows gathered to eat it.

Coming back up the arm Fritz and I saw a doe and snapped her, and I caught a huge pike with the tail of a pound fish projecting from his throat. We got no bass, so we all set out to catch some supper, using some fine minnows Starker had caught at the outlet. Rigged a bobber and fished off our rock point by camp, where I caught a big trout for supper. After supper we caught a big pike and some wall-eyes, all of which we turned back.

CSL: *June 18   We were all lazy this morning and slept until about 6:30. The last hour in bed was spent slaughtering large blood filled mosquitoes that in one way or another had found their way under our netting. Our camp on Darkey was a beautiful one on a high promontory with exceptionally deep water on three sides. Left camp about 8:00 with a strong head wind from the East. The first of five portages to Brent Lake turned out to be a losing proposition but the other four were bona fide portages—the roughest we have struck to date.*

Launched our canoes in a rough bit of water and paddled out to a small Norway pine island where we had lunch.

After lunch we continued on east to the northeast end of the channel connecting the main east & west sections of the lake. A particularly attractive spot because there is less evidence of fire than in any of the country we have struck so far.

Made camp on the westmost of a string of four small islands. Camp is made up in apple pie order because we expect to spend two days here.

In the way of miscellaneous information the deer we saw yesterday was feeding on young horse-tail just coming up out of the water.

Found beaver lodges both in dead water in narrow inland channels and on the open lake shore with a mile or more of open water off shore.

In exploring the details of our island I heard a continued peep-peeping and on investigating found a laughing loon's nest containing one chick and one partially hatched egg with a live chick peeping inside. The egg is very large—about the size of a goose egg. Color a dull brown with a few black specks scattered irregularly. The chick is a slate grey in color with black feet and bill AL: and whitish belly.

During supper the old loons watched us from a distance of sixty yards. But after supper when we all disappeared into the tent where we kept very quiet the hen loon took courage and came right up to within thirty feet of our white tent and just now she has the chick out in the water with her. The rooster is off about forty yards making reassuring small talk to the hen while she takes the chances.

June 19   Heavy rain from about four until seven—we were busy dodging leaks in the tent. After a good rainy weather breakfast Aldo set the pace by shaving and washing clothes. Fritz, Starker and I soon followed suit and the camp was and is still bedraped with garments of many shapes. Weather too uncertain for travel so we spent the forenoon fixing up generally—baked a big batch of tortillas.

Our loon was on the nest and remained there all morning. Her mate dove into the nest evidently bringing food. The nest is just 25 feet from our tent.

An early lunch was ready when we discovered a young bull* moose swimming the channel to the west of our camp. We launched a canoe and raced the moose back to the south shore coming within six feet of his posterior as he heaved himself out of the water into the spruce thicket. Aldo took two pictures.

---

*AL: Had six inch horns with a big knob on the end. Groaned when hard pushed.

While we ate lunch a beautiful white-tail doe browsed along shore just east of camp. She was quite reddish.

Afternoon we explored an uncharted bay south of camp. Aldo caught a pike and two wall-eyes for our supper. Fritz baked a whacking corn bread—and noodles completed the menu.

The loon story is closed. The second chick evidently hatched this morning and the parents proceeded to move their chicks to a safer place. The oldest chick made off at the parents' call but the weaker one was left behind. Fritz and I have just taken it up to another island some distance from camp in hopes that the old loons will find it.

THE LOON ISLAND DECALOGUE

Cuss not mine ancient backlash, for the poor cast we have with us alway.

2. When thou risest up to smite an mosquito, hold thy peace and lay thy shirt on the canopy.

3. Cherish thine hat o'er the portage, that it may be with thee to the end of thy trip.

4. Stack not tortillas without flour, lest they cleave together and thy brother gather up thereof seven baskets full.

5. If thou wouldst bump the tent in a rainstorm, do it over thine own bed.

6. Six days shalt thou paddle and pack, but on the seventh thou shalt wash thy socks.

7. Covet not thy neighbor's share, lest thou cast for a trout and be given a pickerel.

8. To him that eats shall be given a pancake, but from him that is always wanting to cook shall be taken away even the one that he hath.

9. An aluminum cup is made for forbearance, and a hot griddle is the trial of a patient man.

10. See not thy brother's bum cast, and love his campsite as thine own. If there be a rock in the tent, lay thy bed upon it. Ask not for more cheese till thou see if there be any, and peace shall be with thee to the end of thy days.

June 20   Up bright and early, packed up, and underway about 6:30. Eastward along Brent Lake, which has much spruce shore and high bold islands. Saw a bluewing teal and another pair of loons with two tiny chicks trailing them. Down the S.E. arm of Brent and over a beautiful portage into a little unnamed lake where we bumped into another pair of loons, one with the young on her back. Another portage put us into McIntyre Lake. We got as far as the narrows when the heavy sea in the S.W. arm led us to try to portage out of the southeast arm, which was calm. We found an old trail about half a mile long into Sarah Lake. On the trail we found some lovely pink lady-slipper in a swamp, and a mother partridge with a bunch of chicks even smaller than the ones we saw a few days ago. The old hen whined exactly like a puppy dog when we approached the chicks, and played the cripple act to perfection when we started away. She kept ahead of us, leading us almost to the lake.

The portage is through beautiful birch timber with an under-growth of maple brush and hazel. It has never been cleared but has been used at odd times. On it we found some wolf or bear sign with a big gathering of tiger-swallowtail butterflies on it.

Before leaving McIntyre we saw a big light red deer on a rocky point. The water in McIntyre was very high. Could raise no fish.

Cooked lunch near a beaver-lodge in the foot of the N.E. arm of Sarah Lake. More fresh cuttings on the shores (mostly aspen and alder) than any place we have yet seen. In several places recently we have seen old dead pine logs gnawed by beaver—evidently just to exercise their teeth.

All of these waters are now covered with a film of jack-pine pollen, which also makes a line on all the rocks in protected places. It does not seem to gum a line like the willow cotton.

Went south on Sarah to just above the narrows where we made camp on a fine pine island with bold shores and little underbrush. We thought we had gotten away from our nursery duties but soon found we had camped in a regular kindergarten. Carl found a loon's nest with one hatched egg and a pipped one, while Starker found a nest full of little juncos right where we were pitching our tent. We moved into another place, but the young were soon hopping all through the camp while the old birds scolded us constantly, our new hen loon complaining in the channel behind us meanwhile.

Tried the fish but it was an east wind and we couldn't connect with anything but a few wall-eyes, which we had for supper.

During the evening we heard a tree crash across the channel—doubtless the work of beavers. Very few mosquitoes during the night so we all slept fine.

June 21   While we were breakfasting three beautiful loons swam up to within 60 yards several times to look us over. Their motive was evidently curiosity. We have noted that the trill of a laughing call is produced by vibrating the lower mandible, and not by a mechanism of the throat alone. Also, that the "laugh" seems to prevail as a note of alarm or fear, the lonesome call seldom being used when worried or alarmed.

Packed a lunch and started out on the trail of the big bass. Tried a little bottle-necked bay just across from camp but could raise nothing on spoons. Then tried the pike-minnow plug and got results forthwith, removing two gangs of hooks to give the fish a chance. Also caught them on a pork-rind spinner. Those caught on a single hook jumped as much as four times; those on a plug never more than once. No plugs for us if we can help it. Carl also caught two huge pike, one on a barbless spoon and the other on a pork-rind. Each took forty minutes to land—they were so heavy that the light rod acted exactly like trying to lift a railroad tie. Both pike had scars, and one smaller one a healed nick in his back. Both were the same length but the first one was deeper and heavier. It is impossible to squeeze in the gill-covers on these huge fish—they can only be lifted by getting the fingers behind the gills. Even then one's hand would not reach around a much bigger one. Weighed them by using Starker's bow on a paddle, giving the scales three times the leverage of the fish, and multiplying the scale reading by three. Thus we staid within the capacity of the scales.

We named this Battleship Bay after the huge proportions of the big pike. In it was a large beaver lodge recently extended many feet into the lake by adding peeled sticks of aspen, alder, and unpeeled birch. Evidently the birch is not eaten but just cut as building material. The older section of the lodge on the shore end was plastered with gravel and mud,—this was evidently the part used last winter.

Broke my glasses while shaving—luckily had an extra pair.

After a fine nap we all went in for a swim, diving off a steep smooth rock into the deep water. It wasn't nearly so cold after one got in. Then had a big dinner of bean soup, bass, and tortillas. After supper went back to our bay after bass. They weren't biting, but the beaver show was even better. A beaver played around in the mirror-like reflections of the bay, "pomping" down with a huge splash of water only thirty yards from us. Caught a few wall-eyes and returned to camp.

The narrows at the mouth of the bay are full of deer tracks, plainly visible under four feet of water.

Before we went to bed Fritz several times started all the loons within several miles calling by giving the "lonesome" call through his fingers. Some of those which answered him were on McIntyre Lake, away over the hills.

Several times today we thought we could hear a waterfall in the N.E. arm of Sarah. Tomorrow we are going down there to investigate.

June 22   Off for the N.E. arm to see what we can see. Going down the big channel Starker caught a fine lake trout trolling with the rod. We kept him for supper, as we have unanimously concluded they are away ahead of any other fish.

We soon found our waterfall, which is of brown-stained water, coloring the whole extreme end of the bay. Followed it up and found a little lake, only a hundred yards in but 25' higher than Sarah, with its mouth dammed by beaver so that all the shores were flooded. Signs of an old portage to this lake. No suckers in the stream—we looked for some for Starker to shoot with his bow and arrow.

Found no bass in this bay as the water is full of jack-pine pollen which killed our trout, evidently clogging his gills. There is another but older beaver lodge in this bay.

Caught a few bass but they soon stopped biting, so we decided to climb the high hill to the east and eat lunch there. The view was very interesting—also the vegetation and glaciated dome-like granite. Pink lady-slippers were common all over the mountain.

It was a bit warm so we all decided to go swimming. We had a fine swim and seeing a big shoal of minnows we rigged up a dishrag on two sticks and caught a bucketful. This suggested a perch-fishing party, which we tried, but without success. There are no long weeds in any of these lakes and if there are any big perch we haven't seen them.

Now gave the bass a whirl with the minnows. On the way to the bay Fritz and Starker heard a big animal crash into the brush—may have been a moose. Carl and I caught mostly walleyes but Fritz and Starker sighted their bass and dangled minnows in front of them and were very successful. Turned them all back. While fooling with these bass a deer snorted at us from the birch woods. It now threatened rain so we scooted for camp and cooked up a fine dinner. Had the dishes washed before the rain hit us, after which we all holed up in the tent and played the mouth-organ and sang and smoked while the rain beat down and added cheer to the evening. Cleared up and started blowing just before dark, with a fine pale sunset behind the blue clouds. Fritz raised some more loon music by calling them.

June 23   Got underway about eight after taking a picture of Starker's big bass and turning him loose. Had the wind behind

us, so hoisted our shirttail sails and kited down Sarah in a hurry. Starker caught a fine trout trolling and we kept him for dinner. Tried the bass but couldn't raise any. Over a very steep portage into a little lake full of fresh beaver workings. Tried the bass here and saw many little ones but none big enough to strike. Then into another little lake with much fresh beaver work and several lodges, and a fine little lily-padded bay on one end with muskeg shores. This lake was remarkably deep with mud bottom and deep clear blue water. Raised no fish. Then over a very short portage into a lake so flooded by old beaver work that all the shore timber was killed. Here we were so hungry that we ate lunch on a shelving rock. There were many old lodges in this lake but no recent signs of beaver and all the aspen within reach of shore had been cut. It was evidently abandoned. Fritz saw a snowshoe rabbit come down to the lakeshore for a drink. Raised no fish here.

P.S. Mistaken about the fish. After lunch Starker saw a trout pass our point and I soon caught a beauty on a small spoon with a piece of the trout skin caught in Sarah. This fish had only the faintest suggestion of spots and was of a beautiful brown mottled color. We kept him for supper. Now set about to find our portage but couldn't locate it. Spent the whole afternoon cruising around, locating two lakes to the west and one to the

south which we finally concluded was our lake. Meanwhile we had made camp as it was too late to go on. It proved to be one of our prettiest and most interesting camps. A bunch of loons kept inspecting us and providing the music for the evening. After supper I caught another of the beautiful mottled trout. The atmosphere of not knowing quite where we were, also a fine bunch of rootless alderwood, made this an exceptionally nice camp.

June 24   Underway about 7 o'clock after an extra fine breakfast of fried trout, apple sauce, and cornbread. Decided to chance it down the beaver dam and soon identified the next lake (Brown Lake) as the one we were looking for. Frederic's lake with the beaver dam and duck pond runs into it from the west. Portaged on into what we called Blue Lake from the blue water. Fished here and Starker had a strike that seemed to be trout but caught none. Thence over the forked portage into what we thought was the Ranger Station bay but where we soon found we had another long portage to make. Ate lunch here and called it Basswood Jr. from the brown water.

The forked portage was a long one and we rested halfway. There were very big moose tracks on it. The Blue Lake end has been flooded by beaver and we sank up to our knees in places. We observed that a boggy portage was not necessarily a soft one.

At Basswood Jr. we entered the big burn which devastated the "civilized" end of our route about 15 years ago. There is an osprey nest on this lake, and old beaver lodges on its shores.

At lunch today Carl looked wise and trotted out three Tareyton cigarettes, which he with great forbearance had been carrying in his pocket these two weeks.

We had a fair breeze quartering against us all afternoon except one 2 mile stretch at the mouth of Pipestone Bay which we sailed in no time at all. Going up Pipestone we saw a porcupine drinking. After a long drag got over the lower portage just before sunset. Here we saw several canoes—the first human beings we have seen since June 14, ten days ago. Noted basswood growing near the falls—evidently it goes this far north only near water that is open yearlong and hence modifies the temperature sufficiently to enable it to survive.

Camped on a pretty little island within sound of the falls. We were lucky to have such a nice place for our last camp. Had been paddling and portaging 16 hours so we cooked a big dinner and turned in early.

June 25   Up at 4:30 and found a big loon inspecting our camp. Also saw a black mallard and what seemed to be a bluebill. This country has more marshy bays than the rock-bound shores where we had been and hence is better adapted to chicks nesting. After a fine breakfast of bacon and fried noodles we sorted our duffle and started out. Soon reached our last portage where Fritz remarked that there was not only sign of moose, but also elk and Knights of Columbus. Even so we saw a deer on it, in spite of the landing docks, tin cans, and old papers.

Now had a long pull up Fall Lake in the teeth of a very stiff wind. It was quite a tussle, in which Starker had to take a hand to make any progress at all. He did splendidly and we all pulled in to Winton about 9:30. Peterson came over with the truck and we warmed up in Ely and caught the 12:45 train back to work.

It has been a memorable trip—maybe the best we ever made—and we have made some that are hard to beat. It is the first trip we have made together since we went to Drummond Island with Dad about 1906 or 7. How Dad would have loved it! I am reminded of Izaak Walton's terse but lovely tribute— "an excellent angler, now with God."

NOTES ON BIG-MOUTH BASS

6/21 Bait   Wouldn't take spoon but took pike-minnow or pork rind. The ones dressed were empty, indicating that the full fish don't bite. Very moody—at times not rising at all, but would take minnows when not rising to casts if minnows were held in front of them. Little ones would take minnows but not casting lures. We found no good bass fishing to cast lures except in the morning.

6/21 Sporting Qualities   Jumped up to 4 times on a single hook but only once on a plug. Very persistent in following a line and re-striking. Also followed the tied fish string from the boat, not seeming to be shy of boat, people, or noise. Some did not jump at all, even on a single hook.

6/21 Appearance   There is a distinct dark median stripe down each side, and a greenish-bronze cast to the rest of the body, with dark tail.

6/21 Occurrence   Near down snags in shallow water. Seem commoner in bays and protected spots than open lakeshore.

6/21 *Meat & Cooking* A 3¼# fish dressed out only 1¾#, or 54%. Meat not nearly as good as lake trout.

P.S. A party just arrived from Long Lake as we got into Ely had 75 small-mouth which weighed 15# dressed, with heads. They say they caught them on pork minnows.

NOTES ON WALL-EYED PIKE

Location Seem to prefer moving water, although our biggest one was caught trolling in deep still water. Found under snags in Bass Bay on Sarah.

Food Minnows, bees (?)

Bait Any kind of spoon or plug, preferably with pork rind. A sunk spoon is more effective than an unweighted one. Bite minnows freely.

Cooking Hard to scale as a yellow perch. Skin, don't scale them, and then plank. Very fine for chowder. Very pale meat, dead white in color. Not over one 2# or 3# fish should be put in one chowder.

Sporting Qualities Much better fighters than pickerel but not nearly so well as a trout or bass. Eyes turn dead white soon as dead—when caught the eye is merely an opaque film. Make a big fight to start with but soon give out.

Appearance Those in Sarah and some of the other lakes had bright yellow "brindle" flecks and were a handsome fish. In other lakes they were a dull gray color. Also seems to vary in shininess as between lakes.

NOTES ON PIKE

The big pike we caught in Crooked Lake, one had very small oval or round spots with a greenish cast, the other one (bigger one) had longer slashes and a yellowish cast.

All pike seem to prefer the foot of falls but are found everywhere and can't be kept off the lines.

The pike in Sarah Lake, bigger than those of Crooked Lake, had pure white bellies and faintly yellow spots. The length never over twice the width. They lay under down logs in shallow water.

The meat of the one eaten in Brent Lake had a pinkish color when planked—not dead pale like wall-eye meat.

NOTES ON LAKE TROUT

Found in Stomachs   Minnows, crawfish.

Color   Some have a yellowish bronze cast to a clear blue-green. Some have white belly and others are brindled. All fade quickly. So far the yellow ones had white flesh while the green ones have pink or salmon meat. Those caught in "How Come" Lake were mottled brown almost without spots, the flesh of one (female with small roe) was light pink, while the other was blood red when raw and strawberry when cooked.

Size   Up to Trout Lake the only big one was caught deep on a big spoon. Caught several big ones later by casting while wallowing in the evening.

Misc. Points   Bleed profusely from deep-set hooks, even if barbless. Always die on stringers, because they won't stop fighting, or drown themselves. Plugs are no good because they won't sink. In trolling, go slow to get the line deep, using many sinkers. When caught they never jump or break water, but sound furiously. A big proportion are caught on the first cast in any given place.

On certain calm evenings trout come to the surface to feed and would be seen wallowing all over the lake. Other evenings few or none were seen doing this. But will bite whenever wallowing.

The teeth are very sharp and make bad cuts.

Cooking   Skin is thick and hard to brown. In frying planked steaks put meat side down* first. Like other fish the meat "curls up" less if several hours old. Best eating of any fish.

Occurrence   Seem to go with perch. No pike found in† trout lakes, or vice versa. Up to 6/16 no shiners found in trout lakes. Also all trout lakes to 6/16 have green water and pike lakes brown water. 6/22 found with pike in Darkey & Sarah.

Sporting Qualities   All lake trout seem to sound spirally and thus often wrap themselves in leader and line. Often follow the line a long way without striking, returning to it cast after cast.

---

*or skin so the meat is lean on both sides. In planking, skin out the ribs of the body cavity by working from the rear end. The knife follows them more closely in this way. This is true of planking any fish.
† Found pike with trout in Sarah.

ANIMALS SEEN ON WILDERNESS TRIP

SPECIES	REMARKS
Woodchuck	In rocks along rocky shores. Only seen on Basswood Lake.
Pine Squirrel	Not abundant.
Porcupine	Very little evidence except droppings, which were everywhere. Saw one on Pipestone Bay.
Beaver	Eat aspen & alder. Gnaw dead pine. Cut birch for lodges but don't eat it. Lay rocks at uniform intervals on crest of dam. From the dead timber and cuttings we judged beaver had increased in the last 5 or 10 years.
Whitetail Deer	Feeding on red lilies, also new horsetail sprouts. In winter they not only trim cedar boughs to height of 6 feet, but also "ride" the young saplings and break them off to browze the tops. Saw no velvet horns—either none were bucks or they had very recently shed.
Moose	Young bull had 6″ knobs 6/19. Two men by paddling hard could catch up with him swimming.
Chipmunk	Makes the monotonous hollow "chuck-chuck-chuck" that one might mistake for a grouse or other bird.
Snowshoe Rabbit	Winter snow work on alder, willow. Saw one come down to the lake and drink. Forest officers say very destructive to pines.
Bear	Many stumps & logs opened with teeth for ants.
Muskrat	Saw only one. Seem scarcer than beaver.

BIRDS SEEN ON WILDERNESS TRIP

WATER & GAME BIRDS	REMARKS
Herring Gull	Large downy young 6/14
Spotted Sandpiper	
Ruffed Grouse	
Red-breasted Merganser	Young seen 6/19
Hooded? Merganser	
Great Northern Loon	Hatching 6/18–20
Mallard	8 eggs 6/14
Great Blue Heron	
Bluewing Teal	A very few singles seen
Black Mallard	One seen Sarah Lake
Wilson Tern	Only 1, on Fall Lake

OTHER BIRDS	NOTES
Blue Jay	Abundant
House Wren	
Red-hooded Woodpecker	Near Ely farms
Pileated Woodpecker	
Flicker	
Hermit Thrush	
Ovenbird	
White-throat Sparrow	
Crow	
_____ Eagle	
Sparrow Hawk	
Sharp-shin Hawk	
Cooper	
Phoebe	
Least Flycatcher	
Kingbird	
Osprey	
Purple Grackle	Fairly common
Song Sparrow	
Great Horned Owl	
Tree Swallow	Nesting in woodpecker holes
Olive-backed Thrush	
Red-eye Vireo	
Junco	Young leaving nest 6/20
Waxwing	
Turkey Buzzard	
Camp-Robber	Only around small-lake country north of Basswood

PLANTS SEEN ON WILDERNESS TRIP

TREES & SHRUBS	NOTES
White Pine	
Norway Pine	
Jack Pine	Pollen blowing 6/20
Tamarack	
Black Spruce	
Balsam	
White Cedar	
Ground Juniper	
Aspen	Just in leaf 6/15
Large-toothed Aspen	Half in leaf 6/15
Juneberry	Blooming 6/15
Pin Cherry	

Beach Plum
Blueberry
Bearberry
Poison Ivy   Half in leaf 6/15
White birch
Alder
Mountain Ash
Hazel
Scrub Maple
Elderberry
Wild Rose
Sugar Maple   Only near "How Come" Lake
Burr Oak   Only near Pipestone Lake Falls
Basswood   "   "   "   "   "
Red-osier Dogwood

HERBS ETC.   NOTES
Wild Strawberry   Blooming 6/15
Anemone
Ground Pine
Pink Ladyslipper   Blooming 6/16 Trout Lake
Star Flower
Red Columbine
Pink Ladyslipper   Blooming 6/20
Clintonia   "   "
Partridgeberry   "   "
Bracken
Blue Aster
Bleeding Heart   (Pink color)
Wintergreen (?)

WATER PLANTS   NOTES
Red Lily   In mud-bottom bays
Tule
Cattail   In glacial holes on hill
Water Lily
Pondweed
Horsetail   Eaten by deer
Yellow Lotus   First bloom 6/22
Wild Rice   Only 8" high. Scarce.

MISCELLANEOUS OBSERVATIONS

Canoes Turn over at night to keep out dew, and empty all water at once to avoid taking on weight. Keep paddles and skeg clean of "feathers." Take off hat and pack down jumpers and all packs in facing a head wind. Have a nose ring for painter and for lining. Don't step on yoke pads, and place yoke 1 rib forward of centre of canoe. Carry triangular balloon silk cloth 5' on each side in bow for sail. Carry line. We had two 16' Racine light weight 72# each dry.

Packs Don't carry over 60# on a tump, nor over 90# in any pack. Kenwood bags are a little too wide to lie flat crossways. Put extra shirt under shoulder pads for canoe yokes.

Beds & Tents 7 x 9 silkolene wall tent enough for 4 people. Should have bobbinet head-canopy to cover upper end of beds, lower edge weighted with shot, and tied in with tapes. For summer trip wouldn't take sleeping bags or pockets. One feather or wool quilt plus two double blankets for each two people.

Clothing A jumper that buttons in front, or a heavy coat-shirt, is better than a closed overshirt. One extra pair socks, 1 extra suit underwear, and 1 extra kerchief is enough. Extra clothes should be in bag for pillow. No camp or extra shoes are worth their weight. In a rock country have rubber soles on boots—if on wet logs or trout fishing use new sharp conical hobs.

Misc. Have several iodine "vaporoles" in medicine kit, in wooden tubes. Take extra glasses.

Utensils Heavy skillet with griddle lid pays. By no means forget nippers. No aluminum cups.

Fish Lake

AL, EBL, ASL, LBL   July 18–19, 1925
                                                  Cloudy, cool, rain

Fish Lake is said to be carpless.

Probably by reason of this, it displays an aquatic flora so beautiful that it is quite unnecessary to catch fish. At this time there are blooming:

1. The great water lily, with creamy green blooms as big as a small cabbage, and great leaves that stand a foot above water (in the Pot Hole toward Crystal L.)

2. The white water lily, in profusion

3. The yellow lotus (the kind with leaves flat on the water)

4. The small pink lily, with leaves like a mosaic

5. The pink smartweed

6. The sago pondweed

In addition there are three or four mosses (one of which makes floating islands bearing grass), the floating duckweed, ordinary tule. One floating island had just come to the surface, as evidenced by the pale green bases of the fallen tules it bore.

Probably this clear little lake is a sample of virgin Wisconsin. In spite of heavy fishing it seems well supplied,—we had 4 strikes on flies in the evening, landing two, and three in the morning.

Had a pretty camp under the white birches on the east shore. It rained for several hours this morning but we staid dry in the tent.

Explored the hill to eastward—it is full of wild raspberries (now ripe) and hazel, but has no grape vines and no grouse. Whether these two facts are related I don't know. It seems to have been often burned.

Terns were scolding, evidently over their young. They probably nest on the floating islands. Several cormorants visited the lake, seeming to come in from the river. Saw little green and blue herons, night herons, grebes, and on a pond near Roxbury a purple gallinule.

Saw a gray squirrel running out of a field of ripe oats—I didn't know they ate oats.

The water level has gone up—without apparent reason—in Fish Lake, birch groves being flooded out on the west shore.

Canada, 1925

August 8, 1925 at 4 P.M. we ended an unsuccessful argument with the aged Skipper of the Winton Launch, during which we tried to induce him to tow us to the Railroad Portage at the end of Fall Lake. He having a natural monopoly of this transportation system, Saturday was a poor day to persuade him to make an extra trip. So we piled the outfit into the canoe and started up Fall Lake under our own power. Our outfit consisted of:

1	Peterson Pack containing a blanket, axe, and 75 nominal pounds of chuck, the actual weight of the pack being . . . . 95 pounds	
1	Bed Roll with tumpline, consisting of 6 single blankets, 7 x 9 silkolene tent, and 2 rods, actual weight 45	"
1	Duffle Bag, with Cook Kit and miscellaneous tackle . 30	"
1	18' Racine Canoe rated at 90	"
	Total outfit 260	"

Made the 5 miles to the old log landing in just an hour, all four of us paddling most of the way. Saw several mallards and many campers.

We aspired to camp close to Canada tonight but when the monopolist of the motor portage pulled in he discovered a shortage of gas, a flat tire, and other appropriate objections to an extra trip on Saturday evening. So we loaded the stuff back in the canoe and pulled over to a pretty rock point and philosophically pitched camp. We called it Flat-tire Camp but enjoyed it,—until the wind went down about bedtime and the mosquitoes arrived. We spent the night in guerrilla fighting and at daylight they started a general offensive and routed us out.

Aug. 9 It rained a bit during the night and the morning turned out sparkling cool. Some mallards passed over during breakfast. A launch arrived from Winton before eight and took us across the 4 mile portage and on to Bailey Bay west of Prairie Portage. We stopped at the Canadian Ranger Station to get our licenses but nobody home. Henry Chosa, who took us on this trip, is a real character and a good hand. He told us a Minneapolis man was starting to build cottages on the islands of Basswood Lake this fall—so that's the end of the wilderness south of the boundary.

It rained going over the portage from Bailey Bay but we found our outfit carries nicely in a single trip. The lake we came to (Meadow Lake?) runs north for a mile or so and then empties west by a very short portage into another lake which runs west for a couple of miles and then sharp north. Just after the north turn the wind got so bad we camped.

Previously we had landed on a little island to see if it contained

a good camp site and found it loaded with big blueberries. We filled up.

Saw two deer yards in this east arm, where all the shore cedars were trimmed up 6 feet high.

Tried for fish where the Meadow (?) Lake stream empties in. Carl hooked a small pike but lost him.

Our new camp is on a wind-swept rock point. Driving tent-pegs we got all mussed up with blueberry juice.

Nearby is the recent sign of a large bear—evidently been eating raspberries and had visited this blueberry island for his dessert.

It is now 4 P.M. and we have camp all made, a kettle of hominy is on the coals, the boys have hung up a bucket of blueberries. All that's lacking is the fish for supper—Carl is out after him.

We don't know what lake we're on, and don't care . . .

Carl later came in with a nice pike—we fried the planks and found it excellent. After supper trolled deep for trout but no strikes. Explored a quiet bay running south. A beaver was swimming around it. Found a plain portage going south and on the other end of it came upon a big water with sawed logs among

the driftwood—evidently Basswood Lake. A big red buck was
feeding on the shore.

It blew hard all night and we had a comfortable mosquito-
less sleep.

Aug. 10 After a fine blueberry breakfast with loon music we
packed up and hit north. Found the outlet—a little marshy
river in which were a dozen big black mallards. This took us to
a small lake full of water lilies which we called the Pike Pond
because it was full of small pike. Down the river we found it
lost under big boulders but portaged to a big lake nearby. Saw
a camp on it with four people—on asking them we found ourselves in North Bay. So we cut east to a stream coming out of
the Shade Lake chain. At the portage at the head of this stream
we bumped into Carl's friend Jim Harper and Mrs. Harper, just
coming out. Had lunch with them.

Went on through a series of beaver-flooded Lakes—South,
Center, North, and into Shade. Camped in a little bay in the
east end of Shade. Right now we are having a time catching
fish for supper—there are small bass here but we can't get any
strikes.

There are entirely too many signs of old camps here—even
a big crop of regular house flies. A flock of fine black mallards
passing over at sunset I think helped crystallize our desire to
strike off into unfrequented country. So on—

Aug. 11   After a comfortable night, we set off to the north. The sun was just dispersing a soft fog when we carried down into Tray Lake—a fine little white water unspoiled by beaver-flooding. Here we tried both for bass and trout but couldn't raise anything. Then came a long portage into Cray Lake. Just as Carl and I arrived at the end of the portage Starker and Luna set up a shout from a nearby point—they had hooked a fine bass and we all went over to help land him. We all voted to camp here and have some fishing. Found a fine place on the north shore. While Carl and I were doing some chores Starker and Luna set off on a little fishing trip and came back with four fine bass. We then had a swim and some lunch and a nap, and picked a mess of blueberries. There was bear sign in the berry patch. In the evening after a bass dinner we all turned out for a fishing spree. None of us have ever experienced such hot bass fishing. Three times two of us had bass jumping out and shaking the hook simultaneously. Everybody caught bass till their arm was tired. They struck best between sunset and dusk. They were lying in the old beaver-flooded timber along the shore. We put them all back. This would be a glorious fly-fishing lake. We found our scales would not weigh the small fish, of which we caught many which do not show on the record.

Twice we jumped black mallards from up on the bank, each time in the vicinity of blueberry bushes. Next day on Yum-Yum we practically proved they were after berries when we twice jumped them from the face of steep rocks thirty feet above water and covered with blueberry bushes. After all how foolish they would be *not* to eat these fine dew-covered berries dangling from every bank!

Aug. 12   After a very early breakfast we turned out for a last round with the bass. We repeated last night's performance and had a hilarious time. Put them all back.

Packed up and portaged over a little-used trail full of moose sign into Little Tray Lake. Saw bass jumping here but did not stop to fish. Then over a short portage into a lily-covered river which emptied into an arm of Yum-Yum. After trolling unsuccessfully and exploring the various arms of the lake we camped on a fine gently sloping granite point and then set out in earnest for trout. Put the copper line (about 150 feet) on top of the silk casting line and weighted it with an ordinary large sinker.

This let out at an angle of about 30° from horizontal in slow paddling and gave us good depth. In the mouth of the arm from which the portage comes I hooked a fine fish. We were surprised at the lively action of the copper line. When he hove in sight we found he was a fine trout. By towing him we played him out without making any sharp angles between the rod and the line. He proved to be a fine 3½ pounds.

We made tracks for camp and fried him, with macaroni as a side-dish. As we were washing dishes we saw big splashes on the opposite shore and thought it was a moose. Soon we realized however that the splashes were beaver. Carl now gave the fish a round. Caught a pike—we never suspected they got down so deep. Next Carl set another fish which proved to be a big trout. We hung him up and turned in to the patter of rain, all of us dog tired and I with some rheumatism in one shoulder and ribs where I fell on a snag the other day. Beaver splashed around us as we went to sleep.

Aug. 13   Slept late, breakfasting luxuriously in a cool breeze at 6:30. Chored around camp for a while and now are all set for a day's excursion into Kahshahpi Lake.

At the outlet of the lake we found an entrancing rocky glen

with a deep pool covered with multi-colored water-lily leaves. Pale birches and blueberries overhung the mossy banks, and just below the stream gurgled down a cascade of boulders. Overhead hung a great cliff with colored lichens and gnarled pines and cedars. It was quite the loveliest spot I have ever seen. I attempted some pictures but they probably will not do justice without the colors.

We found the portage to be a very old unimproved route blockaded by three beaver ponds and flanked by frequent muskegs under high cliffs. It was much harder going afoot than it would have been by canoe. The direction is west, not south as shown on the map, and the distance is much greater than the map shows. At noon, having not yet reached the lake, we attempted to cut across country westward, but found ourselves in a seemingly endless succession of spruce swamps and granite knolls covered with scrubby pine and blueberries. So we struck back to the lower beaver pond and had lunch and a nap, first however filling up on blueberries which were extra large and sweet.

This whole country is covered with moose and deer sign, but we saw no evidence of grouse. The moose seem to browse the shoots of alder, willow, moosewood maple. There were beds in the tall grass bordering the muskeg. Beaver trails led up into the

woods everywhere, and in the ponds were big lodges so old as to be covered with grass. A flock of grown but flightless black mallards swam around in the ponds accompanied and led by a single merganser.

Carl knocked a squirrel out of a tree with his slingshot but he was not hit squarely and got away. He hit him second shot at twenty yards, indicating that the slingshots may be pretty effective pot-boilers.

This river where it leaves Yum-Yum is in a narrow gorge and seemingly easily dammed. Why then have the beavers not raised the whole lake as in the case of Cray, Shade, etc.? Carl suggests that the very narrowness of the outlet would cause floods to tear out the dam. If this is the case, the beaver seeks the wide dam site, not the narrow one. It will be interesting to observe how this hypothesis works out.

Coming back in the canoe Luna trolled with the copper line and landed a fine trout well down in the bay. We turned him loose, already having a sack of planked trout steak hung in a tree at camp.

We had a pleasant evening cooking a trout chowder with bannocks, and listening to the loons and splashing of beaver. Luna caught a pike right by the campfire. The pike were working on minnows gathered around some rice we had spilled in the water.

Forgot to wind my watch yesterday so had to set my watch by guess, hereinafter known as Yum-Yum Meridian.

Argued till bedtime as to whether to risk the venture into Kahshahpiwigamak or to return by the safe and sane Dell Lake chain into North Bay. Being well fed and full of courage we passed an Order in Council to return via Kahshahpi. The big gamble is the negotiability of the long portage from the southwest arm of Kahshahpi into Rock Lake. We shall see!

Aug. 14   Up before sunup. A soft fog on the lake—much loon music—a beaver cutting a wide circle around the fire as he wended his way lodge-ward for his day's rest. Carl and I flapped flapjacks and then tried to wake the boys. They wouldn't budge until we told Luna there was a jar of jam open, and Starker that a shoal of minnows had gathered and were doubtless followed by an escort of pike. Thereupon they came a-running.

———————

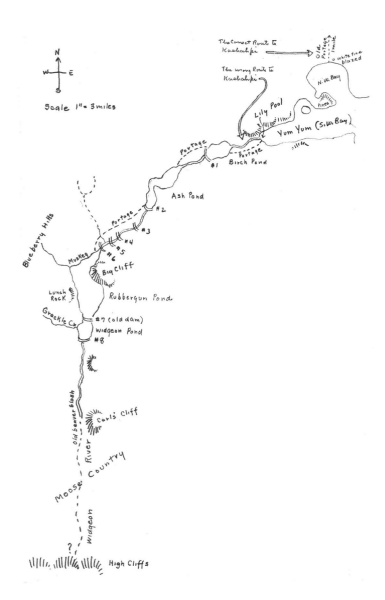

N

W   E

S

Scale 1" = 3 miles

The Correct Route to
Kashahpi

The wrong Route to
Kashahpi

Old Portage
1 mile

white pine
blazed

N.W. Bay

Lily Pool

Pines

Yum Yum (S.W. Bay)

Portage

#1

Portage
Birch Pond

Ash Pond

Portage

#2

#3

Blueberry Hills

Muskeg

#4

#5

#6

Big Cliff

Lunch Rock

Rubbergun Pond

Grackle Cr.

#7 (old dam)

Widgeon Pond

#8

Carl's Cliff

Old beaver Slash

Moose River Country

Widgeon

?

High Cliffs

1:00 P.M. (Y.Y. Mer.) We are back at the Lily Pool on Yum-Yum. We started down the outlet about seven this morning, cutting our own portages into the first two beaver ponds and sliding the canoe over six other dams. We got well below yesterday's explorations but still no Kahshahpi, while Carl went down a mile and climbed a high cliff where he could see the river for several miles more but no lake. Moreover it runs straight south while the map has it heading nearly north.

This country down the river is full of moose sign but the beaver workings are much older than those above—in fact we found old dams from which all wood had rotted entirely away. They were covered with grass and the floods had torn spillways through them.

On the lowest pond reached with the canoe we flushed a pair of widgeons. Saw our black ducks again. I killed a squirrel with the rubbergun, hitting him in the head, second shot, at 25 feet.

———————

On our way back up the now familiar Yum-Yum we took a second look at the northwest bay just to satisfy our curiosity as to the whereabouts of the elusive Kahshahpi portage. We didn't think it probable that Yum-Yum would have two outlets, yet the direction of Widgeon River was so at variance with the map that

something seemed wrong. Sure enough, at the bottom of the Northwest Bay was a blazed white pine and a plain trail headed north. We had missed it entirely on our first exploration because we were looking for a portage *down an outlet* stream, whereas this trail *ran up a hill*. This error was natural enough. The real greenhorn performance was in not smelling a rat sooner on the *wrong direction* of the Widgeon River.

We walked over the newly found portage just to make sure. It runs through several upland muskegs and alder swamps which must be pretty soft during a wet season but otherwise it is an easy route through beautiful shady woods. It emerges on a little arm of Kahshahpi affording a calm easy landing. The rest of the shore in sight was steep cliffs.

There was lots of moose and deer sign on the portage. Coming back a snowshoe rabbit hopped across the trail and stopped in the alders about 25 feet distant. We all popped at him with our slingshots. At the second shot I hit him behind the ear with a marble and knocked him cold. It was such a funny performance to kill a rabbit with a rubbergun that we all roared with laughter.

Soon after a cock partridge hopped out of the trail—the only one seen thus far on the trip. We popped several marbles at him but failed to hit. The grouse seem to have reared no broods this year.

Starker picked up a big pike in Yum-Yum on our way back. Portaged into Leg and Cray and camped at our old bass grounds, feeling very much at home in our old camp. A partridge flew across the lake to the high hill opposite camp as we were cooking supper. Dined on a gallon of bean soup stocked with ham and squirrel. It was delicious. We slept the sleep of the just after a very satisfying failure to camp on the elusive Kahshahpi. Moral: Look at your compass hard and often, and if the country doesn't agree with the map find out who's a liar and why.

Aug. 15   As I sit against a mossy rock writing up the sequel to yesterday's adventures, a cool breeze fans the blueberry bushes which dangle big dewy fruit over the very page of this journal. Starker and Luna, after being prodded through the job of dishes and beds, are organizing the fishing tackle for the day

with thoroughness and enthusiasm. Carl is trying a new way of putting the tumpline on the boys' packs. Gentle waves are lapping the canoe in invitation for the day's travel. Down the lake a loon calls, and back in the aspens a pine squirrel tells us to get the hell out o' here. We will!

Only a few strikes as we tried the bass on the way out. Stopped at Dell Lake and caught several bass and a dozen perch on an improvised bait made out of a small hook, a piece of perch belly, a red rag, and a nail. After we had cleaned the perch for lunch we found the flesh full of encysted parasites and had to throw them away.

Came through to Lily Lake via Wolf Lake. Camped on a fine shelving rock carpeted with wintergreen and moss, where we had a fine swim, a superlative lunch, and a nap with a good many flies.

On down to North Bay by way of a pretty lily-padded stream the banks of which were tramped down by deer and moose tracks. Found a stiff head wind blowing up Basswood so we decided to take the inside passage on the west side of the bay. We found this very interesting country full of pretty camp sites on the smooth shelving rock points, with deep bays full of green grass and lily pads. At the portage of the inside passage a doe and her yearling were browsing pads. The wind blew in our faces so we were able, by keeping quiet when her head was up, to paddle up within 25 feet. Then she got our wind and got out with a snort and a bound, Carl snapping her broadside before she disappeared in the brush. We had gotten between the doe and the yearling and they had a lot of whistling and hesitating to do back in the brush before they finally got together again.

At the end of the passage we bucked a mile of hard wind across the open bay, camping on a lovely pine point on the east shore. A flock of black ducks flushed from the lee of the point as we landed, and we later found all the blueberries cleaned up from the open ground near the shore.

This was quite the prettiest camp we have had. The rocks form a fine fireplace, tables, easy chairs, and landing, while a flat rock in an opening is covered with deep dry moss and duff forming a ready-made bed. The whole point is covered with blueberries. An International Boundary Post, set in the rock,

came very near being in the right position to use as a tent peg. We lived high on fried pike steaks and creamed macaroni with cheese, and turned in at ten after a delightful day, all a little blue at tomorrow's departure for the land of neckties and boiled shirts.

Aug. 16   Up at 3:30 (Yum-Yum Meridian; we afterward found Central time to be an hour slow) and got underway at 5:30—a tolerably good start. Several of our black ducks came back to their little bay as we ate breakfast. It was cloudy and threatening rain so we missed the chance to take pictures of this especially pretty camp. Arrived at the Ranger Station at 7:00 (Yum-Yum = 8:00 Central) and paid for our licenses. Heading on up the bay toward Four Mile Portage we saw a launch, and hailing it found it headed for Winton, so we hopped aboard, thus ending our wilderness trip.

Reunion

AL, Carl, Fritz, Flick
near Stronghurst, Ill.

Nov. 15, 1925
Cold, cloudy, N.W. wind
New wet snow

Carl	Fritz	AL	
7	5	12	Quail
2	1		Rabbit
9	6	12	AL: 38 shells. No doubles. 2 lost birds.

This was more nearly goose than quail weather, but after sixteen bobwhiteless years even a bad day was welcome. Incidentally, this was the first time the three of us had ever been on a quail hunt all together.

Evidently because of the weather conditions, all the birds were bushed up under hedges, grape tangles, and like spots of bare ground. We didn't find a covey in the corn and saw only one track in the snow, and that one was made after we had started a covey to run away down a fence line. Several of the covies rose wild, especially before getting thoroughly scattered, and cold feet made good shooting difficult.

Flick did pretty well, considering his unorthodox education on the western running birds. He made only one firm point on a covey but many on singles, and he did no precipitate flushing even on running bunches. One noticeable fact was that even Flick found none of the singles which flew off with hanging legs, although we searched hard for them. Evidently they lie very close. Between us there were 3 or 4 of these. We also lost several birds that came down straight but were evidently winged and did some hard running.

The first covey we scattered down a hedge and had some comparatively easy shooting. We then drew a blank on several pretty coverts, but found a second bunch in a crab thicket roofed over with a grape vine tangle. These scattered nicely in the corn but somehow we didn't punish them much. On this bunch I made an exceptionally long kill on a towering single but couldn't find him.

In the same locust patch we found a covey of ⅔ grown birds

that we didn't follow very hard because of their small size. This is not very logical, of course. It would have been better to let the big strong birds off easy and harvest the little ones which had a lesser chance of getting through the winter.

By this time it was noon and our feet were in pretty cold storage so we found a dryish place under a box elder tree, shed our boots, and took on some broiled pork chops and toast. There was more comfort than propriety about this camp, the fire being surrounded by concentric rings of the following:

First: Pork chops broiling and sizzling on sticks.

Second: Toast, browning ditto.

Third: Socks, steaming ditto.

Fourth: Boots, likewise steaming.

Fifth: Feet, not only steaming but aching like a newly
     pulled tooth.

Sixth: Hunters and dogs.

After taking on the chops and partially dried footwear it was amusing with what circumspection we went about the old job of knocking wet snow off the brush and weeds. We hit off into

new territory and very promptly two big covies flushed wild and scattered into a woodlot. We got rid of a lot of shells here without hurting the birds very much, partly because most of the birds would not lie and the singles ran badly after scattering. We put more shot into the tree-trunks than into the quail.

Proceeding car-ward Flick located a very large covey which we saw on the ground under a heavy grape tangle but never succeeded in wholly flushing. We got only one bird out of this whole layout.

Almost immediately afterward got a nice covey which flew into posted land, but we got two that headed back toward open territory. By now it was pretty dark, and we went back to the car, first having an unpleasant argument with the owner of said posted land who thought we had purposely skirted his fence to steal his birds.

On our way out at sunset we saw a beautiful bunch sail with bowed wings into the jack oaks, evidently having flown down from the hills for roosting in the extensive jack oak coverts.

All day long we saw cat tracks and I think one fox track. Saw one very large horned owl. Many cardinals.

I think there is no solution for this posted land problem except private leases. I am surprised and reassured at the numbers of covies per farm. A couple of farms now raise 6–8 covies—enough for two men—and with reasonable preservation of coverts and vermin control the number of covies could be increased.

Census   9 covies x 15 birds each =   135 quail
                                                    25 rabbits

P.S. I asked the boys if the bittersweet berry is eaten by wild life. They say cedar waxwings once worked on one of the vines in the yard.

Course of the Fox

where the shot turned him

distance 30 yds

Carlo's course - Carl

edge of upland

fresh den

probable course of fox

my course

aub

fallen limb under which fox lay

draw

Fletche course - Fletr

Id fletchs course / course

Red Fox Day

AL, Carl, Flick   Nov. 16, 1925
Bluffs N. of Hopper Ill.   Cloudy, cool, w. breeze
                                                      2–4:30 P.M.

CSL	AL	
2	2	Quail
	1	Rabbit

| 2 | 3 | AL: 7 shells, 2.3 per bird. No doubles. 1 cripple lost. |

We had hardly left the car at the foot of the bluff when we heard Flick put up quail out of a thicket of saplings on the bank of Allison Creek. Possibly they flushed wild. Carl guessed they would scale the bluff so we started up and soon put up a pair. I was standing on one leg and missed with the right and probably with the left too but Carl in any event got the second one.

We skirted the edge of the bluff into the Allison canyon and I noticed a freshly dug den in the hillside. A few yards further, rounding the point of a hogback, a big fiery red fox darted out of the cover of a fallen limb in the bottom of the draw and started up the opposite slope. I shot about fifteen yards from the place he started. He slipped for an instant and then turned at right angles along the slope and got behind a tree before I could fire the other barrel.

Carl meanwhile was standing on top of the hill where he could see the whole performance, but being some 10 yards further with brush in the way he couldn't shoot to advantage.

Flick, when the fox jumped, was below and behind me but saw him instantly and was soon dashing after him, not returning for a long time. Once we thought we heard him bark and ran forward, but it proved to be a dog in a farmyard below us. The fox was going strong at 150 yards so I don't think he was seriously hurt.

Foxy Thoughts (ex post facto, but not post mortem): I was shooting 2¾" Remington Duck Load 1 oz 7½ c. shot. With such small shot, shooting virtually into his back muscles, the ribs protected by a long angle through the fur, I should have realized that the only chance I had was to deliver such a shock as to knock him over and thus gain time enough to slip in a No. 4 or No. 6 load, both of which I had in my shell vest. Realizing this, I should have pulled both triggers at once at the earliest possible instant. This might have given Flick time to rush in and hold him. I was, as a matter of fact, so dazed by the fact of seeing a fox at all that I shot an instant slower than I would have shot at a quail.

Evidently what happened was that the fox was at work on his den as we came up. He tried to sneak over the hogback and up the draw to get away from me, but seeing Carl on top he squatted under the fallen limb, but had to get out as I rounded the hogback.

Well anyhow the whole episode shows how much excitement a fox can cause by simply carrying away a few birdshot. If we had hung up his hide we would have put on a war dance the rest of the afternoon. He was in magnificent feather and seemed over 4 feet long overall.

———————

Seeing foxes under every bush, we proceeded on our quail hunt. Put up a big covey in the corn on top of a hill with a deserted farm house and orchard on it. We couldn't see them alight because they flew south over the crest of the hill, and spent a long time trying to find them. We finally found they were scattered in the corn around a little pothole but were lying so close that they had to be stepped on before they would get out. The corn was tall and ungathered and hard to shoot in but we managed to garner 3 birds.

Coming home at night Flick again flushed four birds from the thicket at the car and they towered up the bluff over Carl's head, but we didn't see them in time to shoot.

Still seeing and talking red, we mushed home through the deep mud after one of those brave adventurous days that we will smoke pipes about in our old age.

Census   2 covies quail, 20 birds
                 1 RED FOX
                 10 Rabbits

Current River Trip

Nov. 26   Met Carl and Fritz in St. Louis 11 A.M. A cold windy day, gradually clearing up. Reached Leeper 9 P.M. and stayed at Ozark Hotel.

Nov. 27   Arrived Van Buren 9 A.M. and hit the river at 10:30. A fine sunny morning. The river is very fast for a mile or so below town, then calms down somewhat. About noon we had our first excitement when 30 mallards came up the river and began to circle the timber a hundred yards to our left, settling down in a little backwater. We sneaked them, only I going all the way. I got within 30 yards but only got one on the rise; alibi: dark background and brush. They circled and came over us. Everybody missed; alibi: too far. Just as we were leaving five came back, but seeing our boat went on. We landed again to wait when 8 got out unexpectedly below us, one big drake passing within easy range of Carl and myself. Alibi: none. We named this Bungle Bay.

Fritz later killed a green wing that flushed from the bank.

Camped in time for a little quail hunt. Found a small covey in a cornfield and got 4. I killed a huge rabbit going home. We had quail and sweet potatoes—not a bad first night supper, and spent a comfortable night. This camp was full of a dry weed whose pods tinkled as one walked through.

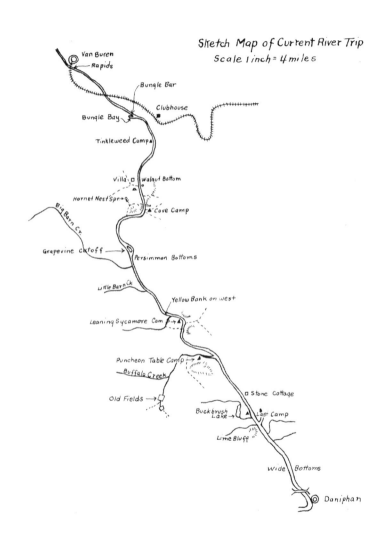

Sketch Map of Current River Trip
Scale 1 inch = 4 miles

Van Buren
Rapids

Bungle Bar
Clubhouse
Bungle Bay
Tinkleweed Camp

Villa Walnut Bottom
Hornet Nest Spr.
Big Barn Cr.
Cove Camp

Grapevine Cutoff
Persimmon Bottoms

Little Barn Ck.

Yellow Bank on west
Leaning Sycamore Camp

Puncheon Table Camp
Buffalo Creek

Stone Cottage
Old Fields
Buckbrush Lake
Last Camp
Lime Bluff

Wide Bottoms

Daniphan

Nov. 28   Up before daylight. No mishap except that tinkleweed seed got in the coffee. Hit the river about eight, stopping here and there to hunt quail. Found 2 covies and did well on them, 9 altogether. Both were in the corn. Killed 2 bluebills (singles) in the river. Camped shortly after noon in a protected cove. Got camp all dolled up. Carl and Fritz then prospected for turkey while I got dinner. The boys report the hills all burned and flinty. Had a comfortable evening, with music and walnuts by the fire. During the night we had a sharp shower that sprayed through the lean-to and got Fritz' bed wet. We had put up the tent so the outfit kept dry.

Nov. 29   Cooked coffee-cake before daylight and made an early start for a turkey trip across the creek. Hunted westerly for about 3 miles getting into better and less burned country with red-haws in the bottoms. No turkey sign. A razorback sow charged Flick when he eyed her offspring too closely. Ate lunch on a high hill and took a little nap in a sunny place. Then went north a mile and thence easterly down a beautiful valley with haws and an incredible crop of thick-shelled hickory nuts and fat squirrels, of which Carl killed one who stuck his chin up between a fork. He tipped him so lightly that we had a footrace when he fell. Here, just as we got into ideal turkey country, we again struck farms. Flick flushed a covey of quail on which Fritz made a double. Killed four altogether.

Back at the Hornet Nest Spring we had seen another covey with two hawks in attendance—a sharp-skin and a Cooper. Did not shoot here as we suspected turkey.

It was a long jog back to the river which we struck at the "Villa" and had to skirt a bluff to get down to the boat. Coon-sign (either pokeberries or black gum berries) in a bayou. The soil in the cornfields is very heavy going after the rain.

We came into camp all fagged out but soon recovered after a monumental dinner. We started with a mallard, a teal, and a big pot of mashed potatoes but this leaving a vacancy we roasted three quail to boot, and then ate walnuts for an hour before we were finally full-up.

The quail we cleaned tonight had whole corn, seeds about radish size, and green leaves (probably *Oxalis*, which is abundant in the cornfields) in the crops.

Had a comfortable night in spite of a sharp frost.

Nov. 30   A hominy-omelet before daylight is a good start toward a fine day. After breakfast we dolled up our faces, washed
handkerchiefs, and made a leisurely start. A fine sunny day to
ride down the river. Ate lunch in a marvelously pretty cutoff
with a deep blue-green current flowing under an avenue of
stately sycamores. We sat in the sun on a little bench and took
a nap and then moved on, in spite of the temptation to stop
and camp. Taking a little quail hunt in a big bottom on the
east side Fritz found a persimmon tree and we spent half an
hour clubbing "simmons" and spitting seeds. Toward evening
we had difficulty in finding a campsite which combined wood,
dryness, shelter, privacy, fishing hole, boat landing, quail and
turkey ground. It was dark before we finally found a suitable
place under a huge leaning sycamore to which we pitched the
lean-to. Luckily we had bean soup already cooked. We ate an
even gallon of it and went to bed.

Dec. 1   After breakfast we idled around an hour setting fish
lines and getting up oak wood. Another fine sunny day, the
threatened rain having passed by. Caught a hideous waterdog
on one line almost as soon as we had set it. There was another
one on it in the evening.

Went on a quail hunt in the corn surrounding our woods. Found only one covey. Shot rather badly in spite of the fact that they scattered in a coral-berry bottom. One field through which we passed was lined with walnut trees with incredible supplies of big nuts lying in the corn furrows. Also found a few butter nuts.

After a rabbit soup by Carl (excellent by the way, mixed with julienne and noodles) crossed the river and after setting a trap went on a quail hunt. Found a covey of 15. They scattered in an oak thicket and we didn't shine at all in getting them out, especially after Flick got excited about a rabbit nearly as big as himself and flushed several birds wild. Then went up the hollow prospecting for turkeys but found no sign. Coming back we picked up a dozen sweet turnips from a patch planted in the corn.

We had set sour-dough at noon and this evening had the finest loaf of hot bread one could imagine, together with broiled bluebills and fried yams. What one can cook on these oak coals is nearly unbelievable. This was a cold night but we weathered it nicely with the help of a cane bed Fritz had built.

Dec. 2   Again made a leisurely start, partly because of needed sock-washing, shoe greasing etc., and partly because it was frosty cold. We dislike to leave our old sycamore.

Stopped at an uninhabited cornfield on the east bank and soon flushed a big covey of 15 (most coveys here are small, even where unshot). They flew almost into my face and I was so rattled that I only slobbered one instead of making an easy double. They disappeared over a slight rise in the corn and in spite of an hour's hunting we found only one scattered bird which Carl hit as he climbed the timber on the bluff and he dropped against a limestone cliff. Flick and Carl did some alpine stuff in retrieving him.

Went on down the river and soon came to the mouth of the Buffalo Fork. Took a walk up to explore for camps. Flick flushed a small covey in the cane on the edge of the corn and Carl and I each got one of the scatters.

Decided to push up the Buffalo to a nice camp about a half mile up. Had to climb over a sycamore snag as we pushed the boat under, just as we did on the Rillito in the Gulf of the Colorado. At the head of navigation we made a magnificent camp, including a table made of a single slab of lightning-riven white oak two feet wide and five long. Cut two backloads of cane for a bed. Had a monumental dinner of roast quail, and noodles with "Krackelchen" made of Swede bread. They are infinitely better than ordinary croutons. Set the traps before supper.

Dec. 3   Cornbread and syrup for breakfast. Shaved and hung out the bedding and got dolled up generally. Some coon hunters came by at daylight and said there were turkey in the ridges back of camp so we renewed our turkey zeal and hit the flints.

Hunted up a draw of Buffalo running southeast. The lower part of it was full of gray squirrels. These are smaller and the fox squirrels and rabbits larger than I have ever seen. This draw looked very good, the day was sunny and fine, and still hunting through the woods was a keen pleasure in spite of the absence of turkeys. Once a crow gave me palpitations by cawing like a gobbler.

We met on the main ridge at the head of the draw and lunched on roast quail under a hickory tree full of fine nuts, of which we ate a large bait. Thence westerly along the ridge and hunted down another draw which opened into some old fields full of springs and surrounded by laden haw trees. It looked good enough to make a turkey's mouth water but there was no sign.

Thence down the main creek hunting quail. After Carl and I had cut for camp Fritz found a big covey and killed three, including a double on the rise, but he lost two because the place was full of cockleburs and Flick wouldn't work.

A wonderful dinner of squirrel julienne with a big loaf of hot sourdough that had raised the lid of the Dutch oven during the day and spilled dough (which we fried for Flick).

A warm night, and we made the most of it in beds just in from the warm sun. Coon hunters and their hounds serenaded most of the night.

Dec. 4   A balmy dawn. The Carolina wrens are singing as I write up yesterday's and speculate upon today's events. I think we shall have a storm. Fritz does too as he is rustling extra wood and stowing away clothes from the clothes-line.

I slipped off the "wharf" this morning while washing in the creek and now write barefoot in perfect comfort. That's how warm it is.

Made a grand quail hunt today. Found four covies, two of them small or partial. We shot badly and lost several down birds due to Flick's getting so tied up with cockleburs that he gave up and couldn't smell.

We found the birds mostly in the corn, the burrier the better. Later in the day they are in the cane fringes or heavy weed patches. They do not frequent the light weed patches or grass as they do further north.

Flick caught a rabbit today all on his own. We were looking for a cripple in a cane patch when Flick made a plunge and we thought we had our bird, but he came out proudly holding aloft a kicking bunny.

As we were eating supper two horned owls turned up within gunshot of camp. One had a distinctly deeper voice than the other. They moved about a great deal from tree to tree. It was a thrilling sight to see one swoop down off the hill against the gray afterglow.

A warm night, threatening rain.

Dec. 5 Up at 5:30 and through breakfast by gray of dawn. I lifted the traps while the boys packed up camp. Our baggage has a shrunken look after three days feasting at our puncheon table.

Made about 8 miles down the river with a north wind behind

us. There is much wide still water in this section which must be paddled. Tried one cornfield on the east bank but found only a single scattered bird. Began to meet people in this section, including one Current River "Steamboat" with a stern wheel.

Camped in a high sandy bottom in tall oak and sycamore timber and rigged up a fine camp in half an hour, including a cane bed. This cane makes excellent bedding if laid butts down parallel with the length of the bed. It has a faint fragrance that is very agreeable.

After a snack of lunch we found a covey in a ragweed patch within 150 yards of camp and got four birds on the rise, losing a fifth down a possum hole. Flick made a brilliant find on one cripple which had crawled under a pile of driftwood within 2 feet of a dead bird we had already picked up. Flick worked much better after a greasing of his under parts last night. He is rubbed pretty raw by the weeds and burrs. I got a scatter from this covey.

We next jumped a covey in a high woods undergrown with cane. These scatters were the hardest flyers I have ever seen. They would go up like a skyrocket to the very tops of the trees and then as suddenly pitch down into the cane again. We must have burned half a box of shells on this covey with only one kill by Carl.

Had roast rabbit (Flick's) and macaroni for supper and spent a pleasant evening recounting past adventures on the Colorado delta. A bit of rain during the night but cold again by morning.

Dec. 6 Our last day of hunting. All shaved in the hope of improving our shooting a bit. It is cool and cloudy.

Tried the quail above camp on the west bank. Found the canebrake covey and did a little better with them, getting three. Hunted a lot of new country that looked ideal but found no birds. Saw a large flock of doves but couldn't get near them. Coming back I unexpectedly flushed a big mallard drake out of the head of the buckbrush lake. I shot through some saplings at him but failed to connect. This is the first mallard we have seen since leaving the cove camp.

In the afternoon we crossed the river and while cutting mistletoe for the girls Flick put up a beautiful covey out of the tinkleweeds but nobody had a loaded gun. We got two however out of a belated rise and later a couple of scatters.

Next hunted some lovely ragweed patches to the south and found a nice covey. Had a hard time finding them again due to overestimating the distance they flew. Finally got them out. Carl put five right over Fritz and me and we scored four clean misses overhead as they pitched down into the cane. Later we retrieved our reputation a bit by killing some singles. It now began to rain and we regretfully left the whistling birds behind us as we left for camp.

Dec. 7   A sad morning packing up and wrestling with tempta- tion to hunt another day. As a parting ceremony Carl smoked his last "Philadelphia Bayuk," I nailed a pair of worn-out pants to an oak tree, and Fritz packed up his favorite dish-mop as parting ceremonies to a famous trip. I sit here on the cane bed, the stripped camp around me and the boys waiting to be off, while the pileated taps an oak limb and the last oak coals of our last camp smoke faintly and die away.

Providentially, it rained all the way down the river to Do- niphan, taking some of the edge off our desire to be hunting instead of leaving.

Arrived at Doniphan 10 A.M., got underway at noon, arrived in St. Louis at 11 P.M. where we broke up the party.

MISCELLANEOUS OBSERVATIONS
CURRENT RIVER TRIP—1926

Tame Squirrels   The big fox squirrels are indifferent to one's noisy approach through the dry leaves. Carl suggests this is because the squirrels and the pigs both live in the same places (namely, the hickory groves) and they are accustomed to hear- ing pigs rustling around all day. We seldom saw fox and gray squirrels on the same ground.

Sexes in Quail   Of 18 birds in camp on Dec. 4 only 7 were cocks. It is rather noticeable that one kills more hens than cocks. Of 7 additional birds killed Dec. 4, 5 were cocks. 4 of these 5 cocks were from one covey.

Canebrakes   Cane does not grow at Van Buren but increases gradually in abundance as one goes down the river. It occurs only in fields which are fenced against hogs during the growing season. Usually this means that it is confined to the wooded edges of fields and to the riverbank. The line of demarcation between the fenced and unfenced ground is always sharp.

Nuts Even the thickest shelled hickories seem to be eaten by hogs, but the walnuts are untouched, evidently because of the unsavory hulls. Squirrels get at the kernels of butternuts by gnawing into the ends and then scooping. The big-nut hickory nuts remaining on the ground at this season are all wormy or empty. How the hogs and squirrels distinguish the poor nuts is a mystery.

Mistletoe is confined almost entirely to the riverbank, the running water evidently ameliorating the winter cold. Fritz saw one bunch in the hills near Doniphan.

Habits of Quail Quail do not seem to use short grass or weeds, even when available. Coveys found in the morning are usually in the corn; those in the afternoon are usually in the cane or ragweed or occasionally in the tinkleweed bottoms. When flushed most coveys go either to the cane or the wooded bluffs. Scatters in timber often skyrocket to the tops of the trees and then pitch down again, when it would be entirely practicable for them to fly through the timber.

Lily River Trip

There were only about twelve hours between the receipt of a letter from Carl saying he was too busy to go fishing and a wire saying he was on his way.

June 24, 1927—a Friday noon—we set sail in Tom Coleman's car and reached Lily, Wisc. (via Oshkosh & Shawano) at noon. Three miles above Lily we went up a wood road along the Little Lily and spent two hours finding out the road was impassable and the creek too small for flies. Then we camped in an aspen grove at the mouth, thus:

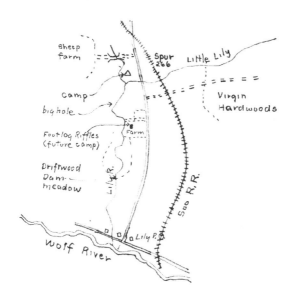

Fished till 8 o'clock and each got a few. Turned in very tired in a sudden rain and had a hot mosquitoey night.

June 25 Out before sunup—so early we had to make sure we had "valid daylight"—a phrase to conjure by the rest of the trip. They bit nicely for a while in the morning. In the evening the wind blew the creek full of mayflies and nothing would bite. The events of the day were a 9½" rainbow caught by Tom, a 10" brook by Starker, and a woodcock seen by Carl.

639

June 26   Slept till 6 o'clock. Each got a few in the morning—21 trout so far. I saw two mother grouse with broods. In evening found a new and very pretty pool and riffle at the upper end of the farm below camp. There are shallow stretches above and below this but it is the nicest place we have found so far. Good camp sites in blue grass pasture full of enormous old white pine stumps.

June 27   In morning we all went to the footlog riffle. Starker and I got a few but Tom and Carl had poor luck. We have about concluded that the big Lily is about the prettiest stream we have ever seen but contains only small fish. Ten inches is the best we have found.

Boiled tea in a shady place by the creek, where a red squirrel tried to run Carl off the bridgehead. At lunch Tom proposed we take a flier at the Rat River this afternoon. Drove to Blackwell via Wabeno and learned from the section boss how to get in to Flanner (Connor?) Lumber Co. Camp No. 14, whence we walked a mile to the Rat, thusly:

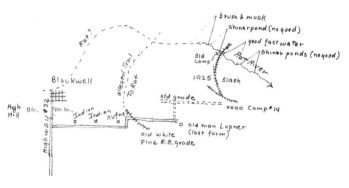

We killed the better part of the afternoon finding out that the quiet ponds were no good and full of shiners, besides being too deep and mucky to wade. For half an hour in the evening we concentrated on the pools in the fast water below the track and caught 7 nice fish averaging 8 inches. The Rat has more water than the Lily but is here narrower, deeper, faster, and badly choked by slash. It is unwadeable.

Had supper at Wabeno and drove to camp and went to bed. Had a bad night on account of "no-see-ums" which went right through mosquito nets and disregarded fly-dope.

June 28   Up early and packed camp. Heard a winter wren sing as we demolished sourdough cakes. A nice breezy morning.

Back at ten, with nobody scoring except Tom who got two ten inchers out of the Little Lily right below camp.

Packed and on the road by noon. Reached Madison 7 P.M.

Total catch about 47 trout, 7 to 11 inches, mostly 7–8.

THE LILY

This pretty river must have been named by some person other than the usual trader or surveyor, and for some reason other than the crass and obvious one that there are lilies in it—for there are none.

The Lily must have been named by some poet-voyageur, and for some more subtle and potent reason—the chance thought, for instance, that not even the Wolf in all his glory is yet arrayed as one of these.

Our poet must have discerned the changeful moods which would have forever mocked the giver of a masculine name to this river. You may come upon her at some dancing shingle where irises and marigolds grow on little mossy islands, and nodding willows dip their branches from wide banks. But within the space of three casts you have passed into a long cool corridor where the current runs swift and dark and deep between the roots of alders and ferns, with here and there a spruce solemnly contemplating your not very solemn attempts to cast a fly. Soon you emerge upon a long pool curving in a wide trouty sweep upon a fallen balsam. What a line you could lay upon that pool, did not the balsam prevent your laying any line at all! Of course you could fish it downstream, but somehow you feel as if that would dampen the gay humor that filled the balsam in its particular place.

The pool gives upon another shingle, on which you may cast high, wide, and handsome, but from which the Lily—except of certain rare and unpredictable evenings—withholds her trout.

One wonders what were the Lily's moods before they took her pines. A dark glory they must have been, in the clearing below the Big Pool—there are stumps which our voyageur could barely have spanned with two lengths of his rifle. What domes those mighty columns must have held against the sky, to be reflected in the Lily! The pines are gone now, but bobolinks hover over their blackened stumps and praise the bluegrass which has taken their place. Odd it is that birds, and rivers, should know what people don't—that bluegrass is the most praiseworthy thing that the white man has brought into this land; the thing that comes nearest atoning for what he has taken away.

The Lily chooses her birds well. In the cool dawn a hundred whitethroats lament in minor chorus that as yet undiscovered tragedy that broke the heart of "Ah—poor Canada." An occasional winter wren breaks in upon them with so jovial a whistle that one is led to think perhaps Canada after all has outgrown her secret sorrow. During the day's fishing anxious mother grouse cluck to their hidden broods and redwings extoll the lush greenness of the little marshes along the Lily's banks. Not until the last evening light is upon the aspens do the thrushes begin. This also is the hour when fishermen go to sleep. Clear at first the ringing cadences, then dimmer with the waning sunset, until at last the windings and unwindings of thrushes' song merge with the windings and unwindings of the Lily and the long lines that fall unerringly upon her trouty pools in fishermen's dreams.

Gila Trip

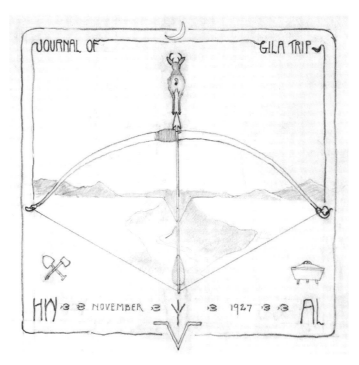

JOURNAL OF   GILA TRIP

HN ·8 8 NOVEMBER 8 ψ 8 1927 8 8 ΑL

Nov. 9   Left N-Bar Ranch with 2 packs 9 AM. Emil* Tipton came with us to take back the stock. Rode down Snow Creek to its mouth where we passed the last autos. A boy on the Middle Fork below Snow Creek had a fine mess of trout up to 9" in length. Saw turkey scratchings near the Trotter place. Arrived at the old Flying V ranch, which Tipton said was the mouth of Canyon Cr., about 2:30, and camped on a watercress spring under two big pines in a little side canyon just north of the old ranch. After lunch Tipton started back with all but one horse while Howard and I spent the rest of the day making camp. Wood scarce due no doubt to the old ranch.

Nov. 10   Up before daylight just at moonset. Got started before sunup. Climbed a high point in the little draw back of camp

*Glenwood P.O., N.M.

Sketch map of Flying V hunting grounds

and made a drive along a nice looking rim but saw no deer and little sign. Concluded that the absence of piñon had caused the deer to move out so we headed east for a high hill that showed piñon through the glasses. Found the true Canyon Creek in a 600' gulch just west of the hill. Boiled tea on the bottom of this gulch. Climbing the other side we promptly began to see lots of deer sign. On a high juniper mesa leading up to the hill we saw that the deer had nearly finished the piñons and were feeding heavily on alligator juniper berries. Made a drive of the Rincon on the west side of this juniper hill. There was a strong S.W. wind which was very favorable. I jumped a yearling which almost ran Howard down. Then in a piñon thicket I jumped 3 very fat does, one of which I found later by the tracks had fawns. All these deer that had a chance jumped *into the wind* rather than up hill.

At 4 P.M. headed down Canyon Creek for camp. Ran into ten deer going to water and feeding on sage in the creek bottom. Could see no horns, but it was a pretty sight.

An Abert squirrel nearly ran into me while we were watching these deer. He was in black phase.

Did not get to the mouth of Canyon Cr. till dark. We thought camp was only a mile or two up the Middle Fork but we encountered a seemingly endless maze of box canyons and S turns in the river. By half past seven we were both pretty nearly all in, and wet from innumerable fordings of the river, so we stopped and boiled some hot water with the sugar left over from lunch. Finally got to camp at 9 P.M. after 3½ hours of steady walking up the Gila. Several deer snorted at us on our way. It was black as pitch till the moon came up about 8:30. Too tired to eat, so we rolled in.

Nov. 11   Spent the morning rustling wood and fixing up around camp, shaving, laundering, and resting from our last night's misadventure. At noon made some tea and took a walk—Howard down the canyon and I to the hills south of the river. Found three squirrels eating Douglas fir cones in one tree and tried to get one shooting straight up with a blunt arrow. Shot too well, as I had to leave an arrow sticking in a limb. The squirrel trotted out his whole collection of profanity and kept it up till I was out of sight.

Found a nice looking juniper mesa with an oak slope below but there were no berries and little deer sign except white-tail. Started back too late and got tangled in a rimrock but near camp. Howard reported nothing seen except some turkey scratchings.

Nov. 12 Started early for Canyon Creek, laying out a "baseline" due east from the old Flying V dugway that climbs out back of camp. Hit Canyon Cr. a little south of where we climbed down yesterday. Found three saddle horses tied on the rim but never located the hunters. Descended one on each end of a rimrock. From a little sharp hogback at my end of the rim I jumped a fine buck. He was lying under a fir. Though only 50 yards away he had only one jump to make before he was out of sight. I saw him again as he ran around the other end of the rim where Howard saw a glimpse of him but did not get a shot. No sooner had the buck disappeared when five does jumped by Howard came on his back track and trotted past me at thirty yards—a nearly sure bow shot.

Crossed the creek and topped out on a flat ridge on the east side. Here was a heavy crop of juniper berries and any amount of deer tracks. We saw 3 bunches of does around this locality but no bucks. Hunted back down another ridge and climbed out again for camp. One must leave Canyon Creek at 3:30 to reach camp by dark. Found a fine pair of shed whitetail horns, 4 points

each side, lying within 4 feet of each other. It is seldom they shed simultaneously. There was no bush or limb on which they could have been rubbed off.

Nov. 13   Sunday, so we piously shaved, cut up wood, set sourdough biscuits, sharpened arrows, and like knick-nacks. A beautiful clear day with a roaring wind. This afternoon we are going to rimrock some bucks.

P.M.: Hunted southeasterly toward Canyon Creek. Met a hunter from Oklahoma. He flushed a deer into a little canyon heading out into the prairie and I tried to drive him to Howard but no luck, as he had evidently topped out over the prairie and dropped into the Gila box. Where the Gila box joins the Canyon Cr. box we found a long knife-like ridge flanked by palisades. It looks promising. We made one drive at the north end of this ridge which put two whitetail does past Howard. Returned via the Gila rim. Walking along this high prairie in the sombre sunset with a howling wind tossing the old cedars along the rim, and a soaring raven croaking over the abyss below, was a solemn and impressive experience. Jumped three whitetails right out on the prairie but it was too late to see horns. They were very pretty bounding over the sea of yellow grama grass with the wind blowing them along like tufts of thistledown. Felt our way down the rocky dugway to camp.

Nov. 14   Decided to make a more thorough exploration of the hills south of the river. Howard went down the box and thence west through the pine ridges. He jumped two blacktail bucks and had 3 shots at one of them.

I took Brownie and rode south to the breaks of Clear Creek at the foot of Lily Mt. Saw a whitetail doe soon after leaving horse. Dropped to the creek and boiled tea in a pretty sunny spot with any number of squirrels all about. Heard a shot to the south, followed by an enormous flock of turkeys sailing across the canyon toward the north slope, where I watched them with the glasses as they topped out. Went down the creek to a small trap where I topped out and hunted back westerly along the rim to the horse reaching him just after sunset. Saw nearly twenty deer along this rim, including two whitetail and one large blacktail buck. One large whitetail was looking back at me at 70 yards. He jumped at the flash of the bow. My arrow stuck in his second jump, so that if he had stood still I would have hit him fairly in the neck. Thus:—

I also jumped the turkeys again and counted about forty as they sailed back to the south side of the canyon. I never saw such a flock, or such a hunting ground.

Nov. 15   Took Howard to Clear Cr. by the "ride & tie" method. Boiled tea in the canyon,—then walked down to the trap. Found a whole herd of whitetail does, yearlings, and fawns down to water and watched them for some time but no bucks. Then started to top out, Howard taking one hogback and I the next. I bumped into two very large whitetail bucks immediately after leaving Howard. One offered a standing rifle shot at 90 yards but brush prevented shooting with the bow.

Just short of the top I suddenly saw a large buck in a pine thicket about 50 yards up the hill, looking me over. I moved to avoid a bush, drew to the barb at point blank, and let fly. The unmistakable thud of the arrow striking flesh told me I had hit—as nearly as I could tell in the fore ribs or shoulder. The buck plunged like a pitching bronco and disappeared over the hogback straight at Howard. I yelled to Howard, who saw him

coming, clearing the oak thicket at every jump. He disappeared in the dip between the two ridges and did not emerge. We apparently commanded all possible exits. We waited from 3:30 to 4:00 for hemorrhage and then I went in on his track to the point where Howard last saw him. The slope was so cut up with other tracks that absolute tracking was impossible. I followed a plunging track to the point Howard designated but there was no sign of blood, while a hurried search failed to reveal any deer. It was getting dangerously late so we hurried back to the horse. Had a tough time getting home in the dark.

When full of hot supper I evolved two hopeful theories: (1) If there had been more than one buck I might have been on the wrong track. (2) If the arrow had not buried deeply why had it not broken off as the buck lunged through the stiff oak brush, and thus been found?

Nov. 16   Back to Clear Cr. to put these pretty theories to the test. I spent all morning at the scene of the shooting, and found there had certainly been at least three bucks, two of which had topped out without being seen by either of us. However there was no blood and no broken arrow on any track. Reluctantly gave up the search. Here is a map of the battle:

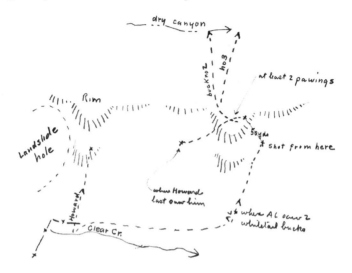

On my way to the battleground I flushed the whole flock of 40 turkeys. They flew north and soon after I heard 2 shots so I knew I had put them into Howard. When he joined me later I found he had had a long shot but no luck.

In the afternoon we hunted the ridge westerly. Saw no white-tail but I got a 70 yard shot at a nice blacktail with 3 points each side. Overestimated the distance and shot over him. When he ran Howard saw another run but got no shot.

We now heard turkeys ahead. Howard went after them and got up on the whole flock at 60 yards but missed. Meanwhile I could see them from the other side but hesitated to shoot at 75 yds. hoping Howard's shot would drive them closer. Finally risked an arrow at 70 yds. but some overhead limbs interfered with trajectory and I only hit a juniper tree. When the whole bunch took wing between us and sailed across the canyon it seemed as if the whole landscape had suddenly turned into turkeys beating upward through the pines. Never again will either of us see such a sight.

A blue evening in camp due to our misses. Got in late.

Nov. 17   Shaved, laundered, sunned, and recorded our mis-
fortunes, which after all netted us some unforgettable pictures
even if no meat. Howard went down on the open flat and practiced with his rifle. Our confidence and ambition is coming back
with clean underwear and warm sunshine. We have three days
left not counting this afternoon.

   P.M.: Walked down the Gila box and climbed west to the
second open mesa. This slope is torn up with turkey scratchings
and deer sign but we found none. Believe they are hanging out
in the pine thickets further back. We worked back to the trail,
Howard seeing 3 does. Got into camp before dark for a change.

Nov. 18   Worked the Clear Cr. ridge again. It is getting so dry that it is hopeless to stalk deer without a wind except early in the morning before the litter has dried out. Saw a few does and fawns only. When we arrived at the ridge a dozen turkeys walked by me, two of them in plain sight, the rest under the rim. I had a 30 yard shot at the two but missed. They did not see me and merely hopped a little when the arrow passed as if it were a falling branch. Had another chance at the bunch* at 70 yards but did not shoot fearing they would fly and lose Howard his chance. When he came up however we could not find them. Didn't see any deer going back along the rim—no wind.

Nov. 19   Took a gamble at the hills across Clear Cr. on the south side. Howard saw 3 turkeys which had been flushed somewhere and lit near him but did not offer a shot and we could not find them later. Worked easterly and found Jackson mesa too flat, with no deer or turkey sign. Worked the break of the creek but found very little sign. I then walked up the creek to get the horse while Howard climbed the ridge. He saw nothing. I saw a doe and fawn while waiting for him at the trail. In late.

---

*This bunch circled me to leeward at 70 yds. feeding peacefully. They can't smell.

Nov. 20 Worked southeasterly across the ridges with great care. Howard jumped a fine buck out of a pine thicket on a point but he was out of sight in 2 jumps. When we got to the ridge I made a new search for the buck I hit on the 15th. Once thought I had a lead when I heard some flies buzzing on the ridge north of where he was shot, but I soon found there were flies working on all the ridges. At sunset worked the rim again but the wind went down on us and there was little chance. Saw only 1 doe. The turkeys had been on this rim during the day and torn it all up.

Found Tipton in camp ready to pack us out.

Nov. 21 Got packed about 9 A.M. Reached N-Bar about 2 P.M. and Magdalena about 10:30 P.M.

Nov. 22 Left Magdalena about 11 A.M. Arr. Albuquerque 4 P.M. Left 5:50 P.M. arr. Chicago 10:10 A.M. Nov. 24 and Madison 5:30 P.M.

PRUDENT PROVERBS

1. A Douglas fir on a hogback under a rimrock is a buck bed. So is a pine thicket on a point.
2. A piñon thicket is a place for does.
3. When the piñon crop is high-graded, juniper berries are in order for blacktail. Some whitetail stay in the oak regardless of nuts.
4. When the edge of a mesa is studded with malpais it is prairie and will produce pine only on slopes.
5. Bucks do not necessarily bed on the same side of a canyon they feed on.
6. Only does water before dark, but both bucks and does feed before dark.
7. When you stop to blow or look, stop in a shade.
8. Deer cannot be stalked in dry country except in a heavy wind or early morning. North slopes stay quiet longest.
9. A startled deer will tend to go (1) uphill (2) into the wind (3) around a point (4) toward cover or rough ground. When he is startled by sight, No. 2 is the strongest; when by scent any of the others may be.
10. A turkey cannot smell enough to make scent a factor in hunting.

Second Gila Trip, 1929

Armaments   Starker: 50# yew bow, started by Geo. Kemmerer, finished by Starker, with 6 footed Alaska cedar broadheads made by him, and 18 birch broadheads left over from my 1927 Gila trip. Harness & rawhide quiver of his own make. Carl: .30-.30 Winchester carbine. Aldo: 60# osage bow; 20 unfooted Alaska cedar arrows with Weniger broadhead points. Harness & quiver same as 1927.

Going In   Madison to Burlington by car Nov 2. Packing Nov 3; left via AT&SF 7:30 P.M. Arr. Santa Fe 2 A.M. Nov 5. By car to Albuquerque and bought chuck list Nov 5. Nov 6: left Albuquerque 8 A.M., arr. Magdalena 12:30 P.M. Arr. Evans Ranch 4:30 P.M. Nov 7: Left 8 A.M. with 4 light packs, arr. Whiterock Tank in a rain 2 P.M. Saw 1 buck antelope, single, in Evans' pasture, and 2 herds of 22 and about 6 (?) on Burnt Canal Mesa. Sent packs back but kept "Tango," a black pony with a white star on his forehead and an artistic temperament. Heavy wind till bedtime (8 P.M.). Carl slept cold and I hard.

Nov. 8   A bright fine morning. Up in dark at 4 A.M. and when sun came out started dolling up camp. We are under a big spreading alligator juniper on the edge of a pretty park full of fine grama grass. It is 200 yards down to Evans' stock tank for water. There is enough oak and juniper wood within 200 yards of camp to furnish the US Army, only they wouldn't appreciate its fine qualities. Our camp is thus:

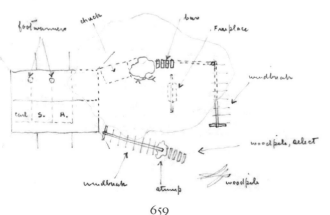

In the afternoon we de-horned a big, dead juniper only 50 yards from camp and piled up half a cord of fragrant wood—also brought in some oak. Also started the sourdough and other like ceremonies, including a pot of beans. Dined on beans and cornbread in a fall of snow which started in the middle of the afternoon and by bedtime was 2" deep. This will make fine prospecting for deer tomorrow. Had music in our snug dry camp after dinner while all the rest of the world outside was white and cold.

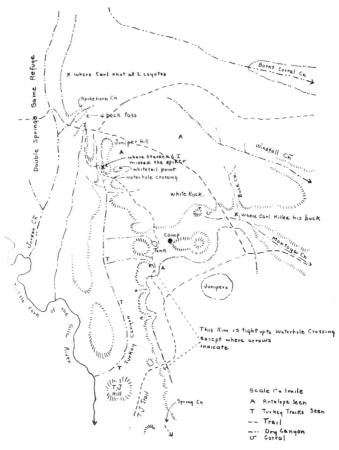

Deer hunters' map of the Whiterock Tank region

Nov. 9   Up before daylight and breakfasted mightily on sour-dough hotcakes. Off about 8 A.M. just as a fog was lifting on the white world. On the mesa prairie just northwest of camp came on the tracks of a big bunch of deer, including at least one large buck, which had drifted west during the night—possibly moving out of the East Gila country because of the hunters congregated there. We backtracked them to where they had topped out of the Whiterock Rincon and decided this would be a dandy pass on opening day.

Carl and Starker then prospected the rolling hills to the northwest where they saw 3 bunches of does totalling 13 (with only 1 fawn and no bucks). They also shot a cottontail but lost him.

I headed northeast along the Montoya drift fence and where it crosses the first little canyon jumped 2 bucks, one very large (at least 8 and possibly 10 points) and one smaller. They bounded north over the prairie to Windfall Canyon. The big one offered me a broadside standing rifle shot before he ran—at 125 yards. At the same time 2 other deer stood watching me on the hill to the east. I never found out what they were.

We met at camp for lunch and then explored southward, locating a pass that would be good but for a drift fence. From the pasture hill back of camp we saw 30 antelope feeding on the mesa to the south. The whole immensity of the Gila basin lay spread before us in a sunset so quiet you could hear a cricket chirp. It was a sight worth the whole trip.

Had a prize dinner of ham, hominy, and sourdough biscuits we had set at noon. Spent the evening planning tomorrow's campaign.

My candle is dripping and the boys are in bed, so no more today.

Nov. 10—Opening Day   Starker and I stayed on the "pass" just north of camp while Carl went further on to Windfall Canyon where I saw the 2 bucks go yesterday. Nothing came our way on the pass except 1 doe and 1 coyote, both routed by the opening bombardment. We got plenty cold however. After boiling some erbswurst we started to drive the little short canyons coming off the rim into Montoya Canyon. The first three yielded noth-ing but just as I was approaching the fourth (now called Buck

Canyon) a big buck jumped out and headed *down* the draw
instead of *up* toward where Starker was stationed. He had not
gone more than 200 yards out of sight when I heard the crack
of a rifle—one shot only. I was just starting to tell myself that
I had presented some stranger with a nice buck when "toot-
toot-toot" came three blasts of our little horn, the agreed-upon
signal for "dead deer—come and help."

Starker and I both heard it and ran up with a loud whoop
to meet Carl emerging from the little draw with the hoped-for
grin on his face.

BUCK DAY ON THE GILA

CSL: *We were late out of camp and the sun was up when I left
Aldo and Starker on the pass above the white rock. It is about a
mile across the mesa to Windfall Canyon where Aldo had seen two
bucks the day before. I followed the old Montoya drift fence and
was still 200 yards from the canyon rim when five bucks hove over
the horizon just east of me and running parallel with my course.
They were looking back and had not seen me.*

*It took them a long time to disappear into the canyon and I
sneaked to the rim about 200 yards above where they had entered.
In a few minutes they all moved out onto an open point just across
from me and not more than 200 yards from me. I watched them for
fully half an hour. They were suspicious but not frightened—four
big bucks and one spiker. Finally they moved back into the canyon
bottom below me but out of sight so I slipped a few yards closer and
waited for an opening.*

*They slowly froze me out and I decided to try a shot. One of the
big ones stepped across an opening and I let go at his shoulder—a
miss. The place was suddenly alive with bounding bucks. Two went
up the canyon and three took right out into the open again across
from me. They stopped on the opposite ridge and looked around
for several minutes, then disappeared into a small draw, but still
were not badly scared.*

*I cut down into Windfall and went up about ⅜ of a mile,
then climbed over the open ridge into the head of their draw and
worked down it very slowly. There was practically no wind. From
bush to tree and tree to rock, always using my glasses, I worked
slowly down. At last there he was, right in the middle of my glass,*

*a fine big buck, about 125 yards away right in the bottom of the
draw and headed my way. Two smaller bucks were behind him.*

*I was kneeling on a flat rock behind a low bush so settled down
to watch and wait. That buck took 30 minutes to move as many
feet and was on the lookout 90% of the time. My knees got stiffer
and my neck likewise but I was determined to stick it out and get
a real shot with no alibis. Finally they practically stopped moving
and I decided the time had come.*

*As I raised the old .30 I realized too late that the buck was head-
on instead of broadside but he was looking right at me and it was
too late to retreat. I aimed low and carefully but missed clean.
Away they went, again across the open hillside.*

*The chest of a ten point blacktail is a ten inch circle. How can
a man miss it at 90 yards? Things looked a bit blue from a meat
viewpoint but I was sure having a whale of a time. No blood sign
on the trail of the fugitives. I worked down the draw to the canyon
and then down the bottom of the canyon. A pipe and a little lunch
in a warm sunny spot while seven does passed up the opposite side.*

*Jumped two bucks right after lunch—they were plenty close but
saw me first—no more running shots for me. Worked down about
a half mile and then climbed out on the south side and worked the
mesa rim back toward the white rock. Three does stampeded out
of a water hole. Farther on another good buck jumped close by but
kept so well to cover I had no chance.*

*Got back to the east fork of the Montoya Box where we were to
have met for lunch, and decided to rest a while and watch. Picked
an opening where I could see across the draw and sat down beside
a small juniper bush. It began to look like the end of a luckless day
and I wondered where the boys were and what their luck had been.
A stone rattled on the opposite hillside and there he was, coming
on the sneak, a big one and straight toward me. I shifted to one
knee and picked out the opening where I hoped he might pass, and
he did, at a walking trot. No time for fancy aiming but he was
close about 70 yards.*

*It was a lucky shot as he dropped in his tracks and never moved.
I covered him for a few seconds and then gave the old horn three
long blasts. And then came the real surprise and treat. Aldo and
Starker answered the horn by voice and soon appeared on the buck's
back track. They had jumped him themselves and drove him right*

into my ambush. It was a lucky break for me and we had a great celebration together while we hung him up and took pictures. Eleven points and in good condition. The liver and heart went back to camp with us for dinner.

Nov. 11   All three of us started with "Tango" to pack in Carl's buck. On the way I caught a glimpse of half a dozen deer we jumped just under the "White Rock" only half a mile from camp. We found the buck as we left him and hardly frozen. Took some pictures and also the following weights (part obtained later but presented here to give his complete specifications).

Weight	Entrails	36#
	Liver & kidneys, est.	8
	Blood, est.	5
		—
	Total drawings	49#
	Head & hide	20#
	Waste, est.	6#
		—
	Total non meat	75#
	Meat, including feet & neck	100#
		—
	Total weight, live	175#
Horns	Widest spread, tip to tip	27"
	Girth at base, steel tape over warts	4½"
	Total points	11
	Ears, tip to tip	22"
	Length track, front 2¼ hind	2"

Carl took the buck into camp while Starker and I went over to Windfall Canyon across the prairie. Carl went to the mouth of Windfall and drove toward us on horseback. He sent two yearlings past me at about 20'. Later some other party drove several bucks past us—too far for a shot. They skipped over the prairie to Buck Canyon where Carl next tried to drive them back but no luck except some does. Carl then rode to camp while Starker and I headed for a high juniper hill to the west. I went in on one side and he on the other. A whole procession of does and 4 big bucks strung past me at about 60 yards but the brush was too thick to shoot. Starker tried one shot but fell short. The whole bunch then showed us their heels as they disappeared over the next ridge to the west.

On the way back to camp we saw some does. Had kidney stew from the buck.

Nov. 12 Carl stayed in camp to skin and butcher his buck. Starker and I went back to where we saw the 4 bucks yesterday. On the way I drove a piñon point for Starker and at the head of the draw saw a deer bedded down under a piñon looking at me not fifty yards off. He was directly into the sun and I could hardly find him with the glass, much less tell whether he had horns. Finally I thought I could see spikes but didn't want to shoot as I would have had to shoot him straight in the face, and besides there was a limb in the way. So I decided to risk walking straight on in the hope of finding a line for a broadside shot. The deer then jumped up and imagine my surprise to see an 8 point whitetail! Of course he kept in the brush. I tried one arrow, but without effect except that the arrow buried half an inch deep in a porous malpais rock.

In the draw where we saw the 4 bucks yesterday we found nothing but some does.

We then went west to the next slope to hunt it back to camp. Just before we got there we heard a shot in the canyon to the north. We ducked for a juniper and waited five minutes but saw nothing, so went on to a kind of saddle. Then a big buck (about 6 or 8 points) came down out of the north and passed right by the juniper where we had been! I tried an arrow but it was too far. The arrow splintered.

Starker then started down the slope, the crest of which I was to follow on the way home. Hardly had he gone when a 4 point buck preceded by a doe came out of the canyon to the north and entered our canyon on Starker's tracks. There had been another shot so I was hoping he would be looking back and would see these deer. They were a long shot for me, as I had moved off 45 yards down the ridge. Soon there was another shot, followed by another 4 pointer. Then another, followed by another 4-pointer with a broken foreleg. This one I should have tried to intercept, but still hoping that Starker was there I did not. Finally two hunters came along—seemingly unaware of all the game they had put up, and I was sure they would stampede all three bucks right by me. Nothing came. Then I blew my horn, and getting no answer, knew that Starker had not been there at all, but had proceeded down the slope as per his instructions! Thus did I miss 4 chances at bucks in 30 minutes!

We got into camp at 2:30 and found Carl had the buck all butchered. We shaved and roasted the ribs over oak coals. They looked fine but were tough,—too early to be good yet. However sourdough bread and macaroni consoled us.

Nov. 13   Starker and I went back to the saddle west of Juniper Hill while Carl rode to Black Mt. to look for turkey. We found everything full of hunters and did not get any shots or good hunts. I found a spikehorn which had been shot in his bed and not claimed, probably because his horns were a little short of the legal 6″ limit. It was very cold standing on the pass.

Nov. 14   All of us went south along the rim to the TJ Points. We could see deer below us under the rim and one outfit we passed were bombarding a buck half a mile away across the canyon. Went down the TJ Trail and on the first hill we drove Carl jumped a very large blacktail buck who eluded two attempts to drive him and finally left the country. In the dry box canyon north of TJ Points we found much turkey sign. Drove this canyon north and got separated. I found a good deer country on the east ridge of this canyon but could not work it alone. Finally located Starker and climbed out the little box below camp, the head of which is full of rich vegetation and has several pools of water. Found Carl had hunted north to the head of the canyon and was in camp. This was a stiff but interesting day.

Nov. 15   General laundry and housecleaning till 10 A.M. Then climbed down the Pothole Box into the big canyon where Carl hunted turkey while Starker and I tried the deer. On the way down the slope Carl jumped a big buck—probably the same one we hunted on the TJ Hill yesterday. He went diagonally across the canyon. Soon after a tremendous bombardment started on the TJ Hill. We got into position and soon a doe came panting up and first nearly ran me down and then Starker. The big buck came back just behind her, but the doe having scented me and seen Starker, the buck was able to exactly split the distance between us and remain out of range of both.

We had intended to work the mesa west of this canyon in the afternoon but we heard other hunters up there. After cooking lunch with Carl we drove south toward the TJ Points. Jumped several deer but there was not enough wind—they seemed to know *both* our locations and to make their getaway accordingly. Just at sunset Starker saw a big buck in the rincon below the TJ Hill. He wanted to follow him up toward the Rimrock, but I was done up and couldn't. Climbed out the TJ Trail, getting into camp late.

Nov. 16   Spent the morning making jerky and cleaning up around camp. Used one whole ham and one shoulder of Carl's buck. We find it dries nearly completely in 1 day when turned over, and ought to be "done" in 2 days. It shrinks 75% in area as well as thickness. In the afternoon we made a little hunt on the Whiterock Hill. In spite of the fact that the hill had been bombarded this morning Carl, who was doing the driving, jumped 3 bucks. One of them was drifting in past the corral in the head of Montoya Canyon. He had 2 open shots at 80 yards and went just over his back both times. Tomorrow we will concentrate on this hill.

Nov. 17   Again worked the home hill but it was very quiet. Saw one buck on the white rock but he offered no shot. In the evening made another hunt toward the Montoya Box where I had a fall off a pine log. Saw some does and yearlings near the mouth of Buck Canyon but saw no bucks. A beautiful quiet evening.

Nov. 18   Carl drove the Malpais Box at the waterhole crossing and put a beautiful buck across the rock face just above it. He had a 70 yard shot nearly straight down off the rimrock and missed him only a few inches.

The three of us then made a careful work of the Juniper Canyon ridge. A fair west breeze had sprung up and we got close to a number of deer. One passed me at 60 yards but in shadow and behind brush. I never made out whether it was a buck or a doe.

At evening we arrived at the point of the ridge. Three bucks which some other hunters had stirred up got up a long way ahead of me and circled to the right. I then took a stand at what I knew was the crossing at the point of the ridge, on which Carl and Starker were working abreast. Soon I heard deer, and made out three small deer coming down the hill diagonally past me, but obscured by brush. When directly opposite me, and about 60 yards distant, they stopped, seemed to ponder the fate of nations, and then to my utter surprise, plunged squarely down the hill and directly at me, but still obscured by brush. As they filed across a very small opening I made out that the first two were does, while the last seemed to be a spiker. I drew on a clear opening under a juniper where I knew they would pass, about thirty yards to my left, and in a moment the two does filed by in that peculiar hesitating trot which makes it uncertain whether the next instant will bring a total stop or a terrified leap. Then came the spiker. I was not yet sure whether his horns were 6 inches (the legal minimum) and devoted the first instant of clear vision to verifying this fact, instead of to a final appraisal of distance and aim, as I should have. Then I shot. The arrow passed over his back and splintered harmlessly on the rocks. I had held only 2' under instead of 3'.

The spiker bounded up the hill. At 120 yards I shot a second arrow, just as a sort of goodbye.

More perfect chances to make a kill do not occur, except in deerhunters' dreams.

A little later Starker came down the hill, looking sheepish. I assumed he was ashamed of my performance, but soon learned that he had missed a similar shot at the same spiker. It was his arrow which pushed them down to my stand.

Nov. 19   A clear still windless day, worthless for hunting. We tried the Juniper Hill country again. Carl and Starker saw a very large buck but could not contrive anything more than a rifle chance. On the way home we drove a point near camp where we had located a buck in the morning and thought the rim rocks would force him to pass the Whiterock Tank. He knew the topography better than we. He cut back below us on the very edge of the lower rim.

Nov. 20   Packed out to Evans Ranch. Kenneth Baldridge had 2 gobblers (15# & 18#) hanging in his camp at Burnt Corral.

Nov. 21   Drove to Albuquerque. Left 8:15 P.M. for home.

MAXIMS OF AN UNSUCCESSFUL
DEER HUNTER

1. A deer never follows anything. If he can cross a ridge, a rimrock, a ravine, or even a prairie, he will do so, especially if it is into the wind.

2. The doe always comes first—the buck after.

3. A whitetail will lie in his bed and let you pass.

4. A deer will not jump from scent except close by, but he will sneak out as far as the scent will carry.

5. In a drive, it's the first run that counts. A drive is no good unless it proceeds slowly enough for each man to sit down half the time.

6. The opposite hillside is always less brushy than the side you are on. It is the best place to shoot.

7. The spikers which run with does and yearlings are an easier bow chance than the big bucks.

8. One windy day is worth a week of calm weather, and a windy evening is best of all.

9. Hunting abreast, into or across the wind, and not over two bowshots apart, is the best formation. Three abreast is better than two. Driving to a stationary man on a "stand" seldom works.

10. Clean your glasses daily, and never hunt without them. Good illumination and clean lenses are necessary to discern horns in shadow, and are both much more important than high magnification. Examine every "doe" twice.

11. Don't be too cautious. You can run up on a trotting or jumping deer, where you couldn't move a foot on a standing or sneaking deer without detection.

12. If in doubt whether to shoot, do so at once, provided only the deer be broadside.

13. Keep a practice arrow (marked for the purpose with a section of rubber tube on the nock) and shoot a few shots daily in the least stony spot you can find.

USE AND CARE OF VENISON AS LEARNED
AT WHITEROCK DEER CAMP

The liver can be braised the first day but should not be broiled until the second. It is the best part of the deer.

The ribs are tough and strong as late as the third day and possibly do not become good until much later.

Roasts and chops may be braised by the fifth day but should not be broiled or fried before the seventh.

All meat cures quicker after skinning.

Jerky may be started five days after skinning. It dries perfectly in two days if cut thin and turned after one day. It shrinks 75% in area and probably more than that in weight (note: find out the shrinkage in weight on next trip).

Jerky should be cut along the grain while the meat is partially frozen. Slices down to ¼ inch thickness are entirely feasible. The shoulders and hams are best for jerky. Remove all fat.

The hide should be stretched on the ground with sharp wooden pegs, Indian style.

A can of tomato greatly improves venison broth tending to be "strong" because of insufficient curing.

Baste all broilings with bacon fat, applied with a pine-needle brush.

A buck with one inch of fat on the rump is moderately fat; a buck with less is thin; two inches of fat is found only in piñon nut or juniper berry years.

Kidneys are very choice but on account of the suet should be braised, not boiled. The heart and neck are good as soup stock and boiled meat.

1936 Mexico Trip

Sept. 1   Left Madison 6:45 P.M. Arrived El Paso 8:30 A.M., Sept. 3.

Sept. 3   Met Clarence Lunt, our guide, and Juan Thatcher, of the Thatcher Baca Company, 317–319 S. Overland Street. Spent a busy day getting licenses, immigration permits, gun-toting permits, etc. The latter, due to the absence of General Rico from his office, did not materialize until 5 A.M. next day.

Sept. 4   Left 7 A.M. on Mexico Northwestern for Pearson. As we stood on the station platform in Juarez a flock of 20 cranes flew over, headed south, and not over 100 yards high. They were silent, and looked small. Little browns? Thatcher says many cranes winter in Chihuahua in a region just south of where we are going. It seems early for migrant cranes to be arriving here.

The slope into the Rio Grande at Juarez is all eaten out and shows the usual erosion. The mesquite flats beyond that are in somewhat better shape. Twenty miles N. of Guzman—the

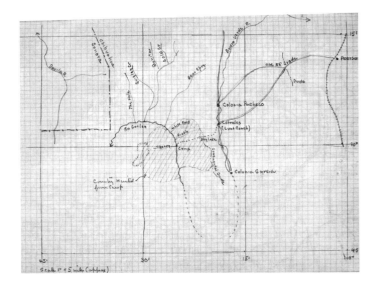

*Remnant of
Laguna Guzman
(once covered
many square
miles)*

lunch stop—are large playas covered with sacaton, and full of doves and mosquitoes.

In one temporary pool a nice flock of ducks were splashing—couldn't make out the species. At Laguna Guzman some rain-pools had an avocet, a blue heron, and some killdeer. Laguna Guzman shows on the map as a large lake, and Mr. Lunt remembers it as such, but he says it has contained no water in the last ten years.

South of Laguna Guzman we passed over great stretches of range, all overgrazed, part of it fenced, and stocked with Herefords. The draws are eroding. The flats have thin sacaton grass. A few jack-rabbits seen between Casa Grande and Pearson.

Had supper at Pearson and set off in Lunt's wagon over the old R.R. grade toward Colonia Pacheco. Moon came up and we drove till one o'clock—then camped.

Sept. 5 Up early and on toward Colonia Pacheco, where we arrived at Lunt's ranch about 11 A.M. Saw on way many "agrarian" homesteads recently granted by the government to settlers. Also saw "check dams" built by prehistoric Indians. On Piedra Verde near ranch a flock of five pintail lit in the creek—Ray and I sneaked them and killed three.

After a fine dinner at Lunt's we set off at 3 P.M. with five

At Lunt ranch

packs. Stopped to look at Lunt's cabin two miles west of his ranch. Here we heard parakeets for the first time. Pressed on to Rio Gavilan, arriving there just before dark. Camped above the mouth of Diablo Canyon on a little flat with heavy grass and weeds. Just as we got camp done it rained pitchforks, so we had to eat later in the dark, and quite wet.

Sept. 6 Up early—a fine bright morning. Harl Johnson rode with us along the rim of the first mesa upstream on the east side. Saw no deer for a long time. Finally Harl spotted a big buck in velvet, lying under an oak. I tried to follow him and drive him over the mesa for Ray—but no luck. Soon after I spotted a spiker lying under three big pines at 75 yards. I shot and missed. We then had lunch and Johnson rode back to camp with the horses while we hunted back. Ray saw several more deer and had a shot at a doe. We met on a pretty little mesa which was full of parakeets, which chattered and flew over us, evidently very curious. We had a good look at their red, green, and yellow colors.

We then practiced a while with blunts and broke nearly all we shot. Then hunted down a point where I missed a doe at about 60 yards. Caught in a shower and hurried our tackle into an overhanging ledge till it was over.

Just before reaching camp another shower hit us and we had to wade the river, thus arriving thoroughly wet. After changing, Clarence got back and we had a good supper of duck, beans, and potatoes. He had seen 11 deer, missing a spiker he wanted for meat.

Heard a whippoorwill at camp.

Sept. 7   Harl and I rode west, Ray and Clarence northwest and down river. Harl and I again rode all morning over beautiful open pine mesas without seeing anything. Then about noon, in the breaks above the first mesa, we began to see many deer. I first stalked to intercept three bucks which were feeding— evidently on pea vines. They took a different route from that anticipated, and finally lay down at 85 yards. I shot and came fairly close, but——. We then saw two bucks lying under an oak and Harl tried to drive them to me but they knew better. At lunch a small bunch of parrots passed, also a few bandtails, and we had a slight shower. After lunch we rode right upon three bucks lying under an oak but by the time I could dismount they were over a rim. In a canyon north of Cherry Canyon we saw a buck, far away, climb into a rim. Rode around and tried a stalk. Never saw him again, but I met a doe with a big fawn which fed right up to me and passed at 40 yards. I shot twice at the fawn, but no hit. The doe couldn't see me but saw Harl and the horses at a distance and milled around all confused.

Crossing Cherry Canyon I decided to walk down it on foot. Soon after I heard Harl shoot twice. I went to him and found he had killed a yearling and a doe for camp meat. He was not sure he had hit the yearling—hence the two deer. Helped him skin out and came into camp. Had liver for supper—not bad, but never at its best the first day. No rain today.

Sept. 8   When Harl drove in the horses a mischievous bay thought he had just as well go home while he was about it. Tried to head him but he got away. At this writing Harl and Ray have gone out while I'm waiting for Clarence who has evidently had trouble heading the runaways. It's a crystal-clear morning with a full breeze, and the sun is pretty on the big sycamores around camp.

Clarence didn't come back—evidently the horses have gone all the way to Pacheco—so I set off down the river alone. A mile

down I was rounding a rocky point when I sighted a yearling at 40 yards, but brush in the way. When he put his head down I got behind the point and climbed over. The sound of the river drowned all noise, but as I climbed I felt a puff of wind from behind and when I put my head over the top there was no deer.

After lunch climbed up a side canyon and saw several Indian check dams. On the way home at dusk I heard a buck snort from the sidehill and there he was looking at me at 80 yards. As I raised to shoot he and his partner—another buck—snorted again and were off.

On arriving at camp found Ray had killed a large gobbler. Harl had sighted him from a distance and Ray stalked up a little canyon within 25 yards and shot him in the head with 7½ shot. He is very large but very thin, and moulting. Harl says they do not get fat until October but are not at their best till January and February.

Sept. 9   Ray, Harl, and I rode east near continental divide, around Park Knoll. Got no shots. Just as we located a good bunch of deer it rained on us. We waited but finally got rained out and into camp wet. Found Clarence back from Pacheco.

Saw a beautiful bunch of parrots in a box canyon.

Sept. 10   Clarence, Ray, and I rode the Salt Canyon mesa country northeast of camp. Just as we started to climb out the trail a doe and a yearling trotted around a point toward us. I got ready for them to top the rise we were behind but they scented us and ran. I should have known better than to trust the wind at such short range.

Rode and hunted all morning. On one pretty mesa we were stalking a rim when I sighted a pronghorn feeding 80 yards ahead. Got a bush between us and got up to 40 yards, where I had a clear broadside shot and missed.

Previously I got up to 80 yards of a doe and shot five arrows at her, but an intervening ridge prevented me from seeing where the arrows fell. I later found all were short.

Then tried the continental divide but saw nothing but one doe.

On the way down jumped eight bucks far away. Tried to intercept them but no luck.

Ray and I hunted the rest of the ridge afoot, seeing nothing, but Clarence who rode to one side with the horses jumped two bucks, one very large. Ray and I followed them and Ray jumped the big one from a thicket and got a running shot at 40 yards, shooting just behind.

Clarence watched this hunt from a distance and says he later jumped two spikers within 25 yards of the route I followed. Evidently they "froze" on me.

This brought us to a fine knoll with mahogany on the south side and a dense oak thicket on the north side. We rode around it and at the base sighted three bucks lying under a juniper at 100 yards. I tried two arrows and Ray one. All fell short. We had guessed the distance as 90 yards.

Riding back up the creek at dusk Clarence nearly ran into a spike buck, the noise of the stream muffling our approach. Further on, at the mouth of Diablo Canyon, a bear met us in a willow thicket on the cobble bar. It was too dark to more than just see him as he made off up the point. Clarence shot with the rifle but fortunately missed.

Sept. 11   This morning at camp saw 2 beautiful trogans—a bird larger than a large jay, scarlet under parts, black head, green back, and black tail edged with white. Their call resembles a mockingbird.

Clarence and Ray rode west. Harl and I rode down the canyon. I tried to stalk a yearling but he winded me. Then I stalked a doe with 2 yearlings—they were near a bunch of horses whose noise and movement somewhat screened my approach. Got a shot at the yearling at 40 yards—but from kneeling position. Missed. Then in the resulting confusion the other yearling offered a 60-yard shot. The arrow stuck in an overhanging limb. Saw an otter track near here.

As we were looking for the arrow a group of local cowmen rode up—with them an inspector who asked us to take him to our camp. He took our venison and had Harl sign an account of our hunting. This trouble arises from the fact that the regulations were changed, unknown to us until our arrival at El Paso, so September is now closed on deer and turkey.

Sept. 12 Harl, Ray, and I rode west. A fine sunny day, not very hot, no rain. As we climbed out of the canyon some parrots were wheeling high in the air—again reminding me of cranes.

Found no deer until noon. As we were eating lunch on a high rim Ray said, "Give me the glasses and I'll spot a turkey." He turned them on the opposite mesa ¾ mile away and immediately located two birds—evidently gobblers—feeding in the pines just above a rim. The canyon was impassable at this

point so we rode toward the head. As we rounded a brushy point Harl saw a deer. Just as we were dismounting 3 turkeys jumped up between us and the deer and coasted noiselessly over the rim. We walked ahead with the bows, Harl following with the horses. From a spot which I had almost stepped on Harl flushed a fourth big gobbler which also coasted noiselessly over the brink. I've never before seen a turkey "lay" before being flushed.

We walked on and put up a bunch of Mearns quail from the same spot.

Going back Ray got a long shot. In camp found Clarence had caught 21 fine rainbow trout 7–11 inches long, which went well for supper and breakfast.

I made a short hunt up the canyon at dusk but saw nothing.

Sept. 13   Made a sunrise hunt down canyon but saw nothing.

After helping Clarence and Harl break camp and pack, Ray and I rode ahead on the trail to the dry lake on the continental divide where we tied the horses and made a foot hunt. Saw nothing. After lunch we rode south along the divide making foot hunts out the points. Saw 4 deer, does and yearlings, but got no shots. Saw a bear track and many rocks turned over.

We regretfully rode down the east slope to Clarence's ranch, where for the first time in 10 days we saw cattle, barbed wire, radios, and roofs. It seems oppressive in the house.

Sept. 14   Rode to Pearson (30 miles), packing the outfit on mules. This was an improvement over the wagon trip we made coming in. We took the old Mormon road (instead of the R.R. grade) going down off the mountain, and marvelled at the work accomplished by these old pioneers without capital and without machine tools. Harl and Clarence reminisced over their early experiences hauling lumber over this road, which is now of course so washed out that it is barely navigable on horseback.

The open valley at the foot of the mountain, Harl says, was one of the old Terrazas ranches, branding 18,000 calves per year until broken up by Villa during the revolution. In those days they often cut hay on these mesas. Today you could hardly keep a goat alive. Harl ascribes this merely to dry years, but I incline to think the sod is gone. Some pretty active erosion is extending up the watercourses.

This was antelope country within Harl's recollection.

In Pearson everything was fine except the flies, which prevented us from eating the otherwise good supper at the hotel. Said goodbye to Clarence and Harl.

Sept. 15   Up early to catch the train to Juarez. By a curious blunder we boarded the "other" bi-weekly train, and suddenly found ourselves steaming off toward Chihuahua City. Got the conductor to stop and dump our outfit on the mesa a couple of miles out of Pearson. I hoofed it in for a car while Ray rounded up some burros and got the stuff back to town. Hired a rattle-trap Chevrolet to take us in for 60-odd pesos. Drove to Columbus via Casas Grandes, Ascension, Laguna Frederico, and Palomas,—the old Mormon route. Arrived just in time to catch the evening train to El Paso, where we arrived about 8 P.M.

Sept. 16   Left about 9 A.M. Arrived Kansas City about 8 next morning. Had to lie over till evening. Arrived Madison about 9 A.M. September 17.

from *Shack Journals, 1935–1948*

(Dates previous to July 1 are approximate)

Jan. 12   Visited place with Ed Ochsner and asked him to lease it.

Feb. 3   Started work on fireplace with Starker & Luna.

Apr. 20–24   Camped with Luna & Carl & Nina. Finished roof. Erringtons there.

Apr. 27–29   Camped with Hamerstroms. Violets and Indian sweet grass blooming.

Bought place through Ed Ochsner.

May 19   Planted food-patch.

June 20?   Yellow lady-slipper in bloom in Lewis woods.

June 30   Completed clay floor with Carl & Donald McBeath. First *Baptisea* in bloom. Spiderwort & *Anemone* in full bloom.

July 5–6   Run out by mosquitoes—went to Baraboo tourist camp for night. Finished battens on front. Sorghum in patch 12″ high. First black-eyed susans in bloom.

July 13   *Baptisea* apparently over with but still some spiderwort and much black-eyed susan. Sorghum 15″ high. Discovered yellow-bellied sapsucker is breeding in elms above shack. Finished battens on north and west side.

*   *   *   *   *

AL, EBL, EL (Ray Roark May 17)   May 17–21, 1936

Ray and I were looking for carp in the woods slough. Just been talking about rattlers, when one started turning up within 2′ of where Ray was sitting. We killed him before we found out it was only a king (?) snake who had been vibrating his tail against a dry leaf.

5/17   Put in screens. Watered pines in nursery and near shack. Very dry hot wind.

5/18   Planted amber sorghum, hemp, millet in food patch.

5/19   Hung screen door. Fran came down from Necedah with 15 tamaracks. Planted them. Drove to portage over river road—many crowfoot violets in bloom.

5/20   Put pegs in shack. Went after spiderwort and violets for garden. Slight rain. Tried catfish—no bites.

5/21   Fixed screens. Made another bluebird house for west entrance. Chickens booming this morning at daylight—this time from south. Warmer & south wind. Regretfully went home.

*   *   *   *   *

AL, Carl, Estella   Nov. 14–15, 1936

A warmish lowering day with scooting clouds and a high wind,—good for ducks only season closed. Built a bittersweet tangle near road on hill. Jumped a large deer in our woods. Nice quiet evening with wind howling outside.

Sunday came clear, cold, and still blowing a gale (from the N.W.). Built a grape tangle on hill. Then felled a large dead oak on bank of creek in woods. To our surprise, when it fell and broke near the top, it began to emit bees and drip with honey. The bees were too active to permit our cutting out the comb—must wait till it gets colder. Made some wood. While doing so, Flick flushed a covey of quail from near our fire. Evidently in woods to escape wind.

Filled hopper today for first time—50# corn.

*   *   *   *   *

AL, Carl, EBL, Estella   Jan. 22–23, '38

Sawed wood on bench near road. Tom Butzen came up Sunday. Found deer had been passing through our woods—evidently spreading due to the thaw. Pump was frozen due to Bert Galistell's failure to drain it—worked till midnight thawing out the ice plug with red-hot steel rods. Made some bands, set trap, caught chickadees at will, but weren't satisfied with the bands so we banded only one—a green band on right leg. His name is "Greenhorn."

Deer had passed within a few feet of corn rack but had not found it.

AL, EBL, Carl, Estella   Jan. 29–30, 1938

Left car and Lewis' and sledded in. Bad stuff—snow too deep for toy sled. Sawed wood on bench near road. Many chickadees in woods but too windy for trapping at shack—caught one but he got away. Snow about a foot deep—too deep for hauling. We are now equipped for regular banding and feather marking. Saw "Greenhorn" in the woods—band seems OK.

*   *   *   *   *

AL, EL, NL, CL, EEL, George Kohler   Feb. 1, 1939

Found the shack a wreck. Somebody had broken in and smashed all cooking outfit, all food, and most furniture. Had taken tools.

Reported case to Sheriff.

P.S.: Two boys were arrested Feb. 7 and pled guilty. Sentenced to 6 mos. each. Recovered tools Feb. 18. *They served 4 weeks, I believe.*

*   *   *   *   *

Notes on History of Alexander Farm

We ate lunch with a farmer—Joe Lewis' brother—who used to live at our place. He couldn't remember ever seeing prairie chickens on our marsh, tho he is a hunter and said there were always chickens on N. side of river and in the big marsh to S. of us.

Mr. Lewis said there used to be a pair of planted white pines easily 50' high in front of the Alexander farm (shack). He doesn't know when they were cut down.

I asked Mr. Lewis whether there were any hard maples on the hill in his time. He said no.

The field east of the shack, he said, always raised good corn. On the sandhill he has raised as high as 60 bushels of rye per acre (except on the sand blow, which never would raise anything). He confirmed the origin of the sandblow as an attempt by a former owner to fill up the "birch pothole" with material from the hill. Mr. Lewis said there always had been partridges in our woodlot.

He said there were no carp in the river in his earlier years—thinks they showed up 20–25 years ago. Used to be lots of buffalo and suckers. Used to spear lots of fish at night in our "creek."

*   *   *   *   *

AL, EBL, Estella   July 12–15, 1940

Weather 7/12–13 Clear and cool. Mosquitoes still bad. Lake level 2.5'. Rain of 0.8" July 10.

　　　　　7/14   Warm, partly cloudy, S.W. wind. Slight shower.

　　　　　7/15   Cooler, clear.

Phenology First bloom: marsh milkweed, sandbur, smartweed, *Veronica*, green foxtail. Michigan lily blooming abundantly in Lewis' hayfield—must have started about July 8–10. Full bloom: harebell, white spurge, elder, bl. eyed susan, yarrow, white morning glory, smooth hawkweed, spatterdock, white water-lily, meadow rue, white campion, fleabane (by 7/12), evening primrose, milkweed (est. 7/8).

In bud *Veronica*, both *Liatris*, ironweed.

Passing out Spiderwort, wahoo, yellow St. John's wort, white *Baptisea*.

Passed out *Anemone*, rose.

Fruits First red raspberry ripe, grapes nearly full size, lambs quarters in green stage. Panic seed fallen. Black raspberries darkish but not ripe yet.

Crops Corn up to 6' high, average 5'. Soybeans 10". Potatoes first bloom. Sweet corn first tassel coming out.

Birds Blue heron IIII marshhawk 1   mallards 1   wood-chuck 0   teal 0   pheasants: young ⅔ grown   quail: still bob-whiting 1, 2, 1, 2, 1   woodcock 1   cowbirds in groups a week ago but few now in groups   Cooper hawk 1.

Panic seed Mostly fallen. Being visited by doves, redwings.

Work New bearings on grindstone; trued up stone with old rasp. Built 2 benches. Built 3½ panels of fence. Looked at a derelict boat across river—found it worthless. Built 2 benches, put one on Chapman hill with birdhouse. Put birdhouse on birch row.

Rabbits   Out 4 hrs., saw 2 rabbits.

Deer   Have fawns with them since last week. Are nipping soybean, smartweed, elder, plum, elm, bittersweet. No longer eating spurge. Saw a yearling on road at night with our lights. Are still nipping lambs quarter. On way out flushed a yearling out of Tom's hay meadow—very bright red.

Plantings   Jackpines now breaking their first bud. Whites and norways which got very dry last year have made less growth this year than last; all others more growth. Length of new needles (and blue color on whites) continues to be the best indicator of thrift. Fertilized white birch has grown 3 times as much as unfertilized control. Red maple on bare cultivated sand shows scorched leaves, just as white oaks; evidently needs partial shade while leaves are near ground. A dozen jacks in birch row were tipped partly over by recent rain and wind: is this because roots are all in one plane from artificial planting? Only one tamarack which formed leaves this spring has died this summer. Fall hazel and dogwood plantings have all survived on good soils, but on poor sand many hazels which leafed out well in spring scorched during hot weather. Spring-planted large wild jack with poor roots has died; fall-planted jack of some size but with good roots is alive. Nannyberry planted in 1936 is still hanging on with only a few leaves; no shoots. Plums planted in 1936 are at last starting to grow—many shoots of 2–2½'.

Cranes   Thought I heard a crane in Baxter's but mosquitoes too bad to verify.

*   *   *   *   *

AL, EBL   April 5, 1941

Weather   Cold, cloudy, turning to clear with south wind about noon. Walked in. Lake level 2.8' (lower than last week), but river up 2" on base of big birch N. of shack,—quite evidently higher than lake. Lake still has mush ice; river cleared Mar. 31 according to Webster.

Gilbert's log cabin   which he wouldn't sell to me last fall under-cut by river and will be lost this week. Gilbert was born there, so must have been built before Civil War. Excellent white pine log work sheathed in a cheap lumber barn.

Phenology*   Soft maple nearly in bloom. Frost out except on N. slopes. First grouse drumming. Leopard frog out on dry grass near shack. Many peepers in voice. Cankerworms in tangle-foot, both sexes.

Migrants   Herring gull 1 (adult).

Birds   Geese 4   woodcock 2 pairs in road   geese 4   mal-lard 4 pairs   song sparrow ○   fewer bluebirds than last week fewer ducks than there should be (later: 2 blacks)   no hawks.

Mammals   Saw 3 rabbits in 2 hrs. Flooded out of bottoms: Gus running them continually. 6 dead on highway. Many deer tracks on road. Rabbits cutting but not eating lower limbs on jacks.

Work   Split wood. Estella washed floor. Burned more down limbs. Told Webster to plow either 12th or 19th.

Banding   1 chick came near shack but wouldn't look at bait.

Trees   Jacks are regaining green color. Not many trees squashed by snow, but quite a few whites tipped by rabbits while lean-ing over. Mice chewed plums slightly. Deer rubbed & killed 1 tamarack.

PS—Big cock in feeder just as we left. Crowing. On way out saw 4 pr. mallard, 10 teal, 1 woodcock.

*   *   *   *   *

AL, EBL, Estella, Nancy C. (Joe Hickey June 6)

June 6–7, 1942

Flood   Found the road at Lewis' entirely underwater. Drove in at Van Housen's. Joe and I swam the lake, paddled the boat across via woods, and ferried the outfit across. Peak of flood came about June 5 and registered about 6.0′, judging by weeds on gauge. On June 6 the lake stood at 5.2′. By afternoon of June 7 had fallen to 3.8′. Heavy rain night of June 6 washed the gardens badly.

*First mole tunnels.

The flood will probably kill the *Carex* in the marsh below Chapman Lake, as did the flood of June 13, 1940. If so, 1943 will bring a crop of smartweed (*Polygonum punctatum*) and *Bidens*. Then, if there is a fall flood, we will again have ducks, as in fall of 1941.

The 6.0' level in the lake reaches into the lower trees in N. end of birch row, covers the S. end of Lake Chapman road. The 5.2' level covers the seat at the waterthrush pool, and stands about 6" deep on the WP planting N. of the birch-row. At 5.2' level a boat may easily cross the road.

Weather   Humid, hot. Mosquitoes bad. Lake level 5.2' on June 6, falling rapidly. Rain of at least 1.5 inch night of June 6.

Phenology   Hereafter phenology is plotted in "Phenology Record" to be later bound with this Journal. First bloom: yellow sweet clover, alsike clover, white clover, squirrel-tail grass, fleabane, wahoo, harebell, white *Baptisea*, gray dogwood, silky dogwood. Full bloom: wildrose, spiderwort, bluets, yellow *Baptisea*, pink phlox, *Anemone canadensis*, *Anemone virginiana*, poison ivy, spatterdock (first bloom?). Passed out: blue phlox, grape, shooting star, *Rumex*, birdfoot violet, black locust. Passing out: columbine, blackberry, *Linaria canadensis*, shagbark hickory, lupine, dewberry, yellow iris at shack. In bud: Solomon's seal, quack grass. Fruit: wild strawberry ripe. *Conifer candles:* Up to 20" in jack pine, 14" in red pine and white pine. White pine at shack (Tree A) 13½" leader, needles 1¾" long. Red pine (Tree B) 9¼" leader, needles 2" long. Buds visible on both.

Birds seen   Mallards 1, 3   ruffed grouse 1 (flooded out of woods; in Starker's grape tangle)   kingfisher 1   blue heron 1   woodcock 1   Joe showed us how to tell note of yellow-throated vireo from red-eye one at lake   quail; 2 pairs   pheasant 1.

Mammals   Rabbits flooded out of bottom. Seen 4 in 3 hours.

Work   Cut lawn. Cult. garden. Planted 3 plants of sand-blow heath (*Hudsonia tormentosa*) in sandblow. Brought these from Black River near Melrose.

*   *   *   *   *

AL, EBL, Estella   Nov. 25–27, 1943

Gus' Last Hunt

We came up to get us a deer. Took the boat up to Anchor's Island, hoping to find it free of hunters. I stood at the lower crossing while Estella and Gus went up the north shore to make a drive. They had no sooner left than I found the fresh track of a deer, crossing the channel from the mainland, and dragging a leg. There was blood. It was clear that somebody's cripple was on the island.

In a few minutes a disgusted-looking hunter appeared. He had followed his cripple to the island but couldn't find her.

When I was talking to the hunter I heard Gus' "big-game" yelp. I knew he had found the cripple, and hurried to join him.

When I got there I found Estella in tears and Gus in the middle of the river. The deer had taken the water and crossed to the north shore. Gus had followed. On a bar in the middle he had come upon the doe and gotten kicked. I had heard the doe give a loud blat, like a half-grown calf in desperation.

Gus is a weak swimmer because of his crooked leg. I doubted whether he would make the far shore, toward which the current carried him. We hurried back toward the boat, but it was too far to enable me to reach him in time. We were overjoyed when he at last reached the north bank.

It took me half an hour to get to the boat and cross the river. When I reached him he had his hind legs in the water, his fore-legs clinging to a sod. He was baying weakly, but was unable to lift his head. I carried him up the bank, but he couldn't stand. His hind quarters were paralyzed, either by exhaustion, or the kick from the deer, or both.

Gus recognized me when I carried him up the bank, but he was soon seized by convulsions. I covered him with my coat, but could do nothing else for him. I had to tell him goodbye, and put him out of his misery.

*   *   *   *   *

AL, Estella, new Flick   Mar. 10–12, 1944

Weather   Installed a thermometer on W. wall of shack. 3/10: S.E. gale, warm, mostly cloudy, snow (2") melting fast. 6 P.M. 40° F. River closed again. Lake level 2.5'. 3/11: 6:30 A.M. 40°

F. Snow mostly melted. S.W. wind. 6:30 P.M. 45° F. Ice started to go out today. 3/12: Lake 2.6'. 7 A.M. 28° F. Colder and clear in P.M.

Seen   3/10: 1 hen pheasant in garden.   2 male bluebirds on sandhill, warbling faintly in the heavy wind.   3/11: 10 Canada geese came down river at noon.   At 7 P.M.: 20 deepwaters (goldeneyes?).   3/12: 1 marsh hawk.   No geese or ducks.

On trip: No redtails, no herons (too early). Possibly 1 gull—couldn't identify.

Phenology   Bluebirds arrived, I think about the first ones. Cardinal at house this morning (nearly zero but cold and clear) started singing at 6:55 A.M. war time.

Order of singing 3/11   Pheasant 6:50, cardinal 7:15. Pheasant may have been induced.

Order of singing 3/12   Cardinal 6:55. No pheasants crowing. (At Madison Monday cardinal sang at 7 A.M. at house.) *Amelanchier* terminal buds have broken out about ¼" near Indian pipe bench.

Rabbits   Saw 2 carcasses on road, one fresh. First seen this year. Saw 1 rabbit in 2 hours. Saw no browsing. Saw no carcasses on road going back.

Deer & misc. mammals   Housecat track in yard. Saw no deer tracks on way in and none on sandhill (snow fell about 4 days ago). Found a mink den and many tracks near Wahoo Pool. One fox track during night, no deer. Saw a meadow-mouse on sandhill and snow tunnels at bridge—doubt if they are scarce. Saw 1 red cedar on island rubbed by deer several years ago. Fresh coon track on island. Barrows says 7 deer below his place.

Work   Sawed up the felled oak on sandhill. Brought in 2 sleds of wood 3/10. 3/11: finished wood. Cut blackberries for pine clump at foot of sandhill. Found a lot of lumber on island. Carried it in and built 3 new benches and hauled them to birch row, sandblow, and "Indian pipe" bench.

Banding   Saw banded chickadee (left) just across slough on island—also several unbanded. Apparently no color on banded bird.

Downy 38–127737 right. Red head. 8:45 A.M. Old bird first banded March 30, 1940.

Hairy 36–224657 right. New bird. Red head. 10:15 A.M. Chickadee trap.

Downy 38–127672 right. New bird. Redhead 10:15 A.M. Sparrow trap.

Hairy 36–224642 left. No red. Last 2 digits worn. 11:30 A.M. First banded 3/12/39.

Hairy 36–224652 right. No red. 12:15 P.M. First banded 11/27/42.

Nuthatch 38–127579 left. 1:30 P.M. First banded Oct. 29, 1943.

Downy 38–127566 right. 3:30 P.M. First banded Jan. 30, 1940 (3rd year).

No woodcock Listened from 7:00 to 7:15 P.M. but heard no peenting. Ideal evening: warm, calm, foggy. Evidently not here yet. No woodcock at daylight 3/12.

Ducks on island opposite shack all day but are evidently unaware of our suet. Not a duck seen in yard.

The Ice Goes Out Saturday about noon Estella and I were carrying driftwood lumber from the island. I heard a groaning from the river and hurried to the bank. The ice had given way in the main channel and apparently had gorged it, forcing the water to flow through the side-channel. This had risen and was now moving its ice. Cakes ten or twenty feet long overrode the sheet ice and doubtless underrode it also. Large slabs upended, showing sand beneath, and plopped back wrong-side-up like great pancakes. Once a whole acre of ice drifted down the free channel above and shaved its edges as against a lathe. An ash tree, leaning out from the bank, was ridden down and drowned by heaving frothing cakes. When this side-channel had choked itself, the water was dammed up and again sought the main channel, where groaning began anew.

In a half day the ice gorge, thus yeeing and hawing, had worked itself half a mile down river. Tonight it rains, and I hear the ice like a distant waterfall. Tomorrow the river will be clear.

A flock of goldeneyes heard it before we did. They arrived tonight, and tomorrow will splash and preen in water.

Going Back got stuck at Gilbert's. Barrows brought team and hauled us out. Says Gilbert place bought by Mrs. Regan of Madison. 3 islands bought by _____ who has logged them, bringing logs across ice. Logs cottonwood, swamp w.o., red birch. Barrows says he found 2 dead deer on his place last fall; he himself crippled a buck he didn't find. Says 7 deer now on his place.

*   *   *   *   *

AL, EBL, Estella   Sept. 14–16, 1946

9/14

Weather   Foggy till 11 A.M. Clear, cool, S.W. breeze. 68° at 5 P.M. Lake level 1.0'; rose 2½ inches since last trip. No mosquitoes.

Seen   Blue heron 1   hawks 0   ducks 0   quail 20+?   king-fisher 1   woodcock 0   pheasant: heard first cackle of year about 5 P.M.

Phenology First bloom: *Chelone* on slough bank. Full bloom: Closed gentian, *Polygonum coccineum*, *H. strumosus*, tall sun-flower, milkwort, yellow *Lactuca* at gate, *Bidens.* Passing out: Prairie goldenrod, cardinal flowers (last bloom), boneset, but-ter & eggs, *Rudbeckia lacinata.* Last bloom: Joe pye, greater ragweed (at Reagan's), vervain, bull thistle, smartweed, *Liatris spheroidea*, *Physostegia.* Out: *M. punctata*, *M. fistulosa*, *A. fur-catus.* Straggle: harebell, E. primrose, small ragweed.

Color   All three pines are losing old needles. Jack pine is partly yellow, partly brown, but seems to go through a yellow stage. Norway turns brown direct. White gets yellow first.

Fall Bloom   Birdfoot violet with 2 flowers in loop of drive.

Fruit   Hickory nuts now peel; a squirrel left one near garden, brought all the way from road. *Crategus* near lake has berries red, full ripe, nearly ready to fall. Jack-in-pulpit berries now deep red, full ripe. A few puffballs, some edible, but not as many as I expected after the good rains. Chokecherry dead ripe. Holly now full red.

Work   Came in from Portage (after speaking at Green Lake last night). Brought in and planted in birch row, at shack, and on sandhill:

20 *Coreopsis palmata* (naked roots)
8 *Viola pedata* (partly earthed roots) ⎫
2 *Aster* sp.? (low, branched, deep blue) ⎭ watered
Cut lawn. Pruned some jacks in haystack planting.

Quail Flushed the covey at S.E. corner of sandblow. There seemed to be more than the ususal 15 (20?) and they divided into two groups, flying west. They started the assembly call almost at once after flushing. Whole bunch called again at sunset, evidently getting scatters in.

Birdsong Heard a y.t. vireo about 8 A.M. at Green Lake, also pewee. Crested called at 6 P.M. No song at sunset, but robin and cardinal called. No woodcock seen but bat first seen at 6:39 P.M.

Katydid Heard a continuous monotone call and traced it down to a katydid on a bluestem plant. No change of tone.

Deer Some tracks on sandhill. Looks like additional stripping of pickerel weed leaves in Lake Chapman.

White Pine Seed Crop Near Marlette (Marquette Co.) saw a heavy crop of cones on a grove of young whites about 25' high. Fred Trenk tells me there is a seed crop throughout the state.

9/15
Weather Fog at dawn, 46° 5 A.M. Later calm, clear, vane S.E.–S.W. 65° at 6:30 P.M. Much warmer at evening.

Seen Blue heron 2, 1 marsh hawk 1 redtail 1 ducks 0 woodcock 1 quail 30+ rabbit 0 pheasant 1 cock 1 red squirrel in wood duck box at shack.

Birdsong Nothing sang at daybreak, but cardinal chirped at 5:06 and woodcock flew (low, headed south) at 5:06. At 5:08–5:11 there was the most beautiful morning assembly-call of quail I have ever heard. They were roosting in the white pines a stone's throw south of the shack. Slight additional calls were heard at 5:11 and 5:30, 5:39. I flushed them about 6:00; they had not moved since 5:08, evidently keeping dry under the pines. There were two groups, which separated on flushing, one going south, the other west; the former larger birds. The former were larger, so I assume they were the home covey.

At 5:43 a pheasant crowed; first cackle yesterday. At 6:40 y.t. vireo sang at soon after a field sparrow gave a single song. The vireo continued through the morning.

Work   Lopped and burned the brush of the down oak; hauled in 1 trunkful of wood. A mole plowed through the pasque rows in nursery last night so I moved 4 clumps to scalps on the hill.

At noon Arthur & Hanna Hasler dropped in. Stayed for lunch.

Trip to marsh   Went to the duckblind and mowed about ⅛ acre just in case we should get some water. The deer trail shows lots of traffic. Much of the smartweed (*P. succineum*) is either frozen or dried up. No water now even in the ditch. Gentians along deer trail much scarcer than last year.

The bur reed at blind seems less dense than last year but there is more "3-square" on the ditch banks. The blind is OK but the spring flood evidently lifted out my seat.

Deer Scrape   At the spot where the deer trail leaves to cross the slough to "the prairie" is a horned aspen, well oxidized. The leaves on the broken limbs are thoroughly brown and dead, but the tree had not been horned on Aug. 18 when I visited the marsh. Hence estimate the work was done within a week of Sept. 1. This is the earliest scrape I have recorded.

Evening Song   Nothing sang. Bat flew at 6:31. No woodcock. Quail were silent.

9/16

Weather   Warmer, 48° at 4 A.M. Calm, south vane. Fog at daybreak.

Seen   Blue heron 11   muskrat 1   first white throat   grouse 1   woodcock 3   rabbit 1   en route home: 5 doves on County A   10 quail on lot near Ringling farm.

Daybreak Song   Woodcock flew at 4:58 (twitter) and 5:00. Robin call 5:05. Song sparrow sang at 5:08 and several times after. White throated sparrow "chinked" at 5:08. Wren scolded 5:13. No chorus of quail as yesterday but several single calls at 5:13 and again 7:20. Bat flew till 5:19, when first crow heard. Pheasant cackled once at 5:29.

Grouse Drumming   Estella heard one four times in our woods. This is extra early.

Red Squirrel Eats Poison Ivy   Estella saw a red squirrel at down oak on sandhill busily eating poison ivy berries which are now ripe. She also saw cedar waxwings eating silky dogwood.

Work   Transplanted a dozen butterfly weeds; part of them replacements of seedlings bitten off by insects. Packed a dozen for Frank Schramm and some for Marie. Hauled in another trunkload of wood.

En Route Home   Saw 10 quail cross the road beyond Ringling Farm—large birds. 5 doves on County A. *Silphium* at church (cemetery) on terminal moraine had just one bloom left.

Some butternuts on County T and also on Baraboo hills already leafless. Others yellow. Red maples on Baraboo canyon already red.

Saw some nighthawks near Baraboo.

*   *   *   *   *

Planting Trip 1948

AL, EBL, Estella, Jean Sullivan   4/16

Weather   Cold, clear, N.W. wind. 48° at sunset. Lake level 2.4'.

Seen   Blue heron 1   Marsh Hawk 0   Mallard 1, 2   No rabbits seen or dead on road.

Geese   I estimate that at least 200 came in to marsh 6:00–6:30. Flock counts 1, 3, 5, 8, 3, 8, 7, 6, 2, 7, 3, 14, 12, 5, 4, 6, 4, 4, 13, 4, 7, 7, 13.

Phenology   Marsh marigold not yet in bloom. Only a few pasques have opened during week. *Geum triflorum* in bud. Could find no pollen on hazel. Tamarack buds breaking green. Ruffed grouse drummed until dark, long after the woodcock peented.

Rabbit   Killed by a raptor, I think horned owl, on the east edge of Clay Hill plantation.

Jackrabbit   Joe Lewis says he saw his first jackrabbit on his farm in spring of 1947. He saw the tracks last winter but did not see the rabbit.

Birdsong   Woodcock peented on east end of Island 7:01 (0.02); at west end 7:05. Not sure that Clay Hill peented. Peenting on sandbar by moonlight at 9:30. Robin sang briefly at 6:30. Field sparrow silent. Woodcock on island still peenting at 10:15. Much goose talk.

4/17

Weather   Cold, clear, calm at daybreak, W. wind after 7:30. Moon. 28° at sunup 5:18. S.E. wind 55° at noon.

Seen   1 grebe in slough   mallard 2   thought I saw a turkey buzzard over woods but couldn't verify   marshhawk 1 ♀   bald-pate 2   scaups 2   wood duck 0   hundreds of juncos on road   blue heron 1, 1.

Geese   Left the marsh, flying very low to S.W., between 5:10 and 5:40. Went out in 11 groups of 25–75 each. One very large group came back and went east at 6:30; we counted about half at 100; estimate 200 total. Total estimate of 300 spent night in marsh. Flock counts: 5, 6, 13, 14, 4, 14, 2, 2, 2, 3, 12, 7, 8.

Daybreak Song   Pheasant, song spar. 4:25 (-0.012); dove, field spar. 4:34 (0.012); robin 4:37 (0.015); woodcock quiet 4:40 (0.015); redwing 4:47 (0.02); cardinal 4:51 (0.03); jay 4:58 (0.06); horned owl quit 5:04 (0.1); crow 5:07 (0.4); sunrise 5:18. Meadowlark sang but failed to catch earliest. Robin sang 4:59–5:05.

Geese P.M.   Estella and Jean sat in the marsh as they came in; they think there must be 1000. Flock counts 15, 9, 5, 6, 6, 2, 1, 1, 5.

Phenology   Bloodroots at big elm bench just up. Hepaticas (yes, ½" high) on N. slope not yet up. Lilac buds opening, 1" long. No Dutch. br. in sight. Mourning cloak butterfly in woods. Green-barked pussy willow still in pollen. Soft maple still in bloom. Columbine 5" high. Golden ragwort 4" high. *Salix discolor* in birchrow first bloom.

Arrivals   Myrtle warbler abundant in woods.

Pasque Age of Bloom   Yesterday I couldn't find the new pasque blooming last week at 2 years from seed. Found it today nipped off (by rabbit?). On steep bank of slough found another 2-year-old pasque just starting to open. Estimate 2 ÷ 50 planted = 4% bloom second year.

Chickadees Saw an unbanded and a banded bird just E. of Wahoo Pool but am not sure they were a pair. The unbanded one quivered its wings but I heard a third chick nearby.

Work Cleared more pines in woods. Estella and Jean made some wood near haystack. Went to Portage to address Tri-County Conservation Club; met warden A.D. Galston. Back 10:30—saw 2 rabbits on road. Galston said 52 deer counted by plane last winter Annecker's Bluff.

Banding Nuthatch 38–127579 left.

4/18

Weather Raining at daybreak. S.E. wind. Didn't go out. Warming with S. wind all day; cloudy 74° at 4:30. Mosquitoes biting at night.

Seen Blue heron 1, 1 marsh hawk o mallard 2 kingfisher 1 wood duck 7.

Phenology Bloodroots in bed by showerbath opened (3) about 11 A.M. One *Hepatica* flower in road thicket near Clay Hill. Toothwort planted last year in bud. Garter snake out. Fritillary butterfly sp.? Shack elm out of bloom. First mosquitoes.

Arrivals Chipping sparrow sang in yard at noon. Thought I heard wren but couldn't verify. No fox sparrows yet.

Geese Went out as usual 5:15–6:00. Came back (perhaps 200) from corn about 9 A.M.—went east, I think to sandbar. Return to marsh began about 4:15. Flock counts: 5, 1, 1, 15, 7, 5, 2, 4, 1, 2, 14, 2, 2, 4, 11, 6, 1, 4, 1, 2, (92); counts 6:45–7:45 (parentheses are est.): 11, 2, 6, 3, 1, 5, 2, 4, 5, 4, 2, 3, 1, 11, 8, 9, 11, 10, 5, 2, 10, (50), (20), 9, 7, 1, 2, 5, 1, 5, 2, 6, (7), 2, 12, 2, 8, 3, 8, 2, (14), 5, 4, (25), 2, 6, 7, 10, (20), 9, 13, 4, 4, 6, 11, 2, 2, (15), (20). Total 444.

Work During rain in early A.M. burned 3 brushpiles near shack. Estella planted onion seedlings in garden. Sowed S. half and centre of garden to 6# alsike clover and 2# timothy. Estella Jr. put in some fence rails. Jim Reagan has plowed garden—paid him $5 on account.

Chickadees are not all paired yet. One group of about 4, at least one banded left, came into suet 5 P.M. with a downy ♂ with a nuthatch.

Pines   Some jack pine terminal buds 4″ long. No clear elongation of white or Norway. Tamarack buds bursting.

Robin   Began song 5:10.

Mammals   Still no spermophile.

4/19

Weather   Part cloudy, warm (60° at 4:30), intermittent S.W. breeze. Warming: 70° at 8:15.

Seen   Marshhawk 1   mallard 2, 7   bluewing teal 2   blue heron 1 *Buteo* (redtail) 1, 1   pheasant 1♂ with 3♀ (Anchor's) rabbits 0 in 2 hrs.

Geese   Went out from 5:10–5:30. Largest flight consisted of 3 groups of about 200 each which went out at 5:15, mostly headed S.W. There were 3 shots at or near Van Housen's at this time. I think my estimates have been low—there are close to 1000 using marsh. About 300 came back headed east 7:20. Flock counts A.M.: 6, 2, 6, 5, 2, 1, 5, 2, 3, 4, 1, 4, 6, 2, 7, 8, 4, 6, 5. (25) went E. 3 P.M. Count 5:00–7:00 P.M.: 5, 5, 9, 2, 3, 2, (35), 8, 1, 7, 5, 7, 7, 6, 7, 2, 3, 2, 10, 3, 8, 12, 5, 16, 2, 7, 10, 5, 4, 6, 4, 4, 9, 6, 7, 19, 8, 3, 3, 2, 7, 3, 12, 3, 3, 2, 14, 2, 3, 10, 7, 2, 3, 5, 13, 13, 4, 3, 6, (17), 5, 5, 1, 1, 1, 3, 2, 12, 3, 12, 9.

Birdsong   Pheasants were almost silent at daybreak. Bobwhite whistled 5:32 (5.0) at sunup; first this year. Song spar. too late, dove and field spar. 4:35 (0.012), bluebird & last woodcock 4:36 (0.013), robin 4:38 (0.014), pheas. 4:44 (0.018), cowbird 4:55 (0.025), crow 4:59 (0.03).

Phenology   European white birch catkins in triangle almost in pollen. First cabbage butterfly (white with black dots). Dutchman's breeches in N. angle of shack in bud. Tree frog calling. Box elder on Co. A partly bloomed out, partly stamens still closed.

Work   Moved 8 or 10 remaining tamaracks from nursery; watered. Potted 6 pasques from nursery for Mark Ingraham. Estella Jr. moved a dozen jacks from birchrow road to Island. Planted lettuce & radishes. Got trees in Baraboo: 200 WP & 200 Red from Nepco nursery, Port Edwards Wis.

Robin   Sang 4:38 (0.014) to 6:10, again at 7:45. Feeding in garden. Sang very briefly 6:33 P.M.—probably too windy.

Chickadees   2 came to suet with a downy ♂ and a nuthatch; one was banded alum. left, yellow right. This was the winter flock we have been catching this spring.

Mole   Killed one with a shovel on lawn about 4 P.M.

4/20

Weather   Cloudy, cold, 46° at 4:30. N.W. wind. Moon set just before dawn. Clearing in P.M., N.W. wind. Warming, clear, 52° at sunset.

Seen   Pileated on elm at gate   mallard 1, 2   wood duck 2 bluewing (in slough) 2   1 rabbit in 3 hrs.   I suspect pileated has been using suet; seen 4 times today near yard   no herons *Buteo* (redtail) 1   r.b. kinglet here singing.

Geese   6 big groups of 50–150 each left the marsh 5:06–5:20, again headed S.W., flying low. Flock counts A.M.: 5, 7, 7, 7, 4, 3, 6, 5, 1, 5, 2, 2, 1. About 300 again flew east 9:00 A.M.—evidently en route from corn to sandbar. Evening flock count: a few flocks in at 6:40: 19, 1, 8, 2, 1, 17. No others up to 8:30.

Daybreak Song   Song spar. 4:32 (-0.012). Field spar. 4:39 (-0.012) dove 4:40 (-0.012) bluebird 4:44 (0.012) robin and last woodcock 4:45 (0.014) cardinal 4:50 (0.02) jay 4:54 (0.03). Robin sang intermittently until 7:30; briefly at 6:40 P.M.—not during day. Woodcock started 7:10 (0.018) on island.

Work   Cut some birch sprouts in birchrow. Planted 50 Norways near gate and Starker's Point. Did some filling of lawn extension N. of shack. Cleared trail through prickly ash thicket above Otter Pool. Cut some birch sprouts in birchrow. Planted 25 more reds and 25 whites near Starker's Point.

Phenology   Gill-over-ground in bloom near Otter Pool. May apple on Wahoo Ridge just up—max. 1″ high. *Antennaria munda* now in bloom. Sandbar willow (early strains) in bloom; this species is very variable. Dutchman's br. and bloodroot in bloom N. slope. *Funkia* leaves 4″ day lily 6″ iris 4″.

Bloodroots close at night, open during day when warm, but not when cold. Those near shower stayed closed all today in windy bed but not on protected N. slope.

4/21

Weather   clear, calm, cold, frost in grass, 36° at 6:00 A.M. S.W. vane.

Seen

Geese   The geese must have returned to marsh after dusk because there was the usual outward flight to S.W. between 5:15 and 5:40 A.M., mostly in small enough groups to be either counted or estimated. Figures below total 871, but there may have been more that went east or north, or that flew too low to reach the skyline. Flocks: 10, (50), (14), (15), 2, (40), 12, 8, 1, 7, 4, 3, (20), 10, (25), 7, 10, 5, 1, 3, 6, 5, 2, 4, 8, 4, (10), 2, (30), 3, (30), 4, 9, 2, 11, (30), 6, (18), 3, 1, (18), (20), 6, 3, 12, 6, (25), 9, (33), (25), 5, 2, (43), 5, 14, 12, 2, (18), 9, 19, 2, 8, (30), 7, 4, 1, 8, 3, 5, 4, 6, (19), 10, 7, 5, 11, 10, 6. Total 871.

Phenology   Eur. white birch, almost in pollen 4/19, is spent today.

Bloodroot in Shower Bed   Closed 6 A.M.

SELECTED LETTERS

To Clara Leopold

Cook Montana
Sept. 12—03

Dear Mama:

Papa has probably described the last few days of our trip so I will write briefly. We passed through a beautiful country yesterday seeing many antelope and one fine blacktail buck. Woke this morning in 2 inches of snow. The air was damp so to keep our feet warm we walked the 23 miles to Cook through the snowstorm. On the way I found a small lake full of beaver sign, cuttings, etc. and obtained fine specimens. Passed the foot of Grand Mountain, but could not see the summit on account of the snow. Also saw fresh bear & elk tracks. Tomorrow we go to Gilbert Ranch (15 miles) and outfit the pack train for the "Hoodoos." According to natives, this storm will be succeeded by a long Indian Summer, which will be very favorable for us. I guess you will be going to Manitou soon, and hope you will enjoy it. Hope you are well. Remember me to the rest.

Your Aldo

To Clara Leopold

Kennedy House
February 10

My Dear Mama:

I have received both Papa's and Marie's account of the Werthmuellers' misfortune. The old people are certainly to be pitied, especially to have it happen just at this time. I guess Elsie has little left after this double fire. What are their plans for the future? Judging from the accounts they have saved nothing at all. Was the building burnt to the ground?

I enclose a copy of the *Lawrence* with an account of the gambling. I have not written often in the last week on account of my busy days falling on that time, nor will I be able for a while on account of my term essay.

I had a fine trip this afternoon. It was clear and cold, without snow, and quite a wind. The Canal being safe, I visited the "far woods" and explored them more thoroughly. In extent they equal the Big Woods, and are fully as interesting. I further investigated the wild white pine, and find that for a square half mile there is a considerable sprinkling of saplings, besides the large trees seen before. There is bracken there in summer, also other ferns. I collected two new species of the strange moss looking like needle wood, besides finding considerable numbers of the species sent you, which, you will remember, I thought quite rare. Also collected a new species of fungus, with a very large fruiting body, some being a semi-circle of 7 inches circumference. You may remember a large white fungus which I found at the Club (Les Cheneaux) 2 years ago, it is of that species. Besides these I saw numbers of very small magnolias, some of which I collected. I will send you a leaf, after it is pressed, perhaps you may identify it having been in the South. In this Far Woods is some of the finest woodcock ground I ever saw. Also found the tracks of a large coon, but as it was late and the snow gone I did not follow. Of course I wouldn't have hurt the coon, but I intend to find his residence. Besides seeing a rabbit (who ran as if half scared to death, being hunted so much), I had much fun with a muskrat. While crossing a creek shortly after starting, I espied a muskrat out on the opposite bank digging in the grass. I stepped behind a tree, and soon he came down to the creek with a large bundle of sod, which, after he had washed it off, he began to eat, and soon went back for another bundle. He repeated this six times, I patiently watching all the while, till at last I grew cold and decided to put an end to the scene. The creek is here only a shingly rapids, and I could have easily killed Mr. Rat, but decided to have a little fun at his expense. While he was out for his seventh load, I ran across the creek, stooping low, and intending to surprise him when he came back. But Mr. Rat had ears to hear, and heard too, so while I was just raising my face above the bank, Mr. Rat came tumbling over, and the fun was at my expense for an instant. I tried to spoon him back from the deep pool with my club, where he had his den, but was not a good enough golf player, so he succeeded in passing me and was soon out of sight. Upon subsequent examination I find muskrats living in the deep places all along every creek, even to the small rills a few feet wide. The difference in this respect between this and our country must be that the winters are not so extremely cold nor the summers so very dry. I could trap great numbers of these muskrats, but have no desire to do so. Perhaps I have told you that in "The Swamp" there are some half dozen rat-houses. Of course the creek rats build no houses, the only evidence of their existence now are the submarine hole-entrances of the deeper pools and an occasional track.

It is amusing to watch the crows going to roost in the evening. They now, the mating season being on, go in one immense swarm, which wheels about and makes a great noise, all the while moving slowly along. Any number of crows could be killed on a windy evening, by keeping to cover in the wake of the swarm and picking off stragglers who, from some distant place, are hurrying carelessly along to join the flock.

Birds were scarce today, besides a red-shouldered hawk and a large flock of horned & p. horned larks, I saw nothing remarkable.

Papa in his letter remarks the advent of a tree-sparrow. They are the commonest bird here now, titmice are also common, and found in the loose "Winter Companies" with other birds. There are undoubtedly great numbers of tree-sparrows as winter visitants in Iowa, but they don't seem to find their way so far into town. I saw great numbers before leaving. Does the little nuthatch continue his visits?

Mr. Robinson has made a new arrangement very convenient to me. If not through with our studies at 9:30 we may study by the parlor lights for a while. I have been down for the last two nights, with visible results in recitations. From now till Monday, however, I have plenty of time.

A novelty in the way of a lecturer today. A full-blooded Indian spoke on "The School of Savagery." His name is Eastman, and he is a graduate of Dartmouth, of fine build and knows his business. Like a true Indian, he talks little, says a great deal to those who have understanding and nothing to those who have not. He ventured no opinions on the present status of his race, holding fast to his subject, or, the education of the young Indian, evidently as it was before the advent of white-demoralization, at least he did not mention the latter. Some words and phrases which I have never heard anywhere else impressed me particularly. He said, after speaking of the Indian's knowledge of nature:

"Nature is the gate to the Great Mystery."

The words are simple enough, but the meaning unfathomable.

Well, I hope you are all well and that Werthmuellers make a favorable insurance settlement. Will write again in a few days, meanwhile, I am

Your Aldo

P.S. Ask Papa if he is acquainted with the cowboy cousin of whom I wrote Carl. As you say, the L's are forging to the front in the Wild & Wooly West, as even Iowa is here called.

February 10, 1904

To Clara Leopold

Kennedy 3/21/04

My dear Mama:

Received yours of the 18th.

I think your description of Iowa weather in March answers here also today, it is raining and muddy. But I congratulate myself in being unlike many people in regard to my opinions on the weather, I don't mind this at all, and as for a sunny March day, I think I appreciate it more than the "balmiest morn of May." I took only a short walk before breakfast this morning, and have been studying rather hard the rest of the day.

I am very sorry that the ducks are being slaughtered as usual, but of course could expect nothing else. When my turn comes to have something to say and do against it and other related matters I am sure that nothing in my power will be lacking to the good cause.

We had quite an excitement here yesterday evening. Some of us were standing on the walk before the house when we noticed that a house about half a mile or more down the road was afire. We all started off at once, on a run, having a sort of race on the way. We were the first ones to arrive of the school. The house was the summer home of one Cook, a Trenton merchant and also owner of the Potteries. It was one of the old fashioned solidly built brick houses which are becoming rare; surrounded by gigantic pines & one of the most magnificent oaks in the country (which by the way, I think is unharmed). The flames spread rapidly and but few things were saved, mostly by the keeper, a nearby farmer. Drummond, the farmer, and I removed a few things such as an ice-chest and tables from the kitchen, where the flames had not spread; also discovered and removed a can of gasoline which might have made trouble. A chemical engine from Trenton arrived after a while but it was only useful in saving the barns and windmill. It was drawn by some beautiful horses and I think made a very quick trip. The house is said to have been very finely furnished but of course was entirely destroyed. The fire started from the furnace.

Your star-flower is very pretty, did you notice the onion smell? By the way there is a kind of wild onion which grows in this country. It is very common on new fields and borders of woods.

I note what you say concerning the opera-glasses. Now I ought to not tell this, but as you ask what Mr. Robinson has done in the matter, I will say that he proceeded as in all such cases to go through the whole house. If you really intend that I should have another, and it certainly is more than I could ask after having received so many new supplies lately for carrying on my studies, I would like to state a few desiderata which while not affecting the price may double the value of the glasses for the purpose in hand. The most important of these is that the instrument should have a large eyepiece, the reason for which I think you will understand; namely, to lessen the chance of the birds escaping from the field of vision. If you remember the character of the lost glasses you will know what to get, they embodied all desirable qualities.

Supper is ready so must end. With best wishes to you all, I am

Your Aldo

P.S. I hope Tante Anna will soon recover from her illness.

Will write Frederic soon.

To Clara Leopold

Kennedy, April 2

My dear Mama:

The glasses came today. Now I will do just as you say and tell frankly what I think of them:—I am very much pleased and find them perfectly adapted to my wants. They magnify finely, the field is clear and outline very distinct. I can assure you that they are most highly appreciated and will also receive the best of care.

I gave them a thorough trial this morning, and happily enough they arrived just in time to help me identify the first new species of the season (i.e. a new species for the eastern states).

The morning was bright (after two days of rain), and I went towards "The Swamp." Between here and the creek I saw nothing extraordinary. But just beyond it is the fencerow with the crow's nest, and there I stopped to make observations. The nest is still empty, perhaps it has been deserted on account of a fire which burned the brush from under the tree. The same fire swept over a large fallow field nearby, and even before I arrived I heard the notes of what I took to be horned larks on the field. As I passed over it, I flushed a great flock of perhaps 200, and, wishing to profit by my new equipment, I followed them to see of what race or races it was composed, this being about the date for the departure of the horned lark proper, while the prairie horned lark breeds at this latitude if not in this region. The flock was very shy, and the more glimpses I had of individuals the more uncertain I became, but luckily I determined to keep on, and after about an hour's stalking I came upon one at twenty yards. You may imagine my surprise when I found it was no horned lark at all, but an old friend of the mountains, the American pipit, or titlark, as it is sometimes called. The bird is of a family intermediate between that of the warblers and thrashers, wrens, etc., and is represented by only this one species in the eastern states. In the west, however, this and another species are found. The actions of the bird much resembled those of the horned larks, but the plumage is white beneath, spotted with olive on the sides, and grayish brown, unstreaked above. The resemblance to a thrasher can be seen when near, also to the water "thrushes," which belong to the family of warblers. Of one thing I am sure, I would have been unable to identify the species without the help of the glasses.

Leaving the pipits, I went to the swamp, but the snipe and bittern had left. I found something, however.

About two weeks ago I had an experience there which I did not write about. I saw a muskrat swimming about as if unable to get away, and an examination disclosed a trap. After some difficulty I released the animal and took the trap. I then looked over the rest of the swamp, and found another, which contained a drowned muskrat apparently several weeks dead. I took this one also. Today I found another, in which the muskrat must have lain half the winter by the looks of the body. This trap I merely concealed in a nearby thicket. So you see I have the three traps on my hands, which of course I will by no means give back to the person who traps in the breeding season, and much less if he leaves the carcasses to rot. At the same time I hesitate to keep the traps myself, so I guess I will take the two former ones back to the swamp, and put them all three away out of doing harm and harm's way. The live muskrat which I released of course had his leg broken but I guess he will recover the use of it. My method of getting him out of the trap might interest you. After trying all manner of stick devices etc., I tried this. Carrying him to the entrance of a hole in the ground, I laid him down and of course he tried to crawl down the hole. This disposed of his wicked teeth; and I merely squeezed open the trap with my hands and Mr. Muskrat continued his course into the earth. It is remarkable that in all my former attempts to release him, in which I necessarily tortured his broken leg a good deal, he uttered not one squeal or noise of any kind, but Papa will tell you how they make use of their teeth when cornered. I took great care, however, and he did not reach me. This affair is rather an unpleasant subject, but I thought I had better tell you about it.

To finish my trip, I went over to the "Far Woods" and examined the woodcock ground, but found no sign whatever, nor any hermit thrushes. The above mentioned tract contains a great deal of skunk cabbage, now in full blossom and buzzing with carrion flies and other insects. Accordingly, the phoebes were there in force, and I actually detected one sitting on a flower and contentedly snapping up all visitors in the way of insects. The cabbage is now beginning to send up its leaves, from one which is unfolded I should say they resemble light green calla leaves more than anything else. Other matters of interest were a young pickerel about five inches long seen in a small ditch which he had evidently ascended from somewhere, and about a dozen more Savannah sparrows seen in various places. They feed out on the open fallow, or sometimes stubble, but when flushed they either alight again and run away or take to trees and brush. Vesper sparrows have become quite numerous, while field sparrows are singing quite frequently. In my opinion the song of the field sparrow is one of the finest to be heard anywhere. Saw another sharp-shin today, sparrow hawks are here in small numbers, but many of the larger species have gone for the summer.

The canal is now filled and canal-boats towed by horses are passing often.

Bedtime now so I must end. Thanking you again for the glasses, and with love to you all, I am

Your Aldo

P.S. had a postal from Mort today sent from New York, saying he is on a trip and will write to me soon.

April 2, 1904

To Marie Leopold

Lawrenceville N.J.
Upper House, Jan. 25, 1905

My dear Marie:—

I ought to have written you long before this, but there always happened to be something to tell which I thought would interest Carl or Mama especially, so I put it off until today.

I was very much pleased to hear Mama say in her last letter that she continued to go roller-skating regularly. I infer from this that you also have accompanied her, or vice versa. Did you get to go ice skating with Carl? We are having ice-weather now after the January Thaw, but the pond has frozen with a rough surface, making skating impossible.

Speaking of weather, I would say that today is the nearest approach to the day on which we broke camp in the mountains which I have ever seen. It has now snowed hard and unceasingly for just 27 hours. The wind is blowing a gale from the north, and the temperature hovers near 0° F. The depth of the snow in the open varies from none at all to three or four feet, and drifts are as much as twenty feet deep. I do not think that the snow will cease before tomorrow morning.

Happily today is Wednesday, so at one o'clock I started out, prepared for the drifts with my knee boots under instead of outside. The plan worked to perfection.

It would take a tenderfoot to declare that he could walk ten miles on an afternoon like this. Progress was in some places impossible. For instance, I headed for the upper Schipitaquin Creek, expecting to cross the divide at random where it consists of a flat plateau. When I reached the plateau, I made about forty yards in ten minutes, and then found myself on the wrong side of a gully fifteen feet deep in snow. The wind blew so that it took all the strength of the thighs to face it, and eyes were good up to ten or fifteen yards against the driving snow and not more than a hundred yards or two in the opposite direction. It was evident that I had better try the road, which crossed about a hundred yards away, running through a cut of varying depth. It seemed all right at first, but before I had gone far I discerned a sort of blank ahead, where I could see nothing at all. At twenty feet I made it out to be a drift, level with the top of the cut, and at least fifteen feet deep. Then I gave up the upper Schipitaquin and going back to the forks, struck into the woods on its banks lower down. It was fine in the woods where the wind could only be heard overhead. The snow was two feet deep there, but it was really a luxury to be out of the wind. When the limit of the woods was reached, I got in the lee of the trolley embankment, and by a hundred yards' run, into the next piece of timber. It was beautiful there, especially along the creek. On some isolated rocks in the creek channel the snow was piled into large cones and domes as much as two feet high and hardly a foot in diameter at the base. There were some chickadees, the forever cheerful, in these woods. It was with reluctance that I started back, but the wind was of a different opinion from myself. As soon as I got into the open, it took no effort at all to go hurtling along at a tremendous pace, and in about one fifth of the time that it took on the way out, I was back on the ridge of the lower creek, and only a few hundred yards from the Pike which leads into town. But on those few hundred yards there was drifted snow, ten feet deep. I devised a plan, however. Going along the ridge a way, I reached the old cemetery, and was soon on the wind-swept stone wall which encloses it and en route to the Pike, grinning at the deep drifts on either side. Once on the pike, it was a great satisfaction to pass a line of three trolley-cars, whose conductors were busy shoveling snow, and making remarks about the weather. Thence there was a mile of open walking to the village, where I arrived in time to write this letter before supper.

I do not remember ever enjoying a bit of winter weather

more than this of today. Neither have I ever heard so many maledictions as were today heaped upon this "blasted Jersey climate" by persons who put on a hat, gloves, overcoat, garters, sweaters, and what not, to go from here to Chapel or to Memorial Hall.

Perhaps these trips are dull reading for you, but today was a day great among the great. I must get to work now, so will end with best wishes to all from

Your brother
Aldo

P.S. My guests the sparrows have eaten four ears of crushed corn on my windowsill today. At this rate the supply which I laid in last fall will not last through the storm.

To Carl Leopold

Lawrenceville N.J.
Hamill House
March 30, 1905

My dear Papa:—

Owing to the fact that we are to be in the Hamill only one week our duffel is all contained in a suit case, so that this letter in pencil is about as much as I can offer in the way of writing. Your very interesting account of the western country came yesterday, also the check for fifty dollars. I still have about ten dollars of the other deposit left.

There was only one bit of bad news in your letter,—that the annual duck-killing has been unusually heavy. I think of it the more, because this very afternoon, after several hours of work on my Laboratory book, I pocketed my glass and note book and set off down the creek, and from a partially flooded field of Winter wheat flushed a pair of fine big black mallards. And whenever I hear the redwings singing from the willows, and the *Hyla*'s piping chorus, I think of some corner of our old swamps, where the same things are going on at the same moment.

I hope your return to the old place will be accompanied by as fine a Spring as we have had here. The weather continues perfect, so warm, in fact, as to bring up a shower nearly every afternoon. After getting my work done yesterday morning I had a fine two-mile walk on the outdoor track, and after dinner an all-afternoon walk. Many birds had arrived—chipping and vesper sparrows, and would you believe it?—a tree swallow. I have been fortunate so far in seeing all the birds at their proper time of arrival, and am now awaiting kingfishers and Savannah sparrows. It often takes many hard and extra miles to reach a country where each bird that is due is liable to be found, but there is a deal of satisfaction if one's efforts for a good record are crowned with success, especially as that does not happen every time. Yesterday, for instance, I thought to find kingfishers on Stony Brook. Striking straight across the uplands for several miles I reached the headwaters. Thence I followed it down and on nearly to Princeton, each step further and further from supper, but still no kingfishers. The course of the Brook is now singularly beautiful, though, with wonderful true-reflections and grass well advanced on the meadows. Moreover I saw two squirrels and three muskrats, and by dint of hard walking got back just in time for supper, so that it was a great day anyhow.

So far the Hamill is a very good change,—Ham & I have a double room together for the week and are well fixed. Have hopes of getting into the Lab tomorrow, so did a lot of writing up directions for experiments today. Am getting a lot of other work done too.

I hope you and Carl Starker will enjoy many of these fine Spring days over in the swamps, just *seeing* things, indeed, I cannot imagine wanting to kill anything now when there is so much to see and appreciate out of doors. And tell Carl to lay in a good stock of these trips around our locality, so that he can live them over again when he goes away, for never will he find a range of country with such beauty and variation of character as our region around home,—swamps, mountains, hills, prairies, uplands and great waters are all there.

But as I have often said,—I mean nothing against this country here by all this. In fact, no one could wish for anything better. With this I will end for today as it is about nine o'clock.

Friday, 10:00 A.M.
Another fine sunshiny day. Have been working this morning, will run before noon, and then have a long walk until evening. I found a poplar tree in bloom this morning, literally draped with

the long tassels of flowers. A great many soft maples are blooming now. They remind me of the lower arm of Eagle Woods,
when we always saw the first ones blooming in the Spring.

Will write again tomorrow about what I see this afternoon.
Hoping you are all well, and are enjoying fine weather.

Your Aldo

P.S. A number of the fellows played golf yesterday,—I guess the
links at home will be in use soon too.

To Carl Leopold

Lawrenceville, May 6, 05

My dear Papa:—

For the next few weeks I may not be able to pay even my
present small attention to writing home, because I have begun
tutoring in Trig. with Mr. Smith, and also must take two hours
per week of English Grammar (all Yale Fellows must take this)
which brings my schedule up to about or over 30 hours per
week, and as I wish to make the most of the tutoring takes a
good deal of time. Not all the time, however, as the following
will show.

Once in a while one will strike a red-letter day anywhere, and
especially in May. And if today was not one, I am off on my
definitions. For imagine yourself in a beautiful piece of brushy,
timbered, hillside, an ideal place for wood-birds, and feeling
rather disappointed because the long trip has so far revealed
nothing. Then you hear a sharp cheep! cheep! note which you
take for an ovenbird and idly follow it up. From out a clump of
newly-leaved kinnikinick springs an olive-green bird too large
for most warblers and too small for anything else, and with
flight of no unusual character but astounding rapidity flies low
over the ground to the next clump. You follow and peer in.
Nothing moves. You look more closely. Perfectly motionless, a
bird with spread tail and greenish back perches on the trunk of
a sapling. He turns! a flash of black and gold! and Ye Gods!—A
hooded warbler! He regards you still motionless, but on the
alert for your slightest movement. Nervously you fumble for
glasses, get them focused successfully, and look and look and
look. A hooded sure enough, and O what a beauty!

This is the second I have ever seen, and neither will I ever forget. The first was three years ago in the black depths of a pin oak swamp back of the Ferry landing, but I can see it all still and could show you the tree. They are really quite rare, very rare for the amateur, so the fortunate observer is not very frequently found.

The other birds which have arrived since Wednesday are the black-throated blue warbler, solitary sandpiper, white-eyed vireo, and scarlet tanager. Also have identified the wild black currant, the very *rare* toothed-sagitate pepperwort, sassafras tree, and thyme-leaved speedwell.

Sunday, May 7

Another perfect day, and a great wave of migrants has arrived. This morning at sunrise I breakfasted on a butterbread and some apples pilfered from the table yesterday, and until chapel-time (10 o'clock) had a regular old bird-trip, going northward to the great orchards now in full bloom, and returning through several woodlands. The meadows were sparkling with the early dew and the songs of bobolinks, and from every woodland the first songs of the wood-thrushes, together with all the vireos, towhees, catbirds, thrashers, tanagers, etc. reminded me of the great chorus that I used to hear in the old bottom-lands along the river. And I had not been in the orchards long, before the new arrivals began to appear. In short, they were—Baltimore orioles, yellow-billed cuckoos, wood pewees, an olive-backed thrush, several gorgeous magnolia warblers, a pair of very talkative chats whose sarcastic remarks could be heard at a quarter-mile distance, a blue-winged warbler and several chestnut-sided warblers. *Parula* and black-throated blue warblers are becoming very common, and with the many myrtles, black-throated greens, and black-and-white warblers form the bulk of these most interesting, mysterious, beautiful, and tantalizing family of birds.

Also found another song sparrow's nest containing five eggs. The young crows in most nests can be distinctly heard by tapping on the trees with a stick. In the line of flowers, I find Solomon's seal and spikenard blooming today; the first hickory blossoms are also out. Watched a cuckoo devour a whole nest of tent-caterpillars on a hickory tree this morning. He seemed to relish the web just as much as the insects and swallowed quantities of both, demolishing the remainder after he had his fill.

There is much work to complete today, which is always done best *now*. So will end hoping that you are all enjoying the May weather together on this peaceful Sunday at home. Tell Mama that the two boxes arrived in safety, but that only the one lives in safety, in fact, the other is quite empty. Best wishes to you all from

Your Aldo

P.S. The trials for the Penn Charter Meet come off tomorrow, the weather having been too boisterous last Thursday. Miller Brooks will probably get the mile.

To Carl Leopold

400 Temple St.
New Haven, Conn.
Sept. 27, 1905

My dear Papa—

With great satisfaction I am able to repeat that everything goes finely. Exam in Algebra A at Winchester Hall this morning. Of eight problems I am quite confident of seven, so that another flunk is unlikely.

At last I have ascertained favorably the only question that has bothered me about Old Eli. That was—Is there a chance for "hikes in the woods" on half-holidays? Well, there certainly is, and I found it out like this—

In the catalog is a map, and way up in the corner it says "East Rock Park." By the map it is a mile and a half from here on Temple Street. So at three today, after I had transacted a lot of trifles, I set off up Temple. There are beautiful residences on the way, with enormous elms & oaks, and carpet-like grass, and squirrels! On one lawn were ten gray squirrels on the ground at once. Then come vacant lots, and then—East Rock. Just like a landlocked portion of the Hudson Palisades, covered with a mixed forest of hardwoods and hemlock, and surrounded by great hills of green. At the base of the cliff is a tidewater creek, bordered by salt meadows and thickets. Roads and footpaths wind around the hills and through the hemlocks, chestnuts, & oaks, nevertheless there are many steep and pathless corners where one would think himself the first colonist, but for the sounds of the city below. And again everywhere are gray squirrels, in incredible numbers, and bands of migrating birds. Rare trees & shrubs like sweet birch and barberry and a host of unknowns make interest for every acre, while good common delicious chestnuts invite clubs and rocks at every turn. In fact if I keep on it will never end, only suffice it to say that I am immensely pleased with it all.

I have already been obliged to cash my second check, although the first fifty dollars were watched very closely. It is to be hoped that expenses will run a good deal lower after I get fully settled. The Room is all in ship-shape, but there will be a lot of text books, and necessarily some clothes. By the way, would you prefer to have me pay my lodging-bill here, or have it come to you? It is paid in advance every four weeks, and will probably come in very soon. I have been fortunate in the choice of this room. It is entirely to my taste, and just as good as some rooms bringing twice as much. Pictures are up and all furnishings in order, so that I am very cozily fixed, and ready for the regular work, which begins tomorrow by a meeting for organization of the class at three in Sheffield Hall. Over in the College proper, i.e. the Academic side, the Freshman-Sophomore rush comes off tonight. There are signs of activity here too. Last night I was awakened by a great noise in the street. It cracked & roared like a cannon, and went to these words—

Hey—fresh—put out that light!
     "   "   "   "   "   " , again & again.
About fifty juniors were there, headed by a cheer-leader, and their combined voices made some noise for sure. The belated Freshmen over in the Row obediently extinguished their midnight oil, and the Juniors apparently departed. Then a daring Freshman who "feared neither man nor devil" lit a match.

Hey! fresh—put out that light! thundered up from the street, and Freshman Row remained black as a dark cat till daylight. (Finish tomorrow).

To Frederic Leopold

Yale—March 25

My dear Frederic—

Today it seems almost as if Spring were coming again—muddy enough for stilts and warm enough for marbles. The snow is melting quite rapidly, and I am hoping that at home too you will soon be able to play baseball and make garden again. Baseball we have here too, but when it comes to gardening weather, I will be wishing I could help you dig again in the rich sweet mellowness of the Spring earth. But if that is not possible we will do the next best—next vacation, cutting the fresh grass and a whole million other delights, all included in "summer."

Do you know, old man, we are going to have high old times next summer! *You and I* are going to try a *new* stunt. We are going to take charge of *Mama* and *Cicero* every alternate day, *both* of us, and there is going to be something doing. On those days things are going to be *moving*. We are going to take them a-blackberrying in the hills of Flint, and a-botanizing in the uttermost parts of the —— country. We will show them where grow the choicest of gooseberries, and hunt out the yellow mayapple on the hillsides. New flowers we shall find in the meadows, and the quails will whistle for us from the green pastures. Of a Sunday we will go a-picnicing, and very often we shall find delight in the reaches of our river. Papa may go along then, and Carolo shall leave his chickens, and with heavy heart accompany us to the islands of trumpet-flower. And he shall not go sadly, although he hath great possessions. Then after many glorious days, we will travel to the Isles of Contentment on the shores of Giche-Gumi, by the shining big sea water.

There shall Mama learn how to cast, and Cicero wax mighty in the craft of the fishers. Day by day shall our two boats toss on the waters, and when the south-wind ripples the Channels, mighty and swift shall the big green pike rise to their casting. Again we shall wander in the sunny clearings and burns, mid the aspens and bracken, and our meat shall be locusts and wild-raspberries. And again sit on the beach where the bearberries are trailing under the beach-plums, and watch the white water beat on the cobbles. Sweet will be the fresh breezes from over the green waters, and grateful the warm sun on the driftwood. Papa may go along then, and Carolo shall leave his sailboat, and with a hungry gun chase partridges with Spud in the Bush. Then shall we seek out the acres of gentian,—Mama shall have bunches of blueness, and for Cicero we will find the wondrous orchid in the cold moss under the cedars, the sweet white *Pyrola* and wintergreen, with harebells and slender *Gerardias* from the Muskeg. And at sundown shall follow a royal old perchfry, and other savory dishes withal, with the flavor of camp-fire. Then when the embers of driftwood burn low, and the new-moon rises over the towering balsams, we will embark one and all and wend homeward over the quiet waters.

So it shall go for many glorious days, and when rumors of school-time come from the Southland, and the wildfowl begin to arrive in the bay, our two charges will have imbibed twenty pounds each of the quintessence of the green earth. Won't that be great?

So long, Kidero, love to all from

Your Brother
March 25, 1906

To Clara Leopold

Diogenes Delight

Branford Township
Connecticut
3:30 P.M.

My dear Mama—

From a pair of very lazy good-for-nothing hoboes:—greetings.

This letter ought to have been written yesterday but what with civilized attire and civilized obligations I didn't have the nerve. For I chafed at civilization yesterday,—I had been out for two days before, just like today, and somehow a stiff collar was very disagreeable.

My Relapse into Barbarism dates from last Friday. All week and for many weeks I had been doing the thirteen-hour day

stunt and when Friday dawned warm and crystal clear I suddenly realized I was about sick of it. So I decided to cut right
& left, and at ten o'clock left our dear old New Haven with a
light heart and my backwoods outfit. Trolleyed to Branford,
walked out a couple of miles thro' a new country and about
noon reached Diogenes Delight.

Diogenes Delight is the south slope of an old moraine, richly
grown over with red cedar & barberry bushes and a carpet of
purple grass. It commands a wild and glorious view over the
hills to the Sound, with Long Island on the horizon. On the
most delightful part of this little paradise I have built my little
fireplace and my windbreak of hemlock boughs, with a deep
fragrant mattress of specially cut purple grass. The order of
procedure here is to cook, eat, and lie in the sun.

Today we (Reynolds and I) are doing just that. And O what
cooking, and what sun! Bill of fare, or rather Grub List, as
follows.

Luncheon of Diogenes
1. Spitted Apples a la Cherry Birch
2. Sizzled Bacon
3. Toasted Whole Wheat Bread

Of course you can't begin to imagine how that wintergreen
flavor from the fresh spits of cherry birch permeates those
delicious baking apples,—baked till they fall off the spit, and
then doused in a cool white snowdrift! And you cannot hear
that contented sizzle of the broiled bacon, nor the sweet nut-
flavor of the whole wheat bread. But it certainly was great—ask
Reynolds.

Now we are lying in the warm sun behind the windbreak
and taking our ease. Reynolds is sleeping very contentedly but
I have been listening to the passing bluebirds and robins and
to the noisy brook down in the hollow, and drinking in the
naturalness of it all with a great contentment. It is variety, the
spice of life, and tomorrow I will tackle the first of the Easter
Exams with so much the more energy. I have enjoyed my few
days loaf, and I am not afraid of any exam, so everything is O.K.

This is being written on a little piece of board from the good
farmer's fence.

The sun is dropping over the hill now and it is time to move in. Reynolds is up and throwing stones like a kid, just for fun. That is the spirit of Diogenes Delight.

Goodbye with much love from

Your Aldo

March 18, 1907

To Carl Leopold

New Haven
Saturday Afternoon
April 13, 1907

My dear Papa—

I had been planning to go for some fresh air this afternoon but the weather is still very backward,—cold and cloudy. Last Wednesday's snow has not altogether disappeared. So instead of going for a tramp I am spending the afternoon getting lessons all up to date so as to steal away for a few hours when fine weather comes next week. I feel rather imprisoned with all this late cold and rain and indoor work.

I have not written you about our new courses of study which we have taken up since Easter Exams. Instead of Mechanics we now have Hydraulics, and instead of Strength of Materials a course in Timber Construction. Spherical Trig is done with, as is also Mineralogy, but instead we have a second Botanical course in Flowering Plants, consisting, later in the season, of mostly Field work.

Hydraulics is very hard and so far quite theoretical. Our instructor, though a pleasant sort of fellow and well versed in his subject, is a very poor teacher and does not keep us working enough from day to day in comparison with what he expects of us at exam time. This you see is a bad combination, and we simply have to tackle the subject and learn it on our own hook or not at all. Might be a lot worse, however.

In Timber Construction we have Tracy. As usual he don't pay much attention to us but nevertheless makes us learn a great deal. So far the course is altogether draughting-work, not hard but taking lots of time. On the whole this subject is very satisfactory.

The new course in Botany is going to be good. It is not

hard work and I always enjoy it and am learning how to make scientific drawings. Our teacher is old "Pop" Evans whom we also have in the other Botany Course.

My weekly schedule is now as follows.

Monday:—German 8–9, Botany 9:30–11:30, Hydraulics 3–4

Tuesday:—French 8–9, Timber Const. 11:30–12:30, Hydraulics 3–4

Wedns.:—German 8–9, Botany 9:30–11:30, Timb. Const. 2–4

Thursday:—French 8–9, Botany Flowering Plants 10–1, Hydraulics 3–4

Friday:—German 8–9, English 12–1, Hydraulics 2–3, Timber Const. 3:15–4:15

Saturday:—French 8–9, Botany Flowering Plants 10–1.

This schedule is easier both in number of hours and amount of preparation required than that of the winter term, but it so scatters our spare moments to such an extraordinary degree that for this time of the year it is really less satisfactory. The subjects requiring overtime all come at the end of the day in the afternoon, so that we will get to see few Baseball games except the Saturday ones, and on that day I will generally have an "engagement back in the hills." However we will manage very well I guess, and there is one good thing about the schedule— it leaves an odd half hour or so here and there for us to step out on "Grub Street" for a game of catch or the like. Gay and I had a good game this afternoon. Then too we can get to bed at very respectable hours, which is a great advantage. Later on I will often skip out to one of my country seats late in the afternoon, to sizzle my bacon and enjoy the summer evening in the open. It is queer to talk about "summer evenings" with this duck weather going on outside.

By the way, I am much interested in your game law work up at Des Moines recently. I don't get time to write about it very often but the Woods Fever is still chronic with me, as is also the desire to someday help out our poor ducks and other game in return for what they have been and will be to me. All this sounds pretty sickly on paper but the time will come.

I am enclosing the last term bill of the year, covering the final third of the total tuition. We have been accustomed to pay these directly by check. Payment due May 1. I have still some of the last check left which will also last me until May.

Have you been able to get out to the golf links this Spring? After the main part of the work on the house is over I am hoping to hear you will go and play very often. I also hope you will take Frederic over into the swamps some sunny Saturday and show him the snipe and teal and all the things I remember so well. After all that is the biggest part of the hunting, just to *see* the game, and together with the fresh air ought to be enough to satisfy any man. It would certainly satisfy *me* to get over there for a look at the old ground some sunny April day.

It is time now that I tackle my lessons again. If this letter causes you and Frederic to pull on your boots and take a trip I will consider it the most successful work I have done this afternoon. You certainly deserve the time off, and perhaps need it too. Goodbye, with love to Mama and all of you. Always

Your Aldo

To Carl Leopold

New Haven
Monday Evening
May 13, 1907

My dear Papa—
Ever since receiving your letter of May 9th I have been very impatient to get time for this reply. Nothing could have happened that could give me more satisfaction than this prospect of a possible trip with you during my free time in June. I say this with all sincerity, and for more reasons than you are aware of. But first about the trip itself.

According to my original plan of going alone or with some one of the fellows, I had intended to carry *nothing*,—absolutely nothing whatever save an extra shirt and a little cash. New England is full of small country "centres" at which food and lodging can be procured with reasonable certainty, and it would also be often possible to reach some small town by nightfall, where accommodations could be secured at a hotel. At present I have topographic maps for a trip up either the Naugatuck or the Hoosatonic river, more likely the latter, in which case the route would extend up the river about to Pittsfield Mass., and thence eastward through the Berkshires to some point on the

Connecticut river (approximately Northhampton), and thence direct up the Connecticut to Northfield, which is just across the Vermont border. In case of the Naugatuck route, I would cross from the head to the Farmington River and thence to the Connecticut and then up the same as before. The country covered in this way, however, is too thickly settled and I have practically given it up in favor of the Hoosatonic Route.

My last exam comes on June 15th, and I will be ready to start by the morning of the 17th if necessary. Northfield conference begins June 28, although it will not be absolutely necessary for me to be there exactly on time. I am due in Milford July 5.

So much for my end of the deal, before the possibility of your joining me arose. I cannot but repeat how very glad I would be if that possibility could be realized. Only yesterday I learned once again that old lesson—be very careful about choosing your companion in the woods. I very greatly doubt if I could find anybody here who was both able to go and at the same time the kind of a man of whom I could be absolutely sure as an agreeable companion. A great majority of people—and they include many men who, in *town*, are very good friends of mine—are unable to enter into the spirit of the open air and the free places; they can not or do not respond or sympathize with natural, simple, or homely things; they are out of place; their conduct though not necessarily offensive still jars against the natural world and against my nerves; they do not know when to speak and when to keep silence,—in short they are blind to the things I see and they see that to which I am for the moment striving to be blind,—they do not fit nor harmonize with anything. You and I are not so, we have always been in the woods together, we understand each other there, and you are still and by far my best companion in the open.

Now although I realize that you cannot promise definitely to come, I will consider in what ways your coming might modify my plans. In the first place, there is no doubt about your ability to stand the trip. I have no intention of making it a walking-race,—on the contrary I want to see the country and the country people and the condition of both, and I want to exercise and rest and breathe the open air. That is my object in the trip. If time falls short, or anything goes wrong, the railroad is always somewhere near. Again as to equipment. You and I always enjoy the camping end of the deal, but for covering a considerable distance *on foot*, it would be impracticable to carry *anything*, especially in a country of open roads. A change of plan could here be considered—i.e. we might spend the time on some fishing water or the like, which would involve more or less outfit. I will leave this open to discussion.

Finally as to why I am so desirous of having you come east at the time. In the first place we would get through just in time for you to go home with Carolo, with a few days to spare. Or Carolo might attend the conference at Northfield—but no, come to think of it, he couldn't get away at the time. Secondly, you would come east some days early and we would see New Haven together. Even with the fellows about to leave, there is much more here to show you than could be done in many weeks, and I have always hoped that some time you and Mama both could come and see for yourselves, as far as a short visit would permit, how and where and with whom we have been spending the years of our dependence upon you—in hopes, at least, the last years of our dependence. And finally there is another reason for which I want this visit with you, that is greater than either or any or all of these. I cannot just explain why, but somehow I have come to feel that you and Mama do not really *know* me thoroughly any more. We have seen each other during vacations and all that; but somehow I know that this is true,—I have felt it for a long time. In some respects your idea of me is too good, I do not at all come up to your belief in me. In other respects I am equally certain that you under-rate me, because your ideas apply to what I *was* long ago and not to what I have become. Please understand that I do not blame anybody, either you or myself, for this, and also that it is only with pleasure that I look forward to the time when we shall see each other face to face and become even better friends than we are already. For on the whole I think things will balance up all right and there is nothing of which I am ashamed. It is for this reason, then, that I hope you can come. We will have a good visit with each other and part with a better mutual understanding which will be a help to all of us concerned. If I have appeared to be too serious in this, remember that in spite of what I have said I know even better than you do that you and Mama are after all my very best friends and that we also understand each other far better than most people who have never been separated seven consecutive days throughout their whole lives. And for my part let me also say something which has long been in my heart an absolute conviction, and which will always remain an absolute conviction. It is this. That never, in any age, at any time, in any land, has a man been given as many chances to make good in life as *I* have been given, and let me also say with Abraham Lincoln, in whose biography I came across these words:—"All that I am, or hope to be, I owe to my angel mother."

As ever
Your Aldo

To Clara Leopold

Sugar Mountain Camp
Halifax Township
Windham County, Vermont
Sunday June 23, 1907

My dear Mama:—

It is Sunday in this camp. Sure enough Sunday. We aren't doing a thing,—writing, lying around in the shade of our big sugar maple, and enjoying a cool breeze from up the valley. Down below in the valley it must be broiling hot, but we are perfectly comfortable on our 1600 ft. perch, and are glad to be taking a day off.

My last letter was mailed Thursday from Westfield. Late Thursday afternoon we took a train from Westfield up the Deerfield River to Shelburne Falls, and left there just before dark in the evening. About a mile out of town we camped on what we called Whip-poor-will Mountain, from the number of those birds that sang for us there. It was quite late, but we managed to get some straw milk and eggs from a farmer and after a supper of baked beans, bread, etc. got settled very comfortably and spent a fine night. It rained early in the night, but we put up our tarpaulin as a dog-tent and remained perfectly dry.

In the morning we struck off up the North River (east branch) and as we were feeling good made very good time all day. Fine country, and much of interest, especially an old country cemetery at Elm Grove. Picked up some supplies at Colerain and also a young chicken en route. At four o'clock crossed the Vermont line at an old deserted tavern and soon after were climbing Sugar Mountain. It is a high climb to our camp, but O how fine after you get here. The country is almost alpine, with sweet fresh pastures and clumps of enormous maples, under one of which is our camp. The breeze blows continually. Fifty yards down the hill a little cold spring, coming out between the roots of a big maple, furnishes us water. We have straw, milk, and eggs from a farm down in the valley. The dog-tent is up, and we are perfectly at home.

Yesterday we spent fishing down in the river. Papa got two dandies, one weighing almost a pound and the other not much smaller. I had a scrub and a swim in a big deep pool and finished up a lot of laundry. In the evening we climbed back up to camp, and had a royal dinner of baked trout, steamed rice, radishes, rye-bread, and chocolate. The baked trout were a tremendous success,—positively the finest fish I ever ate.

This morning we had a new dish for breakfast, namely a soup of chicken giblets, asparagus, rice, oatmeal, and bacon. It was a whooping success, and together with boiled chocolate and toast made a fine meal. You have no idea how well we are living.

The whip-poor-wills are with us here also, as they have been at every camp so far. In the evening after dinner we sit around our little fire and listen to them, and have long talks together. Both of us are enjoying the trip more and more every day, but now the time is coming when we must think of reaching our destination. Tomorrow morning bright and early we go back into Massachusetts and strike off for the Green River, where we shall probably camp and fish tomorrow evening. Tuesday we will make Bernardston or somewhere around there and by Wednesday arrive in Northfield, where Papa will leave by Thursday morning.

We continue to find something every day that we wish you all could enjoy with us, but the main feature of this end of our trip has been this Berkshire country. It is even more beautiful than back on the Housatonic, and up at this elevation is really quite northern in aspect. For instance there are lots of spruces and hemlocks on this mountain, and juncos are nesting near our camp. There is the ruin of an old maple sugar camp nearby which has been quite an interesting study for us.

Papa wishes to write today also, so I will leave the rest of this to him. Perhaps he will be able to tell you what a fine time we are having. Hoping to have more good news from you awaiting us at Northfield.

As ever
Your Aldo

To Clara Leopold

Milford—July 11, 1907

My dear Mama:—

Your letter of July 3 reached me today after being forwarded from Northfield and New Haven. I have only an hour to write this. Today is our first day of surveying and those of us who have had a start in it before are excused from the initial lecture—hence our idleness at this early hour (eight o'clock). It is raining outside,—a regular letter-writing day.

Since work has begun here I like it even better than before. All Monday and Tuesday we have Forest Mensuration. This week it consisted altogether of height measurements and log and board feet contents (estimates) on white pine. We have a beautiful bunch of pine to work on, only half a mile down the creek and one of the finest mixed stands I ever saw. There are pines there—dozens of them—thirty inches through, a hundred feet high, and almost a thousand feet of lumber. One old boy—we call him "The King"—is 35" through, 120' high, containing six and a half logs and 1200 ft. B.M. of lumber. It is the most interesting work I have ever done, this estimating.

Yesterday we spent the day getting the entire cut for a six-acre tract of this mixed forest. I have been very fortunate in getting on a crew with Moon and Maddox—two very fine men—and as we all pull together we put in a very satisfactory day's work. You don't know what a difference there is between congenial and uncongenial fellow-workers on a crew in the woods.

Wednesday afternoons we have free. Last Wednesday was a fine day so Dunkle and I started off on another bass-fishing trip. We did not find the fish—only one 2 lb. bass, 2 dace 1# each, and one 2' shad—but we had a very pleasant time and also have big hopes for a new venture in the shape of a frog-hunt. Of which you will hear more in the future.

Last Sunday—I forgot whether I wrote about it—I made an expedition to a river some miles down the line, and saw a pile-ated woodpecker. On our trip yesterday "Dunk" and I made another observation—we found a strawberry patch. When we came back along that way it was very dark and we were also very thirsty. So after a lengthy debate and infinite precautions, inter-cepted by several false alarms, we made a long crawl through the wet grass and entered the patch. But the way of the trans-gressor is hard. The whole patch had been picked clean during the day and we didn't get enough berries to "sicken a sand-piper" as Dunk put it. But it was lots of fun anyhow.

Yesterday morning we had Dendrology. I find the course very good and even on the half day I learned a lot about dis-tinguishing different trees. There is a botanical library over on Mr. Pinchot's place which I hope to make use of before long.

It promises to clear up a bit now and Tracy is apparently about to put us to work surveying. Tracy is here you know and feeling very good. He made a wonderful talk Tuesday night at the first Campfire Meeting of the year on Yale Spirit.

Roland Clark was elected to the Campfire Committee yes-terday, of which I am very glad, as I put him up for the office. Isn't that good?

Goodbye now—I have a lot more to write about but no time now. As ever

Your Aldo

To Clara Leopold

Sunday Morning
May 3—1908

My dear Mama—

We had planned another sailing-party for today but it has turned out cold and blustery so I will have to stay home and work—as I ought to be doing anyhow. Moreover I have to lead Staff Service in Byers, so I will probably spend my Sunday like a thoroughly domesticated and proper young gentleman.

My civilized aspect however will be only temporary and super-ficial. The fact is that I am getting the woods-fever worse every day, the latest manifestation being a decided disinclination to work. This is really a troublesome condition because if ever I ought to work like a dog it is right now. I have cheerful news concerning my Maltby Report. I have received a *handwritten letter* from Professor Graves commending the "excellence" of the job (that is his word) but at the same time requesting an additional commentary & explanation of the whole business, "sufficiently detailed to be intelligible to a land-owner"—which means a small volume of course.

Last Thursday the whole bunch (35) went to Fairfield (below Bridgeport) and thinned an acre of 20 yr-old white pine & larch plantation, by the "C-grade French" System. It was surely an interesting, instructive, difficult and gooey job. In the first place we took an early tram—"had to git up in the middle of the night" as Pax put it—and then walk 5 miles to the plantation. It was a fine day and the walk was great. Marking, tallying & cutting the pines was also very nice—but when it came to cording them up—ough! The "rosum" sure was thick and gooey. By the time we got through we were "dark black" and so sticky that old Rufus remarked "I do believe, boys, that all we needs to do is to walk through the woods and all this here cordwood will stick right to our pants." A heavy shower cleaned us off somewhat before we got back to town.

The plantation is a dandy—some 30 acres, 30' high and almost impenetrable. We thinned 12 cords per acre and left 30. It is growing 1½ cords per acre per year—a high yield. This is one of the first extensive plantations in America old enough to be "thinned."

I saw many birds walking out and back that day—and it aroused a kind of regret that I can't get out and just loiter around in the woods any more. One really gets to see nothing in hurrying to and from a certain place—only just enough to remember how much there really is to see on a May morning. Still I think that if I should have to loiter around for a week I would be too restless to enjoy it.

I have seen several remarkable birds in the last few weeks— especially night herons, a blue-winged warbler, and a blue-headed vireo, also a Louisiana water thrush. Is the kid showing signs of interest in these things? It would be a great thing for him. I am looking forward to getting acquainted with him next summer. I am going to show him the woods.

You and I are going on expeditions too. I have many of them

planned already. For one thing, you are going to see the Big Hardwoods where Papa and I were, last September. Carolo and I are not going away for more than three weeks at the most.

If we are going straight up to the club early in July, will Papa be able to come early too? He must do it if possible. No I don't care about the Lake Trip—when I get started home I want to see *you* and not scenery.

Goodbye now—love to all.

Always,

Aldo

To Clara Leopold

Jan. 20, 1909

My dear Mama:—

I am writing this to clear up my temper before lunch. I have made a mistake in a lot of my calculations in Timber Testing (done out with great care) and I will have to do them all over. So I am a bit angry with myself. It was my own fault, though, so I have nothing to kick about.

In fact I have had nothing at all go wrong for days. Since the end of last week I have just done heaps and piles of work and enjoyed it all very much. Sunday I made a big start in my Working Plan calculations, with the help of a new labor-saving device, the Slide Rule. We Foresters have never been given a course in the use of the Slide Rule, but it has always been a little ambition of mine to learn how to use one. So when I was confronted with the monotonous heap of calculations incident to my Working Plan Report, I thought I might as well learn right now. So I borrowed Henry's Book and Slide Rule and in a couple of hours was able to dash off additions, multiplications, and divisions at a great rate. I am now also using the Slide Rule in my Timber Testing Calculations, with a great saving in time and patience.

I have decided that I would be foolish to go without a Rule of my own in the future, so I have decided to buy one. They cost only $4 or 5 and if my finances are to be given a boost I think I can afford to get one.

Since Sunday we have been kept busy every minute keeping up to date in our Timber Testing work. It is quite interesting, but I am impatient to get a little ahead and again turn to my Report for a little while.

Yesterday we made a series of tests to establish the relations between the several dimensions of wooden beams and their strength and stiffness. It took me all yesterday evening to deduce the laws of those relations, but the results are very satisfactory so I guess it was worthwhile. I have still to copy the job on the machine and put it into presentable shape. That is where Paxie and Pete get ahead of me,—they figure on doing a job of that kind only once, and to hand it in even though it be in more or less unsystematic shape. They thus gain a lot of time, but in spite of the fact that they laugh at my slowness, I believe my way is best.

We have recently begun a new course in National Forests given by E. C. Carter, Ass't Chief of Silviculture in the Forest Service. He is an odd fellow, but knows his business, and is thoroughly familiar with all the forests. He speaks awfully slowly, however, and it is hard to sit still and listen. He is now treating the forests of District 3 (Arizona and New Mexico). That is where I want to go. Either there, or to the Sierras in California (District 5).

I had an interview with Prof. Graves yesterday. I wanted to see him about getting some lantern slides to illustrate a lecture on "Woods—Kinds & Uses" which I have promised to give at the three local Boys' Clubs, run by the Y.M.C.A. He gave me permission to borrow the slides from the school, and then tackled me on the subject of my work. His procedure, I believe, has possibly some significance in relation to the recommendation he gives to the Forest Service next June as to our several abilities and best lines of work, so I will explain to you in full.

Last year, I had a report to make on the silvical characteristics of "Black Oak in Conn." I collected the data, but did not write up the report because I did not believe it of any value. Well, yesterday Prof. Graves asked me about the report. I explained, and he said all right. "But I tell you what you do. When you get down to Texas, you make a special study of the Distribution of Beech in the Pine Forests, and report on it to me." This is to take the place of the report on black oak, and you bet I was glad to take up the proposition.

Now the significance of this is as follows. When Graves asks for Special Reports he wants them as additions to the library.

Which is to infer that I know how to conduct a silvicultural investigation in a satisfactory manner. Which in turn signifies that he believes my abilities to be in silvicultural lines. Which again indicates that his recommendation will be to put me into the Dep't of Silviculture. Suits me, all right.

Goodbye now, it is late for lunch. As always

Your Aldo

#379 Temple—1/20/09

To Clara Leopold

On Board S.S. Comus—S.P. Line
12 hrs. N.W. Tortugas Light, Fla.
Sunday March 7—1909

My dear Mama—

All but one day of our trip is over. It is great down here on the Gulf—a fine clear hot day with a lazy breeze and a long swell, and the bluest sea—not even the old lake was ever such a dark clear blue. It is a good day to sit in the shade and write this letter. So I shall begin at the beginning and tell you everything that has happened since I wrote last from Shippan.

I left Shippan—almost, yes quite reluctantly—last Tuesday morning. It rained on the way down to New York. With my big Typewriter case and hand-bag I felt quite the traveller. I got down there about noon, and did not have to look about very long before I met Joe Kircher and we had lunch together at the Belmont, where there is very excellent music and good service.

After lunch I left for Tarrytown. Mary met me at the Station and I need not say that I was glad to see her again. Mary is looking quite well but just a little bit serious. Mrs. Lord is well as usual. She certainly is mighty nice and made me feel quite at home.

Mary and I went driving in the afternoon. It had cleared up considerably, but then the weather didn't matter so very much. We got back in time for a most excellent dinner (I have had occasion to remember it since) and in the evening we ran down to the city and saw William Hodge in *The Man from Home*. Mrs. Lord and Mary both enjoyed it I think. It is certainly the best play I have ever seen. I wish you could see it.

The next morning I had to leave rather early, and *very* reluctantly. Somehow I felt as if I were leaving civilization and all the
pleasant things of life behind me. I must say that in a way I still
feel as if I really had. I must own up to a very keen enjoyment
of these occasional glimpses of that kind of life,—of people like
the Lords, of good living, and theatres, and leisurely hours, and
all that. I am perfectly aware, however, that it is because these
glimpses are occasional that I enjoy them so much.

Mr. and Mrs. Lord both asked about Marie and when she
expected to come East. I really think that if she were to stay
a year instead of a month, they would be only too glad. Our
Cicero is quite a part of their family.

So much for the *rest* of the Lords. As for Mary, she is of
course the same as ever. Nobody could be, or at least ever has
been, any more than that.

When I arrived in New York Wednesday morning I piled
my extensive hand-baggage into a cab and went straight to the
landing. It was a busy place, down there among the wharves,
and the preparations for departure were very interesting. We
got started at noon on Wednesday. Connie and I installed ourselves in our fairly comfortable-*looking* stateroom and the trip
began.

Wednesday afternoon, Thursday, and Friday, I shall skip with
as little mention as possible. We had nasty weather. It was cold
and wet and smelly everywhere except on the windy side of the
deck. There it was not smelly, but the coldness and wetness
were rather pronounced. In short, it was absolutely dismal. I
sat on deck and cussed myself for a d—— fool. I envied Paxie
until I was green, and had visions of sitting at home in the bay
window with you, and cussed myself again. Thus it was for three
days and nights.

Saturday morning was like waking up in Heaven. It suddenly turned warm and sunny, the Florida coast hove in sight,
and everybody sat on deck and was ridiculously happy. The sea
was wonderful—deep blue, with snowy white-caps, and a sweet
cool breeze that whistled in the rigging and almost blew the
breath out of one's mouth. We coasted very close to the Florida
shore,—often within a mile. We could see the palms and pine
forests, and the long shining stretches of sandy beach tempted

one to jump overboard and swim ashore and play Robinson Crusoe. I spent the entire day leaning over the rail at the bow, watching the things in the water. There were hundreds of flying fish, large covies of them breaking water every few minutes and skimming off over the waves like big grasshoppers or dragon-flies with gauzy wings. Finally they would drop back into the water with a funny splash. Occasionally we encountered a shoal of sharks—big lazy fellows, "Hammerheads" they called them, 6 or 10 feet long. They would suddenly dart away just under the surface of the water. Every few minutes one would see a big brown-yellow hulk a couple of feet under the water, and once in a while one would poke out its head—a huge sea-turtle. George, but they looked lazy and comfortable! Some of them must have weighed several hundred pounds. In the afternoon we encountered a shoal of porpoises. They were the real treat of the day. They look like a miniature whale, 4 or 5 feet long, with a sharp nose. George how they do swim! They gambol lazily just ahead of the bow, racing with the ship, and every once in a while breaking water with a graceful spring, apparently in pure glee and good spirits. One by one they tired out and gave up the race, but the more enduring ones kept up for over half an hour. I wish I could swim like that!

Then there were all kinds of odd things floating in the sea. Long strings of brown sea-weed, and jelly-fishes, and crazy-looking Portuguese men-o'-war. It was mighty interesting, and I stayed out there in the sun all day. As a result I have a blister-ing sun-burn this morning.

Last night it grew still calmer and warmer, and by the time we had rounded the Florida Keys it was so hot that the staterooms were quite impossible as a place to sleep. I made a partially suc-cessful night of it in a deck chair, with just a bath robe and a blanket. Today it is hotter still, and threatens to get calm with a dead swell. There is less sea-life here in the Gulf. I shall be quite glad to get ashore.

I forgot to mention the wonderful moonlight of the last two nights. It was really almost too beautiful to talk about. I wouldn't have you ever take this trip for anything, but last night I did wish you could have been along. It was a new thing for me—this tropical night-wind, with a vague sweetness that is different from an ordinary balmy night. And the moon is so clear, and has a sort of greenish-silver light. I shall never forget this trip, but I think I shall remember oftener this tropical night, than the miserable storm on the first part of the trip.

Your letter reached me safely the day we left New York. I am hoping to hear again from you all when I land in New Orleans. I have thought a good deal about home on this trip, because I have not quite been able to forget that I *might have been* with you all this time. But I have not been, so there is no profit in speculating on bygone possibilities.

So far I have done not one bit of work. This afternoon I may get out my Dendrology notes and look them up a bit. At least there is nothing much else to do. The passengers, with one or two notable exceptions, are rather bizarre. There is one very interesting man from Lake Champlain—a yachtsman—whom I like very much. We have had some interesting talks. He sailed the Iroquois in the Canadian Cup races last year.

The fellows have divided off into two classes, the Card-Players and the Rest. I am among the Rest. Connie is among the Card-Players. I don't envy them in that stuffy smoky card-room. The Rest of us (since the advent of livable weather) are engaged in walking the deck, watching the sea, and playing Shuffleboard. I have done a bit of each, except the Shuffleboard.

Tomorrow we land. We are 6 hours late, which means that we reach New Orleans late in the afternoon. That means we pass up my dear old native Mississippi by daylight. I will be very glad.

Probably I will not have time to write again until we get settled in camp. That will be toward the end of the week. We will leave New Orleans Thursday morning, stay over Thursday night in Beaumont, proceed on Friday to Doucette, and via the logging railroad to camp. Here's hoping we get there on schedule time.

Goodbye now, and love to you all. This is Sunday noon—and I am thinking of what it would be like to be with you at home. Hoping you are all well and happy I am as always

Your Aldo

To Clara Leopold

Camp—Tuesday Evening
May 4—1909

My dear Mama—

Your letter came yesterday evening, enclosing also the notes from Ballard and Cicero. You can probably guess that the most important news in any of them was about Mary— It had never occurred to me that she might be due for the measles too. It is too bad for Marie's sake too. Please keep me posted as to how she is getting along. Of course I have written, but with this miserable mail service down here, the letter is still lying helpless in the box, and may continue to do so the rest of the week.

In answer to your question—there is no "best way" to send things down here. The registered mail is of course safe, but it stays at Doucette for days and days, until somebody has to go to town on some errand, and gets a chance to bring it out. The regular mail is just a gamble. It is brought out at random at any time, sometimes only once a week. And Express is just like registered mail, only the fool agent doesn't even send one a notice of a package. So that if you have anything *perishable* to send, the regular (?) or rather ordinary mail is the choice of 3 evils.

Did you send that second box of dates? Nothing has showed up. I was careful to write to Woodville too, to have it forwarded. If that gets lost too, I think you had better give up the "box" idea. It makes me feel so awfully mean to have you send all those things and then not even be able to give you the satisfaction of knowing that I received them.

That Gingerbread sent Friday the 23rd arrived last Tuesday, as I have already told you.

Paxie and I came out to camp here on the last log-train Saturday afternoon. Our "home-coming," which we had anticipated with so much pleasure, has really been a bit disappointing, for the reason that on the very day of our arrival, almost everybody whom we really wanted to see either left camp for work at Doucette, or went with a special party up north to Colmesneil to estimate a large tract of timber which the company owns up there. So that now there are only ten men in camp. Connie and Rufus and Paxie and I try to keep cheerful but we do wish the others were here.

A week from Monday Paxie and I will probably join the party working on the North tract. We are very anxious to go in order to see the country and get the experience. Meanwhile we are getting our preliminary training in estimating. Yesterday we spent over on the logging operation getting an idea of how far into the tops the yellow pine here is utilized. We followed the crews of sawyers, guessing the number and dimensions of logs in each tree before felling, and then measuring it up on the ground to check up our mistakes. It isn't so easy to look at one of these pines and guess its diameter within an inch, and its height within a couple of feet. But that is what we must learn before starting out on timber-cruising.

Today we laid out a "practice forty" in some fine timber to the southward. The stunt is to lay out these forty acre plots, get the exact volume of the stand by calipering the Diameter Breast High (D.B.H., remember this) and measuring the height (with a Hypsometer) of *every tree* on the plot. Then we go ahead and make practice estimates of the plot and see how close we come to the actual measured stand. See the stunt?

Well—today we laid out the forty acres and with our crew of five men went over it in strips, measuring the diameter and height of every tree. Golly, but it was an endless job! It was a bright clear dry day—really fine weather—but there was no water within a mile of the forty. And the sun beat down into the open woods, and the air just boiled with dryness. By ten o'clock we were "spitting cotton" and by five this afternoon our tongues felt like a big dry swollen bale of the same material. When we got back to camp I went over and deliberately hooked a lemon from John Briscoe, and went down to the spring, and staid there. The lemon saved the day.

We are also working on our pacing nowadays, in preparation for the estimating work. We have to pace out and back every day over measured courses, and report our results. I have adopted a pace of 5.5 feet (2 steps of course) which runs 240 to the quarter-section and 960 to the mile. I was at first a very poor and variable pacer, but just lately I have begun to improve. I can now pace a quarter within 10 feet every time, and today I generally came within 3 feet. It is very interesting work.

The flea-bag has not yet arrived, but will probably come out in the next mail. So far the fleas have not been so bad as we expected—mostly I guess on account of the cool spell. The mosquitoes are very bad, however. Last night they got me for fair. I have now ordered a Bar from town, and meanwhile borrowed a small piece from Becky which will probably help a lot.

In your letter, you show signs of worrying about me, for fear that we are getting too much work. Please don't do it. I am feeling well most of the time, and I have *not* lost weight. And then we don't work all the time by *any* means. Yesterday for instance we got back from work by four o'clock, and Paxie & Rufus and I made an expedition to a mulberry tree that I discovered one day in the woods. George, but I haven't had so much fun for an age as climbing around after those mulberries! Long black ones, sweet & juicy!

Sunday I spent snooping around by myself, on a kind of preliminary survey for a report that I am going to work up on the Growth of Pine on Old Fields in this part of Texas. I made a stand table of a quarter acre—all by myself—and got a good start. I think I can get up a pretty good report. I shall hand it in in place of that one on the Distribution of Beech that Prof. Graves suggested.

While out after mulberries yesterday Rufus killed a large copperhead. He was a beauty. This is a great place for snakes. Cotton-mouth moccasins are thick. Half a dozen are killed every day by the fellows. Bead snakes, rattlers, king-snakes, blacksnakes are also common. Even the poisonous snakes though are not aggressive. They don't get vicious until stepped on, and then if one wears leggings, as one has to do anyhow on account of chiggers, there is no danger.

You are wrong though about the razorbacks spoiling this country. On the contrary, they keep it cleaner than it would be without them. It is really a very beautiful region. If you could see the full moon tonight, sailing high over the towering pine-trees, you would like it too. I have decided, again and again, that it is worth all the trouble of the mosquitoes and fleas and snakes and pigs, and more too.

Goodnight now, and love to you all from

                                        Aldo

To Clara Leopold

Camp No. 2
Milligan Cienega Sec. 19 T.49 R.28E
September 22, 1909

My dear Mama—

Ranger Wheatley went to Blue after our mail yesterday—I sent with him a so-called note telling you I was very much alive—he returned this evening and brought me just *two* "letters with stamps," one from you and one from Dad. Of course there were bales of government envelopes from headquarters, but they are not *letters.*

I didn't know where to begin on this job, it is so long since I've written. I can't possibly tell you all that has happened, but I will try and give you the main points.

The Apache Reconnaissance Party left Springerville in state on Sept. 8 and splashed 3 days through the rain up slippery hills, arriving at Slaughter's Ranch, the last outpost of civilization, on Sept. 10. When we got there we tried to pull both wagons up a little rise to get a dry place to camp, and both teams of horses sunk in their tracks, exhausted. We camped in the mud, and work began next day.

The next day—thanks be to all the Angels—the rainy season died the death. It cleared, and there has hardly been a white fleck in the sky since. It freezes hard every night, and every morning I get up & look at the fading stars and thank the Lord.

This town is the only surveyed town of the 360 sections covered by this job, and I wish to the devil it weren't. The surveys are 35 years old (where there are any at all) and all the bearing trees have to be chopped out with an axe to read the old blaze-inscriptions. It takes more patience, skill and cussedness to find and identify a corner than to solve a Chinese puzzle.

Moreover the country around Slaughter's is full of magnetic (in one case 38° in 50 paces) so that the needle is useless and all lines must be laboriously run by backsights. Moreover every mile there is a bound-for-China canyon with a river to sweep down a steer in the bottom, ripping and roaring and gnashing its teeth for to swallow some poor Cruiser who loses his footing. But Hell! the weather's fine, and who cares! Golly crickets, the

Lord made the country and so be it! Scenery? If one had time he could spend weeks just gaping at canyons and mountains.

We finished up the north part of the town Sept. 17th and moved 5 miles south here to Milligan Cienega at the foot of the north slope of the Blue Range. (Bow down and take off your hats, gentlemen. Of all the country under Heaven, *this* the Devil himself would let alone to the last.) It is the prettiest country I have ever heard tell of. But wait till you cruise it! One of our men—King—has given out absolutely and has not worked for two days. Luckily (for us and for him) his time is up tomorrow.

And now just let me add—in reply to a solicitous phrase in Dad's letter pertaining to my health—that any man short of 100% husky and well would just plumb evaporate working the way we are working. We start by sunup, and for the last three days I haven't gotten in until three hours after dark, up and down and up and down all day, through thickets and burns and up slopes that bump you on the nose, and over precipices into torrents of ice-water——well, I tell you three months ago I would have lasted just about 1 hour and 13 minutes on this here job. But now, I can wear the legs off the bunch during the day, write official letters most of the night, get up and take a little hunt in the twilight next morning, and then repeat the performance. A sick man had might as well clear out of this country and go to Albuquerque or some other quiet restful place.

So far I have had pretty poor support from the Office. My Appropriation is $500 and I need $2500, and I haven't been able to get a letter. Tomorrow Smith & Ring leave for Springerville to return to School, leaving only Longwell and Pritchard. Pritchard is Guard on this Forest and has just joined us. I need 4 more men, and damn quick, or else the cost of this job will reach 2¢ an acre. You see our Cook and pack outfit costs $8 a day, and that counts up. Today Guthrie arrived to see how things were going, and to my great satisfaction approved all the steps I had taken on my own hook in lieu of the lacking orders from Albuquerque. I think he is quite pleased with the job—he certainly is giving me all possible support.

Our work has been greatly helped by Ranger Wheatley, who knows the country, and besides is a pleasant fellow and a gentleman.

I'm afraid this gives you only a poor idea of the work, but I honestly can't write any oftener. Even now it is cold as the Devil in this tent. But please let me keep on hearing from you all—you don't know what a letter is until mail comes once a week by special messenger, and you are bucking the Universe cussing and planning and fighting and working all the while. Then a letter from a gentle peaceable place like home comes like a message out of another world. Maybe you all think I have forgotten because I don't say very much, but I tell you no. Every night when all the others are snoring in their beds, I finish my letters and then go outside and sit over the embers of the fire till they die, smoking my pipe and thinking. But now has come to me the greatest of sorrows—I have lost my pipe. I would lay down a ten-dollar bill to have it back. It happened the other day, when I hurriedly stuffed it in my pocket to shoot a turkey. By the way, since the 15th you may guess my Sundays have been busy. Wheatley and I have killed 2 timber wolves and 2 turkeys and a lot of grouse, but no deer. Somehow we have bad luck. The party has seen 39 deer but nobody yet has gotten a shot at a buck. Does & fawns are against the law. Our luck will break soon, or else I'm a hoodoo. I go out every morning before breakfast.

I am mostly congealed now—it is freezing cold you know—so goodnight. Will write as soon as I can,—meanwhile don't worry if you don't hear. Always

                                                    Your Aldo

P.S. By the way, somewhere flying around loose in our house are a black silk & a red silk neckerchief that have been around for years and nobody ever uses. I can use them fine if you can send them. There was also a white one which I pinched and am wearing every day. It is just right.

                                                    A. L.

P.S. Ask Dad what's the news about the gun? I have ordered shells, and expect to use it in November when I get back to Springer. Tell Dad if he did not send the scabbard please to fold it up and do so, to Springerville, marked "Hold until return."

                                                    A. L.

To Carl Leopold

Vallecitos N.M. May 20

My dear Papa:

For the last couple of days I've been over on the Canjilon district, and am now on my way back, via the Tres Piedras and Ortiz districts. I will get in to Antonito Monday or Tuesday night.

Fortunately the further west one goes on this Forest, the better the country gets. I was a bit discouraged at first with the looks of the east side.

The Rangers have fine neighbors here—there are only three places on the Forest with any white inhabitants, and I don't believe these aggregate over half a dozen families—on a million and a half acres. Outside of rangers I've seen only one white man on my trip. Everything is Mexicans,—and sheep.

There's going to be the deuce to pay if I ever run the outfit. The country is very plainly overgrazed, and it looks to me as if the previous Supervisors had simply let things slide as they are because of the work and trouble of negotiating a cut. Lots of these Mexicans have been using this range for three or four generations, and when they are cut down they're going to "rare up and fall over backwards"!

So far I have found one good ranger, another one who is able but concerning whom I have not yet made up my mind, and another who is a mere wind-bag. Luckily the last one has seen the handwriting on the wall and is about to go on furlough. He'll never get reinstated while I'm alive. He's built a phone line from Servilleta to Canjilon which is about the rankest piece of slipshod work which I have seen in this little world. Now it's up to us to rebuild it.

There is practically no game in this country. Of course the sheep have run out all the deer; there are a few turkeys, and I saw one place with bear-sign. Two elk were seen here two years ago. There are lots of trout, but I won't have a chance to do any fishing this season.

Spud has made the trip so far but is getting a little limp today. He has learned not to chase sheep, and thinks he is a star horse-wrangler. He is also learning to stay with my saddle.

I am hoping to find lots of letters when I get back to town. That is the most immediate treat that I am able to foresee at this time, unless it be a bath and some mediocre hotel chuck—the ranger's wives can't cook like those on the Apache. I am developing quite a sentimental attitude toward the good old days there.

So long now and love to you all. As always

Aldo

May 20, 1911

To Clara Leopold

My dear Mama—

I guess you are wondering what has become of me—I have been all over this part of New Mexico since I wrote last and it was a big treat to get back to the large stack of letters waiting for me, including *one* from Estella.

As usual I enjoyed your letters more than all the rest put together—they have always got a lot of *real* news in them.

It was awfully good of you to think of the sweetgrass basket for Estella—it is very appropriate and just at the right time—her birthday is on August 24 (you asked once how old Estella is but I'm sure I don't know; about twenty two I guess) and you can either send it direct to her, or to me in advance and I will write. I couldn't have thought of anything nicer to send.

I believe I have neglected to tell you that her brother Luna Bergere is working with us here in a temporary position during the rest of his summer vacation—he is staying with me and it makes it very pleasant for me. He is an *exceptional* young fellow of about 19 or 20 I guess; a perfect gentleman and very good company. He is very husky and very good looking and a willing worker and doing mighty well. We are very good friends and I am pretty sure that without my fishing for it at all, he is and will be pulling for me as hard as he can. Anyhow it is very pleasant to have him here, and it was quite a compliment from Mrs. Bergere and Estella too that they were very anxious to have him with me.

Luna and I opened the box this morning and you should see my little house now. Luna is about as proud of it as I am and it pleased me very much to see how scrupulously spic and span he kept everything while I was gone out in the mountains. The pillows and covers and all are *just right* and with the pictures and books it looks very homelike. In fact it is plenty good enough for you and Marie and I am proud to invite you to come whenever you can. You would be very comfortable and I could move out temporarily into the room over the office. I have made me a *window seat*, and when I add a cellarette and a humidor with a stack of Bock Panatellas my happiness will be complete—almost. I'll have a picture of the house for you before long.

Estella and Anita have been up on the Pecos for a few weeks visiting Mrs. Field at her summer place—Mr. Field is an Albuquerque lawyer and Jamie's senior partner.

Do you want to hear about my trip? Over at Taos I made a PDQ cleanup and was quite pleased with myself—too long to explain but I fired a Ranger and started seven other things to moving where none had moved before. The Taos Mountains are *wonderfully* beautiful. Also saw Mr. Bergere in Taos—he was very nice to me, and furthermore showed me a picture of Estella that I would give three fingers for you to see. It was taken four years ago, in Indian costume, at the Taos Indian Pueblo. The artist colony over there are all crazy about it, and Bert Phillips the Indian artist has a mind to paint it. I am no artist I guess, but I would give anything for a copy, but there are none. It is absolutely beautiful and that's all there is to it.

I had hardly returned from the Taos country when I had to leave for the Chama mountains to inspect the work of our survey-party who are retracing the line of the Tierra Amarilla Grant. Had to track their wagon for 60 miles to get an additional load of supplies to them—lived 2 days off dried beef & crackers with saddle blankets and the stars at night—then worked with the party one day 5 A.M.–9 P.M. and walked the legs off the whole bunch with *riding boots* on while they all had hobnailed shoes—and yesterday returned 50 miles over trackless mountains from Cumbres Colo. And got here 9 P.M. Polly did finely but he was barefooted in front and *hardly* made it in over the rocks. D—— if I have had such a day for a long time—I'll not forget those stifling jungled cañons with a perfect torment of flies, and those cruel rocky ridges still drifted with snow—and poor lame Polly—and yours truly never been in the country before—it reminded me of the gruelling physical labor of the old days on Reconnaissance, and made me think after all that this Deputy business is a kind of gentleman's job after all, and more or less of a cinch. But I've been through the mill—and I can tell every man on the Forest from the Rangers to the Surveyors all about their own job and beat them doing it too. There is a whole lot of comfortable satisfaction in being able to say that to myself. Strangers always size me up as "all right but rather young"—I can see it plain as day light—and it sure does me good to dive in and open their eyes. The surveyors fully expected to walk my legs off I know—and I chuckled with sheer delight when I dragged them all into camp by moonlight and watched them double up exhausted by the fire. After all it's a pretty interesting old world. I am feeling exceptionally well after being out of the old all-day and half-the-night grind in the office for a week or so.

I am glad you are having a pretty pleasant season of it at the club—*don't do too much* and write me all the news. Please give my very best regards to Mrs. Elliot and the Derbys. Is Eunice there? Awfully glad the Clarks are coming—remember me to them too. What news from Carolo? Poor Kiddo! he's an "honest workin man" now sure enough I guess—I must write to him today. D—— but I'd like to see him! Tell Frederic he may be having a pretty good time but he also *missed* one—the little black I bought for him has turned out a *daisy*—bought her for $40 dollars and can sell her for $65 or $75 any day to half a dozen people who want her. Am saving her for *you*—she's pretty as a picture and very easy gaited and gentle as a kitten. If I had any ready money I could make quite a little on the side buying and selling horses, now that I've learned by expensive experience. Am renting the black to Mr. Hall for $8.00 per month.

Goodnight now—supper time and I got to wrangle horses. Love to you all from

Aldo

Tres Piedras
Cassita Mia (My little house)
Sunday Aug. 6

August 6, 1911

To Clara Leopold

Taos—August 16

My dear Mama—

I don't remember whether or no I dropped you a note before leaving Tres Piedras on this last peregrination of mine—anyhow I am over here installing the new Ranger—Hulbert—and we have just been out to the Black Lakes country looking things over—there was a report to the effect that there was a lot of trespass stock out there and a good deal of opposition. The first was a myth and the second due entirely to the fact that our noble predecessors never bestirred their sedentary souls to the point of visiting that remote region. We went out yesterday and stayed overnight at a sheep ranch and came back today—and I believe cleaned up more business in a few hours than has been cleaned up there in the last year. Hulbert is no fool and if I do say it I believe I've given him some pointers as to how much information can be picked up in a day, if a man *takes to it*. Also showed a couple of cowmen, that *some* people in the Service knew just as much about the cow business as *they* did. My training among the cowboys in Arizona is simply *invaluable* to me—and the Sundays I spent in idleness riding around and visiting with the cowboys were the most profitable time I have ever spent. It is my chief joy in life here to meet these old cowmen and sheep men and millmen and see them size me up as "awfully young" and then call their first bluff with what I *know* about their own business. And I believe I can say that I am getting along well with the Rangers too. It is absolutely *absorbing*—this game of handling people, and I'd rather know how to do it than to handle millions of dollars.

You have probably gathered that I am considerably elated with my trip. I am, because I have *had* to throw myself into *work altogether*, or *not at all*, because of the other things on my mind—so I chose the *altogether*. But after all the whole world spins around Saturday, which is day after day after tomorrow, and I am not making the statement with a long face either—a sort of blind conceited confidence has taken hold of me in spite of the fact that I haven't had a letter for two weeks, and it will take more than mere obstacles or delay to shake it in the least. It has been a kind of belated education to me to work with

C. C. Hall, and even *I* can see that he has influenced me a great deal. For instance, he is a *fighting-man* in all things, great and small and all the time; he does not know what "bluffed" or "quit" or "beaten" means. The oilier processes of diplomacy and persuasion are unknown to him, and he rules men not by knowledge, though he has some; not by experience, though he has had a great deal, nor by reason, of which he has little—but by the sheer fighting force of his personality. Enthusiasm and never-say-die, lived and preached by his own self, are the reason and substance of his success. In many things his mind is both prejudiced and crude, but obstacles and impediments alike are swept away by what is stronger than they. Many a time I have called him, to myself, a roughneck, a barbarian, and worse—I have hated him enough to kill him—but it has always come back to his better qualities, which I must admit that I admire enough to find them, as a kind of surprise to myself, growing in *me*. This of course, I would not admit to *anyone* else in the world but you and Dad, but it is a fact, and it stands me in good stead, and I *may* need it badly and soon. At any rate I am becoming an irrepressible optimist this week—which may be conceitedness or not—I don't give a rip if it is.

Odd little town here in Taos. You would find it interesting,—the Indians are very picturesque. We are going up the Pueblo Canyon tomorrow—which they claim as their ground and out of which they have most of the white people bluffed—we may have some arguments.

Goodnight now and love to you all. As always

Aldo

August 16, 1911

To Estella Bergere

My dear Little Girl—

Your sweet little letter of the night of the dance came tonight—it was unexpected—and for some reason or other—I can't tell you just exactly how it *did* make me feel, only it is almost too much for a man sometimes. In a foolish dream I sometimes almost regret the good old days when it wasn't a question of whether this, or when that, or until the other—but just a question of *go*, and *take* you,—away and away into the hills and over the mountains high up to where the eagles live in the crags at the top of the world, and he who dared follow must dare to fight, and to die. I suppose I am saying things I have no business to—but what is a man to do—sit and wait with a smile like a wooden image?

I had the nicest breeziest funniest letter from Luna today—he would make a tombstone cheer up and smile—and he also sent me one whole lot of delectable things to smoke the other day—which was awfully good of him. I owe you a good deal for first suggesting his coming here—and so does the Carson. And I *miss* him—which is more than I can say of most of the people I like.

Tonight before I say goodnight to the little star, I will go out to the big rock of granite which towers behind where the little house is going to be—and I will bow my head and ask the God of the mountains whether *your* mountains have whispered to *my* mountains today—I will not ask him what it was, Estella—but I will make him know it all, and pray that he give you all the happiness that I would give—or *lose*—my life, to give to you. Goodnight—and remember— *Always*

Aldo

August 31, 1911

To the Officers of the Carson National Forest

Burlington, Iowa
July 15, 1913

Greetings:

We take it that the well known proverb "Troubles never come singly," is indeed but a dilution of that modern, but more heartfelt saying, "Everything comes in bunches!" Albeit in this case, not *quite* everything *came*. There was one exception—the Supervisor. He went!

We make bold to assume that the above at least roughly approximates the feelings of your esteemed Deputy Supervisor, who on April 25 last, with the *Pine Cone* ten days overdue, and your humble servant saying "goodbye everybody" from the observation platform of the Chile Flyer, he calmly gazed at the galaxy of "things due," and said things, gently but softly, into the April twilight.

A great executive once said, "Do not make excuses, nor take them." In my opinion, your esteemed deputy is prone to follow in his footsteps. I therefore take it upon myself (not without a guilty smile) to remind you that among the things that "came in bunches" were working plans many and diverse, annual plans manifold, statistical reports and financial statements, and circulars—yea, even unto seven generations! And flocks and herds had their allotments in a thirsty land, and there were fires on the face of the deep. All this and more "came in bunches." By the same token, the *Pine Cone* came not at all.

Obviously, the writer might long ago have been expected to write a *Pine Cone* himself—to help out. But the doctor, at least by implication, had respect unto the proverb:

> Even a fool, when he holdeth his peace, is counted wise:
> When he shutteth his lips, he is esteemed as prudent.

Now, however, I am at least partly back on my feet, and it gives me pleasure to contribute a few lines to the July number.

After many days of much riding down among thickets of detail and box canyons of routine, it sometimes profits a man to top out on the high ridge leave without pay, and to take a look around. Most of us always *have* envied the Lookouts, anyhow. When your "topping out" is metaphorical and prescribed by the doctor—that is a circumstance which merely augments your envy, without decreasing your profit. But be that as it may, I will crave your indulgence while I attempt to describe what I now see from my point of vantage. Peradventure I may generalize a little, but only with the object of arriving at, and pinning down, what seems to me a final specific truth.

National Forest Administration has for its object the actual, concrete, specific application of the well known principles of conservation, to the resources within the National Forests. We are entrusted with the protection and development, through wise use and constructive study, of the timber, water, forage, farm, recreative, game, fish, and esthetic resources of the areas under our jurisdiction. I will call these resources, for short, "The Forest." Our agencies for this development are: first, the Forest Users; second, our own energies, labor, and example; and third, the funds placed at our disposal.

It follows quite simply, that our sole task is to increase the efficiency of these three agencies. And it also follows that the sole measure of our success is the *effect* which they have on *the Forest*.

In plainer English, our job is to sharpen our tools, and make them cut the right way.

Now in actual practice, we are confronted, surrounded, and perhaps sometimes swamped, with problems, policies, ideas, decisions, precedents, and details. We ride in a thicket. We grapple with difficulties; we are in a maze of routine. Letters, circulars, reports, and special cases beset our path as the logs, gullies, rocks, and bog-holes and mosquitoes beset us in the hills. We ride— but are we getting anywhere? To that question I here propose an answer. I here offer a 66 foot chain wherewith to measure our progress. My measure is THE EFFECT ON THE FOREST.

This sounds simple, of course, but after all, day by day, how often do we apply this acid test? Suppose we lay out a few sample plots, and see. I select these as they come to my mind, without effort or guidance, in the hope they may thus attain some degree of fairness.

Plot #1. A question arises as to whether the contract in a two million foot sale shall compel the utilization of White Fir. The Ranger, Supervisor, and District office exchange letters and memoranda, and two men make a field inspection.

Without doubt the resulting decision has a direct, tangible effect on the Forest.

Plot #2. The District Office issues a circular call for estimates of type acreages. The Rangers report, the Supervisor corrects and tabulates, and submits as called for. What is the effect on the Forest?

The data is embodied in the Forester's annual report, which enlightens a limited portion of the public. The final effect on the Forest is very indirect and hard to measure.

Plot #3. A trespass report on ten head of cattle involves heavy field and office work by four men, and a trip to court. The forage consumed and judgement obtained are in themselves negligible. What other effect on the Forest? An example to Users—an indirect effect—doubtless good; but no one knows whether, if balanced against the outlay, the final net effect is a profit or a loss.

Plot #4. A ranger reports on a special use case. He submits only one copy of Form 964. The report is returned and a letter is written requesting two, and the case delayed.

There is a loss of time, fees, forage, and increment on stock; a direct effect. This is balanced against an indirect effect on other future cases, for which the Ranger submits two copies as required.

Plot #5. Hundreds of letters, conferences, and discussions are exchanged concerning the relative merits of #9 or #12 telephone wire.

A wise decision directly affects the Forest in the resulting efficiency of our administrative agency, the telephone.

Plot #6. A mining company is dumping poisonous tailings into a stream. The ranger inspects and reports to the office, and preventive action results.

The effect is direct and tangible.

Plot #7. The experiment station through study and observations evolves a system of silvicultural treatment for a certain type.

Without doubt the effect is tangibly impressed on subsequent sale areas.

Plot #8. A fire burns over two acres and is extinguished by the ranger.

The effect is direct, tangible, and good.

What do these random plots indicate? Briefly as follows:

(a) Effects are direct and indirect.

(b) With the single exception of fire, all effects are applied to our agencies, rather than to the Forest itself.

(c) Effects are good and doubtful, the "doubtful" ones being cases where we can not easily tell that the *net* result is beneficial.

Let us attempt a tabular classification of our plots:

Plot No.	Good Effect		Doubtful Effect	
	Direct	Indirect	Direct	Indirect
1	X			
2				X
3				X
4				X
5	X			
6	X			
7	X			
8	X			
Totals	5	0	0	3

From the above, is it possible to assert that good effects are always *direct* and that doubtful effects are always *indirect*? Perhaps that is on shaky ground, but we can at least assert that fire prevention is the most direct of all our activities, and hence also susceptible of developing the greatest relative efficiency.

A further analysis of our plots will show that indirect effects are mostly under the head of what we call "routine," and further, that most routine results from a striving after *uniformity*. If a ranger in Idaho did not have to handle a grazing case according to the same procedure as his New Mexican fellow-ranger, much routine would of itself be eliminated. No man doubts the wisdom of a policy of uniformity, but do we always remember that uniformity is simply a *policy of Operation* and not a *Conservation Principle*, and as such is not an *end* but a *means* only?

To come back to our original question, how many of us, when we write a letter, talk to a permittee, call for or make a report, recommend an improvement, or decide on our day's work—how many of us stop to try to figure out what will be the *effect on the Forest* of each separate action we take? Are we not more or less in a rut? If so, what puts us there? Principally, the *Operative Policy of Uniformity*, which I have just mentioned. But here is the point: the Policy of Uniformity is meant simply to guide our daily task, and it is *not* meant to confine our minds. And the Forest Officer who lets it do so is burying his talents.

I now come to the point I have been trying to make in the foregoing discussion. I have tried to point out the necessity for clear, untrammelled, and independent thinking on the part of Forest Officers. On this point I wish to submit two propositions:

First: The continued progress of the Service lies in the hands of the men who will thus think.

Second: The men in the best position to observe the faults and merits of our present work, to discern most clearly its effect on the Forest, and to study out the best means for improving that effect, are the *Forest Rangers*.

The Ranger is the man on the ground. He lives there. He is in the position to see the effects of our work at all seasons and under all circumstances, and it is these effects and nothing else, that count. His is the task of applying our principles in detail, and it is not until they are applied in detail that they have any effects. His is the opportunity to apply and measure and hence to study and improve. The Supervisor sees a larger area, but less closely. He may have a better chance at correlating data, and putting together disjointed observations, but most of the *first hand* and hence most vital progress must originate on the Ranger District.

In the foregoing pages I have tried to present a kind of analysis which points out the objects of our work, our agencies for performing it, the circumstances which tend to obscure our vision in trying to improve its effect, and the logically most important source of that improvement. Doubtless my propositions have some weak joints, and the location of my sample plots may be questioned—I hope that they will be. In fact, why not let the *Pine Cone* and our Ranger Meetings be the occasion for constructive discussions by all who "get an idea"?

In the next number—weather permitting—I hope to offer a few thoughts on the evolution of the Service since the "old days"; the resulting good changes to be fostered, and less good changes to be offset; and some outlines of a few specific current Service problems. A man feels better to "get shet" of these things once in a while.

The "Rest Cure," like greatness, is desired by some, while others have it thrust upon them. I wish I may soon be excused from the latter class.

My best wishes are extended to every man on the Carson.

Very sincerely yours,
Aldo Leopold
Forest Supervisor

To the Officers of the Carson National Forest

Burlington, Iowa
January 16, 1914

To the Officers of the Carson:

The time is gradually growing nearer when sheep, bunch grass, mud, troubles, sunshine, hard work, and a supervisor are to return to active duty on the Carson. I hope you will all be glad to welcome the whole consignment, because my part of it will surely be glad to get back.

When I received the December issue of the *Pine Cone*, I wondered whether all of you enjoyed reading it as much as I did. In the near future I want to take up in these columns, in my present capacity of "Associate Editor," the question of further improving the paper in a way to make it of the greatest possible interest and value to the man in the field. But for the present to return to the December issue, I think I am safe in saying that the news that stood out in red letters was the story of Ranger Barker's four lions. That was certainly some shooting. I have mentioned it on several occasions to friends here and the reply was invariably something like this: "Do they ever try to break into your house?" "Aren't you afraid to go out after dark?" et cetera. Barker would be the hero here.

Speaking of lions, there appeared in a recent issue of the *Outlook* an article by Theodore Roosevelt on his lion hunting trip of last summer on the Grand Canyon Game Refuge. Incidentally he mentions in a very complimentary way several Forest Officers whom he met, and has a good word for the work they are doing. He also urges the advisability of providing the Forest Service with a more generous salary allotment.

A subject on which Colonel Roosevelt's article strengthens my already emphatic opinions is the matter of game protection on the National Forests. The moral and aesthetic arguments on this question are readily appreciated by every right minded man, but I do not believe that the economic value of an abundant game supply is often appreciated. Supposing that on the Carson, instead of having possibly 200 deer and 20 black bear on the Forest, that we had 5000 deer and 200 black bear. It is perfectly safe to say that we have the natural range for, and could carry at least that many, or more, without injuring a single existing or prospective interest. Now by the most conservative calculation, such a number of animals could be indefinitely maintained with an annual killing of 1,500 deer and 30 black bears. Now there are nine states resorted to for big game hunting where visiting sportsmen leave $50 to $500 per animal killed in the hands of the local community. A service man from Colorado has recently told me that hunting parties on his Forest paid as much as $100 per day for their outfits while out, and did so gladly where there was any prospect of game. But supposing, to be on the safe side, that our possible 1,500 deer and 30 black bears would bring in $20 and $100 apiece, respectively, to the community, which figures would give ample reduction for that part of the supply killed without cost by the community itself. This would bring $33,000 into the Carson country annually, equal to the net profit on one third of all the sheep on the Forest, and in excess of the money put into the country by the Forest Service, by our present allotments. It would even bear comparison with our total timber receipts under sustained yield, and it might easily be that the sum would in actual practice be doubled, due to my very conservative figures. This question is certainly worth thinking about.

Of course, if there were any question about the demand for good hunting grounds, it would hardly be worthwhile figuring at all, but as a matter of cold facts there are literally hundreds of thousands of well backed people all over the more densely populated part of the United States who would be only too glad to pay much more liberally than I have assumed above, for any hunting where they could be assured of moderate success.

The United States are richer in possibilities for a permanent game supply than their feeble efforts to preserve such a supply deserved. In Europe a man must be very rich to enjoy any hunting at all. Here we have hundreds of National Forests, which if well stocked would afford as good sport for the man of moderate means, as for the rich. The time is coming when the voting public is going to realize this, and the game on the Forests is going to be handled accordingly. But let us realize this right away, and put the Carson in the lead on this question, as far as our funds and time will permit.

> Most sincerely yours,
> Aldo Leopold
> Forest Supervisor

To Clara Leopold

> Jan. 20, 1916
> Albuquerque

Dearest Mütterchen—

You must be thinking that we are an ungrateful lot not to have written you before this, but we have both had a large sized handful since getting back,—Estella in weaning the youngster, and I in giving the Albuquerque Association another spurt. Then too by a peculiar accident we didn't get your good letter with the check enclosed until this morning. It evidently came during our absence and was brought into the house by Mr. Mueller and put *in the desk*, where Estella just found it. I am very grateful for the generous help—we are of course broke as usual, and at the same time badly in need of some more respectable togs to work second shift for the still existing set. We shall remember you when the new ones get to doing duty.

We found a regular second Christmas on our return, what with the bed, cakes, eatables, and other very acceptable trimmings. Your cakes are as usual far in the lead. Tante Tillie also kindly sent us a box.

As for the game movement, I have nothing to report except that its progress is astounding. I don't think that I have many rosy illusions on matters of that kind, but I am simply forced to admit that my most sanguine expectations are being relegated to the scrap-pile as obsolete. It would take me a day to list the letters I have received from all over the country complimenting the *Pine Cone*, asking permission to quote from it, wishing us luck, and offering cooperation. Not the least of these was a letter from Hornaday stating that he is pleased beyond words with our progress, and enclosing $100.00. The Santa Fe Association has raised 164 members in one week. The curious thing is that this thing has been tried time and again right here in New Mexico, and as promptly failed. I therefore can simply state that my plans and methods are delivering the goods.

Tell Carl that I was greatly pleased by his letter, hardly less by his report of good business than by his suggestion of starting something in Iowa. Tell him I shall give the matter special thought and write him complete suggestions as soon as possible.

As you of course realize, each new symptom of success of my venture here in New Mexico is a source of keen personal satisfaction both to myself and Estella. I am confronted also with the serious question of my future plans. This movement brings up opportunities beside which my necessarily limited future in the Forest Service looks pretty dull. At the same time the youngsters are beginning to crowd our rented nest, and we are thinking hard about locating somewhere and building.

Of course the uncertainty of our plans does not jibe very well with the idea of a place of our own. This is what I wanted to see Carolo about. I have to lay out a plan very shortly—at least before spring—or let some of my chances slip. I shall write you fully one of these days.

Love to all of you, and a kiss for the many nice things, including the check.

As always
Aldo

To Clara Leopold

May 11, 1917

Dearest Mütterchen—

Well—our stay at the Canyon is over—and it has been a curiously pleasant and also a very sad one. As I probably have told you, our party included Mr. Sherman, the big boss and a second Abraham Lincoln; Dr. Waugh, probably the foremost Landscape Engineer in the country; Miss Colter, architect and landscaper for the Santa Fe; the Wylders, Pooler, and myself. Also Walter Hubbell, head of the Harvey transportation department.

Our actual field trip in the Canyon was a whooping success. The shrubs and flowers down in the Canyon are a regular botanical garden now—the weather was perfect—the whole party extremely congenial. Sherman and Waugh are both regular humorists—or rather irregular—anyhow I have seldom laughed so hard. Waugh and Miss Colter were naturally also exceedingly interesting on their specialties, which are broad and many. We were out on muleback three days—one day of 24 miles I weathered with equanimity. Moreover the Canyon is best from the bottom—it beats the rim twenty ways for Sunday. My only disappointment was that we saw no mountain sheep.

Since our return we have been arguing long days and nights in the office. Briefly, Waugh has pronounced our Working Plan good as far as it goes, but entirely inadequate. He wants to tackle not only the present proposition but plans the whole Canyon on a huge scale—a dozen hotels—thousands of cottages—a tramway to the bottom—a $100,000 water development—and 1000 tourists a day. The present plan is to be outgrown right away—campaign started for huge appropriations and nation-wide publicity—and meanwhile everything must make way for the grand plan. Engineers are to start work at once mapping and surveying—followed by a prolonged study by a landscape man and the drawing up of a working plan on the new basis. He is opposed to making a National Park since the Park Service is no good, he says.

The whole thing is very inspiring in the abstract, and I believe his scheme is both practicable and justified. But in the mean-while we have the little messy job of clearing the way. We have to hold up the railroad on hundreds of thousands worth of proposed improvements—to make sure first that it harmonizes with the grand plan. Today we had to virtually put three small operators out of business—a pleasant job, as you may imagine. Sometimes I doubt my capacity for following the cold light of reason, even when I earnestly believe I am right. One old livery operator stormed at us all morning, which was not so bad, but this afternoon he brought a frail worn-out wife and four chil-dren to do the tear act, which was worse. There is no getting away from the fact that the "public interest" is sometimes cruel to individuals—and I would rather saw many cords of wood than be on hand when it does.

Tomorrow we go on to Flagstaff (Oak Creek, Lake Mary, etc.) thence I go back home, where I hope to arrive about May 15.

The readjustment of the Service to war conditions has now taken its first decisive step. All of us have been listed in one of three classes:

(1) Those necessary to supervise work that cannot be dropped, like timber sales, meat production, etc. These are to be exempt from draft.

(2) Those whose work can be dropped, but who are quali-fied to handle special war work not only on the Forests but anywhere else,—timber scalers, agricultural experts, range experts, etc. These are to be exempt from draft.

(3) Those who can be spared if necessary.

The expectation is that those exempted from draft will not be allowed to volunteer or leave the Service,—i.e. they are really already drafted for special service. The only sensible plan, of course, would be to create a special Corps of Foresters, like the Corps of Engineers, and handle them as above.

Frank Pooler has just returned from a special trip to Albuquerque and tells me I am listed in Class 2. Just what war specialty I have is not quite plain—but he says he thinks I was listed there as an agriculturalist. Anyhow Class 2 is satisfactory to me, as I would of course be of no account in the army and it might give me a chance to do something in particular. Of course then Class 3 will not be largely drawn upon unless things get really serious, except for such of Class 3 as volunteer.

Well—I must get to bed now—Estella says she and the babies are fine. I had quite a letter from Henry today which I shall send you shortly. Goodbye and lots of love from

Aldo

To Estella Leopold

Grand Canyon
July 18

Dearest Estella—

I am making this sendable to Mother and Carl because I want to tell you of a very interesting little "passear" yesterday and haven't time to write two letters. I used to have the habit of bumping into adventures—and don't seem to be quite over it yet.

Arrived here yesterday morning and strolled down to the office, to find there an old prospector with palsy, a yellow beard, and troubles. His pardner, he said, had left him the day before to look for an alleged lead mine down in the Canyon, and hadn't come back. He went equipped with a gallon canteen of water and a pick. Said mine was supposed to be on Pipe Creek, which is a large scope of country, especially in the vertical dimension.

Well we raised 4 men and 5 mules and 6 canteens and slid off down the trail. It's right summery down there—we absorbed the 6 canteens before we got to the Indian Gardens, where we found more water but no tracks. We had figured he would cut north from there. So we crawled back up, cutting signs on the ledges. Shortly after noon we found the track—cutting north along a ledge at the bottom of the red sandstone. We had to leave all the mules but one—a wise old gray one who must have been born and raised in a stone quarry. The tracking was difficult—only occasional gravelly spots—rest mostly finding the scratches of his shoenails on the rocks. Some day you may see what a ledge is like in the Grand Canyon. Horizontal plan of it is like this

and vertical much the same, not forgetting the mule. We had to save water for our prospective customer and pretty soon we couldn't even keep a piece of pine gum wet in our mouths.

We eased that mule in for about three miles, and then had to leave him. The ledge got to be just a little less straight up and down than the cliffs. Half mile further, lying under a juniper bush, we found our man. He couldn't holler fifty yards, nor get up. He had evidently had convulsions, judging by the dusty path he was kicking toward the brink, which was not far and God knows how deep—a thousand feet at least.

He had been 30 hours without water—a miserable little gallon don't last long down there. We poured orange juice down him, and little dabs of hot canteen water, and when the sun got behind the cliff got mescal poles and eased him back to the mule. From the time we found him—4 PM—until eight, he took a drink every thirty yards. He had a long neck, a large Adam's apple, and drank straight up like a chicken. A pleasanter sight I have not seen in many a day.

He had lots of nerve—which helped a lot. We got back to the mules just before dark. It was a beautiful ride back up. Lightning playing on the Kaibab rim—the juniper thickets hanging like rich moss on the far ledges, and all around the mescal flowers, looking like hundreds of great skyrockets shooting up out of the rocks. Songs of canyon wrens tumbled down from a quarter of a mile straight overhead, and bounced on the rocks off into the blue gulf behind us, toward the pink shadows of mountains far below. Finally we got up into the black firs under the rim, and back—to the dudes who sit up here and think they see the Canyon, but don't.

There is a wild snapdragon down there—acres of it—which some day we must have in the garden. It is a cream-coffee color with maroon pencillings—and sweet as a lily-of-the-valley.

Today we are still drinking water every five minutes. Thirty hours must be bad. The old fellow says he dreamed of reaching the pools at Indian Gardens, and lying down in them under the willows to sleep.

Kiss the boys for me, Dear, and take care of yourself. I am one day behind my schedule but may still make it by Sunday.

Always,
Your Aldo
July 18, 1917

To Austin Carey

March 13, 1922

Personal
c/o Forest Service
Washington, D.C.
Dear Mr. Carey:

It is always pleasant to receive an appreciation of an article, and it gives me special satisfaction to know of your approval of the "Wilderness Policy" proposed in the November *Journal.*

The idea has already received more recognition than I had hoped for. Col. Greeley personally advised me to publish my idea, implying a certain degree of personal sympathy with it; Major Kelley plans to briefly mention and recognize it in the new *Road & Trail Manual,* and the District Forester is willing to entertain proposals for its application in the road and trail plan of the Gila Forest where I hope to work it out incidental to inspection this summer. I quite agree with you that it is a matter best covered by a quiet and gradual agreement rather than by loud publicity.

I hope I have an opportunity to see you again one of these days.

Very sincerely yours,
Aldo Leopold

P.S. Will furnish you with any further material on this subject.

To Estella Leopold

Pecos Ranger Station
June 20, 1923

Stella Dearest—

I got in here last night after just ages away from my mail and was badly disappointed to find a whole bushel of bothersome business mail but not a single letter from you. Evidently your letters had been coming to the house instead of the office and so had not been forwarded. So last night I phoned father to send them on to me and also to find out how the youngsters are—they seem to be all well but it seems a long time since I have seen anybody but strangers.

Darling I wonder and wonder how you are and what you are doing—I'm not used to knowing nothing about you this way and expect your letters here tomorrow. Every day I keep thinking how nice it will be to be with you again. It seems about a year since I have awakened in the morning with you near me—will you be glad Darling when we are together again? I think of you all the time and wish I were with you now.

We had a big rain today and all got pretty wet as we were out on the Glorieta Mesa in a car—the first car-riding I've done in quite a while. Most of last week I was over on the east slope working with Cassidy's Grazing Reconnaissance party—stopped over Sunday at Elliot Barker's and had a nice visit with them. They are very nice and have a perfectly beautiful ranch over on the Sapello. Monday I came across Elk Mountain (snow was 12 feet deep up there but fortunately packed hard) to Panchuela. Saw an awfully pretty pair of bucks in the steep country on Hollinger Cr. The Barkers have invited us to come up next hunting season.

Right now I don't know just where I'm going next but I do know I need a day at laundering and mending and would like to go fishing—but the rain will spoil that for a while. Haven't wet a line yet except that Sunday over at Gallinas—and that's a little brushy creek and doesn't satisfy my hankering for big water.

Many a day sweetheart I've wished you were with me—the flowers are so wonderful—big yellow lady-slippers and little purple orchids all splashed with velvety brown and white. Also shooting stars and violets and columbines. I wish you were here tonight and we were starting out for a week with some good horses and a pack outfit and no destination or time limit. Would you like to do that?

Stella Darling I wish I knew that you were well and having a good time and still thinking of me. Pretty soon it will be time to think of coming home. It will be good to be able to think of just when and where I will give you a big kiss and look at you again. Doesn't it seem a long time to you since we were all home together?

I am feeling quite well and sleeping pretty well and enjoying most of my trip—of course part of the time there are unpleasant things to handle. I wish I could have the boys along—there is always the chance tho that they might be in the way. Maybe I can figure something later to get them out.

Goodnight now little one—I'll be thinking of you a long time tonight and wishing I had you with me. Don't forget I love you and write me often Dearest. Always

Your Aldo

To Estella Leopold

Rito Frijoles
July 1

Stella Dearest—

Arrived here tonight and go on in to town tomorrow. I came on over to that Jemez fire after all and have been making a little round over here since we put it under control a week ago.

Stella Darling I've been wishing for you all the time and wishing it were time for you to come home. I have just one more trip of about five days to make on the Borrego district and three or four days in the office and then I'm through and ready to take you on a fishing trip. I've been thinking of it so much that I've almost promised myself that you actually are coming with me. Are you? I get awfully lonesome to be either alone or with you,—today has been the first time in weeks that I've had a ride by myself. Right now a hermit thrush is singing up on the wall of the canyon—the sunset is lighting up a huge thunderhead hanging over the cliffs to the north. But nobody hears the thrush but me—and nobody else knows the thunderhead as one of "the sun-white majesties that stand at the

gates of dawn." You would. All day we have been passing old
old ruins—unspoiled by archeological labels or tourist trails or
restorations—places to

> Take the wings of the morning
> Pierce the Barcan wilderness
> Or lose thyself in the continuous woods
> Where rolls the Oregon
> Yet the dead are there
> And millions in those solitudes
> Since first the flight of years began
> Have laid them down in their last sleep.

Whitman said of a woman:

> For thee the earth lay preparing quintillions of years
> For thee the revolving cycles truly and steadily rolled
> Without the untruth of a single second.

I incline to think it a little ungrateful that some of the women
here (Whitman's kind as far as brawn is concerned) are not
much aware of the cycles and would have a hard time comprehending what he means by "untruth." Only "the hills—rock
ribbed and ancient as the sun" seem aware of that.

Stella Darling are you really coming to let me take you on a
trip? Every day seems to add another month to the time you
have been gone. I think and think of you—like in the old days
when I had to live on that alone. I hope there is a stack of letters
waiting for me at Santa Fe—and that lots of them will be love
letters—and that you are coming soon.

It is dusk in the canyon now, and the hermit thrush is "trill-
ing sleepily his praise of gardens." The night hawks are out, and
up on the mesa a whippoorwill is calling. I suppose I should
have the faculty of appreciating it—but I can't fit in with people
and hotels in such a place—it is like trying to read Isaiah to
somebody chewing gum.

Goodnight now Darling and remember I love you and want
you to come back soon. I haven't been writing because I have had
no way to either write or send letters—but I think of you always.
Are you well Dearest and will you be glad to come home?

Always

Your Aldo

July 1, 1923

To Starker and Luna Leopold

Aug. 24, 1923

Dear Starker & Luna —

Pretty soon it will be time for you boys to pack the outfit. Do you think you'll remember to fill the canteen?

We've been meeting up with lots of rattlesnakes this trip,—I think 7 or 8 altogether. Some of them were pretty big.

I saw a lot of scattering whitewings in the mountains, and just worlds of big bandtail pigeons. There are lots of bear up in the Sierra Ancha where I've been. Haven't seen any deer—just tracks.

I hear you boys are selling papers. That's fine. When I get back you must tell Daddy how many you sold and how much you made on them and how your bicycle money stands. Also you mustn't forget your license and ammunition when I buy you that gun next year. Wasn't it next year I was to buy you a gun?—i.e. an air gun?

How's Flick? I expect you to have him thinned down and in good shape. See that he gets a raw bone every week or so.

Maybe we'll go on a pack trip deer hunting. Would you like that?

Here at Globe are some of the biggest copper mines in the world. What is copper used for? Look that up and tell me when I get home.

What have you been reading? Are you helping your mother?

Yours always

Daddy

To Raphael Zon

May 19, 1926

St. Paul, Minn.

Dear Zon:

Some of your many friends have taken it upon themselves to remind us that it is now twenty five years since you first began to talk to foresters about the impossibility of practicing forestry by merely talking about it.

This has set me to thinking,—to try and define that quality of your mind which has added so much to the intellectual timbre of our profession.

Stevenson came very close to one aspect of it when he said: "He has in theorizing what I would call the synthetic gusto."

Most foresters think with heaviness, as if they were sawing wood before breakfast. You have shown them how to think joyfully, which is usually the same as thinking well.

I fancy Whitman must have had in mind some previous incarnation of Raphael Zon when he wrote: "Natural history, to be true to life, must be inspired. There ought to be intuitive perception of truth, important conclusions ought to be jumped to—laws, facts, results arrived at by a kind of insight or inspirational foreknowledge that never could be obtained by mere observation or actual verification. In science—some of the most important discoveries seem inspirations, or a kind of winged, ecstatic reasoning, quite above and beyond real facts."

This, my friend, is what we foresters have lacked, and what you have given us for this score of years.

We need a continuance of your gift for another score of years to come.

AL

To Estella Leopold

Delkana Camp No. H
Kaniksu Natl. Forest
June 25, 1926

Stella Dear—

Since you have never been in a logging camp maybe you would like to know what this one is like.

You get here by driving over five miles of "pole road," built of logs like railroad rails only 2–6' up in the air. There are log flanges to keep you from jumping the track. When you meet a truck coming down the road piled high with 2000 feet of white pine logs you feel like jumping the track anyhow.

You drive into the little camp clearing between walls of timber of indescribable grandeur. If "only God can make a tree" then who could make this magnificent forest, which is as much more than trees as America is more than Babbitt.

In the clearing is a street of log cabins, flanked on one side by a fleet of log wagons and on the other by great banks of logs ready to roll down upon the logging trucks.

We arrived in the hot afternoon when the camp was deserted. As we started to climb the mountain to visit the cutting areas a whole string of logs came thundering down the steep chute, which is greased till it nears camp and then curved to dump the logs on the landings. The logs come down with a roar, and when they begin to hit the spikes or "goose necks" set in the chute to retard them, great silky ribbons of sapwood fly from each spike and fall in snowy piles by the chute. The logs slow up and finally stop with beautiful precision just at the landings.

We climb on up the heart-breaking slope—that is heart breaking to the fat men, and enter the burned area. (This sale was made to salvage the timber on this burn.) Here are freshly cut logs, brush, and dead snags heaped in seeming confusion, but through them great teams of percherons are threading their way dragging the logs to the chute, where crews with peaveys roll the logs down skidways into the chute and start them down their long slide to the camp. Ditch-digging is soft compared to the labor of skidding and rolling logs. It is cruelly hot and the men are all in undershirts, blue jeans, and spiked brogans, grimy with sweat and dust. A little spring has been flumed with little troughs of cedar bark and delivers a cool stream all along the chute, from which everybody drinks every five minutes. We climb on up another thousand feet to the upper slopes where the timber is smaller. You can stand still and hear the flat-headed borers chiselling away inside of the logs with a sound like a chorus of crickets. It is a race between the foresters and the bugs. They would ruin all this burned timber within a year, but we have beaten them to it. Likewise there will be no tangle of fallen timber on this burn to catch fire again and burn up the young pines which will shortly sprout from seed held over in the duff. Altogether 15 million feet will be salvaged—enough lumber to build 1500 homes, and we will get $75,000 for it.

After looking over the cutting areas we slide down the mountain into camp just in time to escape the wrath of the cook for being late. 50 men lined up at board tables groaning under surprisingly good food, and every man—jack silent as a tomb.

Conversation at meals is actually forbidden (because it annoys the cooks, and they rule the roost).

After supper all hands sit on the steps of the log cabin street and catch up on smoking, which is strictly prohibited in the woods. The forest men haul out their new toy—a little portable pump for fighting fire that purrs like an aeroplane and throws a 75 foot stream out of a 2 inch hose. With this they wet down the vicinity of the camp, while the teamsters curry and water their sleek horses. Nobody works but some Gyppos who are loading a last few trucks of logs to go down the pole road.

By this time it has turned cool and the thrushes are singing deep in the woods that wall the camp. I don't suppose many of these men hear them, but who knows? The hearers of thrushes may wear hobnails as well as long hair.

Our scaler has just confided that he has 10 grown children in Spokane. He hasn't been home since last 4th of July and is hoping it will rain this fourth so there will be no fires to keep him on the job.

Altogether it is an epic but a hard life in these camps. The city man who buys a truckload of lumber has no idea of what goes into it.

Goodnight now Dear.

Always

Aldo

To Estella Leopold

San Francisco

Aug. 7

Stella Dearest—

I got back late last night and came down to this empty office to get your letters and write you what I had on my mind, but I found a letter from my friend Ed White with the news about the Conservation Commission. Apparently we are entirely sold out and worse off than before we started. I feel pretty sick about it—especially about egging on my friends to do such a terrible lot of work for nothing. When I think of Bill Aberg I almost feel as if I had misled him. Well—it may turn out all right in the end but it's evidently to be a long slow grind just as it was in New Mexico.

Dearest I've been thinking about you a lot and a lonesome Sunday ahead of me doesn't make me want to be with you any less. Two weeks more seem a long time and I'll be glad to settle down to our real work in the woods to make it pass away a lot quicker. I'm expecting Luxford tomorrow and we leave for Fort Bragg tomorrow night on the train.

This last trip ended at Yosemite Park. I can't say whether it was more pleasure to see Yosemite than pain to see the way most people see it. It's a struggle for me sometimes to play ball with the crowd at all. How much to compromise is a question on which there is no such thing as advice, or consolation. Every man is a lone wolf when he faces real realities.

We went through the Sierras for two days. If the Lord ever made another country like that it wasn't on this particular star. Also the great San Joaquin valley, which Walt Whitman no doubt had in mind when he said "I will plant companionship as thick as trees along all the great rivers of America." If he could see a pot-bellied real estate promoter showing his trees I wonder what he would think.

The tourists all gape at Yosemite but what none of them see is the fifty miles of foothills on the way in. They are almost a relief after the highly frosted wedding-cake (and the wedding-guests) on the other end. Especially the quail, and the live oaks "joyously uttering dark green leaves." You never have read my nickel volume of Whitman. We must read some of it together when I get back.

Well Dearest—this is all reaction from too many thoughts, and, I suppose, too many silk stockings. Write me often and take care of yourself. I must get to work now—the morning is half gone.

Always
Aldo
August 7, 1927

To Harold C. Bryant

July 24, 1930

Fish & Game Commission
San Francisco, California
Dear Dr. Bryant:

As you know, I am chairman of a committee of the National Game Conference which is trying to draw a game policy.

No doubt you are familiar with the tentative draft presented at the December meeting.

The recent widespread discussion of predator control policies has made me anxious to include something on this subject and to seek the cooperation of the protectionists in drafting it. With this end in view I wrote to Dr. Witmer Stone asking the A.O.U. to name a representative to serve on the committee. He referred the matter to Dr. Grinnell and Dr. Grinnell has nominated you.

I hope you will be willing to accept this appointment. I sent Dr. Grinnell a new draft of the policy and asked him to forward it to you after reading it, together with his suggestions and past correspondence. I hope you will try to represent the attitude of the ornithologists rather than that of the sportsman in so far as you can conscientiously do so.

An informal meeting of the committee will be held in connection with the International Association of Game and Fish Commissioners at Toronto, August 25 or 26. If you can attend this, fine. If not, will you please send me your criticisms of the revised draft, so that they can be read at the Toronto meeting of the committee?

I congratulate you on your new duties and hope we shall have opportunity to keep in touch with each other.

With kindest regards,

Yours sincerely,
Aldo Leopold
Chairman, Game Policy Committee

To Joseph P. Knapp

Sept. 18, 1930

580 Fifth Avenue
New York City
Dear Mr. Knapp:

I appreciate your courtesy in asking me for further suggestions on the Foundation prospectus as now printed.

As you know, I have nothing but enthusiastic praise for your
fundamental idea of a big-scale program, adequately financed
through a Foundation. I am more than ever convinced, however, that the prospectus is the wrong way to execute your plan.

My suggestions all boil down to one point: the function of
a foundation is to help the country evolve its own system of
game production.

The prospectus commits the Foundation to exactly the opposite course: it selects a system without consulting even the proposed staff or the proposed additional Founders, and proposes
to use the resources of the Foundation to get it adopted by the
country at large.

Possibly it was not the intention of the prospectus to commit
the Foundation to any one system. I can assure you, however,
that the prospectus *is being so interpreted* by sportsmen generally. If this was not the intention, then a corrective statement
is urgently needed.

It so happens that I am personally opposed to the system of
individual game ownership, and to its logical corollaries, open
markets and unlimited bags. While I admit that it conserves
upland game in Europe, it has the opposite effect on migratory
game. Moreover it is open to certain abuses which are important to other conservationists, and should be to sportsmen.
As you know, I personally favor commercializing the shooting
privilege, but *not the game*, thus getting the advantage of private production incentive, without losing the advantage of state
ownership and supervision. However, what I personally favor is
beside the point. Even if the prospectus committed the Foundation to my particular "system," I would still consider it a mistake
for the Foundation to espouse it to the exclusion of all others.

The Foundation should have only one commitment: to see
that any and all promising proposals for the actual practice of

game management are promptly brought to the test of experience, regardless of the theory on which they are based. Some proposals which are based on unsound theory will have to be tried along with the rest. This may teach their proponents that the theory is unsound, but your advance opinion, or mine, will never do so, even if backed by millions of dollars.

By and large, the country has wasted several decades already debating about conflicting theories, instead of trying some of them out. The Foundation, by its advance commitment to one of them, now threatens to prolong the debate indefinitely, instead of ending it by trying all of them, and letting experience be the umpire.

Let me put the whole thing positively in terms of a Foundation "Platform" instead of negatively in terms of criticism of the prospectus. I would suggest something like this:

(1) America has the land to raise an abundant game crop, the means to pay for it, and the love of sport to assure that successful production will be rewarded.

(2) There are many conflicting theories on how to bring the land, the means of payment, and the love of sport into productive relationship with each other. The Foundation does not know which theory is best, but it proposes to devote its resources to bring all promising theories to the test of experience. The public can then choose for itself.

(3) There are some, but not enough, biological facts available on how to raise game. The Foundation proposes to make available the known facts, to promote research to find the additional facts needed to produce game crops, and to promote training of experts qualified to apply them.

(4) The Foundation has only one objective: more game; and only one policy: to help evolve ways and means of getting it which will be mutually satisfactory to all three parties at interest, namely the landowner, the sportsman, and the general public.

> Yours sincerely,
> Aldo Leopold
> In Charge, Game Survey

To Seth Gordon

Oct. 2, 1930

Izaak Walton League of America
541–555 West Randolph Street
Chicago, Illinois
Dear Seth:

I have frequently "crabbed" about the low grade of articles run in *Outdoor America*. It therefore gives me satisfaction to do the opposite for a change.

"The Seven Lean Years" by Dr. Clements is an admirable example of real solid technical material, successfully presented in popular form. I hope you will develop cooperation by a whole flock of Clementses, and soft-pedal some of the other famous writers who have little or nothing to say.

Have you any way to find out the receptivity of the average member to really worthwhile material of this kind? I am personally confident that the average Waltonian *will* read this sort of thing.

Yours as ever,

To Barrington Moore

Oct. 4, 1930

Society of American Foresters
Room 810, Hill Building
Washington, D.C.
Dear Barrington:

The fact that I am not in the government service, together with my experience in relating forestry to game conservation, gives me, perhaps, special qualifications for judging your "Plan for Reorganizing the Conservation Work of the Federal Government."

Your plan is sound as a dollar. It is the only plan I have seen which entirely satisfies me. As a member of the Council, and as a forester in private practice, I endorse it 100 per cent.

I will say further that its adoption is, in my opinion, vital to the future of game conservation, as well as forestry, in this country. I shall outline my reasons for saying this, because I think the people who propose to centre conservation in the Interior Department lack any appreciation of the direction in which both are headed.

1. *The Farmer* holds the key to the future of small game. If anybody doubts this, let them read the "Game Policy" about to be published by the American Game Conference.

2. *The Department of Agriculture* already has the machinery, consisting of 48 Agricultural Colleges and thousands of County Agents, to show the farmer how to make game a paying farm crop. It would cost the Interior Department millions of needless dollars to duplicate this machinery.

3. *The Forester and the Lumberman* hold the key to the future of big game. The Department of Agriculture already has the federal machinery, and is "geared up" to the state machinery, to show the lumberman how to make game a paying forest crop. This machinery might conceivably be transferred to the Interior Department, but that would split the administration of the two kinds of game, which often are intermingled on the same parcel of ground.

4. Federal bureaus *in Washington* are but an insignificant fraction of the human machinery which will really count in the future of either game or forestry. It is the agricultural machinery *already maintained in the field* which matters. To transfer either or both subjects to Interior would throw them *out of gear* with this already existing machinery.

It is true that this agricultural field personnel is not yet working on game. The Arms and Ammunition Industry, which I represent, has, however, invested $50,000 in a Game Survey, and $45,000 in a series of Game Research Fellowships in the Agricultural Colleges, to start the process of "gearing up." To transfer game to another department would jeopardize the whole future of our investment.

Let me put the whole thing another way: Many well-meaning conservationists still think of game conservation as something which is going to be performed by bureaus and appropriations, through game farms, hatcheries, land purchases, and laws. If this were true, it would not matter much what department administers them.

But it is not true. Game conservation, if accomplished at all, can only be performed by private citizens who own land, i.e.

farmers, lumbermen, and stockmen. Bureaus, appropriations, laws, etc., are merely ways to help the landowner. Why build up a second and needless field machinery to help the landowner when one already exists in every county in the United States, with headquarters in the Department of Agriculture?

A little knowledge of conservation is certainly a dangerous thing. I hope the Society will put forth its utmost efforts to burst this plausible but dangerous fallacy of centering conservation in Interior.

> Yours sincerely,
> Aldo Leopold

To Werner C. Nagel

> 421 Chemistry Building
> Madison, Wisconsin
> January 6, 1931

Butler Apartments
Columbia, Missouri
Dear Mr. Nagel:

I am much interested in your desire to study game management, and I wish I were able to give you an unqualified answer as to what to study as preparation. I have been trying to get some of our fellows to express their opinions on this question in published form, but none of them have as yet done so.

All of your work so far is to the point. The following additions occur to me:

(1) Mathematics. At some time or other acquaint yourself with the theory of statistics, including the theory of probabilities.

(2) Unless you have already a working knowledge of soils, I would try to get it.

(3) Ecology. This is of course the rock bottom of game management, but many kinds of courses are offered under this same name. Take any which you think are foundational for game management.

I assume you have a working knowledge of field ornithology and mammalogy. This can rarely be obtained in the classrooms except from the purely taxonomic side, but is essential for the purpose in hand.

These suggestions are necessarily offered in the dark. The only real way for me to be of service to you is to arrange for you to meet personally somebody who is competent to discuss this matter with you. It is not impossible that in connection with Dr. Curtis's proposed program of game research Mr. W. B. Grange of the U.S. Biological Survey may visit Columbia. Do not miss an opportunity to question him personally.

Aside from your formal courses, your general reading is very important. If you can give me a list of what you regularly read, I might be able to make some suggestions for additions.

I do not expect that you will find this letter satisfactory. Keep in touch with me from time to time and I will be glad to be of any service to you that is within my power.

> Yours sincerely,
> Aldo Leopold
> In Charge, Game Survey

To George Latta Barrus

Feb. 19, 1931

Forester
Ridgeland, South Carolina
Dear Mr. Barrus:

I will do my best to answer the questions in your letter of February 10.

1. Stoddard's Quail Investigation, which I consider authoritative, shows that controlled burning at intervals is necessary in the South on lands where a heavy quail crop is desired.

2. A heavy interspersion of plowed strips would certainly reduce the necessity of any kind of burning. How far apart the strips should be would of course depend entirely on the individual case.

3. Stoddard knows of instances where the stand of quail has been reduced through long periods of total protection from fire.

4. I would doubt very much whether fire directly kills enough snakes and rats to make much difference. By regulating the

density of the sedge, however, fire controls the rat population to a large extent. This will be clear from Stoddard's report, entitled "The Bobwhite Quail: Its Habits and Preservation," about to be published by Charles Scribner's Sons.

5. In view of my answer to question 4, this would seem to be beside the point. Controlled burning is not primarily a predator control measure, but a question of density of cover acceptable to quail.

In answering your questions categorically, I hope you will keep in mind that there is no such thing as a categorical answer to biological questions. I would suggest that you study Stoddard's report carefully and learn the *reasons* for his recommendations, after which the necessity for categorical answers will disappear.

Yours sincerely,
Aldo Leopold

To Frederic Walcott

Dec. 10, 1931

Chairman
Committee on Wild Life Resources
U.S. Senate Building
Washington, D.C.
Dear Senator Walcott:

I have received from the Society of Mammalogists committee on Alaskan bears a request that I state my views on the proposed Admiralty Island bear sanctuary.

I personally lack first-hand knowledge of Alaskan conditions but I strongly lean to the belief that where commercial interests conflict with bear conservation, the former have been given undue priority. I favor the sanctuary and will strongly support any policy which your committee or others may evolve to not merely perpetuate the species, but to assure such perpetuation on the largest range in the largest possible numbers.

Yours sincerely,
Aldo Leopold
In Charge, Game Survey

To William T. Hornaday

Soils Building
March 1, 1933

1 Bank St.
Stamford, Conn.
Dear Dr. Hornaday:

I am asking Scribner's to send you, as soon as available, a copy of my *Game Management* which will be off the press some time this month. I would have liked to inscribe it, but that would have entailed delay in shipping it out here and back.

I want you to get it promptly, partly in acknowledgment of the fact that my whole venture into this field dates from your visit to Albuquerque in 1916, and your subsequent encouragement to stay in it.

I do not by any means assume that the book will meet with your approval, or that its appearance is an event of importance. It is of importance to me because it summarizes the chain of thought which I have developed. This is a freer expression than my *Game Survey* because the survey was a compilation of facts, not a discussion of principles, and as such left little room for philosophical interpretation of the facts described. This then should be a better basis for judging whether the tangent I have been following has any long-time merit or not.

Both the publisher and myself will welcome any expression of your opinion, critical or otherwise, which you may care to print, either in your own publication, or elsewhere.

Another and purely personal matter: the time and expense involved in getting out this book have pretty well exhausted what I had laid by while with the Ammunition people. Accordingly I am available for any sort of work, permanent or temporary, regardless of location, which will advance wild life conservation. I would dislike, of course, to tie up with anything politically dominated. I would prefer that my situation be not widely discussed, but if you happen to hear of anything, I would appreciate your telling me about it.

With respectful regard—

Yours sincerely
Aldo Leopold

To Herbert L. Stoddard

March 26, 1934
New Soils Building

The Hall, Route 1
Tallahassee, Florida
Dear Herbert:

I am sending you by express a yew bow, which I have been making for you this winter. I have enjoyed it because it was a way to express my affection and regard for one of the few who understands what yew bows—and quail and mallards and wind and sunsets—are all about.

I cannot assure you that it is a good piece of wood. Staves, like friends, have to be lived with in many woods and weathers before one knows their quality. The fact that the stave is yew, has a specific gravity of .432, came from Roseburg, Oregon, and has been waiting for a job since 1930, is no more a test of how it will soar an arrow than the fact that a man is a naturalist, weighs 160, and has had time enough to season, is a test of the zest or nicety with which he will expend his powers in the good cause. All I can say of this bow is that its exterior "education" embodies whatever craft and wisdom is mine to impart. What lies inside is the everlasting question.

The bow is built for endurance rather than speed, hence the length. Its weight (in a cold cellar) is 50 pounds at 28 inches. This ought to temper down, in your climate, to a heavy American or light York. I doubt if it will hold on the gold at 100 yards, but it might. Should you use it regularly for York, I would advise a lighter string.

If it proves a good piece of wood, it should be re-tillered after a season's use, to catch up any "hinge" which may by then have developed. I will be glad to do this for you. At that time, should it have proven a worthy stick, it may also be shortened to make a straight hunter, or a York.

I have tried to build into this bow the main recent improvements in bow-design, but since some of them are not visible, they will bear mention. The square cross section and waisted handle are of course visible innovations, but probably less important than the new location of the geographic centre. In former days this was put close under the arrow plate, but in this bow it lies as near the centre of the handle as is possible without overworking the lower limb. In a 3½" handle I have found this spot to be 1½" below the arrow plate. Some authorities make it 1¾", but I know from observation that these too-modern bows never appear at two successive annual tournaments, or if they do, they are "on crutches" and ready for premature pensioning to some idle peg on the bow-rack.

The horns whence came these nocks were pulled off the skeleton of an old cow on the Santa Rita ranges by Dave Gorsuch. The slight flaws at the base of the upper nock are the measure of the seasons which bleached her bones before Dave found her. I doubt not that many a black vulture perched on her skull meanwhile, and many a quail and roadrunner, coyote and jackrabbit played their little games of life and death in the hackberry bush hard by her withering hide. Did that stodgy old cow, whilst living, know, or get any satisfaction from knowing, that within her growing horns she was converting her daily provender of desert grama and sun-dried mesquite into an enduring poem of amber light? Does an eagle know, or get any satisfaction from knowing, that in his incomparable pinions he is converting carrion into a structure so perfect that every breeze sings its praises? Does a yew tree glory in fashioning from mere soil and sunlight a wood whose shavings curl in ecstasy at the prospect of becoming a bow? Does a cedar's pride lie in his towering height, or in the fact—unknown to all save archers—that under his shaggy bark lies a snow-white wood that planes with the joyful sound of tearing silk—the sound that bluebills make when they hurtle out of the sky at the invitation of placid waters? These are questions meet for an archer to ask, but for no man to answer.

One cannot fashion a stave without indulging in fond hopes of its future. I hope this one will one day sire a litter of six golds for you, and will many a time hear your gleeful chuckle as you add up the ends for a 500 score. On many a thirsty noon I hope you lean it against a mossy bank by cool springs. In fall I hope its shafts will sing in sunny glades where turkeys dwell, and that one day some wily buck will live just long enough to startle at the twang of its speeding string.

Among my more homely prayers are these: That the nock will never come off just as you start out for the woods or targets, nor the arrow plate spring loose just as you modestly explain to some visiting tyro that the inlay is of mastodon ivory which "stayed put" since the Pleistocene.

And lastly if the bow breaks, with or without provocation, pray waste no words or thoughts in vain regret. There are more staves in the woods than have yet sped an arrow, all longing to realize their manifest destiny. Just blow three blasts on your horn and I will make you another.

Yours as ever,

To Franklin D. Roosevelt

New Soils Building
November 9, 1934

Washington, D.C.

Dear Mr. President:

As a member of your "Committee on Wild Life Resources" I may be entitled to a direct expression of opinion on the proposed transfer of certain conservation bureaus, which I understand is under consideration in Washington.

I was formerly a member of the U.S. Forest Service. I suppose this precludes my being strictly impartial on the question of transferring the Forest Service to the Department of the Interior. I will, therefore, make no attempt to comment specifically upon it.

I have, however, gradually become convinced, after nearly 20 years of watching the annual moves and counter-moves for the juggling of bureaus, of the general futility of such juggling as a means to genuine coordination.

The reason for my skepticism is that whenever better coordination is gained at one point by placing two related bureaus together, it is lost at another by separating two bureaus which have been together. There is, for example, an indisputable need for more mutual sympathy between forestry and parks, and between forestry and public domain, but there is likewise a need for the continuance and further development of the relations between forestry and the various agricultural bureaus. In short, there is usually about as much lost as gained in bureau shifts.

I am skeptical of the genuineness of the coordination obtainable from shifts alone. Real coordination goes much deeper than the mere question of whether two bureaus are in the same or in different departments. Real coordination is an intellectual attribute of bureau chiefs and cabinet officers which cannot either be called into being, or abolished, by moves of this kind.

It is all too true that some bureaus, existing side by side in the same department for decades, have failed to develop any mutuality of thought and action, but as long as their intellectual quality remains constant, the same will probably continue to be true about new relationships established by moving them.

It is, of course, academic to hope that all cabinet officers and all bureau chiefs can attain that catholicity of thought requisite to real coordination. I might, however, have some degree of confidence in the setting up of a conservation coordinator, if the right individual could be found. An interdepartmental planning agency, accountable directly to you, might also be a substantial alternative.

The main point of this letter is to express my skepticism about transfers as a solution worthy of your approval.

> Yours respectfully,
> Aldo Leopold
> In Charge, Game Research

To R. E. Trippensee

> New Soils Building
> February 11, 1935

U.S. Forest Service
Federal Building
Milwaukee, Wisconsin
Dear Trippensee:

I have just learned that some of your timber stand improvement crews are cutting out the ironwoods on National Forest land.

Have you considered this from the standpoint of injury to the grouse range? You know, of course, that the buds of the ironwood are an important winter food. I am afraid that this policy is headed toward the same kind of a conflict as arose in the southern Appalachians where the timber stand improvement crews are taking out the beech "wolf" trees, which are, of course, a principal source of mast.

In my opinion the Forest Service is laying up trouble for itself in riding rough-shod over the game interests in this way. If you are able to secure any reconsideration of this policy, I would be interested to know about it.

> Yours sincerely,
> Aldo Leopold
> In Charge, Game Research

To Robert Marshall

> New Soils Building
> March 25, 1935

Office of Indian Affairs
Washington, D.C.
Dear Bob:

Thanks for the supply of the Wilderness Society prospectus.

I appreciate very much your suggestion about the presidency. I am content to leave the decision in your hands. I have a great deal more than I can carry and would have to drop things to take on anything of this kind, and I could not take it on in any event unless there is an active secretary. I would much prefer not to take it on. In this particular matter, however, I do not feel like flatly refusing to take on the obligation.

What about Sterling Yard? Most policy affecting our interests is made in Washington. It is a long way from here to Washington and I hope at least to avoid very many trips there. It seems to me that Yard would be in a better position.

Let me know what your group decides about this.

> Yours sincerely,
> Aldo Leopold
> In Charge, Game Research

To Robert Sterling Yard

New Soils Building
July 19, 1935

The Wilderness Society
1840 Mintwood Place
Washington, D.C.
Dear Mr. Yard:

I have just learned to my mortification and surprise that the Porcupine Mountain wilderness lying on the west end of the upper peninsula of Michigan is being split by a road from Wakefield to Presque Isle Falls. This is an area of a quarter-million acres of hardwood, hemlock and pine timber which lies in the rough breaks on the south shores of Lake Superior and for that reason has so far escaped "development."

There are two large owners in the area: (1) General Motors (probably through the Fisher Body Company) and (2) Oliver Iron Mining Company. In addition there are numerous smaller scattered lumber holdings. There are probably few or no agricultural holdings.

The attached outline map of the state shows the general location of the area, and the attached road map of the state shows the existing roads and the new road now under construction from Wakefield to Presque Isle Falls. There has already been cut approximately four miles of the 15 miles involved.

The political and economic background for this invasion seems to be as follows: The timber holdings above mentioned cannot be logged until a road is built and the present relief labor program in conjunction with the New Deal conservation program offers a favorable opportunity whereby these private owners can get their main roads built at public expense. Accordingly they have persuaded the county that the tourists must be given access to Presque Isle Falls, which is the scenic center of the area. I am informed that the logging is keeping pace with the road construction, which speaks for itself as to the underlying motivation.

Another side-light on the situation is this: The Forest Service has been dickering with these owners to buy this tract as a National Forest. There is, as you know, a limit to what they can pay for standing timber, which operates to the end that the owner is tempted to reduce his land to slash in order that it may sell the more readily for National Forest purposes. The fact that this slash may be a slightly different kind of slash from that which would ordinarily be produced commercially is merely an incident which by no means obscures the vicious circle thus put into operation.

The Michigan Conservation Department has been far more enlightened on matters of wilderness policy than any other state department I know of, and my guess would be that this invasion of the Presque Isle area is taking place despite their efforts rather than with their help. Since the state has no large land holdings, I assume they are powerless to arrest the process.

All of this, however, does not extenuate the basic fact that the only decent wilderness left in the Lake States is falling victim to the New Deal brand of conservation. I suppose the funds for the road are being fed out through PWA, and it might be of considerable interest to Secretary Ickes, with his well-known sympathy for the wilderness idea, to be aware of how his underlings are using his funds for its defeat.

I do not assume, of course, that the Wilderness Society has facilities for holding up this project, but I do think we could well afford to make a noise about it. It might also be that some of the conservation organizations could help by printing suitable articles.

In order to save time I am taking the liberty of sending copies of this letter to Ernest Oberholtzer, P. S. Lovejoy, and Bob Marshall, and I am asking Oberholtzer and Lovejoy to let you have any facts which might aid in formulating an effective protest. I take it for granted that we have their sympathy on the basic assumption that there should be a protest.

I am sorry to say that I will be in Europe from August 1 to November 1. Should you need any local action in Wisconsin, I would suggest that you keep in touch with the following: (1) Leonard W. Wing, in care of my office. Wing is one of my senior graduate students and intensely interested personally in this area; (2) R. J. Roark, Engineering Building, Madison. Mr. Roark is already a member of the Society and has personally taken trips in this area and knows more about the country than I do; (3) Noble Clark, Agricultural Hall, Madison. Mr. Clark is director of our Agricultural Experiment Station. He formerly lived in this vicinity and knows this country well.

With best regards,

Yours sincerely,
Aldo Leopold
In Charge, Game Research

To Estella Leopold

Oct. 9

Estella Dear—

Just back from a trip to Schorfheide, which is the "National Park" where the Germans are trying to preserve the European buffalo or wisent, also moose, wild horse (no longer genuine), cranes, black stork, etc. This is also the place where the Kaiser did most of his hunting. This is now attended to by Mr. Göring. Very interesting place,—I got especially good information on the life history of cranes. It's astonishing how much like the Wisconsin cranes in their behavior.

Previous to that I was at Wilkendorf—I happen to have some extra prints of the lakes there, and enclose them. I am now through with my trips out of Berlin and proceed to East Prussia as soon as I can get my notes & reading completed. Then I go to Breslau, Silesia, which was not on my schedule but I have learned about a lot of information which I can get there but not elsewhere. Then to Munich, then wind up at Tharandt and Berlin, and then probably will stop in Mecklenburg to see Howard's friend on my way to Bremen. I may not go to Scotland, but just up to Oxford to see Elton.

I've begun to write papers on the trip now—so as to be able to tell where the gaps are and what additional points I must pick up.

Shirley was here in Berlin till yesterday—we heard Lohengrin and Madame Butterfly. I enjoyed Butterfly, but Siegfried was too fat to hug his girl and I can't preserve the illusion of reality under such circumstances. I would enjoy opera if the singers were a little more personable.

I'm glad Marie and mother were there and I enjoyed your account of the shack. Tell Starker or Luna to make some kind of a set-up with Webster to keep an eye on our prairie chickens during the rabbit season. I'd like to give him $10 a year, or more, to take care of them. Did you pay the lumber bill?

Glad to hear of the Riley dinner. Are you still shooting?

Tell John I again saw the big black woodpeckers—corresponding to our pileated—at Schorfheide.

Tell Bill Schorger I met a wood-chemist at University of Dresden who wanted to know if I had ever met the two outstanding Americans in his line: _____ and Schorger! He offered to give me reprints to take to Bill but he hasn't done it.

Well Dear I must get at my knitting—I have a heavy office day. Love to all of you. Always

Aldo
October 9, 1935

To John H. Baker

1532 University Avenue
December 17, 1935

National Association of Audubon Societies
1775 Broadway
New York, N.Y.

Dear Dr. Baker:

I have your letter presenting the questions arising out of your conversations with Mr. Ickes on the poisoning issue.

If all of your questions, especially those for literature, were answered literally, my reply would be a volume which would take some time to prepare and which Mr. Ickes would never have time to read.

For the moment, therefore, I will restrict my reply to a boiled-down presentation of my own views, plus a sample of the *significant* literature on the subject.

A recent paper which in my opinion throws some real light on the problem is the following: Taylor, Walter P., Charles T. Vorhies, and P. B. Lister. "The Relation of Jack Rabbits to Grazing in Southern Arizona." *Journal of Forestry*, Vol. XXXIII, No. 5, May, 1935.

Taylor, in effect, asserts that rodents may be weeds resulting from over-grazing and other land-abuse, just as certain plants, such as burro-brush, are known to be weeds resulting from over-grazing, erosion, and soil-depletion.

If this is true (and I suspect it comes nearer the truth than anything else so far written), then the poisoning problem becomes a problem which cannot be dissociated from the range problem. Rodent pests appear as one of the penalties which we now face as a consequence of fifty years of land-abuse. Poisoning may have to be resorted to during the period of recovery, as a *modus vivendi*. Protection of predators is something which must be tried but which can probably not be relied upon as a self-sufficient rodent control if we are to continue to occupy the country during the period of recovery. Without range restoration we cannot expect natural controls to be more than partially operative. Range restoration, as everybody knows, will take at least one or two generations, even if inaugurated at once. Range restoration, in any ecological sense, cannot yet be said to be inaugurated in any considerable fraction of the West.

I cannot agree that Secretary Ickes will get adequate answers to current problems from scientific and conservation groups. These groups are mainly absentees. Their principles are correct, but they do not realize the rodent problem involves not merely predators and rodents, but the entire organism of nature. They do not realize the predicament of the local landholder who is suffering the consequences of past policies of exploitation, which were often no more of his making than they were of ours. Certainly the Secretary should consult the scientific and conservation groups, but I am afraid all he will get from them is moral support of sound principles. Neither they, nor he, can circumvent the fact that the West is ecologically sick, and that it cannot react normally to human use until it is first made well.

It is hardly necessary for me to say that I am heart and soul for your viewpoint, but I have lived in the West a long time without finding a satisfactory answer to these immediate problems. The only thing I can make out of it is we either have to clear out of these regions we have damaged until they recover (which is of course impracticable) or else accept compromises. The main hope is that intense scientific analysis, plus radical changes in land administration and land economics, can reduce the extent and duration of such compromises.

My main immediate plea is that the Biological Survey, instead of defending its poisoning policy, should itself recognize that poisoning is an unsound but temporarily necessary compromise, and that it measure its success, not by acres poisoned, but by acres which have been removed from the category which needs poisoning. I am afraid that the Survey as an organization has not yet this point of view.

I join you in revolting at making the CCC a poisoning agency. One does not give the children the job of drowning the kittens which result from our own past mistakes in cat-management.

> Yours sincerely,
> Aldo Leopold
> Professor of Game Management

To Karl T. Frederick

December 20, 1935

President
National Rifle Association
Barr Building
Washington, D.C.
Dear Mr. Frederick:

Have you seen the article "Eagle Shooting in Alaska" in the February, 1935, *Rifleman*?

I have just read it, and I confess to a feeling of sadness that a man like Mr. Burch, evidently a keen, intelligent, and decent sportsman in other respects, should be naive enough to boast about his wholesale killing of eagles as "the purest of all rifle sports."

Mr. Burch is a university student. This university is developing, for the use of its students, a wild life refuge on a lake which used to have eagles. We are seriously considering stepping in and erecting near the lake a tall dead snag, in the hope that some day a pair of eagles might again nest there, or at least stop there during migration. These were *our* eagles which Mr. Burch was killing, at the rate of 31 per day, for target practice, on their concentration ground.

Mr. Burch implies as his justification that the eagles prey on fish. The thinness of this rationalization is sufficiently exposed by his own statement that in the region of his eagle hunt "the streams are literally swarming with trout and salmon, and the bays are alive with king salmon and sea bass."

Why doesn't some enthusiastic rifleman go into the concentration ground of the blue geese and shoot them systematically on the ground that they prey on wheat? They do. The only difference I can see is that the Biological Survey lays a closed season on the one, and a bounty on the other. But the basic sportsmanship is the same in either case.

It would help me bolster up my respect for *The American Rifleman* to see an editorial disclaimer of this ugly episode. We gun enthusiasts are constantly complaining of restrictive legislation on firearms. Is it likely that the public is going to accord us any more respect and consideration than we earn by our actions and our attitudes?

My main plea, however, is that young enthusiasts like Mr. Burch take time off to do some straight old-fashioned *thinking* on the ethics of owning and shooting guns. I would infinitely rather that Mr. Burch shoot the vases off my mantelpiece than the eagles out of my Alaska. I have a part ownership in both. That the Alaska Game Commission elects to put a bounty on the eagle, and not on the vase, has nothing to do with the sportsmanship of either action.

I am sending a copy of this letter to Mr. Burch.

> Yours sincerely,
> Aldo Leopold
> Professor of Game Management

To Herbert A. Smith

> 1532 University Avenue
> December 20, 1935

Editor
Journal of Forestry
810 Hill Building
Washington, D.C.
Dear Herbert:

I have just read your editorial, "The Cult of the Wilderness."

First of all, let me express my gratification that the *Journal of Forestry* should at last lift its eyes, editorially, above the daily technical chatter of acres, authorizations, and acts of Congress. Your tracing of the philosophical origins of the wilderness idea is a brand new contribution, and your literary expression very pleasing indeed.

I am intrigued, though, by your assertion that esthetic judgments are not the province of mere foresters, but require the aid of expert professional landscapers. I think I disagree with you. I suspect there are two categories of judgment which *cannot* be delegated to experts, which every man *must* judge for himself, and on which the intuitive conclusion of the non-expert is perhaps as likely to be correct as that of the professional. One of these is what is right. The other is what is beautiful.

The question of the "highest use" of remaining wilderness is basically one of evaluating beauty, in the broadest ecological sense of that word.

Another way to say this same thing is that no one who does not sense the value of wilderness "in his bones" can learn that value through any process of logic or education.

If this is true, then the forester who has no opinion about it, has simply got a "wane" on his spiritual board.

I am not much impressed with your logic in pitting wilderness beauty against landscaped beauty. Why argue whether the domestic fowl is more or less beautiful than the ivory-billed woodpecker? The question is irrelevant. The thing that matters is that the ivory-bill is beautiful, and, like wilderness, irreplaceable. Call this assertion a cult if you will,—that does not change its irrefutable logic.

To fully appreciate what it means to live in a country which has plenty of forests and wild life, but which has lost all its wildness, one must go to Germany and see the annual exodus of hunters and hikers to the still partly-wild Carpathians.

But thanks again for your thought-provoking editorial.

                              Yours sincerely,
                              Aldo Leopold
                              Professor of Game Management

To Raphael Zon

1532 University Ave.
May 18, 1936

Director
Lake States Forest Experiment Station
University Farm
St. Paul, Minnesota
Dear Raphael:

I am much interested in your swamp project. It so happens that the Committee on Wildlife Studies of the National Research Council has recently broached to the National Resources Board a similar but nation-wide study of the drainage problem, so I need not say that I sympathize with your proposal.

Your statement makes it clear enough that the survey should be conducted with regard to all rather than any one possible function of swamps. To find a man intellectually capable of such an approach might not be so simple. His sympathies might be all right, but his technique, knowledge, and penetration might not. This is just another one of those land utilization problems which are constantly arising nowadays and which demand a kind of human being that does not yet seem to exist, at least not in any numbers.

That, however, is no reason for not trying.

One incidental comment: Your prospectus does not mention the esthetic function of swamps as a habitat for rare and odd species, especially flowers and other plants. I have been particularly struck by the unconscious ruthlessness of foresters in relation to swamp trees like tamarack and white cedar. The first is certainly being slowly exterminated in southern Wisconsin and the latter in northern Wisconsin, but this does not worry foresters because they have no "economic" niche. A whole biotic community is, of course, going over the brink with these two trees. If there be any doubt as to the correctness of my contention, I suggest the doubter take a look in the forest nurseries of the Lake States and see if either is present. Likewise in the research programs to see if either is present.

I plead guilty, of course, to being a crank on such questions, but you asked for a frank comment and I am giving it to you. I would enjoy discussing the whole thing.

With best regards,

> Yours sincerely,
> Aldo Leopold
> Professor of Game Management

To Ray P. Holland

July 1, 1936

Editor
Field & Stream
578 Madison Avenue
New York, N.Y.
Dear Ray:

Your editorial, "Rabbits—or Hawks," displays an attitude which seems to me so extreme and unreasonable that I have gone through it a second and third time for some evidence that you are "spoofing." Finding none, I am forced to choose between three possible interpretations.

The first, and kindest, is that a sportsman like yourself can accumulate a vast hoard of knowledge of wildlife without gaining any understanding of its principles.

The second is that all scientists who have studied predation during the past century, in both America and Europe, have either been unanimously biased, or else so uniformly incompetent that they all made exactly the same error.

The third is that you know your public and are playing to their prejudices, even though the actions thus incited may be wrong.

As to No. 1: Yes, of course the buteo hawks feed largely on rabbits and other rodents. And have you any comprehension of what would happen if they didn't? Do you know that the English heaths were once high forest and have been reduced to cow-pasture, largely by rabbits? Do you realize that in the Upper Mississippi states last winter the rather moderate stand of rabbits, plus mice, nearly wiped out thousands of small isolated coverts needed for nesting quail, pheasants, and Hungarians?

Have you ever planted bird-coverts and had them riddled by an ordinary stand of rabbits? If so, you might understand that removing the natural checks to see if it will make more rabbits is exactly equivalent to pulling the trigger on a gun to see if it is loaded.

You will no doubt regard this as exaggeration, but that is because you don't understand biological gunpowder.

I agree with you that there are many regions which could stand more rabbits without any risk. *And you can get them* without any risk, simply by leaving winter corn and winter cover. All my game demonstration areas show a prompt increase in rabbits the year after feeding and cover-fencing begins, and that without any hawk-shooting. Isn't it reasonable to ask rabbit-hungry sportsmen to at least *try* this method before they resort to pulling biological triggers?

As to No. 2: I am not one of those who give credence to the alleged impartiality of science or scientists. The only unbiased man I can think of is one who has never worked hard for anything. As a game researcher, I am biased in favor of a landscape which shows a reasonable abundance of all wildlife, game and non-game, and I admit it. So you can't make me angry by alleging pro-raptor bias. But when you challenge the competence of research conclusions, I have to smile a little. I believe that we researchers are still a long way from fully understanding predator-game relations. But I also believe we understand much more about it than you do, and more than any other man who has not opened stomachs, analyzed pellets, and watched the feeding of young in nests day after day and year after year for the express purpose of learning something.

As to No. 3: It is clear to both of us, I guess, that we who plead for moderation and restraint in raptor-control are outnumbered. All you need is more guns in the hands of the populace, and more editorials like yours, and the hawks will be "controlled," law or no law, including the buteos. But just suppose that after they become dangerously reduced, as they are in Europe, the "execution" should prove to have been a mistake? It is possible, you know, for a large number of people to be mistaken, especially about questions of blame for events they do not like but cannot explain. I need hardly remind you that a good supply of ropes, plus an inflammatory speech, can make people act in ways which would put even a hawk to shame. But actions thus incited are not necessarily just or right.

I suppose it is mutually understood that your remark about "hawks wearing halos" is all twaddle. You know that no sober scientist claims that any predator abstains from killing for any reason except lack of ability or lack of need. It seems strange, though, that we sportsmen, who have so many convincing demonstrations of our own lack of ability to score even with a shotgun, should refuse to credit the gunless buteos with the ability to miss a fat strong bird making a getaway into good cover. Having missed, we then refuse to credit them with sufficient laziness to stick to the rodents, which on the average outnumber the birds by 1000 to 1, like mudhens on an empty duck lake. If you were indolent, clumsy and hunting solely for meat, how many ducks would you shoot? And where does the halo come in?

Twaddle, too, and somewhat shopworn, is your editorial trick of implying that the Hawk and Owl Society is composed of elderly ladies who know nothing about the subject. I, for one, am a member, and I could name dozens of others who are just as fond of their shooting as you are, although perhaps not quite so worried about the future of rabbits.

                                                        Yours sincerely,

To Raymond J. Brown

                                        1532 University Avenue
                                        November 16, 1936

Editor
Outdoor Life
353 Fourth Avenue
New York, New York
Dear Sir:

I note with surprise the article on airplane hunting of eagles, by Leland Elam, in your December issue. My surprise arises, not from the fact that there are people who would use airplanes in hunting, but from the fact that so high-grade a sporting magazine as yours should advertise their exploits without editorial disclaimer or censure. I don't think any such article would have passed Colonel McGuire unchallenged.

I suppose, since it got by you, that I will have to explain what I mean. Airplane hunting is exactly like poisoning—it is too deadly to be defensible, even when employed against a predator. If it became general, the golden eagle might soon become extinct. Do you want that to happen?

I have no doubt that these eagles picked up lambs, and I do not blame a sheep man for resorting to rifle, or even trap, to defend his property. I do object to use of airplanes—especially by a third party who was quite evidently in search of sport, rather than protection. And I think there is a growing group of sportsmen who would back my view.

Unsportsmanlike predator-killing is *always* rationalized as defense of property,—usually somebody else's property. This excuse is getting too thin to pass muster among thinking conservationists.

Since you printed this article on a method of hunting which at least some of your readers consider unethical, will you now print either this protest or your own views on the question involved?

Yours truly,
Aldo Leopold

To T. D. Peffley

1532 University Ave.
May 11, 1937

P.O. Box 891
Dayton, Ohio
Dear Mr. Peffley:

I am intensely interested in your situation, because the scientific idea of predation, if it can be "sold" to sportsmen at all, should be salable to the I.W.L.A. I say this as a sportsman and as a long-time member.

The information you ask for is voluminous, and much of it I have only in the form of library copies which I cannot send you. Hence I am sending you only some samples.

I will, however, attempt to give you a comprehensive summary of why we game managers think that "vermin campaigns" are ordinarily not only useless, but actually harmful to conservation.

Reasons for Doubt

1. We seldom find any considerable numbers of game birds in the pellets, nests, or stomachs of hawks and owls, nor of other "vermin." There is a vast array of data. As a sample see Errington and Breckenridge: "Food Habits of Marsh Hawks in the North-Central United States," *American Midland Naturalist*, Vol. 7, No. 5, September, 1936, pp. 831–848.

2. When we do find evidence of material predation, it is (a) where birds have expanded beyond the carrying capacity of the food and cover, or (b) where they have been left unfed during a blizzard, or (c) where half-tame artificial stock has been turned loose, or (d) when goshawks have come down out of Canada in winter. For point 2a, see Errington and Hamerstrom, "The Northern Bob-white's Winter Territory," Research Bulletin 201, Agricultural Experiment Station, Iowa State College, Ames, p. 417.

3. We constantly find evidence that hawks and owls eat great numbers of the mice, gophers, and rabbits which (a) compete with the birds for food, which (b) destroy more bird-cover than anybody realizes, and (c) some of which (gophers) eat eggs and chicks. I do not have extras of the documents detailing these three points, but you will find (a) in Stoddard's *The Bobwhite Quail* (Scribner's), (b) in Hilbert R. Siegler's "Winter Rodent Damage to Game Cover," *Journal of Mammalogy*, February, 1937, pp. 57–61, and (c) in David Gorsuch's "Life History of the Gambel Quail in Arizona," University of Arizona Bulletin Vol. V, No. 4, May 15, 1934.

4. In so far as we have measured predation losses, we find no differences between areas or years where abundant, or areas or years where scarce. Example: See Errington's "Bobwhite Winter Survival in an Area Heavily Populated with Gray Foxes," *Iowa State College Jour. Science*, Vol. VIII, No. 1, 1933, pp. 127–130.

5. We have obtained satisfactory increases of pheasants and quail by food and cover improvement alone, without any "vermin control." For example, see Riley Area in "The University

and Conservation of Wisconsin Wildlife," by Leopold et al., Table 2, p. 32.

6. Even defenseless half-tame stock, both fish and game, can sometimes be safeguarded by means other than shooting. See McAtee's "Excluding Birds from Reservoirs and Fishponds." I have no extras, but you can easily get one by asking the U.S. Biological Survey, Washington, for Leaflet 120.

7. Where effective predators have been eliminated, there is often serious injury to game mammals, and to their range, through over-browsing and malnutrition. For example, see the literature on German deer (Leopold: "Deer and Dauerwald in Germany," enclosed), on Pennsylvania deer (Gerstell: many papers in the *Pennsylvania Game News*), on Kaibab deer (many papers by Goldman, Locke, Hall, Rasmussen, and others).

It should be noted, though, that overstocking by game birds does not injure the range as far as we know.

8. Conversely, where effective predators remain in natural abundance, we often have abundant game mammals without any of the troubles due to irruptions or overbrowsing. See Leopold, "Conservationist in Mexico," marked copy enclosed.

9. Some species of hawks and owls (duck hawk) and some of the larger carnivores (cougar, wolf, wolverine) are in as great danger of local extermination as game is. I have no extras of the documents, but will be glad to detail them if you care to look them up.

Personal Convictions

All of the foregoing propositions are supportable by physical evidence. It should be admitted, though, that the game manager's view is in part determined by personal conviction on certain questions of abstract principle, not easily proven either pro or con.

One of these is that the opportunity to see predators has just as high a sport value as the opportunity to see game, and if we can have a reasonable amount of game without blanket vermin control, then those who practice it are, wittingly or unwittingly, disregarding the rights and interests of others.

Practical Considerations

No game manager has ever said that all predator-control is useless or wrong. Most game managers agree, however, that "campaigns" (i.e., the artificial whipping up of control activities by bounties, prizes, or competition) are inherently devoid of discrimination in what, where, when, or how much to control.

They also agree that discrimination is usually obtainable only where control, if any, is based on research.

They also agree that poison, dynamite, and other wholesale weapons are open to the same objection as campaigns, in addition to being questionable ethics.

Finally, game managers draw a distinct line between predators which are easily vulnerable to over-control (lion, hawks, owls) and those which are "tough" and resistant to abuse (crow, coyote, weasel). The danger of mistakes lies, of course, mainly in the vulnerable species, but a bad principle followed in one class easily spreads to the other.

Let me know what conclusions your group reaches. Our crowd does not want to shove either opinions or evidence down anyone's throat. If American conservationists cannot achieve wisdom by conviction, they cannot achieve it at all. Moreover we game managers have no monopoly on wisdom. We know we do not yet understand predation problems, but we believe our fragments of advice are more reliable than the advice of those who know all about it.

> Yours sincerely,
> Aldo Leopold
> Professor of Game Management

To Robert Marshall

> 1532 University Avenue
> July 10, 1937

U.S. Forest Service
Washington, D.C.
Dear Bob:

When I visited the "Irish Wilderness" of Missouri in 1929 there was nearly a county of woods substantially roadless.

I have recently seen a map of recently constructed and projected state and federal highways in this area. The largest remaining fragment is 14,000 acres. This is officially labelled as a wilderness area and turkey refuge. I hear it is being fenced.

I need hardly point out to you that aside from the Superior and the Porcupine—whose history I need not recount—this was the only large wild spot in the Upper Mississippi Basin.

There must, of course, be pros and cons in this question which I am unfamiliar with, and cannot easily find out about. Except as a private citizen, it is also none of my business. On the surface, though, it looks like another case of chopping up a wild area and then labelling one of the chips a wilderness.

I don't want to burden you, or Lyle Watts, with a report on the question I have raised. I don't even expect a letter. I would, however, like to make sure that somebody with a sympathetic view of all the conflicting interests has given these plans a "once-over" to make sure that the road engineers have not been running wild. I have a special affection for this area, and to an old Service man it is disquieting to feel that conversion into a National Forest or Park always means the esthetic death of a piece of wild country.

> Yours sincerely,
> Aldo Leopold
> Professor of Game Management

To Henry P. Davis

> 1532 University Avenue
> January 17, 1938

American Wildlife Institute
Investment Building
Washington, D.C.
Dear Henry:

Yes, of course, I could present the farm conservation project in as much detail as you like at any time. Its basic idea can perhaps be expressed most clearly in this way:

We cannot sell game management to the farmer without reorienting his entire education. It is not sufficient that some farmers like to shoot. Until the average farmer likes not only to shoot, but also to observe, study, argue about, and enjoy not only game but all the other natural phenomena on his farm, we will have no sound basis for any kind of farm conservation venture.

We have spent the last fifty years weaning the farmer from all such interests. We have made him a mechanic, an engineer, an accountant, everything else but a naturalist and wildlife ecologist.

Farm boys come to me here and after taking a course in wildlife management and wildlife ecology, it becomes their consuming interest and would remain so regardless of whether they were paid for it or not. This leads to the idea of testing a farm community by and with its consent and through its own governance, to try to make the entire coming generation of that community mindful of wild things.

I was given courage to broach this project when I noted with what enthusiasm the mature generation of farmers at Riley welcomed the idea of some very sketchy nature studies offered to their children by myself and my students. I think sample communities could be found where the older generation would play ball heartily with this idea of changing the intellectual complexion of the younger generation by and with their help.

Of course, this is human engineering, and it is beyond my powers to predict either success or failure. No one should support such a project without appreciating its length, its magnitude or its difficulties. We would be bucking the whole current of human affairs, which are still trending in the exactly opposite direction. I would not want anyone to subscribe without having had the opportunity for at least an evening to impress them with the difficulties as well as the opportunities involved. I was much interested in the replies, but I think a much more thorough presentation of the idea should be made in person. Should you care to venture, I am of course at your disposal.

Yours sincerely,

To A. M. Brayton

Old Entomology Building
Madison, Wisconsin
March 9, 1938

Wisconsin State Journal
Madison, Wisconsin
Dear Colonel Brayton:

Your signed article in yesterday's *Journal*, written in support of the crow banquet of the Dane County Sportsmen's Association, contains several statements which I think should not pass unchallenged.

You state that "the crow is the worst marauder in the homes of game and song birds. . . . It is estimated that each year an average crow destroys a thousand game and song bird eggs."

I do not know how many eggs an average crow eats, but my group of students have, during the past five years, accumulated some actual figures on what proportion of game bird nests fall victim to crows.

Since 1934 Arthur S. Hawkins has studied 200 nests of Hungarian partridge and pheasant in Jefferson County, of which 40 per cent hatched successfully. Of the nests destroyed, 80 per cent were destroyed by haymowers, and 20 per cent by predators, of which crows accounted for about 6 per cent. Crows often found and ate the deserted eggs exposed by haymowers.

In 1935, 1936, and 1937 my students and I studied 60 pheasant nests in Dane and Jefferson counties, of which 29 were destroyed by haymowers, and 3 by crows. Part of the nests exposed by haymowers and deserted by pheasants were found and eaten by crows.

In 1931 Paul L. Errington studied 69 quail nests in Sauk and Dane counties. Of these 34 hatched successfully, 14 were destroyed by mowers, 8 by other human activities, and 5 by gophers, skunks, and dogs. Crows destroyed no "live" nests, but did eat the eggs exposed by haymowers.

In 1933, 1934, and 1935 F. N. Hamerstrom, Jr., studied 503 pheasant nests in Iowa, of which 103 hatched successfully, 179 were destroyed by mowing and burning, 35 by flooding and weather, 38 by miscellaneous predators, and 28 by crows. Crows of course ate many of the deserted eggs exposed by haymowers.

It appears, then, that crows destroy some nests, but the claim that the crow "is the principal marauder in the homes of game birds" is an exaggeration of the facts at least for this region. Most of the eggs eaten are from nests previously destroyed by mowing.

Again you state: "Crows start their ravages in the middle south where the nesting season is earliest. As the nesting season develops further and further north, they follow it. Robbing birds' nests is their main business."

The crow migration at Madison starts early in February and is over by March 15. The earliest game bird nests start about May 1, but the bulk of the first layings not until May 20.

In the "middle south" the earliest game bird nests come about April 15. The crow migration is over in February. It appears, then, that an interval of nearly two months separates the crow migration and game bird nestings. Only the resident breeding crows of any region have any chance to eat game bird eggs, and the crow migration has nothing to do with it.

I realize, of course, that the crow banquet was held in a spirit of good-natured exaggeration. I take no exception to this Münchausen spirit—it is appropriate to the occasion, and harmless if it be clear to your readers where the "whoppers" end and where the serious argument begins. Your allegations as to the biological role of crows, however, have the ring of serious argument. If they were meant to be, I think they badly distort the picture.

In my opinion the marsh and fencerow fires which will befog the sky of Dane County next month will destroy far more game than crows. The haymowers which follow in June will destroy still more. The nearly universal grazing of marshes and woodlots which takes place all summer will, by removing the winter food and cover, destroy still more. The WPA crews which are at this moment, for lack of something better to do, debrushing all the roadsides of Dane County are destroying more game than crows. Your editorial pen, and also the educational influence of the Dane County Sportsmen's Association, could do much good by attacking these destructive influences. To lay the blame for our prevailing scarcity of game so exclusively on the crow seems to me a kind of intellectual witch-burning which does more harm than good.

Let it be clear that I take no exception to crow hunting. I hunt crows myself. I do so because I like to shoot and because the crow is one of those species which can be shot pretty heavily without changing next year's supply. Why befog and befuddle this perfectly good sport, for which no one need apologize if pursued in moderation, by presenting it to the public as a crusade to save the nation? Even the redoubtable Baron Münchausen confined himself to less transparent means of self-flattery.

> Yours sincerely,
> Aldo Leopold
> Professor of Game Management
> University of Wisconsin

P.S. You might be interested in the following nest studies made outside Wisconsin.

Logan Bennett of Iowa State College, in 1933 and 1934, studied 240 duck nests of eight species. Of these, 7 were destroyed by crows.

E. R. Kalmbach of the U.S. Biological Survey, in 1934 and 1935, studied 512 duck nests in Canada. Of these, 156 were destroyed by crows.

> A. L.

To a Wildflower Digger

This letter is addressed, through the columns of *The State Journal*, to that unknown person who last week dug up the only remaining yellow ladyslipper in the Wingra woods.

While your name is unknown, your action sufficiently portrays the low estate of either your character or your education. On the chance that the latter rather than the former is at fault, I address to you this letter. I address it also to all whose gardens at this season suddenly blossom forth with new wildflowers lifted from other people's woods.

When John Muir came to the Madison region two generations ago, the woods and marshes were studded with millions of ladyslippers of a score of species. Today, what with drainage, fire, cow, plow, and wildflower diggers—like yourself—a dozen of these species are extinct, and the remainder are so rare that the average citizen has never seen one.

Now John Muir got something pleasant and valuable from his wildflowers. He became a great man, and it seems likely that his wildflowers had something to do with it. It is reasonable to suppose that the present generation might get something pleasant and valuable from them, too—if there were any. But no one, even yourself, is going to get anything valuable from this ladyslipper languishing in your backyard.

The University of Wisconsin has got the notion, perhaps a foolish one, that the privilege of seeing a ladyslipper woods has got something to do with education. For this reason it is acquiring an arboretum. It wants to take its botany students out there and show them what Wisconsin looked like in its youth—in John Muir's youth. It hopes that this will make them dissatisfied with what Wisconsin looks like now. But now, thanks to you, the Wingra woods is one step nearer looking like all the rest of the state. Perhaps, after all, our students would learn a lot if we took them out there and said: "Here is where we used to have a ladyslipper."

Then, if you will consent to the invasion of your privacy, we would like to take them to your backyard and show them where you have planted it, and how it is thriving in its new home.

In respect of thriving, here are some things you may not know:

Only one man has ever succeeded in germinating the seeds of this species in artificial surroundings. It takes a high-powered chemist to reproduce the conditions necessary for its germination. Wild woods sometimes allow of reproduction, but backyards never. After the seedling has been born, it takes four years to reach the age of flowering. Do you think your ladyslipper will reproduce its kind in your backyard?

One of our ambitions for the arboretum is to apply the newly discovered chemistry for germinating the species, i.e., to start a "ladyslipper nursery" out of which the Wingra woods, and all other Wisconsin woods not yet grazed to death, may be abundantly restocked. To this end we have hired the only living man who knows how to do it, and he is ready to make the attempt. But now you have taken his source of seed. We can find other plants, to be sure, but it will not be long, what with the thousands of other wildflower-diggers like yourself, before the goose with golden eggs is dead. We had better hurry.

I invite your attention to the fact that this ladyslipper is not the only public property which you might lift for the embellishment of your home. There are numerous paintings in the Memorial Union which you could cut out of their frames while nobody is looking. They are, I admit, less beautiful than your flower, but their loss could be more easily replaced. In the historical museum are any number of things as irreplaceable as your flower—why not add some of them to your collection?

I anticipate your reply and tell you why not: because you, and also your friends and neighbors, would recognize your act as vandalism. You do not recognize your theft of the ladyslipper as vandalism. I will leave it to you to decide whether it is.

Yours truly,
—Aldo Leopold
Research Director,
University of Wisconsin Arboretum

June 7, 1938

To Carl O. Sauer

Division of Wildlife Management
424 University Farm Place
December 29, 1938

University of California
Berkeley, California
Dear Professor Sauer:

I was much pleased to learn from Starker that you are interested in deciphering the ecology of the northern Sierra Madre. I would like very much to join with you in some attempt to make fundamental measurements there before the terrain is manhandled and before the opportunity is lost.

To my mind, the most important item is to decipher the soil-water-streamflow relation and compare it with the "modified" terrain of similar geologic formation on this side of the line. As you know, there are rather explicit historical records of the former condition on this side (James Ohio Pattie, for example). By comparing the ecology of an unspoiled terrain with the known history of a similar spoiled terrain, some important deductions would probably result. Speaking in economic terms, I don't think the Forest Service and the Soil Conservation Service know what to do with the mountain country of southern Arizona and southern New Mexico because it is so severely modified that no one knows what the original equilibrium consisted of. In the Sierra Madre we could find out.

In order to correctly decipher the soil-water-streamflow relation, many special studies of the ecology of particular plants and animals would be necessary.

One which interests me particularly is the deer-wolf-coyote relation. The Chihuahua Sierra is the only deer range I know of which is free from irruptions of deer. There are always plenty of deer but never too many. Every deer range in the United States is exhibiting irruptive behavior the minute that wholesale poaching is withdrawn. As a result deer are eating themselves out of house and home as rapidly as "conservation" is transferred from the office into the field. The European deer ranges are long since spoiled. Why the peculiar stability of Chihuahua deer? The most credible guess is that the full assortment of native predators (wolf, lion, bobcat) is still present. But no one knows the detailed mechanism of the deer-predator equilibrium. My group here has discovered some of the details of a similar quail-predator equilibrium, but no large mammal has ever been explored from this angle.

Another peculiarity of the Chihuahua deer range is that coyote are not present at high altitudes; only wolves. Coyotes, however, have invaded all the high country on our side, and the invasion has coincided roughly with the elimination of wolves. Are the two phenomena related? Have we simply traded a wolf problem for a coyote problem? Is the instability of our deer herds related to either or both? The Biological Survey is spending millions yearly on coyote and wolf control without having asked itself these questions. No answer is to be found in theory alone. There must be an unmodified biota to work with, and we have none on our side of the line.

All ecologists know, from both theory and observation, that plants determine animals, but the converse theorem (namely that animals determine plants) is "known" in theory and laboratory only. Elton is one of the few ecologists who has pointed out a convincing case in nature (*Animal Ecology*, Case 8, pp. 23–24). It seems not impossible that some of the distinctive birds and mammals of the Sierra Madre may ultimately be found to play an important role in the biotic equilibrium. In any case these distinctive birds and mammals are in urgent need of ecological study in order to arrive at a sound basis for conservation policy. I have in mind particularly the Merriam turkey, the Imperial woodpecker, and the thick-billed parrot.

Do you think that Carnegie might be interested in setting up some comprehensive effort to unravel these ecological problems which cluster about the Mexican border, and which are of both scientific and economic importance to both countries? I happen to be acquainted with the head of the Mexican Department of Forests and have a high opinion of him. I would be glad to sound out his attitude if there were a prospect of possible action. I assume that if anything were done, Mexico should participate in both the planning and execution of the venture.

Sincerely yours,
Aldo Leopold
Professor of Wildlife Management

P.S. I am sending you some papers which bear on the foregoing questions.

To Henry DeWitt Smith

Division of Wildlife Management
424 University Farm Place
May 9, 1939

Rahway Road
Plainfield, New Jersey
Dear Henry:

I have just received word that a family in Silesia, on whose estate I was a guest when I was in Germany, has been "liquidated" in the manner now prevalent.

My particular friend has in some manner made his way to British East Africa, but his brother (age 30) is still in Breslau, and desires if possible to emigrate either to the U.S. or to Bolivia.

He is trained as an electrical engineer, but I am told has considerable engineering experience, including automotive engineering. I did not meet this young man, but judging from his brother I would guess him to be of the highest grade as to personality, physique, education, etc. Incidentally his brother shows no visible trace of the ancestry now considered damaging. Neither did their father, whom I met, and who was Professor of Oceanography at the University of Breslau, and one of the organizers of the International Institute for Oceanography. The old gentleman died before the present troubles became acute.

I am writing this to ask you to keep your eye out for possible openings for this young man. I suppose openings in South America would be more probable than openings here. I am making inquiries as to conditions I have to meet as to (a) getting out; (b) getting into the U.S., including quotas; (c) degree of assurance of employment required by either country. I will write you later as to the limiting conditions which may appear.

Incidentally, this young man hopes to be able to bring with him about 56,000 gold marks, the remnants of his personal fortune.

His name is Ard Heinrich Schottlaender. I have written him to give me details of his professional status.

There is, of course, nothing you can do at this stage of the game except to keep an eye out for situations which might bear promise of opening up later. I of course have no illusions about whether anything can be done.

We are well, happy, and busy, but I pretty nearly lost my job in the course of an economy wave in our Legislature. It is not yet certain that my work will be continued, but the chances now look better. Love to Ellen.

Yours as ever,

To the Editor, Baraboo News-Republic

Division of Wildlife Management
424 University Farm Place
November 6, 1939

Baraboo News-Republic
Baraboo, Wisconsin
Dear Sir:

On Sunday, November 5, a reputable citizen of Baraboo, while hunting rabbits on my farm in Fairfield Township, was found pulling pine trees out of one of my plantations.

His plea was that he did not realize that the trees had been planted; he thought they were wild ones.

My pine plantations are scattered over a hundred acres of land. At the request of the Baraboo Rod & Gun Club, I have left my land unposted. This is the third time that planted pines and planted wildflowers have been destroyed by Baraboo hunters, fishermen, or picnic parties. In the hope of getting better cooperation from the local public, I take this means of informing people about my operations.

My land is a worn-out sand farm useless for any crop except forests and wildlife. The Baraboo region contains thousands of acres of such land. Your Rod & Gun Club has been urging farmers to develop such land for forests and wildlife, but the number who have done so could be counted on one hand.

I bought my land in 1934. My family and I have spent nearly every weekend for five years planting or tending trees, feeding birds, restocking native wildflowers and shrubs, and otherwise developing the place for conservation purposes.

Rabbits destroy my trees, hence rabbit hunters are welcome on my premises, if they will respect my plantings and if they will refrain from shooting the hawks and owls which help me keep the rabbits down.

I have several rare or uncommon kinds of wildlife, most of them protected by law, which I rigidly protect and which I must ask my "guests" to spare: ruffed grouse, woodcock, quail, wood duck, pileated woodpecker, otter, and raccoon. Needless to say I also protect my deer.

In short, I am trying to do what all conservationists want done, but my operations are at the mercy of the local public. If the local public wants landowners to do more of this sort of thing, they had better learn that pine trees growing in a row in the bottom of a plow furrow are not "wild," and that even wild pines are sometimes treasured by their owners.

> Sincerely,
> Aldo Leopold
> Professor of Wildlife Management

To Jay N. Darling

424 University Farm Place
November 21, 1939

c/o *Register-Tribune*
Des Moines, Iowa
Dear Jay:

Otto Doering, Kenneth Reid, and I had a session November 18 for the purpose of going over wilderness situation. I was asked to report our conclusions to you. In one respect they depart from yours.

There are, we concluded, three jobs to be done:

1. Decide on the *legal framework* for areas. (Should areas be set aside by statute or by proclamation?)

2. Set up "watchdogs" to prevent and forestall "nibbling" (gradual loss of areas through road, power, resort and other developments).

3. *Plan for particular wildlife species* (viz., grizzly bear) which need wilderness areas to survive.

Legal Frame. Wilderness areas are a radical departure from pioneering tradition. It will take a long time for the public to understand and accept all the implications of a wilderness policy. Even the conservationist who says he is "for" them may waver as these implications develop with time.

Most wilderness areas now on the map represent not a unanimous conviction, but a temporary "balance of power" between pros and antis. Some of them are in fact "stalemates" induced by purely temporary economic accidents such as the fall of stumpage rates or livestock prices.

Should an attempt be made to convert such areas to a statutory (as distinguished from a proclamation) basis, the latent opposition would be stirred up. The net result would be a radical shrinkage in the total area.

Time, presumably, will tend to strengthen the pro-wilderness forces. If the issue is called now, each case must be fought out on our present strength. On the other hand, if the issue is deferred, each case can be fought out on our future (and presumably greater) strength. A statute would precipitate the issue now. It might be possible to pass such a statute, but only at the cost of a large loss in areas. It therefore seems wiser not to press for a general statutory basis for wilderness areas at this time.

This need not preclude particular statutes for particular cases where the pro-wilderness strength is sufficient to assure success.

Watchdogs. The Wilderness Society has a system of local representatives who are supposed to keep a weather eye on "nibblings." Its weakness is that they report only by mail; they do not meet each other to discuss techniques; they are very diverse in skill and experience; the Society lacks mass strength. The I.W.L.A. might serve as a *meeting place* for such a corps of "watchdogs," and as a cooperator and supporter of the Wilderness Society.

It was decided to confer with R. S. Yard to discuss this possibility.

Plans for Species. Despite the rather large area (14 million acres) now withdrawn, the history of animal species dependent on wilderness shows a continued shrinkage. In the case of the grizzly bear this shrinkage is radical and dangerous. There is, as yet, no such thing as a planned system of strongholds for the grizzly, or for any other wilderness species.

Two defects in administration lie behind this. One is the lack of inter-bureau cooperation. (To take care of a species, joint action between U.S.F.S., U.S.B.S., N.P.S., and often S.C.S. and Indian Service, is often called for.) The other defect is that no bureau (to my knowledge) has as yet used land exchange or land purchase facilities to clean up and round out its wilderness holdings.

There may be legal inhibitions behind this. (Is a clean-up of alienations in a wilderness area a proper purchase of N.F. land?)

The only way to smoke out the reasons for this failure is for the public to insist that inter-bureau planning for particular species be done, and if it is not done, to ask why. But for the public to get down to cases, it must be represented by somebody equipped by experience and training to analyze cases.

This leads to this thought: Should not the conservation associations (I.W.L.A., Mammal Society, A.O.U., Ecological Society, etc.) have a joint committee on wilderness with an *executive officer* to do actual work? Might not the I.W.L.A. organize and help finance such a joint group?

Quetico-Superior Area. We discussed how the foregoing conclusions might apply to the Quetico-Superior, which by common consent is the special charge of the I.W.L.A.

It was agreed that the key move toward any future course is an appropriation bill to clean up interior alienations. Reid has asked the Forest Service for data on which to base such a bill.

The present legal status of "roadless area" cannot even be changed to "wilderness area" until the area has been freed of private land.

I am sending copies of this to Kenneth Reid and Mr. Doering, and request that they send a copy to Bob Yard if they think proper.

With best regards,

Yours sincerely,
Aldo Leopold

To Gifford Pinchot

424 University Farm Place
January 4, 1940

Milford
Pike County
Pennsylvania
Dear Chief:

I applaud your proposal to write a history of the Service, and especially your proposal to preserve historical materials in the Library of Congress. It is unlikely that any one book, even from your pen, will capture all the angles of the story, and perhaps a generation or two must elapse before its values can be truly weighed by anyone.

Unfortunately I have not kept a diary, and any attempt of mine to comply with your request as a whole would soon become a book rather than a letter. I am trying to single out what more limited contribution from me would be most useful to you.

I take it you want to write a critical as well as a factual account of the Forest Service idea. If so, I am quite sure that my best contribution would be on the critical side. Do you want me to attempt a history of Forest Service thought, as exemplified in the Southwestern Region, up to World War I or thereabouts?

Actually the year 1920 marks a turning point from (what shall I call it? a certain viewpoint, as yet unnamed) to an ecological mode of thinking. I am willing to attempt this, although I make no promises as to the value of the result. Of course I would illustrate this abstract treatment with local concrete events. Let me know whether this might fit in.

> Yours cordially,
> Aldo Leopold
> Professor of Wildlife Management

To A. M. Brayton

August 31, 1940

Wisconsin State Journal
Madison, Wisconsin
Dear Colonel Brayton:

I wonder if you realize that the conversion of the University Bay marsh into a boat harbor, which you advocate in your Friday issue, has important bearings on conservation?

One of the fundamental premises of conservation is that marshes are an important part of the organism we call land, and as such are not to be lightly "amputated" from the landscape. Land, like any other organism, consists of interdependent parts. It is a fallacy to think we can amputate one part and retain normal health in the land as a whole.

If you doubt this, I suggest you listen in on the Hydrobiological Symposium being held on the campus next week. It is ironical that the university faculty should be telling the world about the indispensability of marshes during the very week that the city of Madison is arranging the demise of the University Bay marsh.

I admit at once that the University marsh is a small place, and that its demolition will have no measurable physical effect on the land-health of the county or the region. But the sum total or cumulative effect of these small demolitions is another matter. One of the effects has been the ruin of five counties in central Wisconsin.

University Bay is a moral, rather than physical, issue. If the university expects Wisconsin farmers to heed its advice to be cautious about demolishing marshes, it had better watch what example it sets on its own campus.

An esthetic issue is also involved. The university marsh, which you call "one of the few uninviting spots on Lake Mendota," is the sole bit of natural landscape remaining on the campus. If, in the eye of Wisconsin citizens, "dockage and sightly buildings" are more inviting than a natural marsh, then we had better spend our money, if we have any, on a new department of esthetic education, rather than on new dockage for boats.

I am heartily in sympathy with the proposal to encourage boating on the lake. If University Bay is the only possible place for dockage, then I suppose the marsh will have to go. But let the sacrifice be made sadly rather than gladly, and let it be made clear that we sacrifice this area not because it is a marsh, but despite the fact that it is. And finally, let the university, in token of its regret, set up a research fellowship for marshland conservation, or some other concrete evidence of its attitude toward the fast-vanishing marshlands of the state.

> Sincerely yours,
> Aldo Leopold
> Professor of Wildlife Management

To Morris L. Cooke

> 424 University Farm Place
> September 30, 1940

c/o Friends of the Land
710 Denrike Building
Washington, D.C.
Dear Mr. Cooke:

I almost passed up the chance to read your "Total Conservation." You know, the usual task of clearing desk.

It's a masterly job and very well written. This is the sort of thing that should come out in our prospective journal, *Land*. If you get it into print, will you please send me a separate?

Unless you've already done so, also please send the present mimeograph to:

Geo. S. Wehrwein, Agricultural Hall, University of Wisconsin, Madison, Wis.

J. R. Whitaker, Peabody College, Nashville, Tenn.

L. E. Pfankuchen, South Hall, University of Wisconsin, Madison, Wis.

Horace Fries, Bascom Hall, University of Wisconsin, Madison, Wis.

Rudolf Bennitt, Wildlife Conservation Bldg., University of Missouri, Columbia, Mo.

Doubtless you have sent one to Jay Darling.

I take issue with you on one point. You assume, by implication at least, that the "total" job can be done without rebuilding *Homo sapiens*, or, to put it conversely, by government initiative alone. I do not believe it can. I doubt whether it is true that "the steps to be taken (by the S.C.S.) might effect virtually complete stabilization of the agricultural lands of the United States." The steps are *toward* this end, but they will not reach it until we have a new kind of farmer, banker, voter, consumer, etc. This is the real "blind alley" which all planners of conservation overlook.

> Yours sincerely,
> Aldo Leopold
> Professor of Wildlife Management

To Robert Sterling Yard

Wilderness Society
1840 Mintwood Place
Washington, D.C.
Dear Bob:

The "open-mindedness" of the Forest Service in respect of the Glacier Peak area is something for us to regard with apprehension.

I have always been puzzled about which of two basic attitudes the Forest Service is taking. Either the Forest Service:

(1) Concedes the basic rightness of a wide variety of forest

land-use, including the extreme of wilderness use. It shares our enthusiasm for wilderness reservations, and makes a positive effort to make and keep them, despite the accumulated momentum of universal economic "development."
          Or
(2) It concedes only the "nuisance value" of the wilderness movement. It has no enthusiasm for wilderness reservations, and heeds only the need of playing the wilderness factor against the other opposing factions. It is without conviction, pro or con. Under this alternative, the accumulated momentum of universal economic development may be surely counted upon to whittle away on the wilderness area system, bit by bit. New areas are periodically proclaimed, but old ones are whittled away just a little faster. The end result is that the Forest Service acquires merit with the uncritical as the champion of wilderness, but the wilderness system approaches zero.

I fear that Chris Granger, whether he realizes it or not, in this and other cases is proclaiming No. 2 as the real attitude of the Forest Service. At least he creates in my mind the "need for a sign" that No. 2 is *not* the real attitude. It is the natural attitude for the weary administrator, and I fear will be characteristic of all the bureaus as their personnel gains age and experience, and loses capacity for quixotic ideas.

                                    Yours sincerely,
                                    Aldo Leopold
                                    January 3, 1941

To Robert Sterling Yard

                                    424 University Farm Place
                                    February 26, 1941
The Wilderness Society
1840 Mintwood Place
Washington, D.C.
Dear Bob:
     I hadn't seen the *Post* editorial, nor did I ever have a political discussion with Bob Marshall. I had heard of his leanings, and his unlimited confidence in government ownership is visible in "The People's Forests." In my own dealings with Bob,

he differed from others only in seeing, thinking, and speaking more clearly and sensibly than his fellows.

The fact that the *Post* calls George an "orthodox Stalinist" does not, of course, prove that he is, especially in the modern sense. I suspect both boys may have been Marxians rather than Stalinists—a very big distinction—and products of the "popular front" era when communism put on a respectable front to hide its more devious manipulations, and became outwardly indistinguishable from parlor socialism. (You doubtless know all this history, but if not, you will find it in "Out of the Night.")

Be that as it may, George's presence on the board need not hurt the Wilderness Trust; certainly my confidence would be unshaken as long as you and Olaus Murie are on the job. I wouldn't do anything; just see how George works out. If he devotes himself to the job and doesn't muddy the water, we needn't shy at political labels, especially those pinned on by the *Post*.

With best regards,

> Yours as ever,
> Aldo Leopold
> Professor of Wildlife Management

To Robert Sterling Yard

> 424 University Farm Place
> March 27, 1941

Wilderness Society
1840 Mintwood Place
Washington, D.C.
Dear Bob:

HR3793 provides, as I expected, for a national Forest Purchase Area, with the implied assortment of resorts, roads, and silviculture in the Porcupines. Of course this would be better than to have the area skinned by lumber companies.

If there is a Bureau wide enough between the eyes to actually *buy* land for non-use, or a Congress far-sighted enough to allow them to, then I'll have to start all over in my appraisal of contemporary affairs.

I see no chance for a real wilderness in the Porcupines, except by private gift. Even with such a gift, what Bureau could be entrusted with administration?

It would be an interesting challenge, wouldn't it, to have somebody hand FDR the Porcupine area with the proviso that it be kept roadless, resortless, planeless, and no cuttings! Whom would he hand it to? To raise this issue clearly might be worth the price of acquisition—the actual area would be velvet.

Is there in the United States the combination of a long purse and deep understanding of wilderness values? I never heard of such a man.

Thanks much for so promptly dispelling my worries about an impending transfer.

> Yours as ever,
> Aldo Leopold
> Professor of Wildlife Management

To Richard J. Costley

> 424 University Farm Place
> September 13, 1941

203 Vivarium
Wright and Healey Streets
Champaign, Illinois
Dear Dick:

This letter is to summarize my opinion about the need for Spanish in the execution of your research on irruptions of deer.

Your research is an attempt to deduce the nature of the mechanism behind deer irruptions by comparing the unhealthy herds with healthy ones. By "healthy" I of course mean that capacity for self-adjustment in a population which insures against both over-population and under-population.

My trip through the West this summer further convinced me of a fact which I have long suspected: there are no really healthy deer herds left in the United States. You can find on this side of the border examples of almost any kind of ecological distortion, but I cannot think of any herd which I could conscientiously call normal.

On the other hand, I know from my own experience that the under-settled parts of Northern Mexico contain numerous healthy herds. On these ranges all of the natural predators are still present in practically their original numbers. There are plenty of deer but never too many, and the deer stand up under a rather heavy kill without loss of density or distortion of sex ratio or deterioration of weight or antlers. I never heard of epizootic diseases or any considerable degree of parasitism.

No one has ever censused such a normal herd nor described its make-up in terms of sex and age classes or its mechanism of population replacement. In my opinion your study cannot be complete in any scientific sense, nor can it achieve its full value as a guide to conservation policies, until you have studied these Mexican deer herds at first hand.

No corresponding opportunity exists in Canada because the deer belt in Canada is very narrow except on the coast, and the cover conditions make censusing very difficult.

Anyone doing biological work in the back country of Mexico must know Spanish, not only to extract information from local residents, but also to search the literature for historical evidence on past conditions.

I therefore hope that the University will permit you to substitute Spanish for French as one of the languages required for your doctorate.

> Yours sincerely,
> Aldo Leopold
> Professor of Wildlife Management

To Mrs. Frank K. Quimby

> 424 University Farm Place
> October 3, 1941

Wisconsin Conservation League
Park Hotel
Madison, Wisconsin
Dear Mrs. Quimby:

I didn't think I did particularly well, but I am glad you thought so. I give you the following summary of what I said.

For the Conservation League to put up a united front, it must reduce to a minimum the sources of internal friction between conservation groups. Such frictions are still frequent and serious, but might be reduced by franker discussions at meetings, including meetings of county units.

For example, a Wisconsin fish hatchery this spring shot 300 kingfishers to protect the trout in the pools. In such an instance, the sporting group is obviously riding rough shod over the non-sporting groups. If we could have a joint discussion over which we need the most—more trout or more kingfishers, we might develop an attitude of mutual tolerance for the other fellow's viewpoint. My own opinion is that kingfishers have decreased even more rapidly than trout and that the killing was unjustified.

Another case. Of five horned owl nests kept under observation by my students last spring, three were "shot up" during pest hunts staged by local sportsman's groups. Again the question is which do we need the most, more horned owls or more mice and rabbits? In my opinion the question almost answers itself, but we seldom have frank discussions of such questions. Probably the sportsman's groups are not even aware that any other conservation group objects to further reduction of horned owls. The attached summary of game censuses on University study areas shows, furthermore, that it is possible to produce excellent stands of pheasants where horned owls and all the predators are uncontrolled. Probably the average sportsman does not realize this, and might listen to it if he were told.

In addition to the need for more tolerance and sympathy between groups, there is need of more self-education in natural history by all members of all groups. Some conservation questions simply cannot be comprehended until a certain level of competence in natural history is reached. An example is the problem of excess deer. This has not yet hit Wisconsin as seriously as it has hit some other states, but there is every reason to expect that it will.

I recounted in detail the natural history basis for excess deer problems in the West and pointed out how sportsmen had simply failed to appreciate what was going on until the range was already spoiled. The reason for this failure was their lack of personal knowledge of range plants.

Yours sincerely,
Aldo Leopold
Professor of Wildlife Management

To Harold A. Stassen

424 University Farm Place
April 9, 1943

State Capitol
St. Paul, Minnesota
Dear Governor Stassen:

I am one of those far-scattered citizens who have a hopeful eye on you for a new kind of leadership in public affairs.

In this connection I wait with interest and anxiety your attitude toward Senate Bill 21 and House Bill 137, which in my opinion would wreck the Quetico-Superior National Forest, and its wilderness area.

In past years I put in much work on the wilderness area and therefore feel entitled to speak, even though not a resident of Minnesota.

I am no federalist; I have often been accused of an anti-federal bias in conservation matters. But even I get my hackles up when Minnesota, in a sudden burst of enthusiasm for state forests, proceeds to plant two of them in manner and in a place nicely calculated to obstruct the completion of the Quetico-Superior Forest. Minnesota has millions of acres of cutovers crying for state attention. Why not put the state forests where they will help rather than hinder the general forestry program?

I can't avoid ascribing this sudden upsurge of anti–Forest Service feeling in Minnesota either to the mistakes of other federal bureaus for which the Forest Service is not responsible, or to backstage manipulation by power interests, or to some unknown motives of hatred or revenge which have no proper place in conservation planning. This is more than a Minnesota matter, and I look to you to remind your citizens of that fact.

Yours truly,
Aldo Leopold

To E. E. Alvar

January 10, 1944

2408 West 2nd Street
Duluth, Minnesota
Dear Mr. Alvar:

No one has greater admiration for the capercailzie and the black grouse than I do. I have seen both on their native range, and I have read much of the literature, both in English and German, concerning them.

Despite my appreciation of these birds, I had better tell you bluntly that I would oppose introducing them to Wisconsin, even though the effort were assured of success. As to the effort having any assurance of success, I wish you would read John C. Phillips' "Wild birds introduced or transplanted in North America." U.S.D.A. Technical Bulletin No. 61, Apr. 1928, 63 pp. (Available at Government Printing Office, Superintendent of Documents, Washington, D.C. for ten cents.) You can find this in any good library, and if you can't find it, I will loan you my copy. I think you will see from it that repeated attempts in many northern states to plant these two species have met with nothing but failure.

In my opinion Mr. Bowers of the Fish and Wildlife Service has made a very evasive statement when he says "The Service is vitally interested in undertakings of this character designed to acclimate exotic game species which will fit peculiar ecological niches without endangering the status of our native species of game." Mr. Bowers should know that nobody living can truly evaluate ecological niches, nor can anybody give assurance that native species will not be interfered with should the experiment succeed.

This may strike you as a harsh letter, but I think you would prefer to have me give my opinion to begin with, rather than beat around the bush. There was a time in my own education as a sportsman when I would have heartily favored your proposal.

The photographs are very good indeed, and I much enjoyed looking at them.

Please let me hasten to say that I am not assuming that I have anything more than one vote in this question. I am not trying to decide anything for anybody else.

I hope to have the opportunity to meet you in person and to go into this question in more detail.

> Yours sincerely,
> Aldo Leopold
> Professor of Wildlife Management

P.S. I didn't notice until after writing the above that you had given me the pictures, which I can use nicely for teaching purposes. Thank you very much.

To Evan Kelley

October 13, 1944

Dear Evan:

Your formal retirement now impending does not fool me a bit. Stopping work is something of which you are constitutionally incapable. They may reduce your salary, but they will never make you quit working.

I am moved to state on this solemn occasion that I learned to work from you. I thought I knew how to work before you showed up in District 3, but I now realize that I was entirely mistaken. I was just playing with my job until you demonstrated how to heave with both shoulders, and especially how to steady the heaving process to make it more effective. For this personal instruction I shall be forever grateful. My career, such as it is, in the field of wildlife conservation, might well be described as applying Evan Kelley's methods in fire control and operations to wildlife management.

I wish for you many additional and happy years of working at what you please rather than at what pleases somebody else.

With profound personal gratitude and best wishes,

To Jay N. Darling

October 31, 1944

Register-Tribune
Des Moines, Iowa
Dear Jay:

I apologize for keeping Bill Vogt's MS. so long. Same old story: snowed under. A MS. of my own which I expected to finish in a month took me all summer and fall and isn't done yet.

Without a doubt Bill's MS. has something which puts it ahead of all parallel efforts to date. Without a doubt it could be adapted for use this side of the border, although I would rather hate to see the deletion of the Mexican atmosphere he has given it. For secondary schools at least there might be some virtue in the teacher (or her pupils) making their own "adaptation" to U.S. conditions.

There is an important omission which I think should be taken care of, and which could be without lengthening or complicating the treatment. Bill omits entirely two of the three functions of organic matter in and on soil:

(1) "Millions of little dams." This is adequately handled.
(2) Organic matter *anchors* plant foods so they can't leach down or wash away. This is omitted.
(3) Organic matter *anchors* soil moisture so soil doesn't dry up. This is omitted.

The perennial question of scientific correctness vs. simplicity is one that puts cockleburs even on Bill's socks. I am not content with Bill's catechism about birds: "protect them so they will eat the bugs in your garden." This is the Mosaic philosophy of retribution. I think the argument would actually be better psychologically, not to mention ecologically, if based on indigenous culture and pride. To wit: Mexico has her own birds, just as she has her own folklore. To know, enjoy, and protect them is part of the national culture. Other countries have found this out too late; let Mexico show the world how to do better. Incidentally, birds help control insects and rodent pests. They are part of the "web of life."

I actually fear the present argument on insects and rodents; it is based on hate, although I can readily see Bill didn't mean it to be, but was striving for simplicity. It should be brought out somewhere that the only thing to hate is too many, too few, or in the wrong place. Hate should never attach to species or classes.

Of course I am carrying coals to Newcastle: Bill himself is the leading exponent of my thought. It is no simple matter to write truth for those accustomed to dogma.

I particularly like Bill's thread of analogy: "the face of the land." That is sound allegory.

Did Bob Mann tell you of the park association setting up a fund for education? I think this is a trend. Such funds should be used to capture the few available Bill Vogts, put them in a room, lock the door, and then say "Take your time." The only trouble with this MS. is that it had to be done in a hurry.

Incidentally, productive writing on conservation for the masses has to be done before the age of 50. After that one accumulates too many ifs and ands.

I hope you are well. I am sending Bill a copy of this.

Yours ever,
Aldo Leopold

P.S. How did you like Hochbaum's "Canvasback"?

To Starker and Betty Leopold

Aug. 22

Dear Starker and Betty—

Every time we get one of Betty's fine letters I have a number of thoughts. First, how grateful we are for keeping us so thoroughly posted. Second, that I may have gotten jolly-well spoiled in what I expect from acquired daughters. Third, how much I value her hospitality of mind.

We are particularly pleased, Betty, that you are actively painting and even selling paintings. I wish I could see the recent ones. By the way, George Sutton spent a couple of evenings with us, had much to say of Starker's work, and examined attentively your pewee and also Albert Hochbaum's chicks.

I'm glad, Betty, that you had a separate visit with Bill Vogt. Of course we can't understand his domestic difficulties, having never met Juana—probably we wouldn't understand them even if we had. Did you notice, Starker, that Doug Wade reprinted

Bill's "Hunger at the Peace Table"? Does Bill know it? Copy
enclosed. This will reach many who do not read the *Post* (a
curious reversal of the usual argument).

I can well imagine the lessons in patience which Starker is
getting from a dilatory officialdom. I used to say that education
in the niceties of profanity originated entirely from mules, but
I imagine Starker would now dispute that.

Your mother and I have been duly tempted by your repeated
Xmas invitations. The trouble is partly financial. The old house,
a rattletrap to begin with, is soaking up a lot of post-war maintenance. It is partly a matter of time. I have worked furiously
all summer on a single paper, after scheduling 2 papers plus
the essays. Now I am up against the annual squeeze of being
unprepared for the winter's courses and new students. The influx of G.I.'s has very decidedly begun, and can't all be diverted
elsewhere. Fred Greeley, who was shot down and lived in the
Belgian underground, shows up today for formal work. His
wife (nee Perk Hannaford) knows Bill Vogt. We are very fond
of both of them. The skipper of a Canadian destroyer, who is
doing a blackduck study in New Brunswick for his thesis, shows
up early in Sept. He is full of ribbons, which is all right, but
also full of 1910 notions of wildlife research, which may be more
difficult. Albert is helping me by mail to plant a little ecological
humility. It may prove to be an interesting case.

Libby Jones and I have sweated all summer over the phenology paper, which I thought would be a pushover. I'm anxious for you to see it. We seem to have evidence that there are
"length-of-day" plants, *and also birds*, which do their stuff on
the same date each year regardless of weather. Then there are
weather plants, and birds, which jiggle all over the calendar.
Meaning? One interesting sidelight: the Germans knew this
long ago!

V-J left Bill Elder in a pickle: either spend another year at
Chicago, or arrange a job on a few weeks' notice (before fall
Semester). I guess Bill will have to stay.

The prospects for gun powder this fall are puzzling. There
are no grouse. Pheasants may have brought off some squeakers
after the cold rains of May & June, but how many is problemati-
cal. I see none at the shack (i.e. Flick doesn't) nor has there been

any crowing since June. There was duck-water on the marsh in June, but of course it is low now. Some heavy rains *soon* would make the grade; I've learned that late rains do no good because the migration is already diverted elsewhere. Woodcock are plenty and I am under pressure (from Tom Coleman, for ex.) to shoot them more heavily, but I just can't see any really heavy pressure against our "pets." I shot 2 limits last year, but only because there was nothing else for the dog before the pheasants opened.

The summer at the shack has been almost entirely spent on wildflowers, and largely on seedings. I had excellent germination on some mixed prairie seedings made last fall on white grub-killed spots which could be peeled bare. This summer we have seeded violets, lupine, butterfly weed and (next trip) prairie *Desmodium*. Our butterfly weed this year was a knockout—5 years after seed (1941).

Well, must hit the ball now. Love to both of you and to Fritz. Betty, thanks again for your letters, and even more than that, your attitude toward the world.

> Yours ever
> AL
> *August 22, 1945*

To G. N. Sale

September 26, 1945

c/o Department of Forests
P.O.B. 1167
Jerusalem
Dear Mr. Sale:

I am much interested in your inquiry about excess deer and elk. You have laid your finger on two critical questions.

The answer to the first is that irruptive big game herds preceded the war and are not a war-time problem in the sense of being induced by war conditions. The first irruption occurred in 1924. The enclosed reprint gives you something in the way of a historical outline.

Your second question cannot be answered so briefly. In general the wolf has had a raid against him; almost universal bounties; publicly paid trappers; the livestock industry and unfavorable ecological conditions in the sense of shrinking wilderness and rapidly extending motor roads.

Big game, at the same time, has had the advantage of nation-wide protective laws, refuges, predator control and favorable ecological conditions in the form of wide-spread lumbering, followed by fire protection. In addition there is a rather subtle point in public psychology. The public can visualize and understand a wolf pulling down a deer, but they cannot visualize and understand a deer ruining his own winter food supply by the selective overbrowsing of trees and shrubs, nor does the public understand that when excess deer are artificially fed the overdraft on food plants is not decreased but rather increased.

Yours sincerely,
Aldo Leopold

To William Vogt

January 25, 1946

Pan American Union
Conservation Section
Washington 6, D.C.
Dear Bill:

The only thing you have left out is whether the philosophy of industrial culture is not, in its ultimate development, irreconcilable with ecological conservation. I think it is.

I hasten to add, however, that the term industrialism cannot be used as an absolute. Like "temperature" and "velocity" it is a question of degree. Throughout ecology all truth is relative: a thing becomes good at one degree and ceases to be so at another.

Industrialism might theoretically be conservative if there were an ethic limiting its application to what does not impair (a) permanence and stability of the land (b) beauty of the land. But there is no such ethic, nor likely to be.

To pass to one very small point: Jewish agriculture in Palestine does not prove what you say. It only proves one well known fact in soil science: that in semi-arid countries the subsoil contains nutrient salts, hence you can farm it. Too bad Lowdermilk left this out of his book.

Bill, your outline is excellent. That the situation is hopeless should not prevent us from doing our best.

Yours ever,
Aldo Leopold

To Nina Leopold Elder

Thursday

Nina Dear—

You know my (doubtless indefensible) habit of saying nothing about what matters most. Well that, and that alone, accounts for my silence on matters of "F_1." (I do not share your mother's bias against that little pleasantry.) As a matter of cold fact there is nothing in the world more important to me than the hope that your qualities of heart and mind may be handed on to another generation. I couldn't get along without them, and it is reasonable to suppose that our successors will need them as badly as I do, or more so. From the present trend of events, I would guess more so.

We are having an extraordinarily perfect May, save only no rain. The extra earliness has now slowed down a bit, and strangely enough some birds like oriole & tanager were not early at all, but the plants are all early. It's the first year in 10 when lupine bloomed the first week in May. I was at the shack alone, and felt guilty having no one to share the sight (except Flick, who had his eye on spermophiles).

Another change: we have no canker worms. The geese left April 28, i.e. the last of them. We have a pair of teal, and at least one of wood duck. I got a look at the woodcock brood 2 weeks running: at 7 days, they sprouted their first pin-feathers and at 14 they could fly 20 yards. The census shows only 8 "pairs" as against max. of 14. I missed your help on the census.

Giving 40 118'ers an hour's oral each is proving a marathon. I guess I'll get thru it, but by the skin of my teeth. But you ought to see the project work some of those "laymen" are handing in! I've never had the like. Much work of professional grade. My own students are by no means distinguishable from half a dozen others.

Joe urges me to tackle the book at once, but I think I shall first do at least the phenology paper. Revised tables in final form will reach you in a few weeks. My own notions of the quality of the paper have gone down a bit. Long pondering on inherent errors is a wholesome discipline. If only one could foresee the ultimate needs of a 10-year job! Bill should try to think of coons in terms of 1957. I've been much interested in the growth of the coon idea, and am anxious to talk it over with you and Bill.

Must write my 118 exam now. Love always.

AL

Tell Bill I have scores of new flock-counts on geese if you can use them. Sorry Soper dropped out. Go ahead anyhow.

May 9, 1946

To J. Hardin Peterson

June 13, 1946

House Committee on Public Lands
Washington, D.C.
Dear Congressman Peterson:

I am writing you in connection with H.R. 5401 sponsored by Congressman Angell of Oregon, which, I understand, makes it mandatory for the National Park Service to reduce the wolves in Mt. McKinley National Park.

You have probably already heard that the Park Service attempted to remove some wolves on its own initiative, but it was found that almost all of the wolves had moved out of the Park, doubtless temporarily and presumably in response to the caribou herd temporarily moving out.

In my opinion it is bad public policy to saddle a technical bureau with mandatory legislation of this kind. The Park Service has already shown its willingness to reduce wolves when damage to the mountain sheep made it necessary to do so. It would be calamitous, however, for the Park Service to be forced to reduce wolves at a time when they are virtually absent, because such legislation would contradict their basic function of preserving the fauna of the National Parks.

I feel entitled to speak on this question because the Wisconsin legislature recently imposed some mandatory action on the State Conservation Commission, of which I am a member. The Legislature re-enacted a wolf bounty when our own technical field men had demonstrated that wolves were in danger of extermination in the state. It thus contravened our basic function of preserving the fauna of the state.

Adolph Murie, who as you know has been the technical advisor of the Park Service on the big game and predators of Mt. McKinley, is widely respected as one of the most competent men in his profession. In my opinion his judgment is a much better guide to public policy on Mt. McKinley than mandatory bills arbitrarily imposed from a distance.

I hope you will see fit to kill H.R. 5401.

> Sincerely,
> Aldo Leopold
> Professor of Wildlife Management

To Noble Clark

April 9, 1947

101 Agriculture Hall
Dear Noble:

I appreciate Professor Buchholtz taking the pains to analyze the weed spray situation.

At bottom the issue resolves itself into one with which you are already familiar: does the research man have any responsibility for the misuse of his research findings, or can he relegate all the responsibility to the user and the public? It still seems to me that special advocacy of such a dangerous weapon without reservations or cautions is tantamount to assuming that all of your responsibility lies with the user and the public.

Let me say in the same breath that this assumption is the prevailing one but, of course, that does not make it the right one. Professor Buchholtz suggests that wild flora be relegated to the woodlot. This is partially unsatisfactory from an ecological standpoint because only certain tolerant species grow in woodlots, and the sentimental value of wild flora consists principally of the interspersion with cultivated fields.

I hope Professor Buchholtz understands that my criticisms are made in a friendly spirit and with the full realization that my view point is that of a very small minority.

One can of course escape the fact that such questions are a matter of degree. Intensive agriculture has nearly extinguished many valuable wild plants. They have been pushed aside to such a degree that many are disappearing from the average farm. It seems to me that this question of degree is more important than abstract logic.

Yours sincerely,
Aldo Leopold

To J. S. McDiarmid

May 13, 1947

Minister of Mines and Resources
Winnipeg, Manitoba
Dear Sir:

As a conservation commissioner in a state which has already "burned-out" its local breeding ducks, I have read with particular interest and satisfaction the printed news release about the Delta Marsh circulated by a group of sportsmen in Portage la Prairie.

This idea of a self-imposed deferment of shooting pressure strikes me as a very enlightened and hopeful development which I hope will have the official encouragement of your office. I am also thinking that it might be applied to some of our Wisconsin areas such as Horicon Marsh, upon which we are confronted with the problem of restoring breeding stock. If any of your conservationists have any doubts about the reality of the burning out phenomenon, I extend to them a standing invitation to come down here and look at it. We are spending state money in five figures per year on several marsh restorations, from which the total annual crop of ducks is measured in terms of a few hundreds. Each duck in short, is costing us more than $10.00 to produce, and were it not for muskrats, these projects would hardly have a leg to stand on.

I hope your province will comprehend this situation before and not after the burning out process is completed.

Yours sincerely,

To M. W. Smith

July 8, 1947

Ducks Unlimited
1204 Flour Exchange
Minneapolis 15, Minnesota
Dear Mr. Smith:

As you know, I have long felt anxiety lest Ducks Unlimited offset its good work in marsh restoration by overclaims on the question of duck population.

When Tom Main dropped out I hoped for an improvement, but the June "Ducko-logical" now convinces me that there is no change. Your staff continues its incredibly expert job of taking a given set of facts and so twisting the emphasis as to create an overall impression that is false.

The overall impression one gets from the June Duckological is that things are not so bad after all, and that by opening day we may again expect a pretty good flight.

The overall impression that I get from my personal connections in the breeding belt is that with the single exception of Alberta, the shortage of breeding ducks is almost catastrophic. My connections are well scattered from the Atlantic to the Rocky Mountains, and they are field men. I believe what they tell me, and I do not believe the overall impression given by the June "Duckological."

The present waterfowl crisis is so close to my heart that I cannot support any organization that withholds the truth about it. This, then, is the withdrawal of my membership in and my moral support of Ducks Unlimited.

I am sending copies of this to Stanley Johnson, C. A. Gross, and Bert Cartwright. I assure you that I have come to this decision with great reluctance, and that I appreciate the many courtesies which you have extended to me.

Yours sincerely,
Aldo Leopold

To William H. Carr

July 15, 1947

1034 North Jacobus Avenue
Tucson, Arizona
Dear Mr. Carr:

The news of Arizona's recent legislation putting black bear on the vermin list is a source of real disappointment to me because I had harbored the illusion that the Southwest had outgrown such an uncivilized idea toward bears. The extermination of the grizzly from the state without any support from anybody to save a remnant from one of the wilderness areas was a black mark for the state, but it is water over the dam, and not worth crying about now. To extend the same attitude to the black bear is, however, discouraging.

I am, of course, perfectly aware that individual bears often need removing, and likewise that bears may become too thick at certain times and places; and that the whole population may need a reduction by such local regulations is quite a different matter from outlawing the species on a state-wide basis.

Here in Wisconsin we gave the black bear almost complete protection for a decade, and three years ago they became so numerous in some spots that we opened the season, and also allowed farmers to trap in defense of their own bee hives and livestock. As a result the population is now back to a normal and harmless level. During the height of the crisis we also were threatened with extremists who wished to outlaw the bear completely. Fortunately, their view did not prevail.

I congratulate the Federation on fighting this issue and I know enough Arizona cattle men to be absolutely certain that the livestock interests are not unanimous in this matter. I fervently hope that some more reasonable form of local control can be worked out and accepted by both parties to the dispute. If I understand the present legislation correctly, it is a disgrace to the state.

Yours sincerely,
Aldo Leopold

To Philip Vaudrin

December 19, 1947

Oxford University Press
114 Fifth Avenue
New York 11, New York
Dear Mr. Vaudrin:

I am sending you under separate cover the manuscript for the essays.

In looking these over myself I can see that those comprising part I, "A Sauk County Almanac," do not yet conform perfectly to the almanac idea. They were written before this particular arrangement was in my mind. In printing there should doubtless be some indication of the month for each individual essay.

The manuscript does not yet contain the autobiographical notes referred to in the foreword, page ii. I also have in mind that the volume when published should end up with an index, which of course cannot be prepared until the page proof step is reached.

The blank yellow pages are for notes by critics, whose advice I am now seeking.

There are some gaps in page numbers due to changes in length in the process of revision.

I might also add that Charles Schwartz of Missouri is doing a series of illustrative sketches. He is the author of *The Prairie Chicken in Missouri*, and in my view is a competent artist.

Yours sincerely,
Aldo Leopold

P.S. I am uncomfortably conscious of the possibility that there still remain, in occasional spots, phrases or sentences that are trite or pretentious. I hope to get these out if I can get my critics to spot them for me. I have never had the time to do the self-editing which any job of this sort needs. I am ready to devote next summer to this, should you decide there is enough solid framework to merit publication.

To Carl Russell

Superintendent
Yosemite National Park
Yosemite Valley, Calif.
Dear Carl—

I have been meaning to write you, to express to you and to Newton Drury, my anxiety about the possible further motorization of the Park, particularly the proposed high-speed highway through Tioga Pass.

I realize, of course, the pressure you are under. This letter is just to express my fervent hope that the pressure will be resisted, and to assure you of my moral support for any such resistance. I know that the reasons for my view need no explanation to you, or to Newton Drury. I think the Park Service has already acquiesced in far too much motorization, and that the time to call a halt on that process is now, while there are still some wilderness values left to conserve.

I was reminded of this situation upon hearing my friend Harold Bradley describe his winter ski trip to Tioga.

With personal regards,

Yours sincerely,
January 19, 1948

To Charles Schwartz

January 28, 1948

131 Forest Hill
Jefferson City, Missouri
Dear Charlie:

My family, my staff, my students, and myself are all full of admiration for your drawings. The more I study them the more I like them. In addition to their over-all merit, I like the accuracy of your details even down to the species of grasses suitable for each.

There is much debate over which one is the best. Everyone likes particularly the buffalo skull, but hates to see the fluttering woodcock against the sky relegated to second place.

The thought occurs to me that these drawings are vulnerable

to fire during this interval. What would you think of a set of photographic reproductions to be scattered in several repositories, not all of which could burn at once? This would have the incidental advantage of showing the publisher how strong will be the pictorial aspects of the essays. If you are agreeable, I will proceed with this. Let me know.

I will send you shortly two additional essays with the page marked to show the point of insertion in the manuscript. One of these called "Good Oak" calls for a series of very simple sketches to divide the successive themes treated in the text. I would like your reaction to this idea of topical sketches. You of course will need to see the manuscript first.

I have not heard from the two publishers who are now reading the manuscript.

With personal regards and thanking you again for the drawings,

Yours as ever,
Aldo Leopold

To W. A. Wood

February 9, 1948

Director
Arctic Institute of North America
Audubon Terrace
Broadway at 156th Street
New York, 32, N.Y.
Dear Mr. Wood,

I appreciate the invitation to become an associate of the Arctic Institute.

I cannot accept because I cannot endorse more than a part of the Institute's objectives.

That part dealing with scientific exploration I heartily approve, but the avowed objective of "future development of the Arctic" (page 6 of your prospective) I cannot endorse.

My reasoning is this: the economic resources, while larger than originally supposed, are nevertheless limited. On the other hand the native wild fauna is of outstanding value, and to me this value is the greater of the two.

All polar history shows the fauna to be exceptionally vulnerable. With the single exception of Alaskan seals, I know of no instance in which development and faunal conservation have been successfully reconciled in the polar regions. (If I am mistaken in this, please correct me.)

The hope that conservation will follow the scientific program sponsored by the Institute is no guarantee that it will follow; indeed history shows the contrary. Scientific expeditions to the polar regions may be credited with their full share of faunal depletion.

For these reasons I think the governments involved, including my own, should demonstrate their capacity to conserve the polar fauna before development is encouraged to proceed. (I of course know that they will not do this, but that does not change the ecological ethics involved.)

If any illusions persist as to what development means in the polar regions, I recommend Robert Cushman Murphy's recent volume *Logbook for Grace*.

I appreciate the kind intention of your letter, and I am sorry I cannot go along.

Yours sincerely,
Aldo Leopold

To Manly F. Miner

February 9, 1948

Jack Miner Migratory Bird Foundation, Inc.
Kingsville, Ontario
Dear Mr. Miner:

I am intensely interested in your letter and welcome its length. I am asking all of my students to read it, but I am specifically asking them not to embarrass you by quoting it. I hope you will not take exception to this.

On this issue of teaching a student to be practical, there are of course differing definitions of the word. I would like the privilege of telling you, however, about my strivings in this same direction. These are not intended to imply that training at Wisconsin is better than elsewhere. They are offered you simply as a straight statement of fact.

First of all, every candidate for a degree in wildlife is required to spend at least half of his training period in the field, where he is required to find the answer to a definite problem. The answer constitutes his thesis, and the thesis must be original enough to be publishable.

Today I have two students trapping, banding, sexing, and aging pheasants in zero weather with eight inches of snow. Another student sat in a tower on the pheasant area from before day light until after sun up noting the beginnings of mating behavior in pheasants. Another student is in southwestern Wisconsin studying foxes with our most expert fox trappers and hunters. These laymen tell him what he does not know about foxes, and he benefits greatly by their advice. He gets the carcasses after they have skinned the foxes, and he autopsies these carcasses to the number of several hundred each winter.

Another student is writing his report on the new method of aging rabbits. At the moment he is at a desk, but he had to spend two winters trapping and banding rabbits and two summers hunting for nests and marking litters by tattooing their ears. These marked young were recaptured the following winter by the students hunting as a group. Last winter these group hunts collected 400 rabbits.

Another student is in Manitoba where he spent the whole summer in the field studying nesting waterfowl. Another is on Pelee Island in Lake Erie trapping, banding, sexing and aging pheasants. I will not prolong the descriptions of these samples, but I think you can see that you and I have the same fundamental concept: namely knowledge of wildlife comes from out doors, and often at the cost of discomfort and hard labor. Brain work must follow, but it has no significance without field work.

I will later send your letter to my student on Pelee Island, who may some time have the opportunity to call on you. His name is Allen Stokes. Possibly he has already stopped to see you.

With kind regards and thanking you very particularly for your welcome advice.

Yours sincerely,
Aldo Leopold

To Luna B. Leopold

March 9, 1948

Box 3166
Honolulu, T.H.
Dear Luna:

We always get a kick out of Bruce's conversations and this was especially so of your last letter.

I hasten to reply to your questions about the increase in woody plants in your photographs comparing 1899 with 1937. This is exactly what I would expect on overgrazed slopes. At least there are many instances in which overgrazing has had this effect. The one most familiar to you is the present increase in red cedar and creeping juniper in the sandy region around Prairie du Sac, which is undoubtedly due to the weakening of the sod by overgrazing, thus exposing the soil and weakening the grass composition. Of course only unpalatable woody plants can take advantage of this situation.

Probably the most important and spectacular encroachment by woody species is in South-central Texas, where juniper and mesquite are usurping very large areas of overgrazed grass range or range formerly overgrazed. I saw a perfect instance on the King Ranch where the encroaching species is mesquite and where they are using bulldozers to cope with the situation. North of San Antonio is the same thing, but the species is juniper (red cedar).

A small scale instance of great historical value is the region of mesquite which crosses the Jornado del Muerte above Las Cruces in New Mexico. This follows the old Spanish trail where passing wagons and pack animals had the same effect as overgrazing.

In Northern Arizona on the benches of the Verde Valley between the Prescott and Tusayan National Forests are several hundred thousand acres of former grama range, now thickly dotted with juniper. This encroachment followed the overgrazing by sheep.

Do you have my paper on grass, brush, and fire in the Arizona brush fields? This describes a similar situation in the Tonto, but with a more complex mixture of species. If you do not have this paper, the reference is as follows: "Grass, brush, timber, and fire in Southern Arizona." *Jour. Forestry* XXII:6:1–10 (Oct. 1924).

I am less familiar with the details of sage brush, but I have always heard range managers in the north state that it increased with overgrazing.

I am much pleased that you are making headway with your photographs, and hope that you will call on me whenever I can kick in any suggestions or information.

Yours ever,
Aldo Leopold

To Ernest C. Oberholtzer

March 15, 1948

1218 Flour Exchange
Minneapolis 15, Minnesota
Dear Ernest:

Thanks for your good letter bringing me up to date on developments in the Quetico-Superior.

The best news to my ears is the fact that Sig Olson is now giving the project full time. That is excellent and heartening.

I am much pleased that the shore-highway has been delayed.

I had heard about the dispute about reimbursing the counties. That one looks like a hard nut to crack.

I recently heard several comments by Canadian officials giving me some insight as to their general attitude. I am told that Canadian officials do not consider the Quetico as a high grade or valuable area, and when I try to pin down why, I infer it is because it is short on game. This is a revealing circumstance indicating that wilderness travel as such is not yet scarce enough to have any value up there. Most of the discussions end with the question "if you want to withdraw wilderness, why don't you pick a good one?" This is the fateful wait-until-next-time attitude that has already pushed most wilderness areas into the ocean.

A former student of mine, Tony de Vos, is now located at Port Arthur, representing Ontario in technical wildlife matters. I told him to drop in to see you when opportunity offered. He is the author of a manuscript on the vanishing species of the world, and I think you will like him. He may need some moral support from your region.

With best regards,

Yours as ever,
Aldo Leopold

P.S. I am taking the liberty of sending a copy of this to Olaus Murie.

To Ernest Swift

April 14, 1948

Director
Conservation Department
State Office Building
Madison, Wisconsin
Dear Ernie:

Professor Andrew Weaver has reminded me of a project that has been on my mind for a long time: the acquisition of at least one of the two boyhood farms of John Muir as a state park. The purpose of this letter is to recommend that it be added to the list of possible park projects of the state Conservation Department and the state Planning Board. Before deciding either way on this proposal, Commissioners and officers of the Forests and Parks Division should read Muir's book *The Story of My Boyhood and Youth*, and this should of course also be in the Department library. It is a necessary background.

One reason I have hesitated to recommend this project in the past has been that the Muir farm is undoubtedly badly depleted floristically and otherwise, and hence any possible restoration at this time might be a pretty drab affair compared to the original farm described in Muir's book. It now occurs to me, however, that this area might fall half way between a state park in the ordinary sense and a "natural area," the objective being to restore the flora to something approaching the original. To this end the cooperation of the Botany Department would be needed, and the superintendent would have to be a botanist with a general enthusiasm for this restoration job. He should also of course be equipped with the requisite knowledge of history and literature.

In more general terms, such a state park should be something more than a mere stopping place for tourists lacking something to do. It might be made a public educational institution in the ecological and intellectual history of Wisconsin just as Devil's Lake ought to be an educational institution in the geological history of Wisconsin. I think the time is now right for the Commission and the Department to develop this enlarged function of state parks.

Yours sincerely,
Aldo Leopold

To A Sand County Almanac *Reading Committee*

I would like your help in a critical scrutiny of the essays. If you are able to undertake this, I have a copy ready to send you with yellow sheets opposite every page for easy entry of critical comments.

What I need, of course, is the most critical attitude you are able to muster. Which are the weak ones? What is ambiguous, obscure, repetitious, inaccurate, fatuous, highbrow?

For the job as a whole I would appreciate your opinion on the following:

1. Is there sufficient unity?
2. Should there be more (or less) emphasis on esthetic description, ecological information, particular species or groups?
3. Have I omitted some idea you think I could do, or included something I should better let alone?

By way of background, I might say that Charlie Schwartz is doing the drawings, and Oxford Press is the publisher now interested.

c. April 1948

Chronology

1887 Born Rand Aldo Leopold in Burlington, Iowa, on January 11, the first of four children of Carl and Clara Starker Leopold. (His first name, subsequently never used, is the surname of his father's business partner.) Mother is twenty-seven years old, the daughter of a prominent Burlington businessman and civic leader. Educated in Boston, she is a devotee of opera, the piano, skating, gardening, German cooking, and literature. Father, twenty-nine, is co-partner in what will become the Leopold Desk Company (its motto: "Built On Honor To Endure"). A conscientious businessman, he is also an enthusiastic outdoorsman; Aldo will later call him a "pioneer in conservation." With "Oma" and "Opa" (Clara's parents), the family lives in a comfortable home atop Prospect Hill, a bluff overlooking the Mississippi River. German is Aldo's first language.

1888– A sister, Marie, is born in 1888, and a brother, Carl Jr., in
1902 1889. Attends Prospect Hill School beginning in 1892. With his siblings, explores local bluffs and river bottoms. Acquires an Irish terrier, Spud. In 1893, family moves into a new house, next to the grandparents'; they garden extensively on their three-acre property. Brother Frederic is born in 1895. For six weeks each summer and early fall, family travels to Marquette Island, Michigan, at the northern end of Lake Huron, where they are members of the Cheneaux Club. Aldo enthusiastically explores, camps, sails, and learns to fish there. At eleven, writes in his school notebook, "I like to study birds," and lists thirty-nine species he has identified. At twelve, in 1899, begins hunting with his father at the Crystal Lake Club on the Illinois side of the Mississippi River, and at upland sites on the Iowa prairie. In 1900 receives from his parents a copy of Frank M. Chapman's *Handbook of Birds of Eastern North America*. Studies history, geography, natural science, and the classics. Reads German literature, poetry, *Outing* magazine, Jack London, Ernest Thompson Seton, Ralph Waldo Emerson, Henry Wadsworth Longfellow, Henry David Thoreau, Stewart Edward White. Attends Burlington High School.

1903   In August vacations with his family in Estes Park, Colorado, later travelling with his father to Yellowstone National Park; they spend several weeks hunting outside the park in "beautiful country" in nearby Montana. Adds many new species to his list of birds, now numbering 261.

1904   On January 6, arrives in Lawrenceville, New Jersey, and enrolls at The Lawrenceville School, hoping eventually to study forestry at Yale University. Writes long letters home and explores the local countryside on daily "tramps."

1905   Graduates from the Lawrenceville School in May. Enrolls in Yale's Sheffield Scientific School.

1906   Begins coursework in the Yale Forest School, founded in 1900 under the leadership of Gifford Pinchot and Henry Graves. Attends lectures by Jack London, Jacob Riis, and Ernest Thompson Seton; reads Cicero, Milton, Byron, Darwin's *Vegetable Mould and Earthworms*, and Theodore Roosevelt.

1907   During the summer, hikes with father in the Green Mountains and the Berkshires, then attends the Yale Forest School camp on the Pinchot estate in the Pocono Mountains, near Milford, Pennsylvania.

1908   Completes Bachelor of Science degree. His motto, in the Yale yearbook, is "To hell with convention!"

1909   Completes classes in late February and receives Master of Science degree in forestry. Expresses interest in working in District 3 of the U.S. Forest Service (USFS), comprising the Arizona and New Mexico Territories ("That is where I want to go"). With other members of his graduating class, travels by ship to New Orleans and spends ten weeks in training at a forestry camp near Doucette, Texas. Takes Civil Service exam and in July travels to Albuquerque to begin work: he is appointed Forest Assistant on the Apache National Forest, headquartered in Springerville, Arizona. In August, takes over as head of a forest reconnaissance crew, mapping land and surveying timber. Early in this assignment, on September 22, he and a fellow ranger shoot into a wolf pack and kill the mother wolf (an incident memorialized thirty-five years later in the essay "Thinking Like a Mountain"). After miscalculations and complaints from his crew, his reconnaissance work becomes the subject of an official investigation, but he is cleared of intentional wrongdoing.

1910   Leads another reconnaissance crew surveying the northern third of the Apache Forest; calls it "the best summer I ever had."

1911   In March, on a visit to the USFS district office in Albuquerque, meets and begins to court Estella Bergere (b. 1890), the second daughter of a large, prominent New Mexico political and ranching family. In May, begins work as Deputy Forest Supervisor on the Carson National Forest in northern New Mexico. Founds, edits, and illustrates the *Carson Pine Cone*, a U.S. Forest Service newsletter.

1912   In August is promoted to Forest Supervisor. After courting her primarily by mail, marries Estella at the Cathedral of Saint Francis in Santa Fe on October 9.

1913   While at work in the mountains of northern New Mexico in April, suffers a near-fatal attack of acute nephritis. Ordered by doctors to avoid physical exertion, and warned of the possibility of relapse, convalesces over the next eighteen months, dividing his time between New Mexico and Iowa. Reading occupies much of his time, including works of Thoreau, Emerson, Samuel Johnson, Theodore Roosevelt, and wildlife advocate William Temple Hornaday. First child, son Starker, born in Burlington on October 22.

1914   Returns to work in September, and is assigned to the office of grazing in District 3 headquarters in Albuquerque; family relocates to Albuquerque. Father dies on December 22.

1915   In June is given responsibility for oversight of USFS work in District 3 on recreation, publicity, and game and fish conservation. Makes the first of several trips to the Grand Canyon (then under Forest Service jurisdiction) to prepare a working plan for management of the area. Son Luna is born on October 8. Begins effort to organize "game protective associations" throughout the Southwest. Meets William Temple Hornaday in Albuquerque on October 12. Hornaday gives him a copy of his recent book, *Wild Life Conservation in Theory and Practice*. Publishes the first issue of *The Pine Cone*, the official paper of the New Mexico game

protection movement, in December; edits and writes much
of the content over the next five years. Also publishes the
Game and Fish Handbook, an internal USFS document providing guidance for game and fish management on USFS
lands.

1916   Travels and lectures throughout New Mexico promoting
            game conservation.

1917   In January receives a letter from Theodore Roosevelt: "It
            seems to me that your association in New Mexico is setting
            an example to the whole country." Daughter Marie Adelina
            (Nina) Leopold born on August 4. Resumes hunting dur-
            ing the summer after a hiatus of several years. On August
            16, begins a "Hunting & Fishing Journal," the first of many
            such field journals he will keep throughout his life.

1918   In January accepts a position as secretary of the Albuquer-
            que Chamber of Commerce. Maintains active role in game
            protection while advocating for civic improvements in Al-
            buquerque.

1919   Rejoins the Forest Service in August as Assistant District
            Forester in Charge of Operations, overseeing personnel,
            business organization, finance, timber management, fire
            control, grazing, roads and trails, and other functions for
            the twenty million acres of USFS land in the Southwest.
            During his regular field inspections, studies the interrela-
            tionship of historic and contemporary grazing, soil erosion,
            vegetation change, and climate in the ecological function-
            ing of southwestern watersheds. In December, meets with
            USFS landscape architect Arthur Carhart in Denver to
            discuss wilderness protection on federal lands. Son Carl is
            born on December 18.

1920   Recommends erosion control demonstration projects on
            the Prescott National Forest in Arizona: "What is needed
            is a series of actual demonstrations, to test and improve
            techniques and to serve as examples to private interests."

1921   Publishes articles "A Plea for Recognition of Artificial Works
            in Forest Erosion Control Policy" and "The Wilderness
            and its Place in Forest Recreation Policy" in the *Journal
            of Forestry*; the latter, his first important publication on the
            theme, calls attention to the loss of roadless wildlands in
            the Southwest.

1922   After an inspection of the Gila National Forest in New Mexico, recommends the designation of a 755,000-acre portion of the forest as a wilderness area, submitting an official proposal on October 2. Later that month, embarks with brother Carl on a three-week hunting and camping trip through the Colorado River's upper delta. Recalls this trip in his later essay "The Green Lagoons."

1923   Drafts essay "Some Fundamentals of Conservation in the Southwest," which includes his earliest sustained exploration of the ethical dimensions of human relationships to land. In December, USFS publishes his *Watershed Handbook*, summarizing insights on watershed management derived from his national forest inspection tours.

1924   The Forest Service approves his Gila National Forest Recreational Working Plan, with its proposal for establishment of the Gila Wilderness Area, on June 3; it is the first such area in the country. In June, accepts a transfer to Madison, Wisconsin, where he will serve as Assistant (later Associate) Director of the USFS Forest Products Laboratory. Travels with brothers Carl and Frederic and son Starker into canoe country of the Superior National Forest in northern Minnesota (the future Boundary Waters Canoe Area).

1925   Begins to publish articles in various national journals and magazines on the theme of wilderness values and wilderness protection; these continue for the next several years. Concurrently begins to publish more regularly on the subject of game management.

1926   Inspired by Saxton Pope's *Hunting with the Bow and Arrow*, takes up archery, which becomes a family hobby; constructs his own bows and arrows from exotic woods and attends tournaments.

1927   Daughter Estella born January 8. Travels to California in August and visits Yosemite National Park. Leads efforts to reform state conservation administration and forestry policy in Wisconsin. Returns to New Mexico and Gila Wilderness Area in November for a two-week pack trip and bow hunt.

1928   In June resigns position with the Forest Products Laboratory and leaves the USFS to conduct state-wide game surveys as a private consultant, under the auspices of the Sporting Arms and Ammunitions Manufacturers' Institute

(SAAMI). Conceived at first as a national effort, the work will come to focus on the upper Midwest. Conducts surveys of Michigan, Minnesota, and Iowa over the summer, and of Ohio in November. Chairs committee, formed in December, to formulate a national policy on game conservation.

1929   Travels to Mississippi in January, conducting game surveys there as a test in the application of his methods outside the Midwest. In February and March delivers a series of lectures on game management at the University of Wisconsin in Madison. Oversees early wildlife research projects at the Universities of Minnesota, Michigan, and Wisconsin. Conducts game surveys of Illinois, Indiana, Wisconsin, and Missouri. Makes another hunting trip to the Gila Wilderness Area.

1930   In December, presents a new American Game Policy at the 17th American Game Conference in New York; the policy is adopted and receives wide coverage in national publications (including *Time* magazine).

1931   Publishes *Report on a Game Survey of the North Central States*, a summary of the survey work of the previous three years. In July, attends the Matamek Conference on Biological Cycles in Quebec, where he meets Charles Elton, a leading animal ecologist from Oxford University. Consults with state of Iowa in preparation of a comprehensive, long-term conservation plan. In November receives Izaak Walton League gold medal in recognition of game survey work.

1932   Returns to Iowa to continue work on state conservation plan. In March, SAAMI discontinues its support for his research; advertises his services as a "consulting forester," but ends the year without a regular source of income. Completes manuscript of textbook *Game Management*.

1933   Is employed temporarily in the spring and summer by the USFS in the Southwest, overseeing erosion control projects of the new Civilian Conservation Corps. *Game Management* is published in May. Delivers "The Conservation Ethic" as the John Wesley Powell Lecture at a meeting of the Southwest division of the American Association for the Advancement of Science. In July, accepts an appointment as the new chair of game management in the Department of Agricultural Economics at the University of Wisconsin (the *New York Times* calls it the "one and only 'wild-game chair'"). Works to set up several local cooperative conservation programs in Wisconsin, including the nation's first watershed-scale soil and water conservation project, at Coon Valley. In September, gives the first of an occasional series of radio talks for farmers on Madison station WHA.

1934   Begins teaching and accepts first graduate students at the University of Wisconsin. At the end of January, as one of three members of the President's Committee on Wild Life Restoration, meets Franklin Roosevelt; committee report is submitted in February. In March, addresses the subject of "Conservation Economics" at the University of Wisconsin, making comments critical of New Deal conservation programs. Declines an invitation to become director of the U.S. Bureau of Biological Survey. On June 17, delivers dedicatory address at the University of Wisconsin Arboretum, site of pioneering research and demonstration in ecological restoration. In October, at the invitation of Robert Marshall, becomes a founding member of The Wilderness Society.

1935   In January makes first visit to the Wisconsin River farm that will later provide the setting for many essays in *A Sand County Almanac*. Purchases the eighty-acre property in April, and renovates an abandoned chicken coop as the family "Shack," adding a clay floor, fireplace, and roof. Begins a "Shack Journal." Delivers address "Land Pathology" on April 15—the day after the historic "Black Sunday" dust storms. Writes "Why the Wilderness Society?," a manifesto for the recently organized group, and meets Robert Marshall. In August, travels with five other foresters on a fellowship to Germany and Czechoslovakia; they spend three months touring state forests and land estates. Consults with foresters and game managers, works in the archives of the Forest School at Tharandt, and hunts with German aristocrats. Returns to U.S. on November 15, meeting Estella in New York; they see Paul Robeson in *Showboat*.

1936   Attends the First North American Wildlife Conference, in Washington, D.C., in February, and plays key role in creation of the new professional organization of wildlife biologists, The Wildlife Society. Publishes articles "Deer and *Dauerwald* in Germany" and "*Naturschutz* in Germany"; his experiences in Germany also prompt the writing of the

article "Threatened Species," on the needs of "near-extinct
birds and animals." Begins a series of biweekly seminars fea-
turing his students and invited speakers. In March, installs
an outhouse at the Shack; son Starker nicknames it "the
Parthenon." The next month, family plants two thousand
pine trees, and other trees and shrubs, initiating extensive
restoration efforts on the Shack property. In the years to
come, visits the Shack regularly, often weekly, with family,
friends, and students, recording field observations of the
Shack environs in a series of detailed journals. Travels in
September to Chihuahua, Mexico, with friend Roy Roark,
on the first of two pack trips he would take to the Rio
Gavilan in the Sierra Madre Occidental. Drawing on this
trip, composes the essay "The Thick-Billed Parrot of Chihuahua," later included in *A Sand County Almanac* as
"Guacamaja."

1937   Based on recent studies of sandhill cranes and field experience in central Wisconsin, writes and publishes "Marshland Elegy." In December makes a second trip to the Rio
Gavilan with brother Carl and son Starker. (Will later recall:
"all my life I had seen only sick land, whereas here was a
biota in perfect aboriginal health. The term 'unspoiled wilderness' took on a new meaning.") The trip also prompts
his essays "Conservationist in Mexico" and "Song of the
Gavilan."

1938   In the spring, his graduate students take possession of an
empty Victorian house owned by the university, at 424
University Farm Place; it becomes the new office for Leopold and his students. Begins bird-banding at the Shack,
and makes notes in his journal about the "sky dance" of the
woodcock. Publishes increasingly on the social, cultural,
and economic dimensions of conservation. Helps to launch
the Delta Duck Station (later Delta Waterfowl Research
Station), near the south shore of Lake Manitoba, and develops conservation and land management plans for the
Huron Mountain Club in Michigan's Upper Peninsula. In
November, publishes the first of a series of short wildlife
conservation articles for farmers in the *Wisconsin Agriculturalist and Farmer*; he will continue the series until 1942,
writing forty such articles, several of which he will incorpo-
rate in *A Sand County Almanac*.

1939   Offers a new undergraduate course, Wildlife Ecology 118, which uses case studies to teach students how to "learn to read the landscape." In Milwaukee in June, delivers his address "A Biotic View of Land" to a joint meeting of the Ecological Society of America and the Society of American Foresters. Serves as president of The Wildlife Society. Becomes chair of a new Department of Wildlife Management at the University of Wisconsin. In September, investigates wildlife conditions on sites from Colorado and New Mexico to Texas and Georgia as a consultant for the Soil Conservation Service.

1940   Begins making flock counts of geese arriving at the Shack. Over the summer, makes two trips to the Delta Station. Shares early drafts of essays with his student Albert Hochbaum, director of the station and a leading waterfowl biologist and wildlife illustrator.

1941   Over the summer has first discussions with Hochbaum about preparing a collection of his ecological essays; writes new essays throughout the year. In July and August travels extensively across the inland West for three weeks, inspecting progress on wildlife research programs. Writes "Cheat Takes Over" after touring California's Modoc National Forest and adjacent rangelands. Visits Zion National Park. After the attack on Pearl Harbor, son Carl enlists in the U.S. Marines; Luna enlists in the Army shortly thereafter. Daughter Nina marries Bill Elder, a zoology student, in September.

1942   Becomes involved in controversial deer management issues in Wisconsin, remaining embroiled in these issues for the remainder of his life.

1943   Appointed to Wisconsin Conservation Commission.

1944   Continues collaboration with Albert Hochbaum on essay collection. At Hochbaum's prodding—"I think your case . . . is all the stronger if, in one of these pieces, you admit that you haven't always smoked the same tobacco"—drafts "Thinking Like a Mountain" on April 1. Prepares first full version of essay collection in June and submits manuscript to two publishers, Macmillan and Knopf. Macmillan rejects the manuscript, while Knopf offers encouragement.

1945   Teaching load grows with the return of students after the end of the war. In the fall, begins to experience painful symptoms of trigeminal neuralgia.

1946   Serves as chair of The Wildlife Society's Committee on Foreign Relations. Prepares and delivers early version of "On a Monument to the Pigeon" as an address to the Wisconsin Society for Ornithology.

1947   Elected honorary vice president of the American Forestry Association and president of the Ecological Society of America. In June, speaks on "The Ecological Conscience" at the annual meeting of the Garden Club of America in Minneapolis. In July, overhauls the manuscript of his essay collection and, drawing upon earlier essays, composes "The Land Ethic." Charles Schwartz, an illustrator with the Missouri Conservation Department, is enlisted to provide illustrations for the collection. On September 27, undergoes surgical procedure at the Mayo Clinic to relieve symptoms of trigeminal neuralgia. Knopf rejects essay collection manuscript in November. Continues to compose new essays and drafts new foreword. Submits revised manuscript, entitled "Great Possessions," to Oxford University Press in December.

1948   Asked by U.S. Secretary of the Interior to serve as advisor to the United Nations' International Scientific Conference on the Conservation and Utilization of Natural Resources. On April 14 receives call from editor at Oxford University Press notifying him that his manuscript has been accepted. On April 21 succumbs to a heart attack and dies while helping to fight an escaped grass fire on a neighbor's farm near the Shack. Is buried at Aspen Grove Cemetery in Burlington, Iowa.

Note on the Texts and Illustrations

This volume contains the complete text of Aldo Leopold's *A Sand County Almanac* (1949), including Charles W. Schwartz's original illustrations, and presents selections from Leopold's other works in three sections: "Other Writings on Ecology and Conservation," "Selected Journals," and "Selected Letters." The text of *A Sand County Almanac* has been taken from the posthumous first edition, published by Oxford University Press. The texts of Leopold's other works have been taken, in cases where he published them, from the periodicals and books in which they first appeared. For those works he left unpublished, texts have been newly prepared from his manuscripts and typescripts in the Aldo Leopold Papers at the University of Wisconsin, Madison, and (in the case of one letter) from a manuscript privately held by the Leopold family. Many items in the present volume, including a speech, an essay, several journal selections, and almost all of the selected letters, are believed to be published for the first time.

A Sand County Almanac, and Sketches Here and There. Leopold's decision to write what would become *A Sand County Almanac* seems to have been precipitated by Harold Strauss, an editor at Alfred A. Knopf, who sent him a letter on November 26, 1941, "seeking among biologists for a good book on wild-life observation." Such a book, Strauss explained, would need to be "warmly, evocatively, and vividly written"; it would "have room for the author's opinions on ecology and conservation," so long as they were "worked into a framework of actual field experiences." Replying on December 3, Leopold at first imagined such a book as "a job for a team." By December 29, however, he wondered if Knopf might be interested in publishing "a series of ecological essays, illustrated," that he himself would gather and prepare "as a Christmas book for next year."

The series of essays Leopold envisioned ultimately took much longer than a year to produce. On July 18, 1942, he explained to Strauss that his collection was not yet "large enough to take seriously as a publishing project," but that he was at work on several additional essays. On May 7, 1943, he wrote to one of his recent graduate students, Albert Hochbaum, to renew plans for their "joint venture": Hochbaum, an artist and field biologist, had agreed to illustrate the collection. Writing between Madison, Wisconsin, and the Delta Marsh Field Station on Lake Manitoba, where Hochbaum was leading a waterfowl research program, the two exchanged essays and drawings and Hochbaum offered his reactions to the evolving manuscript. ("This is the kind of criticism that I really need and seldom get," Leopold acknowledged.)

By June 8, 1944, Leopold felt ready enough to send thirteen "sample" essays, along with several of Hochbaum's illustrations, to Clinton Simpson, Strauss's successor at Knopf. Two days earlier, he had sent the same essays—"Marshland Elegy," "Song of the Gavilan," "Guacamaja," "Escudilla," "Smoky Gold," "Odyssey," "Draba," "Great Possessions," "The Green Lagoons," "Illinois Bus Ride," "Pines above the Snow," "Thinking Like a Mountain," and "The Geese Return"—to Wellmer Pessels, an editor at Macmillan. He suggested "Thinking Like a Mountain, and Other Essays" as a possible book title, having decided against "Marshland Elegy, and Other Essays."

Pessels conveyed Macmillan's rejection on July 20. Though she found the essays "beautifully written," her firm doubted their commercial appeal: "we do not feel that a volume of essays on outdoor topics would find a wide enough market to warrant our use of paper at this time." Simpson responded on July 24 with similar, though less definitive, bad news: the essays "do not seem altogether suitable for book publication in their present form," he wrote. Unlike Macmillan, however, Knopf left open the possibility of publication at some point in the future: "readers who like nature will enjoy such writing, and [we] hope that we can work out with you a successful plan for a volume." In particular, they suggested Leopold focus on "one region of the country," and consider "making a book purely of nature observations, with less emphasis on . . . ecological ideas." These "ecological theories," they argued, "are very difficult indeed to present successfully for the layman."

Leopold continued working on the essays for another three years before he felt ready to offer Knopf "a new manuscript," on September 5, 1947. In the meantime, he had extensively revised and expanded it, adding especially to its Wisconsin sections. On January 19, 1946, he had sent five sample essays ("Thinking Like a Mountain," "Great Possessions," "The Green Lagoons," "Smoky Gold," and "Odyssey") to the University of Minnesota Press. Helen Clapesattle, an editor at Minnesota, suggested he send his manuscript when it was finished—an offer he did not ultimately pursue. On January 3, 1947, he had written his son Luna to encourage him to enlist Charles W. Schwartz as an illustrator for the book. (Hochbaum had dropped out as illustrator sometime after March 1945, and Herbert Sanborn, another candidate, had proven unsatisfactory.)

On November 5, 1947, Simpson all but rejected "Great Possessions," as Leopold had since titled his collection: it would need "a more fundamental kind of revision" than Leopold had achieved, and "a complete . . . rewriting," before Knopf would be willing to consider it again. Praising Leopold's "nature observations," Simpson reiterated Knopf's dissatisfaction with the book's "ecological argument," which, Simpson reported, "everyone finds unconvincing." Within a few weeks of Knopf's rejection, however, Leopold received an invitation from Philip Vaudrin, an editor at Oxford University Press, to submit his work for review. (Luna Leopold had corresponded with Vaudrin about the book a year earlier.) On December 2, the publisher William Sloane sent another request, having learned of the essays from Leopold's friend William Vogt. Leopold sent copies of his collection to both publishers on December 19. Sloane's response was delayed because the carbon copy they received was "very difficult to read." Oxford, however, promptly accepted it.

On April 14, 1948—a week before he died, fighting a wildfire on a neighbor's farm—Leopold came to an informal agreement with Oxford to publish "Great Possessions." Vaudrin promised to convey some "very minor criticisms" that had been raised among his otherwise enthusiastic colleagues. Leopold himself planned to work on revisions to the book over the summer, and he drafted a letter (see page 845 in the present volume) soliciting criticism from colleagues and friends: he listed Alfred Etter, Frances and Frederick Hamerstrom, Joseph and Peggy Hickey, Albert Hochbaum, Robert McCabe, Lyle Sowls, Alice Harper and Allen Stokes, and William Vogt as intended recipients. (He had also shared copies of the manuscript with Vogt, his wife Estella, and his secretary Virginia Kiesel Spence.) He aimed to complete his revisions by the end of October, and Oxford hoped to publish it in the fall of 1949.

In the wake of Leopold's death, Vaudrin wondered if publication could proceed. Revising the book would be "a job which he alone would have been able to manage, I should have thought," he wrote Joe Hickey on April 22. Alarmed that Oxford might renege, Hickey and others in Leopold's Madison inner circle moved quickly to make certain that "Great Possessions" would be published as he had hoped. "We have decided on a plan of action," McCabe wrote Luna Leopold on April 24. The same day, Hickey sent a memo to what he called "The Reading Committee" (adding Estella Leopold, Luna Leopold, and Charles Schwartz to the list Leopold had already prepared) and circulated a copy of Leopold's typescript: "we must close our ranks and get this book into print." He assured Vaudrin that Leopold's readers would be able to complete the task by the end of October. By May 4, all had agreed that Luna Leopold would serve as "final editor," reviewing the committee's suggestions. Hickey, in consultation with Estella and Luna, would help to negotiate contractual matters. Separately, an "illustrations subcommittee" would work to ensure the best possible presentation of Schwartz's drawings, for which Leopold had already expressed his admiration (see pages 838–39 in this volume), but which Oxford had not yet seen.

The members of Leopold's "Reading Committee" suggested numerous changes, large and small, to the unfinished text of "Great Possessions," but they did so with a keen sense of respect for Leopold's intentions. "[W]e should not try to 'improve' what Aldo has written," Frederick Hamerstrom advised, calling the book "a beautiful thing": "better to leave in it a few things that might perhaps have been said differently than to risk taking liberties (no matter how well intended) with Aldo's own way of expressing things." Acting as editor, Luna Leopold adopted the committee's suggestions sparingly. He corrected hyphenation and spelling, factual errors, and repetitious phrasing; in a few cases, he altered "dated" references (omitting "Tarawa" and "black markets," for instance, from a list of conversation topics in "Illinois Bus Ride"). His most significant alterations were to the arrangement of the essays within the collection. He moved "The Land Ethic" from the beginning to the end of Part III, and "The Alder Fork" from Part II to Part I. "Prairie Birthday," an unpublished essay not included in any of Leopold's various submissions to publishers, was added to Part I. Vogt objected to a title, "Ave Maria": "Did A.L. mean matins? Hail Marys are not restricted to the dawn. Why bring in the sectarian at all? Did A.L. mean it, unknown to me? Or was this a slip into the literary? It seems to me a false note." Estella Leopold explained that she and her husband "listened to the 'Ave Maria' record by his request many evenings," but agreed the title could be revised, and Luna decided on "The Choral Copse." "The White Mountain," similarly, became "On Top." The change in the overall title, from "Great Possessions" to *A Sand County Almanac*, was suggested not by the committee but by Oxford, on the grounds that Leopold's proposed title did not give the book's potential audience a sense of the contents. Leopold might have resisted some or all of these revisions, and may indeed have revised more extensively, had he lived. He did not intend "Great Possessions" as a finished work, and he was edited posthumously only by those whose comments he had already solicited or would have expected in the ordinary course of affairs.

Twenty-one of the forty-one pieces ultimately included in *A Sand County Almanac* had been previously published elsewhere, though sometimes only in part, and often in significantly different form. The following list provides further details about the publication history of each. Leopold's extant typescripts often bear a date indicating when a particular work was drafted or subsequently revised; such dates appear in italics. *A Sand County Almanac* is abbreviated *ASCA*, which here indicates that the work first appeared in print in the published volume:

January Thaw: *ASCA. July 12, 1947; August 28, 1947; December 1, 1947.*
Good Oak: *ASCA. January 25, 1948.*
The Geese Return: *Wisconsin Agriculturalist and Farmer* 67.7 (April 6, 1940): 18 (as "When Geese Return Spring Is Here"). *June 1, 1944; August 25, 1946.*
Come High Water: *ASCA. April 1, 1945; June 5, 1947.*
Draba: *ASCA. March 16, 1943; June 2, 1944.*
Bur Oak: *Wisconsin Agriculturalist and Farmer* 68.7 (April 5, 1941): 10 (as "Bur Oak Is Badge of Wisconsin"). *August 1, 1946.*
Sky Dance: "Wildlife Conservation on the Farm," an unpaginated collection of reprints from *Wisconsin Agriculturalist and Farmer*, c. September 1941? (as "Sky Dance of Spring"). *July 21, 1947.*
Back from the Argentine: *Wisconsin Agriculturalist and Farmer* 69.10 (May 16, 1942): 10 (as "The Plover Is Back from Argentine").
The Alder Fork—A Fishing Idyl: *Outdoor America* 10.10 (May 1932): 11.
Great Possessions: *ASCA. September 1, 1943; June 2, 1944.*
Prairie Birthday: *ASCA. December 27, 1947.*
The Green Pasture: *ASCA. August 15, 1945.*
The Choral Copse: *ASCA. October 21, 1947; March 4, 1948* (as "Ave Maria").
Smoky Gold: *ASCA. October 27, 1943; June 4, 1944.*
Too Early: *ASCA. November 22, 1943; June 1947.*
Red Lanterns: *ASCA. July 8, 1947.*
If I Were the Wind: *ASCA. November 21, 1943.*
Axe-in-Hand: *ASCA. November 27, 1947.*
A Mighty Fortress: *Wisconsin Conservation Bulletin* 8.2 (February 1943): 25–27 (as "A Lesson from the Woodlands"). *August 13, 1947.*
Home Range: *Wisconsin Conservation Bulletin* 8.9 (September 1943): 23–24.
Pines above the Snow: *Wisconsin Conservation Bulletin* 8.3 (March 1943): 27–29. *April 5, 1944; July 10, 1947.*
65290: *ASCA. September 11, 1941; July 20, 1947* (as "65287").
Marshland Elegy: *American Forests* 43.10 (October 1937): 472–74.
The Sand Counties: *ASCA. June 2, 1947.*
Odyssey: *Audubon* 44.3 (May–June 1942): 133–35.
On a Monument to the Pigeon: *Silent Wings: A Memorial to the Passenger Pigeon* (Madison: Wisconsin Society for Ornithology, 1947): 3–5 (as "On a Monument to the Passenger Pigeon"). *August 25, 1946; April 10, 1947.*
Flambeau: *American Forests* 49.1 (January 1943): 12–14, 47 (as "Flambeau: The Story of a Wild River").
Illinois Bus Ride: *ASCA. January 1, 1944; July 10, 1947.*
Red Legs Kicking: *ASCA. Undated.*

On Top: *ASCA. Undated* (as "The White Mountain").

Thinking Like a Mountain: *ASCA. April 1, 1944.*

Escudilla: *American Forests* 46.12 (December 1940): 539–40. *November 30, 1946.*

Guacamaja: *The Condor* 39.1 (January–February 1937): 9–10 (as "The Thick-Billed Parrot in Chihuahua").

The Green Lagoons: *American Forests* 51.8 (August 1945): 376–77, 414. *January 11, 1944; November 25, 1946.*

Song of the Gavilan: *Journal of Wildlife Management* 4.3 (July 1940): 329–32.

Cheat Takes Over: *The Land* 1.4 (1941): 310–13.

Clandeboye: *ASCA. July 10, 1944; July 10, 1947.*

Conservation Esthetic: *Bird-Lore* 40.2 (March–April 1938): 101–9.

Wildlife in American Culture: P*roceedings, 7th Annual Midwest Wildlife Conference, Des Moines (December 4–6, 1941)*: 19–25; *Journal of Wildlife Management* 7.1 (January 1943): 1–6.

Wilderness: published in part as "Wilderness As a Land Laboratory," *The Living Wilderness* 6 (July 1941): 3. See also pages 454–56 in the present volume.

The Land Ethic: published in part in "The Conservation Ethic," *Journal of Forestry* 31.6 (October 1933): 634–43 (and see pages 325–39 in the present volume); in "A Biotic View of Land," *Journal of Forestry* 37.9 (September 1939): 727–30 (and see pages 438–46); and in "The Ecological Conscience," *Wisconsin Conservation Bulletin* 12.12 (December 1947): 4–7 (see pages 524–32 in the present volume).

In 1966, Oxford University Press published a revised and enlarged edition of *A Sand County Almanac*, which, among other changes, removed further "dated references" and incorporated eight additional essays and sketches first published in *Round River: From the Journals of Aldo Leopold* (New York: Oxford University Press, 1953), edited by Luna B. Leopold. Both the first and the revised editions have been reprinted on multiple occasions. The text of *A Sand County Almanac* in the present volume has been taken from the first edition, published by Oxford University Press on October 20, 1949; all of Charles Schwartz's illustrations have been included.

Other Writings on Ecology and Conservation. In addition to *A Sand County Almanac*, Leopold published two books—*Report on a Game Survey of the North Central States* (1931) and *Game Management* (1933)—and several hundred shorter works. He also left an extensive collection of unpublished writings. "Other Writings on Ecology and Conservation" gathers fifty-six of these published and unpublished items, written from 1917 to 1948; they are presented in approximate chronological order of composition, and include speeches, articles for popular magazines, sketches and vignettes, professional papers and conference presentations, drafts and fragments, and a book chapter (from *Game Management*). Two items, it is believed, appear here in print for the first time: "Address before the Albuquerque Rotary Club" (1917) and "Scarcity Values in Conservation" (c. 1946). The remaining items left unpublished during Leopold's lifetime have appeared in posthumous collections, including *Round River* and *The River of the Mother of God, and Other Essays* (1991), edited by Susan L. Flader and J. Baird Callicott.

A list of sources from which the texts of these works have been taken appears below. For the thirty-three published items, Leopold's original publications have been preferred over earlier manuscript or subsequent print versions (with one exception, as noted below). For the twenty-three he left unpublished, the last and most complete of his manuscripts or typescripts have been preferred. Some of Leopold's unpublished writings were evidently left unfinished; others include sentences or paragraphs he subsequently revised and published in other contexts. (He incorporated "The Conservation Ethic," "A Biotic View of Land," and "The Ecological Conscience," for instance, in a new essay in *A Sand County Almanac*, "The Land Ethic.") Items from the Leopold Papers—accessed in facsimile at http://digital.library.wisc .edu/1711.dl/AldoLeopold—are cited by the abbreviation *LP*, followed by their archival subseries and box number, their page number(s) in the online edition, and (in italics) their date of composition:

Address before the Albuquerque Rotary Club on Presentation of the Gold Medal of the Permanent Life Protection Fund: Typescript, *LP* 8B8, 666–73. *c. July 1917*.

Boomerangs: *The Pine Cone* (April 1918): 3. An unsigned item attributed to Leopold, who was principally responsible for the writing and production of *The Pine Cone* from 1915 to 1924.

Wild Lifers vs. Game Farmers: A Plea for Democracy in Sport. *Bulletin of the American Game Protective Association* 8.2 (April 1919): 6–7.

A Turkey Hunt in the Datil National Forest: *Wild Life* 3.3 (December 1919): 4–5, 16.

The Wilderness and Its Place in Forest Recreational Policy: *Journal of Forestry* 19.7 (November 1921): 718–21.

Blue River: Manuscript, *LP* 6B16, 367. *June 11, 1922*.

Goose Music: Manuscript, *LP* 6B16, 399–407. *c. June 1922*.

Some Fundamentals of Conservation in the Southwest: Typescript, *LP* 6B16, 32–49. The original typescript of this essay in *LP* is missing its final page. The missing text, amounting to half a sentence, has been taken from a typescript copy (*LP* 6B17, 1467) apparently prepared after Leopold's death. *c. March 1923.*

A Criticism of the Booster Spirit: Typescript, *LP* 6B16, 354–66. *November 6, 1923.*

Pioneers and Gullies: *Sunset Magazine* 52.2 (May 1924): 15–16, 91–95.

Grass, Brush, Timber, and Fire in Southern Arizona: *Journal of Forestry* 22.6 (October 1924): 1–10.

The River of the Mother of God: Typescript, *LP* 6B16, 374–81. *c. December 1924.*

Conserving the Covered Wagon: *Sunset Magazine* 54.3 (March 1925): 21, 56.

The Pig in the Parlor: *Service Bulletin* (U.S. Forest Service) 9.23 (June 8, 1925): 1–2.

Wilderness as a Form of Land Use: *The Journal of Land & Public Utility Economics* 1.4 (October 1925): 398–404.

Mr. Thompson's Wilderness: *Service Bulletin* (U.S. Forest Service) 12.26 (June 25, 1928): 1–2.

The American Game Policy in a Nutshell: *Transactions of the Seventeenth American Game Conference, December 1–2, 1930* (Washington, DC: American Game Association, 1930), pages 281–83.

Game and Wild Life Conservation: *The Condor* 34.2 (March–April 1932): 103–6.

A History of Ideas in Game Management: *Game Management* (New York: Charles Scribner's Sons, 1933), pages 3–21.

The Virgin Southwest: Typescript, *LP* 6B16, 89–107. *May 6, 1933.*

The Conservation Ethic: *Journal of Forestry* 31.6 (October 1933): 634–43.

Conservation Economics: *Journal of Forestry* 32.5 (May 1934): 537–44. At 344.12 in the present volume, "supervision" has been emended to "assumption" following a holograph emendation to the copy of the printed text in *LP. March 1, 1934.*

The Arboretum and the University: *Parks & Recreation* 18.2 (October 1934): 59–60. *June 17, 1934.*

Land Pathology: Typescript, *LP* 6B16, 452–59. *April 15, 1935.*

Coon Valley: An Adventure in Cooperative Conservation: *American Forests* 41.5 (May 1935): 205–8.

Why the Wilderness Society?: *The Living Wilderness* 1.1 (September 1935): 6.

Wilderness ("To an American conservationist . . ."): Manuscript, *LP* 6B16, 335. *c. December 1935.*

Wilderness ("The two great cultural advances . . ."): Manuscript, *LP* 6B16, 340. *c. December 1935.*

Threatened Species: A Proposal to the Wildlife Conference for an

Inventory of the Needs of Near-extinct Birds and Animals: *American Forests* 42.3 (March 1936): 116–18.

Naturschutz in Germany: *Bird-Lore* 38.2 (March–April 1936): 102–11.

Conservationist in Mexico: *American Forests* 43.3 (March 1937): 118–20, 146.

Conservation Blueprints: *American Forests* 43.12 (December 1937): 596, 608.

Engineering and Conservation: Typescript, *LP* 6B16, 490–500. *April 11, 1938.*

Natural History, the Forgotten Science: Typescript, *LP* 6B16, 511–17. *April 26, 1938.*

A Survey of Conservation: Typescript, *LP* 6B16, 518–29. *c. 1938.*

The Farmer as a Conservationist: *American Forests* 45.6 (June 1939): 294–99, 316, 323. An earlier version appeared in Stencil Circular 210, Extension Service, College of Agriculture, University of Wisconsin, Madison (February 1939), pages 1–8.

A Biotic View of Land: *Journal of Forestry* 37.9 (September 1939): 727–30. *June 21, 1939.*

Lakes in Relation to Terrestrial Life Patterns: *A Symposium on Hydrobiology*, ed. James G. Needham, Paul B. Sears, Aldo Leopold, et al. (Madison: University of Wisconsin Press, 1941), pages 17–22. *September 4–6, 1940.*

Wilderness As a Land Laboratory: *The Living Wilderness* 6 (July 1941): 3.

Yet Come June: Manuscript, *LP* 6B16, 636. *December 23, 1941.*

The Round River: A Parable of Conservation: Typescript, *LP* 6B16, 655–65. Published posthumously in *Round River: From the Journals of Aldo Leopold* (1953) as "The Round River—A Parable." The *Round River* text adds a concluding paragraph drawn from other unpublished writings by Leopold, and includes line art at three points to illustrate energy flows between component parts of the biota. The *Round River* text may have been based on an authorial version of the essay no longer known to be extant, but is more likely to have been altered after Leopold's death. The present volume follows *Round River* in adding line art not present in the extant typescript. *c. 1941.*

The Grizzly—A Problem in Land Planning: *Outdoor America* 7.6 (April 1942): 11–12.

The Role of Wildlife in a Liberal Education: *Transactions of the Seventh North American Wildlife Conference, April 8–10, 1942* (Washington, DC: American Wildlife Institute, 1942), pages 485–89. *April 9, 1942.*

The Last Stand: *Outdoor America* 7.7 (May–June 1942): 8–9.

Land-Use and Democracy: *Audubon* 44.5 (September–October 1942): 259–65.

The Prairie: The Forgotten Flora: Typescript, *LP* 6B18, 918–21. *November 6, 1942.*

What Is a Weed?: Typescript, *LP* 6B16, 1494–98. *August 2, 1943.*

Post-war Prospects: *Audubon* 46.1 (January–February 1944): 27–29.

Conservation: In Whole or in Part?: Typescript, *LP* 6B16, 732–45. *November 1, 1944.*

The Outlook for Farm Wildlife: *Transactions of the Tenth North American Wildlife Conference* (Washington, DC: American Wildlife Institute, 1945), pages 165–68. *February 8, 1945.*

The Land-Health Concept and Conservation: Manuscript, *LP* 6B18, 340. *December 21, 1946.*

Scarcity Values in Conservation: Manuscript, *LP* 6B16, 754–56. *c. 1946.*

Deadening: Manuscript, *LP* 6B16, 751. *c. 1946.*

Wherefore Wildlife Ecology?: Manuscript, *LP* 6B16, 746–48. *c. Spring 1947.*

The Ecological Conscience: *Bulletin of the Garden Club of America* (September 1947): 45–53. *June 1947.*

The Deer Swath: Typescript, *LP* 6B16, 799–800. *February 29, 1948.*

The texts of items taken from Leopold's manuscripts and typescripts in the present volume (including twenty-three of the "Other Writings" listed above, all selections from Leopold's journals, and all but 3 letters) are newly prepared clear texts. Leopold's holograph corrections and cancellations have silently been accepted. Slips of the pen, missed keystrokes, and inadvertently misplaced or omitted punctuation have silently been corrected. Letter cases, often ambiguous in Leopold's handwriting, have been regularized to capitals at the beginning of sentences and for proper names. Titles of works, taxonomic binomials or partial binomials, and journal entries in other hands have been printed in italic type.

Selected Journals. Leopold kept journals of various kinds for most of his life, including a sketchbook (1899–1913), ornithological records (1902–6), official U.S. Forest Service diaries (1909–16), a commonplace book (c. 1914–early 1930s), hunting and fishing journals (1917–45), archery journals (c. 1926–35), and the Leopold "Shack Journals" (1935–48). The present volume contains the complete text of twelve selections, written from 1920 to 1936, from the hunting and fishing journals, and thirteen entries from the "Shack Journals," written from 1935 to 1948. Where entries in the manuscript "Shack Journals" have been omitted, this fact is noted with a line of five asterisks.

Several of the selections included here—"'Gettin' Ganders on the Rio'," "Fish Lake," "Lily River Trip" (apart from the sketch entitled "The Lily"), "1936 Mexico Trip," and excerpts "*from* Shack Journals,

1935–1948" (apart from one entry, "Gus' Last Hunt")—are believed
to be previously unpublished. "The Lily," "Gus' Last Hunt," and the
remaining journal selections were first published, after Leopold's death,
in *Round River*, often in significantly different form. Three journal
selections—"Canada, 1924," "Canada, 1925," and "Reunion"—are
untitled in Leopold's manuscripts, and titles have been supplied following the *Round River* text.

Leopold appears to have written his journals almost exclusively in
camp or at the Leopold family shack near Baraboo, Wisconsin, making
subsequent textual revisions only rarely. He did return to the journals
after their initial composition, however, to add photographs, illustrations, travel ephemera, and other ancillary documents such as lists
of equipment and provisions, tables of game taken or species seen,
graphs or charts of data collected, and published maps. In the case of
two of the selections included, "'Gettin' Ganders on the Rio'" and
"1936 Mexico Trip," he replaced his original manuscript with a typed
copy. The present volume includes representative examples of these
photographs and ancillary documents, which are published here, in the
context of the journals they illustrate, for the first time. Leopold sometimes invited others to write in his journals; their entries have been
printed in italics, preceded (where the author is known) by their initials. In a few instances, he took advantage of a blank page or space in
an otherwise already completed part of a journal to add new material.
Such later entries have been moved in the present volume so that they
follow rather than interrupt the regular dated sequence of entries. On
a few occasions in the "Shack Journals," Leopold includes parenthetical
cross-references to data on journal pages not included in the present
volume; such references have silently been omitted. The text of the
journal selections presented here is a newly prepared clear text taken
from Leopold's original journals in the Leopold Papers (*LP* 7B2–3).

Selected Letters. The final section of this volume contains a selection
of ninety-four letters written by Leopold from 1903 to 1948. Three of
these letters appeared in print during Leopold's lifetime: two, to the
officers of the Carson National Forest, in *The Pine Cone* on July 15,
1913, and January 16, 1914, and one, to an anonymous "wildflower
digger," in *The Wisconsin State Journal* on June 7, 1938. Texts of these
published letters have been taken from the original periodicals; a
newspaper headline presumably added by *The Wisconsin State Journal*
("You Dug Up the Last Yellow Ladyslipper; You Might Steal Paintings and Treasures, Too") has been omitted. One letter (to Herbert
Stoddard, on March 26, 1934) was published after Leopold's death in
Stoddard's *Memoirs of a Naturalist* (1969). The remaining ninety letters are printed here in their entirety, it is believed, for the first time,

though some have been quoted in posthumous books and articles. Texts have been taken from manuscripts and typescripts in the Leopold Papers and in one case (To Clara Leopold, September 22, 1909) from a manuscript held privately by the Leopold family.

This volume presents the texts of the original printings and manuscripts chosen for inclusion here, but it does not attempt to reproduce features of their typographic design, such as the display capitalization of chapter openings, or holographic features, such as variations in the length of dashes. The texts are presented without change, except for the correction of typographical errors, slips of the pen, and other manuscript and typescript accidentals noted above. Spelling, punctuation, and capitalization are often expressive features, and they are not altered, even when inconsistent or irregular. The following is a list of typographical errors corrected, cited by page and line number: 11.28, Phillip; 28.4, 1763; 31.3, moonlight; 91.31, known; 99.4, dimunition; 122.16, *numenon*; 122.20 (and *passim*), numenon; 129.21, Alexander Pattie; 156.6, polychoke; 188.20, land-users'; 194.2, its; 205.11 (and *passim*), pinon; 205.26, consists; 208.14, to tho; 208.35, Maeos; 208.35, beter; 209.9, mater; 217.5, sand bar; 217.9, goulish; 217.12, ecstacy; 220.16, artic; 222.23, womens'; 224.12, upom; 224.27, rate; 224.39, if it; 226.18, down hill; 226.27, ranges,; 227.20, Douglas and Huntingdon; 227.36, dessication,; 228, 3–4, dessication,; 228.25, effect; 229.16, De Vargas; 229.19, Douglas; 231.18, uillustration.; 233.6, compount; 233.12 (and *passim*), Esekiel; 233.20, draft; 234.2 (and *passim*), Onpensky,; 234.23, "There; 235.18, Jeanette; 235.30, oceans; 236.33, Burrough's; 243.22, covetous trifles; 243.28, obseqiousness; 244.10, Carlisle,; 245.22, commerical; 257.16 (and *passim*), pinon; 257.21, (Arctostaphylos pungens); 263.1, principle; 267.4, Clarke.; 269.9 (and *passim*), Mamon; 290.1–2, about not; 316.14, (1922); 317.7, bolstering such; 318.4, Alexander Ohio Pattie; 318.33, Couzens; 321.9, spring; 323.35, dimished; 326.15, near-program; 326.17, Ezekial; 327.36, which in; 328.40, Couzens; 329.36, impliments; 329.37, former's; 330.25, most; 334.17, is; 336.29, then.; 338.16, at books?; 338.33, pointed the; 340.22, butter:; 342.4, is an; 342.33, determines; 342.40, grading,; 344.4, hinderlands; 348.14, great; 349.17–18, hookery; 360.39, tatooed; 367.21, Pocohontas; 369.16, adsorbed; 371.20, before before; 372.2–3, "Naturshutz"; 372.8, Parker's; 373.32, expense all; 374.17, Ehrlkönig; 375.10, the more; 394.17, Arizona should; 413.28, reasons; 415.20, refused; 419.14, then continue; 444.21, population.; 453.2, aquiculturists; 459.19, ro receive; 460.26, or; 465.3, Clarke,; 484.32, vaguries; 485.3, bare; 488.15, *Veronia Baldwini*; 497.13, Mediteranean; 499.7, severly; 508.27, runways; 508.36, Anopheles gambiae; 508.39, DDT); 512.2, Compte; 512.6, pschology; 514.13–14, point being; 515.32, supercede; 521.3, There degrees; 525.31, in the preserving; 526.39, come;

528.20, phychiatric; 529.16, even-aged;; 531.4, show; 533.17, outdoors men; 533.23, sky line; 533.19, bird-hunters; 533.29, bird-hunter; 534.3, sportsmen; 534.12, orrurence; 534.12, illusive; 534.13, I ate; 534. 17, trade; 534.26, illude; 596.19, Isaac; 632.3, "crackelchen"; 711.25, chicadees,; 715.29–30, become; 816.13, it made.

Notes

In the notes below, the reference numbers denote page and line of this volume (the line count includes chapter headings but not blank lines). No note is made for material included in standard desk-reference works. Items from the Leopold Papers at the University of Wisconsin, Madison, are cited by archive subseries, box, and page number in the digital edition, accessed at http://digital.library .wisc.edu/1711.dl/AldoLeopold. Quotations from Shakespeare are keyed to *The Riverside Shakespeare*, ed. G. Blakemore Evans (Boston: Houghton Mifflin, 1974). Biblical references are keyed to the King James Version. For further information about Leopold's life and works, and references to other studies, see David E. Brown and Neil B. Carmony, eds., *Aldo Leopold's Southwest* (Harrisburg, PA: Stackpole Books, 1990; repr. Albuquerque: University of New Mexico Press, 1995); J. Baird Callicott, ed., *Companion to* A Sand County Almanac: *Interpretive & Critical Essays* (Madison: University of Wisconsin Press, 1987); J. Baird Callicott and Susan L. Flader, eds., *The River of the Mother of God and Other Essays by Aldo Leopold* (Madison: University of Wisconsin Press, 1991); J. Baird Callicott and Eric T. Freyfogle, eds., *For the Health of the Land* (Washington, D.C.: Island Press, 1999); Susan L. Flader, *Thinking Like a Mountain: Aldo Leopold and the Evolution of an Ecological Attitude toward Deer, Wolves, and Forests* (Columbia: University of Missouri Press, 1974); Richard L. Knight and Suzanne Riedel, eds., *Aldo Leopold and the Ecological Conscience* (New York: Oxford University Press, 2002); Curt Meine, *Aldo Leopold: His Life and Work* (Madison: University of Wisconsin Press, 1988); Julianne Lutz Newton, *Aldo Leopold's Odyssey* (Washington, D.C.: Island Press, 2006); and Thomas Tanner, ed., *Aldo Leopold: The Man and His Legacy* (Ankeny, IA: Soil Conservation Society of America, 1987).

The Library of America and the editor wish to thank the Aldo Leopold Foundation (www.aldoleopold.org), a not-for-profit conservation organization founded in 1982 by Aldo and Estella Leopold's five children, for its generous assistance in the preparation of this volume, and for its ongoing efforts to inspire an ethical relationship between people and land through the legacy of Aldo Leopold.

A SAND COUNTY ALMANAC

1.4 *Charles W. Schwartz*] Before illustrating *A Sand County Almanac* (1949), Schwartz (1914–1991) worked as a biologist for the Missouri Conservation Commission and published *The Prairie Chicken in Missouri* (1944); afterwards he illustrated the posthumous *Round River: From the Journals of Aldo Leopold* (1953), and published books including *The Wild Mammals of Missouri* (1959).

3.1 Foreword] On September 5, 1947, Leopold sent a version of the collection ultimately published as *A Sand County Almanac*, then titled "Great

Possessions," to Alfred A. Knopf, where it was rejected. He later wrote a new foreword for the book. The original foreword, dated July 31, 1947, is reprinted below from a typescript in the Leopold Papers (6B16, 790–98):

These essays deal with the ethics and esthetics of land.

During my lifetime, more land has been destroyed or damaged than ever before in recorded history. As a field-worker in conservation, I have seen, studied, and measured many samples of this process.

During my lifetime, the stockpile of scientific facts about land has grown from a molehill into a mountain. As a research ecologist, I have contributed to this pile.

During my lifetime, the thing called conservation has grown from a nameless idea into a mighty national movement. As a sportsman and naturalist, I have helped it grow—in size—but so far it has seemed almost to shrink in potency.

This concurrent growth in knowledge of land, good intentions toward land, and abuse of land presents a paradox that baffles me, as it does many another thinking citizen. Science ought to work the other way, but it doesn't. Why?

We regard land as an economic resource, and science as a tool for extracting bigger and better livings from it. Both are obvious facts, but they are not truths, because they tell only half the story.

There is a basic distinction between the fact that land yields us a living, and the inference that it exists for this purpose. The latter is about as true as to infer that I fathered three sons in order to replenish the woodpile.

Science is, or should be, much more than a lever for easier livings. Scientific discovery is nutriment for our sense of wonder, a much more important matter than thicker steaks or bigger bathtubs.

Art and letters, ethics and religion, law and folklore, still regard the wild things of the land either as enemies, or as food, or as dolls to be kept "for pretty." This view of land is our inheritance from Abraham, whose foothold in the land of milk and honey was still a precarious one, but it is outmoded for us. Our foothold is precarious, not because it may slip, but because we may kill the land before we learn to use it with love and respect. Conservation is a pipe-dream as long as *Homo sapiens* is cast in the role of conqueror, and his land in the role of slave and servant. Conservation becomes possible only when man assumes the role of citizen in a community of which soils and waters, plants and animals are fellow members, each dependent on the others, and each entitled to his place in the sun.

These essays are one man's striving to live by and with, rather than on, the American land.

I do not imply that this philosophy of land was always clear to me. It is rather the end-result of a life-journey, in the course of which I have felt

sorrow, anger, puzzlement, or confusion over the inability of conservation to halt the juggernaut of land-abuse. These essays describe particular
episodes en route.

My first doubt about man in the role of conqueror arose while I was
still in college. I came home one Christmas to find that land promoters,
with the help of the Corps of Engineers, had dyked and drained my boyhood hunting grounds on the Mississippi River bottoms. The job was
so complete that I could not even trace the outlines of my beloved lakes
and sloughs under their new blanket of cornstalks.
    I liked corn, but not that much. Perhaps no one but a hunter can
understand how intense an affection a boy can feel for a piece of marsh.
My home town thought the community enriched by this change, I
thought it impoverished. It did not occur to me to express my sense of
loss in writing; my old lake had been under corn for forty years before I
wrote "Red Legs Kicking." Nor did I, until years later, formulate the generalization that drainage is bad, not in and of itself; but when it becomes
so prevalent that a fauna and flora are extinguished.

My first job was as a forest ranger in the White Mountains of Arizona.
There I conceived a large enthusiasm for the free life of the cow country,
and I admired the mounted cowmen, many of whom were my friends.
Through the usual process of hazing and horseplay, I—the tenderfoot—
acquired some rudiments of skill as a horseman, packer, and mountaineer.
    When the advent of motor transport began to shrink the boundaries
of the horse-culture, I realized that something valuable was being lost,
but I bowed my head to the inevitability of "progress." Years later, I tried
to recapture the flavor of the cow-country in "The White Mountain."

It was in the White Mountain country that I had my first experience
with government predator-control. My friends the cowmen shot bears,
wolves, mountain lions, and coyotes on sight; in their eyes, the only
good predator was a dead one. When some particularly irksome depre-
dation occurred, they organized a punitive expedition, or even hired a
professional trapper for a month or two. But the overall outcome was a
draw; the predators were kept down, but they were not extinguished. It
occurred to no one that the country might eventually become bearless
and wolfless. Everyone assumed that the fewer varmints the better, and
within limits this was (and is) true.
    Then came paid government hunters who worked on salary, took
pride in their skill, and (in the case of wolves and grizzlies) were often
able to trap a given unit of range to the point of eradication in the state,
and the sum of a dozen "clean" states was national extermination. To be
sure, there was a face-saving policy about leaving some predators in the
National Parks, but the actual fact is that there are no wolves, and only a
precarious remnant of grizzlies, in the Parks today.

In "Escudilla," I relate my own participation in the extinguishment of the grizzly bear from the White Mountain region. At the time I sensed only a vague uneasiness about the ethics of this action. It required the unfolding of official "predator control" through two decades finally to convince me that I had helped to extirpate the grizzly from the Southwest, and thus played the role of accessory in an ecological murder.

Later, when I had become Chief of Operations for the Southwestern National Forests, I was accessory to the extermination of the lobo wolf from Arizona and New Mexico. As a boy, I had read, with intense sympathy, Seton's masterly biography of a lobo wolf, but I nevertheless was able to rationalize the extermination of the wolf by calling it deer management. I had to learn the hard way that excessive multiplication is a far deadlier enemy to deer than any wolf. "Thinking Like a Mountain" tells what I now know (but what most conservationists have still to learn) about deer herds deprived of their natural enemies.

In 1909, when I first moved to the southwest, there had been six blocks of roadless mountain country, each embracing half a million acres or more, in the National Forests of Arizona and New Mexico. By the 1920s new roads had invaded five of them and there was only one left: the headwaters of the Gila River. I helped to organize a national Wilderness Society, and contrived to get the Gila headwaters withdrawn as a wilderness area, to be kept as pack country, free from additional roads, "forever." But the Gila deer herd, by then wolfless and all but lionless, soon multiplied beyond all reason, and by 1924 the deer had so eaten out the range that reduction of the herd was imperative. Here my sin against the wolves caught up with me. The Forest Service, in the name of range conservation, ordered the construction of a new road splitting my wilderness area in two, so that hunters might have access to the top-heavy deer herd. I was helpless, and so was the Wilderness Society. I was hoist of my own petard.

It was at this time that I wrote several papers, now combined in the essay "Wilderness."

Ironically enough, this same sequence of proclaiming a wilderness, erasing the predators to increase the game, and then erasing the wilderness to help harvest the game, is still being repeated in state after hapless state. The latest instance is in the Salmon River, in Idaho.

I have always felt a deep love for canoe trips on wild rivers. In 1922 my brother Carl and I essayed the then wildest stretch of river in the Southwest: the Delta of the Rio Colorado. We were the third party to navigate the Delta, and the first to do it by canoe. Of my many ventures into wild country, this was the richest and most satisfying. I have tried to recapture its flavor, in retrospect, in "The Green Lagoons."

Twenty five years later, while serving on the Wisconsin Conservation

Commission, I was impressed by the fact that Wisconsin youth were about to lose one of their last wild rivers: the Flambeau. Most other canoeing rivers in the state had already been harnessed for power. I joined with Conservation Commissioner W. J. P. Aberg and Deputy Director of Conservation Ernest F. Swift in an effort to rebuild a small stretch of cottageless river on the Flambeau State Forest. The defeat of this venture, after it was half completed, by the Wisconsin Legislature, is described in "Flambeau." What is a wild river more or less among farmers thirsty for cheap power?

I moved to Madison, Wisconsin, in 1924, to become Associate Director of the Forest Products Laboratory. I found the industrial *motif* of this otherwise admirable institution so little to my liking that I was moved to set down my naturalistic philosophy in a series of essays: "The Land Ethic," "Conservation Esthetic," and others.

It was at this period that I made a series of vacation trips to the Sierra Madre in Chihuahua, Mexico, in company with my brother Carl, my friend Raymond J. Roark, and my son Starker, by then grown. The Sierra Madre was an almost exact counterpart of my beloved mountains of Arizona and New Mexico, but fear of Indians had kept the Sierra free from ranches and livestock. It was here that I first clearly realized that land is an organism, that all my life I had seen only sick land, whereas here was a biota still in perfect aboriginal health. The term "unspoiled wilderness" took on a new meaning. I recorded these impressions in "Song of the Gavilan" and "Guacamaja."

In 1928 I undertook a game survey for the sporting arms industry, and in 1931 I became Professor of Wildlife Management at the University of Wisconsin. During the ensuing decade several ventures were undertaken which bear upon this autobiography.

During the thirties, in company with my friends Franklin Schmidt, Wallace Grange, Frederick Hamerstrom, and Frances Hamerstrom, I did much field work in central Wisconsin. "Marshland Elegy," "The Sand Counties," "Red Lanterns," and "Smoky Gold" express my abiding affection for this region, called poor by those who know no better.

In 1938, with the help of my friend Hans Albert Hochbaum, I helped to organize a waterfowl research station at Delta, Manitoba. I became acquainted with the great marshes of the Canadian wheat belt, and I was shocked to learn how rapidly they were drying up. It was evident that the whole continent was gradually losing its principal nursery for wild fowl. "Clandeboye" is a descriptive sketch of a part of the Delta marsh that seemed to me particularly wild and delightful. I am told that Clandeboye still has water, but it has now acquired roads, empty bottles, and limit-shooting gunners from the States.

One of the penalties of an ecological education is that one lives alone in a world of wounds. Much of the damage inflicted on land is quite invisible to laymen. An ecologist must either harden his shell and make believe that the consequences of science are none of his business, or he must be the doctor who sees the marks of death in a community that believes itself well, and does not want to be told otherwise. One sometimes envies the ignorance of those who rhapsodize about a lovely countryside in process of losing its topsoil, or afflicted with some degenerative disease of its water systems, fauna, or flora.

A group of sketches written during the period 1935–1945 deals with this theme of lethal illness, visible only to the ecologist, in the still-lovely landscapes of various states. "Illinois Bus Ride," "Odyssey," "Cheat Takes Over," and perhaps "On a Monument to the Pigeon" belong in this group. I have been told that "Odyssey" is a complete summary of the fundamentals of ecological conservation.

In 1935 my education in land ecology was deflected by a peculiar and fortunate accident. My family and I had become enthusiastic hunters with bow and arrow, and we needed a shack as a base-camp from which to hunt deer. To this end I purchased, for a song, an abandoned farm on the Wisconsin River in northern Sauk County, only fifty miles from Madison.

Deer-hunting soon proved to be only a minor circumstance among the delights of a landed estate in a semi-wild region, accessible on weekends. I now realize that I had always wanted to own land, and to study and enrich its fauna and flora by my own effort. My wife, my three sons, and my two daughters, each in his own individual manner, have discovered deep satisfactions of one sort or another in the husbandry of wild things on our own land. In the winter we band and feed birds and cut firewood, in spring we plant pines and watch the geese go by, in summer we plant and tend wildflowers, in fall we hunt pheasants and (in some years) ducks, and at all seasons we record phenology. All of these ventures are family affairs; to us a landless family, relying on other people's wildlife, has become an anachronism. My experiences at the shack are recorded in "Great Possessions," and a dozen other essays arranged calendar-wise as "A Sand-Country Almanac."

Whatever the philosophical import, or lack of it, in these sketches, it remains a fact that few writers have dealt with the drama of wild things since our principal instruments for understanding them have come into being. Thoreau, Muir, Burroughs, Hudson, and Seton wrote before ecology had a name, before the science of animal behavior had been born, and before the survival of faunas and floras had become a desperate problem. Fraser Darling and R. M. Lockley have expressed, for the British Isles, some fragments of the wildlife drama as illumined by these new viewpoints, but in America, parallel attempts have been few. I salute Sally Carrighar's *Beetle Rock*, Theodora Stanwell-Fletcher's *Driftwood Valley*, and Louis Halle's *Spring in Washington* as among the best of these. My hope is that *Great Possessions* may add something to what they have ably begun.

These essays were written for myself and my close friends, but I suspect that we are not alone in our discontent with the ecological status quo. If the reader finds here some echo of his own affections and of his own anxieties, they will have accomplished more than was originally intended.

I take the reader first on a round of the seasons at my shack in Sauk County, Wisconsin, and next on a hop-skip-and-jump tour of the North American continent. In both journeys I sketch the observations and experiences which have impressed me most deeply.

At the end of the volume I try to sum up, in more coherent form, the basic logic of the ecological concept of land.

6.2   microtine] Of or relating to the subfamily Microtinae (now Arvicolinae), including lemmings, muskrats, and voles.

6.7   freedom from want and fear] Two of the four "essential human freedoms" proposed in Franklin Delano Roosevelt's January 6, 1941, State of the Union Address.

11.2   alphabetical conservation] In the "alphabet soup" of agencies established under the New Deal, those charged with conservation included the Civilian Conservation Corps (CCC, 1933) and the Soil Conservation Service (SCS, 1935).

11.6   Babbittian] Materialistic and complacent, like the character George F. Babbitt in the novel *Babbitt* (1922), by Sinclair Lewis (1885–1951).

11.26–29   even in 1915 . . . proposition.'] A 1910 Wisconsin constitutional amendment authorizing state forestry was struck down by the Wisconsin Supreme Court in 1915 in *State ex rel. Owen v. Davis*. In a message to the Wisconsin legislature later that year, Governor Emanuel L. Philipp (1861–1925) commented: "The scheme of reforesting these lands wherever the same have been cut over is at best a poor business proposition and a burden upon the taxpayers of the state."

12.7–8   1910, when a great . . . conservation] See *The Conservation of Natural Resources in the United States* (1910), by Charles Richard Van Hise (1857–1918), a professor of geology who served as president of the University of Wisconsin from 1903 to 1918.

13.5–7   Babcock Milk Tester . . . Dairyland.] In 1890, Stephen Moulton Babcock (1843–1931) of the University of Wisconsin Agricultural Experiment Station developed a simple method for determining the fat content of milk; his "milk testers" were invaluable to the dairy industry. The slogan "America's Dairyland" was added to Wisconsin license plates in 1940.

20.33   the unity of nations at Cairo in 1943.] At the Cairo Conference in November 1943, Winston Churchill, Chiang Kai-shek, and Franklin Roosevelt agreed to cooperative actions "in harmony with those of the United Nations at war with Japan."

28.3–11   Jonathan Carver . . . the vallies.] See *Travels through the Interior Parts of North-America, in the Years 1766, 1767, and 1768* (1778), by Jonathan Carver (1710–1780).

46.11–13   the fugitive Black Hawk . . . famous march.] Beginning in late June 1832, Black Hawk (1767–1838) led a retreat of approximately 1,000 Sauk, Fox, and Kickapoo warriors and civilians from northern Illinois to the Wisconsin River near present-day Roxbury, Wisconsin. On July 21, 1832, they were met by a militia under the command of Henry Dodge and fought what has come to be known as the battle of Wisconsin Heights. After escaping across the Wisconsin River, the band was decimated in the Bad Axe Massacre along the Mississippi River on August 1–2, 1832.

82.33–34   wind . . . the Flatiron corner.] Wind currents around the sharply angled Flatiron Building, a Manhattan skyscraper (1902), were featured in New York guidebooks and postcards, notably for their tendency to lift women's skirts.

86.38–87.4   Bengt Berg . . . Nights.'] See chapter II of *To Africa with the Migratory Birds* (1930) by Bengt Berg (1885–1967), first published in Sweden as *Med tranorna till Afrika* (1922).

98.13–14   Mr. DuPont's nylons . . . bombs] Nylon stockings were introduced by the DuPont corporation, led by Pierre S. du Pont (1870–1954), in 1939. Vannevar Bush (1890–1974) headed the wartime Office of Scientific Research and Development, which oversaw military-scientific cooperation on many new technologies, including the atomic bomb.

99.13   pre-Babbittian] See note 11.6.

101.13   'Bide-A-Wee'] Scottish: stay a little. A common name for guest houses and hotels.

101.15   Paul Bunyan] A legendary lumberjack. Probably originating in Québecois and logging-camp folklore, Bunyan stories became widely popular in the early decades of the 20th century through the writings of James MacGillivray (1873–1952) and William Laughead (1882–1958).

102.37   co-operative REA] The Rural Electrification Administration, formed under the New Deal in 1935, offered loans to local REA cooperatives, subsidizing rural access to electricity.

113.16   'Frijole Cienega'] Spanish: Bean Spring.

117.5   peace in our time] A false or dubious assurance of security. (The phrase, ultimately drawn from the Anglican *Book of Common Prayer*, is commonly associated with British prime minister Neville Chamberlain, who on his return to London from the September 30, 1938, signing of the Munich Agreement ceding the Sudetenland to Germany proclaimed "peace for our time.")

117.8–9   Thoreau's dictum . . . world.] See Thoreau's essay "Walking," first published posthumously in *The Atlantic Monthly* in June 1862.

119.12   *bailes*] Spanish: dances.

122.15–16   a philosopher] Immanuel Kant (1724–1804) introduced the concept of the noumenon in the *Critique of Pure Reason* (1781) and other works. When Leopold first published "Guacamaja" (as "The Thick-Billed Parrot in Chihuahua," *The Condor*, January–February 1937), he attributed the idea to Russian philosopher Pyotr D. Ouspensky (1878–1947).

122.22   piñonero] Pinyon jay (*Gymnorhinus cyanocephalus*).

127.10   When Kipling smelled . . . Amritsar.] Leopold may be remembering "The Fires," a prefatory poem to Rudyard Kipling's *Collected Verse* (1907), which he copied into his *Personal Notebook* (c. 1914–early 1930s). Kipling praises the powers of wood-smoke in his essay "Some Aspects of Travel," published in *The Geographical Journal* in April 1914.

129.20   in 1829, Sylvester Pattie] See *The Personal Narrative of James O. Pattie, of Kentucky* (1831), by the fur trapper James Ohio Pattie (1804–c. 1850), whose father, Sylvester, collapsed while crossing the California desert and subsequently died.

138.36   the back forty] Colloquially, any remote or barren piece of land. Under the Land Ordinance of 1785, western public lands were divided into regular lots for sale and settlement; a quarter of a quarter-section, in the resulting survey system, made a forty-acre parcel. The "back forty" referred to the parcel farthest from the farmstead.

139.36   Lake Agassiz] A glacial lake that, at the end of the last glacial period (approximately 10,000 years before present), covered parts of present-day Manitoba, Minnesota, North Dakota, Ontario, and Saskatchewan.

148.17   CCC's] See note 11.2.

149.22–24   Daniel Boone . . . bloody ground,'] Boone (1734–1820) first visited present-day Kentucky on a hunting trip in 1767, and in 1775 he helped to negotiate the Treaty of Sycamore Shoals, by which the Cherokee sold tribal lands in Kentucky and Tennessee to the Transylvania Company. Kentucky has since been referred to as "the dark and bloody ground," a phrase attributed to Cherokee chief Dragging Canoe (Tsiyu Gansini, c. 1738–1792).

154.28   poly-choke] A trademarked adjustable shotgun choke.

154.29   Super-Z shells] A brand of rifle ammunition.

156.4   Bugle Ann] The title character, a hunting dog, in *The Voice of Bugle Ann*, a 1935 novel by MacKinlay Kantor (1904–1977), filmed in 1936.

157.8   'one-gallus'] Poor, rustic (literally, having one suspender).

158.15–16   Elliott S. Barker . . . one of the two best books] *When the Dogs Bark "Treed": A Year on the Trail of the Longtails* (1946).

159.22–24   Errington . . . animal analogues.] In extensive field studies, Paul L. Errington (1902–1962) attempted to demonstrate density-dependent characteristics in the population ecology of the muskrat. Under the stress of overcrowding, the muskrat's own behavior, rather than predation by mink, kept populations in check. In "Predation and Vertebrate Populations" (*Quarterly Review of Biology* 21.2–3 [1946]), he suggested that his results called for "modification of conventional views as to the struggle for existence, the ruthlessness of natural testings, and the nature of predation." Later, in *Of Men and Marshes* (1957), he noted that "the common propensity of man and muskrats for growing savage under stress appears to be basic."

161.34   a forty] See note 138.36.

162.4   forty-niners] Participants in the California gold rush of 1849.

163.25   'illimitable woods . . . Oregon.'] See lines 52–53 of "Thanatopsis" by William Cullen Bryant (1794–1878), first published in 1817.

163.31–32   Where nameless men . . . alone.] From the penultimate stanza of "To the Man of the High North" (collected in *Ballads of a Cheechako*, 1909), by Robert W. Service (1874–1958).

167.24–26   J. E. Weaver . . . supplanted it.] A professor of plant ecology at the University of Nebraska, John Ernest Weaver (1884–1966) published extensively on the roots of native prairie plants and agronomic crops; see *The Ecological Relations of Roots* (1919) and *Development and Activities of Crop Plants: A Study in Crop Ecology* (1922).

167.32   Togrediak] "Togrediak" is obscure and possibly an error. Leopold may have misremembered the name, or his secretary may have mistranscribed his original manuscript, which is no longer known to be extant; he died before *A Sand County Almanac* was published, leaving the error uncorrected.

170.13–14   empires . . . a thousand years] In Nazi propaganda, the Third Reich was sometimes described as a "Tausendjähriges Reich" or thousand-year empire.

174.2–3   Boone and Kenton] Daniel Boone and Simon Kenton (1755–1836), early explorers of Kentucky.

185.5–7   Professor Weaver . . . dust bowl] See note 167.24–26.

187.1–8   Robinson's injunction . . . leave.] See "Tristram" (1927), a long poem by Edwin Arlington Robinson (1869–1935).

OTHER WRITINGS ON ECOLOGY AND CONSERVATION

193.26–28   the great philosopher's . . . *stony way.*] See the essay "American Civilization" (1862) by Ralph Waldo Emerson (1803–1882).

194.34   our paper] The New Mexico Game Protective Association published *The Pine Cone* from 1915 to 1931.

195.16–17   O. Henry's story . . . feuds.] See "A Technical Error," first collected in *Whirligigs* (1910).

195.36–39   Coronado . . . *thigh.*"] See the narrative of Pedro de Castañeda (fl. 1540) in George Parker Winship, ed., *The Coronado Expedition, 1540–1542* (1896).

196.37–38   Cervantes . . . pursuit."] See Thomas Shelton's translation (1612) of the *First Part* (1605) of Don Quixote (book III, chapter XII), by Miguel de Cervantes Saavedra (1547–1616).

206.22–23   dogeying, sleepering, and smearing brands] Forms of cattle rustling. "Dogeying" is apparently a usage unique, in print, to Leopold, but the theft of "dogeys" (orphaned or stray calves) was common, as were various methods of separating animals from the herd in order to facilitate subsequent theft. "Sleepering" involved the cutting of an earmark in a "slick" or unmarked calf without properly branding it, so the calf could pass cursory inspection but could later be given a new earmark and brand and stolen. "Smearing" or "running" brands—deceptively altering an original brand—was also a notorious rustling method.

210.8–9   the Hornaday campaign in 1916] William T. Hornaday (1854–1937), author of *Our Vanishing Wild Life* (1913), *Wild Life Conservation in Theory and Practice* (1914), and other books, was director of the New York Zoological Society and president of the Permanent Wild Life Protective Association. In 1916, he campaigned for the Chamberlain-Hayden bill, which would have established game sanctuaries within the National Forests. Hornaday and Leopold first met in Albuquerque in 1915.

213.9   "The truth . . . long run."] See the essay "Changed Conceptions of Science" in *Some Influences in Modern Philosophical Thought* (1913) by Arthur Twining Hadley (1856–1930): "the right is that which will prevail in the long run."

220.4   Sousa's band] John Philip Sousa (1854–1932) led the popular Sousa Band from 1892 until his death.

220.4–5   iron men] Silver dollars.

220.33   an Angelus] *The Angelus*, a painting (1857–59) by Jean-François Millet (1814–1875).

220.33–35   "I, the Lord . . . created it."] See Isaiah 41:17–20.

222.30   the "Four Hundred"] A phrase coined by Samuel Ward McAllister (1827–1895) to refer to New York's social elite.

225.28   ___%] Leopold left this article unfinished; it is printed here without alteration.

227.19–20   These studies . . . Douglass and Huntington] Andrew Ellicott Douglass (1867–1962) published his first dendrochronological paper on the growth of Arizona *Pinus ponderosa*: see "Weather Cycles in the Growth of Big Trees," *Monthly Weather Review* 37 (1909): 225–37. In 1914 he contributed a chapter on Arizona trees to *The Climatic Factor: As Illustrated in Arid America*, by Ellsworth Huntington (1876–1947). With Huntington, he visited the giant sequoias of California in 1915, publishing data on these trees in *Climatic Cycles and Tree-Growth: A Study of the Annual Rings of Trees in Relation to Climate and Solar Activity* (1919).

229.4–5   "dust . . . shall come."] A refrain line in section 5 of "The Windy City" by Carl Sandburg (1878–1967). The poem was first collected in *Slabs of the Sunburnt West* (1922).

229.20–22   Munns . . . scars.] Edward Norfolk Munns (1889–1972) reported his findings in an unpublished manuscript, "Predicting Forest Fire Conditions from Sunspot Cycles" (1922), and later in *Report of a Conference on Cycles* (1923).

229.25–27   "embalmed in books . . . business men."] See Chester H. Rowell, "The Press As an Intermediary between the Investigator and the Public," *Science* 50 (August 15, 1919): 150.

230.28   GOS Range] Located on the Gila National Forest near Silver City, New Mexico.

230.39   *"Studies . . . 192__.] See Theodore S. Woolsey Jr., *Studies in French Forestry* (1920).

233.12–15   Ezekiel . . . *your feet?*] See Ezekiel 34:18.

234.2–8   Ouspensky . . . inanimate nature.] See chapter XVII of *Tertium Organum* (1911; in English translation, 1922) by Pyotr D. Ouspensky.

235.18–32   Jeannette Marks . . . *tomb of man.*] See "Swinburne: A Study in Pathology" (*The Yale Review*, January 1920) by Jeannette Marks (1875–1964); "The Yellowstone National Park" (collected in *Our National Parks*, 1901) by John Muir (1838–1914); and lines 37–45 of "Thanatopsis" by William Cullen Bryant.

236.10–11   Hadley's . . . run"!)] See note 213.9.

236.17–26   —all that tread . . . sleep.] See lines 48–57 of "Thanatopsis" by William Cullen Bryant.

236.33–34   John Burroughs' . . . itself?] See "Each for Its Own Sake," the third essay in *Accepting the Universe* (1920), by John Burroughs (1837–1921).

236.35   "the derisive silence of eternity."] See the essay "Walking Tours" in Robert Louis Stevenson's *Virginibus Puerisque, and Other Papers* (1881).

237.1   *A Criticism . . . Spirit*] A speech Leopold delivered at the Ten Dons club, Albuquerque, New Mexico, November 6, 1923.

237.15–16   paraphrasing Decatur . . . my ____!"] At an April 1816 dinner in Norfolk, Virginia, naval officer Stephen Decatur Jr. (1779–1820) is reported to have offered the toast "*Our country*—In her intercourse with foreign nations may she always be in the *right*, and always *successful, right or wrong*."

240.11–13 Pile the bodies . . . cover all.] The opening lines of "Grass" (from *Cornhuskers*, 1918), by Carl Sandburg.

240.14–16 Machiavelli . . . little account."] See chapter XVIII of *The Prince* (1532).

241.30–31 the Bursum Bill] Legislation proposed in July 1922 by New Mexico senator Holm O. Bursum (1867–1953) would have extinguished aboriginal title to Pueblo lands. A Pueblo assembly resolved to oppose the bill, and issued "An Appeal for Fair Play and the Preservation of Pueblo Life" in the *Santa Fe New Mexican* on November 6, 1922; reformer John Collier (1884–1968) helped to organize and publicize Pueblo opposition.

242.15 "Et tu, Brute?"] Latin phrase supposed to represent the last words of the betrayed Julius Caesar, as in Shakespeare's *Julius Caesar*, III.i.77.

243.19–20 "I love thy rocks . . . hills"] From the second verse of "America" ("My Country, 'Tis of Thee") by Samuel Francis Smith (1808–1895).

243.29 Ich Dien] I serve: a motto, sometimes borrowed by other individuals and organizations, on the Prince of Wales' heraldic badge.

244.10–11 Carlyle . . . do it."] See "Labour," book III, chapter XI, of Carlyle's *Past and Present* (1843).

244.28–30 "lest we laugh . . . wit."] See chapter 10 ("Old Maids") of the novel *Shirley* (1849), by Charlotte Brontë (1816–1855).

245.10 "The Franciscan,"] An Albuquerque hotel completed in 1923 and since demolished; it was designed by Henry Charles Trost (1860–1933) in the "Pueblo Revival" style.

245.11–18 What vigor . . . stand!] The opening stanza of "Portrait of an Old Cathedral" (1920), a sonnet by Louis Untermeyer (1885–1977).

245.33–34 "the virtue . . . profit by them."] See "The Expert and American Society," an unsigned editorial in *The New Republic*, May 4, 1918.

259.25–27 Bates . . . denudation itself.] See "Forest and Streamflow Experiment at Wagon Wheel Gap, Colorado: Final Report on Completion of the Second Phase of the Experiment," *Monthly Weather Review*, Supplement No. 30 (1928), by Carlos G. Bates (1885–1949) and Alfred J. Henry (1858–1931).

265.6 all her ways . . . peace.] See Proverbs 3:17.

265.32–34 MacMillan . . . climbed] Donald B. MacMillan (1874–1970) brought a radio transmitter aboard the schooner *Bowdoin* during his 1923–24 expedition to the Arctic. In June 1924, members of the British Mount Everest Expedition nearly reached the summit of Mt. Everest, but abandoned the attempt after two climbers disappeared.

266.5–7   "for this the earth . . . rolled."] See section 7 of "I Sing the Body Electric" by Walt Whitman (1819–1892). The poem was first published without a title in *Leaves of Grass* (1855) and given this title in 1867.

266.20–22   "chose rather to live . . . remote lands."] See "A Report of the Voyage and Success Thereof, Attempted in the Year of Our Lord 1583, by Sir Humphrey Gilbert, Knight," written by Edward Hayes (c. 1550–c. 1613) and initially published in the first edition of Richard Hakluyt's *Principall Navigations* (1589).

267.6   Auroch bull] *Bos primigenius primigenius*, a wild ancestor of modern domestic cattle, extinct in 1627.

270.3–4   the potato bug . . . itself.] See note 236.33–34.

271.32–35   "We pitched our tents . . . wagons."] See "The Ballad of William Sycamore" by Stephen Vincent Benét (1898–1943). The poem first appeared in *The New Republic* on November 8, 1922.

272.14   a diamond hitch] A method of tying loads to pack animals, favored in the southwestern U.S. and for travel over rough terrain.

272.32–35   Shakespeare's . . . too-much."] See *Hamlet*, IV.vii.117–18.

274.36   When Secretary Wilson . . . rule] James Wilson (1835–1920), who served as Secretary of Agriculture from 1897 to 1913, expressed the guiding principles of the Forest Service at its founding, in a letter of February 1, 1905.

276.3   D–6] District 6 of the Forest Service (the Pacific Northwest).

276.25   townships] Public land survey townships: 23,040 acres or six miles square.

278.33–34   *"Where nameless . . . alone."*] See note 163.31–32.

280.27–29   Ouspensky says . . . self-directed.] See *Tertium Organum* (1911; translated 1922).

280.29–31   John Burroughs . . . itself.] See note 236.33–34.

285.12   Joliet . . . Champlain] Louis Joliet (1645–c. 1700), Robert de La Salle (1643–1687), and Samuel de Champlain (1574–1635), French explorers of the Great Lakes and the Mississippi.

285.19–20   Kit Carson and Jim Bridger] Christopher Houston ("Kit") Carson (1809–1868) and James Felix Bridger (1804–1881), legendary "mountain men."

285.20   Rendezvous] Within the context of the North American fur trade, a rendezvous was a large, festive annual gathering at which furs were exchanged for money and supplies.

285.21   Forty-Nine] See note 162.4.

286.9–13   Herbert Hoover . . . employed.] As Secretary of Commerce from 1921 to 1928, Hoover (1874–1964) pledged federal support for the recreation movement; Leopold may be paraphrasing his December 11, 1929, address to an advisory committee of the National Conference on Outdoor Recreation.

287.2 D–4] Forest Service district 4 (including Nevada, Utah, southern Idaho, and western Wyoming).

288.22–23 Voltaire . . . exclusions."] See Voltaire's letter of April 15, 1743, to Luc de Clapiers, marquis de Vauvenargues (1715–1747), as quoted in *The Story of Philosophy* (1926) by Will Durant.

292.2–3 Mr. T. T. McCabe's . . . *exposé*] See "More Game Birds in America, Inc.," *The Condor* 33.6 (November–December 1931): 259–61.

296.10–11 "glaciation hypothesis"] In chapter 4 of his *Report on a Game Survey of the North Central States* (1931), Leopold observed a correlation between successful introductions of ring-necked pheasants and Hungarian partridges and the furthest advance of continental glaciers during the final ("Wisconsin") stage of the last ice age, approximately 12,000 years before present. He hypothesized that without the soils deposited by glaciation (or some food supported by such soils), these exotic species may not be adaptable in North America.

296.13 Hungarians] The English, Hungarian, or Gray partridge, *Perdix perdix*, a common game bird.

297.13 the A.O.U.] The American Ornithologists' Union.

300.6 Taverner (1930)] See P. A. Taverner, "The Law and the Prophets," *Du Pont Game Conservation News*, no. 57, May 1, 1930, pp. 296–298.

300.35 (Pratt, 1923)] See G. D. Pratt, "The Egyptians as Sportsmen," *Bulletin of the American Game Protective Association*, October 1923, p. 9.

300.39–301.2 Solon forbade . . . arts."] As quoted in *Geer v. Connecticut* 161 U.S. 519 (1896), which cites vol. 4, p. 128, of the *Répertoire universel et raisonné de jurisprudence* (1812–25) by Philippe-Antoine Merlin (1754–1838).

301.3–17 Xenophon . . . endurance."] See chapter 12 of the *Cynegeticus* ("On Hunting") of Xenophon (c. 430–354 BCE).

305.19 Malcolm and Maxwell (1910) and Johnson (1819)] See George Malcolm and Aymer Maxwell, *Grouse and Grouse Moors* (1910) and Thomas Burgeland Johnson, *The Shooter's Companion* (1819).

307.27 Malmesbury mentions] Leopold cites Frederick George Aflalo, ed., *Half a Century of Sport in Hampshire* (1905), as his source for the shooting journals of James Edward Harris, 2nd Earl of Malmesbury (1778–1841).

308.27–28 Palmer's admirable *Chronology*] See T. S. Palmer, "Chronology and Index of American Game Protection, 1776–1911," *U.S. Department of Agriculture, Biological Survey Bulletin*, no. 41 (1912).

309.21–22 Phillips (1928)] See J. C. Phillips, "Wild Birds Introduced or Transplanted in North America," *U.S. Department of Agriculture Technical Bulletin*, no. 61 (April 1928).

312.21–38   He wrote in 1909: . . . preserved."] See Roosevelt's foreword to the 1909 Duffield & Company edition of *The Master of Game* (1406–13) by Edward of Norwich, Second Duke of York (1373–1415).

313.20–23   "For it the Earth . . . this wonder,"] See note 266.5–7.

316.4   Bailey (1915)] See the sections "It Is Kindly" and "The Keeping of the Beautiful Earth" in *The Holy Earth* (1915) by Liberty Hyde Bailey (1858–1954).

318.3–4   the journal of James Ohio Pattie] First published as *The Personal Narrative of James O. Pattie, of Kentucky* (1831).

318.33   Cozzens . . . 1859(?)] See *The Marvellous Country, or, Three Years in Arizona and New Mexico* (1873) by Samuel Woodworth Cozzens (1834–1878), who crossed the Puerco in 1858.

318.35   Abert] See "Report of Lieut. J. W. Abert, of His Examination of New Mexico, in the Years 1846–'47" by James William Abert (1820–1897), in W. H. Emory, *Notes of a Military Reconnaissance, from Fort Leavenworth, in Missouri, to San Diego, in California* (1848).

320.8–9   Doniphan . . . good quality."] See John T. Hughes, *Doniphan's Expedition; Containing an Account of the Conquest of New Mexico* (1847).

321.24   "bony-tails,"] *Gila elegans*, bonytail chub.

325.1   *The Conservation Ethic*] When first published in the *Journal of Forestry* (October 1933), this essay was preceded by the following abstract:

> The gradual extension of ethical criteria to economic relationships is an historical fact. Economic criteria did not suffice to adjust men to society; they do not now suffice to adjust society to its environment. If our present evolutionary impetus is an upward one, it is ecologically probable that ethics will eventually be extended to land. The present conservation movement may constitute the beginnings of such an extension. If and when it takes place, it may radically modify what now appear as insuperable economic obstacles to better land-use.

328.39–40   Coronado, Espejo, Pattie, Abert, Sitgreaves, and Cozzens] Explorers Francisco Vásquez de Coronado (1510–1554), Antonio de Espejo (c. 1540–1585), James Ohio Pattie, James William Abert, Lorenzo Sitgreaves (1810–1888), and Samuel Woodworth Cozzens.

329.23–27   "Whether you will . . . you leave."] See note 187.1–8.

329.34–35   Canute commanding the tide] Cnut the Great (c. 985–1035) is reported, in Henry of Huntingdon's *Historia Anglorum* (1129–54), to have commanded the tide to halt; when it did not, he acknowledged the limitations of his power and yielded authority to God.

334.22–23   Wilson called . . . mankind."] See Woodrow Wilson's June 30, 1916, address to the New York Press Club on the Mexican border crisis; the phrase is from the opening of the Declaration of Independence.

337.22–23   Whitman's dream . . . *America.*"] See "For You O Democracy," first included in *Leaves of Grass* in 1860.

338.38–39   "as a man thinketh, so is he."] See Proverbs 23:7.

339.3–5   the Senator from Michigan . . . bread.] On February 11, 1933, responding to another senator's protests about the cost of a bill intended to assist the unemployed in Army camps, James J. Couzens (1872–1936) noted: "We appropriate millions for the problem of migratory birds and, though it is hard to believe, there is complaint now heard when we wish to appropriate money for the care of migratory boys."

340.1   *Conservation Economics*] Originally presented as a speech at a meeting of the Taylor-Hibbard Economics club, University of Wisconsin, March 1, 1934. When it was first published in the *Journal of Forestry* (May 1934), this essay was preceded by the following abstract:

> The "New Deal" expenditures for conservation indicate that from now on damage to land is to be repaired at public expense. Misuse of land thus becomes a direct liability against the public purse. In the light of this new premise, this paper critically examines current programs for public land acquisition and for regulation of private land practice. It suggests prevention rather than cure of misuse, and the fusion of conservation laws into some single system for rewarding the private owner whose land-use serves the public interest.

341.2   Copeland Report on forestry] See *A National Plan for American Forestry* (1933), a congressional report produced at the request of Senator Royal S. Copeland (1868–1938) and under the supervision of Earle H. Clapp (1877–1970) of the U.S. Forest Service.

342.30   Article X of the Lumber Code] The Lumber Code was one of many sets of industrial regulations produced in the wake of the National Industrial Recovery Act of 1933. Article X, which went into effect in June 1934 after extensive negotiation, required a number of conservation and sustainable management practices of the timber industry. Some companies voluntarily continued these practices after the act was ruled unconstitutional in May 1935.

343.27–29   like Whitman . . . himself."] See section 6 of "I Sing the Body Electric" (1855/67).

343.40–344.1   "leisure for all" . . . Mr. Hoover's dream] See note 286.9–13.

344.5   the CWA] The Civil Works Administration (1933–34), organized under the Federal Emergency Relief Administration to provide employment for manual laborers.

344.7–8   like Shakespeare's . . . too-much."] See note 272.32–35.

344.33   "wolf trees"] Large, old trees that "prey" on younger and smaller trees around them, by inhibiting their growth.

345.39   the AAA] The Agricultural Adjustment Act (1933).

346.24 the Clarke-McNary Law] A 1924 act that provided for the enlargement of the National Forests, fire and flood control measures, and the reforestation of private lands.

352.1 *The Arboretum and the University*] A dedicatory address at the opening of the University Arboretum, June 17, 1934.

353.1–2 "rugged individualism,"] A phrase popularized by Herbert Hoover, who in 1928 campaign speeches contrasted "the American system of rugged individualism" with European "doctrines of paternalism and state socialism."

355.1 *Land Pathology*] An address delivered at the Madison, Wisconsin, chapter of Sigma Xi, a scientific honor society, on April 15, 1935.

359.25–26 the recent Lumber Code . . . Courts.] See note 342.30.

369.27–28 The recreational value . . . Koch] See, for instance, *Arctic Village* (1933) and *The People's Forests* (1933) by Robert Marshall (1901–1939), and "The Passing of the Lolo Trail," *Journal of Forestry* 33.2 (February 1, 1935), by Elers Koch (1880–1954).

370.7–9 Weaver at Nebraska . . . crops.] See note 167.24–26.

371.8–9 "where the yellow pines . . . crest."] See the opening lines of "Apuni Oyis" (in *Riders of the Stars: A Book of Western Verse*, 1916) by Henry Herbert Knibbs (1874–1945).

371.10 *rudel*] German: pack, herd.

374.8–9 Shakespeare's . . . too-much."] See note 272.32–35.

374.17 the *Erlkönig*] A poem (1782) by Johann Wolfgang von Goethe (1749–1832) about a malevolent forest creature of the same name; it was frequently set to music.

378.8–9 certain ornithologists . . . Woodpecker] In 1935, a joint expedition of Cornell University and the American Museum of Natural History led by Arthur A. Allen and including Albert R. Brand, James S. Tanner, and P. Paul Kellogg filmed and recorded rare ivory-billed woodpeckers in the Singer Tract, a virgin hardwood forest in northeast Louisiana.

378.10–11 "dark and bloody ground"] See note 149.22–24.

380.20 Jay Darling's . . . ranges"] Jay N. ("Ding") Darling (1876–1962), chief of the U.S. Biological Survey, urged preservation of ancestral wildlife ranges in a January 1935 address before the twenty-first American Game Conference.

381.19 "Thus, and not . . . hills."] See "The Sea and the Hills" (1902) by Rudyard Kipling (1865–1936), and also his novel *Kim* (1901), which used parts of the poem as epigraphs.

386.11–12 An analysis . . . Forestry.] See "Deer and *Dauerwald* in Germany," published in the *Journal of Forestry* in two parts, in April and May 1936. (*Dauerwald* is usually translated as *permanent* or *sustainable* forest.)

387.4–6   Naturschutz . . . ruling party.] See the Reichsnaturschutzgesetz (Reich Conservation Act) of 1935.

387.15   iltis] *Mustela putorius*, the European polecat.

395.35–36   our own Act of June 11, 1906] Under the 1906 Forest Homestead Act, land "chiefly valuable for agriculture" within the National Forests was opened for settlement.

401.5–6   this idea grow . . . Louisiana] Mark Leigh Alexander (1863–1923), the first commissioner of the Louisiana Department of Conservation.

401.22–23   Secretary Ickes' . . . scheme] Interior Secretary Harold L. Ickes (1874–1952) sought to create a federal Department of Conservation, and to take over the administration of the Forest Service, which had previously operated under the Department of Agriculture, as part of an executive reorganization in January 1937; his scheme ultimately failed.

406.36–37   Olmstead's report on the Gila River] *A Report on Flood Control of the Gila River in Graham County, Arizona* (1919) by Frank Henry Olmstead (1858–1939).

407.2–3   Lowdermilk's formulation . . . runoff.] Walter Clay Lowdermilk (1888–1974), who had studied flooding problems in China beginning in 1922, conducted many experiments on the relationship between plants and runoff. Most notably, see "Factors Influencing the Surface Run-off of Rain Water" (*Proceedings: Third Pan Pacific Science Congress*, 1926) and "Further Studies of Factors Affecting Surficial Run-off and Erosion" (*Proceedings of the International Congress of Forestry Experiment Stations*, 1929).

407.8–10   Weaver's discovery . . . stability.] See note 167.24–26.

411.1   *Natural . . . Science*] A speech given at the University of Missouri, April 26, 1938.

412.12–13   an industrial chemist . . . pigeon] Arlie William Schorger (1884–1972), a friend of Leopold's; his book *The Passenger Pigeon, Its Natural History and Extinction* was published in 1955.

412.30   a study . . . Ohio housewife.] See *Studies in the Life History of the Song Sparrow* (1937), by Margaret Morse Nice (1883–1974).

420.1–2   I worked this summer for a club] Leopold prepared a land-management plan, *Report on Huron Mountain Club* (1938), at the request of club members.

423.19–20   Paul Sears . . . Fraser Darling] See *Deserts on the March* (1935) by Paul Sears (1891–1990); *Oceanic Birds of South America* (1936) by Robert Cushman Murphy (1887–1973); *Animal Ecology* (1927) by Charles Elton (1900–1991); and *A Herd of Red Deer: A Study in Animal Behaviour* (1937) by Frank Fraser Darling (1903–1979).

425.32–33   When Van Hise . . . use,"] A paraphrase of Van Hise's arguments. See note 12.7–8.

429.23–24   Our godfather the Ice-king] The "Wisconsin" glacier, an ice sheet that covered large areas of North America up to about 10,000 years before the present.

434.2–3   John Steuart Curry, Grant Wood, Thomas Benton] Curry (1897–1946), Wood (1891–1942), and Thomas Hart Benton (1889–1975), midwestern American regionalist painters.

443.36–38   Professor Weaver . . . dust bowl] See note 167.24–26.

444.29–30   new Kaibabs] The "Kaibab crisis" of the mid-1920s prompted Leopold to revise his ideas about predators and game management. Deer herds on the Kaibab Plateau in northern Arizona were protected by law within the Grand Canyon Game Preserve beginning in 1905, and saw many of their natural predators removed by government hunters. Instead of thriving, the deer overran the carrying capacity of their range, and the population collapsed. Subsequent research has revealed more complex chains of cause-and-effect, but has also verified many of the basic findings of Leopold and his contemporaries.

448.14–15   the Townsend Club] An organization whose members advocated the "Townsend Plan," a government-sponsored old-age pension plan proposed by Dr. Francis Earl Townsend (1867–1960).

458.4–5   Paul Bunyan discovered it] See James MacGillivray, "The Round River Drive," *Oscoda Press* (Oscoda, Michigan), August 10, 1906, and note 101.15.

461.25–26   Franklin Roosevelt . . . ship canal] Construction of the Gulf-Atlantic Ship Canal (later referred to as the Cross Florida Barge Canal) began in 1935 with funds from the Emergency Relief Appropriations Act and continued intermittently, over fiscal and environmental objections, until 1971.

462.11–12   moved to California . . . wrath.] See *The Grapes of Wrath* (1939), a novel by John Steinbeck (1902–1968) about a family of Oklahoma tenant farmers forced to emigrate to California after their farm mortgage is foreclosed.

477.8–12   "Children are like . . . Paul Sears] See Paul Sears, "The ABC of Conservation," in *The Foundations of Conservation Education* (1941).

481.15–16   NRA . . . the Supreme Court] The National Recovery Administration, a New Deal agency established under the National Industrial Recovery Act of 1933 and charged with reregulating industrial practices, was judged unconstitutional by the Supreme Court in 1935.

484.35   *Kinzie . . . Waubun.] Originally published in 1856 as *Wau-bun, the "Early Day" in the North-west.*

485.8   Mr. McCormick] Cyrus Hall McCormick (1809–1884), founder of the McCormick Harvesting Machine Company.

489.4   to be] Leopold left this essay unfinished; it is reprinted here without change.

508.36–37   *Anopheles gambiae* to Brazil] *Anopheles gambiae*, an African mosquito species-complex responsible for the transmission of malaria, had reached Brazil in 1930 and caused several epidemic outbreaks of the disease.

512.34   Hugh H. Bennett] Bennett (1881–1960), the author of *Soil Conservation* (1939), headed the Soil Conservation Service within the U.S. Department of Agriculture from 1935 to 1951.

524.1   *The Ecological Conscience*] Presented at a Minneapolis conservation meeting, June 1947.

527.24–25   a newspaper . . . herd-reduction.] *Save Wisconsin's Deer*, published by the Save Wisconsin's Deer Committee and edited by Roy Jorgensen, director of publicity for the Manitowish Waters Chamber of Commerce, appeared from August 1944 to October 1945, when it changed its name to *The Badger Sportsman*.

SELECTED JOURNALS

543.6   *Mythical Straits of Annian*] In early maps of the New World, a supposed sea route across the North American continent, akin to the Northwest Passage; also spelled "Anian."

543.11–15   "*Many voyages . . . Humphrey Gilbert*] See note 266.20–22.

545.14   W–D] Worm-drive, a gear arrangement.

548.8   tambien] Spanish: also.

550.18   "muchos venados."] Spanish: many deer.

551.2   "carrillo"] Spanish: small cart.

553.33   cachanilla] Spanish: arrowweed, *Pluchea sericea*.

556.9   Cocopa] An Indian people living in the southwestern U.S. and northwestern Mexico, especially on the lower Colorado River and its delta.

557.13   CSL] Carl Starker Leopold.

558.23   paseo] Spanish: trip, voyage.

567.10   calabasa] *Cucurbita foetidissima*, a wild gourd.

567.14   chemise] Chamise or chamiso (*Adenostoma fasciculatum*), a flowering evergreen shrub.

567.23   sandias] Spanish: watermelons.

568.1–3   "*Choosing . . . Gilbert*] See note 266.20–22.

572.18   Sorio] Probably *zorillo*, the western spotted skunk (*Spilogale gracilis*).

580.19–20 "all our ways . . . peace."] See Proverbs 3:17.

596.19–20 Izaak Walton's . . . with God."] See Walton's tribute to Sir George Hastings (d. 1641) in *The Compleat Angler* (1653).

603.10 tump] Tumpline, a backpack secured with a strap across the head or chest.

605.2 AL, EBL, ASL, LBL] Aldo Leopold, Estella B. Leopold, A. Starker Leopold, Luna B. Leopold.

611.22 the record.] Leopold kept a statistical "Record of Fish Caught" for this and other trips, not included in the present volume; see Leopold Papers 7B2, 129.

636.11 "Philadelphia Bayuk,"] A popular cigar brand.

640.8 footlog] A log footbridge.

643.11 Howard] Howard F. Weiss (1883–1940), a former director of the Forest Products Laboratory at the University of Wisconsin and author of *The Preservation of Structural Timber* (1915).

661.37 erbswurst] A dehydrated paste made from pea flour and bacon and packaged in tube form; literally "pea sausage."

662.12 CSL] Carl Starker Leopold.

672.6 sacaton] *Sporobolus wrightii*, a perennial grass.

672.25 Ray] Raymond J. Roark (1890–1966), an engineering professor at the University of Wisconsin and author of *Formulas for Stress and Strain* (1938).

681.4 Ed Ochsner] Edward D. Ochsner (c. 1872–1944), a taxidermist and woodsman from Prairie du Sac, Wisconsin.

681.7 Erringtons] Paul L. Errington (see note 159.22–24) and his wife Carolyn Errington (1908–2011).

681.8 Hamerstroms] Frederick (1909–1990) and Frances Hamerstrom (1907–1998), Leopold's students and colleagues, noted particularly for their efforts to study and preserve the prairie chicken in Wisconsin.

681.13 Donald McBeath] Donald Y. McBeath (1910–2001), one of Leopold's former graduate students who had worked planting experimental food patches at the University of Wisconsin Arboretum.

682.26 Tom Butzen] Thomas F. Butzen (1890–1948), a work crew foreman at the University of Wisconsin Arboretum.

682.29 Bert Galistell's] Albert F. Gallistel (1888–1964), superintendent of buildings and grounds at the University of Wisconsin.

683.9 George Kohler] George O. Kohler (1913–2006), a University of Wisconsin biochemist whose work focused on the nutritional properties of grass juice.

686.26   Nancy C. (Joe Hickey] "Nancy C." was probably Nancy Cuno, a school friend of Leopold's daughter Estella. Joseph J. Hickey (1907–1993) was one of Leopold's graduate students and a leading ornithologist.

687.9   WP] White pine.

693.19   Fred Trenk] Fred B. Trenk (1900–1969), an extension forester for the University of Wisconsin.

694.7   Arthur & Hanna Hasler] Arthur Davis Hasler (1908–2001), a limnologist and professor in the zoology department at the University of Wisconsin, and his wife Hanna Prüsse Hasler (1908–1969), a homemaker.

694.15   "3-square"] *Schoenoplectus americanus*, also known as three-square bulrush, a flowering sedge.

695.8   Frank Schramm . . . Marie.] Frank H. Schramm (1900–1995), a family friend, and Marie Leopold Lord (1888–1983), Leopold's sister. Both lived in Burlington, Iowa.

696.1   7:01 (0.02)] The parenthetical number is a measure of light intensity in footcandles, decreased by a factor of 100. Leopold's "Shack Journal" data on light and birdsong were assembled posthumously by Alfred E. Eynon and published as "Avian Daybreak and Evening Song in Relation to Time and Light Intensity," *The Condor*, July–August 1961.

699.2   Mark Ingraham] Mark H. Ingraham (1896–1982), a professor of mathematics at the University of Wisconsin who served as Dean of the College of Letters and Science beginning in 1942.

700.12–13   *Seen . . . Geese*] Leopold died on April 21, leaving this entry incomplete.

SELECTED LETTERS

705.28–29   A full-blooded . . . Eastman] Charles Eastman (1858–1939), a physician, social reformer, and popular lecturer, was the author of *Memories of an Indian Boyhood* (1902); his talk on "The School of Savagery" stressed the importance of outdoor skills in the formation of character.

711.1   Schipitaquin] More commonly spelled Shipetaukin.

716.23   Old Eli] A nickname for Yale University, after Elihu Yale (1649–1721), for whom the original college was named.

718.15   *Cicero*] Leopold's nickname for his sister Marie. His brother Carl (1889–1958) was sometimes "Carolo," and his brother Frederic (1895–1989) "Kidero."

726.7–9   Abraham Lincoln . . . mother."] See Josiah G. Holland, *The Life of Abraham Lincoln* (1866).

729.15   Mr. Pinchot's place] Gifford Pinchot (1865–1946) hosted the Yale Forest School's summer field camp on his family estate, Gray Towers, near Milford, Pennsylvania.

733.35   William Hodge . . . *Home*] Hodge (1874–1932) played the title character in the popular play, which opened in Chicago in 1908 and was written by Booth Tarkington (1869–1946) and Harry Leon Wilson (1867–1939).

750.14–15   Even a fool . . . prudent.] See Proverbs 17:28.

755.14–16   the *Outlook* . . . Refuge.] See "A Cougar Hunt on the Rim of the Grand Canyon," *The Outlook*, October 4, 1913.

760.13   *To Estella Leopold*] Estella Leopold forwarded this letter to Leopold's mother, with the added note "Aldo wants you to read this. Most interesting, don't you think? E."

760.18   "passear"] Leopold probably means *paseo*, a trip or ride, from the Spanish verb *pasear*.

762.21   the "Wilderness . . . *Journal.*] See "The Wilderness and Its Place in Forest Recreational Policy" on pages 212–16 in the present volume.

764.38–765.1   "the sun-white majesties . . . dawn."] From the opening lines of "The Unknown Soldier," a poem by Angela Morgan (c. 1875–1957) recited at a November 1921 special memorial exercise at the Tomb of the Unknowns in Arlington National Cemetery.

765.4–11   Take the wings . . . last sleep.] See lines 50–57 of "Thanatopsis" (1817) by William Cullen Bryant.

767.3–4   Stevenson . . . synthetic gusto."] See "Talks and Talkers" by Robert Louis Stevenson (1850–1894), first published in the *Cornhill Magazine* in April 1882.

767.8–16   Whitman . . . real facts."] The text quoted is from a description of Whitman by his friend John Burroughs; see his journal entry for August 26, 1865, in Clara Barrus, ed., *The Heart of Burroughs's Journals* (1928).

767.35   "only God can make a tree"] From the last line of the poem "Trees" (1914) by Joyce Kilmer (1886–1918).

769.31–35   Ed White . . . Bill Aberg] Leopold had worked successfully with White, an engineer at the Forest Products Laboratory in Madison, Wisconsin, and William J. P. Aberg (1889–1968), a Madison attorney, to establish a state Conservation Commission in Wisconsin, but Leopold was not chosen to head the agency as he had hoped.

770.17–19   Walt Whitman . . . America."] See note 337.22–23.

770.24   wedding-cake] Leopold may be alluding to Bridalveil Fall, one of Yosemite's picturesque attractions.

770.25–26   the live oaks . . . leaves."] See "I Saw in Louisiana a Live-Oak Growing" by Walt Whitman. The poem appeared, untitled, in *Leaves of Grass* (1855) and was given this title in 1867.

771.15 Dr. Grinnell] Joseph Grinnell (1877–1939), editor of *The Condor* and director of the Museum of Vertebrate Zoology at the University of California, Berkeley.

772.1 *Joseph P. Knapp*] Knapp (1864–1951) was cofounder of the More Game Birds in America Foundation, later renamed Ducks Unlimited.

780.1 *Herbert L. Stoddard*] Stoddard (1889–1970) was author of *The Bobwhite Quail: Its Habits, Preservation, and Increase* (1931) and would later publish *Memoirs of a Naturalist* (1969).

781.9 Dave Gorsuch] David M. Gorsuch (1894–1959), author of *Life History of the Gambel Quail in Arizona* (1934).

784.25 Sterling Yard?] Robert Sterling Yard (1861–1945), executive secretary of the National Parks Association since 1919, led The Wilderness Society from 1937 until his death.

785.20–21 The attached . . . road map] These maps are not known to have been saved along with the typescript of Leopold's letter.

786.17–18 PWA . . . Secretary Ickes] The Public Works Administration, founded under the New Deal in 1933 and led by Interior Secretary Harold L. Ickes.

786.27–28 Ernest Oberholtzer . . . Bob Marshall] Ernest C. Oberholtzer (1884–1977), a founding member of The Wilderness Society, appointed by Franklin Roosevelt in 1934 as chairman of the Quetico-Superior Committee; Parrish Storrs Lovejoy (1884–1942), chief of the game division for the Michigan Department of Conservation; Robert Marshall, author of *The People's Forests*.

787.14 Mr. Göring] Hermann Göring (1893–1946) took the title of Reichs-jägermeister (Reich Master of the Hunt) soon after the Nazi accession to power in 1933, and built an elaborate hunting lodge at Schorfheide near Berlin.

787.27 Elton] Charles S. Elton, author of *Animal Ecology* (1927).

787.31 Shirley] Hardy L. Shirley (1900–1996), a silviculturalist at the Lake States Experiment Station.

787.31–32 Lohengrin . . . Siegfried] *Lohengrin* (1850) and *Siegfried* (1876), operas by Richard Wagner (1813–1883); *Madame Butterfly* (1904), an opera by Giacomo Puccini (1858–1924).

788.4 the Riley dinner.] Beginning in 1931, Leopold collaborated with Madison sportsmen and farmers in Riley, Wisconsin, to improve the local game crop. See his "History of the Riley Game Cooperative, 1931–1939," *The Journal of Wildlife Management*, July 1940.

790.23 Mr. Burch] Lucius E. Burch, Jr. (1912–1996), a Memphis trial lawyer; he later renounced his eagle-hunting and served as chairman of the Tennessee Fish and Game Commission.

797.3   Colonel McGuire] John A. McGuire (1869–1942), founder and publisher of *Outdoor Life* from 1898 to 1929.

797.24   *T. D. Peffley*] Talmadge DeWitt Peffley Sr. (1891–1967), an automobile dealer, was president of the Ohio division of the Izaak Walton League of
America.

797.32   I.W.L.A.] Izaak Walton League of America.

799.12   Gerstell] Richard Gerstell (1910–2001), chief of the research division
of the Pennsylvania Game Commission.

799.14   Goldman, Locke, Hall, Rasmussen] See, for instance, E. A. Goldman and S. B. Locke, "The Mountain of Twenty Thousand Deer," *American
Forestry* 29 (1923): 649–82; E. Raymond Hall, "The Deer in California," *California Fish and Game* 13.4 (October 1927): 233–59; and D. Irvin Rasmussen,
"Biotic Communities of the Kaibab Plateau, Arizona," *Ecological Monographs*
11 (1941): 229–75.

799.20   "Conservationist in Mexico,"] See pages 394–400 in the present
volume.

801.9   Lyle Watts] Lyle F. Watts (1890–1962), chief of the U.S. Forest Service
from 1943 to 1952.

802.13   at Riley] See note 788.4.

806.23–24   Only one man . . . surroundings.] See "Germination and Seedling
Development in Five Species of Cypripedium," *American Journal of Botany* 30
(1943): 199–206, by John Thomas Curtis (1913–1961).

807.33   James Ohio Pattie] See note 129.20.

809.20   *Henry DeWitt Smith*] Smith (1888–1962), a mining executive,
attended Yale at the same time as Leopold and was listed as a "special cooperator" in his *Report on a Game Survey of the North Central States* (1931).

810.22   whether anything can be done.] After failed attempts to emigrate to
Brazil and to Ecuador, Schottländer was deported from Breslau (now Wrocław)
in May 1942 and was probably killed in a German extermination camp at Belzec
or Sobibor.

812.7   Otto Doering, Kenneth Reid] Otto Charles Doering (c. 1891–1955),
president of the Izaak Walton League, and Kenneth Alexander Reid (1895–
1956), general manager.

818.34   the *Post* editorial] See Benjamin Stolberg, "Muddled Millions: Capital-
ist Angels of Left-Wing Propaganda," *Saturday Evening Post*, February 15, 1941.

819.3   George] George Marshall (1904–2000), Robert's brother.

819.10   "Out of the Night."] See *Out of the Night* (1941), the autobiography of
Jan Valtin (Richard Julius Hermann Krebs, 1905–1951), a German communist
who emigrated to the United States in 1938.

819.13   Olaus Murie] Olaus J. Murie (1889–1963), a cofounder (with Leopold and others) of The Wilderness Society, was the author of *Alaska-Yukon Caribou* (1935), *Food Habits of the Coyote in Jackson Hole, Wyoming* (1935), and later *The Elk of North America* (1951), among other books.

826.6   Bill Vogt's MS.] See *El hombre y la tierra* (1944), published in Mexico by the Secretaría de Educación Pública and written with the support of the conservation section of the Pan American Union.

827.20   Hochbaum's "Canvasback"?] *The Canvasback on a Prairie Marsh* (1944), by H. Albert Hochbaum (1911–1988), a former graduate student of Leopold's.

827.31   George Sutton] George Miksch Sutton (1898–1982), ornithological author and illustrator.

827.37–828.1   Doug Wade . . . Table"?] William Vogt's "Hunger at the Peace Table," first published in the *Saturday Evening Post* on May 12, 1945, was reprinted in the *Bulletin of the Audubon Society of New Hampshire*, of which Douglas E. Wade (1909–1987) was editor, in June–August 1945.

828.25–26   Libby Jones . . . phenology paper,] With Sara Elizabeth Jones, Leopold published "A Phenological Record for Sauk and Dane Counties, Wisconsin, 1935–1945," *Ecological Monographs* 17.1 (January 1947): 81–122.

828.33   V–J] Victory over Japan, announced on August 14, 1945.

828.33   Bill Elder] William H. Elder (1913–2006), one of Leopold's students, married his daughter Nina Leopold in 1941.

829.5   Tom Coleman] Thomas E. Coleman (1893–1964), a Madison, Wisconsin, manufacturer, was a longtime hunting partner and ally in conservation initiatives.

830.23   left out] Leopold was responding to Vogt's draft outline for a proposed Inter-American Conservation Congress that Vogt was organizing. The conference was held in Denver in September 1948.

831.2–3   Lowdermilk . . . his book.] See *Palestine, Land of Promise* (1944).

831.13   "F₁."] A term from genetics and selective breeding ("Filial 1," the first generation produced by crossbreeding).

831.34   118'ers] Leopold taught Wildlife Ecology 118 beginning in the spring of 1939.

832.4   Joe] Probably Joe Hickey (see note 686.26).

832.9   Bill] Bill Elder (see note 828.33).

832.15   Soper . . . anyhow.] Probably J. Dewey Soper (1893–1982), author of *The Blue Goose: An Account of Its Breeding Ground, Migration, Eggs, Nests, and General Habits* (1930) and *The Life History of the Blue Goose* (1942). Nina

Leopold Elder and William Elder collaborated on the paper "Role of the Family in the Formation of Goose Flocks," published in the *Wilson Bulletin* in September 1949.

833.20   *Noble Clark*] William Noble Clark (1891–1988), associate director of research programs for the College of Agriculture and Life Sciences at the University of Wisconsin.

833.24   Professor Buchholtz] Kenneth P. Buchholtz (1915–1969), assistant professor of agronomy at the University of Wisconsin, published a pamphlet, "Killing Weeds with 2, 4–D," in 1946, and later *Weeds of the North Central States* (1968).

835.32–33   Stanley Johnson, C. A. Gross, and Bert Cartwright] Ducks Unlimited officials: Johnson served as chairman of the southern Wisconsin committee, Gross as Wisconsin chairman and later president, and Cartwright as chief naturalist for Ducks Unlimited Canada.

836.1   *William H. Carr*] Carr (1902–1985) was chairman of the Arizona Wildlife Federation and author of *Stir of Nature* (1930) and *Desert Parade* (1946), among other books.

838.7   Newton Drury] Newton B. Drury (1889–1978), director of the National Park Service from 1940 to 1951.

842.6   Bruce's] Bruce Leopold (b. 1945), Aldo's grandson.

843.18   Sig Olson] Sigurd F. Olson (1899–1982), an ecologist, canoe enthusiast and guide, academic, and popular writer on wilderness subjects, later the author of *The Singing Wilderness* (1956).

844.16   Andrew Weaver] Andrew T. Weaver (1891–1965), chairman of the speech department at the University of Wisconsin.

845.11   *To . . . Reading Committee*] Leopold drafted this letter sometime between November 28, 1947, and April 14, 1948—after Oxford University Press first expressed an interest in his book but before they had agreed to publish it. He apparently left the letter unsent, but he listed a number of trusted colleagues and friends to whom he planned to send it, along with copies of his manuscript. The list included Robert A. McCabe, Frances and Frederick Hamerstrom, Joseph and Peggy Hickey, Albert Hochbaum, Lyle K. Sowls, Alfred G. Etter, William Vogt, Alice Harper, and Allen Stokes. On April 24, 1928, a few days after Leopold's death, Hickey informed this "Reading Committee" of Leopold's wishes. He considered Luna Leopold, Charles Schwartz, and Estella Leopold as implicit members of the group and copied them in his correspondence.

General Index

Game refuges, 203–4, 210, 305–6, 309–10
Game research fellowships, 775
Game Survey, 773, 775, 777–79
Game wardens, 194–95, 209–10, 302, 305, 307–8, 373–74, 385–86
Gaul, 328
Gavilan River, 131–35, 673–75
General Motors Corporation, 785
Georgia, 310, 315, 384, 396, 780
Georgia Quail Preserves, 310, 366, 507, 777–78
Germany, 147, 150, 276, 326, 371–74, 381–93, 417, 423, 429, 444–445, 472–73, 787–88, 792, 799, 809–10, 824, 828
Gerstell, Richard, 799
Gila National Forest, 215, 230–31, 259, 287, 762
Gila River, 215, 247, 318, 321–22, 324, 406, 643–70
Gilbert, Humphrey, 543, 568
Gilbert, Isham, 686, 692
Glacier National Park, 463, 465
Glacier Peak, 817
Glaciers, 87, 91, 436
Globe, Ariz., 766
Glorieta Mesa, 763
Golden Rule, 171–72
Goldman, E. A., 799
Gómez Yarrias, Y., 545
Good roads movement, 269, 272–75, 283
Gordon, Seth: letter to, 774
Göring, Hermann, 787
Gorsuch, David, 781, 798
Governmental conservation, 179–80, 254, 267, 312–13, 332, 341–42, 344, 348, 359–60, 362, 401–4, 421, 424, 430, 482, 775–76, 782–83, 786
Grand Canyon, 318, 322, 758–62
Grand Canyon National Game Preserve, 755
Grand Canyon National Park, 759
Grange, W. B., 777
Granger, Chris, 818
Graves, Henry S., 730, 732, 739
Great Depression, 10, 291, 293, 331, 340, 430, 466
Greece, 230; ancient, 171–72, 300–1, 325–26, 409

Greeley, Fred and Perk, 828
Greeley, William B., 274–75, 762
Green Lake, 692–93
Green River, 727
Green River Soil Conservation District, 105
Grinnell, George Bird, 771
Gross, C. A., 835
Grouse in Health and Disease, 307–8
Guano deposits, 182, 450
Gulf of California, 125, 127, 129, 322
Gulf of Mexico, 220, 342, 733, 735–36
Gullies, 253, 319–21, 328, 346, 348, 363–65, 397
Gus (dog), 420–21, 686, 688
Guthrie, John D., 741
Guzmán, Mexico, 671–72

Habitat, gains/losses in, 507–8
Hadley, Arthur T., 236
Halifax, Vt., 726–28
Hall, C. C., 746, 748
Hall, E. Raymond, 799
Hamerstrom, Frances, 681
Hamerstrom, Frederick, 681, 798, 803
Hamilton, Alexander, 405
Hanno, 266–67
Hasler, Arthur and Hanna, 694
Hatcheries, fish, 146, 156, 166, 822
Hawk and Owl Society, 796
Hawkins, Arthur S., 452–53, 803
Heil, Julius P., 11
Heismann, M., 392
Henry, O. (William Sydney Porter), 195
Henry, W. H., 13
Henry IV, 303
Henry VII, 304, 306
Henry VIII, 303–4, 306–7
Herrick, C. A., 499
Hickey, Joseph, 686, 832
Hidalgo (ranchero), 557–58, 566–67, 572
"Highest use" principle, 212, 214, 279, 792
Hiking, 148, 164, 213–14, 719–21, 723–29
History, 10, 16, 43, 46, 86, 89, 106, 152, 157, 159, 162, 169–70, 173–75, 182, 184, 188, 215, 224, 230, 326–30, 429, 443, 485
Hochbaum, Albert, 827–28

Index of Animals and Plants

THE LIBRARY OF AMERICA SERIES

THE LIBRARY OF AMERICA, a nonprofit publisher, is dedicated to publishing, and keeping in print, authoritative editions of America's best and most significant writing. Each year the Library adds new volumes to its collection of essential works by America's foremost novelists, poets, essayists, journalists, and statesmen.

If you would like to request a free catalog and find out more about The Library of America, please visit www.loa.org/catalog or send us an e-mail at lists@loa.org with your name and address. Include your e-mail address if you would like to receive our occasional newsletter with items of interest to readers of classic American literature and exclusive interviews with Library of America authors and editors (we will never share your e-mail address).

To subscribe to the series or to order individual copies, please visit www.loa.org or call (800) 964.5778.

This book is set in 10 point ITC Galliard Pro, a face designed for digital composition by Matthew Carter and based on the sixteenth-century face Granjon. The paper is acid-free lightweight opaque and meets the requirements for permanence of the American National Standards Institute. The binding material is Brillianta, a woven rayon cloth made by Van Heek-Scholco Textielfabrieken, Holland. Composition by David Bullen Design. Printing and binding by Edwards Brothers Malloy, Ann Arbor. Designed by Bruce Campbell.

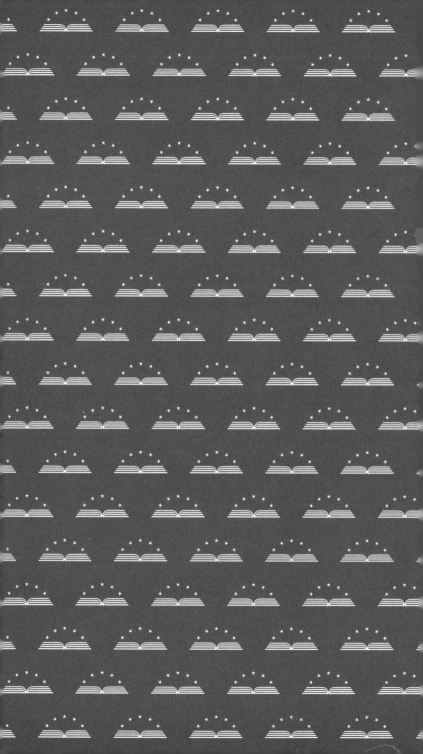